History of British Intelligence

British Spies and Irish Rebels
British Intelligence and Ireland, 1916–1945

Paul McMahon

History of British Intelligence

ISSN 1756-5685

Series Editor
Peter Martland

With the recent opening of government archives to public scrutiny, it is at last possible to study the vital role that intelligence has played in forming and executing policy in modern history. This new series aims to be the leading forum for work in the area. Proposals are welcomed, and should be sent in the first instance to the publisher at the address below.

Boydell and Brewer Ltd, PO Box 9, Woodbridge, Suffolk, IP12 3DF, UK

British Spies and Irish Rebels

British Intelligence and Ireland, 1916–1945

Paul McMahon

THE BOYDELL PRESS

First published 2008
Printed in paperback 2011
The Boydell Press, Woodbridge

ISBN 978-1-84383-656-8

The Boydell Press is an imprint of Boydell & Brewer Ltd
PO Box 9, Woodbridge, Suffolk IP12 3DF, UK
and of Boydell & Brewer Inc.
668 Mt Hope Avenue, Rochester, NY 14620, USA
website: www.boydellandbrewer.com

A catalogue record for this title is available from the British Library

The publisher has no responsibility for the continued existence or accuracy
of URLs for external or third-party internet websites referred to in this book,
and does not guarantee that any content on such websites is,
or will remain, accurate or appropriate.

Papers used by Boydell & Brewer Ltd are natural, recyclable products
made from wood grown in sustainable forests

Designed and typeset in Adobe Myriad Pro and Adobe Warnock Pro by
David Roberts, Pershore, Worcestershire

Printed in Great Britain by
CPI Antony Rowe, Chippenham and Eastbourne

Contents

List of Illustrations

Map of Ireland p. 10

Following p. 116

1 Flying the flag – a combined RIC and British Army patrol during the Irish War of Independence (The National Archives, CO 904/168)

2 General Sir Nevil Macready, Commander-in-Chief of the British Army in Ireland, with Lord French, who narrowly avoided assassination by the IRA

3 The less fortunate Field Marshal Sir Henry Wilson, shot dead on the steps of his London home by two IRA men

4 Brigadier-General Ormonde de l'Epée Winter, codename 'O', British spymaster in Ireland, 1920–1

5 Winter the keen sporstman – on his gelding Post Entry, winner of many races

6 Sir Basil Thomson – head of the Special Branch and director of domestic British intelligence after the First World War (Metropolitan Police Historical Collection)

7 Thomson's more pliant successor, Major-General Sir Wyndham Childs, who was nicknamed 'Fido'

8 David Neligan, the 'Spy in the Castle' – DMP detective, IRA mole and head of the Garda Special Branch after the establishment of the Irish Free State

9 A uniformed Michael Collins, the mastermind behind the IRA intelligence war (courtesy of National Library of Ireland)

10 The equally dynamic Winston Churchill, on his way into the Anglo-Irish negotiations, October 1921 (Getty Images)

11 Irish communist, Roddy Connolly, with Lenin at the second Comintern congress in Petrograd, 1920

12 Éamon de Valera with Clan na Gael leader Joseph McGarrity, the McGarrity family and Harry Boland, 1919

13 Inspector-General Sir Charles Wickham with the Northern Ireland Minister for Home Affairs, Sir Richard Dawson Bates, at the opening of the RUC Depot in Enniskillen, 1936 (Police Service of Northern Ireland Museum)

Following p. 372

28   David Low cartoon in the *Evening Standard*, 8 November 1940, a time when the British government exerted strong pressure on Dublin to allow British forces to use Irish ports and airbases

29   Director of Naval Intelligence, Rear-Admiral John H. Godfrey – the intelligence chief with most interest in Irish affairs during the first year of the Second World War (courtesy of the Imperial War Museum, A20777)

30   The avuncular John Betjeman, British press attaché in Dublin from 1941 to 1943, with close links to SIS (Getty Images)

31   Hermann Görtz, the most successful German spy landed in Ireland during the Second World War (Irish Military Archives, G2 1722)

32   Ernst Weber-Drohl, the most bizarre German spy landed in Ireland, in a publicity photograph for his strongman act (Irish Military Archives, G2 1928)

33   Sir Charles Tegart, one of Britain's more experienced imperial intelligence officers – he was associated with SIS operations in Ireland during the summer of 1940

34   Jane Archer, the shrewd SIS officer responsible for Irish affairs between 1941 and 1945

35   No. 30 Merrion Square, Dublin – British Passport Control Office and hub of the clandestine SIS Irish network during the Second World War

36   Colonel Dan Bryan, the head of Irish military intelligence (G2) who penetrated SIS operations in Ireland (Irish Military Archives)

37   British propaganda poster targeting Irish-Americans who supported southern Ireland's neutrality, 1941 (Irish National Archives)

Acknowledgements

This book is the product of a decade's research, pondering and writing. It first sprouted while I was an undergraduate at University College Dublin; it grew to maturity during languid doctoral days at Cambridge University; it was hewn and crafted during a career break spent in New York and in London; and it received a final polishing in the tropical heat of Aceh, Indonesia. Over this time, I have accumulated many debts of gratitude. I would like to thank my supervisors in Cambridge, Professor Christopher Andrew and Dr Neville Wylie, and an early mentor in Dublin, Dr Richard Aldous. My appreciation goes to all the librarians and archivists who guided me towards the sources, especially those responsible for government and military records in London, Dublin and Washington, D.C. I also received generous help from Dr Emily Wilson, Professor Eunan O'Halpin, Professor Keith Jeffrey, T. Ryle Dwyer, Dr Mark Hull and the Rev. Brendan Bradshaw. The initial research for this book was made possible by financial assistance from St John's College, Cambridge, the Foreign Office Chevening Scholarship programme, the Economic and Social Research Council, the Arts and Humanities Research Board and the Robert Gardiner Memorial Fund. At a later stage, Dr Peter Martland, Chris Lane, Simon Duke, Dr. Joe Ó'Longaigh, and my father, Liam McMahon, undertook the heroic task of reading through long, and sometimes painfully raw, versions of the text (although any errors that remain are solely my responsibility). I would like to thank Carmen and Naomi for putting up with me while in difficult writer mode, and my brother for always providing good advice. Finally, I would like to thank the characters who people this book – the spies, the rebels and all the others who became entangled in the complex Anglo-Irish relationship. I have pulled into the light some who may have preferred to stay in the shadows, but I hope I have done them justice in my portraits.

Abbreviations

AARIR	American Association for the Recognition of the Irish Republic	HO	Home Office
		IMA	Irish Military Archives, Dublin
		INF	Ministry of Information
ACA	Army Comrades Association	IRA	Irish Republican Army
AIDA	American Irish Defence Association	IWM	Imperial War Museum
AOC	Air Officer Commanding	JIC	Joint Intelligence Sub-Committee
BOAC	British Overseas Airways Corporation	JP	Joint Planning Sub-Committee
BSC	British Security Coordination	MEPO	Metropolitan Police
BTNI	British Troops in Northern Ireland command	MI5	Security Service [British domestic intelligence]
'C'	Chief of Secret Service (SIS)	MI6	Secret Intelligence Service [British foreign intelligence]
CCA	Churchill College Archives	MOI	Ministry of Information
CID	Criminal Investigation Department	NAI	National Archives of Ireland
CIGS	Chief of the Imperial General Staff	NI	Northern Ireland
		NID	Naval Intelligence Division
CO	Colonial Office	NLI	National Library of Ireland
COS	Chiefs of Staff	NMM	National Maritime Museum
CPGB	Communist Party of Great Britain	OSS	Office of Strategic Services
		PG	Provisional Government (Dublin)
D Branch	British secret service in Dublin, 1920–1		
D/EA	Department of External Affairs	PGI	Provisional Government of Ireland Committee (London)
D/FA	Department of Foreign Affairs	PREM	Prime Minister's office
D/J	Department of Justice	PRO	Public Records Office
D/T	Department of Taoiseach	PRONI	Public Records Office of Northern Ireland
DMI	Director of Military Intelligence	RIC	Royal Irish Constabulary
DMP	Dublin Metropolitan Police	RSS	Radio Security Service
DNI	Director of Naval Intelligence	RUC	Royal Ulster Constabulary
DO	Dominions Office	SIS	Secret Intelligence Service [British foreign intelligence]
FO	Foreign Office		
FS	Free State	SOE	Special Operations Executive
G2	Irish military intelligence	TNA	The National Archives, UK
GC&CS	Government Code & Cypher School	UCD	University College Dublin
		USNA	United States National Archives
GHQ	General Headquarters		
GOC	General Officer Commanding	UVF	Ulster Volunteer Force
HD(S)E	Home Defence (Security) Executive	WO	War Office
		X-2	Office of Strategic Services counter-espionage branch
HHW	Henry Wilson Papers		

In memory of Nora, my mother

Introduction

'Simply put, intelligence is knowledge and
foreknowledge of the world that surrounds us.'[1]

I N July 1920 an Anglo-Irish intelligence officer named Charles Tegart made the long sea journey from India to London. The son of a Church of Ireland minister, Tegart was born in County Derry, spent much of his childhood in Dunboyne, Co. Meath, and studied briefly at Trinity College Dublin, before joining the Indian police force in 1901. Over the next two decades he established a reputation as a resourceful and ruthless opponent of Indian nationalist revolutionaries. He was particularly famous for his disguises – a colleague once saw him dressed as a Bengali gentleman talking with pimps and prostitutes in the red-light district of Calcutta.[2] At the personal request of the British Prime Minister, Tegart was released from the Indian police in 1920, so that he could deploy his counter-revolutionary skills in Ireland. His task was to design a new intelligence system that would be capable of defeating the separatist campaign of Sinn Féin and the Irish Republican Army (IRA), then at its most intense. Twenty years later, after a spell in Palestine fighting Arab rebels, Tegart returned to the vexing Irish problem. With Europe falling to Hitler's advancing armies, British intelligence chiefs worried that neutral Ireland might be the next country to face German attack. At their request, Tegart travelled to Dublin in May 1940 to investigate conditions. His reports were disturbing. He claimed that 2,000 IRA leaders and German agents had been landed in Ireland by U-boat since the outbreak of the war. Together with members of the German legation in Dublin, they were 'buying up estates' on the west and south coasts, 'rooting up hedges' and 'leveling suitable fields' to make landing grounds for German aircraft. These 'Quislings' were 'awaiting the signal to declare a revolution at the moment that German troops land'. A German force of no more than 2,000 troops 'could probably capture the whole country' in days.[3] Tegart's reports were transmitted to the new Prime Minister, Winston Churchill, in London. Convinced that his picture was 'a true one', British ministers made a desperate offer of Irish unity in an effort to persuade the Dublin government to join the war, while British military chiefs planned a pre-emptive invasion of southern Ireland.[4]

Tegart's interventions in 1920 and 1940 mark the high points of Irish threats to Britain in the first half of the twentieth century. At one end was Ireland's violent struggle for independence, which began with the Easter Rising in 1916; at the other was southern Ireland's clearest declaration of that independence – its neutral stance during the Second World War. In between, there was a period of difficult evolution that saw the partition of the island, civil war in the south, Anglo-Irish diplomatic disputes and recurrent republican violence. The British government struggled to understand or to come to terms with these challenges. One reason was its difficulty in obtaining good intelligence on Ireland. Because the country did not fall neatly into the normal structures of British intelligence, it was subject to neglect and confusion. The attitude of the British government veered between ignorance and alarm. Indeed, ignorance often bred alarm. 'What frightens Intelligence people', one Irish army officer observed, 'is not what they know but what they don't know and what they suspect.'[5] This only changed in the middle of the Second World War, when Britain developed excellent intelligence on Irish affairs, largely because of highly secret co-operation with the indigenous authorities in Dublin. The early failures, uncertain development and eventual success of Britain's intelligence engagement with Ireland are the subject of this book.

There is often confusion over what 'intelligence' means. In popular culture, the term is synonymous with spies and spying, a black art of statecraft. Scholars of intelligence have sometimes used equally narrow definitions: for some, it is limited to the collection of information by *covert* means, for example, using secret agents or the breaking of codes; others interpret it as the study of specialist (often secret) intelligence *agencies*. This book adopts a broad definition, which incidentally conforms to the meaning of the word when it first entered use in the sixteenth century: intelligence is the collection and processing of all information, whether open or secret, pertaining to the security of the state. British intelligence gathering in Ireland between 1916 and 1945 involved plenty of covert operations, specialist intelligence agencies and colourful spies; but information also flowed into government from diplomats, private correspondents and the press. Once there, it mingled with a cacophony of preconceptions, prejudices and political opinions that conditioned how the British perceived Ireland. It is necessary to examine all these inputs, and the way they were processed, to understand how British policy-makers learnt about Irish threats. By using this broader definition, a study of intelligence ultimately becomes a study of governmental *knowing*.[6]

Tegart's 1940 reports touched on all the threats to national security that had preoccupied the British government since 1916. The most important was the threat posed by Irish *militant republicanism*, a movement that advocated the use of force to achieve a united Irish republic, free of British control. It had a political wing, in the shape of Sinn Féin and other mutating political parties, but at its core was a paramilitary organisation, the IRA. It posed a direct subversive threat in Ireland, first to the British administration before 1922, and thereafter to the two Irish administrations in Belfast and Dublin; it carried out terrorist acts on English soil in 1919–23 and 1939–40; it had an important international dimension and could affect Britain's relations with its allies, particularly the United States of America. The second major threat to British security was *foreign subversion* in Ireland by Britain's enemies: first Germany during the First World War, then the Soviet Union and the international communist movement after 1917, then Germany again in the 1930s and 1940s. Such activities, as well as threatening the Irish government, could be directed at Britain in the form of sabotage, espionage, and propaganda. Closely linked to this was the third major threat to preoccupy British intelligence: Ireland's potential *role in war*. Ireland possessed naval and air bases vital to Britain's communications and was an important source of military manpower; it also offered a tempting 'back door' for invasion of the British Isles and a base for subversive activities against Britain. This would be of critical importance at the end of this period, when Britain was fighting for its survival.

It would have been impossible to write this book a decade ago. Historians have pointed out that intelligence is often the 'missing dimension' in traditional accounts of domestic and foreign affairs, often because government files on this subject have remained closed.[7] However, the past ten years have seen the British and Irish governments open a vast amount of material on intelligence and security matters. Frustratingly, much remains classified; the historian is sometimes forced into the role of detective, piecing together evidence from incomplete sources. But there is now enough material in official and private archives to tell the story of British intelligence and Ireland for the first time. It is an engrossing tale, full of conflicting loyalties and unexpected paradoxes, which reflect the complexity of the Anglo-Irish relationship during these years.

As well as unveiling Britain's intelligence relationship with Ireland, this book explores some broader themes. On one level, it throws further light on the evolution of the British intelligence community. The latter had many early deficiencies, and it was not until the Second World War that it developed into the sophisticated system that survives today.[8] The story of British intelligence and Ireland largely follows this arc, although Ireland's anomalous political status often made it an unique intelligence case. At another level, this subject can also help us better understand the development of British policy towards Ireland and the 'high politics' of Anglo-Irish relations. Intelligence on (and misperceptions of) national security threats had a major impact on British decision-makers during this period, especially at times of crisis. Bad intelligence could lead to bad policy. Finally, this book contributes to the historiographical debate over the realities of twentieth-century Ireland. The historian F. S. L. Lyons has identified a clash of four cultures in modern Irish history: nationalist, northern unionist, southern unionist and English.[9] This book focuses on the attitudes of the English (who had much in common with northern and southern unionists). Their views on the nature of Irish politics and society are often very different from orthodox nationalist interpretations. Post-modern approaches to history underscore the value of studying such alternative narratives in order to appreciate the complexity of the past. Thus, by looking at British intelligence, and British perceptions of Ireland, we not only learn something about Britain and how Britain thought; it can also tell us something about Ireland and how Ireland *was*.

B RITISH spies had been fighting Irish rebels for centuries before 1916. They dealt with the same threats that preoccupied London in 1940: secret republican organisations, enemy agents and the possibility of foreign invasion. In contrast to the twentieth century, the earlier British intelligence system proved capable of handling these threats. Irish revolutionary movements were crushed and Britain's foreign enemies gained little advantage from their would-be ally. However, it will be seen that the pre-twentieth-century experience contained legacies that help explain the difficulties of Tegart and his colleagues between 1916 and 1945.

The triumph of British spies over Irish rebels was epitomised by the experience of the United Irishmen in the 1798 rebellion. This uprising had all the hallmarks of later Irish revolutionary movements: an oath-bound secret society (the United Irishmen), republican ideals, a commitment to physical force and a willingness to obtain assistance from Britain's foreign enemies – in this case France. One of the principal reasons for its failure was the good intelligence available to the government. Some of this intelligence came from continental Europe, where Theobald Wolfe Tone was conspiring with French revolutionary leaders to mount a military expedition to Ireland. The British Prime Minister, Pitt the Younger, directed a number of informants on the Continent and encouraged the heads of British diplomatic missions to cultivate agents, especially among counter-revolutionary elements in France.[10] The British secret service recruited a Swiss agent who posed as a disaffected Irishman, infiltrated United Irishmen circles in Paris in 1798, and uncovered the French plans for an invasion of Ireland.[11] In Ireland the government at Dublin Castle oversaw an equally ambitious intelligence effort. Officials throughout the 32 counties – magistrates, custom officials, stamp officers – reported information on suspicious individuals, cargoes and publications. The staff of the Irish post office regularly intercepted, read and copied the correspondence of suspected subversives. Both Dublin Castle and the British military recruited some notorious informers at the highest level of the United Irishmen: Thomas Reynolds provided information on a meeting of the organisation's Leinster Directory that led to their round-up on 12 March 1798; two months later the United Irishmen leader Lord Edward Fitzgerald was arrested on information disclosed by a Dublin barrister, Francis Magan. The government's best source was Samuel Turner, a member of the Ulster Revolutionary Committee, who presented himself in the house of Lord Downshire in London in October 1797 and gave full details of the preparations for rebellion, including critical information on the 'French connection'. The Castle's excellent understanding of the ramifications of the conspiracy allowed it to take decisive action against the rebels in the spring of 1798. One historian, in a recent article on this topic, concludes that 'Dublin Castle emerged as victor in the intelligence wars of the 1790s'.[12]

After 1798 the British government made political reforms and instituted an effective security apparatus to minimise the risk of another rebellion. Following the Act of Union in 1801, the Irish parliament was abolished and Irish MPs moved to Westminster. Though separate administrative departments remained at Dublin Castle, Irish affairs were put under the control of a member of the British cabinet – the Chief Secretary. The internal security and policing system that emerged under this regime was very different from the rest of the United Kingdom. In the 1780s the first police service in the British Isles had been established in Dublin, and in 1836 this was reconstituted as the Dublin Metropolitan Police (DMP). As an unarmed force, it shared some features with the contemporary London Metropolitan Police, but it differed in that it was under central, not local, control and possessed a detective division (the G Division) that played a significant role in investigating political crime. Also in 1836 the Royal Irish Constabulary (RIC) was formed to police the rest of the country. This was very unlike anything to be found in Britain: it was a heavily armed, semi-military force, subject to military drill and discipline, under tight central control, and possessing a Crime Special Branch that dealt with subversive political movements.[13] The RIC, which developed a reputation for loyalty and efficiency, provided a model for imperial policing in many parts of the world. Throughout the nineteenth century Ireland was at the forefront of modern developments in state counter-subversion and domestic intelligence collection.

The two police forces were notably successful in infiltrating and suppressing the Irish revolutionary movements that emerged during the nineteenth century. When the Young Ireland group planned a rising in 1848, the government was kept fully informed through its spy network and was able to take precautionary measures. Ten years later a more serious organisation emerged on both sides of the Atlantic – the Fenians. With parallel branches in Ireland and the

United States of America, and further members in Britain, it secretly plotted revolution. Yet, as before, all these branches were quickly riddled with informers. The Dublin Metropolitan Police pre-empted a planned revolt in 1865 by raiding the Fenian headquarters and arresting most of the leaders; they were convicted of treason felony and sentenced to penal servitude. When a desultory rising was finally attempted in March 1867 Dublin Castle was forewarned by its spies and able to crush it with ease. Over the next two decades a law officer from Dublin Castle, Robert Anderson, recruited and maintained a number of long-term agents deep within the Fenian movement. The most remarkable was Thomas Billis Beach (alias Henri Le Caron), who successfully penetrated the Fenian Brotherhood in America, rose to a senior position in the organisation and provided regular intelligence to the British government for over twenty years. When his role was finally revealed, it came as a complete shock to his erstwhile comrades. The American Fenian leader John Devoy, after conceding that Beach was 'the champion spy of the century' expressed regret that he had been allowed to die peacefully in his bed when the Irish nation was 'thirsting for his blood.'[14]

Until this time the security system in Ireland was far more sophisticated than in Britain. Liberal Victorian distaste for Continental-style 'political policing' precluded the development of a domestic intelligence agency in Britain. The re-emergence of the Fenian threat in 1881 forced a change in this attitude. The successors to the 1860s Fenian movement were two elaborate, oath-bound, secret societies: the Irish Republican Brotherhood in Ireland and Clan na Gael in America. Intent on waging war in England, they began a short-lived bombing campaign in 1881. A year later a group called the 'Invincibles' assassinated the Chief Secretary, Lord Frederick Cavendish, and the Under-Secretary, Thomas Burke, while they walked in Dublin's Phoenix Park. In 1883 the Fenian bombing campaign was renewed on a greater scale in English cities, with bombs exploding at the Local Government Board in Whitehall, the Houses of Parliament, the office of *The Times*, several railway stations and even a public urinal within Scotland Yard itself.

Although this revolutionary violence had little political impact, it produced a major institutional change within British security. 'This is not a temporary emergency requiring a momentary remedy', the Home Secretary, Sir William Vernon Harcourt, wrote. 'Fenianism is a permanent conspiracy against English rule which will last far beyond the term of my life and must be met by a permanent organisation to detect and control it.' In March 1883 he created a 'Special Irish Branch' within Scotland Yard under the veteran detective Superintendent 'Dolly' Wilkinson. The Special Irish Branch and the police forces in Ireland mounted an extensive security operation against the global Fenian organisation: police officers were stationed at British ports, in European cities and in the United States; more informers were recruited on both sides of the Atlantic. Due to this crack-down the terrorists were thoroughly defeated by early 1885. However, rather than disbanding the temporary security apparatus, in 1887 the government merged RIC officers who had been stationed at British ports with the Special Irish Branch to form a new, permanent organisation – the Special Branch of the Metropolitan Police. It was given responsibility for monitoring *all* political crime in Britain. Thus, it was the experience of Irish republican revolutionaries that led to the creation of the first British domestic political surveillance agency. As a future chief of the Special Branch noted: 'Without the Irish there would possibly have been no Special Branch.' [15] The organisation continued to have a strong Irish influence for many years. Subsequent recruits tended to be drawn from the Irish police or Anglo-Irish families, because they had more experience of counter-subversion and showed fewer scruples than their English colleagues about engaging in 'political policing'. Similarly, although the 'Branch' diversified into monitoring anarchist groups, the Irish republican movement remained one of its chief targets.[16]

The British intelligence system was effective in crushing Irish separatist movements throughout the nineteenth century. This was one of the reasons for the decline in support for militant republicanism in the 1890s – to many would-be Irish rebels, success appeared impossible. The other reason was the policy of the British government. The Conservative Party instituted a policy of 'killing Home Rule with kindness', and, through reforms in land ownership, local government, and education, removed many of the social grievances that had fuelled political radicalism.[17] Anglo-Irish relations improved, and the majority of nationalist Ireland put their faith in the constitutional politics of the Irish Parliamentary Party, demanding not republican separation but Home Rule, a relatively limited form of self-government within the British empire.

Yet the long-running battle between the British state and Irish rebels left some important legacies. First, it shaped Irish attitudes towards British intelligence activities. Nineteenth-century Irish histories cited the work of informers as one of the main reasons for the collapse of the 1798 rebellion. W. J. Fitzpatrick included an appendix titled 'Informers Everywhere' in his 1872 book *The Sham Squire and the informers of 1798*; he concluded that 'secret conspiracies can do no good … informers will always be found to betray them'.[18] Irish society developed a special abhorrence of informers, and the 'British Secret Service' entered Irish folklore as an all-knowing, all-powerful sinister force. One DMP officer described how the British authorities were commonly perceived at this time:

Their web was spread wide and of a fine mesh: they kept a lynx eye on every Irish organisation, big or small. It is well known that for centuries the Castle succeeded in penetrating Irish leftwing circles with the aid of secret services, police, informers, and that crack regiment, St. George's cavalry (i.e. gold sovereigns) ... In every age an Irish Judas was hidden in the undergrowth.[19]

A new generation of Irish revolutionaries in the twentieth century, well aware of this history, would place much greater emphasis on guarding their secrets against British spies.

A second legacy of this turbulent past was to shape British perceptions of the Irish race. The Fenian bombing campaign, the Phoenix Park murders and persistent agrarian disturbances reinforced deep cultural stereotypes in Britain about the Irish people that were of far older provenance. In the early modern period, dehumanising portrayals of the 'mere Irish', and contrasts between English 'civilization' and Irish 'barbarism', were used to justify English conquest of the island. In the mid-Victorian period, political violence combined with mass emigration from Ireland to British cities to produce a wave of anti-Irish sentiment, best typified by the representation in *Punch* cartoons of Irishmen as drooling, crazed apes, or Frankenstinian monsters, bristling with weapons. The extent to which this racial and colonial stereotyping reflected opinion in Britain has been the subject of lively debate by historians, which reflects the difficulties of categorising national mentalities.[20] Naturally, there were varying representations of the Irish in British culture; even within *Punch*, there were positive, romantic images of the Irish as a 'pure' race unsullied by modern civilisation or as a beautiful feminine Hibernia. Nevertheless, there is convincing evidence that the negative stereotypes were far more numerous than the positive, and that most people in Britain perceived Ireland as an uncivilised, violent 'Other'. Even when Ireland was portrayed positively in the form of a feminine Hibernia, she was invariably menaced by a gun-yielding, simianised Caliban – the embodiment of militant republicanism and land agitation – and in need of Britannia's protection. Between 1860 and 1890 an indelible image of Irish savagery was stamped on the minds of the British reading public.[21] As we shall see, these stereotypes would distort British policy towards Ireland well into the twentieth century.

The final legacy of the nineteenth century tussle between Irish rebels and the British state was to reinforce the separateness of the Irish security system. The Irish police forces were very different from their British counterparts, and Dublin Castle handled political subversion in its own way. Even the Special Branch in London remained distinct from the new British domestic and foreign intelligence agencies established in 1909 (which would gradually evolve into MI5 and the Secret Intelligence Service – or MI6, as it is popularly known). This was all very well so long as the Irish security system was effective and at the forefront of modern techniques. But by the start of the twentieth century this was no longer the case. The Irish police had become complacent and conservative. When outside British agencies were introduced, there was organisational confusion and a clash of cultures. As violent revolution reshaped the country between 1916 and 1923 the British government struggled to fit the Irish anomaly into its developing intelligence system; it would continue to do so until the Second World War.

PART I

The Irish Revolution, 1916–23

CHAPTER 1

Losing Southern Ireland

E VER since the first failed Home Rule Bill in 1886, nationalist Ireland, led by the Irish Parliamentary Party in Westminster, had patiently sought to achieve self-government through constitutional means. In 1910, for the first time in a generation, this appeared within reach. In that year a closely fought general election handed the Irish party under John Redmond the balance of power in the House of Commons. The Irish formed an alliance with the Liberal Party on condition that Home Rule would be part of the government's programme; over the next three and a half years, the reluctant Liberal Prime Minister, Herbert Asquith, slowly pushed a Home Rule Bill through parliament. He faced stiff opposition. The Protestant unionists of Ulster cried that Home Rule was 'Rome Rule' and were prepared to go to any length to stay out of a self-governing Ireland. They were supported to the hilt by the Conservative Party. Matters moved towards civil war when unionists raised a 100,000-strong Ulster Volunteer Force (UVF), which imported arms and was prepared to fight against the government if the Bill was passed. In reaction to this, nationalists formed the Irish Volunteers, eventually comprising 105,000 men, who threatened to fight if the Bill was *not* passed. The country now boasted two hostile amateur militias that recruited, drilled and procured weapons. In the end the spiral towards violence was interrupted by the outbreak of European conflict in August 1914. The Home Rule Bill was finally passed – with the proviso that north-east Ulster would be excluded – but its implementation was postponed until the end of the war.

It was assumed that the war would be over quickly. Although the fate of the Ulster counties was still uncertain, it appeared that the bulk of Ireland would be enjoying self-government before long. To nationalist Ireland, a great victory had been won, the culmination of decades of parliamentary agitation. John Redmond called on the country to support the war effort, and most Irish Volunteers – renamed the National Volunteers – followed his lead. However, within seven years Ireland had gone through a dramatic revolution. Redmond was dead; the Irish Parliamentary Party had ceased to exist; the moderate nationalist consensus in favour of Home Rule was no more. Instead, a majority now backed a party that had been on the fringes of Irish politics since 1905 – Sinn Féin. Demanding full independence from Britain, Sinn Féin swept the elections in 1918 and 1921.

Even more surprisingly, much of the country was prepared to support, or at least acquiesce in, a campaign of republican violence. An IRB-controlled faction of the Irish Volunteers had broken away from Redmond in 1914 and staged a rising at Easter 1916; between 1919 and 1921 the organisation, now known as the 'Irish Republican Army', waged an effective guerrilla war against the forces of the crown. The British government agreed to a truce in 11 July 1921 and signed an Anglo-Irish Treaty with Sinn Féin leaders on 5 December 1921, granting Dominion status and substantial independence to the southern twenty-six counties. Sinn Féin and the IRA had not obtained a full republic, but they had achieved far more than any previous separatist campaign in Irish history.[1]

The Irish revolution provided a template for separatist campaigns that the British state would face in many parts of the world during the twentieth century. It had a military aspect – a guerrilla insurgency against the security forces. It had a political dimension – the radicalisation of the general population. It posed a major challenge for the British intelligence system. Two types of intelligence were essential if the British state was to have any chance of victory. The first was *tactical* intelligence: information on the identity, location, strength, and intentions of the militants, which could be used for military operations, arrests and criminal prosecutions. The second was *political* or strategic intelligence: information on the state of opinion in Ireland, and the overall strength of the separatist movement, which was necessary for wise policy-making and the achievement of a favourable political solution. The British intelligence system did not always perform well on either of these dimensions. It was hampered by its own internal weaknesses, the effectiveness of its Irish opposition and the constraints imposed by British policy and the Irish political environment.

The rise of Sinn Féin

THE first stage of the Irish revolution was essentially a political process, whereby the advanced nationalism of Sinn Féin squeezed out the Irish Parliamentary Party and established itself as the credo of Catholic Ireland. Yet its catalyst was a military rising at Easter 1916. The rising was planned in great secrecy by a cabal within the IRB Supreme Council, led by long-time revolutionaries and a new generation of quasi-mystical republicans. They sought to exploit the 8,000 radical Irish Volunteers under Professor Eoin MacNeill, who, refusing to support the British war effort, split from John Redmond's mainstream organisation in 1914. In 1916 the IRB plotters co-opted a small paramilitary labour organisation in Dublin – the Irish Citizen's Army – led by a talented socialist organiser named James Connolly. This was very much an international conspiracy. From the United States of America, Clan na Gael urged on the militant wing within the IRB and the Irish Volunteers. The Clan also acted on behalf of the revolutionary leaders in Ireland to secure military assistance from Germany. The public figurehead of this international alliance-making was Sir Roger Casement, a British colonial civil servant turned revolutionary, who travelled from New York to Berlin at the end of 1914. His objectives were to recruit an Irish Brigade from prisoners of war in Germany and to persuade the German government to launch a military invasion of Ireland. He failed on both counts: the German government refused to send its own soldiers to Ireland, and all but sixty Irish prisoners of war rejected Casement's appeals. However, the Germans did agree to send a major shipment of arms (including 20,000 rifles) and to smuggle Casement ashore by submarine. This was to coincide with a general rising in Ireland set for Easter Sunday, 23 April 1916.[2]

It was the job of the British intelligence system in Ireland to uncover and pre-empt this plot. However, the security and intelligence apparatus in Ireland was less equipped to deal with this threat than at any time during the previous century. The more liberal regimes before the First World War had discouraged active surveillance of nationalist groups and cut secret service funds. The zeal and efficiency of the Irish police forces in intelligence work had declined because of complacency, bureaucracy and the expectation that major police reform would accompany Home Rule. By 1914 there were only twelve plain-clothes detectives in the G Division of the Dublin Metropolitan Police. They spent most of their time attending public meetings and watching the movements of political activists; they did not attempt to place long-term secret agents inside revolutionary groups (though they had a string of casual informers or 'touts'). In the rest of the country the Crime Special Branch of the Royal Irish Constabulary consisted of a small bureau of three officers in Dublin, together with part-time duty by a sergeant in each county and a constable in each district. They refrained from plain-clothes activity and aggressive agent recruitment, and relied on an antiquated record-keeping system. The failings of the police forces were evident to the British army. On the eve of the First World War its Irish Command drew up a paper condemning the RIC and DMP intelligence system and urging the government to create a proper Irish secret service to provide intelligence on militant groups. But Dublin Castle took no action: the liberal Chief Secretary, Augustine Birrell, and the Under-Secretary, Sir Matthew Nathan, were complacent about the republican threat and reluctant to interfere with Sinn Féin agitation or Volunteer organising.[3] Thus, whereas the Irish policing system had been at the forefront of innovation in intelligence-gathering techniques during the nineteenth century, by the twentieth it had fallen behind.

It is ironic that the intelligence system in Ireland went into decline just as the modern British intelligence community came into being. Before the 1900s there was no permanently established 'British Secret Service'. The collection of foreign intelligence through secret means was hastily improvised, usually in times of war; domestic intelligence gathering did not go beyond the limited activities of the Special Branch. This changed in the first decade of the twentieth century because of the perceived threat – based as much on fiction as fact – from a newly potent Imperial Germany. A series of bizarre invasion and spy scares, whipped up by the populist press, swept the country: many otherwise sane individuals, in the government and outside, believed that the Germans were not only poised to launch a surprise invasion of Britain, but had also recruited tens of thousands of spies and saboteurs among the German community residing in the country. (One of the first and most influential novels in this genre was *The Riddle of the Sands* by Erskine Childers. He would go on to become Sinn Féin Director of Propaganda and a major target for British intelligence, before facing execution by the Irish government during the Civil War.) Responding to this clamour, the London government established a Secret Service Bureau in 1909.

The new Bureau had two sections, which would evolve into the major institutions of British intelligence. The first was tasked with domestic counter-espionage and, despite numerous titles, would eventually become known as the Security Service or MI5. Its head until 1940 was Captain (later Colonel Sir) Vernon Kell, a meticulous army officer who spoke five languages, thanks to a cosmopolitan, well-travelled upbringing. The second section was tasked with foreign espionage and became known as MI1c, the Secret Intelligence Service (SIS) or MI6. (To avoid confusion, this book will use the appellation SIS throughout.) Its chief until the end of the First World War was Commander (later Captain Sir) Mansfield Cumming, a retired naval officer who went by the codename 'C' – a designation that all heads of SIS have used since. He was known for his habitual cheerfulness and his passion for mechanised transport: he was the owner of a small fleet of boats; he learnt how to fly in his early fifties; and when he lost a leg in a motor accident during the First World War, he took to propelling himself around the corridors of the War Office on a child's scooter. Cumming also had an Irish connection: in the late 1880s he served as private secretary to the Earl of Meath, and then as agent on his estates in Ireland, where he had some success in winning over hostile tenants.[4]

Before 1914 the two new agencies had an amateur ethos, tiny staffs and meagre budgets – their achievements were limited. But after the start of the war they expanded rapidly and carved out permanent institutional niches in the British government. The entire British intelligence community underwent a similar process. The naval and military intelligence departments – with headquarters in London and local units attached to army commands and fleets around the world – saw dramatic expansion in size and function. There was also a change in how politicians viewed intelligence. Intelligence chiefs began to enjoy much greater influence in policy-making, and the government was willing to sanction much more aggressive intelligence techniques: most notably, Britain began systematically decrypting and reading the diplomatic communications of foreign powers. It has not stopped since. The British intelligence community increased its scope, developed a professional cadre, and made some notable contributions to the eventual Allied victory.

The expanded and professionalised British intelligence agencies began to play a greater role in Irish affairs after 1914, though the unusual status of the country meant that their involvement was limited and not always productive. The army was the first to increase its intelligence capabilities, appointing Major Ivor H. Price, a former RIC County Inspector, as Intelligence Officer to the Irish Command. His chief contribution to Irish intelligence derived from his responsibility for wartime censorship in Ireland, especially the imposition of postal censorship on suspected individuals. Postal censorship was the primary source of information for domestic intelligence agencies in Britain during the First World War. However, its operation in Ireland was on a small scale: whereas the MI5 postal censorship bureau in Britain was 1,453 strong by the end of 1915, its Irish equivalent consisted of just ten men. As a result, only a small proportion of correspondence could be inspected; some important leaders of advanced nationalism, such as Pádráig Pearse, were not on the list. Apart from postal censorship, Price had few other sources of intelligence of his own. He did not build up any sort of secret service in Ireland, instead relying on the reports from the RIC and DMP. Though exhibiting greater concern about the revolutionary threat than many in Dublin Castle, he never fully got to grips with the leadership structure of the Sinn Féin movement.[5] This was confirmed after the rising, when he interrogated Eoin MacNeill, the titular Chief of Staff of the Irish Volunteers. 'Price made a number of statements', MacNeill later recorded, 'designed to convey the impression that he was in possession of much inner knowledge.' The actual impression, MacNeill continued, 'was distinctly the contrary. In fact, in view of the open character of the Volunteer organization, the ignorance shown by the Intelligence Department was surprising.'[6]

Another agency with a developing, if tangential, interest in Ireland was MI5. This was partly driven by the personal interests of one of its senior officers, Captain (from 1915 Major) Frank Hall. A 'classic Ulster imperialist' from near Warrenpoint in Co. Down, Hall had organised the anti-Home Rule Ulster

Day demonstrations in September 1912 and served as Military Secretary of the Ulster Volunteer Force. He was an accomplished unionist gunrunner, importing machine guns from London in 1913 and taking charge of the landing and distribution of UVF rifles smuggled into Larne Harbour a year later.[7] On the outbreak of war he switched from subverting the British state to protecting it: he joined MI5. Hall first took on Irish affairs as something of a sideline, but in May 1915 he was made head of a dedicated Irish section (G3), which investigated 'all cases of suspected espionage, sedition or treachery in Ireland'. In September 1916 this section was spun off as a new MI5 branch (D Branch) and given responsibility for the Dominions (Canada, South Africa, Australia, and New Zealand) as well as Ireland.

The First World War files of MI5 are strangely reticent about the agency's involvement in Ireland. To some extent Hall was concerned about the threat of rebellion, examining intelligence on the foreign intrigues of Roger Casement and circulating it within MI5.[8] However, MI5 was mostly focused on German spies, not Irish rebels. For example, Hall tracked two German agents in Britain who travelled to Ireland in 1915: one was Anton Kuepferle, a naturalised American of German descent, who spent two days in Ireland after being sent to Britain by the head of the German secret service in New York; he was arrested and put on trial, but committed suicide before a verdict was reached.[9]

MI5 took a back seat on Irish affairs to two other British intelligence departments – the Special Branch of the Metropolitan Police and the Naval Intelligence Division (NID). They were headed by two of the most flamboyant and powerful intelligence chiefs in wartime Britain. The Special Branch was led by Basil Thomson. A son of an Archbishop of York, he had enjoyed an extremely varied career in the Colonial Service and then at home: he had been Prime Minister of Tonga (at the age of only twenty-eight), private tutor to the Crown Prince of Siam and governor of Dartmoor prison. 'My first native friends were cannibals', he recalled of his early colonial experiences, 'but I learned very quickly that the warrior who had eaten his man as a quasi-religious act was a far more estimable person than the town-bred, mission-educated native.' He became head of the Special Branch in 1913.[10] The Special Branch had traditionally dealt with Irish republican organisations outside of Ireland, but Thomson was also an aggressive empire-builder who attempted to carve out a role as intelligence supremo in the British government. He would play a major role in Irish affairs until his removal in November 1921. His ally, the Director of Naval Intelligence, Captain (later Admiral) Reginald 'Blinker' Hall, has been described as 'the most successful intelligence chief of the First World War'. His great influence in government was due to his control of the outstanding naval cryptanalytic department,

Room 40, which succeeded in breaking Germany's naval and diplomatic codes, although he also masterminded a bewildering range of other covert activities around the world.[11] He was renowned for his high-speed blinking (which gave him his nickname) and his piercing gaze: 'Hall can look through you and see the very muscular movements of your immortal soul while he is talking to you', an awed American ambassador to London wrote. 'Such eyes as the man has! My Lord!'[12]

Hall and Thomson threw themselves into operations in Ireland during the early stages of the war, when they became convinced that German U-boats were sheltering on the Irish coast, communicating with 'Sinn Féiners' and landing spies. This was part of a wave of 'spy mania' that partially infected politicians and intelligence chiefs.[13] Hall's characteristically bold response was to despatch a 510-ton steam yacht, the *Sayanora*, to snoop around the Irish coastline. It was crewed by members of the Royal Navy, who did their best to imitate Americans. A British major posed as its owner, and advertised his pro-German sympathies by sporting an up-turned moustache, Homburg hat and strong Teutonic accent. They set out to make contact with Irish republicans and to discover German intrigues, but they achieved little apart from exciting the suspicions of Irish loyalists: one dignitary rushed to London with a story that he had seen the *Sayanora* planting mines on behalf of the Germans in Westport Harbour. In addition to this far-fetched scheme, the Admiralty developed a secret coastwatching network among Irish residents.[14] Although details remain vague, it seems that its members were mainly drawn from the dependable loyalist class, organised by notables such as the Governor of the Bank of Ireland. They started the work under their own initiative, before being taken on by the Admiralty, which put the network in the hands of W. V. Harrel.[15] Little information regarding German activity in Ireland could have come from this network, for the simple reason that, apart from the IRB negotiations in Germany, such intrigues hardly existed. (Both the development of a secret coastwatching service among southern loyalists and the despatch of undercover ships to the Irish coast would be repeated in the Second World War, when London was gripped by similar fears about U-boat activity around Ireland.)

The limited and ineffective involvement of British intelligence agencies, the decline in the capabilities of the Irish police forces and the strict secrecy of the Irish rebels all meant that the government had very little intelligence on the preparations for rebellion being laid in Ireland. Only two significant informers – codenamed 'Chalk' and 'Granite' – appear in Dublin Castle records from this period, both run by DMP G detectives. Their information in the weeks leading up to the Easter Rising was incomplete and sometimes contradictory: for example, Chalk quoted orders from a rebel leader to the effect that they were 'going out on Sunday. Boys, some of us may never come back'; but just a few weeks earlier Granite had reassured his handlers that there was 'no fear of any rising by the Volunteers'.[16] In contrast to their success with republican movements in the nineteenth century, the authorities never penetrated the inner circle of the IRB. As a result, they did not understand the manœuvrings within the Volunteer leadership in the weeks leading up the rising.

The British intelligence system had better luck in uncovering the foreign dimension of the revolutionary plot. The first evidence of the contacts between Irish revolutionaries and Germany came on 29 October 1914, when a 24-year old Norwegian-American named Adler Christensen walked through the doors of the British embassy in Christiania, Norway. He informed the surprised British Minister, M. de C. Findlay, that Sir Roger Casement had just arrived from New York *en route* to Berlin, where he planned to organise a German expedition to Ireland. Over the next two months Christensen returned to Norway and handed over letters, plans and charts belonging to Casement. Findlay accepted them eagerly, and, in a signed note, promised the Norwegian £5,000 for information leading to the capture of Casement. Findlay's reports on this supposed intelligence windfall were passed to the British Prime Minister and other members of the cabinet.

Christensen was Casement's translator, messenger, travelling companion and sexual partner. He was also a liar, a blackmailer and a fantasist. At some point, while concealing much of the truth, he revealed his contacts to Casement, who decided to allow the liaison to continue in order to ensnare the British Minister. Once he had collected enough evidence, Casement triumphantly revealed the story to the press, published Findlay's note and (erroneously) claimed that there was a British plot to murder him. The affair was a public embarrassment for the British government and the British Minister to Norway. Yet Christensen also passed on some valid information on Casement's activities, including copies of actual messages to rebel leaders in Ireland and the United States, together with names and addresses of correspondents – these individuals were immediately placed under postal censorship. The Christensen case prompted MI5 to open a personal file on Casement, which was soon populated with reports from returning prisoners of war describing the Irishman's unsuccessful attempts to recruit an Irish Brigade.[17]

The best intelligence on the foreign dimension of the Irish republican movement came not from Europe but from the United States, and specifically from the telegraph cables that passed between that country and Germany. Clan na Gael, led by John Devoy, managed the IRB's relationship with Germany in the run-up to the Easter Rising: messages from Ireland were typically passed by secret courier to Devoy, who handed them to the German embassy in Washington DC, from where they were sent by enciphered telegram to Berlin. Because the transatlantic cables passed through British territory, the codebreakers of Room 40 obtained copies of all these messages, and were invariably in a position to provide Captain Reginald 'Blinker' Hall with timely decrypts. These revealed that the Irish Volunteers were preparing for a rising, that a German ship was bound for Ireland laden with arms, and that Roger Casement would be landed by submarine – all on Easter weekend 1916. British intelligence chiefs, therefore, knew what to expect, and this contributed to the failure of the German intervention. The Royal Navy intercepted the German ship, the *Aud*, on 21 April (Easter Friday), after she arrived off the coast of Kerry. Casement was captured by the local RIC on 22 April, just hours after stepping ashore. He was immediately whisked off to London for interrogation by the intelligence chiefs most active in Irish affairs – Captain Reginald 'Blinker' Hall of NID, Basil Thomson of the Special Branch and Major Frank Hall of MI5.[18]

However, the quality of Britain's foreign intelligence was stymied by the inability or unwillingness of British intelligence chiefs to use it properly. Though he had received some warning from the Admiralty about the impending arrival of a German ship, the commanding admiral of the Royal Navy in southern Ireland did not take vigorous measures to intercept it; the *Aud* was able to cruise around the Kerry coast for two days before being detected. If the IRB had organised a proper reception, it would have had time to land its arms. The capture of Casement by the RIC was quite fortuitous: they had received no special instructions on the matter. Worst of all, the Chief Secretary and the administrators at Dublin Castle, who had primary responsibility for Irish affairs, were left woefully ill-informed: they did not receive any special warnings based on the decrypted German messages in the weeks before the rising, and they received no details from the interrogation of Casement on 23 April (Easter Sunday).[19] In a later report on the organisation of intelligence, Basil Thomson admitted that there was 'certainly a danger that from lack of co-ordination the Irish Government may be the last Department to receive information of grave moment to the peace of Ireland.'[20] The reluctance of British chiefs to share intelligence with Dublin Castle was partly because they did not want to jeopardise a precious source (Room 40's decrypts); it was partly because the lack of communication between the Irish intelligence system and British agencies meant that neither side fully understood the implications of the information in their possession; but it has also been suggested that British intelligence chiefs deliberately withheld information from Dublin Castle because they wished the rising to go ahead. Casement later revealed that his interrogators refused his request to be allowed to make a public appeal to the Irish Volunteers for the rising to be cancelled: one of his questioners had responded, 'It's a festering sore, its much better it should come to a head.' Thomson denied this accusation, but his explanation for their actions over the Easter Weekend is not very convincing; it is possible that British intelligence chiefs did manipulate the situation to ensure that an insurrection took place, thereby making a repression of the Irish militants unavoidable.[21]

As a result, when approximately 2,000 Irish Volunteers occupied key sites in central Dublin on the morning of Easter Monday, the civil and military authorities in Ireland were taken completely by surprise. Dublin Castle had interpreted a last-minute order from Eoin MacNeill over the weekend, cancelling the Sunday manœuvres, as a sign that the Volunteers had called off whatever demonstration they had in mind. In fact, this was a belated attempt by MacNeill to thwart the plans of militant leaders whom he no longer controlled. It caused much confusion, especially outside Dublin, but the IRB military committee did not call off the rising – they merely postponed it by one day. The inaction and passivity of the Irish authorities in the face of this threat is astounding. The Chief Secretary and Irish Commander-in-Chief were both in London during the Easter Weekend and made no efforts to return, even when they learnt of the sinking of the *Aud* and the capture of Casement. The officials remaining in Dublin Castle dithered over taking action against the separatist leaders on Sunday and eventually decided to postpone the matter until the next day. On Easter Monday, rather than garrisoning the capital, army officers went off to the horse races at Fairytown.

The complete lack of preparedness is illustrated by the insecurity of Dublin Castle on the morning of Easter Monday. It was defended by a tiny garrison: one unarmed DMP constable, six soldiers at the main gate, and a reserve of twenty-five in the adjacent Ship Street Barracks. A Volunteer force, under the command of Captain Seán Connolly, made a half-hearted attempt to take the Castle in the first hour of the rising. They shot the police constable, overpowered the six soldiers, who were quietly cooking their lunch in the guardroom, and entered the main courtyard; they could have pushed on to the take the entire complex if they had known how weakly defended it was. However, they decided to retreat when the military intelligence officer, Major Price, then meeting with officials to discuss the round-up of Volunteer leaders, ran into the yard blazing away with his revolver. Price may not have been the most effective intelligence officer, but his courageous action almost single-handedly saved Dublin Castle, the seat of British rule for 700 years and the most strategically important building in the capital.[22]

The Easter Rising represented a serious intelligence failure for the British state. Some exoneration lies in the extreme secrecy with which the rising was planned; the rebel leaders were a minority within a minority within a minority, and their furtiveness was one of the reasons why the rebellion went off at half cock. Yet it also reflects the poor performance of the British intelligence system. In contrast to the previous century, Dublin Castle was unable to place informers within the inner circles of the revolutionaries; this explains its inability to unravel the mystery behind the orders and counter-orders emanating from Irish Volunteers headquarters over the Easter weekend. British intelligence chiefs did have access to good intelligence on the foreign dimension of the Irish republican plot, but did not share or use this information wisely. Even when signals were available, the Chief Secretary and his civil servants chose to disregard them, preferring inaction to the risk of alienating nationalist opinion. During the nineteenth century, attempts at revolution had been foiled by a combination of pre-emptive intervention and military deterrent, which turned ambitious plots into inglorious squibs. A similar policy in 1916 may have had the same effect. Instead, the rebels were able to occupy Dublin for six days and mount an heroic, if doomed, defence that would have a dramatic effect on Irish politics.[23]

AFTER the Easter Rising, Irish militant leaders laid down their guns and instead concentrated on turning Sinn Féin – erroneously credited with instigating the rebellion – into the political voice of nationalist Ireland. British policy played directly into their hands. The complacency of the pre-Easter 1916 era was replaced by a ruthless crack-down that transformed the rebels into martyrs and built support for the separatist cause. Martial law was declared by the newly established Military Governor, General Sir John Maxwell; sixteen Irish leaders, including Casement, were executed; and some 1,850 individuals, many innocent, were deported to England and interned under Defence Regulation 14b. This may seem lenient, given that Britain was in the midst of a world war; but in the Irish context it was an over-reaction.[24] Over the next two years the failure to achieve a Home Rule settlement killed the Irish Parliamentary Party, while the death of a republican hunger striker (Thomas Ashe) after clumsy forced feeding provoked further public anger. The position of Sinn Féin, by now a powerful mass movement, was cemented by the government's decision in March 1918 to impose conscription. The whole of nationalist Ireland rose against this measure. Though the government chose not to follow through on its decision, the damage had been done. Sinn Féin swept the board in the December 1918 elections, winning 73 of the 105 seats. Its dominance outside Ulster was complete.[25]

What the British government needed in 1917 and 1918 was not tactical intelligence on the activities of the Irish Volunteers, but political intelligence on the momentous shifts in Irish opinion. This might indicate how British policy was going wrong. By and large, this was provided by the RIC and DMP, which made good reports to Dublin Castle on the deteriorating situation in the country. Regional military intelligence officers, newly established under martial law, provided a similar function.[26] However, intelligence chiefs in London, now more influential than ever, were more concerned with tracking down minor Germany intrigues and proving that German manipulation lay behind the Sinn Féin movement. In the second half of 1916, MI5 produced evidence that the German secret service was stepping up its activities in Ireland. It discovered that an active German spy centre in New York was recruiting American journalists for missions in Ireland: one such person, George Vaux Bacon, toured the country between 25 November and 8 December, met with 'Sinn Feiners' and was 'definitely' engaged in espionage.[27] On numerous occasions between 1916 and 1918 London became convinced that German arms were being landed in Ireland; that German U-boats were a frequent presence on the Irish coast; and that the Germans were communicating with Sinn Féin leaders and disseminating propaganda in preparation for another major insurrection. A good example is contained in Basil Thomson's diary entry for 18 February 1917: he confidently asserted that there were two ships *en route* from Kiel, carrying 60,000 rifles, 6 million cartridges and 10 machine guns.[28]

Though there were some continuing contacts between Irish-American leaders and German representatives in 1916 and early 1917, the role of Germany was greatly exaggerated – Sinn Féin was an indigenous nationalist movement that drew strength from the grievances of the Irish people and the blunders of the British government, not a foreign conspiracy. The British misconception was caused by reliance on faulty intelligence sources. In February 1917 the British lost their best source of information on the foreign dimension of the republican movement – Room 40's decrypts of German diplomatic communications from America. In that month the United States broke off diplomatic relations with Germany; the German ambassador was recalled; and the messages ceased. Instead, Thomson and the two Halls began to rely on reports from spy-obsessed loyalist residents in Ireland. It appears that MI5 worked with the Special Branch to establish an informal intelligence-gathering network in Ireland in 1916. Few details about this shadowy agency have survived. It mainly consisted of private individuals loyal to the crown, who reported on local conditions, though it may also have employed more sophisticated techniques: Thomson describes in his memoirs how one of his agents 'secreted a powerful dictaphone in the secret meeting room of the Sinn Féin executive' at the time of the Irish Convention in

1917.[29] Information from these sources was circulated in highly secret reports marked 'Q', which was also the personal codename used by Major Hall of MI5.[30] These biased, informal sources produced a steady stream of alarmist information on German intrigues in Ireland, which the London intelligence chiefs replayed to British ministers and the Dublin Castle executive. The intelligence chiefs declined to reveal their sources, gave no indication that their information might be less reliable than before, and therefore produced warnings that the government felt obliged to act on.[31]

The 'German plot' arrests in May 1918 are a striking illustration of the apparent manipulation of intelligence in order to prod the Irish authorities into more forceful action. On 12 April 1918 a former member of Casement's tiny Irish Brigade, Joseph Dowling, was arrested after he landed from a German U-boat in Co. Clare. He claimed that the Germans were planning to send a military expedition to the country. Over the following weeks, 'Blinker' Hall and Thomson first persuaded the British cabinet that a coup was imminent and then pressed this notion on the Dublin Castle executive. As a result, it was decided to arrest practically the entire Sinn Féin leadership: 150 were picked up and interned in English jails on the night of 17–18 May. The measure backfired dramatically. The Irish leaders had been tipped off about the raid by informers within the police, allowing some of the most militant physical force advocates, such as Michael Collins, to evade arrest. In contrast, many moderate political leaders chose not to escape, as they realised that their arrest would provide a political windfall. They were entirely correct; when the British government was unable to provide convincing evidence of a 'German plot', nationalist Ireland concluded that it had been invented as retribution for the defeat of conscription. It helped Sinn Féin to its sweeping electoral victory, in which a number of those interned successfully stood as parliamentary candidates.[32]

Contrary to Irish opinion, the 'German plot' was not deliberately invented by British ministers; they sincerely believed that the threat was real. Between 1916 and 1918 British ministers did not recognise that Sinn Féin was a popular, indigenous movement, and instead clung to the notion that it was a German conspiracy; this delegitimised it and produced a vain hope that the problem would die away if the German intrigues were crushed. This was part of an overall failure to understand the political situation in Ireland and the likely implications of British policies. There was little urgency about thrashing out a political settlement acceptable to nationalist Ireland, and decisions such as the introduction conscription were entirely counter-productive. These political developments, rather than the security response to the Easter Rising, really killed the Irish Parliamentary Party and gave life to Sinn Féin.[33] It was the job of the intelligence system to challenge the prejudices and wishful thinking that lay behind the British cabinet's decisions – to better educate policy-makers about the reality on the ground. Instead, the intelligence chiefs in London, obsessed with minor German intrigues, were as much a cause of obfuscation as enlightenment.

By the end of 1918 the British government was faced with an extremely difficult situation. The bulk of southern Ireland had become alienated from the state and backed a radical Sinn Féin party that demanded full independence. After the dramatic military sacrifice of the Easter Rising, Sinn Féin had confined itself to political agitation and electioneering, but in 1919 the shooting would start in earnest: the Volunteers, now more popularly known as the Irish Republican Army (IRA), would wage an insurgency against the police and the British army. The British intelligence system and the British government would find it even harder to bring this under control.

The intelligence war

The period between January 1919 and July 1921 is known as the 'Anglo-Irish War', the 'Tan War' or the 'War of Independence'. It had a political dimension. After the general election in December 1918 Sinn Féin representatives abstained from Westminster and instead met in Dublin on 21 January 1919 to form their own parliament (or Dáil). They claimed to be the legitimate government of the country, despatched envoys across the world to obtain international recognition for the republic and attempted to set up a counter-state by establishing rival judiciary, police and government departments. However, these peaceful, political moves were overshadowed by an escalating campaign of violence by the Irish Republican Army (IRA). The first shots of the war of independence were fired on the same day that the Dáil first met in Dublin, when Seán Treacy and Dan Breen led a party of Irish Volunteers in an ambush of policemen at a quarry at Soloheadbeg, Co. Tipperary, killing two RIC officers. The ambush was carried out by a small number of Volunteers acting on their own initiative, and much of the violence that followed was of a similar pattern. It was conducted by a militant IRA hardcore, determined to use physical force, who were barely under the control of the IRA headquarters, let alone the Sinn Féin political leadership. They were not responsive to public opinion, and their actions initially conflicted with the wishes of the people. In 1918 support for Sinn Féin was not support for violence. However, by 1921 this too had changed. A large proportion of nationalist Ireland began to see the IRA as an army of liberation struggling against a foreign oppressor: violence had been partly legitimised.[34] This was the critical stage in the collapse of British rule in Ireland.

The War of Independence was largely an intelligence war. The Irish insurgency was like many others, in that a small group of militants used violence while much of the population was uneasy with the means, even if supporting the political ends. To mount a successful counter-insurgency campaign, the state required information on the identity of the fighters, their location, their intentions and the sources of their weapons – that is, good tactical, operational or criminal intelligence. It was essential to collect this in a way that targeted the militants without alienating the majority, so that the way would be left open for a political compromise. A surgical instrument, not a blunt instrument, was required. As a result, covert intelligence and counter-intelligence operations – involving undercover officers, secret agents and informers – would play a major role in deciding the outcome.

The importance of intelligence has long been recognised by historians, but there has been little research on how the British intelligence system worked in Ireland. Irish historians have traditionally referred in blanket terms to the 'British Secret Service', without differentiating the organisations or individuals involved. Many assume that the IRA – under the leadership of Michael Collins – was wholly successful in neutralising British intelligence, largely because writing on this subject has been based on Irish sources, in particular the memoirs of IRA leaders.[35] However, the release of British government documents over the past decade now makes it possible to tell the full story of the intelligence war between the IRA and the British state.

There were four distinct phases in this war. The balance swung from side to side, as each responded to advances in the tactics and organisation of the other. There was no simple triumph. The IRA had the upper hand in the covert struggle, but the British eventually obtained good intelligence through overt security measures, which allowed them to place substantial pressure on their opponents by 1921. Nevertheless, by forcing the British to resort to heavy-handed, politically damaging tactics (the blunt instrument), and merely by surviving, the IRA emerged as the ultimate victors.

T HE first phase of the war, from January 1919 to January 1920, resulted in the destruction of the intelligence capacity of the Irish police and Dublin Castle. This was a deliberate strategy of the IRA – the War of Independence was an intelligence war because the IRA determined to make it so. The mastermind behind this focus on intelligence was Michael Collins. Known to his colleagues as the 'Big Fella', he was a youthful Corkman with a genius for administration, a ruthless desire for power, and a boisterous, charismatic style of leadership: even his British enemies admitted that 'he combined the characteristics of Robin

Hood with those of an elusive Pimpernel.[36] He had an immense capacity for work, combining at various times the roles of IRA Adjutant General, IRA Director of Organisation, Dáil Minister for Finance, and acting Dáil President. His most influential role was as IRA Director of Intelligence, a position that he formally assumed in January 1919. Collins was determined that the Sinn Féin rebellion would not be thwarted by informers as in the past. He later summarised his credo:

> Without her spies England was helpless. It was only by means of their accumulated knowledge that the British machine could operate. Without their police throughout the country, how could they find the man they wanted? Without their criminal agents in the capital how could they carry out that 'removal' of the leaders that they considered essential for their victory?[37]

His policy was to 'put out the eyes of the British', and he devoted much of his energy to counter-intelligence. In this he had much success. 'For the first time in the history of separatism we Irish had a better intelligence service than the British', one IRA member wrote. 'This was Michael Collins's great achievement and it is one for which every Irishman should honour his memory.'[38]

Collins's first step was to build up an extensive network of casual informants who could scrutinise the actions of the crown forces. 'There were spies everywhere', the British army lamented, 'and a very large percentage of the population were ready to act as extra eyes and ears for Sinn Fein and for the IRA even if they were not prepared to fight for them.'[39] 'Hotel waiters, tramway conductors, bus drivers, tap-room loafers and members of the Cumann na mBan [a republican women's organisation] were all willing agents', one British intelligence chief recalled.[40] The most important informants were in the postal, telegraph and telephone services. A highly developed IRA organisation copied most official communications passing through these channels: on two occasions in 1920 Collins captured Dublin Castle's mail bags, with the connivance of local postal officials.[41]

The next step in the IRA strategy was to actively penetrate the opposing security and intelligence organisations. Initially, this effort was focused on the Irish police forces. Pro-Sinn Féin officers in the RIC and DMP were persuaded to stay on, rather than resign, so that they could supply information: for example, when one man told Michael Collins that he intended to leave the RIC, he received an immediate response that 'under no circumstances' was he to resign, and that if he did so he would be 'looked upon as a coward'.[42] Numerous other RIC officers, some within the Crime Special Branch, secretly worked for the IRA throughout this period. Collins also had priceless moles deep within the DMP and Dublin Castle. Ned Broy, a confidential typist at DMP headquarters, provided high quality information from 1917 until 1921, including the tip-off for the 'German Plot' arrests in 1918. David Neligan was a detective in the DMP G Division who met with Collins and pointed out officials for assassination. (He subsequently wrote a colourful book about his experiences.) Two other detectives, Joe Kavanagh and Jim McNamara, also provided information. Perhaps the most celebrated example of Collins's achievement came in April 1919, when Broy smuggled him into the G Division document room, where he spent the whole night examining police files on the Irish Volunteers – his own file made particularly fascinating reading![43] While much attention has focused on Collin's activities in Dublin, the IRA in other parts of the country were equally successful in penetrating the security forces: Florence O'Donoghue, for example, built up an impressive system in Co. Cork.[44]

The IRA used the information collected from these sources to go on the offensive. This campaign began with the boycott and ostracising of the RIC. In 1919 there were 11,000 armed officers and men in the RIC, situated in 1,299 barracks. Mostly sons of farmers, 70 per cent Catholic, they were well respected, closely integrated with the community, and had excellent knowledge of local events.[45] But now Sinn Féin decried them as the instruments of British repression and called for 'that terrible weapon, the boycott, immensely cruel' to be used against them: 'No one would speak to them or to their wives and children', a contemporary wrote, 'shopkeepers would not serve them, nor undertakers bury them.'[46] The societal consensus essential to all police work unravelled. This, combined with IRA intimidation, meant that members of the populace, even loyalists, became unwilling to give information to the police. One RIC Divisional Inspector complained: 'Before the war we knew everybody and what he was doing ... Now we know nothing! The people are dumb.'[47]

His words of warning – 'Beware of a silent Irishman. He is dangerous' – were prescient. The IRA quickly escalated from social warfare to more violent tactics. Much of this violence targeted police officers with an official intelligence function. In 1919 Collins created his infamous 'Squad', a group of hardened gunmen tasked with carrying out targeted assassinations on the streets of Dublin. Collins first turned them on the G Division of the DMP: five were killed or wounded in 1919 and 1920. Outside Dublin many of the assassination attempts on the RIC were aimed at Crime Special Branch officers, especially those who actively pursued Sinn Féin or IRA leaders. Because of inadequate record-keeping, when one of these men was killed or quit the force, he often took with him all the intelligence that had been built up over many years.[48] The attack on the intelligence apparatus was part of a wider IRA campaign against the RIC and the institutions of the British state. Regular RIC officers were assaulted and killed, weapons and ammunition were stolen, outlying barracks were raided and burnt to the ground. As a result, the RIC vacated 434 isolated barracks (approximately one-third) and concentrated in better-defended locations, abandoning large areas of the country. The RIC became detached from local communities and devoted much of its energy to simply defending itself from attack.[49]

By the end of 1919 the IRA had been successful in 'putting out the eyes of the British'. The British army lamented that 'the police source of information, at that time the only one on which the authorities could rely, was dried up and the intelligence service paralysed'.[50] This led to a doomed attempt at intelligence reform by the Dublin Castle authorities. The driving force behind the security policy was Field Marshal Lord French, an Anglo-Irish landowner and famous wartime military commander who had been appointed as Lord Lieutenant to Ireland in early 1918 with 'virtually dictatorial powers'.[51] At the end of 1919 he despondently concluded:

> Our secret service is simply non-existent. What masquerades for such a service is nothing but a delusion and a snare. The DMP are absolutely demoralized and the RIC will be in the same case very soon if we do not quickly set our house in order.

He set up a secret committee in December 1919 to advise on how to improve the intelligence system.[52]

This committee recommended two main steps. The first could be termed the 'Ulsterisation' of the Irish police. Chief Commissioner T. J. Smith of the Belfast police, a highly partisan Orangeman, was brought to Dublin as acting Inspector General of the RIC. One of his colleagues from Ulster, Detective Inspector W. C. Forbes Redmond, was made Assistant Commissioner of the DMP and put in charge of the G Division, which he attempted to revive through the importation of officers from Belfast. This coincided with an effort to sideline prominent Catholics in Dublin Castle, such as James MacMahon (the Under Secretary) and Joseph Byrne (RIC Inspector General). They were seen as, at best, insufficiently opposed to Sinn Féin, and, at worst, traitorous. It is possible to detect a 're-Orangeing' of Dublin Castle in this period, as French surrounded himself with staunch loyalists.[53] The British government, preoccupied with the Paris Peace Conference and other crises, allowed the management of Ireland to fall to an unrepresentative group of Anglo-Irish Ascendancy and Orange figures – a last, futile stand of Irish unionism.

Lord French's other initiative was to call on the assistance of intelligence chiefs in London. In April 1919 he had unsuccessfully requested the loan of the head of MI5, Captain Vernon Kell.[54] When he turned to the newly knighted Sir Basil Thomson in early 1920, he received a more favourable response. Thomson was happy to expand his Irish activities because he was attempting to build an intelligence empire in Britain. In May 1919, in response to hysteria over the threat of Bolshevik revolution, he had been appointed as the head of a new Directorate of Intelligence. Incorporating the Special Branch, it was given responsibility for combating all domestic subversion and for analysing all intelligence on revolutionary movements for the British cabinet. Thomson despatched a number of agents to Ireland in early 1920. For a time, they were frequent passengers on the mailboats between Holyhead and Kingstown (now Dún Laoghaire). A regular Special Branch detective on these boats recalled stumbling across one undercover agent after he noticed how a man 'changed his complete make-up on the ship, put on a false moustache, parted his hair in the middle, changed his suit and hat, and landed in Ireland a totally different citizen from that he had been when he left England'. When challenged, the newly disguised man produced credentials from Scotland Yard. 'By jove', the detective remarked with a laugh, 'you and I are in the same business!'[55]

Both these attempts to bolster the intelligence system met with immediate, bloody and effective IRA responses. The rebels had some success in uncovering and eliminating the agents despatched by Sir Basil Thomson. The most famous case involved John Charles Byrnes, who went under the alias John Jameson: the First Lord of the Admiralty, Walter Long, later told the British cabinet that he was 'the best Secret Service man we had'. The thirty-four-year-old had the appearance of a well-travelled seafarer: he was small, with a very muscular build, and his arms were covered with a series of tattoos. Byrnes had made a career of deception. He had originally infiltrated the Sailors', Soldiers, and Airmen's Union in London as an undercover agent of A2 Branch, a highly secretive British military agency created after the war to combat Bolshevik agitation in the armed forces. He was then borrowed by Sir Basil Thomson for use in Ireland. He first won the confidence of IRA leaders in London, who asked him to travel to Dublin. There, he was able to secure an audience with Collins – a considerable achievement that could have had dangerous implications for the IRA leadership. Yet his identity was soon revealed by a leak from Dublin Castle. Detective Inspector Redmond boasted to a group of DMP detectives that a British agent in Dublin for no more than two days had been able to meet Collins; when this was relayed by IRA moles, the connection with Byrnes was made. (There is also some evidence that an IRA mole within Scotland Yard may have tipped Collins off about Byrnes's previous activities as an A2 Branch agent.) Byrnes was shot dead by the

Squad on 2 March 1920. One of his executioners, Paddy Daly, later recalled the incident:

> I told him that we were satisfied he was a spy, that he was going to die, and that if he wanted to say any prayers he could do so. The spy jumped to attention immediately and said, 'You are right. God bless the King. I would love to die for him.' He saluted and there was not a quiver on him.[56]

Byrnes's unhappy experience appears to have been typical of Thomson's agents in Ireland. The army concluded that 'a small amount of general and political information was collected through this source but none on which any action was possible'.[57]

The second aspect of the IRA response was a direct assault on the leadership in Dublin Castle. In its most daring act the IRA narrowly failed to assassinate Lord French. Detective Inspector Redmond was killed by Collins's Squad in January 1920 while walking back to his hotel in Harcourt Street; his movements were known because he had unfortunately chosen Jim McNamara (one of Collins's secret DMP helpers) as his confidential clerk. On 26 March 1920 Alan Bell, a member of Lord French's secret intelligence committee and former RIC district inspector, was taken off a tram on his way to work and shot dead. He had been investigating Sinn Féin finances, as well as the attacks on French and Redmond.[58] After this, the DMP 'for political purposes ... practically ceased to function' and became a neutral force in the ensuing struggle.[59] The remaining detectives in the G Division stayed well out of trouble. One colleague described how two officers tasked with investigating the IRA 'spent each day on a pub crawl and did no investigating as they wanted to stay alive ... they drank steadily from 10 a.m. until 6 p.m. – all whiskey – only stopping briefly for lunch.'[60]

The first phase of the IRA campaign brought about the destruction of the Dublin Castle intelligence system, severely weakened British rule in many parts of Ireland and allowed Sinn Féin to go a long way towards creating its own 'counter-state'. This led to a new security response between January and April 1920: the authorities decided on a policy of coercion towards the Sinn Féin movement. In this second phase the British army, which hitherto had stood aside from the fight, began to play a leading role. Army units accompanied the RIC on patrol, carried out raids and guarded barracks. They took the lead in the arrest, conviction and internment of prominent Sinn Féin and IRA members: 317 persons were detained between January and April 1920.[61]

Army officers were immediately faced with the problem of a lack of intelligence. They admitted that their information 'as to who was or who was not mixed up in the Sinn Féin movement was practically nil'; at the same time, it was clear that police intelligence was little better.[62] As a result, from early 1920 the army began to develop its own intelligence system, 'filtering through from the smallest units and detachments up to the central office at G.H.Q.' in Dublin.[63] The intelligence staff at GHQ was augmented, with Brigadier-General (later Colonel) J. E. S. Brind taking charge and Colonel S. Hill-Dillon, formerly of MI5, as his assistant. They created a registry and card index system, with the aim of devising 'an Irish Republican Army List'. Intelligence officers, assigned to divisions, brigades and battalions, were expected to recruit informers and liaise with the police. Their degree of activity depended on the level of IRA violence and the proficiency of the RIC in their districts. Unsurprisingly, the 6th Division in Munster, which was the most troubled area in the country, had the greatest need for intelligence: it expended £2,032 in secret service funds in the twelve months after 1 April 1920. Its divisional intelligence officer, Captain J. O'G. Kelly, was particularly industrious and was commended for his 'fearlessness and keen intelligence'. In contrast, the 5th Division (in the central part of the country) spent £320 and the 1st Division (in the north) just £14, which illustrates the lower level of IRA violence and the better state of the RIC in those areas.[64] The army had come late to the show, and lacked basic knowledge at first, but out of necessity gradually built up a wide-reaching intelligence system.

The most striking feature of the military intelligence system was the extent to which it relied on the responsibility, ability and zeal of relatively junior intelligence officers at the battalion and company level. They were mostly young, rarely had any intelligence training and were usually new to their areas. Blending staff work with improvised detective activity, they were compelled to build up 'a sort of local secret service'. This meant 'considerable personal risk' and also the use of techniques of disguise and agent-handling not on the Sandhurst curriculum.[65] A youthful Kenneth Strong, a Scotsman who went on to serve as Eisenhower's intelligence officer during the Second World War, was thrown into this work as a Company Intelligence Officer with the Royal Scots Fusiliers. He described how he received £5 per month to pay secret agents:

> My agents were not of very high calibre. Sometimes a railway porter who noted suspicious train travellers; sometimes a shopkeeper who might report unusual purchases of food or medical supplies; a bartender who had noted the arrival of strangers in the neighbourhood. My area of responsibility was so small that unusual happenings soon came to the notice of local inhabitants. Contacts with my so-called agents had to be personal and this could be an exceedingly dangerous undertaking for the informant. To get to a rendezvous I would disguise myself, usually as the

owner of a small donkey cart, but my English accent was against me and I had several narrow escapes.[66]

The army somewhat defensively concluded that 'the results obtained in Ireland were remarkable ... considering how few of the officers employed on intelligence duties had had any previous experience or training, and when it is remembered that the system grew up almost haphazard and depended more on enthusiasm than on any instructions from above'.[67]

In most of the country, military intelligence officers, though donning occasional disguise, were attached to uniformed units and generally operated alongside them. The situation was different in the capital, where Dublin District Command was responsible for a large, sophisticated and purely clandestine secret service. This had its origins in the summer of 1919, when a small group of officers began undercover intelligence work against the IRA on their own initiative. In March 1920 they were taken under army control and formalised as the 'Special Branch' of Dublin District Command. Two months later their activities were expanded and placed under the control of a high-ranking intelligence officer, Lieutenant-Colonel Walter C. Wilson, a former English rugby international who was wounded twice on the Western Front, before serving on the British military missions to the United States and the Baltic states. With MI5 assistance, he formed a school of instruction in Hounslow (near London) from where recruits, mostly retired army officers, were sent to Dublin. These men operated in plain clothes, took up normal lodgings and attempted to blend in with the normal life of the city:

> Men were placed successfully in most of the steamship companies trading with Dublin, on the railways, as journalists or farmers and even in the I.R.A. They made friends with Dublin citizens of every class and both sexes, they mixed with crowds and they were arrested with officers and men of the I.R.A.

Some frequented the Cairo Café on Grafton Street and became known to the IRA as the 'Cairo Gang'. Although taken over and legitimised by the regular army, the Dublin District Special Branch maintained a distinct and independent ethos. The army later admitted that it was a 'peculiar organization, as secret service organizations generally are': it was built up by 'enthusiastic amateurs', it had its own 'constitution', and 'in the event of its official head taking action to which the original creators objected, they did not hesitate to raise their objections in unmistakable fashion'. Its members did not just collect information, but also took daring action, sometimes outside the law – an army history euphemistically noted that the organisation was 'partly pure intelligence and partly executive'.[68]

One member, Captain R. D. Jeune, has left a memoir describing his experience. Jeune had served as an interpreter with the 1st Indian Cavalry Division in France in 1914 and 1915, and then commanded the 94th and 24th Trench Mortar Companies on the Western Front, participating in the battles of the Somme and Ypres. After the war he took part in the British Military Mission in Poland. On his return he joined up with the 'rather hastily improvised Intelligence Organisation' for Ireland and after a short course of instruction at Hounslow was sent to Dublin in early summer 1920. He recalled how the first batch of men initially posed as Royal Engineer officers, but this 'rather futile procedure' was soon dropped, and a variety of covers were later adopted. Their work consisted of 'getting to know the town thoroughly, tailing "Shinners", and carrying out small raids, with a view to collecting all possible information which would lead us eventually to stamping out the revolt'. One of Jeune's more memorable actions involved a surreptitious night raid on the house of the Sinn Féin leader Arthur Griffith, from which he carried off a number of 'subversive documents'. Jeune noted with some satisfaction a report in the Irish press the next day that Griffith's house had been raided by 'expert Cracksmen'.[69]

The Dublin District Special Branch grew rapidly during 1920: it consisted of seven officers on 1 June, fifty-one in July, and eighty-two in August, peaking at ninety-seven in November. In the course of the 1920–1 financial year it accounted for £20,000, which dwarfed the military intelligence effort in the rest of the country. The police authorities acknowledged that these officers were 'of great value in collecting intelligence in Dublin' and comprised the most important source during the summer and autumn of 1920 – they were commended for achieving 'admirable results ... in the face of grave personal risk and danger'.[70] Even their Irish opponents conceded that they were 'crack operators' and 'brave men who carried their lives in their hands'.[71] In effect, the Dublin District Special Branch replaced the shattered G Division of the DMP and became the state's secret service in the capital. This is illustrated by the dwindling of the DMP's share of the secret service fund to just £405 for the 1920–1 financial year.[72]

The gradual increase in the security role of the army was part of an attempt at coercion by the Dublin Castle administration in the first four months of 1920, leading to the incarceration of a large number of prominent IRA members. However, this had little impact on the IRA campaign, which graduated to larger attacks on police barracks and government offices: for example, over the Easter weekend 300 barracks and twenty-two income tax offices were burned.[73] The government's coercive measures also proved unsustainable. IRA prisoners went on hunger strike, demanding treatment as political prisoners, and this led to mass demonstrations culminating in a general strike. Dublin Castle backed down and released all those captured on 14 April 1920, much to the chagrin of the British army and local police forces, which had put so much effort into the initial round-up.

The botched handling of this episode, along with the continuing rise in IRA violence, demonstrated to London the incompetence and powerlessness of the Dublin Castle leadership. In the spring of 1920 the British government finally turned its full attention to the incipient rebellion on the other side of the Irish Sea. Whitehall's most senior civil servant, Sir Warren Fisher, was sent to carry out a review of the administration. He produced a damning report. He found 'absolute chaos in Ireland' and a Castle administration that simply did not administer: 'The Government strikes one as almost woodenly stupid and quite devoid of imagination', he scathingly concluded.[74] The result was a radical reform of the Irish administration, a thorough review of security policy and new initiatives to bolster intelligence collection. This third phase of organisational experimentation would last from May to November 1920.

The first step was a radical overhaul of the leadership of the Irish administration. At the top, the bluff, Canadian-born Liberal MP, Hamar Greenwood, became Chief Secretary for Ireland. Of limited ability, he never fully grasped the challenge in Ireland and was always one step behind events – one contemporary described him as 'a Canadian bagman and a windbag at that'.[75] Far more impressive was the troika of high-flying Whitehall civil servants handed control of Dublin Castle. Sir John Anderson was made Joint Under Secretary. He was widely regarded as one of the most brilliant administrators of his generation; he would go on to make the uncommon switch from civil servant to minister, serving as Home Secretary and Chancellor of the Exchequer during the Second World War (and lending his name to the famous Anderson air raid shelter). Alfred W. Cope became Assistant Under Secretary. Widely known as 'Andy', and a protégé of Prime Minister Lloyd George, he began as a detective in the Customs and Excise department before attaining a high rank in the Ministry of Pensions. The third member of this remarkable team was Mark Sturgis. A debonair aristocrat, educated at Eton and Christ Church, Oxford, his love of horses and high society was allowed full expression during his time at Dublin Castle.[76] One contemporary described him as a 'level-headed, cool man' who mixed easily in all circles.[77]

This complete overhaul of the civil administration was accompanied by two radical changes to the leadership of the security forces in Ireland. In March 1920 General Sir Nevil Macready was chosen as the new Commander-in-Chief of the British army in Ireland. His previous experiences made him ideally suited for this position: he had commanded troops in aid of the civil power in England and Belfast, before serving as London Metropolitan Police Commissioner.[78] Macready had little love for Ireland: 'I loathe the country ... and its people', he once commented, 'with a depth deeper than the sea and more violent than that which I feel against the Boche.'[79] His main goal was to protect the army, arguing that it should be either given the tools to fight a proper war against the IRA, or kept out of it altogether. Nonetheless, he was politically unbiased and aware of the futility of trying to solve a political problem with coercion alone. Macready refused control of the Irish police, a decision that he later regretted. Instead, the police was placed under the command of another new introduction from England, Major-General Hugh Tudor. Unlike Macready, Tudor had no experience of police work and little aptitude for the job, and he was selected by the Secretary of State for War, Winston Churchill, because the two had served together on the Western Front.[80] Tudor became a hawk on security issues and failed to recognise the political dimension of the Irish problem; history has not been kind to him.

These men directed the campaign against the Irish separatist movement until the signing of the Anglo-Irish Treaty (and, excepting Tudor, they would exert great influence on British policy towards Ireland for some time afterwards). On their appointment, they initially made an attempt at conciliation. It was hoped that moderate Sinn Féin could be induced to work the Government of Ireland Act, a new Home Rule settlement then passing through parliament. However, this attitude only bolstered the morale of Sinn Féin, weakened that of the crown forces and led to an escalation of violence during the summer of 1920. IRA tactics shifted from attacks on individual policemen and raids on police barracks to ambushes against army or police patrols conducted by 'flying columns' – groups of about twenty-five armed men on full-time active duty, supported by local IRA companies. This was the ideal form of offensive and defensive warfare. 'By trial and error', according to one historian, 'the IRA had stumbled on the type of warfare ... extensively copied since from Latin America to Vietnam, in which the advantage of a committed and motivated force, local knowledge and support outweighs the numerical superiority and vast armed resources of the occupying force.' Its impact can be seen in the casualty figures for crown forces: in the first six months of 1920, just 60 policemen and soldiers were killed by the IRA; 495 died in the following twelve months.[81]

In July 1920 the worsening military situation led the government to consider a policy of rigorous coercion. Two options were available. The simpler was to impose martial law on the country and ask the military to suppress the rebellion. But this was politically unacceptable. Instead, it was decided that the civil administration and the police would retain responsibility for the maintenance of

law and order. Yet, though the veneer of civil primacy over security was maintained, the RIC in fact became heavily militarised. They were granted many of
the powers of martial law by the Restoration of Order in Ireland Act of 9 August
1920. As it was almost impossible to obtain recruits in Ireland, large numbers of
ex-servicemen from England were encouraged to join the RIC. Eventually numbering some 9,500, these new men were barely trained and hastily equipped:
because of their khaki army trousers and dark green police tunics, many Irish
derisively nicknamed them the 'Black and Tans', after a Limerick Hunt. From
July 1920 they were joined by the Auxiliary Division, a group drawn exclusively
from British ex-officers and paid a highly attractive £1 a day. Comprising 2,214
men, they were divided into mobile, heavily armed companies, operating virtually independently of the rest of the RIC.[82] 'They were a thoroughly dangerous
mob', David Neligan recounted, 'and far more intelligent than the Tans.'[83]

The decision to wage a 'police war' had significant consequences for the
organisation of intelligence. In May 1920 Colonel Ormonde de l'Epée Winter
was appointed as Deputy Chief of Police and Director of Intelligence for Ireland.
It was clear that Irish intelligence was deficient, and that there was a lack of co-
ordination between the RIC, the army and Thomson's Directorate of Intelligence
in London. Winter was given the task of creating a unified intelligence system
under police control. The military was initially happy to cede this role to Winter
and intended to graft their existing system onto his: Macready said that the way
was open for Winter to make himself 'top dog' in Irish intelligence.[84]

Winter had a fairly conventional career: public school, the army and then
India, where he was mainly concerned with pursuing gentlemanly sports such
as tiger-hunting and pig-sticking. This was followed by service on the Western
Front.[85] He had no particular experience of intelligence work, but he made up
for this by conforming to the stock image of the spymaster: he had greased black
hair, wore a monocle, permanently kept a cigarette dangling from the lips and
surrounded himself with a dense cloak of secrecy – he preferred to be known
by the codename 'O'.[86] 'He looks like a wicked little white snake', one colleague
recorded, 'is clever as paint, probably entirely non-moral, a first-class horseman,
a card genius, knows several languages, is a super sleuth, and a most amazing
original.'[87] His 'non-moral' and 'original' character is illustrated by some of the
extraordinary projects that he flirted with after finishing his work in Ireland. In
the 1920s he offered his services to an Eurasian adventurer named Cherif Tidjani
who, under the instructions of Abd-el-Krim, the leader of the Riffs, was trying to
mount an insurrection against the Spaniards in Morocco. When this fell through,
he was approached by a Slovak party and asked to give advice on how to organise
a successful revolution against the Czech government; the plot collapsed when

the Slovak leader was arrested and sentenced to fifteen years' imprisonment. It is ironic that a man who had been at the forefront of the campaign against the Irish rebellion was so eager to lend his experiences to rebels in other parts of the world.[88]

On his arrival in Dublin, Winter threw himself into a number of ambitious 'cloak and dagger' schemes in an attempt to produce quick results. One of his first ideas was 'to photograph the entire population of Ireland back and front' to aid the identification of rebels.[89] This proved impractical, but he did set up a photographic section in his central Intelligence Bureau that tried to build up a photographic index of all suspected rebels – this led to the apprehension of some active IRA men.[90] Of less value was Winter's importation of fifty bloodhounds from England: he admitted that 'their employment seldom achieved satisfactory results.'[91] Similarly, a joint attempt with Sir Basil Thomson to encourage people to send anonymous information to an address in London backfired: it was manipulated by 'irresponsible jesters or active rebels', and merely produced 'accusations against well-known loyalists.'[92] With obvious relish, Winter also became personally involved in undercover detective work. On one occasion, he boasted to his colleagues about donning a wig and false moustache and 'pinching' Michael Collins's 'war chest' from a Dublin bank – Sturgis correctly remarked that this was probably illegal and 'hardly his job.'[93]

The cornerstone of Winter's intelligence offensive against the IRA was a secret service operated from a newly created 'London Bureau'. (This replaced the network started by Sir Basil Thomson, who conceded that Winter should have control over all future agents sent from England, thus ending his brief overlordship.) Winter's London Bureau was born in July 1920 from an alliance with the Indian secret service. It was initially headed by Charles Tegart, a famous Indian policeman regarded as 'one of the most expert Criminal Investigation officers in the British Empire'. The Prime Minister personally requested the Secretary of State for India to release Tegart for this purpose. He was assisted by G. C. Denham, a young policeman who travelled from Singapore at short notice over the summer. At the outset, Tegart warned that he did not have an ' "Open Sesame", some quick & ready method of establishing an Intelligence system in Ireland', pointing out that the suppression of the Indian revolutionary movement was 'the result of five years plodding and patient investigation'. He wanted to collect all papers on the subject first, sift through them, create card indices, compile history sheets on the 'enemy organisation', and only then suggest 'lines for attacking it'. This did not fit with Winter's desire to quickly despatch as many undercover agents as possible to obtain immediate results.[94] Their relationship soured, and, just four months after arriving, the Indian intelligence officers broke with

Winter and returned to their original organisations, leaving ill-feeling all around. The Bureau was next taken over by a military officer named Jeffries (with the rather unimaginative codename 'J'), who had been an undercover member of the army's Dublin District Special Branch. He was assisted by Major Cecil Aylmer Cameron, who later took over control of the operation. Cameron had run a military intelligence network in the Low Countries during the war. In keeping with many British intelligence professionals in this period, he was a rather unstable character: he had been imprisoned for insurance fraud along with his morphine-addicted wife in 1911 and would commit suicide in 1924.[95]

The Bureau recruited Irishmen living in Britain, supplied them with a special secret ink considered 'immune from discovery' and sent them to Ireland. Each agent then corresponded with the head of the London Bureau via a cover address. Sixty agents were despatched during the eight or nine months that the scheme lasted. Winter later boasted that 'only one of these agents met with a violent end', also that the network collected information that saved lives and prevented ambushes. However, a number of the agents were unreliable, and it is unlikely that they provided much important intelligence from within the Sinn Féin movement. This may account for their lack of casualties. The army certainly took a dim view of their effectiveness.[96]

The activities of the London Bureau, together with the rapid expansion of military intelligence, led to an influx of 'sleuths' in the summer of 1920, especially in the capital: Winter later recalled that 'an attempt was made to flood the country with agents, who would supply the ordinary information usually available to the Police under normal conditions.'[97] This coincided with a concerted crack-down by the heavily reinforced RIC and army, acting under the Restoration of Order in Ireland Act. There was an improvement in the intelligence available to the crown forces and many IRA men were forced to go 'on the run'. Captain Jeune of the Dublin District Special Branch recalled that 'in November, information was coming in well and we were beginning to get on top of the IRA, who were becoming desperate.'[98]

The increased intelligence effort did not go unnoticed by Michael Collins, who took a number of steps to neutralise the threat. At least one agent of the London Bureau was killed by the IRA, although his identity is not recorded. According to Winter, his death was due to his own 'carelessness', as he had left incriminating documents written in normal ink in his hotel room.[99] A much luckier, if completely untrustworthy, London Bureau agent, about whom many details survive, went by the name of F. Digby Hardy. (His real name was J. L. Gooding.) A lifelong fraudster, who had been in and out of prison since 1886, Hardy was serving a five-year jail sentence in England when he wrote to Lord

French, offering to work as a secret service man against the IRA. He was released and sent by the London Bureau to Ireland, where he met with Arthur Griffith. According to Winter, he betrayed his masters and 'proved himself a villain of the first water': he offered to lure Sir Basil Thomson to a meeting on Kingstown pier so that he could be assassinated by the IRA. Rather than take up Hardy's proposal, the Sinn Féin leaders decided to use him for propaganda purposes. Griffith invited press reporters to a secret meeting on 16 September 1920, convinced Hardy that the journalists were senior IRA leaders and urged him to present his proposal. Hardy duly explained to the assembled group his plot to kill Thomson, describing him as 'the man responsible for all the dirty work in Ireland'. At this point, Griffith dramatically exposed Hardy as a 'scoundrel', provided evidence of his prior criminal convictions, and warned him to leave Ireland immediately. The press wrote this up in full, and it led to the belief in Ireland that the British were willing to allow any criminal out of jail to fight Sinn Féin.[100] Having managed to offend both sides in the bloody intelligence war, Hardy was fortunate to escape from this episode alive.

The IRA had even greater success in penetrating the new intelligence system being created by the British military. Collins and his lieutenants bribed some British officers to provide information, although they were never fully trusted.[101] A more reliable source were the civilian clerks used by the British army – many of them worked for the IRA. The most important were two female clerks in Dublin and Cork. Lily Mernin, a young typist who worked in British army GHQ, provided daily copies to Michael Collins of confidential documents, including details of premises about to be raided, and names and addresses of undercover army officers. Her counterpart in Cork was Josephine Marchmount, a typist working for the British 6th Division headquarters. She provided a steady stream of secret army documents between 1919 and 1921, many of which can now be found in O'Donoghue's private papers.[102] In addition to these moles at the heart of the British army, the IRA could rely on the extended network of casual informers – lodgers, bartenders, cleaning ladies, cooks, post office employees, telephone operators and sailors – to uncover British intelligence operatives.

Through these means, IRA headquarters was able to identify members of the army's Dublin District Special Branch. It was decided to kill a large number of these men on Sunday morning, 21 November. The primary objective was to relieve some of the pressure from the IRA; but it was also a calculated political gesture to demonstrate that the IRA was capable of large-scale operations in the heart of the capital. Planning was entrusted to a twenty-seven-year-old Dublin man named Seán Russell (who would mastermind an IRA bombing campaign in England two decades later). Men from Collins's Squad and the Dublin IRA carried out attacks on at least twenty individuals in twelve different locations. Twelve military officers were shot dead in hotels and lodgings houses, often in their beds, sometimes alongside their wives. Four officers were wounded. (On the same morning, two officers of the Auxiliaries were killed by an IRA party guarding the assassination squads. A landlord was also shot dead.) There have been some erroneous conclusions about the identity of those killed, which reflects continuing confusion over the organisations active in Irish intelligence at this time. Two of the British officers were victims of mistaken identity, and the role of two others is unclear. However, eight were certainly intelligence officers, either part of Dublin District Special Branch or Winter's intelligence department. The reputation of this day as 'Bloody Sunday' was fully earned later that afternoon when the police raided a Gaelic football game in Croke Park in search of the gunmen and opened fire, killing eleven spectators and one player.[103]

One of Collins's principal intelligence officers, Frank Thornton, boasted that 'the British Secret Service was wiped out on the 21st November, 1920'.[104] Although this is an exaggeration, the Dublin District Special Branch was 'temporarily paralysed'. Several of its most efficient members were murdered and the rest were brought into the Castle and the Central Hotel for safety. 'This ... greatly decreased the opportunities for obtaining information and for re-establishing anything in the nature of secret service', the army later recorded.[105] Captain Jeune recalled that 'those of us who had survived were shut up under guard in a hotel, from where it was impracticable to do any useful work'. To some extent the organisation was broken up: Jeune left Ireland at that time and did not return, while Jeffries left Dublin to take over Winter's London Bureau.[106] Therefore, at least in the short term, the IRA action had the intended effect on the intelligence situation.

Its political effect was also dramatic, especially when coupled with events in Co. Cork: the most violent incident of the guerrilla campaign occurred one week later, when an IRA ambush at Kilmichael wiped out an Auxiliary patrol, leaving seventeen dead.[107] This led to a fourth phase in Britain's struggle against the IRA – a period of sustained coercion that lasted from December 1920 until the truce on 11 July 1921. In December martial law was proclaimed in the south, while in the rest of the country there was a major crack-down. The death penalty was enforced for carrying arms, curfews extended, and internment of IRA suspects introduced. Large-scale sweeps by troops and police in rural areas, and systematic house-by-house searches in urban quarters placed considerable pressure on IRA flying columns. 600 IRA men from all districts were immediately rounded up, and by the end of June 4,500 were interned in camps at Ballykinlar, Spike Island, Bere Island and the Curragh. The military believed that 'from this time the initiative may be said to have passed to the crown forces for the first time since May, 1920'.[108]

There were also changes in the organisation and effectiveness of British intelligence. After spending six months engaged in 'cloak and dagger' detective work, and a frustratingly slow search for staff and office space, Winter finally began to build up a countrywide system that sought to integrate army and police intelligence activities. The result was a complicated system, consisting of a Central Bureau under his direction and nine 'Local Centres' in Dublin, Belfast, Dundalk, Athlone, Galway, Kildare, Limerick, Clonmel and Cork (with a 'sub-centre' in Derry). Military intelligence officers with police rank staffed these offices, recruited a network of local agents and made sure that information was exchanged between the RIC and army. During the first half of 1921 this system was unhurriedly rolled out through the country. In December 1920 Winter took over control of the Dublin District Special Branch from the army and renamed it the D Branch – it effectively became the Local Centre for Dublin. (Lieutenant-Colonel Wilson resigned in protest and was replaced by one of Winter's men, David Boyle.)[109] In January 1921 Winter created the first Local Centre in Belfast. Other Local Centres were not set up until March or April; the last, in Clonmel, was only formed in July one week before the truce. Winter's share of the Secret Service Vote gives some indication of the growing scale of his operation: in January 1921 his expenditure was only £655, in contrast to the £3,380 spent by the army's Dublin District Special Branch; by June 1921 he accounted for £10,000 per month, along with an additional undisclosed sum from RIC funds. By this time his intelligence staff had grown to 150, not including the undercover officers of the D Branch, or the many informers they employed.[110]

The flow of intelligence, and the pressure on the IRA, increased again in the early months of 1921. In Dublin the D Branch was rebuilt. Former or serving British military officers continued to man the senior ranks, but with money plentiful, a wide assortment of 'sub-agents' or 'touts' were recruited, often with little discrimination. One observer described them as 'poor wretches who were on the look-out for easy money'.[111] In a new innovation, Winter formed an RIC 'Identification Squad' and set it to work in Dublin. Led by Sergeant Igoe, it consisted of handpicked RIC officers, two from each county, who could recognise Sinn Féin and IRA leaders from their districts. Dressed in plain clothes, they wandered the streets of the capital and were able to make some arrests.[112] During this period raids on Dáil and IRA offices in the capital led to the capture of large quantities of important documents, including those of Michael Collins.[113] British activities in Dublin made it extremely difficult for the Dáil departments and IRA headquarters staff to function. The discovery of reports from IRA moles in

Dublin Castle among the captured documents also led to a tightening of British security.

In the south-west, after martial law was imposed, military intelligence officers recruited more local informers and benefited from a brief surge of information given by the public. The Divisional Intelligence Officer, Captain Kelly, had forty-five agents working for him in January 1921, of whom twenty-three were considered reliable: one gave information that resulted in the death of wanted members of an IRA Active Service Unit.[114] The RIC, strengthened by the Black and Tans and Auxiliaries, and accompanied by military units, began once more to assert itself. Winter recalled that 'the ordinary channels of general police information were once again opened (and) the necessity to flood the country with minor agents gradually disappeared.'[115]

As before, this led to a response by the IRA – a combination of more audacious penetration of the British secret service, targeted assassination of active intelligence officers and ruthless killing of any members of the public suspected of giving information.

Perhaps the most impressive feat of Collins's organisation was its penetration of Winter's highly secretive D Branch. For sheer audacity, David Neligan's actions stand out. Neligan had been a valuable IRA mole within the DMP G Division, but could provide little information after the DMP was cut out of the security picture in 1921. As a consequence, he decided to volunteer to work as a D Branch agent. After a light grilling by Alfred Cope, he was directed to Winter's office, where his application was processed by Major Poges, 'a hardy-looking fellow of about fifty with a pugnacious expression.' The principal method of vetting was to ask Neligan to swear on the Bible a curious oath of fidelity to the secret service:

> I ... solemnly swear by Almighty God that I will faithfully perform the duties assigned to me as a member of His Majesty's secret service: that I will obey implicitly those placed over me: that I shall never betray such service or anything connected with it even after I have left it. If I should fail to keep this oath in every particular I realise that vengeance will pursue me to the ends of the earth. So help me God.

Neligan was given an automatic pistol and ammunition, a crash course on secret ink (urine was suggested), a curfew pass signed by the British army commander in Dublin and the codename 'No. 68'. He was assigned to Kingstown, in the suburbs of Dublin. Poges told him to resign from the DMP and to take a job 'as cover'. 'Join the I.R.A., old boy', the Major recommended, 'and if you catch Collins it will be £10,000 for you.' In the end he received £7 per week. He was also shown a sign of recognition 'somewhat like those of the Freemasons', which he could use when identifying himself to other agents.

Neligan's day-to-day handler was Captain Catchpole, a young 'foxy-faced, dapper, handsome' English military intelligence officer, who met him frequently on the Kingstown pier. He had an unusual style of language, a mixture of expressions picked up during service in India ('pukka', 'gun-wallah') combined with 'a share of London thieves' argot ('rumble', 'grass', 'crib'). 'A likeable fellow', Neligan wrote, 'he regarded his duty as a job of work, and did not engage in any high-falutin' sentiments, unlike some of our bombasts'. Neligan spent his time as a British secret agent concocting reports showing the IRA to be on an unstoppable march to victory. Though complete 'fairy-tales', they were well received by his British handlers. His reward was promotion to 'paymaster' for his area after the truce. Even when Neligan joined the police force of the new Irish government after the signing of the treaty, his former double role was not suspected. He received a note of thanks from Henry Tudor and was awarded an annual pension of £65 per annum for his services.[116]

At least one other man, an ex-officer of the British army, succeeded in gaining acceptance to the secret service organisation in Dublin on the instructions of Michael Collins. More incredibly, senior members of the IRA intelligence staff used their contacts with these double agents to pass themselves off as 'touts' and socialise with members of the British network. When Frank Thornton and Tom Cullen (two of Collins's closest lieutenants) joined three English agents for fish and chips at a saloon on Marlborough Street, they were taken for Englishmen who had brilliantly adapted to the local environment. 'Cor blimey, how did you learn the Irish brogue?' one of the Englishmen asked. 'We're here in Dublin for the last twelve months and we can't pick up any of it, yet you fellows seem to have perfected it.'[117]

Collins used the knowledge collected from his men within Winter's undercover intelligence organisation, as well as the steady flow of information from casual informants, to continue to target British intelligence officers in Dublin. The Squad killed Captain Cecil Lees, a top intelligence officer drafted out of Asia to work with Colonel Hill-Dillon (and rumoured to use torture on suspects).[118] Collins's assassins also came very close to killing Colonel Winter himself: ambushed on 2 June 1921 after driving out of Dublin Castle, Winter claimed that he was shot through the hand as he put a cigarette to his mouth.[119] Outside Dublin the IRA was instructed to compile a list of 'aggressive' military Intelligence Officers with a view to targeted assassination. Hits were scored in some cases.[120] Even where the IRA missed, this constant danger took its toll on Winter's intelligence staff: five of its members had committed suicide by May 1921 (and at least another two senior officers took the same course over the next few years). Mark Sturgis remarked that 'there seems a curse on the place.'[121]

The third and bloodiest aspect of the IRA counter-intelligence involved the ruthless execution of suspected informants. When an individual was suspected of passing information to the authorities he was passed invented details about future IRA activity. If the crown forces were then seen to act on this information, his guilt was assumed, and retribution was swift and brutal – a bullet in the head, a corpse by the road, and beside it a sign, 'Traitor. Shot by the IRA.' When pressure on the militants increased in early 1921, and it became obvious that information was being passed to the crown forces, suspects rarely received even this rudimentary form of trial. Hundreds were executed on the flimsiest of suspicions in a wave of killing across the country, particularly vicious in Co. Cork. We now know that almost all those killed were innocent, and that gunmen were using the threat of informers as a pretext to attack those seen as enemies to Irish nationalist society – Protestants, ex-soldiers, tramps, anyone who was regarded as an outsider.[122] Yet the IRA counter-espionage was effective because of its sheer brutality. It terrified local communities, and any possible informers among them, into silence. For example, information from Captain Kelly's agents completely dried up in February, even though only one was killed.[123] It had a particularly powerful effect on the 300,000 Protestants in the south who would have been expected to support the crown forces – in fact they played almost no role in the campaign against the rebellion.[124]

The four phases of the intelligence war between 1919 and 1921 had seen the advantage swing back and forth between British spies and Irish rebels. Did one side come out on top? In terms of *covert* intelligence methods – the use of undercover officers and informers – the IRA was the clear winner. The crown forces received little operationally useful information from their array of agents and touts. This was the opinion of the Company Intelligence Officer in Co. Cork, Kenneth Strong. He recorded that his agents were 'not of very high calibre' and that he never managed to capture 'a Sinn Feiner of any importance' during his service in Ireland.[125] Moreover, the intelligence agencies failed to recruit or place agents within the enemy's ranks. In its internal history of the rebellion the army concluded:

> Irish persons who were prepared to act as genuine secret service agents, i.e., as Sinn Feiners or as I.R.A. were difficult to find. ... Secret Service was on the whole a failure in Ireland. For many reasons it was practically impossible to place a man in any inner circle.[126]

Penetration of the republican leadership had distinguished the successful suppression of revolutionary conspiracies during the nineteenth century – it was markedly absent from the 1919–21 period.

Yet, though *covert* British intelligence activities were largely nullified, there were alternative *overt* methods by which intelligence could be collected. From the autumn of 1920 the country was saturated by British troops and a militarised RIC, which employed patrols, curfews, random searches, house raids, arrests and internment. These security measures produced two good sources of intelligence. The first was captured documents. The IRA and Sinn Féin leadership had a tendency to commit things to paper, as they sought to prove their credentials as a *de facto* government and army. Raids on houses, especially in Dublin, unearthed much of this; it gave the crown forces a good picture of the organisation and personnel of their opponents.[127] The second, and more operationally useful, source of information was Irish prisoners: the army concluded that 'the best information, i.e., that on which the most successful operations, where the heaviest loss was inflicted on the I.R.A., were based, was that given by I.R.A. deserters and prisoners under interrogation.' 4,500 men had been interned by this stage, and many more were subject to arrest and temporary detention. Some prisoners gave information to escape punishment; others gave information unwittingly to skilled interrogators; torture, though officially deemed counter-productive, was used in many cases.[128] Prisoners also yielded intelligence through 'Moutons' or stool pigeons placed in cells; through the censorship of the secret mail that the IRA operated from internment camps; and through listening sets placed in cells (although the latter gave 'unsatisfactory results', according to Winter's bizarre explanation, because 'a microphone of English manufacture' was 'ill adapted to the Irish brogue').[129] In April 1921 General Macready estimated that 80 per cent of all British intelligence was a by-product of overt security measures such as raids, arrests and engagements with IRA units.[130]

By the spring of 1921 this intelligence allowed the crown forces to put severe pressure on the IRA. The number and ambition of IRA operations reached a peak in March 1921, declining thereafter. By July 1921 there were fewer than 2,000 active fighters left in the field. Arms and ammunition were running dangerously low: IRA documents captured in May 1921 showed that the organisation had only 569 rifles, 477 revolvers and twenty bullets per rifle (although its armoury did boast 220 pikes and six swords).[131] There has been much debate over how strong the IRA's position was in the summer of 1921. Recent historical research indicates that the IRA was in serious trouble and would have experienced a difficult summer if the government had stepped up the repression. Thus, British intelligence and British security measures, though not producing outright victory, had some success in containing the insurgency in 1921.[132]

However, this success came at an enormous political cost. Patrols, raids, restrictions and arrests were indiscriminate measures that caused intense resentment among local communities. By 1921 they were carried out by heavily armed groups – mostly British soldiers or ex-soldiers – who were often undisciplined and hostile to the native population. They were also liable to engage in brutal reprisals and atrocities, sometimes with the tacit approval of senior commanders: suspected 'Shinners' were assassinated by plain-clothes 'death squads'; town centres were 'shot up' and burnt down; prisoners were tortured and killed 'while trying to escape'.[133] This played into the IRA's hands. The historian Charles Townshend has remarked that the IRA campaign was primarily 'armed propaganda' and that 'the purely military effect of guerrilla warfare' was 'subordinate to its political and psychological effect'. One of the chief objectives of IRA operations was to invite a violent reaction by the crown forces, so this could be exploited to win support for the republican cause.[134] The British duly obliged. Rather than adopt a surgical approach that might separate extremists from moderates, they used the bluntest of instruments based on nothing more sophisticated than the possession of superior force. To some extent, they were forced into this response by their inability to collect intelligence through discreet, covert means; it was because the security forces struggled to identify and apprehend IRA attackers that they resorted to heavy-handed security measures and vicious reprisals. Thus, defeat in the covert intelligence war precluded a sophisticated 'hearts and minds' strategy.

The British were unable to target and neutralise Irish radicals, as they had throughout the nineteenth century. Why was this? One reason was the quality of the Irish opposition: Irish revolutionaries paid more attention to security and waged a more effective counter-intelligence campaign than before. Yet the British intelligence system also suffered from major weaknesses. The calibre and suitability of intelligence officers was often low. Both Winter and Macready frequently complained that London was not sending the capable intelligence officers they needed.[135] Most of the officers assigned to this role lacked experience and were forced to improvise on the job. Security in both the police and military systems was shockingly lax, with sensitive documents circulating far too easily and officers openly boasting about their agents' exploits. People died as a result. Nationality was also a serious handicap. Because of the difficulties of recruiting Irishmen, the majority of the intelligence practitioners were British. They automatically aroused local suspicion, especially in rural areas. Many British operatives did not help themselves. David Neligan observed that his handlers in Winter's D Branch stood out due to their 'dapper' London-cut suits. 'When you come here again', he advised one agent, 'wear your oldest clothes and a battered old hat. With that rig-out you have on, your fair hair and your English accent, anyone would cop you a mile away.'[136] It also meant that most intelligence officers began with little knowledge of conditions in Ireland.

Other problems related to how the intelligence system was organised and led. A bewildering variety of groups became involved in Ireland. For example, in the autumn of 1920 covert intelligence activities were carried out by the remnants of the RIC Special Crime Branch; the army's undercover Dublin District Special Branch; the system of army Battalion and Company Intelligence Officers; Winter's London Bureau; Winter's staff in Dublin Castle; the Auxiliaries; and what was left of the agents despatched by Sir Basil Thomson earlier in the year. The army later admitted that 'the systems which were evolved grew up haphazard and without co-ordination.' Friction and lack of co-ordination between the police and army was particularly bad. RIC sergeants were suspicious of military intelligence officers, and reluctant to share information; the military was disgusted at what it saw as the indiscipline and incompetence of the police. It was Winter's job to bring about co-ordination by creating an integrated police and military intelligence system. However, he failed to achieve this. His scheme took an inordinately long time to develop, and, when implemented, it proved 'extraordinarily complex and involved'. It added yet another organisation to the intelligence firmament. Now, as well as military intelligence and the Crime Special Branch of the RIC, there was the network of Local Centres, which ran agents and sent back reports independently of those pre-existing organisations.[137] One of the greatest weaknesses was the absence of a central registry where all information could be collated, cross-checked, carded and indexed (which lay at the heart of MI5's wartime achievements). As early as December 1920 General Macready stated that Winter was 'not the man for the job'. John Anderson concurred that 'his show is thoroughly bad and I don't see it getting any better'. Tegart and Denham, the Indian intelligence experts, concluded that Winter was 'amateur' and operating entirely 'on wrong lines'.[138] There have been some recent attempts to defend Winter, but earlier negative judgments on his performance still stand.[139]

By March 1921 the inadequacy of the intelligence system had come to the attention of politicians in Westminster. A deputation of MPs led by Sir Samuel Hoare (who had served in SIS and MI5) urged the government to create a military dictatorship in Ireland by giving the Commander-in-Chief full control over the army and the police. The MPs claimed that 'an efficient Intelligence Service' was 'a factor only second in importance to the factor of unity of command'. They judged the existing intelligence system as 'bad'. They complained that 'the more highly developed methods of intelligence have not been applied to Ireland' and that 'the real experts in the field of intelligence' who had distinguished themselves in the First World War had not been employed. They called for a reformed, unified intelligence system under complete military control.[140] These MPs had obviously received secret briefings from senior army figures, as this was exactly what General Macready was planning at this time. It was decided that, if hostilities continued, martial law should be declared in the whole country and the army should have complete control over the security effort, including intelligence. Lieutenant-Colonel Charlie French, who had held the second most senior military intelligence position during the war, was earmarked as the new Director of Intelligence. Winter would be removed or demoted.[141] Intelligence in Ireland had gone through a succession of changes and never achieved a settled form; it was on the verge of one last major overhaul when hostilities ceased.

Intelligence and policy-making

The British intelligence system suffered from many weaknesses: inexperienced officers, amateur techniques, poor security, lack of co-ordination. However, its task was made much more difficult by the policies of the British government. The root cause of the unfavourable political environment in Ireland was not the behaviour of the crown forces but the failure of leaders in London to achieve a political settlement that would satisfy Irish nationalist demands. Between 1916 and 1918 the inability to implement Home Rule, rather than military repression, killed the Irish Parliamentary Party and gave life to Sinn Féin.[142] After 1918 the British government quixotically persisted with a Home Rule measure (the Government of Ireland Act), even though Irish demands had now shifted to much more substantial form of autonomy. Recent research indicates that a peace agreement could have been achieved in December 1920 along the same lines as the settlement a year later, but for the British cabinet's refusal to concede the principle of Dominion status – the most bitter and bloody period of fighting could therefore have been avoided.[143] The failure to achieve an acceptable political settlement and the perceived bias towards the unionist minority alienated the Irish majority and made many turn to violence as a means to achieve political goals. As a result, the task of the British intelligence system was difficult from the outset: the army later recognised that 'the bulk of the people were our enemies and were therefore far more incorruptible than has been the case in former Irish movements'.[144]

Similarly, some of the weaknesses of the British intelligence system were caused by the inept security policies adopted by Dublin Castle and the British government. The political decision to maintain a veneer of civil control and fight a 'police war', in a highly militarised context, was the principal reason for the intense friction between the army and police throughout most of this period. The repeated vacillation between coercion and conciliation prevented the development of a long-term, coherent intelligence strategy.[145] Winter concluded that 'one of the outstanding difficulties in the suppression of political crime in Ireland was the fact that the British nation was not at war with Ireland, whilst Ireland was at war with the British nation'.[146] Britain's constitutional and security policy towards Ireland was always one step behind the developing political situation – which meant that the intelligence system was doomed to a similar fate.

Almost all commentators have united in denouncement of British policy towards Ireland from 1916 to 1921. It has been called 'a disaster'; with 'scarcely even the semblance of coherence'; stemming from a persistent 'refusal to acknowledge the depth of the crisis.'[147] A striking feature was London's poor understanding of the Irish situation. There was a persistent desire to characterise the Sinn Féin movement as a minor, temporary, unrepresentative phenomenon that could be eradicated – a curable disease with which the Irish people were afflicted. Thus, during the First World War Sinn Féin was condemned as a 'German plot' orchestrated by a foreign enemy. When the war ended, Germany was replaced by Bolshevism – Sinn Féin was now part of the 'Red Menace' threatening the British empire. The IRA was characterised as nothing more than a 'murder gang', a small fanatical, psychopathic or criminal minority that was terrorising the majority into submission. It was claimed that IRA gunmen were motivated by money, even that they were imported from the gangs of New York and Chicago. Sinn Féin victories in the 1918 and 1921 elections were dismissed as the product of wholesale intimidation. The usefulness of these characterisations was that they robbed the Sinn Féin project of political legitimacy and excused British politicians from having to face up to the reality of Irish nationalism. Instead, all attention could be focused on the suppression of the 'murder gang' and the restoration of law and order.[148] These opinions were most prevalent among the Conservative Party. It was by definition the 'Unionist Party', hostile to the very idea of Irish independence, deeply committed to Irish unionists, especially in Ulster, and worried about the effects of Irish independence on the British empire. The Conservative Party was the dominant partner in a coalition government with the Liberals from 1915 to 1922 and exercised an unfortunate veto over Irish policy, blocking a possible Home Rule settlement in 1916 and preventing any sort of imaginative political settlement during the War of Independence. Conservative misconceptions and intransigence did much to radicalise the Irish population and precipitate a mass rebellion.[149]

It was the job of a well-functioning intelligence system to overturn misconceptions in London and inform policy towards Ireland. Good political intelligence was as important as operational intelligence to tackling the Irish insurgency. However, the political intelligence provided by security agencies in Ireland was of mixed quality. The Irish police between 1916 and 1918, and some of the civil and military leaders drafted into Ireland in 1920, provided accurate assessments of the rise of Sinn Féin, the radicalisation of the population, the limitations of coercion and the need for a political settlement. But other intelligence sources produced material of more doubtful quality. The Dublin Castle administration between 1918 and 1920 had a distinctly Orange tinge and was out of touch with nationalist feeling. 'It listens solely to the ascendancy party', one senior British civil servant wrote, 'and ... never seemed to think of the utility of keeping in close touch with opinions of all kinds.'[150] With the exception of Macready, the pervading view of the British military was one of strong support for the Union, antipathy towards nationalist Ireland and a desire for a full policy of coercion to crush the murderous rebels. This was certainly the view of Field Marshal Sir Henry Wilson, the Chief of the Imperial General Staff, who did everything possible to sabotage peace efforts aimed at placating Sinn Féin.[151] Colonel Winter's intelligence staff and Thomson's Special Branch in London were obsessed with the conspiratorial nature of the Sinn Féin movement – for example, links with Bolshevism – and did not exhibit a very sophisticated understanding of the political situation. For example, in December 1920 the civil and military intelligence agencies expressed confidence that they could crush the revolt: David Boyle, the head of the D Branch, predicted victory within six weeks. This influenced the cabinet's decision to shut down peace initiatives at that time.[152] The intelligence officers were mostly English, had spent little time in Ireland, and had only a limited feel of the political situation – it was perhaps natural that they should stress the merits of strong security measures rather than the uncertain benefits of political conciliation.

In some ways, however, it did not really matter what the British intelligence organisations were saying about political conditions in Ireland. Studies of notable intelligence 'failures' in the twentieth century reveal that in most cases the problem is not an absence of intelligence but the way in which intelligence is *used*: signals are missed, good intelligence is not distinguished from bad information, policy-makers see what they want to see.[153] If this is the case for well-developed intelligence systems in the contemporary era, then it applies to an even greater extent to the British government system in 1916–21. At this time there was no effective system for collating and analysing this information, passing it to politicians and shaping their policy-making assumptions. The situation with regard to Irish affairs was particularly bad. The existence of multiple intelligence agencies (the military, the Dublin Castle administration, Thomson's

Special Branch and other *ad hoc* sources), all reporting on Ireland and often with different views, made it difficult enough for cabinet members. But 'official' intelligence was joined by reports from individuals and groups who had contact with prominent government figures through family, friends or the network of the British establishment. These individuals were often rabidly unionist and hostile to all forms of Irish independence. The problem was that these different sources often provided wildly diverging pictures of the situation. In such a confused intelligence bazaar, policy-makers tended to fall back on their own preconceptions and prejudices, choosing those reports that suited them. Thus, the racist stereotyping, the antipathy to the 'native' Irish, the insistence on empire and union, the sheer unwillingness to come to terms with the fact that the Irish people might honestly desire independence from Britain – all of these came to the fore. Policy was ultimately based more on the political preferences and personal prejudices of the ministers involved than any 'objective' analysis of the actual situation in Ireland. Everyone had a set opinion on Ireland, and these opinions dictated political decisions.

Some army chiefs recognised how the lack of an intelligence system led to misunderstanding of the Irish situation and hence to ineffective policy. Macready frequently complained of the 'complete ignorance' of cabinet ministers of Irish conditions, and urged them to visit the country: he pointedly remarked that even the Irish Chief Secretary was a rare presence in his own land.[154] The commander of the 5th Division argued that 'the Government never realized the true state of affairs in Ireland' and 'never devised a suitable and clear policy, or made any attempt to convince the country of the need for putting one into force'. This was because 'there were political circumstances which clouded the judgment of some of the Government's responsible civil advisers', and because there was no established system of intelligence to expose political optimism and form sounder judgments. He concluded that 'the first lesson we learn therefore is the necessity for a thoroughly good intelligence system so that the Government's advisers may be in a good position to appreciate the situation justly and to put it squarely, fully and honestly before the Cabinet'.[155] This was highly perceptive but ahead of its time – such a system would not fully exist until the Second World War.

It was only in the summer of 1921 that the government was shaken out of its complacency and forced to reformulate old assumptions. The bankruptcy of British policy was becoming impossible to ignore. The Government of Ireland Act had become a charade. Its one redeeming feature was that it led to the establishment of a separate parliament for the six counties of Northern Ireland, and therefore clearly separated the issue of north and south. But in the south the Act was irrelevant. The elections in May 1921 had led to the unopposed return of

Sinn Féin in all seats but four, and Sinn Féin refused to have anything to do with this meagre gesture towards Home Rule. At the same time, while the IRA was undoubtedly under considerable pressure, the violence showed no sign of ending; it was realised that the existing security regime was not capable of restoring order. This led to some stark choices. General Macready bluntly told the cabinet that they had 'only two policies, to go "all out" or "get out"'. By 'all out' he meant imposing crown colony government and martial law, reinforcing the army with twenty battalions and granting the military sweeping powers to finally crush the IRA. However, this bleak proposal was impossible for two reasons. First, Macready admitted that Irish public opinion was so hostile to Britain that his scheme offered no long-term solution; as soon as the repressive measures were relaxed, the rebellion would spring up again. Second, such a Cromwellian scheme was simply not practical given public opinion in Britain, a full democracy since 1918, and in the rest of the world. There is evidence that Macready himself did not actually support it, but put it forward to show the British government that coercion alone was impossible and that they would have to come up with a political solution. In a sense it was a *reductio ab absurdum* of the British position.[156]

As a result, there was a gradual change in the attitudes of the government and attention shifted to political initiatives. The cabinet finally brought itself to agree to an offer of Dominion status to the southern twenty-six counties of Ireland – a far greater measure of independence than contained in the Government of Ireland Act. It also decided to make an unconditional truce with Sinn Féin. There was a flurry of peace initiatives between London and Dublin during these summer months before a truce came into effect on 11 July 1921. Negotiations on a comprehensive political settlement began with Sinn Féin soon after. The 'murderers', the 'gunmen' and the 'fanatics' were now accepted as the representatives of Catholic nationalist Ireland.

T HE revolutionary events of 1916 to 1921 compelled the British government to make concessions to Irish nationalism that would have been unthinkable at the start of the period. Deficiencies in intelligence played a significant role in producing this situation – the experience of British intelligence was in marked contrast to its success in suppressing Irish revolutionary movements in the previous century. One reason was that Irish separatists were more determined, better organised and paid more attention to internal security. Many IRA intelligence officers (including Michael Collins) had a natural gift for intelligence work; some would pit their wits against clandestine British operations in the Second World War with similar success. On the other hand, the British intelligence system was less effective: the old Irish system organised around the RIC and DMP fell into decline before 1916 and was then smashed by the IRA campaign; the new British agencies and personnel that became involved displayed poor organisation, amateurish techniques and ignorance of Irish affairs. Colonel Winter's effort to create an integrated, professional intelligence system was not a success. The British lost the covert intelligence war and were forced to resort to overt, indiscriminate intelligence methods, which, though yielding information, alienated the Irish population. Of course, the British intelligence system was also hampered by the misguided decisions of policy-makers in Dublin and London, and the frustration of much of the Irish people at the failure to introduce self-government. Yet, through its inability to educate policy-makers, and its unpopular heavy-handed measures, the intelligence system also played a part in causing this political context. The humiliating consequence was that southern Ireland was lost from the United Kingdom. The question now was whether it could at least be kept in the empire.

CHAPTER 2
Alarms, Excursions and Civil War

T HE truce on 11 July 1921 stopped the war between the IRA and the British state, but it neither ended the violence in Ireland, nor resolved the political fate of the country. It was followed by five months of prevarication, manœuvring, high tension and frustration, as the British government negotiated a peace settlement with Sinn Féin leaders, first through correspondence, and then, from 11 October, in conference in London. Eventually, after a Lloyd-George ultimatum and some anxious brinkmanship, an Anglo-Irish Treaty was signed on 5 December 1921, which granted southern Ireland Dominion status. The settlement split the Sinn Féin and IRA organisations. The moderates formed a government, set about raising a National Army and worked with London to implement the treaty. A significant republican minority condemned the treaty as a betrayal, and seized control of parts of the country. This confrontation, and the security vacuum it created, led to escalating political and criminal violence throughout the twenty-six counties in the first half of 1922. Open civil war finally broke out on 28 June 1922, and continued for the next eleven months. More Irish people died during the Civil War than during the War of Independence; the RIC, DMP and British army also suffered casualties, despite the continuance of the truce. Moreover, on a number of occasions it seemed to London as if the moderate faction in Sinn Féin might lose control or throw their lot in with the extremists, which would force Britain to launch a full reconquest of southern Ireland. The Anglo-Irish settlement remained fragile: as General Macready later recalled in his memoirs, 'there were moments when the reoccupation of the island seemed to hang on a thread.'[1]

Southern Ireland's violent transition from rebellious province to independent state was a uniquely confusing period for the British government and its intelligence system. The British security apparatus, slowly built up during the previous two years, was first suspended and then dismantled: there were soon no British representatives across much of the twenty-six counties. The new Sinn Féin administration was neither willing to share intelligence openly, nor trusted by British officials. At the same time, London was bombarded by rumours and warnings from unofficial sources, especially from loyalist Irish residents threatened by the new political regime. Because of a lack of good intelligence the

British cabinet struggled to assess the intentions of the Sinn Féin leaders and the strength of republican opposition to a compromise settlement. Sentiment lurched between cautious optimism and deep despair: Macready referred to a persistent 'atmosphere of "alarms and excursions"' at this time.[2] This led to misjudgements that almost brought down the Anglo-Irish settlement and reignited the War of Independence. It was not until 1923, when the pro-Treaty administration in Dublin gained the upper hand over the rebels and began co-operating with Britain on intelligence, that London developed a more accurate and reassuring picture of Irish affairs.

Intelligence and the 1921 peace process

T HE Anglo-Irish peace was at its most fragile during the five months between the agreement of the truce and the signing of the treaty. There were grave suspicions of the *bona fides* of the Sinn Féin leaders, and many suspected that the IRA was simply using the truce as an opportunity to rearm. British military and intelligence officers played a large part in generating these perceptions. Indeed, Irish leaders accused them of deliberately sabotaging the peace process (just as similar accusations were made against British 'securocrats' in Northern Ireland during the 1990s). There is some truth in this: intelligence material severely shook the Anglo-Irish negotiations and challenged those British policy-makers who looked forward to an easy settlement of the Irish problem.

One immediate impact of the truce was a dramatic reduction in British intelligence capabilities. Under its terms, both sides were to cease intelligence operations. For the first three months, the British largely respected this provision. General Macready wrote that 'unfortunately the Chief Secretary ... had practically broken up the Police Secret Service very shortly after the truce, a step which would have resulted in much unnecessary loss of life had activities recommenced.'[3] Inactivity led to indiscipline, and a series of scandals befell Winter's organisation: three senior officers were dismissed after they were discovered in a conspiracy with the army to oust Winter; another intelligence officer, who had 'broken down from insomnia', was involved in an ugly hit and run incident – he took out a government car against orders and ran over and killed a tram conductor. 'It is difficult to see how this staff has carried on under such conditions,' Cope wrote exasperatedly, 'we have to keep a constant eye on these people for unless we do, they run amok.'[4] The one advantage of this period was that the Irish rebel leaders had come out in the open and could be more easily observed. Colonel Winter found himself rubbing shoulders with one of the most wanted IRA men,

Dan Breen, while placing a bet at the Galway Races. 'I wonder if he had an automatic in his pocket at the time?' Winter mused in his autobiography. 'I know I had!'[5]

The British intelligence system tried to assist the British negotiators by furnishing information on the Irish leaders. In July 1921 intelligence officers drew up briefing sheets on the key personalities. For example, the President, Éamon de Valera, was described as a 'school teacher type, idealist, feels Ireland is in bondage, strong on the wrongs to Ireland'. He would 'probably speak at length on the "bad treatment" of Ireland by England', 'the broken promises' and 'the support given by England to the 600,000 Protestants of Ulster', but he would accept less than a full republic. The report warned that the British must show patience in dealing with the Irish delegates, as they had been under severe strain during the conflict. 'All of them will probably be found to be children in statesmanship and politics', it was noted. 'They have no real experience of politics. They have no opportunity of maturing under responsibility.'[6] Once face-to-face negotiations began in October 1921, Winter's London Bureau conducted clandestine activities targeting the Irish delegation. A detailed report exists from an 'informant' who had conversations with senior members of the Irish delegation on 30 October and 1 November. These individuals obviously trusted the informant, as they were quite frank as to their views and their future negotiating tactics. The identity of the informant is unclear, but there have been persistent rumours that John Chartres (a member of the Irish delegation who was formerly associated with British intelligence) passed information to the British – he may be connected to this report.[7]

In October 1921 the British also made a limited effort to restart their intelligence activities in Ireland. Military intelligence officers discreetly monitored IRA activity and attended public Sinn Féin meetings.[8] Winter's organisation was partially revived, and intelligence officers were recalled to Ireland. The remnants of the D Branch produced sporadic material from informers at this time: for example, Winter reported on a private meeting of the Dáil and quoted one of Michaels Collins's conversation in the Gresham Hotel on Sackville Street.[9] Sinn Féin leaders even complained that Dublin was 'flooded with spies', now that they had 'come out of cover'.[10] This was an exaggeration. British intelligence activities were unobtrusive, shied away from aggressive penetration of Sinn Féin circles, and mostly consisted of collection of gossip from Irish society. Moreover, the British no longer engaged in the overt security operations that had yielded the bulk of intelligence, in the form of captured documents and interrogation of prisoners, before the truce. As a result, the flow of intelligence largely dried up: Colonel J. J. Brind, a senior member of the army staff, concluded that 'owing to the very nature of the agreement, but little information has been received in comparison with that obtained prior to 11th July'.[11]

In many ways British concern about the Irish situation was inversely proportional to the quality of intelligence available: gaps in knowledge were filled with worst-case, often politically motivated, interpretation. There were two main issues that taxed the British intelligence system. The most challenging was predicting whether the Sinn Féin movement would accept a compromise settlement – its political intentions. There was considerable uncertainty on this issue, although all opinions were pervaded by extreme distrust. A more tangible challenge was detecting the activities and assessing the strength of the IRA – its military capabilities. Though information on this subject was incomplete, enough evidence emerged to confirm suspicions that the IRA was using the truce to strengthen its power. Consequently, there was a steady stream of disquieting intelligence on the situation in Ireland throughout the truce period.

To understand British intelligence assessments, we must first look at the attitude of British military and intelligence officers towards the truce. They had not been consulted over the truce policy, belittled its chance of success and worried that it would weaken the British position.[12] Less than a week before the truce was agreed, the Director of Intelligence, Colonel Winter, dismissed the peace hopes as 'but snow on the dusty desert's face':

> There will be no peace settlement – of that you may be quite sure – at the present moment. But I do hope, sincerely, that the proceedings will not be too long dragged out. It will only afford them more breathing space, and more time to negotiate the purchase of arms ... This is not merely an impatient diatribe, but just to put in black and white my view that, at the present juncture, there will be *no* peace. And that is all there is to it.[13]

The truce was the work of Westminster politicians working through senior civil servants in Dublin Castle, who held secret talks with Sinn Féin leaders. Alfred 'Andy' Cope (the Assistant Under Secretary) was the key figure: when asked to whom 'the honour of the peace' should go, Mark Sturgis was adamant that it should go to 'Andy first, last and all the time' – he was 'the author of the whole thing'.[14] An Englishman of 'tidy build' and 'suave manners', who 'dressed in the height of fashion', Cope had risen from humble origins as the son of the bottle manufacturer from south London. He could appear to his colleagues as highly strung, prickly and unwilling to delegate, but he had an immense capacity for work and would play a crucial role as liaison between the British government and Sinn Féin in 1921 and 1922, developing a close friendship with Michael Collins.[15]

Cope's role earned him the hatred of many British military and intelligence officers. One member of Winter's staff remarked that 'Cope was universally detested by everyone in the Castle, it being generally supposed that he was going to sell us all to the rebels'.[16] Rumours that he was working on behalf of Sinn Féin were raised by Tory MPs in parliament, and formed the basis of a 'spy campaign' in the ultra-conservative *Morning Post* newspaper in September 1921.[17] The enmity towards Cope reflected opposition to the truce policy among military and intelligence officers. A view quickly began to take hold that the British had thrown away a winning position. When the Military Secretary at the War Office met with commanding officers in Ireland during the truce, 'they all, without exception, said that the rebels were beaten, and that if, instead of agreeing to an armistice, the Government had stuck it out for another fortnight, they would have been glad to surrender'.[18] The inevitable inference was that the truce was a mistake: the British politicians had been hoodwinked by Sinn Féin.[19] These feelings of resentment and betrayal were encapsulated by the Chief of the Imperial General Staff, Field-Marshal Sir Henry Wilson:

> This plan of inviting over Valera [*sic*] and anybody he likes to bring with him leaves me in the same condition as the coster who wheeled his barrow to the top of Hampstead Hill, where a passing bus knocked it over and all the oranges rolled to the bottom of the hill. He looked up at the bus driver and said, 'there ain't no bloody words for it'. How anybody in their senses, or out of them, can hope to get peace in Ireland by this means passes my understanding.[20]

As time passed, the retrospective conviction that they had the IRA beaten, but had been betrayed by the politicians of Westminster, would become a powerful myth within military and unionist circles.

Many of the comments by intelligence and military officials in this period reveal deep suspicions that Sinn Féin had no intention of compromise and was simply using the truce as a tactical ploy to develop its armed forces, ready to resume guerrilla warfare when conditions were more suitable. Sir Basil Thomson expressed this view forcefully, and it was prevalent among the armed forces: for example, the admiral commanding the Royal Navy in Ireland gloomily concluded that 'the rebels will try to prolong negotiations until the end of winter and then force a break'.[21] Intelligence reports also identified the splits within the Sinn Féin movement. At one level these were caused by ideological differences between doctrinaire republicans and leaders willing to compromise. At another, they were caused by the leadership's lack of control over their followers. Winter stated that there was a group of extremists and fanatics who are against 'anything'; a group of members of the I.R.A. who have risen to a higher position than they had ever hoped to attain; and those men, who are purely adventurers, enjoy the pastime of 'killing the peeler' and who, being indolent, are more prosperous in war than in peace.

Ultimately the fracturing political landscape, prolonged negotiations and conflicting intelligence reports meant that the security chiefs could never confidently predict the outcome of the Anglo-Irish negotiations. 'The chances of the negotiations resulting in peace increase with the passing of time', Winter wrote in early August, 'but the question still hangs precariously in the balance, the chances being, approximately, slightly over evens that a settlement will be arrived at.'[22] By December he was more pessimistic. General Macready demonstrated a slightly greater optimism, certainly compared to his fellow military officers, but he was by no means confident of peace and 'would not trust these devils an inch' until a pact was 'signed, sealed and delivered'. This remained his view until the day before the treaty was signed: the situation was 'odds even', he wrote on 4 December.[23] Fundamentally the intelligence chiefs hedged their bets because they did not know which way the Sinn Féin leadership would go – in the words of Sir Basil Thomson it was simply 'impossible to forecast'.[24]

If Sinn Féin intentions never allowed a consistent interpretation, British intelligence came to a more confident appraisal of IRA activities and capabilities. The actions of the IRA during the truce immeasurably increased the frustration of the crown forces. Gunmen emerged from their life on the run to be feted as heroes by the populace. (They frequently donned newly made military dress: British army officers complained that Dublin tailors were unable to tend to their sartorial needs, 'owing to large contracts for I.R.A. uniforms'.)[25] IRA units paraded and drilled openly, and there were sporadic clashes with members of the security forces. Perhaps worst of all, both the IRA and the Irish media 'flaunted the achievement of the I.R.A. in having vanquished the Crown Forces'. Colonel Brind complained that 'although no one knows better than the members of the I.R.A. themselves what their condition was 3 months ago, they are gradually being convinced by the boastful speeches of their leaders' that they were victors.[26] General Macready lamented that 'the position of the police and soldiers was humiliating in the extreme'; it was 'a period which was almost more trying to the police and troops than when active operations were in progress.'[27]

The cause of greatest concern was not the triumphant displays of the former fugitives, but evidence that the IRA was using the truce to increase its military strength. According to the British interpretation of the truce, the IRA was to refrain from recruiting, training, raising funds and importing arms. But the IRA comprehensively broke all these terms: the organisation swelled in size as it drew in thousands of new recruits; IRA units were busy training, drilling, parading and turning themselves into a proper military force; 'levies' were imposed on the population, often compulsory, to raise money for the fighters. The British army also learnt that the IRA was intensifying its intelligence-gathering activities, often with the assistance of the women of Cumann na mBan: General Macready warned that they would 'fraternise to this end, possibly to the extent of being more than sisters to some members of the Crown Forces'.[28] Republican activities outside of Ireland (in Britain, America and continental Europe) provided some of the most worrying signs of IRA audacity, as British intelligence uncovered many plots to import arms and ammunition. (See chapter 3.) A senior army officer concluded that 'owing to the withdrawal of all check on importation and smuggling of weapons and ammunition, considerable progress has been made in the arming and equipping of the rebel forces'.[29]

Intelligence, though of doubtful quality, was also available on how these guns might be used. In November and December, Winter's intelligence service produced a number of very alarming reports on the IRA's intended plan of campaign. According to Winter, it would involve the destruction of communications and transport links, concerted attacks on small RIC barracks and the seizure of military, police and leading loyal citizens, 'to hold as hostages so that for every I.R.A. shot two loyalists will be shot'. It would be a very dirty war: Winter warned that 'when the majority of people in small towns are loyal, gas will be used, which is being ... manufactured in laboratories owned by the Christian Brothers, and other like institutions'.[30] The second front for the IRA campaign would be Northern Ireland. Winter provided a steady stream of reports that the southern IRA was massing for an attack on the border. 'A reliable informant states', he wrote just days before the treaty was signed, 'that fifteen thousand I.R.A. men are now ready and equipped to tackle the North at a moment's notice, the same number of men – as a reinforcement – will be ready in a few days' time.'[31] This mirrored a shift in political attention towards Northern Ireland, as sectarian violence flared and negotiations stalled on the issue of partition.

Intelligence of this sort led to a unanimous feeling that the IRA had been able to use the truce to alter the military balance. This was powerfully argued in September 1921 in two reports by Colonel J. Brind, the senior military intelligence officer in Dublin, who warned the cabinet that 'advantage has been taken of the truce to convert the I.R.A. which was 3 months ago little more than a disorganised rabble into a well disciplined, well organised and well armed force', which existed for one purpose – 'the establishment of a Republic of Ireland'.[32]

The worrying implication was that the British plan of campaign devised before the truce, requiring 80,000 troops, would no longer be adequate. Macready later recalled that 'the whole situation had changed since the Prime Minister's surrender', because the IRA had been allowed to reorganise and the British intelligence services had 'lost touch with their objective'. If the negotiations had broken down in December 1921 a force of 150,000 men would have been necessary to pacify the country.[33] With Britain stretched by imperial responsibilities, and the government under pressure from public opinion, this was highly unpalatable; it led to the exploration of other methods to pacify Ireland, such as raising militias from the loyalist population or instituting a blockade of rebel districts – none offered a good solution.

There was an unanimous conclusion within the intelligence community that the IRA was preparing for a resumption of war. Whether the Sinn Féin leadership intended to wage this war was still uncertain, but knowledge of these secret IRA activities only reinforced the deep distrust about Sinn Féin purposes. It gave ammunition to Conservative politicians who argued that Sinn Féin had no intention of compromising over the republic. It also confirmed the military-unionist thesis that the truce had been a mistake and that the politicians, through cowardice or wishfulness, had thrown away a certain victory.

How accurate were British intelligence appreciations of the Irish situation? The answer is mixed. As for the assessments of Sinn Féin intentions, it is clear that intelligence personnel underestimated the forces leading towards peace. Similarly, there is evidence that intelligence personnel exaggerated the increase in IRA capabilities during the truce period. Too much credence was given to fantastic reports of poison gas manufactured by the Christian Brothers and thousands of IRA men massed on the northern border. Indeed, the principal historical work on the truce period argues that the IRA saw a *decline* in its strength during the peace, as the truce produced indiscipline, slackness and splits at all levels.[34] At the same time, the pessimism of the British intelligence chiefs had some basis. Even if IRA capabilities never reached the levels assumed, there is no doubt that the IRA did view the truce as an opportunity to rearm and strengthen its organisation. The nominal strength of the IRA leapt to 72,000, local IRA units drilled openly, the institutions of the republican state reappeared, and efforts to import arms and ammunitions were successful. It may be necessary to revise some of our perceptions of IRA capabilities in this period. In addition, the intelligence agencies were quick to recognise the very real splits within Sinn Féin: the treaty would, after all, lead to civil war.

The reports emanating from the British intelligence system could have had a fatal impact on the peace process. That they did not was due to the existence of a counterbalance of opinion that maintained an unashamedly positive belief in the *bona fides* of Sinn Féin and the ultimate outcome of the truce policy. This was consistently espoused by the civil authorities in Dublin Castle, in particular Alfred Cope and Sir John Anderson. It was communicated to the cabinet through weekly reports from the Chief Secretary for Ireland, Hamar Greenwood (which Cope and Anderson wrote). Greenwood's reports frequently contradicted the gloomy assessments of Macready, Winter and Thomson by asserting that the IRA was respecting the truce and that Sinn Féin leaders would make the necessary compromises.[35] This led to heated and highly personal clashes with the intelligence and military chiefs, who directly challenged these opinions. Macready informed Greenwood that his reports were 'not only optimistic', but 'by no means a statement of fact'; he privately complained of 'having to run in harness with a lot of double distilled blithering idiots like Hamar and his satellites'.[36] Winter also commented on how 'the results of the truce negotiations are viewed in Government Official circles with considerable optimism, whilst nearly all the reports from our informants tend to show that hostilities are likely to be resumed.'[37]

These two opposing interpretations of the Irish situation battled it out from July to December 1921. To some extent, they had natural adherents among the politicians: there was a staunchly unionist group within the Conservative Party – known as the 'diehards' – that was deeply uncomfortable with negotiating with Sinn Féin; conversely, the Liberal Prime Minister, Lloyd George, was determined to see the policy through to a successful conclusion. The civil optimists were (just) able to keep a check on the more alarmist prognostications of the intelligence and military chiefs. However, the steady stream of alarming intelligence reports fostered considerable distrust, misgiving and apprehension through all sections of Whitehall and Westminster. It is perhaps not recognised just how close the process came to collapse. On three occasions codewords warning of an imminent resumption of hostilities were issued to the British army in Ireland – on 16 August, 21 October, and 5 December 1921. The most serious crisis came in October, when the discovery of IRA gunrunning plots in Germany and Britain coincided with the receipt of 'secret advices from Ireland' (probably from Winter) warning that the Irish delegates were 'impossible people' and unwilling to compromise.[38] On 22 October the Secretary of State for War expected 'a break': he told a colleague that 'our army is likely to have work soon' in Ireland.[39]

The assessments of the intelligence and security community can throw further perspective on Lloyd George's actions on 5 December, when he presented a dramatic ultimatum to the Sinn Féin delegation: he told them to choose between peace on the terms offered or 'war in three days', demanding an answer by 10 pm that night. It explains why Lloyd George was determined to put a deadline on the negotiations; the longer the talks continued the more opportunity it offered to the IRA to rearm and strengthen, tipping the military balance further in its favour. Paradoxically, a close reading of military reports at this time reinforces the view that Lloyd George's ultimatum was partly bluff. Because of the shift in the military balance and the decline in intelligence capabilities, the British army was in no position to wage 'war in three days'; massive reinforcements and reorganisation would be required before a campaign of coercion could be launched. Therefore the most likely result of an Irish refusal on 5 December would have been an indeterminate period of militarisation and manœuvre before any shooting began. Finally, it is clear that Lloyd George did not have any confidence about whether the Irish delegation would accept his terms or not. The intelligence and advice received by the British delegation was full of contradiction and uncertainty, with reports of various splits within the Sinn Féin movement. The British government did not know which way the decision would go – peace and war were truly in the balance until the last hours. There was palpable relief when the Irish delegates accepted what was on the table and signed the Anglo-Irish Treaty that night.

Withdrawal or reconquest

T HERE were great hopes in London that the treaty would provide a final answer to the Irish question. However, rather than bringing harmony to Anglo-Irish relations, it was followed by seven months of drift and uncertainty that were almost as challenging for the British government as the period of negotiations. Under the treaty, Ireland would be partitioned and the southern twenty-six counties would become the 'Irish Free State', enjoying substantial autonomy, but remaining within the British empire and owing a weak form of allegiance to the British crown. Though welcomed by the majority of Irish people, this compromise split the Sinn Féin movement. After a month's debate the Dáil ratified the treaty on 7 January 1922, but the margin of victory was slim – just seven votes. The President, Éamon de Valera, along with two other members of his seven-man cabinet, came out in opposition. It was left to Arthur Griffith and Michael Collins to form a Provisional Government in Dublin; they set about the slow, difficult task of building the institutions of the new state out of the ruins of the old. At a military level, a majority of the IRA opposed the treaty. The anti-Treaty faction publicly rejected the authority of the Provisional Government at an Army Convention in Dublin on 26 March 1922 and placed the IRA under the control of a newly elected Army Executive, led by republicans such as Rory

O'Connor and Liam Mellows. This anti-Treaty branch of the IRA earned the sobriquet 'Irregulars', while the Provisional Government set about recruiting a new 'Regular' National Army to enforce its authority.

The splits within the Sinn Féin and IRA organisations produced a growing number of confrontations and violent outbursts in 1922. The withdrawal of British security forces led to a scramble for control of evacuated barracks, which fell into Regular or Irregular hands according to the allegiance of local IRA units. In much of the south and west, this led to complete republican control; where there were splits among local IRA units, there were tense stand-offs.[40] The British army, RIC officers and Protestant loyalists were also subject to violent assault and assassination. Some of these attacks had the political object of provoking hostilities with Britain, most were motivated by private feuds and vengeance stemming from the War of Independence, others were purely criminal in nature – for example, an RAF lieutenant carrying the regimental pay was shot dead during a robbery in Kildare town.[41] There was a partial breakdown of law and order because of the dangerous security vacuum created by the split in Sinn Féin and the withdrawal of British forces.

The British government looked to the Provisional Government to assert its authority and fill this vacuum. It was hoped that elections could be quickly held, thereby granting a clear mandate to the new administration. An Irish Free State constitution could then be drawn up in line with the treaty. In the meantime the Provisional Government would build up its military and police forces with assistance from Britain, using force to quell republican resistance. However, the Irish leaders were not prepared to obey British wishes. With the possible exception of Arthur Griffith, few embraced the Anglo-Irish Treaty on principle – it was simply the best that could be obtained under the circumstances. They were determined to do everything possible to avoid civil war, and would quite happily abrogate the treaty, or bend it out of recognition, if they could get away with it. Thus, at the Sinn Féin Árd Fheis on 22–3 February 1922 Collins agreed with de Valera to postpone the planned elections until June. The Provisional Government prepared a draft constitution that was republican in nature and in complete contravention of the treaty. Behind the scenes the Chief of Staff of the National Army, Richard Mulcahy, collaborated with the Irregulars to attack Northern Ireland. The leaders of the Provisional Government were caught between pressure from Britain to implement the treaty and the calls of their erstwhile comrades to reject the agreement and rejoin the fight for independence. They twisted and turned in every direction in an attempt to reconcile these two forces, before their options ran out in June 1922.[42]

The most immediate and visible impact of the Anglo-Irish Treaty was the dismantling of the civil and military arms of the British state in southern Ireland. The administrative departments of Dublin Castle were handed over to the Provisional Government in January 1922. The Dublin Metropolitan Police was also transferred to the new authority; but the Royal Irish Constabulary, which had actively fought against the IRA, was disbanded. Its men were concentrated in a small number of camps, the recent British recruits (the 'Black and Tans' and Auxiliaries) were quickly evacuated, and its Irish members were given three options: stay in Ireland, join the new Royal Ulster Constabulary, or be resettled in other parts of the British empire. 'Three hundred of the best' joined the newly created gendarmerie in Palestine, thus continuing the Irish influence on imperial policing.[43] The British military underwent a similar process of contraction and withdrawal. Battalions were concentrated in a few garrisons and then moved to Northern Ireland or back to Britain. By 14 February 1922 there were no British troops west of the River Shannon; after 17 May 1922 the only detachments remaining consisted of a large force stationed around Phoenix Park (west of Dublin) and small, isolated garrisons in three ports retained by Britain under the treaty (Queenstown, Berehaven and Lough Swilly).[44] All over the country the Union Jack was hauled down and replaced by the Irish tricolour.

The intelligence system built up between 1919 and 1921, and then suspended during the truce period, was also 'disbanded by order of the Cabinet'.[45] Colonel Winter, the police Director of Intelligence, was removed to London in February and given responsibility for the resettlement of RIC men outside Ireland. His intelligence system was broken up and the agents and touts dismissed.[46] Though the British army did retain a presence in the country, the military intelligence system was also wound down. General Macready issued instructions to British officers that he would 'not permit anything in the nature of secret service to discover what is going on in their area'. Instead, they were told to liaise with the new Irish authorities: 'the policy of His Majesty's Government' was 'to trust ... the Provisional Government', Macready wrote. He added that British officers could 'neither force this on them, nor attempt any substitute in the nature of secret service, but must endeavour to win their trust by a perfectly frank attitude'.[47] Macready told the War Office in early February:

> I need not emphasise the point that I am now like a man who has lost his sight, as my Intelligence Service is completely scrapped, and I am entirely dependent on anything I may get either from the Ulster Government or from the funny men in Dublin.[48]

Following a deterioration in the situation in March 1922, there were some half-hearted attempts to restart military intelligence activities in southern Ireland.

A conference of British ministers on 3 April 'agreed that the War Office should be authorised to expend £2,000, if required, for the re-establishment of Intelligence Services in Southern Ireland.'[49] The man who had been earmarked to take over the intelligence system in 1921, Lieutenant-Colonel Charlie French, was brought back to Dublin. Army headquarters issued new instructions to intelligence officers, asking them to step up unobtrusive intelligence gathering. They were prohibited from secret service methods such as 'shadowing' or 'sleuthing', but were told to get out and about in their areas, keep their eyes and ears open, and attend public meetings – 'it should be done perfectly openly, plain clothes of course, & if it can be combined with a visit to friends, or a fishing trip, so much the better.'[50] However, General Macready made clear to British ministers that they should not expect too much from this policy. 'We have reached a stage where no amount of money can produce the information we require', he warned in April 1922. 'We cannot as things now stand, re-establish the system of intelligence which existed in Ireland up to three months ago, or anything like it.'[51]

Even this limited and unobtrusive attempt to increase the flow of intelligence had tragic consequences. On 26 April 1922 three intelligence officers of the 6th Division and a military driver were abducted by the IRA at Macroom in Co. Cork. The men had been acting on the instructions issued that month to increase intelligence work. The Brigade Intelligence Officer (Lieutenant R. A. Hendy) 'wished to see the state of affairs at Macroom' and took with him two battalion officers (Lieutenants G. R. Dove and K. L. Henderson), 'making the excuse of lunching with a mutual friend on the way'. The three men entered an inn at Macroom, where they were drugged by local members of the IRA. They were taken to Macroom Castle, held there for two days and then taken to a lonely corner of bog and shot. The incident made the military more wary about engaging in any sort of undercover intelligence work. It was also the catalyst for the withdrawal of the remaining four battalions from Cork city on 17 May 1922, leaving the garrison in Dublin as the only substantial British military presence in southern Ireland.[52]

Following this withdrawal, the sources of intelligence outside Dublin were very limited. The British government was forced to rely on a motley bunch of official and unofficial sources. The first official source was the Royal Navy. Naval officers were stationed at Queenstown (soon renamed Cobh) in Co. Cork and at Kingstown (now Dún Laoghaire) in Co. Dublin. Destroyers based in the southwest sailed around the Irish coast, patrolling for gunrunners, evacuating loyalist refugees, collecting information and making sporadic reports on some of the most remote areas of the country.[53] Second, the Special Branch of the London Metropolitan Police – now headed by Major-General Sir Wyndham Childs – continued to provide some intelligence. Most of its activity was focused on republican activities outside Ireland, but through censorship of correspondence, its network of informers in Britain and continuing relationships with agents in Ireland, the Branch also picked up information on internal Irish matters. In addition to the Royal Navy and the Special Branch, Whitehall also received information from the press and Irish residents. Both had weaknesses. Newspapers were prone to inaccuracy, sensationalism and political bias: Macready stated in April 1922 that 'the greatest evil at the moment is the exaggeration of the Press'.[54] British contacts with Irish residents tended to be with loyalists, who were often deeply embittered by their treatment and not representative of Irish opinion. Naval officers, British policemen, newspapers and southern loyalists provided an unpredictable flow of local gossip, insider information, political rants and alarmist rumour that was difficult to digest in Whitehall.

Under the new Anglo-Irish relationship envisaged in the treaty, the primary source of intelligence on southern Ireland should have been the Provisional Government. Yet the nature of this source also caused problems. First, the new government took some time to build its administrative, military and intelligence structures. A large part of the country was in the hands of the anti-Treaty IRA and contained no Free State representatives. The Provisional Government was itself, therefore, sometimes ignorant of the situation in outlying areas. Second, the Irish leaders inevitably pursued their own interests and could not always be relied on to provide objective information. The intelligence they provided on the political situation was often too optimistic: it was designed to appease British concerns over the precarious position of the treaty, so that power (and military supplies) would be transferred to the new Irish government as quickly as possible.[55] The Provisional Government kept the British at arm's length and did not share intelligence openly until the Civil War began.

The dismantling of the old intelligence system, and the absence of a good replacement, produced an information vacuum that left much room for conjecture and argument in London. The two opposing interpretations of the Irish situation that had emerged during the peace negotiations diverged even further in 1922. The civil departments responsible for Irish affairs (the Irish Office and the Colonial Office), and the senior civil servants and politicians who had been the architects of the treaty policy, believed that the 1921 agreement would put an end to the Irish problem. Making southern Ireland a Dominion within the British commonwealth would satisfy nationalist demands, remove the cause of bitterness towards England and foster closer relations between the two islands, with Ireland playing a full and loyal part in shaping and defending the empire. It was even hoped that the north would eventually take its place in a united Irish Dominion, thereby counteracting any latent republican tendencies in the south. The splits and violence in Ireland in early 1922, though regrettable, were an inevitable consequence of the dramatic political upheavals and the difficulty of constructing a new administration. An immediate election was the answer, as it would grant a firm mandate to the Provisional Government. This view was perhaps best personified by Lionel Curtis, who occupied the unusual post of special adviser on Irish affairs in the Colonial Office. An Oxford fellow, Curtis was a prolific writer on imperial affairs and a leading member of the 'Round Table' symposium, the federalist imperial movement founded in 1909. He had consistently championed the offer of Dominion status to southern Ireland. He assisted the British delegation during the treaty negotiations as part of the Prime Minister's staff and then moved to the Colonial Office in February 1922, where he played a leading role in managing the transition to the Irish Free State.[56]

An antithetical and more pessimistic interpretation was common in London at this time. Its proponents condemned the 1921 treaty as an ill-judged surrender that would lead to the persecution of Protestants in the Free State, attacks on Northern Ireland, and the crumbling of the entire British empire. A 'diehard' faction in the Conservative Party, led by John Gretton (an Irish Protestant brewer) and Lord Salisbury, consistently voted against legislation related to the treaty in 1921 and 1922. They were supported by publications such as the *National Review*, the *Spectator* and, above all, the *Morning Post*, under the editorship of Howell Arthur Gwynne.[57] These views were also prevalent in the armed services, and were epitomised by Britain's most senior army man, Field-Marshal Sir Henry Wilson. An Anglo-Irish landowner with Ulster roots – an ancestor fought under William of Orange – he was Chief of the Imperial General Staff until February 1922, after which he was elected MP for Co. Down. His diaries reveal his fury on discovering that a treaty had been signed:

> The Agreement is complete surrender
> 1. A farcical oath of allegiance
> 2. Withdrawal of our troops
> 3. A Rebel Army ...
> The British Empire is doomed.[58]

Seeing 'nothing in front of poor Ireland except chaos', he advocated a complete reconquest of the island. 'There is only one solution to the Irish problem', he wrote, 'it is a very simple one and has been astonishingly effective for 115 years, to wit, the government of Ireland by England.'[59]

These differing perceptions of Ireland were reflected in the two most important British officials left in Dublin – Alfred Cope and General Nevil Macready. With the departure of more senior civil servants, Cope took over the running of

Dublin Castle and acted as chief British liaison to the Provisional Government. In opinion he was closely aligned with Lionel Curtis. He placed the rosiest interpretation on developments in Ireland, defended the Provisional Government at every turn and trivialised opposition to the treaty, asserting that the republicans were a weak minority.[60] A very different account of events was given by the military Commander-in-Chief, General Macready, who, though not a typical diehard, was on very friendly terms with Field-Marshal Wilson. From the beginning, he foresaw that the treaty would lead to further violence: 'I think it quite possible', he wrote, 'that Collins and Co. will have to fight for their lives, not only with ballot boxes, but also with automatics and rifles.' [61] He became more and more pessimistic about the ability and will of the Provisional Government to stand up to its opponents, predicting a republican victory by force or through elections. His overriding concern was to get the British troops out of the country, as they were nothing more than an 'irritant'. They could then leave the Irish to settle their differences – 'if not we can reconquer the country'.[62] With such contrasting interpretations of the situations, it was inevitable that Cope and Macready would clash repeatedly over policy. Relations deteriorated to such an extent that Macready made a failed attempt to have his rival removed. On 15 April 1922 he wrote a damning letter to Cope's superiors in London:

> I hope you will not mind if I say that I think Cope is a danger in the present situation ... it is impossible to rely on his statements, which vary from hour to hour, according as he visualises the situation, and there is no doubt that on account of the nervous strain he has undergone for the last two years he is unable to sift the facts and come to a considered judgment ... it is my strong and considered opinion that, owing to the state of his nerves, he is out of place and a danger to Ireland at the present moment.[63]

This intervention was hardly like to improve relations between the two men; they remained at loggerheads for the rest of the year.

Winston Churchill, Secretary of State for the Colonies, was the chief arbiter between Cope and Macready, and between the competing interpretations of the Irish situation that battled for influence in London. Churchill had been deeply involved in the Irish question for some time, first as Secretary of State for War and then as a member of the British delegation during the treaty negotiations. After the treaty was signed Hamar Greenwood was gradually sidelined, and Churchill was given overall responsibility for Irish affairs: more than anyone else in the British government he shaped the development of the emerging Irish state. His opinions on Ireland were complex: as a signatory to the treaty he felt a personal commitment to carry out the British side of the bargain, and he subscribed to the ideals of liberals such as Lionel Curtis; but temperamentally, and on issues of empire, he had much in common with the diehards, and he was not prepared to tolerate a republic in southern Ireland.

Churchill is a good bellwether for the shifting attitudes of the British government towards Ireland in 1922. In the first months after the signing of the treaty, Churchill, like the majority of the British government, held an optimistic view of Irish affairs. He endorsed the prediction of Hamar Greenwood that 'the treaty of Peace will be accepted by the Irish people throughout the world as a lasting settlement and will open a new chapter in the history of the relations between Ireland and this country'.[64] He pondered over the ceremonies that the new Dublin government would hold for the King's representative and 'talked merrily about British troops returning the salute of the Free State Army on the march'.[65] However, by 2 March 1922 the mood was very different. Sir Henry Wilson noted with satisfaction that Churchill was despondent and 'at last' realised 'the coming crash in Ireland'.[66] This was partly caused by developments in Ireland, which proved the depth of the treaty split in the Sinn Féin movement. It was also produced by a string of alarming intelligence reports, many unreliable, from British officials and informal sources. Two months later, after more disquieting reports, Churchill and the British cabinet had swung even further towards the pessimistic, diehard interpretation of the Irish situation. This drove them to a policy decision that almost had a catastrophic effect on Anglo-Irish relations.

British optimism was first punctured by a wave of attacks on members of the crown forces. Between the signing of the treaty and the start of the Civil War in June 1922, twenty-three RIC officers and eight soldiers were killed.[67] One of the most controversial incidents involved the shooting of a British army officer, Lieutenant Genochio. His body was found on 17 February 1922 near the grounds of Cork Asylum. He had been shot twice in the back. He had left the officers' mess after dinner two days earlier, dressed in plain clothes, and carrying his revolver and identity badge. According to the local IRA and the Provisional Government, he was arrested by the republican police for participating in robberies. They claimed that £15, a lady's hand bag, and some gold watches and chains were found in his possession, and that he was shot while attempting to escape, after his captors had called on him to halt a number of times.[68] An internal British army enquiry concluded that he was not engaged in any criminal activity; instead, he had been targeted by the IRA because he had been 'very active in rounding up rebels' during the War of Independence. They claimed that he had attempted to escape, but had fallen, and was deliberately shot while lying on the ground.[69] The truth about Genochio was and remains 'shrouded in mystery'.[70] However, the case left no doubts about the power of the republicans in Cork and the impotence of the crown forces and the Provisional Government. Neither the remnants of the RIC nor the dwindling British garrison in Cork could obtain any information on what had happened. The recently formed Dublin government did not want to help, as it feared its orders would not be obeyed; the IRA liaison officer in Cork would do nothing, as he did not recognise the Dublin government. It was impossible to hold a normal public coroner's inquest, and the Military Enquiry had to adjourn because there was no evidence.[71] 'Any civilians who might know anything of course refrained from giving evidence', General Macready exasperatedly wrote, referring in particular to 'a lady, who saw the whole thing', but was 'nearly off her head' and knew 'perfectly well that if she gave evidence she would probably be murdered'. 'I hope in London you make no mistake about it', he reported to the War Office, 'that the "Republic" exists in Cork and the surrounding country'.[72]

Of equal concern to London was a string of raids on British military and police facilities by IRA units in search of arms and ammunition. The most audacious involved the capture on the high seas of one of His Majesty's ships, the *Upnor*. On 29 March the vessel left Cork harbour for England, carrying a large quantity of small arms. It was intercepted off the Cork coast by a local IRA unit in a commandeered tug, the *Warrior*. The captured steamer was taken to Ballycotton Bay and some 300 men unloaded the military supplies and transported them away in a fleet of lorries (many borrowed from Murphy's Brewery). Throughout their detention the crews of both vessels were 'treated with consideration': the local hotel was forced open and a bottle of whiskey purchased to sustain them through the night. The operation was only disturbed the next day, when the vice-admiral at Queenstown became suspicious and despatched two destroyers to search for the vessels. Having learnt this news, the IRA raiders abandoned the *Upnor* to be looted by locals.[73] This daring act of piracy highlighted the impotence and blindness of the remaining British forces in Ireland. The naval commander in Cork, Vice-Admiral Gaunt, was harshly criticised for not protecting the shipment, and threatened with court martial.[74] In a long letter to the Admiralty he defended himself by pointing to the lack of intelligence:

My sources of Intelligence were practically nil; my Intelligence Officers, since the evacuation of troops has commenced, find nearly all sources of information have dried up because people who, before would or might speak now consider that the Rebels are the winning side and they will not endanger themselves. I have had no information from the Military and General Macready informs me that he now gets no information. The Provisional Government has given me no information whatever. ... The R.I.C.

have been withdrawn and the Free State Police – whom I am informed are Republicans – consist of three of four young men in mufti with no regular beats and who made themselves scarce upon the occasion of the seizing of the tug.[75]

Together with the Genochio incident, it revealed that the scattered British armed forces remaining in southern Ireland were more of a target than a deterrent to Irish republicans.

The *Upnor* raid showed that the anti-Treaty IRA meant business. Churchill told the cabinet:

The Queenstown episode clearly shows that we are in contact with revolutionaries who will stop at nothing, who are capable of brilliantly conceived operations, and who have facilities and resources at their unhampered disposal both in money and arms of a kind and on a scale never previously experienced.

It was a bad blow to the Provisional Government, as it led to the capture of 449 rifles, 748 revolvers, 39 machine guns and over 300,000 rounds of ammunition. It made the republican section of the Cork IRA by far the most heavily armed party in the district.[76] Coming on top of a string of IRA attacks and raids, it demonstrated that the republican IRA was firmly in control of much of the southwest of the country.

British concerns over the republican threat were heightened by a number of spurious intelligence reports that warned of a *coup d'état* by the Irregular IRA at Easter. These reports arrived simultaneously from police, military and naval sources. According to the Special Branch, rumours were prevalent in England that the extremist section of the IRA was 'contemplating a big coup to depose the Free State Government during the Easter holidays'.[77] Military intelligence assessments, reporting that at least 75 per cent of the IRA in Munster was anti-Treaty, warned of an 'an outburst in the near future'.[78] The most alarming reports came from the naval intelligence officer at Queenstown, Captain G. M. Crick. Perhaps stung by criticism of his inaction during the *Upnor* incident, he provided an amazing report based on a local informer who had 'usually proved reliable and well-informed'. It began with a startling statement:

The split in Sinn Fein is practically 'entirely bluff'. At a secret session of the All-Irish Conference which was held in Paris in January last it was decided to work up this split outwardly as much as possible in order to lull England into a sense of false security, and that when the time was considered ripe (when the Crown Forces had all left the country), to declare a republic. … The Sinn Feiners are delighted that the British Press is so convinced that the two factions are going to fight one another. It has been their aim to encourage this idea in every possible way, and they say that 'England will wake up one morning and discover that instead of fighting each other, they have joined forces, and it will be too late for England to do anything then'.

Crick warned that 'the Extremists' were 'evidently contemplating a "coup" of some description in the immediate future'. The 'Free Staters' would not put up any opposition but bow to 'force majeure'.[79]

IRA activity in southern Ireland and the string of alarmist intelligence reports led to serious anxiety in Whitehall at the end of March about a possible Easter coup. General Macready was urgently called over to London for consultation. He later wrote:

I was over last week for two days and I cannot remember ever having seen such a gale blowing as was raging in Downing Street and the War Office. Even the old days of the Agadir business and the Declaration of War in '14 was as nothing to the wild excitement consequent on the capture by Mr. Barry of one of His Majesty's ships of war.[80]

Soon after, Churchill wrote a detailed and highly secret report for his ministerial colleagues that was 'not reproduced, owing to its great secrecy' and does not appear in the normal cabinet papers.[81] He reported that he was 'becoming increasingly anxious' and apprehended 'either an attempt at a *coup d'état* in Dublin or the proclamation of a Republic in some part of the country'. Although he did not doubt the goodwill of the Provisional Government, its leaders had not stood up to the extremists on any important occasion. 'There is no doubt that the Irish have a genius for conspiracy rather than government', he concluded. 'The Government is feeble, apologetic, expostulatory: the conspirators, active, audacious and utterly shameless.'[82] A Conservative MP with close links to senior party figures also recorded that 'so far as Ireland is concerned, things are going from bad to worse'. 'It looks almost a certainty that in a few weeks, possibly before you get this letter', he told a correspondent on 11 April 1922, 'an Irish Republic will have been declared in the South and West of Ireland.'[83]

In the end the Easter weekend proved something of a damp squib. Anti-Treaty forces peacefully occupied the Four Courts in Dublin, the centre of the Irish judiciary, as a headquarters for their activity, but there was no countrywide uprising against the Provisional Government. It seems that intelligence officers mistook plans for the takeover of the Four Courts for preparations for a major coup. Opinion in London briefly became more optimistic after Mark Sturgis returned from Ireland in the middle of April 1922 with a reassuring report that things were 'worrying along in a favourable direction'.[84] Yet within a month Churchill and his colleagues had swung back towards even greater despair. This time the cause was not only the political and military split within the Sinn Féin movement, but the rising wave of apolitical, criminal and sectarian violence in southern Ireland. There was a catalogue of house raids, bank robberies, car thefts, cattle driving, intimidation, boycotts and attacks on persons, often directed at loyalists and Protestants. At least eighteen civilians were killed in the first six months of 1922.[85] This violence was fuelled by sectarian animosity, personal grudges, land hunger and a breakdown in policing and civil order. The most gruesome murders took place in rural Co. Cork, where ten local Protestants were shot dead between 27 and 29 April: in Churchill's words, this was 'little less than a massacre'. It provoked a flood of Protestant refugees from the south of Ireland.[86]

The British government received a deluge of alarmist warnings and appeals from loyalist residents in Ireland who believed that the events in Cork were the harbinger of a general slaughter. A deputation of loyalists received by Churchill on 25 May reached far back into Irish history and drew explicit parallels with the massacre of thousands of Protestants in 1641 and 1798. They claimed that the same conditions existed now: 'the last relic of Government' had collapsed; there was 'no effective police'; it was 'possible for any man who was armed to rob whom he pleases'; there was 'nothing to prevent the peasants expropriating every Protestant and every loyalist':

> The temper of the country is now like that of a savage country. Murder, arson, robbery, and even mutilation of the dead are common. The slight-est spark may, at any moment, kindle the flame and cause a massacre. ... A massacre is now only a matter of time.[87]

A loyalist woman from Co. Cork asked, 'when will the British Government real-ise that they are really dealing with savages and not ordinary normal human beings?'[88]

The leaders of the diehard faction in Westminster passed on similar warnings to British ministers. In June 1922 Colonel John Gretton transmitted urgent infor-mation to the government that pointed 'to the probability of serious happenings during the first few days of July'. He reported that the Gaelic Athletic Associa-tion, a 'thoroughly Republican body', was organising 'a kind of Olympic Games in Dublin', which would facilitate a large mobilisation of gunmen in Dublin. A 'more alarming portent' was the decision by the Franciscan order to hold a great pilgrimage to Multyfarnham Abbey in Meath for the first time in many years. Gretton explained how the Franciscans, who 'all through Irish history' had been 'the agents of sedition and outrages on Protestants', had met at Multyfarnham Abbey in 1641 to organise a Protestant massacre. According to Gretton, the conjunction of these incidents within one week led to 'grave apprehensions' that a concerted attack was planned against Irish loyalists.[89]

Due to the withdrawal of British officials and soldiers, the London government was over-reliant on these types of reports from outside Dublin. They were either sent directly to Whitehall, or seeped through the matrix of family and friendship that linked the British establishment with the Anglo-Irish class. The sources were invariably Protestant, loyalist and unionist – and prone to exaggeration. Although 1922 witnessed despicable attacks on loyalists and a weakening of law and order, there was no apocalyptic massacre or collapse into anarchy. Southern loyalists – conditioned by centuries of ascendancy and sectarian division, angry at their betrayal and abandonment to the 'savages' by the British government, and fearful that all of this would culminate in a doomsday of Protestant annihilation – did not make the most reliable intelligence agents.

These reports certainly had an impact on British ministers. Churchill opened an important cabinet meeting on 16 May 1922 by stating they were 'witnessing in Ireland a process of rapid social disintegration'. Lord Birkenhead 'feared from information which had reached him that the deterioration was so rapid that the election might not take place in time to arrest it'.[90] The Royal Navy was told to prepare for a general evacuation of loyalists from the Irish coast.[91] Even Lionel Curtis, normally such a champion of the Free State, was shocked by the reports that he received. He drafted a long, threatening letter for Michael Collins that ended with ominous words: 'A time has come when unless drastic steps are taken ... there will presently be no hope for the restoration of order in Ireland except in sheer force ruthlessly applied from without.'[92] This was a not so veiled threat of British reintervention in southern Ireland.

The prospect of military intervention was further increased by changing perceptions of the Provisional Government. Up to May 1922 the British government had sometimes criticised the passivity of the Irish leaders, but had never doubted their *bona fides*. London counted on them eventually using force to crush their republican opponents and to restore law and order. But now that trust began to evaporate. The question became not *when* the Provisional Government would fight the rebels, but *if* they would fight them at all; or if, instead, they would give in to republican demands and sacrifice the treaty in order to avoid the one contingency that the British saw as necessary to safeguard it – civil war. Rather than fight the rebels, the Provisional Government might join them.

This change in British perceptions was partly caused by the Provisional Government's public acts. In the first half of May, Michael Collins made very visible attempts to heal the rift in Sinn Féin and the IRA, culminating in the announcement of an electoral pact with Éamon de Valera on 20 May that guaranteed republicans and Free Staters the same proportion of parliamentary seats then held.[93] A week later the Provisional Government presented its draft constitution to the British government for approval. On seeing the draft, Lloyd George exploded. 'We are back where we were on the first day', he told his ministers on 27 May 1922. 'It is a complete evasion of the treaty and a setting up of a republic with a thin veneer.' 'And with the King as lackey', Churchill added.[94] Two days later, Irish ministers were handed detailed revisions of the constitution with a demand that they be accepted – they were asked to choose between de Valera and the treaty.[95]

Another cause of British suspicion was the discovery of the Provisional Government's secret plots in Northern Ireland and Britain. On 15 May 1922 the IRA launched an offensive in the six counties with secret backing from Michael Collins and senior figures in the headquarters of the National Army. The Northern Ireland administration first suspected, and then was able to prove, Dublin's complicity in the IRA campaign. This was passed to London, along with a stream of intelligence that was in line with diehard unionist conspiracy theories.[96] Around the same time the Special Branch discovered secret attempts by Collins to purchase military supplies in Britain. The chief agent was Frank Fitzgerald, brother of the Director of Publicity in the Provisional Government – his complicity was 'proved up to the hilt'.[97] Detection of these plots reinforced perceptions of the Irish leaders, and especially of Michael Collins, as born conspirators, incapable of responsible government or honest relations with Britain.

One obvious consequence of this loss of faith in the Provisional Government was Churchill's decision in May 1922, against Cope's advice, to suspend the supply of munitions to Dublin. He refused to issue arms 'on a large scale until he was satisfied that they would be used effectively against the Republican party'.[98] In the same month, Churchill called a meeting of the British signatories to the treaty for the first time since December 1921. He gave a very gloomy assessment:

> He said that the situation was increasingly unsatisfactory. He did not think
> we should be confronted with any sudden breakdown and clear issue, but
> rather that the Free State would slide into an accommodation with the
> Republicans. ... Looking back on the political history one could see how
> we had been sold.

Churchill's views were shared by most of his colleagues. Austen Chamberlain was 'losing confidence in Mr Collins'; Lloyd George suggested that they 'may have to face re-conquest'.[99] The dark atmosphere was reflected in the diaries of a contemporary politician, Leo Amery. He wrote on 31 May 1922: 'The Irish situation has now reached the critical point and I fancy we are within a few days of a complete break-down of the famous treaty.'[100] In preparation for this event Churchill held conferences with military chiefs to draw up a plan for the full reconquest of Ireland.[101]

Britain was brought to the brink of military intervention by the greatest crisis of this period – the assassination of Field Marshal Sir Henry Wilson on 22 June 1922. Wilson was shot dead by two London IRA men on the doorstep of his house in Belgravia, London. Because he was a well-known figure, the killing had a dramatic effect on the British public and politicians in Westminster. 'It is enough to make anyone despair of Ireland and curse the Irish as a hopeless and impossible race', the future Prime Minister, Neville Chamberlain, wrote.[102] Recent research indicates that the assassination was an independent act by local IRA men, incensed by Wilson's support for the Northern Ireland government.[103] However, suspicion immediately fell on the Irregular headquarters in the Four Courts in Dublin. The British government came under severe political pressure from Conservatives to destroy this rebel nest, regardless of the attitude of the Provisional Government. In a series of secret and fevered conferences between 22 and 24 June British ministers agreed to take this action. This was a serious misjudgement, which, if carried out, would have changed the course of Irish history. A close analysis of the events of these days reveals that it was produced by flawed handling of Irish intelligence and a poor understanding of the political situation in Ireland.

British ministers made the decision to attack the Irregular headquarters on the basis of a single secret intelligence report received on the same day as Wilson's death. It was provided by a Special Branch agent in Dublin whose identity remains unknown. The head of the Special Branch frankly admitted that they had 'no organisation whatever in that country', so the agent must have been a casual informant, either a remnant of the networks created before 1922, or someone who had subsequently come forward to volunteer information.[104] His report was explosive, stating that the Irregulars in the Four Courts were responsible for the Wilson murder, and warning that the attack marked the start of a wider campaign of violence against British interests: in Britain and Ulster this would take the form of further assassinations; in Dublin there would be attacks on British soldiers, using machine guns and a field gun in the Four Courts, in an attempt to restart hostilities and reunite the IRA. British ministers were convinced that the 'information from Secret Service sources ... indicated the probability of the renewal of activity and outrages by the extreme section of the I.R.A.' within days. When the new Chief of the Imperial General Staff, Lord Cavan, was asked 'whether in a purely military enterprise, he would take action on the unsubstantiated report of a good agent', he declared 'the secret service report good enough information'. Moreover, it was pointed out that 'if, a fortnight hence, trouble arose all over Ireland and in Great Britain, and it became known that the Government had received this warning, people would cry out "Why didn't you take action?" ' As a result, on 23 June British ministers decided that the British army should use tanks, artillery and aeroplanes to capture the Four Courts and 'take prisoner the whole garrison'. It was naively thought that the Provisional Government, though bound to protest, 'would not unlikely be uncommonly glad to have this difficult situation cleared up for them'. British ministers ordered General Macready to carry out this attack on the following day, 24 June, a Sunday.[105]

The only reason that the attack did not take place was that the army refused to obey the order. Macready had briefed the conference on the ease of carrying out the operation when in London on 23 June, but on his return to Dublin that evening he had second thoughts. He sent his staff officer, Colonel Brind, to London to explain why an attack was not a good idea. First, the army cast doubt on the value of the intelligence supplied by the Special Branch. Brind stated that 'it was unusual to rely on single agents. He knew nothing personally of this particular agent, who was not a military agent, though he was thought well of by Scotland Yard.' He 'did not attach much importance to this particular report', as it had a 'marked similarity' to other unreliable pieces of intelligence received during the previous few years. Second, Brind warned that a British attack on the Four Courts would have fatal consequences for the position of the British military in Ireland and for Anglo-Irish relations. It would prompt violent retaliation against loyalists and British troops in Ireland, cause a complete rupture in relations between Britain and the Provisional Government, and 'draw the two wings of the I.R.A. together'. As things stood, the Provisional Government had stated their intention to clear the Four Courts following the Irish election and now 'might act'. On the basis of these military objections, the operation to take the Four Courts was cancelled. Instead, the British cabinet authorised Churchill to make a stern speech in the House of Commons and to give the Provisional Government a final ultimatum.[106]

An attack on the Four Courts by British troops would have wrecked Britain's Irish policy at one stroke. It would have achieved the very object that the republicans sought – a pitched battle between Irregulars and British troops that would have rallied the pro-Treaty IRA behind the republican cause. The decision to carry out this operation reveals how intelligence could be misused by the government. Cabinet ministers, and not intelligence or military personnel, pushed forward the Four Courts operation. It was a political decision, motivated by feelings of anger over the Wilson assassination, disenchantment with the Provisional Government and a determination to strike at the republicans. Ministers seized on the intelligence report from the Special Branch informant and used it as a pretext for action, without properly assessing its accuracy or understanding its context. (The army's reservations about the report should have arisen earlier.) Even more damning was the ignorance and indifference towards the consequences of the Four Courts operation for Irish politics. It was a culmination of four months of alarmist, politicised, partial intelligence that swung opinion towards a pessimistic interpretation of the Irish situation and led to desperate acts. Macready recollected in his memoirs how he never ceased to congratulate himself for 'staving off what would have been a disaster from every point of view, except the actual capture of the buildings':

> Anything more fatuous than the idea of such an enterprise, which would have undone everything for which the Government had striven throughout the past year, it was difficult to imagine. ... It can only be imagined that panic and a desire to do something, no matter what, by those whose ignorance of the Irish situation blinded them to possible results, was at the root of this scheme.[107]

Macready continued that this episode 'flavoured strongly of Mr. Winston Churchill's feverish impetuosity'. It bears all the hallmarks of his approach to intelligence and Ireland. He was fascinated by secret intelligence and too eager to use raw reports as the basis for major policy decisions. He was also capable of wild changes in mood towards Ireland. By May 1922 his advisors were appalled that he wanted 'to pull the whole plant out of the ground'; they tried to 'get Churchill sent on a holiday'.[108] Lloyd George 'compared Winston to a chauffeur who apparently is perfectly sane and drives with great skill for months, then suddenly he takes you over a precipice. He thought there was a strain of lunacy.'[109] Churchill has received widespread praise from historians for his skilful and patient handling of Irish affairs, but his actions in May and June 1922 indicate that he was not always a safe pair of hands.[110]

From intelligence target to intelligence partner

THE folly of the British government's proposed action was demonstrated just two days after Churchill's speech in the House of Commons. At 4 am on 28 June 1922, under the orders of Michael Collins, the forces of the Provisional

Government launched their own attack on the Four Courts, thus starting the Irish Civil War. They bombarded the republican positions using borrowed British artillery, and, despite greater difficulty than expected, compelled the surrender of the garrison two days later. By 5 July the National Army had cleared Irregular units occupying much of Sackville Street (now O'Connell Street), the main thoroughfare of Dublin. After the fighting ended in Dublin, attention turned to the rest of the country. The Provisional Government issued a 'call to arms', rapidly expanded its armed forces with the aid of limitless British supplies, and began to push into republican-controlled areas. The crucial strategic point of Limerick fell, and gradually the Provisional Government forces converged on Cork and Kerry. Cork city was taken after an ambitious landing from the sea, and soon republican garrisons had been cleared from all the south-west. By the end of August 1922 the republicans no longer offered open military resistance. The Provisional Government had gained physical control of its territory.

The state of public opinion throughout the country, the resources at the command of the Provisional Government and the support of Britain meant that the outcome of this military phase of the Civil War was never in much doubt. However, the government struggled to cope when the Irregulars switched from pitched battles to guerrilla warfare. Flying columns were formed to harass Free State forces; political and military leaders were assassinated; arson attacks were directed at the property of treaty supporters and loyalists. Though the situation was quiet in some counties, in others, such as Co. Kerry, the Irregulars were equal to the government forces and could launch major operations. The Provisional Government faced a counter-insurgency challenge similar to that encountered by the British in 1921. It was not helped by the state of the National Army, which was dogged by the inadequacies of its officers, the ill-discipline and inexperience of its troops, the weakness of central command and a poorly functioning supplies organisation.[111] In addition, the Provisional Government was weakened by the death of its two most prominent figures: Arthur Griffith died from a heart attack on 12 August 1922; the most charismatic leader of the Irish revolution, Michael Collins, was shot dead in a republican ambush in his native Co. Cork ten days later.

The man who became President of the Dáil and Chairman of the Provisional Government was William T. Cosgrave. The oldest member of the cabinet, he had a lower profile than his predecessors: a contemporary profile in the *Irish Times* described how he dressed in 'sombre hues', wore a bowler hat and looked 'rather like the general manager of a railway company'.[112] However, with the able support of Kevin O'Higgins (Minister for Home Affairs) and General Mulcahy (Minister for Defence), the Provisional Government took ruthless steps to crush the revolt. When, following the June elections, the Third Dáil met for the first time on 9 September 1922, Cosgrave and Mulcahy stated their determination to stand by the treaty and to use all necessary means to crush the republicans. A Public Safety Bill was introduced, giving them sweeping powers, including the imposition of the death penalty by military tribunals. The first execution of Irregulars was carried out on 17 November, and over the next six months seventy-seven people were officially executed. Many more were murdered by security forces sometimes capable of outdoing the Black and Tans for savagery. Although legally and morally questionable, these actions were effective in crushing the republican revolt. Between February and April 1923 the republicans lost public support, struggled to obtain military supplies and became increasingly demoralised. The final blow came with the killing of the Irregular Chief of Staff, Liam Lynch, on 10 April 1923. His successor, Frank Aiken, realised that continuing the war was futile. He gave the order to dump arms and cease fire on 23 May 1923.[113]

The conditions in southern Ireland after the outbreak of fighting made it harder for the British government to gather good intelligence, especially outside Dublin. London relied on an even more eclectic mix of official, commercial and civilian sources for information. There were also continuing oscillations in British government perceptions of the situation. Initially London welcomed the Civil War with relief, as it appeared to represent an irrevocable commitment by the Irish leaders to the treaty. However, in August and September 1922 the intensification of guerrilla warfare and a series of alarming reports from Ireland created a mood of despondency in London and fears of a republican victory. This proved short lived. The actions of the Cosgrave regime removed any lingering concerns and established a more optimistic interpretation of events; this consensus was not subsequently challenged. The focus of the British government shifted from collecting intelligence *on* southern Ireland to encouraging full collaboration on intelligence and military matters *with* the Irish authorities. Cosgrave's government went some way to becoming the loyal and trustworthy partner that the British had been searching for. This was reflected in the constitutional developments of this period. In September 1922 the Irish Dáil finally approved the draft Irish constitution, and on 6 December 1922 the British parliament formally ratified the treaty and established the Irish Free State. The last British troops left Dublin days later. After a long and difficult birth, independent Ireland had taken its place in the world.

WHILE fighting was confined to Dublin, the British government received detailed intelligence on developments from British officials with ringside seats. Alfred Cope, who was in constant contact with the leaders of the

Provisional Government, provided a blow-by-blow account of the battle in hourly telegrams to London.[114] Military intelligence officers attached to the British garrison in Dublin also discreetly observed the fighting from the streets and buildings around the Four Courts. They were not impressed by what they found. One officer, out to 'see the fun', managed to get into the Bridewell prison, where he came across a young National Army soldier firing shots with amazing inaccuracy at a rebel not more than 150 yards away. The British officer initially gave some hints to the soldier, who had little knowledge of how to use a rifle. When this failed to produce any improvement, the officer finally said: 'Here, give me your rifle.' But the Irish soldier refused indignantly. 'Indeed I will not', he replied, 'you might kill the poor boy!' This anecdote was retold by British army officers to highlight the 'comic opera' nature of the fighting and the reluctance of the Provisional Government forces to use lethal force.[115] However, the army also reported on the successful conclusion of the fighting and the return to normality. On 6 July Colonel Brind and a fellow staff officer could safely walk down Sackville Street, inspecting the ruins and watching the firemen pull down the 'skeleton walls of the burnt buildings', before stopping for a shampoo and a hair cut, and ending the afternoon with tea at the Shelbourne Hotel.[116]

When the fighting moved outside Dublin the situation was very different. The British government found it impossible to gain a good picture of what was happening. 'Very little information is to hand regarding other parts of Southern Ireland', General Macready told the cabinet, 'on account of the absence of an organized Intelligence Service.'[117] This lack of knowledge was not confined to the British. The Provisional Government also struggled to collect good information on the outlying areas, as there was a deliberate campaign by Irregulars to destroy railways, roads, and telephone and telegraph lines. Moreover, in this period the press became even more unreliable than before. Journalists suffered from lack of information and a tendency to sensationalise the fighting. In addition, the Irish authorities imposed an ever stricter censorship that magnified government successes and denigrated the strength of the Irregulars. In effect, the press became a mouthpiece for Free State propaganda: Macready lamented that 'the news published in the Press, being heavily censored, in no way represents the actual condition of affairs.'[118] The unreliability of the press, combined with the lack of official British representatives outside Dublin, threatened to turn much of southern Ireland into *terra incognita*. It forced Whitehall to rely on an eclectic range of sources for its information on the progress of the Civil War: British businesses, the Royal Navy, intercepted Free State army signals, loyalist residents, the Northern Ireland administration and the Special Branch in London.

The economic intimacy of the two islands meant that British companies had numerous representatives in southern Ireland. They sometimes became entangled in the Civil War, providing eye-witness accounts that found their way, via company directors, to the Colonial Office. For example, a wireless operator with the Clyde Shipping Company reported how he was forced by Irregulars to dismantle a wireless set from a ship in Waterford and set it up in the local barracks: he gave details on the strength and disposition of the garrison.[119] An employee of the Queenstown Dry Docks, Shipbuilding and Engineering Company, stationed at Passage, had an excellent vantage point for observing the landing of Free State troops and their capture of Cork city in August. At times he was almost too close to the fighting: he described how one of his colleagues, 'old Buckly', was reading a newspaper in his office when a bullet 'went clean through it' – 'he picked up the bullet and it was quite hot.' This observer gave an optimistic report on the progress of the war in Cork:

> The Irregulars ran out of Cork like a lot of sheep, and the defence of Cork itself was a complete fiasco. They (the Free Staters) had a tremendous reception in Cork and the back of the whole Republican movement is broken. All round the country they are handing in their arms or else leaving them behind for the other fellows to pick up.[120]

The most important intelligence provided by commercial interests came from the two large stations that lay at the end of the transatlantic telegraph cables in Co. Kerry – one in Valentia operated by the Western Union Company, and the other in Waterville operated by the Commercial Cable Company. These installations were of considerable strategic importance, as they controlled the bulk of Britain's transatlantic communications. In the pre-truce period they had been spared from destruction because of the vital expenditure they contributed to the local economy and the moderating influence of a local doctor and priest. But as the Irregulars were forced back into Co. Kerry, the stations became pawns in their bitter struggle against government forces. Waterville was captured in July by republicans, and all outgoing cables were censored by Erskine Childers. It was relieved by the National Army, but was thereafter menaced by marauding bands of Irregulars, who controlled much of the surrounding countryside. The station at Valentia came under similar threat. By early August its equipment had been seriously damaged, and its personnel (200 men, women and children) were practically under siege, with food running short. The superintendents of both stations passed constant information to their headquarters in London using the cables under their control, while the Colonial Office liaised closely with senior executives in each company. The cable stations provided a window on the course of the Civil War in one of the most remote and disturbed parts of the country.[121]

British naval destroyers were also despatched to Valentia and Waterville to help protect the cable stations. This was indicative of the increasingly active, if discreet, role played by the Royal Navy during the Irish Civil War. By August 1922 there were three light cruisers, eleven destroyers and nine minesweepers and auxiliary vessels stationed in Irish waters.[122] These vessels had a number of duties. They provided protection to the Treaty Ports at Queenstown and Berehaven, the cable stations and, on occasion, private property. They evacuated coastguard personnel and loyalist civilians from disturbed areas near the coast: for example, children from a Protestant orphanage at Clifden were rushed to safety by HMS *Watchman* and HMS *Danae* after their building was burnt down by the IRA.[123] The Royal Navy quietly assisted Provisional Government forces by providing transportation, wireless communication, ammunition, fuel and the use of searchlights. Its most important duty was patrolling Irish waters in order to prevent gunrunning to the republicans. These activities sometimes brought the Royal Navy into direct confrontation with armed Irregulars, as there was a standing IRA policy to shoot at British ships in an effort to invite retaliation and bring 'the old enemy back'.[124] 'One's orders are to reply heavily with every available gun', a naval commander wearily noted, 'but as in these cases the sniper is probably behind a bush and the only apparent target is a cottage, some children and cows, it is a little hard.'[125] Despite these dangers the Royal Navy was a constant presence around the coasts and ports of the south and west of Ireland in 1922.

The spin-off of naval involvement was some good intelligence. Naval officers were the best source of information on the Civil War outside Dublin: they were practically the only remaining British officials outside the capital; they were concentrated in the counties where the Civil War was fought and won (Cork and Kerry); and they had access to other remote coastal areas that saw much republican activity – west Galway, Mayo, Sligo and Donegal. This intelligence gathering was channelled through one man: the Senior Naval Officer at Queenstown, Captain Hugh C. Somerville. The brother of the writer Edith Somerville (co-author of *The Irish R.M.*), he was a member of a well-known loyalist family from Co. Cork. He provided invaluable, regular intelligence reports on the progress of the Civil War in the south and west of the country in 1922. He drew on the reports of naval commanders on their tours up and down the Irish coast. He was well positioned to observe the landing of Free State troops at Queenstown during the capture of Cork city. (On one occasion he played an active role, boarding a ship that had been left by the Irregulars to block the river channel and disconnecting an explosive device.)[126] Somerville and other naval officers also used their local contacts to build up a network of pro-Free State informants around the coast. For example, the Harbour Master at Fenit provided details of individuals involved in republican gunrunning.[127]

This was not the only surreptitious activity carried out by the Royal Navy in this period. Together with the British military, it actively intercepted, decrypted and read the signals communications of the Free State army.[128] Due to the breakdown of land communication, the Irish forces relied heavily on radios; consequently their messages were easily picked up by naval and military listeners. On many occasions the British did not have to go to this trouble, as the Free State troops frequently sent their messages via British-controlled equipment, using radios on Royal Navy ships or the cable stations in Co. Kerry; this practice was enthusiastically promoted as it provided direct access to the communications of the Irish army. Many of these messages were sent *en clair*. Even when encrypted, the Irish ciphers were usually simple, inexpertly used, and easily broken by British cryptanalysts. Occasionally Irish signals security was so lax that material fell into British laps without the slightest effort: some letters and telegrams addressed to the Free State army headquarters in Dublin were inadvertently delivered to the nearby British headquarters instead! The confused transition between British rule and Irish independence, therefore, could have its intelligence advantages.[129]

The final sources of information on the Civil War – individual residents in southern Ireland, the Northern Ireland administration and the Special Branch of the Metropolitan Police – were more problematic. Whitehall continued to receive a stream of letters and visits from individuals in southern Ireland. Because they usually passed through the web of family, social and political contacts that linked the two islands, they came disproportionately from the Protestant Anglo-Irish community, which suffered most during the Civil War and could be biased. In the middle of 1922 the Northern Ireland government turned its extensive security and intelligence apparatus on the south, and actively spied on the twenty-six counties. Though the information collected was often equally biased and unreliable, it was passed to London with a measure of official imprimatur. Finally, the Special Branch in London continued to gather an assortment of gossip on conditions in southern Ireland through its informants in the Irish community in Britain and by reading the mails of republican suspects. It picked out the most shocking reports on conditions in Ireland, and distributed them to British ministers and civil servants. These three sources of information were susceptible to inaccuracy and alarmism; they would have a negative effect on British assessments of the Civil War in August and September 1922.

I NITIALLY, however, the British government was greatly buoyed by the actions of the Provisional Government. Civil war was exactly what the British wanted, as it created an irrevocable split between the supporters of the treaty and the republic. Lionel Curtis wrote that the Provisional Government had 'crossed the rubicon and definitely ranked themselves on the side of the constitutional government by opening fire on their old comrades'.[130] The attack on the Four Courts brought a complete change in the attitudes of British ministers, after the extreme despondency just days before. This was especially evident in the response of Winston Churchill. He immediately authorised the transfer of a small arsenal to the Dublin government, overruling the reservations of the British armed services.[131] He wrote warmly to Michael Collins that the action he had taken 'with so much resolution and coolness was indispensable if Ireland were to be saved from anarchy and the treaty from destruction.'[132] Referring to the explosions that had destroyed the ancient records of the Four Courts, he added a typically Churchillian flourish: 'The archives of the Four Courts may be scattered but the title deeds of Ireland are safe.' [133] Even General Macready grudgingly admitted that 'the Provisional Government had made a much better fight than might have been expected'. (He also took comfort in the fact that 'retribution overtook a large proportion of the gunmen at the hands of their own countrymen and former abettors in murder.')[134] There was a wholehearted shift back to the early optimism that had underpinned the British government's treaty policy. It was thought that it would only be a short period of time before the republicans were crushed and southern Ireland could take its place as a loyal Dominion within the commonwealth.[135]

This optimism was severely shaken in August and September 1922. This was partly due to unfavourable developments in Ireland. The shift to guerrilla warfare posed a major threat to the Provisional Government and highlighted the inadequacies of its armed forces. Alfred Cope, the British army and the Royal Navy all tracked this worrying trend. The Dublin government was also hit by the double blow of losing its two most prominent leaders. British attitudes to the death of Michael Collins were decidedly mixed. The most notorious gunman of the 1920–1 period, and implicated in the 1922 attacks on the north, many were glad to see him go. 'Personally I felt a sense of relief when I heard that Collins had paid what you just described as a debt he owed', Curtis wrote to Churchill. 'I don't believe that the P.G. [Provisional Government] would ever have shaken off the habits of conspiracy in which they were tied, so long as he remained at their head.' He later remarked that 'Collins's early death alone saved the treaty.'[136] Griffith's death provoked greater consternation in London, as he had been cast as the only Sinn Féin leader who believed in the Free State concept. Macready stated that it would 'have serious consequences', because he was widely trusted and respected.[137] Moreover, Griffith and Collins were signatories to the treaty, had personally conducted talks with the British ministers over the previous eight months, and had popular appeal in Ireland – in contrast, little was known about William Cosgrave.[138]

In addition to actual events in Ireland, the British government also received very gloomy reports that perpetuated the pessimistic unionist perspective of Irish affairs. Most notably, this came from the loyalist community in southern Ireland. A steady stream of letters from southern loyalists lambasted the fighting ability of the National Army, questioned the determination of the Provisional Government to quash republicanism and described a litany of attacks on Protestant women, property and churches across the country. These reports were passed to government officials by Tory politicians such as Lord Salisbury.[139] In October 1922 a deputation of southern unionists, led by W. M. Jellett, MP, visited the Colonial Office and handed in a seven-page document that was infused with the language and imagery of the apocalypse.

> Four months ago Ireland was on the brink of economic paralysis and political anarchy. Since then the crash has come. Southern Ireland has sunk to the nadir of her fate. ... The destruction of the last few months is simply staggering. It far exceeds that of 1798. We have to go back to 1641 to find anything like a parallel. Throughout the 26 southern counties of Ireland, murder, pillage, rapine, and arson stalk unchallenged. The full force of the cyclone fell on the loyalists first. It has now swept beyond them, and threatens to submerge all who have anything to lose.

According to this deputation, they were faced with a combination of republicans, Bolsheviks and 'all the elements of Irish lawlessness – the egoist, the landless man, the unemployed desperado, the village bully, the anarchist, in fact all those who are discontented'. The Free State was 'left with a weak and fading Government' and 'untrained and undisciplined' military forces that were 'wholly unable to establish ordered conditions'. With the collapse of the economy, Ireland was now 'faced with the question of famine'. Soon there would be 'little to distinguish rural Ireland in the twentieth century from the steppes of Russia in the stone age'. The report was ultimately an exposition of the unionist creed and a polemic against the treaty policy:

> Southern Unionists have always believed, and still believe, that the policy of the Union is the only policy that can save Ireland from herself, and secure the foundations of the Empire. It is but poor consolation to them,

amidst the ruins of their homes and the wreckage of their country, to contemplate that what they have always said would happen under the policy
of Home Rule had happened, and worse than they ever dared to predict ...
To the impartial observer there would appear to be now only two alterna-
tives before this distracted country, either the speedy restoration of Imperial control, or the perpetuation of chaos, misery, and murder, with the
certainty that a Republic will be established in the near future on the ruins
of a land so recently thriving and prosperous.[140]

A similarly bleak interpretation of developments in southern Ireland was evident within the unionist community in Northern Ireland. Unionist newspapers
portrayed conditions in the twenty-six counties in the worst possible light.[141]
Unionist politicians wrote directly to Churchill and other British politicians
about how the Free State was an 'impossible proposition' doomed to 'anarchy
and chaos'.[142] The security forces of the Northern Ireland government produced
alarmist intelligence, full of conspiracies about a likely combination of republicans and Free Staters against the north. The northern intelligence service enjoyed
close relations with the British military in Belfast and shared its information
freely; these assessments, therefore, found their way into the British military
intelligence system.[143]

The reports of southern and northern unionists were part of a concerted diehard unionist campaign against the Free State and against Britain's Irish policy.
A memorandum from the delegation led by Jellett was reborn as a Conservative
Party pamphlet. These views, along with gruesome stories of loyalist persecution, were repeated almost daily in the right-wing *Morning Post*. This campaign
had two aims. The first was unrealistic: to topple the Lloyd George government,
destroy the treaty settlement, bring about the British reconquest of Ireland and
re-establish the Union. The second was more achievable: gaining financial compensation from the British government for damages suffered by Irish loyalists. A
number of associations were formed to agitate on this issue. With contacts and
sympathisers in the media, parliament and government, they earned a great deal
of publicity for their cause.[144] While persecution of loyalists did occur, there is
no doubt that these campaigners exaggerated its extent and underestimated the
intention of the Free State government to treat loyalists fairly.

These pessimistic views also began to creep into the reports of the British
army in Ireland. After some early hopes, General Macready became increasingly despondent about the situation. The remaining British troops in Dublin
were subjected to daily attack and insult by Irregulars, suffering a number of
casualties: for example, an intelligence officer was shot dead on 30 August when

he flagged down a car after a minor road accident.[145] The shift to guerrilla warfare did not augur well, as the might of the British empire had failed to defeat such a campaign in 1920–1. Above all, British military officers had the lowest possible opinion of the Free State armed forces. British reports portrayed Irish troops as poorly trained, badly led, disorganised and undisciplined, with many cases of drunkenness. One informant stated that non-commissioned officers who had previously served with the British army were murdered by their men if they started enforcing discipline; it was then put down to an ambush or an accident.[146] There were considerable doubts about the loyalty and zeal of the Irish army: according to Macready, the 'fundamental difficulty' was 'the reluctance of the Free State troops to kill the Irregulars'.[147] Macready even had 'a strong suspicion' that Michael Collins 'was shot by his own men. A .303 bullet does not stick in a man's head at short range!' When the Free State army started to take more aggressive action against the rebels, the British army disdainfully noted how it resorted to murder and intimidation, thus losing the confidence of the people.[148] By September 1922 Macready feared that the Irregular campaign would 'reduce the whole country to a state of terrified impotence'. Pointing to rumours of peace initiatives before the opening of the Dáil, he suspected that the Provisional Government would cave in to republican demands.[149] This once again raised the spectre of British military reintervention in southern Ireland: Macready had little doubt that it was 'a case of "when" not "if" ' that the British army would be called on to 'destroy the gunmen'.[150]

The confluence of worrying events and bleak intelligence reports produced a wobble in London towards a more pessimistic view of the Irish situation. Churchill was so concerned that he called a rare meeting of the British signatories to the treaty on 7 September 1922. He read out a despondent letter from an Irishman in Clonakilty, Co. Cork that described how the country was 'ruined' and famine at hand – the letter had been obtained by the Special Branch through its monitoring of suspect mails. Macready, who also attended, gave a very pessimistic analysis of the situation.[151] The result of this disturbing meeting was a telegram from Curtis to Cope:

> Mr. Churchill directs me to tell you that reports received here from several different quarters point to the conclusion that the P.G. forces are making no real headway against the republicans, and suggest that negotiations are on foot with Breen for an understanding before Saturday or soon after. Mr. Churchill wishes you to report fully on the situation for his information by to-morrow morning.[152]

At this point Cope played a crucial role in steadying British nerves. The actions of the Provisional Government in the summer of 1922 had strengthened his position. Soon after the attack on the Four Courts began, Churchill had sent him a warm note: 'I consider the events of the last three days and the action of the Irish leaders constitute a striking vindication of the judgment and instinct which you have displayed in Irish affairs.' He promised to submit Cope's name to the king for special recognition. (Cope replied that he was 'deeply touched' by this 'very kind message'; his old colleague, Mark Sturgis, telegrammed, 'Congratulations old boy.')[153] Cope, who continued to enjoy the closest relations with the Irish government, was henceforth restored to a position of great influence over British policy. When he received the disturbing telegram from Lionel Curtis on 7 September he immediately took steps to refute the accusations. He asserted that the Provisional Government was sticking by the treaty and would not compromise with the republicans, and that the Irish army was 'steadily improving.' 'All things considered I think the present situation is quite hopeful', he wrote. 'The Prov. Gov. [sic] is gaining strength and confidence.' Cope also explicitly set out 'to confute the statements made in *Morning Post* and Die Hard Circles that the condition of Ireland is one of anarchy.' He reported that loyalists were not especially victimised, law and order was returning, there was no risk of famine.[154] His positive analysis was supported by Lionel Curtis when he made a personal visit to Dublin on 17 September 1922. The reports from Cope and Curtis, combined with the ruthless steps taken by the Provisional Government to crush the republican revolt, dispelled any lingering British concerns about the fate of the treaty. From October 1922 the needle swung strongly towards a more hopeful interpretation of the Irish situation – and stayed there. There was never any further doubt that the Provisional Government would win the Civil War and establish the treaty settlement; as a result, the prospect of British military reintervention disappeared.

This optimistic consensus survived some potentially tricky changes in the British government. On 19 October 1922 the coalition government under Lloyd George collapsed, following a revolt by back-bench Conservative MPs at the Carlton Club. A Conservative administration was formed under Andrew Bonar Law, which went on to win a majority at a general election one month later.[155] This did not augur well for nationalist Ireland. The new cabinet, to quote A. J. P. Taylor, was 'strikingly Conservative, even obscurantist, in composition.'[156] Its Prime Minister had led opposition to the Liberal Home Rule Bill in 1912–14 and it contained ministers, such as Lord Salisbury, who had been on the fringes of the diehard movement since 1921.[157] The power shift brought some immediate changes to British representation in Dublin. Alfred Cope, who had suffered public attacks by figures close to the new government, resigned and was replaced by his assistant, N. G. Loughnane. In contrast, military officers reacted warmly to these political developments: according to Macready, they 'looked forward to the advent of a Government who would relive them from an indefinite prolongation of the "watching brief," and from the startling surprises to which they had momentarily been liable under the wayward direction of Mr. Churchill.' [158] Following Macready's advice, the new administration decided to evacuate the remaining British troops from around Dublin. This was carried out with great pomp and ceremony on Sunday 17 December 1922.[159] Yet there were no major changes to British policy towards Ireland. The new government pragmatically accepted that they had no option but to implement the treaty settlement: even Lord Salisbury said that the Provisional Government should be 'treated with liberal patience.'[160]

In early 1923 the new government expressed satisfaction at developments in Ireland. The military withdrawal put an end to the army's negative, corrosive influence on British perceptions of southern Ireland. Henceforth the officials of the Colonial Office would have unchallenged supremacy in shaping British policy towards the Free State. Anglo-Irish relations had improved greatly, and William Cosgrave was soon regarded as a substantial improvement on the wayward Michael Collins. The new Secretary of State for the Colonies, the Duke of Devonshire, expressed wholehearted confidence in the Free State authorities when he looked back on his first six months in office in April 1923:

> Throughout this period [Cosgrave] and his government have in every detail shewn the most scrupulous fidelity to the terms of the settlement. ... The various sources of secret information at our disposal not only in this office but also in the War Office, have yielded no single indication of bad faith on the part of the Free State Government. The members of this Government have risked their lives and suffered loss in their own property and families in order to make good their obligations under the treaty to establish a constitutional government in Ireland. The most conclusive proof of all is that they have not hesitated to execute some of their former comrades.[161]

The improvement in relations between Dublin and London led to a change in intelligence priorities. The focus shifted from collecting intelligence *on*, and planning military operations *against*, the Irish Free State, to collaborating *with* the Free State on military and intelligence matters. During the Civil War there were two types of assistance that Britain could offer: tactical military and naval support on southern Irish territory, and joint action against republicans abroad. The Dublin authorities were cautious about accepting this help, as it might provide ammunition for republican propagandists who claimed that the Free State was a puppet of the British government. The legacy of the War of Independence also caused suspicion on both sides. Consequently, in the first months of the Civil War, Anglo-Irish co-operation was *ad hoc* and not particularly effective: the Provisional Government attempted to go it alone. By the end of 1922, however, it had reached a much deeper level, because of changes in attitudes on both sides of the Irish Sea.

The British armed services provided discreet assistance to the Free State in its prosecution of the Civil War. The role of the British army was limited to the transfer of arms, ammunition, vehicles and other war equipment. British army officers never developed close relations with, nor any measure of respect for, their supposed imperial partners. Assistance was usually given begrudgingly and only after stern orders from ministers in London.[162] The Royal Navy co-operated more easily with the Free State armed forces. 'One gets the impression that the Navy are more inclined to help in Ireland than the Army, who are, of course in a more difficult & delicate position', one Whitehall official remarked.[163] Captain Hugh Somerville in Cork enjoyed good relations with local Free State army commanders, who kept him fully briefed on the course of the war. Naval ships helped to prevent republicans moving by sea, and gave direct assistance to the Irish army on land: for example, when the Free State garrison was attacked at Cahirciveen, HMS *Waterhen* used searchlights and fired a star-shell, which 'effectively stopped the battle'.[164] The most important type of assistance requested by the Dublin government was help with stopping Irregular gunrunning. In the summer of 1922 arms and ammunition flowed through American and European republican networks to Britain, from where they were smuggled to Ireland by sea. The Provisional Government requested that the Royal Navy institute a 'vigilant' patrol on the south and west coasts of the island, urging that 'special observation' should be made 'on small crafts such as trawlers and fishing vessels picking up contraband at sea'.[165] As a result, the Royal Navy deployed six minesweepers and four fishery trawlers, the latter disguised as normal working vessels, to join the force of destroyers and cruisers already in Irish waters. They carried out many searches of vessels in the summer of 1922.[166]

Yet the ineffectiveness of this naval patrol highlighted the restricted nature of Anglo-Irish security collaboration. Up to the end of July, though seventy-six vessels had been stopped and searched, not one shipment of munitions had been discovered.[167] The Admiralty made a number of efforts to end what they regarded as an onerous and futile commitment, complaining that they were 'maintaining a vigilant and expensive patrol on the West Coast of Ireland with barren results'.[168] In October 1922 the number of Royal Navy ships in Irish waters was halved, and the regular gunrunning patrol came to an end. The reason for its failure was that most gunrunning was being carried out by small coasting vessels that mingled with other sea traffic and landed at many creeks along the coast.[169] It was impossible to search them all. Instead, intelligence was required on specific shipments of arms so that individual vessels could be targeted. This, in turn, required undercover intelligence operations against the republican organisation in Britain.

Here, too, co-operation between the British and Irish organisations was initially lacking. In the summer of 1922 the Irish government under Michael Collins was reluctant to co-operate with its old enemy. It tried to go it alone, tapping into the old IRB and IRA networks to create an Irish clandestine intelligence system in Britain. Some of these men had been tasked before the start of the Civil War with secretly procuring weapons for the Provisional Government; these efforts continued into August 1922, much to the chagrin of the British authorities, who stumbled across at least three individuals active in this way.[170] Even when these Irish agents had success in penetrating the Irregular organisation, the lack of co-operation with the British police reduced their effectiveness. First, they could take little action against the Irregulars because they had no law enforcement powers.[171] Second, their secretive activities confused and diverted the British police's own attempts to suppress republican plots. One officer from the Criminal Investigation Department in Dublin (Arthur Nolan) was arrested after he was discovered on the Glasgow–Liverpool train with twenty-seven automatic pistols, a revolver and a machine gun. He had confiscated these weapons from Irregulars in Scotland, and intended to return them to his superiors in Dublin, but the British police understandably feared that he was smuggling on behalf of the republicans. He languished in police custody until Alfred Cope secured his release. The Special Branch complained that 'in these days, it is difficult to differentiate between Irishmen ... who are Free Staters one day and Republicans the next and all the time have none too friendly feelings towards England'.[172]

The inadequate information-sharing between the Irish and British security forces was highlighted by two incidents in 1922. In July the Provisional Government learnt that a republican courier named M. J. O'Connell was arriving on an ocean liner from America with despatches for Éamon de Valera. Irish officials urgently approached Cope to enquire whether the Royal Navy could discreetly arrange for the courier to be intercepted. They suggested that the British prevent the ship from landing in Ireland and redirect it to England, possibly by citing an imaginary minefield. However, due to delays in communication, the message arrived too late: by the time Captain Somerville in Cork began to consider the problem, a republican launch had already met the ship and escorted O'Connell away.[173] The second incident involved the arrival of another suspect ship – the ss *Wicklow Head* – from Germany in early September. Information that this ship was carrying arms for the Irregulars first came from the police in Northern Ireland. It was passed through the Admiralty to the Colonial Office, then to Cope in Dublin, and finally to the Provisional Government, which again asked the Royal Navy to intervene. The ship was detained by the HMS *Doon* and thoroughly searched, although no arms were found. This incident revealed the slow and convoluted mechanisms for sharing time-sensitive information between Belfast, London and Dublin. It led Lionel Curtis to begin an initiative to improve intelligence co-ordination:

> Hitherto all this kind of intelligence work has centred in London. Henceforth there are to be three organisations, one here, one in Belfast and one in Dublin. The London and Dublin departments have already got at cross purposes over those Dublin detectives who were arrested by our police. I now find that there is no liaison between the Intelligence services here [in London] and in Belfast. ... These different Intelligence Services ought not to develop into water-tight compartments. They must learn to keep in touch with one another.[174]

Although Curtis' dream of perfect co-operation was not realised, steps were taken after the *Wicklow Head* incident to establish co-ordination between the Free State and British intelligence organisations. As Curtis hoped, the death of Collins removed a conspiratorial and Anglophobic influence; the Cosgrave administration proved far more willing to work with London. It agreed to approach the British in the first instance for all its military supplies and to inform them of any moves to purchase arms from other sources – there would be no more intrigues.[175] Of even greater significance was a decision by the Irish cabinet on 6 September 1922: the minutes record that 'sanction was given to the Army to co-operate with the authorities in places outside Ireland for the arrest of persons engaged in gun-running or other activities, on behalf of the Irregulars'.[176] This was a euphemism for active intelligence co-operation with the British authorities.

The effects of this decision were soon evident outside Ireland. The Dublin government disclosed its intelligence activities in Britain and asked for official recognition. Irish agents were issued with firearms permits and began 'secretly and efficiently' passing information on Irregular arms trafficking to the British police for action.[177] In addition, the new Irish Director of Intelligence, Diarmuid O'Hegarty, travelled to Britain, saw the police authorities, and made arrangements for co-ordination that had 'very satisfactory results'. Subsequently, 'two good officers' were sent by O'Hegarty to London and Liverpool 'to get things into shape there'.[178] By the end of 1922 there was increased liaison between Irish army intelligence and Scotland Yard, and between Irish agents in Britain and the local police. There was similar co-operation between Dublin and London to counter Irregular activities in the United States and continental Europe. By the spring of 1923 the Free State and Britain were working together closely, if secretly, to starve the Irregulars of arms, ammunition and financial support from abroad. As we shall see in the next chapter, this had a major effect on the ability of the Irregulars to prolong the Civil War.

T HE British state's intelligence relationship with Ireland had changed entirely in the two years since July 1921. From posing a domestic security problem, the twenty-six counties now had many of the characteristics of a foreign country. From relying on an extensive intelligence and counter-insurgency apparatus, the British government, with few official representatives in the new state, was now dependent on informal, *ad hoc* sources of information. From treating the Sinn Féin movement as an enemy to be fought, London was now co-operating and sharing intelligence with former Sinn Féin leaders in Dublin. For much of this period of transition, the British government struggled to understand the fluctuating Irish situation. The intelligence vacuum caused by the dismantling of the old structures was partially filled by rumour, biased reporting and politicised interpretation by officials and ministers in London. In an 'atmosphere of "alarms and excursions"', British perceptions swung towards despairing extremes, and British policy makers flirted with decisions that could have brought the entire Anglo-Irish settlement crashing down. However, by 1923 British policy and Anglo-Irish relations had achieved much greater stability. A major cause was the willingness of the Irish authorities to engage in intelligence and security co-operation with the British state, albeit secretly. This played an important part in confirming the new Free State as a trustworthy partner in the British commonwealth.

CHAPTER 3

An International Conspiracy

I N March 1923, as the Irish Civil War entered its last stage, an American attorney named John T. Ryan boarded an ocean liner for Germany. Ryan was a leading figure within Clan na Gael, the secret American counterpart to the Irish Republican Brotherhood. He had fought in the 1898 Spanish-American war, arranged German help for the Easter Rising in 1916 and represented the Sinn Féin movement in Germany between 1920 and 1922.[1] On his return to Germany, he carried $100,000 in Clan na Gael funds, together with instructions to arrange a major arms shipment for the anti-Treaty Irregulars in Ireland. If it proved impossible to smuggle the supplies by ship, Ryan hoped to purchase a decommissioned German submarine. Once in Germany, Ryan exhibited the ideological flexibility that was a hallmark of Irish revolutionaries. He worked closely with the German Communist Party, which had aided previous IRA gunrunning schemes. At the same time he approached the right-wing paramilitary groups that had sprung up in the chaotic political atmosphere of post-war Germany, making at least one overture to Adolf Hitler and his National Socialist Party. Though the German government was officially opposed to the export of arms to Irish rebels, there is evidence that Ryan had friends in high places and received assistance from at least one cabinet minister.[2] In addition, he could call on the support of the IRA organisation in Britain, which transmitted correspondence to and from Ireland and provided a channel for the smuggling of small packages of arms.

Ryan's activities illustrates the extent to which the Irish republican movement was an international conspiracy. Given the distribution of the Irish race, this was hardly surprising: by 1911 one-third of all people born in Ireland were living elsewhere.[3] Republican networks in Britain, the United States of America and Europe provided crucial support to the fighters at home, in the form of funds, war material and propaganda. Irish revolutionaries sought assistance from Britain's foreign adversaries, principally Germany and the Soviet Union. The foreign dimension also provided a field for offensive action against British interests, through physical sabotage (terrorism on English soil) and diplomatic sabotage (interference with Britain's relations with other countries). The international aspect of the militant republican movement has been neglected in histories of the Irish revolution – there is no comprehensive treatment, just occasional asides in works that focus on Irish events – yet it posed a serious threat to Britain and was a preoccupation of the British intelligence community and government.

Dealing with this international conspiracy was in some ways easier than tackling the insurgency in Ireland, because it conformed more naturally to the duties, powers and strengths of the established British intelligence system. The Special Branch of the London Metropolitan Police was responsible for investigating republican activity in Britain. It also co-ordinated intelligence on Irish activities abroad, which mostly came from the secret foreign intelligence service (referred to here as SIS for the sake of consistency) or the diplomatic service under the Foreign Office. Overall, British intelligence performed quite well outside of Ireland. However, there were also failures caused by a lack of co-ordination, an inability to separate baseless scares from accurate information, and the limited range of responses available to the British state, both on home soil and abroad. Moreover, the experience of the Civil War would show that the British authorities could only fully neutralise the threat of militant republicans outside Ireland with the active assistance of the government *inside* southern Ireland. This was a lesson that would be brought home even more strongly during the 1930s and the Second World War.

Irish rebels in Britain

THE most active arena for republican activity outside Ireland was Britain. Irish republicans saw the British government as controlling Ireland's destiny and wished to apply pressure at the source of British power. The existence of a large, sometimes alienated, Irish immigrant community provided an ideal pool of supporters. (According to the census, in 1921 there were 523,767 Irish-born persons in Britain.)[4] Britain first became a major field for republican activity during the War of Independence. One dimension of the Irish campaign was open and political. An Irish-Self Determination League, numbering 27,000 members, conducted propaganda against British policy through rallies, publications and speeches. The second dimension was secret and military. Built on the foundations of an older IRB structure, IRA companies were formed in Scotland, London, Newcastle, Liverpool, Manchester, Birmingham and Sheffield. They comprised approximately 1,000 men, although only a proportion could be relied upon for active operations. IRA activities received enormous coverage in the British press, but the impression remains that the IRA never worked out a coherent strategic rationale for operations in Britain. Its activities were *ad hoc*, only gathered steam in the middle of 1921, and did not reach their full potential.[5]

The IRA may have perfected the techniques of twentieth-century popular insurgency in Ireland, but it lacked either the will or the imagination to fully pursue modern urban terrorist methods in 'enemy' territory.

Michael Collins was a driving force behind this IRA campaign, as he had worked in London for almost ten years and knew the country well. He used his IRB contacts in Britain to mastermind a number of dashing prison escapes: the most famous – involving keys smuggled in a cake – was the freeing of Éamon de Valera from Lincoln Gaol in February 1919.[6] Collins also brought the increasingly vicious counter-intelligence war to Britain. On 14 May 1921 the homes of fifteen English Auxiliary officers were targeted: five relatives were attacked and one killed. On 2 April 1921 the body of an English agent, Vincent Fovargue, was discovered on a golf course in Middlesex with a note pinned to his jacket: 'Let Spies and traitors beware – I.R.A.' Fovargue was a member of a Dublin IRA battalion who had betrayed his comrades to the British authorities and fled the country, before being tracked down by Collins's network. IRA leaders in Dublin also considered kidnapping and assassinating leading British politicians, though no attempt was ever made because of the practical challenges and the expected negative political impact. Britain was also a critical link in the IRA's international gunrunning networks. Not only was it the source of large quantities of stolen explosives, arms and ammunition, but it was also a conduit for much of the material secretly imported from America and continental Europe. This material was smuggled to Ireland in trawlers, merchant vessels and on the mail-boats from Holyhead, often beneath the undergarments worn by women of Cumann na mBan.[7]

Prison escapes, assassinations and gunrunning were clandestine in nature, but the final element of IRA activity in Britain was designed to attract maximum publicity. Starting in November 1920 there was an escalating campaign of damage to property. This included incendiary attacks on farms, warehouses, factories, cotton mills and railway signal boxes, as well as widespread cutting of railway, telegraph and telephone lines. *The Times* described how one wave of incidents from the Tyne to the Tees on 26 March 'lit up the district for miles around' in an 'extraordinary burst of illumination'. The attacks were carried out by small groups of IRA men operating close to their homes at night or at weekends. Casualties were usually avoided, but the IRA units were heavily armed, and shooting did sometimes occur: one policeman, two IRA men and one civilian watchman were killed during these operations. The damage caused was valued at over £1 million. The publicity impact was also massive: questions were frequently asked in the House of Commons, and, on average, *The Times* ran a story on the British IRA every second day from January to June 1921.[8]

The British state met this threat through a combination of normal legal and policing measures and special initiatives. The powers available to the police and the courts were bolstered by the Restoration of Order in Ireland Act passed in 1920. The decentralised and autonomous local police forces were the 'front line' in applying these laws against the IRA. Although they increased patrols and security measures, they were generally unable to prevent attacks. Their effectiveness was rather in the response. Once attacks occurred, the police rounded up Sinn Féin activists in the area and gathered incriminating evidence through subsequent interrogations and searches of property. The Liverpool police were the most effective, arresting four successive captains of the city's IRA company. Local police forces concentrated on the prevention, detection and investigation of particular illegal acts, rather than the penetration and surveillance of subversive movements. Pure intelligence work was the preserve of the Special Branch of the London Metropolitan Police. (After the end of the First World War MI5 rarely paid any attention to the IRA, except where it touched on espionage matters.) 'The Branch' reached its maximum strength and influence between 1919 and 1921 as part of a powerful Directorate of Intelligence under Sir Basil Thomson. Though responsible for combating all forms of subversion, including communism, Irish republicanism continued to be one its chief duties. Plain-clothes officers attended public meetings, suspects were followed, informers recruited within Irish circles, homes and individuals searched for documents. The most valuable source of information, as it had been for the British intelligence community during the First World War, was the secret, systematic interception of suspects' mail. Unlike in Ireland, where the IRA used its own courier networks, Irish separatists in Britain relied on the Royal Mail for communication, thus providing a steady stream of information for the Special Branch. The combination of Special Branch intelligence and local police action certainly had some impact on the IRA organisation: over 200 people were arrested and charged, convicted or interned on IRA-related offences before the truce in July 1921. At times this crippled local IRA companies.[9]

Yet the IRA was always able to reform and engage in further acts of violence. The intensity of attacks increased steadily during 1921 and reached a peak in June with 101 incidents. It forced the government to sanction a number of extraordinary security measures, especially in the capital: fifty prominent individuals received bodyguards; barriers were erected around Whitehall and Westminster; the army was called out to patrol telegraph lines and other vulnerable points; checkpoints were erected on all roads out of London each night, and motorists were stopped and questioned by armed police.[10] If the IRA stumbled on its British campaign through instinct and accident, it is clear that the British authorities

were improvising a response. They would not be the first democratic government in the twentieth century that struggled to suppress a violent campaign
by non-state actors. There was considerable relief when the truce brought this
campaign to an end.

In the uncertain period between the truce (July 1921) and the signing of the
Anglo-Irish Treaty (December 1921), when negotiations frequently teetered on
the brink of collapse, it appears that the IRA leadership realised the power of its
terrorist weapon and planned to greatly increase the level of violence in Britain
should hostilities restart. This came to the attention of the Special Branch. Sir
Basil Thomson warned that the failure of the peace negotiations was 'almost
certain' to be followed by reprisals in England, claiming that Michael Collins had
'been organising and arranging for this purpose' while attending the peace conference in London.[11] When this information reached Sir Henry Wilson (Chief of
the Imperial General Staff), he attempted to leak it in order to discredit the Sinn
Féin delegation.[12] The British authorities certainly overestimated the strength of
the IRA in this period. The Special Branch told the cabinet on 17 November 1921
that the organisation was 'computed by observers to be approximately 19,000 in
England and Scotland', 'most ... in possession of a considerable amount of arms'.
This was an exaggeration: the IRA in Britain still consisted of approximately
1,000 men, and few possessed weapons.[13]

Apart from planning a future campaign, the main activity of the IRA in Britain
during the truce period was acquiring and smuggling war materials. The Special
Branch uncovered some of these efforts. It issued a warning to wholesale chem-
ists after learning that they were receiving orders from Ireland for chemicals
which could be used for the manufacture of high explosives. It tracked closely
efforts to obtain arms from servicemen. When six machine guns and twenty
rifles were taken from barracks at Chelsea and Windsor, the Special Branch
discovered that the IRA had been assisted by one Sergeant Michael Roche of
the Irish Guards, who owed 'his downfall to the twin failings of drink and bad
company':

> There is no doubt that in this country there is a conspiracy to attempt to
> corrupt members of the H.M.'s Forces, particularly those of Irish national-
> ity. They are waylaid in public-houses and bribed with drink, and invited
> to parties, etc., with the sole object of inducing them to make attempts to
> steal arms and ammunition.[14]

The Special Branch's greatest success during the truce period was the discovery of 'a wide conspiracy, spreading from South Wales to the Tyneside and
engineered by the local organisers of the Irish Self-Determination League.'

Its ringleader was J. P. Connolly of Cardiff, who collected stolen explosives and arms for shipment by trawler to Ireland. Through interception of Connolly's correspondence, the network was uncovered and broken up, with members receiving lengthy terms of imprisonment. Raids on their property uncovered large quantities of arms and explosives, as well as documents that supplied 'ample proof of a widespread and deeply laid conspiracy' under the direction of Liam Mellows, the IRA Director of Purchases. The Special Branch was able to thwart some IRA gunrunning operations, but it recognised that arms, ammunition and explosives were still 'undoubtedly being shipped in not inconsiderable quantities to Ireland.'[15]

The flamboyant empire-builder Sir Basil Thomson directed the security effort against the IRA until he was removed from his post in November 1921 – the cabinet was unhappy at his independence and wished to bring the Special Branch back under the control of the Commissioner of the Metropolitan Police. His successor, Major-General Sir Wyndham Childs was of a very different character: he was known by the nickname 'Fido', because of his doggedly obedient attitude towards his superiors. He had had a long working relationship with General Sir Nevil Macready, serving under him in South Africa and then dutifully following him to army positions in Britain and France. Childs also had some connections with Ireland. He was 'partly Irish' by birth, an 'Ulster man by conviction', intimately involved with the Curragh Mutiny in 1914 and had guarded Sir Roger Casement when the latter was placed in the Tower of London awaiting trial for treason in 1916.[16] He accepted the leadership of the Special Branch in December 1921 (as Assistant Commissioner of the Metropolitan Police) with little enthusiasm, believing it to be a 'thankless task'. This was partly because of the challenge of dealing with the Irish republican movement. He wrote in his memoirs:

> The political situation in Ireland was distinctly impossible, and had a very definite repercussion on us at Scotland Yard. London was full of gunmen, plotters, intriguers, and members of the I.R.A. – indeed, they boasted of the existence of a battalion in London, though as a matter of fact, the organization actually consisted of very few men, most of whom were terrorized into joining companies of the I.R.A. That the I.R.A. organization in London was very extensive, however, was a matter of public knowledge.[17]

The period between the signing of the treaty on 5 December 1921 and the outbreak of civil war on 28 June 1922 was uniquely confusing for the British authorities, as the treaty split worked its way through the different Irish organisations in Britain. On the political side, the Special Branch noted that most of the Irish Self-Determination League membership, including its president, supported the treaty. However, its vice-president, Art O'Brien, who had for long 'been an extremist and exercised a sinister influence over the younger Irish men and women', came 'prominently to the front' by backing de Valera. When he was supported by other ISDL leaders, especially in Scotland, a struggle ensued to control the league. O'Brien won, but only at the price of destroying the organisation. There was a bitter split, and much of the rank and file drifted away: the Special Branch reported in March 1922 that there was 'nothing but apathy and confusion', the ISDL was 'almost dead'. The police estimated that 'more than 90% of the Irish in Great Britain' supported the Free State. The remaining minority were 'cranks and roughs', 'mainly young men and women led by fanatics and intriguers', and 'not among those who count socially, politically or in the commercial world'.[18] Though these extremists were monitored closely, the British government could take some comfort from the fact that the bulk of the Irish community welcomed the treaty settlement.

The Special Branch was more concerned about the military wing that operated behind the scenes. It was aware that the majority of active IRA members in Britain had come out against the treaty (just like in Ireland). By March 1922, they were 'organising drafts of young men' and sending them to Ireland to strengthen the Irregular army.[19] But their most important activity continued to be smuggling arms, ammunition and explosives.[20] The Special Branch had sporadic success in intercepting the trickle of supplies. Their greatest coup came in the last weekend of April 1922, when they broke up a Midlands gunrunning conspiracy. Six men were 'caught red-handed' while trying to steal a considerable quantity of .303 ammunition near Birmingham; six others were arrested over the next few days. IRA documents were discovered, many concealed in a sofa in a house in Liverpool, which disclosed an extensive conspiracy to obtain arms and explosives for the 'mutinous section of the I.R.A.'[21] The smashing of this network was a temporary setback to republican activity in Britain, but the Special Branch was under no illusions about its limited ability to prevent gunrunning: Britain was the primary channel for IRA arms smuggling in 1922 and 1923.[22]

Although IRA activities in Britain during the first half of 1922 were underground and discreet, there was a risk that the IRA would resume its campaign of destruction, or, worse still, turn to political assassination. Rumours to this effect were circulating in the first half of 1922. Childs recalled how 'life was somewhat anxious, for Irishmen in London were pursuing their usual tactics by sending threatening letters and "death warrants" to all persons of importance connected with the Government'. Childs himself received a 'death warrant' in his early days in office, 'duly signed with skull and cross-bones'; he confessed that it gave him 'a little bit of a thrill down the back'. The Special Branch tended to disregard these threats and rumours, but Childs was under no illusion that 'if anything went wrong' his head 'would be on a charger'.[23] This is exactly what happened when Field-Marshal Sir Henry Wilson was assassinated on the steps of his home in London on 22 June 1922. The killing led to serious criticisms of the performance of the British domestic intelligence system and produced a brief panic over the risk of further IRA attacks.

Wilson was shot dead by two active figures in the London IRA: the battalion commander, Reginald Dunne, and a regular Volunteer, Joseph Sullivan. Both had been born and raised in London, serving in the British army in the First World War – O'Sullivan had lost a leg at Ypres. After learning that Wilson was unveiling a war memorial on the morning of 22 June 1922, the two men waited by his house in Eaton Place in Belgravia and shot him as he walked up the steps to his front door. They were immediately pursued by Wilson's butler and local workmen, soon joined by some police officers. Largely because O'Sullivan's wooden leg inhibited a quick escape, the men were caught, beaten and overpowered, though not before they had shot two police constables.[24] Dunne and O'Sullivan were brought to trial and hanged in Wandsworth prison on 10 August. There have been persistent claims, supported by one leading historian, that the men acted under orders from Michael Collins.[25] However, the most recent research indicates that they acted independently and on the spur of the moment, incited by stories of bloody pogroms against Catholics in Northern Ireland. Sir Henry Wilson, by then an Unionist MP, was believed to be actively involved with the security policy of the Belfast government and, therefore, fell victim to republican patriotic fury.[26]

The shooting of Sir Henry Wilson was the first political assassination in Britain since the murder of Sir William Curzon Wyllie by an Indian nationalist in 1909.[27] Like the Fenian dynamite campaign in the previous century, it had a dramatic impact on public opinion, catapulting Irish terrorists into prominence. Fingers were immediately pointed at the British authorities for failing to protect the life of such a prominent citizen. In a debate in the House of Commons on the day of the assassination, MPs accused the police of not reacting to warnings that Wilson's life was in danger. The Home Office replied that no credible warnings had been received. The Home Office also defended its decision to remove special protection from individuals in January 1922. It explained that the information in its possession indicated that the IRA would try to procure arms and explosives, and might possibly resort to an incendiary campaign, but 'there never was any fear of organized murder by Sinn Fein in this country'.[28] The Special Branch can be excused for not having discovered the plot to murder Wilson – it was carried out with minimal planning by Dunne and O'Sullivan. However, the police's knowledge of the London IRA was revealed to be poor: even though Dunne was the most senior IRA officer in London, the Special Branch admitted that he had not come to their attention before.

The assassination of Wilson caused panic within the government, as it was believed to be part of a wider conspiracy in Britain – the first shot in a concerted IRA campaign of murder. This was based on incriminating documents found in the possession of the two assassins and on an intelligence report from an unidentified Special Branch agent in Dublin. The effect of this misconception on policy towards southern Ireland has already been discussed. It also led to heightened security measures in Britain. Thirty 'dangerous Irishmen under observation by the police in London' were immediately arrested and brought in for questioning. The gallery of the House of Commons was closed. The police instituted a 'conspicuous watch' on passengers landing in British ports from Ireland, in the hope that this would become known and act as a deterrent to travelling assassins.[29] Police protection was also reinstated for public figures considered under threat: by October 1922 this included twenty-one ministers and thirty-four others with connections to Ireland. (Colonel Winter, the former Director of Intelligence, received police protection for another eighteen months.) The Special Branch, 'exhausted' by this effort, had to draft in 150 policemen from the uniformed branch to serve as bodyguards.[30]

The assassination of Sir Henry Wilson also led to a deluge of threatening letters and anonymous warnings of further attacks. A typical example was received by Winston Churchill:

> There are four thousand Republican Brotherhood in London out to wreck the British Government by murdering its members. The Prince of Wales is to be the next victim. Unless every S.F. is driven out of London it is the beginning of the end for England. Do not say you have not been warned as you have by one who knows and has heard all under the seal of confession for I am a Parish Priest.

The Special Branch found it hard to determine whether these letters had any significance. It noted that 'anonymous letter writing and anonymous warnings' were 'some of the most primitive methods of antagonistic organisations to "stampede" the police and exhaust their energies in fruitless work, thereby ensuring better facilities for carrying out some serious attack'.[31]

One of the main constraints on the Special Branch when dealing with republican activities in Britain was that it could not rely on assistance from the new government in southern Ireland. Under Michael Collins the Irish regime was reluctant to work with the 'old enemy' and preferred to go it alone, sending clandestine agents in Britain to penetrate the Irregular network. This was not only ineffective, but also diverted the attention of the British police forces: they sometimes investigated and arrested Free State agents without knowing which side they were on.[32] Moreover, in the summer of 1922 the Special Branch was distracted by the Dublin government's secret attempts to purchase arms in Britain. The most serious case was an 'intrigue' to obtain 10,000 rifles and dozens of Hotchkiss machine guns from the British Disposal Board. The chief agent was Frank Fitzgerald, brother of the Director of Publicity in Dublin and an experienced pre-Treaty IRA gunrunner. (He received £10,000 from National Army headquarters in June 1922 and a further £9,704 over the next two years. There were accusations of financial impropriety, as few goods were actually delivered. Another Irishman who worked on these deals claimed that the money was 'lavished upon champagne for prostitutes in the night clubs of London'.) The Special Branch tracked Fitzgerald's activities from an early stage and waited until six machine guns arrived at a London warehouse in August 1922 before raiding the premises. Lionel Curtis planned to present Collins with irrefutable evidence, 'shame him' into dropping these underhand methods and get him to deal with the British 'squarely', although Curtis was also anxious that there should be no publicity, as the publication of 'so disgraceful an intrigue' would make it difficult for Churchill to maintain a friendly attitude towards the Provisional Government in parliament. 'Our task', Curtis wrote, 'is not to destroy but to reform them.'[33] At this stage, the new Irish government in Dublin was still an intelligence target rather than an intelligence partner.

The death of Collins and the new approach of the Cosgrave administration soon changed this. Cosgrave was willing to collaborate with the British government on intelligence and security matters. Free State agents in Britain were accredited and given firearm permits. The Director of Intelligence in the Irish army began to liaise with the Special Branch in London. By the end of 1922 the two governments were working together to suppress Irregular activity in Britain. Unlike before, the intelligence collected by Free State agents was now acted upon. This had a noticeable impact on the quality of British domestic intelligence and the ability of the British police to thwart IRA activities. On 4 October four IRA men were arrested for attempting to steal arms from an army drill hall in Edinburgh, and were sentenced to fifteen months in prison. The greatest successes came in Glasgow and Liverpool, the two major centres for republican gunrunning, when dozens of arrests and weapon seizures between November 1922 and January 1923 led to the capture of senior IRA officers and the break-up of the IRA smuggling networks. The crack-down caused paranoia within Irregular ranks in Britain: the Special Branch reported that they could not 'trust even their own people' and feared 'the presence of Free State agents among them'.[34]

It was fortunate that the Irish and British governments took the decision to co-operate more fully over intelligence, because in the winter of 1922–3 republicans made a concerted effort to improve their organisation in Britain. In September 1922 a Cork IRA man named Pa Murray was appointed 'Officer Commanding Britain' and sent to his new territory. By February 1923 he had revitalised the organisation and developed good smuggling networks.[35] The Special Branch was concerned at the impact of this new leadership on the IRA:

> It is definitely known that Republican activities in this country are on the increase. The new 'officer commanding' sent here some time ago has been visiting Scotland and the North of England for the purpose of putting the Irish Republican Army back on something like its old footing. Recruits are being sought and new companies established in various centres, and all are being urged to become efficient and ready for any emergency that may arise.[36]

The revival in the military organisation was accompanied by a similar resurgence of republican political activities in Britain. The vast majority of the Irish community supported the Free State, but the Civil War left them disillusioned, apathetic and silent. This left the field open for anti-Treaty extremists, who were organised, fanatical and vociferous. From December 1922 public rallies were held in London and other cities: anyone who might be inclined to voice support for the Free State was deterred by the presence of a 'chucker out section' – 'half a dozen young men in shirt sleeves standing by a table, placed just inside the door, upon which a number of heavy blackthorn sticks were displayed'. The key figure in this campaign was Art O'Brien. He led the ISDL and gave fiery speeches at its rallies; he was the channel for money from the United States to de Valera; he was also President of the Gaelic League, using its weekly meetings at the Minerva Café in Holborn to recruit young men for the IRA.[37]

The growing boldness of Irish republicans in Britain in the early months of 1923 led to a major crack-down by the British authorities in conjunction with the Free State government. On 13 January 1923 the Colonial Office telegrammed to Dublin that there was 'increased evidence of Irregular activity on this side closely connected with activities in Ireland', which made an 'immediate conference of greatest importance'. The Free State Director of Intelligence was sent to London, where he conferred with the Special Branch to devise a plan to crush the Irregular organisation.[38] The plan came into effect in the early hours of Sunday 11 March 1923. In a series of raids across Britain, 114 men and women were arrested, brought by special train to Liverpool, and conveyed to Dublin on a naval cruiser, where they were promptly interned in Mountjoy Prison. Childs boasted how 'the whole plan was carried out with the greatest secrecy, and even when the arrests became known, the Press had not the slightest idea what was up.'[39] When justifying this action to the House of Commons, the Home Secretary referred to 'the existence of a quasi-military organisation' involved in a plot to murder persons and destroy property in Britain. This was somewhat disingenuous. The real reason for the deportations was the involvement of republicans in gunrunning, combined with concern at the rise in the temperature of political agitation in Britain. This crack-down was carried out mainly to assist the Free State government in its prosecution of the Civil War. It was the culmination of Anglo-Irish security co-operation during this period.[40]

The government's action soon turned into a legal fiasco. There was a storm of protest on behalf of the deportees from Labour members of parliament, who argued that the government had no power to deport British citizens to Ireland for internment without charge or trial. In April 1923 the most prominent deportee, Art O'Brien, applied for a writ of *habeas corpus* in London; it was granted a month later after the case went to the House of Lords. As a result, in May 1923 all the deportees were brought back from Ireland and released, although six of the most notorious extremists, including O'Brien, were quickly rearrested, convicted on charges of criminal conspiracy and imprisoned. All the deportees demanded compensation from the government, which set up tribunals to hear their claims. During these tribunals, accusations of ill-treatment against the British police were rebutted, but credible allegations of drunken brutality were made against prison guards in the Free State.[41] Because of their treatment in Dublin, the deportees received substantial compensation for their two months incarceration – £54,099.17.0. in total, or an average of £475 each.[42] The whole affair was costly and embarrassing to the British government: like efforts in the 1970s and 1980s, it showed that extradition of political prisoners between the British and Irish states could quickly become mired in political and legal controversy.

Yet, despite the legal complications and the release of the deportees after just two months, the deportations had the desired effect. Although Pa Murray and some other senior figures were not picked up, the IRA organisation was crippled. One IRA officer reported to the Chief of Staff in Ireland: 'I am afraid the chances of operations in Britain are now negligible if not altogether impossible.'[43] The Special Branch satisfactorily concluded that 'the recent deportations entirely disorganised the Irish Republican Army in this country, and completely upset their plans', just as they had been gathering their forces to strike a major blow against the Free State. The political movement was similarly affected.

It was 'practically at a standstill' and 'all the usual weekly meetings were cancelled owing to the absence of the real leaders', most of whom had been deported.[44] The Home Secretary later opined that the 'internment practically brought the rebellion in Ireland to an end'. This is an exaggeration, but the actions in Britain did starve the Irregulars of military supplies at a critical moment.[45] The episode demonstrated that British action could help the security of the Irish state, but it also showed that the British government could only stamp out republican activity on its territory with the active co-operation of the Irish authorities.

Enemies and allies in America

THE co-operation of the new authorities in Ireland would also be essential to the suppression of militant republican activities in the territory of Britain's most important ally – the United States of America. The United States was home to a vast Catholic Irish-American community that was politically organised, hostile to Britain and strongly in favour of Irish independence. Its support was critical to the achievements of the Irish republican movement between 1916 and 1923; indeed, without American intervention there might have been no Irish revolution. This support took two forms. First, Irish-Americans injected the Irish question into domestic American politics, pressing their government to recognise Ireland's right to independence and opposing pro-British diplomatic and trade initiatives – they sought to force London into making concessions on Ireland by holding Anglo-American relations to ransom. Second, Irish-Americans provided direct assistance to revolutionaries in Ireland in the form of funding and weaponry. This was largely organised by Clan na Gael, the secret oath-bound organisation that emerged during the Fenian era as the American counterpart of the Irish Republican Brotherhood.

Because Irish-American activities posed a serious threat to British interests, they were an important subject of investigation for the British intelligence system in North America after 1914. The ability of the British to tackle this problem varied across three separate periods: during the First World War a well-developed British intelligence system, with the support of the American authorities, had some success in uncovering and limiting Irish-American revolutionary plots; during the War of Independence the uncooperativeness of the American authorities meant that the British struggled to stem the flow of money and arms from the United States; in the Civil War Irish republican activities were eventually countered, largely because of the transfer of responsibility to Free State representatives, who had greater success in gaining assistance from American officials.

The role of Irish-Americans in arranging German support for the 1916 Easter Rising has already been described. This was part of a wider alliance between Irish republicans and imperial Germany, organised through the United States. The *quid pro quo* for German military assistance was Irish-American support for the Germans' covert and overt campaigns against British interests in the United States. In an attempt to prevent supplies reaching Britain, Irish-Americans helped to foment strikes in munitions factories and to place explosives in factories and ships. The Clan na Gael leader John T. Ryan, who received money from the German military attaché, was identified as the 'paymaster' of a 1914 plot to blow up the Welland Canal in Canada. Irish-Americans were also at the forefront of political movements agitating against American entry into the war and against the provision of munitions and financial loans to the Allies. This was partly a natural position, driven by long-standing opposition to Britain, yet it was partly inspired and funded by German propagandists. The chief recipient of German largesse was Jeremiah O'Leary, a prominent lawyer and political leader in the New York Irish community, whose American Truth Society campaigned alongside German propaganda organisations: the American authorities believed that most of the $191,000 that mysteriously appeared in his bank account between 1914 and 1917 came from German sources.[46] After 1916, and especially after American entry into the war in April 1917, the relationship between Irish-Americans and Germany cooled. However, the Easter Rising and the rise of Sinn Féin provided new momentum to Irish-American agitation. Judge Daniel F. Cohalan and John Devoy founded a mass movement, the Friends of Irish Freedom, to raise money for the Irish cause; Irish republicans on the run were fêted after being smuggled across the Atlantic. The radicalisation of public opinion in Ireland was mirrored by an intensification of demands for full Irish independence in the United States.

These Irish activities came under the eye of the extensive British intelligence system that developed in the United States during the First World War. At first, the only British intelligence presence in the country was a small agency in New York that focused on Irish and Indian affairs. Created at the time of Fenian violence in the nineteenth century, it reported to the Chief Commissioner of the Dublin Metropolitan Police. It consisted of a single officer, who was able to recruit some agents close to the Clan na Gael leadership.[47] After the war started, the British government significantly increased its intelligence activities in the United States. Under the instructions of Captain 'Blinker' Hall, the naval attaché, Guy Gaunt, built up a network of agents among Central European émigré nationalists and employed a private detective agency, Pinkerton's, to watch ships suspected of supplying the Germans. Room 40 of the Naval Intelligence Division supplied priceless decrypts of German diplomatic communications. In late 1915 Britain's foreign intelligence agency (SIS) created its first American station under the control of the thirty-year-old Sir William Wiseman, a former member of the Cambridge University boxing team and holder of an ancient baronetcy, who had enjoyed a successful business career in North America before serving on the Western Front. He built up a position of great personal influence with President Wilson and his advisers, gaining better access to the American president than any other British official during the war. He was also personally responsible for collecting intelligence on Irish affairs, running a network of informants in the Irish-American community. The British were given extraordinary license by the federal government to operate clandestinely on American soil. This was because the American domestic intelligence system was underdeveloped, fragmented and preoccupied with internal feuding. Britain, the senior partner in the Anglo-American intelligence relationship throughout the war, knew more about German covert action in the United States than the Americans themselves.[48]

The British intelligence community was able to collect good information on Irish-American conspiracies during the war; indeed, America was sometimes the best source of information on republican plots back in Ireland. British intelligence officers tracked the movements of Sir Roger Casement when he visited the United States before his mission to Germany: according to one SIS report, his 'eccentricity was much commented on ... some saying that he was mad'. As already described, Room 40 provided advanced warning of the shipment of arms on the *Aud* and Casement's landing by submarine in Ireland. During the latter's trial for treason, the British naval attaché showed Irish-American leaders copies of Casement's diary – which described his homosexual practices – in order to dampen agitation for clemency. This had some effect: 'there is the loveliest three cornered fight going on', the British attaché wrote on 22 August 1916, 'all cussing one another and all making it personal and entirely forgetting the original cause of the row. I have dropped out of it, not that I ever appeared really, but it is going to complicate the Irish question in the U.S.A., from the villains side of it.'[49]

After the United States joined the war, the British persuaded the American authorities to crack-down on Irish propaganda. In August 1917 a number of 'Soap Box orators' operating under the banner of the Friends of Irish Freedom were arrested. In November 1917 Jeremiah O'Leary was charged with publishing articles in violation of the Espionage Act; his newspaper, *The Bull*, was closed down. The most dramatic case occurred after the arrest of a German agent, Madam Maria K. de Victorica, in New York in May 1918. Five Irish-Americans, including John T. Ryan, were indicted on espionage and treason charges; Ryan was forced to flee the country and remained in exile for four years. In October 1918 the British made an effort to convince the federal government to carry out a full suppression of the Irish republican movement. British intelligence officers supplied a well-informed, seventeen-page report on Clan na Gael that described its constitution, history and aims. Pointing to continuing Irish intrigues with Germany and the damaging effect of Irish agitation on Anglo-American relations, the British pressed for a full-scale public investigation of Irish-American organisations across the country. At least one American agency, the Military Intelligence Division, was in favour of this step.[50]

Unfortunately for Britain, the end of the First World War changed the terms of the debate. As long as she was at war, the United States was willing to take action against a movement that had conspired with the enemy and attacked a key ally; but once the conflict was over, it was no longer clear that Irish republican activities, though damaging to Britain, were against US interests. The joint proposal by British intelligence and the American Military Intelligence Division to investigate the Irish movement was shot down by the US Department of Justice. A special assistant to the Attorney General wrote:

> The Military Intelligence, spurred on, we believe, by British intelligence officials in this country, have from the beginning pressed for the point of view that Irish activities in America, directed against England in favor of the independence of Ireland or Irish revolutionary movements in Ireland, should be suppressed in this country. This Department has consistently declined to agree with this view and has consistently held that the only Irish activities that fall within the purview of the federal law or federal jurisdiction are those activities directed at influencing Irishmen in America towards seditious activities against the United States or disloyalty to the United States. In short it is only with the disloyalty of Americans in the United States with which we are concerned.[51]

In addition to uncertainty over whether Irish revolutionary activities broke American law, there were political considerations. The Department of Justice believed that it would be difficult to secure criminal convictions in court because of widespread popular support for Irish independence; they also worried about the electoral consequences for any administration that was seen to be acting on behalf of the British empire. When the Bureau of Investigation (the forerunner of the FBI) took over responsibility for domestic intelligence from the Military Intelligence Division at the beginning of 1919, it was extremely reluctant to investigate or start prosecutions in any cases related to the Irish republican movement. At a lower level, state and local police and justice officials were often outwardly sympathetic to the Irish revolutionary movement. As a result, during the Irish War of Independence the United States provided a favourable environment for Irish republicans to agitate, organise and support the insurgency at home – to use modern language, it was a safe haven for an international terrorist conspiracy.[52]

Between 1919 and 1921 the Sinn Féin and IRA movement took full advantage of this. Irish-American leaders organised a mass political campaign to press President Wilson to recognise the Irish republic and to place Irish independence on the agenda of the Paris Peace Conference. Huge rallies were held around the country and pious resolutions introduced in Congress. The importance of the United States was confirmed when Éamon de Valera, president of the still theoretical Irish republic, arrived in New York on 11 June 1919 after escaping from an English jail. He stayed in the country for the next eighteen months. After clashing with the established leaders of the Friends of Irish Freedom – Devoy and Cohalan – he sponsored the establishment of a new political organisation, the American Association for the Recognition of the Irish Republic (AARIR). Despite its clumsy title, it soon eclipsed its rival, growing to a membership of 965,000. De Valera also worked with Irish-American groups to raise approximately $12 million – a major sum – for the Dáil government and for victims of the War of Independence.[53] Some of this money went to IRA fighters and their dependents. The IRA benefited more directly from the assistance of Clan na Gael. The splits in the open political movement were mirrored in the underground organisation: a 'Reorganised Clan' under the leadership of Joseph McGarrity, a wealthy wine and spirits merchant from Philadelphia, split from Devoy, aligned itself with de Valera, and received the backing of the IRA. Inspired by the fighting in Ireland, it grew in strength: by January 1921 it could count on 18,000 members. Clan na Gael proved more resourceful than ever in smuggling funds, arms, ammunition and fighters to the IRA.[54] The Irish separatist movement never achieved all that it desired from the United States – there was no official recognition of the republic – but the motivated, organised and well-financed Irish-American organisations were a vital help to the insurgency in Ireland and a major headache for the British government.

The British intelligence system was less able to deal with this threat than during the First World War, as the end of the conflict was followed by a rapid worsening in Anglo-American relations and a decline in the Anglo-American intelligence relationship. Sir William Wiseman left the country after he lost the confidence of the President. The American government forced SIS to wind up its station in August 1919, because of a campaign, led by Irish-Americans, against the influence of British intelligence officials in the country. SIS soon established a new operation in New York, under the cover of the Passport Control Office, which continued to track Irish separatists, but political sensitivities and budget cuts meant that its activities were on a small scale.[55] Instead, the British government began to rely more heavily on its General Consul in New York, Harry Gloster Armstrong. Born in 1861, Armstrong had been a captain in the Irish Fusiliers and a Shakespearean actor in London's famed Haymarket Theatre, before joining the diplomatic service. Though *Time* magazine later referred to him as 'the grand old man of foreign consuls in the U.S', he did not shirk from clandestine activity: he hired private detectives to investigate suspect Irish-Americans in New York, recruited agents within Clan na Gael circles, and scrutinised the manifests of ships plying between America and Ireland.[56] Through the work of SIS and the General Consul, the British had some success in gathering intelligence on Irish organisations and intercepting shipments of arms and ammunition.[57] However, much more got through. The zeal of the British Consul was not enough to compensate for the limited nature of Britain's clandestine intelligence activities in the United States and the unwillingness of the American authorities to co-operate fully.[58]

The partial successes and persistent challenges surrounding the British state's response in America are illustrated by events in the port of Hoboken, New Jersey, in June 1921. American customs officials disrupted Clan na Gael's most audacious gunrunning operation when they seized 495 Thompson machine guns from the ss *Eastside*, a coal ship preparing to leave for Ireland. Irish republicans had been the first major purchasers of the newly invented 'Tommy gun' (which would become a favourite of gangsters and police forces during the 1920s, and a key prop in Hollywood crime movies for much longer). They made careful plans for a specially picked engine crew to obtain employment on the *Eastside* and smuggled the arms on board by night. The plot was thwarted not by British or American intelligence officials, but by the curiosity of the ship's mess boy, who opened one of the bags and saw the muzzle of a gun sticking out. He informed the captain, and a search by the shipowners on 13 June uncovered the full stash, which was handed over to US Customs officials two days later. Although this was a lucky development for the British, the way this discovery was handled reveals a lot about the freedom enjoyed by Irish conspirators in the United States. An Irish republican, claiming that the guns had been stolen from his warehouse, was able to obtain a warrant for their recovery from a sympathetic local magistrate. Using this, the Hoboken police arrested federal Customs officials as they were loading the arms onto a truck and took the weapons to the police station. Gloster Armstrong reported that 'political machinery' had been put into action through the mayors of New York and Hoboken to make sure that the guns were returned to the Irish revolutionaries. Although the danger was averted the next day when Customs authorities secured a warrant from a federal judge, it was a near thing.[59]

The progress of the federal investigation into the gunrunning plot also revealed the near impossibility of bringing any of the Irish ringleaders to justice. A young attorney of the Bureau of Investigation, who was given the task of preparing a case, initially showed some vigour, indicting seventeen people, including the general manager of the gun manufacturer, Colonel Marcellus Thompson. However, it soon became clear that he had overstepped his mark. The Assistant Attorney General dismissed the unfortunate attorney from the department and dropped all charges, ostensibly because he deemed it impossible to obtain a conviction. (There may also have been political pressure – Thompson was the son-in-law of a Republican Party grandee then serving as ambassador to London.)[60] Moreover, not only was no one ever charged in connection with the *Eastside* incident, but Clan na Gael won custody of the guns four years later. Most were subsequently smuggled to Ireland, where they would be used by the IRA for the next half century: their distinctive 'rat-tat' sound could be heard on the streets of Belfast during the 'Troubles' of the 1970s.[61]

The *Eastside* incident was not the last gunrunning plot orchestrated by Clan na Gael: Irish-Americans played an important part in sustaining the anti-Treaty republican movement during the Irish Civil War. As in Ireland and Britain, this support came from a minority. The bulk of the Irish-American community, including the Friends of Irish Freedom, welcomed the Anglo-Irish Treaty and backed the new Free State government. However, a republican hardcore retained control of the AARIR and Clan na Gael, throwing what was left of these organisations behind de Valera and the Irregular IRA.[62] Their attempts to influence events in Ireland through political campaigns in the United States gained little, as the treaty split broke the power of the Irish-American movement and destroyed sympathy for Irish nationalism among the wider population: the Free State representative in Washington told his superiors that 'one has got to face the fact that Irish effective influence in the U.S.A. in international affairs is silenced for some years'.[63] Instead their significance was in the direct financial and material assistance provided to the republican cause in Ireland. Clan na Gael transferred at least $280,000 to Ireland between January 1922 and August 1923.[64] Perhaps a further $100,000 was sent by the AARIR and other republican fund-raising groups in the United States.[65] From May 1922 Clan na Gael smuggled arms and ammunition to the Irregular IRA, usually in small consignments via Britain: this was the principal source of weaponry for the rebels by the end of 1922. Once again Irish-America provided critical support to an armed insurgency in Ireland: without it the Irish Civil War would have been shorter and less bloody.[66]

Nonetheless, Irish republicans found it more difficult to operate in the United States than before. One reason was that the British government found it easier to collect intelligence, possibly because the numerous splits and feuds weakened the movement's security. The chief source of intelligence was the British Consul in New York, Gloster Armstrong, who gained access to some well-placed informants within Clan na Gael: for example, he was able to obtain the secret circulars sent by Joseph McGarrity to Clan members.[67] Drawing on these sources, he was able to uncover some gunrunning plots. His greatest coup materialised on 2 June 1922, when a Royal Navy destroyer off the coast of Kerry stopped an American steamer (the ss *Seattle Spirit*) and discovered 240,000 rounds of ammunition packed in forty barrels marked 'Neutral Lard'. The navy had acted on the basis of detailed intelligence from Armstrong, who had been tracking the consignment of ammunition for the previous six months and telegrammed a warning when it was loaded onto the *Seattle Spirit* in New York.[68] Further insight into republican activities in the United States came from police action in Britain. The arrest and deportation of 114 republican suspects in March 1923 led to the discovery of a bundle of correspondence between anti-Treaty leaders in Ireland and America – Britain had been the staging post for the transatlantic communication. These documents revealed important details on republican fund-raising, IRA gunrunning schemes and the interminable feuding between different groups in the United States.[69]

The way in which London handled these documents reveals the importance of a new player on the American scene – the Free State government. The Foreign Office decided that the Free State representative in Washington, Professor Timothy Smiddy, should be asked to carry out 'detective work' on leads contained in the republican communications. He should also approach the American authorities and ask them to prosecute the Irish-American ringleaders. Smiddy, a professor of economics from Cork University, had been engaging in the darker arts of foreign diplomacy for some months. Troubled by fears for his own safety, discovery of republican gunrunning and an obsession with links between the Irregulars and Bolsheviks, he had decided to create his own 'secret service' in December 1922. Rather than building one up from nothing, he employed a private firm, the William J. Burns International Detective Agency. This was a fortunate choice, as it was intimately linked with the Department of Justice – the agency's founder was then serving as Director of the Bureau of Investigation.[70] Smiddy's detective agency kept suspect properties under observation, shadowed individuals, carried out illicit searches and recruited informants.

Its most impressive achievement was the infiltration of an undercover operative, 'New York Investigator Z-25', into the heart of Clan na Gael.

Smiddy was initially treated with some coldness by British diplomats and American officials because the Free State, as a Dominion, was not entitled to have accredited diplomats in foreign countries. However, this changed in April 1923. The British ambassador vouched for Smiddy in conversations with the State Department, thereby making 'formal' the latter's relationship with the federal government. At the suggestion of British officials, Smiddy approached the Department of Justice and asked them to prosecute extremists implicated in the documents found in Britain.[71] In addition, Gloster Armstrong began to share his reports freely with the Free State representative.[72] In the final weeks of the Civil War the British worked jointly with Free State officials to counter Irregular activity in the United States.

The adoption of a lead role by the Free State stimulated greater co-operation on the part of American officials. Smiddy worked with the Bureau of Investigation to track down a leading republican, Seán Moylan, after it was discovered that he had come to America on a false passport.[73] When Smiddy's deputy met with William Burns, the Director of the Bureau of Investigation, the latter 'was very obliging and most anxious to help in every way'. He told the Irishman 'to come as often as I wanted, and if others did not attend promptly just to let him know what I wanted and he would see to it that I had results immediately'.[74] Smiddy also developed a good relationship with the head of the New York Police Department bomb squad, Lieutenant James J. Gegan.[75] The Free State government was able to extract greater assistance from the American authorities when dealing with republican rebels than British had received two years before.

This seriously hampered the ability of Irish-American militants to give support to the Irregulars in Ireland. By spring 1923 Clan leaders were feeling the pressure. Joseph McGarrity complained that he had 'a small army of detectives or maybe thugs covering all his movements'.[76] It led to a curtailment of arms smuggling in the final months of the war: McGarrity told his comrades in Ireland that their 'future supply must be arranged from Europe with great saving and better material'.[77] After reaching a zenith in 1921, the Irish-American republican movement was no longer able to sustain its counterparts on the other side of the Atlantic. This was partly brought about by the weakening of the Irish-American organisations, partly by the more effective security response of the Free State, British and American authorities, working closely together. By the end of the Civil War, rather than relying on support from Britain's erstwhile American ally, the republican movement would look for help to Britain's current and former enemies – the Soviet Union and Weimar Germany.

The 'Red Menace'

T HE Bolshevik revolution in 1917 had repercussions far beyond the borders of Russia. As well as providing inspiration to socialists, it put Russia under the control of a regime that was committed to fomenting a world-wide worker's revolution. In 1919 the Soviets established the Third International (soon renamed the Communist International, or Comintern) to provide financial support and ideological direction to communist organisations in other countries. Much of the Soviet energy was directed at the British empire: Russian propagandists were sent to India; professional agitators and funds were secretly despatched to Britain to help the newly created Communist Party of Great Britain (the CPGB). These developments horrified the British government, which first tried to topple the Bolsheviks by intervening militarily in the Russian Civil War. When this failed, there were moves to normalise relations, through a trade agreement in 1921 and *de jure* recognition for the Soviet Union in 1924. However, evidence of Soviet subversion in the British empire ensured that relations were always close to a complete breakdown. Soviet interference was regarded with so much concern because 1918 was the beginning of a period of great labour and social unrest in Britain. A post-war economic slump, the rapid demobilisation of the army, and the increased organisation and militancy of workers led to a wave of strikes and protests. The threat of a crippling strike by a 'Triple Alliance' of mining, railway and transport workers hung over the country for almost a decade. To some observers, Britain seemed on the brink of its own socialist revolution.[78]

At the end of the First World War the Director of Naval Intelligence, Admiral 'Blinker' Hall, addressed his staff: after congratulating them for their part in defeating Germany he warned that they now had 'to face a far, far more ruthless foe, a foe that is hydra-headed, and whose evil power will spread over the whole world, and that foe is Russia'.[79] From 1918 until the mid-1930s the Soviet Union and the international communist movement were the chief targets of the British intelligence community. Domestically, the Special Branch of the Metropolitan Police took the lead in monitoring communist subversion in Britain, while MI5 confined itself to tracking Soviet military espionage and communist propaganda within the armed services. Both agencies infiltrated numerous agents into the British communist movement and kept a close watch on the correspondence of leading agitators. Foreign intelligence on the Soviet threat was primarily the responsibility of the Secret Intelligence Service (SIS). Its first chief, Sir Mansfield Cumming, remained as 'C' until 1923, when he was replaced by the former Director of Naval Intelligence, Admiral Sir Hugh Sinclair (nicknamed 'Quex'), who occupied the post until 1939. Most SIS intelligence on the Soviet Union came from its stations in the Baltic states, Germany, eastern Europe and the Low Countries. In addition to SIS, the British government could call on the Government Code & Cypher School, which had been formed from a merger of the wartime naval and military cryptanalytic units; it successfully intercepted and decrypted Soviet communications between 1920 and 1927. Finally, the much larger diplomatic system of embassies and consulates, controlled by the Foreign Office, also played an important role in providing information on foreign countries.[80]

British intelligence on the 'Red Menace' had two main weaknesses. First, with regard to foreign intelligence, British officials, especially in SIS, gave far too much credence to wild rumours and deliberate forgeries, often emanating from White Russian émigré communities around Europe. The most fantastic reports were circulated in the raw, with little analysis as to their veracity, and they sometimes had a major influence on British policy.[81] Second, Britain's domestic intelligence exaggerated the power of the Soviet Union over communist groups in Britain, magnified communist influence within the mainstream British labour movement and overestimated the threat of socialist revolution in Britain. Intelligence chiefs had an instinctive, almost pathological, hatred of socialist doctrines: Sir Basil Thomson famously described Bolshevism as 'a sort of infectious disease, spreading rapidly, but insidiously, until like a cancer it eats away the fabric of society, and the patient ceases even to wish for his own recovery'.[82] They had a ready audience on the Right of British politics. Politicians in the Tory Party and sections of the military, publicly backed by the hysterical *Morning Post*, outdid the intelligence chiefs in anti-Bolshevik scaremongering. 'Bolshevism' became a political swear-word used against the political and social changes set in motion by the First World War.[83]

Both these weaknesses – an exaggeration of the communist menace and a gullible acceptance of unfounded secret reports – would be evident in the British government's understanding of communist influence in Ireland between 1917 and 1923. Developments in Ireland certainly gave some cause for concern, as there were real links between the Soviet Union and Irish groups. At one level, Sinn Féin and the IRA made some half-hearted efforts to gain the co-operation of the Soviet government. A Sinn Féin representative in the United States of America, Patrick McCartan, discussed a draft treaty with a Soviet representative in May 1920, advanced a loan of $20,000 to the cash-starved Russians and travelled to Moscow in February 1921 to discuss a formal agreement. At the height of the Civil War, in early 1923, de Valera used a socialist journalist named Kathleen O'Brennan to approach the Soviet foreign minister in Switzerland with a request for financial aid and military supplies. Neither of these efforts met with success and the republican movement received little tangible assistance from the Soviet Union or the Comintern. Having signed a much-needed trade agreement, the Soviets did not want to further upset their relationship with Britain; they also saw the Sinn Féin movement as a purely nationalist, and largely bourgeois, struggle.[84]

There were more tangible links between Moscow and the small communist movement in Ireland, as both shared the same political vision – the establishment of an Irish Worker's Republic on socialist lines. In the two years after the 1917 revolution the Irish Labour Party, the main workers' union and the small Socialist Party of Ireland all expressed admiration for Bolshevik achievements and looked to the Soviet Union for help. There followed a 'race to Moscow' by various Irish radicals seeking official imprimatur. It was won by the youthful Roddy Connolly, who had fought in the GPO in 1916 beside his father, James Connolly. In July 1920, while just nineteen years old and on the first of many trips to Moscow, he met Lenin at the second world congress of the Third International. (He later remarked that the Russian leader spoke with a Rathmines accent, acquired from an Irish tutor.) Together with a small cadre of Irish communists, Connolly established the Communist Party of Ireland in October 1921, with official backing and financial support from the Comintern. Connolly and his Comintern mentors, hopeful that the nationalist revolution in Ireland could be turned towards socialist ends, made determined efforts to capture the Sinn Féin/IRA movement, especially during the Civil War. This period did see unprecedented social unrest. Factories and farm land were seized, workers went on strike, soviets were declared, and the red flag hoisted – in 1922 there were over 80 workplace occupations. Certain IRA leaders, especially on the anti-Treaty side, were sympathetic towards socialist doctrines.[85] However, the mainstream labour movement eventually backed the treaty and Free State, and most Sinn Féin and IRA leaders took active steps to prevent any socialist takeover of the separatist movement. All commentators agree that the Irish revolution was a strangely conservative one – it sought political change, but socio-economic continuity. In Catholic, rural Ireland, communist ideas never stood much chance of gaining widespread acceptance.[86]

This reality was not evident to right-wing politicians and intelligence officers in London obsessed with the Red Menace. From the time of the Russian revolution, there were frequent attempts to ascribe developments in Ireland to a Bolshevik conspiracy. It was a thesis advanced in a bestselling 1920 book on Irish affairs, entitled *Red Terror and Green*, by the secretary of the London branch of the Irish Unionist Alliance.[87] It was supported by a drip feed of information from Britain's foreign intelligence activities describing Soviet intrigues in Ireland.

It reached a very public culmination in May and June 1921, just before the truce. The way this was handled indicates the limitations of British intelligence and how intelligence could be leaked for political ends.

The British received two separate pieces of information on links between Sinn Féin and Moscow in the middle of 1921. The first came from SIS espionage activities in April in Reval (now Tallinn), Estonia. An agent, 'B.P.11', with supposed access to telegrams and letters in the Bolshevik mission in Estonia, claimed that £50,000 had been supplied to two Soviet 'germ cells' in Dublin by the head of the Russian Trade Delegation in London. The term 'germ cell', SIS remarked, was 'used by the Bolsheviks to denote the small Communist groups which they insinuate into unions and movements of any character suitable to their purpose.' Three communists had also been sent to Ireland by Moscow. In total, the enormous figure of £400,000 was earmarked to promote revolution in Ireland, under the direction of Maxim Litvinov, the deputy commissar for Soviet foreign affairs. This was extraordinary if true, and the Foreign Secretary, Lord Curzon, was keen to use it as the basis for a protest to the Soviets about their continuing subversive activities: 'surely the evidence is damning and sufficient', he minuted to his officials. Unfortunately SIS could find no confirmation of the information, and Sir Basil Thomson cast doubt on it, as there was no evidence of payments to Dublin from the Russian Trade Delegation.[88] The source, agent 'B.P.11', was later discredited and dropped. The whole report would appear to have been an elaborate forgery – a problem that affected many SIS operations in the 1920s.[89]

The second piece of information was more incontrovertible, although out of date. In April 1921 a raid on a house in Dublin netted a hoard of Sinn Féin documents, including a copy of McCartan's 1920 draft treaty with the Soviets, and correspondence between McCartan and de Valera on the subject. In contrast to his reaction to the SIS material, Sir Basil Thomson pounced on this material as solid evidence of an alliance between Sinn Féin and Moscow. Sinisterly, this document was leaked to the *Morning Post* and published with great fanfare in May. It was also the subject of a number of questions in the House of Commons by diehard Conservatives led by Colonel Gretton. The Soviet government denied that any such treaty existed (they were right – it was a draft discussed by two officials distant from their capitals) and took legal action against the newspaper. To defend its position, the British government published the draft treaty as a White Paper, entitled 'Intercourse between Bolshevism and Sinn Fein.'[90] This incident shows how individuals within the security forces were prepared to leak documents in order to discredit Sinn Féin, even at a time of sensitive peace initiatives. The alternative 'triple alliance' of intelligence chiefs, diehard Conservative MPs and the *Morning Post* would come together on numerous occasions in the 1920s to campaign against perceived government weakness towards British communists and Irish rebels.

During the Anglo-Irish peace negotiations in autumn 1921 the British government received further intelligence on Soviet intrigues in Ireland. The most startling evidence involved an exotic alliance between Irish republicans, Soviet communists, and Indian and Egyptian nationalists. It came to the cabinet's attention from an unexpected source: the intelligence service of the India Office run by Major John Wallinger. Berlin was a major focus of his attention, because it contained Indian revolutionaries who had sought assistance from imperial Germany during the war. In the course of his German operations Wallinger also stumbled over extraordinary information about Irish activities. According to his report, an Irish communist (named as 'I. J. Beaumont', but probably Seán Beaumont) had been sent to Moscow to press the Comintern to give assistance to the Sinn Féin movement. There he met with Indian revolutionaries and put forward a scheme to create a committee 'composed of mixed Irish, Indians, Egyptians and Mesopotamian Revolutionaries for the purpose of taking action unitedly against the British Government'. The proposal was further discussed in Berlin on 18 September 1921 at the house of Virendranath Chattopadhyaya (considered by the Raj as 'the doyen of Indian revolutionaries living abroad'). A 'United Committee of Action' was formed to co-ordinate an international campaign of revolutionary violence against the British empire: 'the chief aims of this Committee would be to simultaneously set fire to Government buildings, docks, jettys, English warehouses and police stations, and to destroy railway lines, and bridges and telegraph wires and to loot post-offices and treasuries, and to paralyse Government in every possible way.' Sinn Féin, with the assistance of the Comintern, was the driving force behind this committee. It was to furnish instructors on sabotage techniques to India and Egypt, and would provide most of the finance for the campaign.[91] Sir Basil Thomson gravely informed the cabinet in October 1921 that Irish extremists were trying 'to encourage all anti-British Revolutionaries to emulate the methods of Sinn Fein' – they were 'imbued with such hatred' that they would 'work for the downfall of the British Empire'.[92]

British observers also tended to see the increasing anarchy in the Irish countryside between the signing of the truce and the start of the Irish Civil War as symptomatic of dangerous Bolshevik tendencies. Lord Midleton, an Anglo-Irish landowner, warned of 'the general spirit of Bolshevism' that stalked the country.[93] In September 1921 Sir Basil Thomson described an incident at Bruree, County Limerick, where the bakery and mill were seized by workmen, who 'hoisted a Red Flag over the entrance' and sold bread at one pence below market price – a notice over the entrance boldly stated 'Bruree Soviet Workers' Mills. We make bread, not profits.' Thomson pointed to this as an 'example of the effect of Communist propaganda from Moscow'. The Special Branch also learnt of Roddy Connolly's visits to Moscow and discovered that the Communist Party of Ireland was receiving a quarterly subsidy from the Comintern. It concluded that 'the Bolsheviks hope to make Ireland the jumping off ground for a European revolution'.[94] British military intelligence officers warned that the CPI was 'largely responsible for the revolutionary actions … and many of the disturbances in Ireland' during the first months of 1922.[95] This was certainly an exaggeration. The CPI had little influence on events in Ireland.

British concerns about the Left in Ireland extended to the mainstream labour and union movement. The British government's greatest fear was that the labour movement would side with the republicans and come out against the treaty. This explains the lengths to which London was prepared to go to stop the return to Ireland of the famous strike leader, James Larkin. Larkin had founded the Irish Transport and General Workers' Union and led thousands of workers in the bitter Dublin strike of 1913. When the employers won this battle he moved to the United States, where he became involved with the radical International Workers of the World (known as the 'Wobblies'). A figure of great suspicion to both British and American intelligence agencies during the First World War, he was sentenced to five years' imprisonment by an American court in 1920 on a charge of 'criminal anarchy'.[96] The case was controversial, and there was strong pressure from the Irish-American community for Larkin's release. When this appeared imminent on two separate occasions in March and May 1922, the British intervened with the American government. Churchill telegrammed to the British ambassador in Washington that 'Larkin's appearance on the scene' could 'definitely turn the scale in the direction of civil war'; the ambassador hurriedly interceded with the State Department, which asked the Governor of New York to refuse Larkin's release. Churchill's anxiety to prevent Larkin returning to Ireland indicates the level of concern in London over the destabilising influence of militant labour in the already chaotic Irish situation.[97]

When the Irish Civil War broke out in June 1922, British observers immediately applied the Bolshevik label to the anti-Treaty side. The Special Branch was aware that the Communist Party of Ireland under Roddy Connolly had come out against the treaty earlier in the year and was trying to forge an alliance with Irregular leaders. To its credit, the Special Branch realised that, though the Irish communists had 'a very great opinion of themselves', they were 'of no importance with the real Irish Republicans'. When Roddy Connolly sallied forth during the Four Courts fighting, expecting to be received with open arms and given an important command, the IRA leaders put him filling sandbags, and he had 'bolted at the first opportunity.'[98] British intelligence chiefs were more concerned about potential links between the anti-Treaty republicans and the Soviet Union. As early as May 1922 the Special Branch reported that republican leaders were in talks with representatives of the Soviet foreign minister, Georgy Chicherin.[99] More conclusive proof came in early 1923 from Free State officials in Switzerland, who discovered that Kathleen O'Brennan had passed communications from de Valera to Chicherin. In a sign of the close Anglo-Irish intelligence co-operation of that time, British representatives in Geneva and Paris assisted the Free State to investigate this matter. Cosgrave subsequently spoke in public about the intrigue in an effort to discredit the republicans.[100]

The attachment of the Bolshevik tag to the Irregulars was given more credence by developments in Britain. Once the Civil War started, the Irish Communist Party partially relocated there. Its paper, *The Workers' Republic*, was printed in Fulham. Roddy Connolly moved to London and gave speeches to communist meetings about the tactics of urban warfare: a member of one audience remarked that 'as Connolly had taken an active part in the revolution in Ireland, especially in street fighting, he would be a capital man to lead the revolutionary force here when the time arrived'. Connolly also acted as a bridge between British communists and Irish republicans in Britain. In early 1923 the Special Branch provided a number of reports of an 'entente' and a 'very favourable understanding' between the two groups. British communists offered to help smuggle arms and ammunition to Ireland, and to instigate strikes to prevent the movement of war material to Ireland for use against republicans. For their part, Irish republicans agreed to support the labour movement in Britain and to fight alongside militants in the event that striking workers were attacked by the forces of the state. They also intervened in electoral politics: before the general election at the end of 1923, the IRA in London was asked to 'rally the Irish vote' for two radical Labour Party candidates (Shapurji Saklatvala and George Lansbury), which gave rise to 'alarmist reports' of Irish gunmen 'on the war path against the Liberal Candidates'.[101] The increasing co-operation between British communists and Irish republicans in Britain in 1923 was one of the reasons why the Home Office was keen to round up and deport over 100 extremists in March of that year.

Between 1917 and 1923 the British intelligence system uncovered most of the intrigues practiced by Irish communists and most of the approaches made by Irish republicans to the Soviet Union. This was largely a by-product of the successful intelligence effort against *British* communists: much came from intercepted correspondence sent from Ireland to British leaders, or from informants within the CPGB. This source was so rich because British communists played an important role in fostering the development of a communist movement in Ireland and mediating between Irish groups and Moscow. This was recognised in December 1922, when the CPGB was given formal oversight of the CPI at the Comintern world congress. However, if the British intelligence system was successful in revealing Irish intrigues, its failing was that it did not always understand their significance. There was a tendency to exaggerate the role of the Soviet Union, the influence of Irish communists, and the propensity for Bolshevik revolt in Ireland. It took some time to realise how unfavourable conditions were within Ireland and within the mainstream republican movement for radical left-wing ideas. Just as with British concerns about the Red Menace in general, the misconceptions of intelligence chiefs were outdone by the exaggerations of politicians and military officers on the diehard unionist end of the political spectrum. They lazily assumed that the revolution in Ireland was part of a world-wide Bolshevik threat to British civilisation fostered by the Soviet Union. Evidence of contacts between Dublin and Moscow, and of labour militancy in Ireland, was pounced on and magnified out of all proportion. This served to further delegitimise the Sinn Féin movement and reinforced perceptions of the Irish as easily influenced, prone to political instability and possessing a strain of savagery – just like the Russian Bolsheviks.

Gunrunning in Europe

ONE of the main reasons for British concern over the involvement of Russian communists in Ireland was that they might be a source of military supplies for the IRA. Guns, ammunition and explosives were three ingredients essential to a successful insurgency campaign. In 1916 the Irish Volunteers had placed all their hopes on a single ambitious gunrunning operation from abroad; it failed when the German ship, the *Aud*, was intercepted by the Royal Navy. Over the next three years Irish separatists chose a different course: they looked within Ireland for arms and ammunition, raiding police and military barracks and disarming members of those forces. By 1920, however, this source was drying up because of the strengthened security measures adopted by the crown forces. In addition, IRA stores were being rapidly depleted through combat operations and the discovery of arms dumps. As a result, the IRA began to look abroad once again. Britain and the United States provided the most regular supplies, often small quantities smuggled through on passenger ships or merchant vessels. But continental Europe had the potential for major shipments that could substantially alter the military balance in Ireland.

The Irish were fortunate that post-war Europe offered good conditions for the quasi-legal purchase and smuggling of weaponry. The head of the Special Branch, Major General Sir Wyndham Childs, described the situation:

> Europe was, to my knowledge, chock-a-block with arms of every shape, form and description. Owing to the rates of exchange, automatic pistols in any quantity could be bought for something like five shillings, and I knew perfectly well that they were being shipped to Ireland in large quantities either via this country or direct.

According to Childs, the Irish were just one of many eager clients for this trade: Moroccans, Chinese, South American states, the Red Army in Russia and the frontier tribes of India were all desperate to obtain arms and 'the ways of the professional gun-runner were both devious and ingenious'.[102] The chief arms bazaar of Europe was Germany. It was awash with material left over from the First World War, and the political instability of the Weimar Republic meant there was little control over how it was used. The Social Democrat government was assailed on all sides: communists attempted to seize control in various state capitals; ex-soldiers formed volunteer forces known as Freikorps to combat this threat; extreme right-wing groups such as Hitler's Nazi party attacked parliamentary democracy and searched for a *völkisch* community.[103] There were a number of groups on the Left and the Right with access to weapons that were willing to help Irish revolutionaries, because of the money on offer and because they had a common enemy in the British empire.

Michael Collins despatched a number of secret emissaries to Germany in 1920 and 1921 to secure military supplies. The pivotal figure was Robert Briscoe (a future Lord Mayor of Dublin), who had worked in Germany before the war, spoke the language fluently, and had useful business contacts there. He travelled to Germany in the middle of 1920 and teamed up with another Irishman, John Dowling (whose brother Joseph had joined Casement's ill-fated Irish Brigade and had landed from a U-boat on the Irish coast in 1918), and the American John T. Ryan, Sinn Féin's 'ambassador' to Berlin. They established contact with Major Hassenhauer of the Orgesch, one of the many secret, right-wing organisations of disaffected military personnel that resented the Allied presence in Germany. Over the next year Briscoe succeeded in acquiring large quantities of arms. At first they were smuggled to Ireland in small batches by individual couriers travelling on regular shipping. By the summer of 1921, however, because of the severe shortage of munitions in Ireland, he was instructed to organise large-scale shipments. His activity was in no way interrupted by the truce signed in July 1921; indeed, gunrunning initiatives were accelerated, as the IRA was determined to use the truce to strengthen its military capabilities. In September 1921 a flamboyant sea captain, Charles McGuinness, joined the German scene, determined to purchase a boat and sail it to Ireland. Other Irish representatives in Germany at this time included a communist polo-playing ex-British army officer, Billy Beaumont, who was in contact with the Comintern; a future IRA Chief of Staff and Nobel Peace Prize winner, Seán MacBride; and one Michael Cremin, sent by IRA headquarters to check on all the others. These men were well funded: Briscoe and McGuinness, for example, had £30,000 to spend in 1921. Because of police intervention, internal squabbling among the Irish representatives, and their unfortunate choice of German associates, their achievements were mixed. However, some shipments did get through.[104]

The Special Branch had primary responsibility for co-ordinating all British intelligence on IRA activities in Europe. Under Sir Basil Thomson, it also operated its own undercover agents in Germany and other countries. This did not please the Secret Intelligence Service (SIS) which sought, and in 1922 won, a monopoly on foreign intelligence activity. SIS stations in a number of European capitals came across Irish republican intrigues. In Germany, Britain exercised considerable power through the Inter-Allied Commission of Control that was formed after the German surrender in 1918. It contained military officers and provided a cover for SIS and other British intelligence activities. In the early 1920s it was preoccupied with uncovering and preventing the smuggling of arms in contravention of the Versailles treaty. In theory the British could exert pressure on the German authorities to stop this activity, and it appears that the Weimar government was anxious to avoid friction on this issue: the British ambassador in Berlin wrote that members of the German government were 'quite as hostile to this traffic in arms as anybody else' for their lives were 'in constant danger owing to this traffic which places weapons in the hands of dangerous characters'. Yet the Weimar state was so weak that gunrunners could often operate unmolested. In addition, the British often did not have sufficiently precise information to allow the German government to take action. 'The experience of the Commission of Control here', the British ambassador wrote, 'is that nine out of ten denunciations are false and that in the tenth case the amount of arms said to exist is exaggerated tenfold.'[105]

The same problem afflicted British intelligence on Irish republican activities abroad before July 1921: information was sporadic and often unreliable. The SIS network in particular was capable of producing quite fantastic pieces of information without giving much thought to their credibility. Perhaps the most bizarre was a report in early 1920 from an anti-Bolshevik former army officer in Finland. He avowed that Finnish activists were 'instituting a propaganda campaign in the interests of the Sinn Fein movement' under the leadership of one Raukanheims. Moreover, the informant claimed that Raukenheims had been 'one of the organizers of the attempted assassination of Lord French' outside Dublin in December 1919 and was 'directing an organization of Germans, Swedes and Finnish Officers' fighting with the IRA in Ireland! This remarkable claim was accepted with considerable gullibility by British intelligence (and by the American military intelligence officers to whom it was later passed).[106] The Irish conspiracy was also seen to spread further a field; the British Consul General in Algeria investigated a Belgian individual suspected of arranging gunrunning from north Africa.[107] The British intelligence system chased plenty of false leads during the War of Independence, but failed to discover many real IRA gunrunning operations. Just a month before the truce Winston Churchill admitted that 'it was doubtful whether our secret service system, both on the Continent and in America, was efficient enough to be able to give the full information regarding cargoes leaving foreign ports that it would be necessary to have'.[108]

During the peace negotiations between July and December 1921, British intelligence stepped up its effort against IRA intrigues in Germany, with greater success. This was possible because intelligence activities abroad, unlike those in Ireland, were not constrained by the truce terms. The most unexpected but best source of information was the intelligence service run by Major John Wallinger, which targeted Indian revolutionaries in Berlin. Alongside the more outlandish claims regarding an alliance between Irish, Indian and Egyptian revolutionaries, his report on 8 October 1921 contained impressive detail on IRA gunrunning intrigues in Germany. It stated that 2 million marks had been given by the IRA general staff to a 'Mr. Thompson' (the alias of Charles McGuinness); that he and Beaumont had succeeded in purchasing arms from the Orgesch organisation; and that the Orgesch had 'offered them two small submarines hidden somewhere, in order to regularly smuggle arms from the high seas to the Irish coast' – the Irishmen were awaiting extra funds to allow them to avail of this offer. In the meantime, with a cavalier disregard for German political alignments, the Irish were working with the German Communist Party to arrange for fishing boats to transport the arms. In addition, Indian nationalists had introduced the two Irishmen to 'a certain famous explosive expert in Berlin, so that they may purchase quite a new and disgustingly powerful incendiary bomb, together with its formula, so that it may be manufactured and used in Ireland'. The intelligence report also identified other IRA representatives active in Germany at that time, either by real name or by one of their many aliases; this included Robert Briscoe, John T. Ryan and a 'Mr. Baker' (probably either Dowling, Cremin, or MacBride).[109]

It is clear that the British intelligence services were closing in on the Irish networks in Germany in the autumn of 1921. Most of the information in the British report came from a single 'informant' within Indian nationalist circles under Wallinger's control. References to samples of Beaumont's handwriting indicate that intercepted correspondence was a fruitful source of information. British intelligence officers were also capable of covert operations on German soil. Robert Briscoe later recalled how four British secret service agents traced IRA funds to a bank in Berlin and made enquires as to the holder of the account.[110] On at least one occasion a dictaphone was placed in a hotel room where Irish representatives were holding a meeting. The level of detail in the Wallinger report, in particular the verbatim description of conversations, makes it possible that a similar operation was attempted in this case. Finally, the British benefited from the indiscretions and poor security of the Irish arms smugglers, who were sometimes incautious in their choice of associates. For example, an Irish agent approached a member of the American military mission in Germany and asked if he could assist with the supply of arms; after listening carefully to what the Irishman had to say, the American promptly walked across to the British headquarters and told them everything.[111]

Poor Irish security would lead to Britain's major success in thwarting IRA gunrunning plots during the truce period. In October 1921 one of the Irish representatives approached an officer of the Orgesch organisation, told him that he wanted to purchase arms, and took him to Hamburg port to show him the vessel that was waiting. Unfortunately, this Orgesch officer happened to be a liaison officer with the British; he unfolded the matter to the British authorities, who tipped off the German police.[112] The ship involved was almost certainly the *Anita*, which had been purchased by Briscoe and McGuinness. It was crewed with German communists and loaded with arms, ready for a voyage to Ireland. On 21 October it was searched by the German police, and a large quantity of revolvers, rifles and ammunition discovered.[113] This caused consternation in London, where the Anglo-Irish peace talks had started just ten days earlier. Lloyd George angrily presented the Irish delegation with evidence of the arms seizure and asserted that these were not 'real negotiations', but were being 'spun out' to enable the Irish to 'equip' their forces.[114]

Charles McGuinness was arrested by the German police and tried for violating customs regulations, but, because of German sympathy for the Irish cause, he escaped with the light fine of 2,000 marks. Together with Briscoe, he quickly procured another ship, the *Frieda*, and this time crewed it with Orgesch members. Laden with arms, it sailed from Hamburg, berthing at Waterford on 11 November 1921 after a hazardous ten-day voyage. It carried at least 200 rifles and 10,000 rounds of ammunition.[115] Thus, although the British intelligence system did uncover some of the activities of republican representatives in Germany in the autumn of 1921 and intercepted at least one shipment, it did not prevent arms and ammunition reaching the IRA.[116]

The seven months that followed the signing of the treaty were uniquely confusing for two reasons: it took some time for the treaty split to work its effect on Irish representatives in Germany; the Provisional Government duplicitously tried to smuggle arms from Germany for use against Northern Ireland. For the first few months of 1922 IRA arms purchasers in Germany continued much as before, with the blessing of Michael Collins. Just before the treaty was signed, Briscoe and McGuinness had set up a commercial shipping line and purchased another vessel, the *City of Dortmund*, to operate between Hamburg and Ireland. This venture combined business and patriotism: it carried general goods but was also used to smuggle arms and ammunition. (The two men later boasted that the *Dortmund* was the first vessel to fly the Irish tricolour.) This was not the only vessel used by Irish gunrunners. McGuinness, Briscoe and Ryan also secured a two-masted steel schooner, the *Hanna*, which departed from Bremen on 24 March 1922 and landed at Ballynagaul in Co. Wexford nine days later. It carried a cargo of about 6 tons of arms, consisting of ammunition, Mauser rifles and Parabellum pistols. The weapons were transferred to the Tipperary No. 1 Brigade and from there to IRA units in Northern Ireland. This was a joint operation between the pro-Treaty headquarters (under Michael Collins) and the anti-Treaty faction, part of a combined policy towards the north. It was the last consignment of arms from Germany for a unified IRA. After this point the deepening split within the republican movement in Ireland was replicated in Germany. Most of the key figures involved with purchasing arms (such as Robert Briscoe and John T. Ryan) sided with the anti-Treaty Irregulars, but their gunrunning activities were placed on hold, as it was unclear how the situation would develop in Ireland.[117]

The British intelligence community's response to these IRA intrigues reflects the fluctuating health of Anglo-Irish relations during this period. Initially, British information was placed at the service of the Provisional Government, as it was assumed it would share the British objective of stopping gunrunning. In January 1922 SIS and the Inter-Allied Commission of Control became aware that the *City of Dortmund* was smuggling arms to Ireland. A British officer managed to sneak on board the vessel at Hamburg and open some cases, although without result. Instead the Provisional Government was informed, and its troops investigated the cargo when the ship arrived in Dublin on 26 January. Nothing was found and Michael Collins adopted an air of unconcern, stating that the report was probably incorrect.[118] In the second week of May his attitude had changed, and the Provisional Government complained that arms were being shipped to the Irregulars from Germany. This led the British Foreign Office to send a formal note of protest to the German government.[119] But just a month later, Anglo-Irish co-operation had broken down and gunrunning reports were handled very differently. When SIS officers in Hamburg reported in June 1922 that another ship, the *Stella Maris*, was regularly carrying arms to Cork, the Royal Navy was ordered to intercept the vessel in Irish waters without any reference to the Dublin government. On 14 June a British destroyer fired two shots across the bow of the *Stella Maris* off the Cork coast, escorted her into harbour and searched her for two days. No arms were found, and its German owners and their Irish customer, the Belfast Bottling Company, complained to the British government about the disruption to its trade. The Provisional Government also issued a formal protest because the British had acted unilaterally. British handling of the *Stella Maris* incident reflects the level of distrust towards the Provisional Government. It came at a time when London doubted whether the Provisional Government would defend the treaty and (rightly) suspected that imported arms might be used against Northern Ireland.[120]

With the start of the Civil War in late June 1922, the Irish and British governments slowly began to tackle the gunrunning issue together. Co-operation was certainly necessary as the Irregulars were beginning to actively look abroad for arms and ammunition. Robert Briscoe, Michael Cremin and Seán MacBride travelled to Germany once again, this time under the direction of Liam Mellows, the Irregular Quartermaster-General. Small quantities of arms and ammunition were smuggled on regular shipping lines, either directly to Ireland or via Britain.[121] The Provisional Government requested the Royal Navy to institute a special patrol around the Irish coast to stop this. When yet another report of suspected gunrunning emerged, the southern Irish authorities were informed and the offending ship (the *Wicklow Head*) was intercepted by the Royal Navy, which escorted it to Dublin for search by Free State officers. (Once again, nothing was found.) Co-operation was incomplete and permeated by mutual mistrust before September 1922, but after Cosgrave's assumption of the premiership, this began to change. Henceforth the two governments worked side by side to quash the republican revolt. The Irish authorities relied on the extensive British intelligence and diplomatic network on continental Europe to monitor suspected Irregular arms smugglers. Similarly, the British government passed on reports of gunrunning from representatives abroad to the Irish government for investigation.[122]

Some of the reports furnished by London continued to be of a fantastic nature: for example, in November 1922 British military officers in Germany reported that 200,000 rifles, with 1,000 rounds of ammunition each, were awaiting shipment to Ireland from Genoa.[123] The British intelligence system still found it difficult to separate unsubstantiated rumour from fact. However, from the autumn of 1922 the British did have some tangible success in intercepting Irregular shipments. In November 1922 the Special Branch investigated steamers trading between Hamburg and London and exposed some smugglers among their crews: the police found one pistol (along with a quantity of cocaine) and were convinced that other weapons had been thrown overboard to avoid discovery. Four months later, English customs officials seized 142 'Peter the Painter' German automatic pistols on board the SS *Glenapp*, sailing from Antwerp to London. They were in the possession of Woo Kong Dai, a Chinese steward, who was arrested and convicted for illegal importation of arms. He claimed that the weapons were bound for China, but the Special Branch was satisfied they were for transhipment to Ireland. This class of pistol was much sought after by the Irregulars because it could be converted into a rifle.[124] As a result of increasing pressure on the republican movement in Britain in early 1923, republican gun-running channels began drying up. It appears that only small quantities of arms were imported from Germany and other European countries in the latter stages of the Irish Civil War.[125]

By early 1923 the Irregular forces in Ireland were suffering from a lack of weapons and ammunition, while their networks in the United States and Britain were being successfully disrupted by the Irish, American and British authorities. As a result, republicans placed all their hopes on one last attempt to ship a large quantity of material from Germany, either by ship or, more imaginatively, by submarine. This was to include artillery. Irregular IRA military strategists laboured under the ridiculous fantasy that the introduction of a few field guns would allow them to march on Dublin and achieve victory. 'One such piece could be moved around among our strong forces and this would completely demoralise the enemy and end the war', the IRA Chief of Staff, Liam Lynch, wrote. This was a last-gasp effort, made more in desperation than anything else, and it says little of the calibre of the Irregular leaders.[126] The mission was organised by the Irish-American wing of the republican movement and led by John T. Ryan. He travelled to Germany in March 1923, and was followed by the IRA envoy to the United States, Seán Moylan, and a third man, Joseph McVeigh. With $100,000 in funds, the Irish mission made contact with a range of political groups in Germany with access to weapons; everyone from communists to the Orgesch movement, even including Hitler's nascent National Socialist party in Munich. There is evidence that they had the tacit recognition of certain elements within the German national government. However, their plans were discovered when the round-up of republicans in Britain on 11 March 1923 led the Special Branch to capture a priceless hoard of high level correspondence between IRA and Sinn Féin leaders. This material was passed to the Irish government, which made enquiries at its end, while the British intelligence system and the Commission of Control moved to thwart the republican mission in Germany. In the end, although Ryan and Moylan did manage to set up the purchase of ammunition, if not artillery, they concluded that it would be impossible to get a shipment to Ireland without detection. The plot came to nothing.[127]

T HE Irish republican movement was a truly international conspiracy, bringing the fight to English soil, drawing support from the Irish-American community in the United States, seeking alliance with the Soviet Union and looking to Europe for supplies of arms and ammunition. It engaged Britain's domestic and foreign intelligence agencies, as well as the intelligence system in Ireland. To some extent the British intelligence system was able to tackle the foreign dimension of Irish militant republicanism more directly and with greater success than the insurgency in Ireland. A surprising number of republican plots were detected, and many were thwarted. Yet the experience of the revolutionary period demonstrated that Irish militants would always be able to operate abroad, and London would always be susceptible to unfounded scares about international conspiracies, so long as intelligence was lacking on the situation in Ireland. Britain's response to the international dimension of the republican movement was only fully effective when it had the active co-operation of the Dublin government. This lesson would be reinforced in the following two decades of Irish independence.

There was another field of operations for the republican movement that posed a separate set of challenges and required the co-operation of the other indigenous Irish authority – the unionist government of Northern Ireland. The northern six counties, still part of the United Kingdom but with its own parliament, went through its own bloody revolution in this period, with vicious sectarian violence in Belfast and an IRA attempt to destroy the administration. The British government faced the unwelcome prospect of being dragged into the maintenance of law and order in the six counties. Developments in Northern Ireland also threatened to wreck Britain's relations with the new state in the south. British intelligence and military personnel were presented with unique and complex challenges in Northern Ireland that presaged many of the problems encountered when the province erupted again in 1969.

CHAPTER 4

Security and Sectarianism in Northern Ireland

O NE of the more entertaining paradoxes in Irish history is that the north-east of Ireland, which had fought so strenuously against Home Rule for half a century, was the only part of the country to get it. On 23 December 1920 the British parliament passed the Government of Ireland Act, which partitioned the six counties from the rest of the island and established a Home Rule parliament in Belfast. Elections were held in May 1921, and the King opened the first session of the Northern Ireland parliament in Belfast on 22 June 1921. Over the next six months, powers were gradually transferred to a new government controlled by the Unionist Party. Its leader, and the Prime Minister of Northern Ireland until his death in 1940, was Sir James Craig. The son of a millionaire whiskey dis-tiller, and a man with deep Ulster roots, Craig had been a chief organiser of the unionist campaign in 1913 and 1914, before taking up junior positions within the London government during the First World War. He was an able administrator, a skilful politician, and more moderate than many of his partisan loyalist col-leagues, but he possessed a strong antipathy towards Irish republicanism and an unyielding determination to protect the interests of the unionist community in the north. His objective during 1921 and 1922 was to create a strong, independ-ent 'statelet' that would be insulated from the revolutionary events in southern Ireland and policy changes in London.[1]

The birth of Northern Ireland was a difficult one. The emerging Sinn Féin government in the south refused to accept this settlement of the Irish problem. It waged a continuous propaganda and diplomatic offensive, seeking to under-mine the unionist administration and to compel the British government to undo partition. The constitutional future of the six counties was a major sticking point in the Anglo-Irish negotiations during the second half of 1921. An overall set-tlement was only reached by postponing a resolution of the issue: the delegates agreed to form a Boundary Commission after ratification of the treaty, which would redraw the border. The backdrop to these political manœuvrings was hor-rific bloodshed. Protestant loyalist gangs attacked Catholics, especially in Belfast; the IRA resorted to assassination, arson and kidnapping, partly in self-defence, partly in an attempt to bring down the unionist administration; the new Sinn

Féin government in the south covertly supported the IRA campaign. Between July 1920 and July 1922, 557 people were killed: 303 Catholics, 172 Protestants and 82 members of the security forces.[2] The Belfast government and its armed forces struggled to control the violence; indeed, through sectarian actions, they sometimes contributed to it. As a result, the survival of Northern Ireland was in some doubt until the middle of 1922.

Events in Northern Ireland were of great concern to British policy-makers. They threatened to drag the British government into taking responsibility for maintaining peace and security in Northern Ireland, an unappealing prospect given the level of animosity between the unionist and nationalist communities. In addition, the decisions that Britain took in regard to Northern Ireland threatened to destroy relations with the new government in Dublin, which might bring down the entire treaty settlement.

For the British intelligence community, Northern Ireland posed two main challenges. The first was deciding whether the British should develop their own intelligence system in the province, or whether they should rely on the new Northern Ireland government to handle the security situation. The second challenge was understanding what was actually happening in the province, in particular assessing the nature of the endemic violence. Was it caused by organised IRA subversion against the state, supported by the government of southern Ireland? Or was it the result of a sectarian pogrom against Catholics, backed by the unionist government? It was difficult to come to a firm conclusion because of the conflicting versions of reality presented by nationalist and unionists groups in Ireland. Until May 1922 London wavered on both these issues, but then it backed the Northern Ireland administration and worked with it to develop a joint intelligence system. The final months of 1922 saw full responsibility for security and intelligence shift to the Belfast authorities – the British were happy to get rid of this difficult problem.

A security vacuum

THE northern six countries had initially dodged the storm of Irish revolutionary violence. The IRA campaign of violence that began in January 1919 made little impact in the province. Because the majority of the population was Protestant and strongly unionist, neither Sinn Féin nor the IRA could draw on mass support. When violence did erupt, it was mostly sectarian in nature. It began in July 1920, sparked by the killing of RIC District Commissioner Smyth, a native of Co. Down, by the IRA in Cork. This was followed by riots and the expulsion of 8,000 Catholic workers from the Harland & Wolff shipyards and other industries in Belfast. Over the next twelve months, violence flared up from time to time, as the IRA carried out sporadic attacks on the security forces, and Protestant mobs retaliated by attacking Catholic areas. However, the violence was on a much smaller scale than in southern Ireland, and never posed a serious threat to the state.[3]

The security and intelligence apparatus that emerged in response to this violence was also very different from the south. Local police forces took the lead; neither the British army nor imported British ex-servicemen played much of a role. The Royal Irish Constabulary, which escaped the ostracisation and attacks suffered by its colleagues in the southern counties, continued to function as the principal law-enforcement and information-gathering agency. It was bolstered by a local armed militia, created on the initiative of northern unionists who did not trust the Dublin Castle administration, the British army under General Macready or the London government. In the summer of 1920 they revived the old Ulster Volunteer Force to protect the unionist community against republican gunmen. Though its recognition was initially resisted by Dublin Castle officials and the British army, Craig was able to persuade senior politicians in London to give it official sanction and to integrate it into the province's security apparatus. In September 1920 it was transformed into a Special Constabulary composed of A (full-time), B (part-time) and C (reserve) units.[4] The pervasiveness of the Special Constabulary, together with the loyalty of the majority of the population, ensured that the IRA could not wage an effective guerrilla campaign in the six counties.

The real challenge to the security of Northern Ireland came after the truce brought peace to the south on 11 July 1921. Over the next twelve months a wave of violence threatened to bring down the nascent Belfast administration and plunge the whole island into a sectarian civil war. The announcement of the truce sparked fierce outbreaks of rioting during unionist celebrations on 12 July. Over the coming months Catholic homes, groceries and public houses were burnt down; Catholics retaliated by bombing trams packed with shipyard workers. There was a short lull in January 1922, but the next month rioting, sniping and bomb-throwing flared up on the fault-lines between Catholic and Protestant working-class neighbourhoods. Hundreds of families were expelled from their homes. 'Practically a state of anarchy exists in Belfast', the local American Consul wrote on 8 March 1922. 'Human life is unprotected from any who may wish to take it. There are certain quarters of the city in which shooting proceeds by day and night.'[5]

Sectarian violence in Belfast was intertwined with IRA action on the border. In the early hours of 8 February 1922 IRA units from Monaghan crossed the border, kidnapped forty-two unionists and took them back to the south. They were used as hostages to secure the release of IRA prisoners: two had been sentenced to death for the murder of prison guards at Derry Gaol, while others had travelled to the north as members of the Monaghan Gaelic football team to free their condemned comrades. Three days later a bloody clash between B Specials and the IRA at Clones railway station, just south of the border in Monaghan, left four Special Constabulary and one IRA officer dead. There were further IRA hostage-taking raids across the border in March. The IRA took action on the border in retaliation for attacks on Catholics in Belfast, but this usually provoked further aggression by Protestant extremists in the city. The American Consul likened the situation to an 'Italian vendetta': 'The blood feud exists between the two elements of the population, and a single attack or a personal dispute between the two opponents develops at once into an outbreak participated in by all of similar sympathies.'[6]

Violence in Northern Ireland was caused by political circumstances: the truce and then the treaty caused enormous insecurity and anger among northern unionists, while emboldening nationalists and the IRA to strive for the removal of partition. But it was also made possible by the breakdown of the security and intelligence system in the six counties. This began after the truce. The Dublin Castle administration, whose primary goal was to maintain good relations with Sinn Féin, attempted to restrict the use of the Special Constabulary and the RIC against the IRA in Northern Ireland. As we have seen, aggressive intelligence activity was suspended under the terms of the truce. The IRA took the opportunity to openly train and organise within the six counties and along the border, further provoking unionist alarm. Incensed at Dublin Castle officials for neutering the police forces, Craig demanded that complete control of internal security, including the RIC and the Special Constabulary, pass to the Northern Ireland government. This was executed on 22 November 1921, just two weeks before the signing of the Anglo-Irish Treaty.[7]

This was something of a poisoned chalice, as the security forces of Northern Ireland were temporarily incapable of dealing with the challenges facing them. The greatest problem was that the six counties lacked a proper police force. The RIC had become demoralised, disorganised and passive during the truce period: in General Macready's opinion they were 'perfectly useless' and 'a pure waste of money'.[8] It was decided to replace them with a newly formed Royal Ulster Constabulary. This took much longer than the British government hoped, because of difficulties in incorporating former RIC men into the new organisation: unionists were suspicious of the loyalty and calibre of the primarily Catholic local force, suspecting that the most pro-Sinn Féin or incompetent officers had been transferred from the south to the relative quiet of Northern Ireland; RIC officers were not eager to join because they feared that Catholics would face discrimination under the Protestant regime. The RUC was not formed until 5 April 1922, and recruitment thereafter was slow: by the summer there were only 1,000 officers out of a planned 3,000.[9]

In the absence of a functioning regular police force, the maintenance of law and order in the first half of 1922 fell largely to the Special Constabulary. By November 1921 this was a large force, consisting of 3,453 'A' Specials, 15,944 'B' Specials and 1,084 members of the 'C' Specials.[10] These numbers steadily increased over the next six months. Yet, despite its size, the Special Constabulary was not well suited to quelling the violence that afflicted the province. The force suffered from poor training, indiscipline and sectarian bias. Its preferred form of policing was often the terrorisation of the Catholic population. Rather than preventing Protestant mob violence against Catholics, the Specials sometimes joined in themselves. General Macready lambasted the Specials as 'a whole lot of indisciplined scallywags': he wrote that 'so far as regards organisation and discipline' they were 'not greatly in advance of the Black and Tans'. The recently elected MP for North Down, Field-Marshal Sir Henry Wilson, was invited to develop a scheme for the reorganisation and improvement of the force. He selected a friend, Major-General Arthur Solly Flood, to serve as Military Adviser to the Northern Ireland government. But it would be some months before basic controls and disciplines were established.[11]

The conjunction of vicious sectarian fighting and a collapse of policing meant that the Northern Ireland government turned increasingly to the British army to restore order. The role of the British army in early 1922 provides an interesting precursor to its involvement in Northern Ireland in 1969. British troops patrolled the streets of Belfast, set up semi-permanent posts on the faultlines that separated the two communities, and attempted to keep the two sides apart.[12] As in 1969, the attempt by British troops to act as 'honest brokers' in an environment of sectarian violence aroused the gratitude of the Catholic community and the enmity of sections of the Protestant population. General Macready warned in March 1922 that loyalists had began 'to make a dead set' at the British troops, 'simply because they have carried out their duty impartially without regard to politics or religion'.[13] In the first week of January a member of the Norfolk Regiment was shot dead by an 'Orangeman' during rioting in the city: thus, the first British soldier to be killed in Northern Ireland since the establishment of the new state died at the hands of a loyalist. The unfortunate Norfolks were also shot at by members of the Special Constabulary, urged on by a Protestant crowd.[14] (In total, two soldiers were killed – one by Protestants and the other by IRA gunmen – and twelve wounded in the six months after the treaty.)[15] The army's role in Northern Ireland was deeply unpopular with the British troops. They were being used as police, caught between two antagonistic sectarian communities in 'the slummy streets of Belfast', a punch bag for both sides, unable to impose order.[16]

A major cause of the inability of the British army to suppress sectarian violence in Belfast was the lack of good intelligence. British troops reacted to rioting and shooting when it occurred, but rarely had information that would allow them to prevent it, or to apprehend the perpetrators: the commander of the army in Northern Ireland, Major-General A. R. Cameron, complained that 'the soldier is only a kind of scarecrow really'.[17] The British military, because of its limited role in Ulster's security before 1922, did not possess its own intelligence system at this time. Neither could it rely on the local police forces. The dismantling of the RIC and delays in forming the RUC led to a breakdown of the traditional police intelligence system. The British army complained of 'the total lack of a Criminal Investigation Department of any value whatever', dismissing police reports as 'in many cases inaccurate', 'badly arranged', 'highly exaggerated' and almost without exception 'of little value'.[18] The burden fell on the Special Constabulary, but it lacked the training and impartiality essential for security intelligence work: the British army concluded that 'information was not reliable because almost every Protestant saw a Sinn Feiner and potential murderer in every Roman Catholic'.[19] At a meeting on 10 March 1922 between Winston Churchill, Sir James Craig and the local army commander, Major-General Cameron, it was recognised that 'an establishment of efficient Intelligence would be the best means of combating existing disorders' in Northern Ireland.[20]

The absence of a good intelligence system in Northern Ireland made it impossible for the British army and the local police to stop the violence on the streets of Belfast and on the border with the south. It also made it difficult for the British government to understand what was happening in Northern Ireland: it struggled to obtain reliable information on the causes and nature of the crisis. British policy had been 'to trust the Government of the Six Northern Counties, and the Provisional Government in the South of Ireland' to provide intelligence.[21] However, the problem was that the two Irish governments provided diametrically opposed representations of the situation in the north. With every incident came two accounts of what had happened.

Put simply, Sir James Craig and the Northern Ireland government characterised the violence as *political*; it was part of an IRA plot to destroy the six counties administration.[22] They blamed southern gunmen for causing the trouble and accused the Provisional Government of secretly orchestrating and supplying the campaign. They turned attention from Belfast to the border at every possible opportunity, playing down the number of Catholic casualties in the city and citing IRA attacks on the frontier as the initial cause of sectarian rioting. Moreover, unionists warned that border skirmishes were the prelude to a full-scale invasion of the north by the IRA, backed by the full force of the Free State – this was their doomsday scenario.[23] On the other hand, the Provisional Government, and its most passionate spokesman on the northern issue, Michael Collins, gave an entirely different analysis of events. They blamed the Ulster security forces for the clashes with the IRA on the border. Moreover, they tried to shift attention to the violence in Belfast. What was occurring there was no less than a 'pogrom' against the Catholic minority, the aim of which was to drive the Catholic community from the province. It was being encouraged by unionist politicians and a thuggish, partisan Special Constabulary. Any IRA activity in the six counties was simply defensive. The violence was not political, but *sectarian*.[24]

The conflicting assessments provided by Collins and Craig reflected the perceptual chasm that opened up between the nationalist and unionist communities in Ireland during the revolutionary period: the same event, viewed from opposite sides of the political divide, could be interpreted very differently. However, the pronouncements of each government were also designed to advance political goals. It was in the interests of the northern authorities to portray the unrest as a southern IRA plot. It deflected attention from the sectarian violence perpetrated by their followers and from their inability to maintain order; it persuaded the British government to provide millions of pounds to fund their security forces; it made the proposed Boundary Commission appear unjust. Similarly, the Provisional Government exaggerated the persecution of the Catholic community and the sectarianism of the northern authorities because it assisted its goals of bringing down the unionist government and proving that partition was unworkable. There was clear duplicity on Dublin's part. Collins and National Army leaders secretly collaborated with the anti-Treaty faction to build up the IRA organisation in Ulster: the kidnapping raids in early February were carried out with their approval.[25] As one historian has written, 'the north and south were to all intents and purposes openly at war' during this period.[26] This placed the British government in a trying position. It had taken the decision to dismantle its intelligence capability and to rely on the two Irish governments, but now these governments were in violent conflict when it came to events in the six counties.

The differences between the northern and southern Irish governments were to some extent mirrored within different parts of the British governmental machinery in London. The strongest supporters of the Northern Ireland government were politicians within the Conservative Party. Craig and his patrician Minister of Education, Lord Londonderry, used their old political alliances and social networks to by-pass the normal Whitehall channels and impress their views directly on sympathetic leaders such as Arthur Balfour and Bonar Law. They had some success in getting their views across, for example, securing a promise in March 1922 that London would pay the costs of the Special Constabulary for six months.[27] On the other hand, the civil officials behind the treaty policy – men such as Alfred Cope, Sir John Anderson, Lionel Curtis, Mark Sturgis and Hamar Greenwood – tended to side with the Dublin government's interpretation of events. They classed the violence in Belfast as sectarian, not political or IRA-inspired. They were extremely critical of the failure of the unionist government and the Special Constabulary to restrain Protestant mobs. They absolved the Provisional Government from responsibility for the border raids, claiming they were the work of autonomous IRA units. Above all, civil officials in London were very suspicious of what they saw as the militarisation of the Special Constabulary, warning that the northern government 'was developing an army under the name of police' that could potentially be used against imperial troops.[28]

The British army took a more balanced position – one of disdain towards both Irish governments. British military reports accused the Provisional Government of colluding in the IRA attacks on the border: referring to one incident on 19 March 1922, General Macready informed the cabinet that it was 'difficult to believe that the whole affair was not known to the IRA leaders in Dublin, if not actually planned by them.'[29] Yet Macready, who had been sent to Ulster in 1914 to resist an Orange rebellion, had just as much contempt for the northern government in Belfast: 'I hate the Ulstermen rather more than the Southern Irish', he commented.[30] He dismissed Craig's warnings of a mass republican attack on the north as 'all tosh', 'hot air telegrams' got up for 'political reasons'.[31] He produced figures of casualties in Belfast that showed 'in spite of any arguments Craig and his Cabinet may use' that 'the balance for making trouble' was 'due to so-called PROTESTANTS'. However, he departed from the views of the leading British civil servants when advocating a solution. He resisted calls for greater British intervention and, instead, backed Craig's scheme to build up the Special Constabulary (despite frequently criticising its indiscipline and partisanship). The overriding desire of senior British army officers was to avoid getting dragged into the maintenance of security in Northern Ireland.[32]

The man who had to deal with the conflicting representations of the Belfast and Dublin governments, as well as the different advice tendered by the civil and military branches of His Majesty's Government, was Winston Churchill. As

Secretary of State for the Colonies he was responsible for both parts of Ireland. If the British army attempted to act as an honest broker between the communities in Belfast, Churchill undertook the equally difficult task of mediating between James Craig and Michael Collins. Lacking good intelligence sources of his own, and unsure of what was happening in the six counties, Churchill gave equal weight to the representations of the Belfast and Dublin governments and spent his energy on cajoling, persuading and pressuring the two sides onto a precarious middle-ground.[33] The culmination of his frantic Irish diplomacy was the signing of a pact between Collins and Craig on 30 March 1922. It was triggered by a particularly gruesome murder in Belfast six days earlier, when five members of the McMahon family, and one friend, were shot dead in their home in the early hours of the morning. It was widely suspected that members of the Special Constabulary were responsible for this incident.[34] It came at a time of many warnings from British civil and military officials of the danger of full civil war between north and south.[35] At this point British ministers decided that if the two Irish governments could not arrive at a peace agreement, the British army should take over the security of Belfast and the border region. Churchill used this decision, as well as the threat to withhold funding and arms from the Special Constabulary, to force Craig to come to conference with Collins.[36] The resulting Collins–Craig Pact, which gave the Dublin government a say in the security arrangements of the north, represented a strong intervention by the British government to force a compromise agreement between the two parts of Ireland. It was the last time that such pressure would be put on the government of Northern Ireland until the early 1970s.

In the following month Churchill continued to mediate between Craig and Collins in a desperate attempt to ensure that the provisions of the pact were implemented. However, amid renewed sectarian violence and public recrimination between Belfast and Dublin, the pact quickly unravelled; by 20 April it was a 'dead letter'.[37] The collapse of the pact was followed by a change in the attitude of the British government towards Northern Ireland. Henceforth the British government sided with the representations of the Belfast authorities, threw its full support behind their security policies, and isolated the province from its relations with the south – it no longer tried to be a neutral mediator between Collins and Craig. It also worked with the Northern Ireland government to develop an extensive intelligence system in the six counties. This shift in policy was brought about by signs that the IRA was planning a full assault on the north with the connivance of the Dublin authorities.

Cracking down on the IRA

FOLLOWING the breakdown of the Collins–Craig Pact and a renewal of sectarian bloodshed in April 1922, the IRA prepared for a major offensive against the north. Michael Collins and the pro-Treaty army headquarters in Dublin secretly supported this plan by providing personnel, arms and finance. (Other members of the Provisional Government, such as Griffith and Cosgrave, were kept in the dark.)[38] The IRA offensive began on the night of 17 May 1922, when twenty-one men raided the Belfast police headquarters at Musgrave Street. An intense firefight broke out, leaving one Special Constable dead and another wounded. This was followed by a wave of attacks on the police forces and a sustained incendiary campaign against unionist property. There were 606 violent incidents during May, and 604 in June. Claims for compensation arising from malicious injuries totalled £794,678 in May, and £760,018 in June, compared with £252,578 in April. IRA gunmen also carried out a number of grisly murders: six loyalists were massacred in Altnaveigh, Co. Armagh, by republicans dressed as police officers; an Ulster Unionist MP, William Twaddell, was assassinated in Belfast on 22 May. In all, the northern authorities attributed twenty-four murders to the IRA in this period.[39]

Although the IRA campaign achieved little, fizzling out by the end of June, it had a dramatic effect on British attitudes towards Northern Ireland. It seemed to give proof to what the unionist government had long asserted: that violence in the six counties was caused by republican terrorists supported from southern Ireland. Evidence of southern involvement first emerged a week before the start of the IRA offensive, when the RUC captured important IRA documents in Belfast. They were passed to the British army, which quoted them in its weekly intelligence summary for the London cabinet: the military chiefs concluded that 'organisers from outside the Six Counties' were 'responsible for most of the aggression displayed by the local I.R.A.'[40] By June more document captures confirmed to the northern police that the Dublin government was 'fully cognisant of the activities and outrages in the Six Counties.'[41] On the basis of this evidence, Lionel Curtis wrote to Churchill on 23 June 1922 that it was 'scarcely possible to doubt that the I.R.A. Headquarters in Dublin under General Mulcahy' was 'responsible' for the organisation of the IRA in Northern Ireland.[42]

Dublin's support for the IRA campaign was not sustained. On 3 June 1922 Collins and the Provisional Government 'decided that a policy of peaceful obstruction should be adopted towards the Belfast Government'; they abandoned their attempts to use force against Northern Ireland.[43] However, this was not evident to the northern unionist administration: it feared that the IRA campaign was no less than a preliminary skirmish before a full-scale invasion. Craig informed Churchill that the anti-Treatyites and Free Staters were secretly preparing for the establishment of a republic and a joint onslaught on the north.[44] This view was supported by intelligence from the Military Adviser, Major-General Arthur Solly-Flood. In a series of 'Secret Notes on Southern Ireland' in May and June 1922, he presented a conspiratorial history of developments since the treaty, asserting that there was a 'secret deal' between Collins and de Valera to build up their strength under cover of the Free State 'until the situation was ripe for the two forces to unite and strike at the Empire.'

> The triumphant Republicans now boast that in a year's time they will be in such a strong military position that they can laugh at England, 'if', in the words of Cathal Brugha, 'there is still such a place on the map'. Throughout the whole of these proceedings there is constant and abundant evidence that the Irish Republicans are in close touch with foreign Communists, Bolshevists, and internationals to promote revolution in England and bring about the destruction of the Empire.[45]

These views were echoed in a secret circular issued by Solly-Flood on 24 May to senior police officers, in which he warned that it was only 'a question of time before open hostilities between the North and South break out.'[46]

The northern authorities were responsible for foisting a series of unfounded invasion scares on the British government during May and June 1922. An excellent example is provided by events in Derry. Here we can trace the origins of a particular piece of 'intelligence' and the route it took to London. On 23 May the Dean of Derry, Richard King, wrote an urgent letter to Craig, calling his 'attention to the entirely inadequate provision made to secure this City from attack by large forces collected on the border with that openly avowed purpose'. Warning that they were on the brink of 'one of the most cruel and most tragic disasters in the whole bitter history of our Country', he demanded that naval vessels and aeroplanes be sent to the city to protect it – he had 'not the least doubt' that the IRA attackers possessed the latter. The source of the Dean's information was a small number of loyalists who were forced to flee from the Donegal side of the border. The Dean himself may not have been entirely reliable, as his appeal to the local police authorities had elicited little response. Rather than treating this letter with the scepticism it required, Craig relayed its contents in a 'Secret & Urgent' message to Churchill. 'This is S.O.S. on behalf of Derry City, which is in grave danger', Craig dramatically began. 'I have reliable information that a Force is mobilising in Donegal to launch an attack when word is given from higher authority.' He urged Churchill to send a cruiser and a gun-boat immediately to the city. Craig had taken the second-hand rumours supplied by one individual and transmitted them to London as 'reliable' intelligence. Churchill, in turn, accepted the warning at face value; he ordered that Royal Navy ships be despatched to Derry.[47]

There was little basis to this crisis, as the British army discovered when it sent officers to Derry to investigate.[48] The situation led Ulster District Command to issue special instructions to army intelligence officers. It said that the authorities at the War Office were 'periodically greatly troubled by false scares':

> For instance, the recent reports of I.R.A. concentrations in Co. Donegal were so exaggerated by persons having direct access to the authorities in LONDON, that it was actually believed that LONDONDERRY would fall if a warship etc, were not sent up immediately!! Many of these scares are started and kept up by the Ulster Press in order to deliberately affect public opinion at home. Others owe their origin to 'windy individuals', sometimes the police, sometimes prominent civilians with no military knowledge.

Military officers were instructed to send telegrams contradicting any 'glaring announcements in the press' so that the army headquarters would 'be able to gauge the true worth of these scares, and compete with them'.[49] Yet Northern Ireland ministers continued to by-pass the military intelligence system and appeal directly to politicians in London to take action on the border. On 4 and 8 June 1922 Craig successfully persuaded Churchill to order a British military attack on Irregular and Free State armed forces on the southern side of the border villages of Pettigo and Belleek. Seven men from the Free State army were killed in an artillery barrage.[50]

British action on the border, taken at the insistence of the unionist authorities, threatened to cause a breakdown in Anglo-Irish relations at a time of sensitive negotiations on the draft Irish constitution. When Michael Collins came to London, he accused the British of carrying out a premeditated 'massacre' of his innocent troops at Pettigo, and was 'thoroughly distrustful' – one civil servant recorded that his tone was one of 'great gravity and of a menacing character'.[51] Events in the six counties in May and June 1922, and the way in which they were interpreted by the Belfast government, contributed to the intense mistrust felt in London towards the Provisional Government. They also brought about a major change in British policy towards Northern Ireland. Whereas London had previously placed itself in the position of neutral arbitrator between Dublin and Belfast, the British cabinet now backed Craig to the hilt, insulating the north from policy towards southern Ireland.

This change in British perceptions was most evident in London's support for Northern Ireland's security policy. In April 1922 Major-General Arthur Solly Flood, Military Adviser to the Northern Ireland government, had assumed 'supreme command' of the northern police forces and developed a detailed scheme for their expansion: this included massively increasing the numbers of Special Constables, equipping them with heavy weapons and transport, and developing a headquarters staff of 200 military officers. During April 1922 Solly-Flood and the leaders of the northern government had been turned down when they pressed London to provide the finance, military officers and hardware necessary to realise this scheme.[52] However, by 12 May, with evidence of the impending IRA attack mounting, the attitude in London had changed. Craig returned from conferences with Churchill and the Chancellor of the Exchequer in an upbeat mood. He told his colleagues that 'the British Government were quite clear in their assurance that they would see Ulster through any attack from the South' and that 'Ulster's position was much better appreciated in Great Britain than was previously the case'.[53] When the IRA offensive spluttered into action, Lord Londonderry travelled to Britain to ensure that the promises of assistance were put into immediate effect. Much to the pleasure of the Northern Ireland cabinet, he secured commitments on the funding for the Special Constabulary for the next year, the provision of army officers to augment Solly-Flood's staff and the supply of arms and equipment: 'the Cabinet agreed that Lord Londonderry had rendered splendid service'.[54]

IRA activity also prompted the British government to make serious efforts to improve the collection of intelligence in Northern Ireland. As noted, this had been a major reason for the inability to suppress violence in the early months of 1922. General Macready brought this to the attention of Winston Churchill and Lord Londonderry at an important conference in London on 22 May 1922.[55] The British government responded in two ways: first, by increasing the intelligence capabilities of the military; second, by supplying officers to a newly created Criminal Investigation Department in Belfast.

In the summer of 1922 army chiefs decided to build up a military intelligence system in Northern Ireland. This was done not only because their role in internal security might continue, but also because there was widespread pessimism about the ability of the Provisional Government in Dublin to establish the treaty – it was likely that the army in Northern Ireland would have to lead the reconquest of the south. The Ulster District army headquarters wrote:

> By May 1922, the situation had materially changed. The nucleus of the
> Free State Army was an uncertain element, cases had occurred where

supposedly loyal Free State Officers and men had thrown in their lot with the Republicans, and it was a matter of difficulty to decide which were really Free State and which definitely republican. The situation in Ulster had also become changed. The I.R.A. forces in the Six Counties had been carrying out a programme of arson and promotion of civil strife in order to show that the Government of Northern Ireland were unable to govern. At this date their campaign reached its height, and the military forces had been greatly augmented.[56]

New instructions were issued to intelligence officers, stating that 'with the possibility in the near future of renewed hostilities with the I.R.A., as a whole, the G.O.C. would like further steps taken to ensure that an effective Military intelligence organisation' was 'in operation.'[57] Three senior intelligence officers were appointed at District HQ, assisted by four clerks, while intelligence officers were appointed in each brigade HQ and battalion.

A comprehensive report on the army Intelligence Branch in Northern Ireland, prepared when it was wound up in 1926, provides a fascinating description of the 'nuts and bolts' of a military intelligence system.[58] The officers who built this system had little experience and therefore proceeded on the basis of trial and error, guided only by a few army manuals on field intelligence. One of the first challenges they faced was transportation. Intelligence officers were therefore issued with motor cycles, subsequently converted into combination machines with sidecars because of the poor state of the roads. These proved 'invaluable', although because the motor cycles were often laid up for repairs, it was recommended that in the future 'intelligence officers be conversant at least with the rudiments of motor-cycles maintenance'. Typewriters were issued to each officer and 'though they had no previous knowledge of the art, it was soon learnt'. A dark-room and bromide printing machine were rigged up at headquarters and used for the reproduction of photographs and documents. An extensive system of cards, personal dossiers, photographs and indices was constructed, which allowed officers to compile an IRA and Free State army 'Order of Battle'. This information was used by an expert draughtsman to produce maps showing the location of IRA units, plotted against the religious composition of each area.

The 1926 report also describes the challenges the British army faced in collecting intelligence in closely knit Irish communities. It explained that IRA activity corresponded to the distribution of the different religions in the province. Not all Catholics were 'ipso facto, to be branded as "rebels"', and not all Protestants were 'to be hailed as patriots', but areas which contained a Catholic majority were far more likely to contain IRA units. It added that few, if any, Protestants would be found living in districts more than 400 feet above sea-level. These were the most dangerous areas: they were wholly Catholic, sparsely populated, often close to the border and therefore ideally suited to guerrilla operations. They were also impervious to penetration by British military intelligence:

> it is advisable to state as far as Ireland is concerned, that the possibility of a British Officer disguising himself and wandering round in search of information has not yet emerged from the realms of romance. Even were he to succeed in eliminating such things as a straight back and a regulation walk – not to mention an English accent and an English way of thinking – he would still be faced with the almost insurmountable task of explaining his presence as a stranger in a district where strangers are rare, and who, when they do appear are at once regarded with great suspicion and probably put down immediately as detectives in search of illicit stills.

The only agent who could 'hope for any reasonable chance of existence' was a 'native of the district', but the problem then arose of how he would communicate his information: an army officer could not visit his house, and use of the post would arouse the suspicions of the local post office employees, as the inhabitants of these districts were 'not prone to voluminous letter-writing'. The only possibility was to exploit an agent's regular visits to a market town by utilising as an intermediary someone with whom he would come into contact, for example, a shopkeeper. In more densely populated and mixed areas, the running of an agent would not pose such difficulties. However, it would still take a considerable amount of time to build up an intelligence network.

> All Irishmen, whether Roman Catholic or Protestant, consider a newly arrived Englishman to be either a fool or a knave, or possibly both. With luck an Englishman who can be classed in neither of these categories, may persuade an Irishman to realise the fact, but the latter will not consider himself able to arrive at a definite conclusion before a very close acquaintance lasting at least three months.

On this basis, the army concluded that it would take it 'the best part of a year' to build up a system of agents in Northern Ireland. It would be no easy task.

Furthermore, any attempt to do this would have provoked the 'jealousy' of the Special Constabulary, who would have accused the military of going 'behind their backs'. Because the power to act on information lay with the Special Constables, it was essential that the army maintain the closest liaison with them. Also, the running of agents would entail the use (as intermediaries) of Protestants who would rather deal with Special Constables than British officers. For all these reasons, the army decided to leave the organisation of a system of agents in the hands of the Special Constabulary. However, it was recognised that Special Constabulary officers would not be content to be continually giving information and receiving nothing but thanks in exchange: the military intelligence officer could not 'spend his time sitting under the tree of knowledge and eating such of the fruit as might drop into his lap'. It happened that the military intelligence officer could perform a very valuable task, 'namely the collating and recording of all information' obtained by the police officers, 'who, as a general rule, relied entirely on their memory'.[59] Therefore, the Ulster police and the military enjoyed close co-operation through a mutually beneficial division of labour: the police collected information and focused on the pursuit of individuals inside the six counties; military intelligence collated and analysed information, built up a complex filing system, and focused on the broad features of the security situation in the north and all facts concerning the IRA in the south. The army staff in Northern Ireland had a good foundation for this activity, as they received duplicates of the most important intelligence records, dating back to 1916, from British army headquarters in Dublin.[60]

The intelligence needs of the British army were served by a complete reorganisation of police intelligence in Northern Ireland. The inadequacy of the surviving Royal Irish Constabulary had been obvious for some time. Therefore, when Solly-Flood drew up his proposals for the reorganisation of the security forces, the establishment of a new 'Secret Service', or Criminal Investigation Department (CID), had a prominent part. The CID was created in early May 1922. Controlled by Solly-Flood, it consisted of a headquarters in Belfast and branches in each of the six counties. It was only able to develop when London agreed to loan personnel to the north, as it was composed primarily of British army and civil intelligence officers: for example, of the twenty-three officers in the CID in October 1922, eighteen were from Britain, four from Northern Ireland, and one from southern Ireland. Many had served in the south during the War of Independence, either with the army or Colonel Winter's intelligence organisation: for example, the director of the CID, Colonel Haldane, was a senior figure on Winter's headquarters staff in 1921.[61] These intelligence officers, demobilised following the treaty, were at a loose end – the Belfast CID provided well remunerated employment at an opportune moment.

Solly-Flood and the officers of the CID prided themselves on implementing 'scientific' intelligence methods – i.e., the full battery of techniques that had been perfected during the First World War. The CID certainly had a wide range of activities. In Belfast it built up a network of agents and 'touts' similar to the system created in Dublin in 1920–1. Across the province a small unit of three officers and a clerk operated a censorship on mails and telegrams to and from republican suspects. Because post office staff were distrusted, this was a 'travelling censorship', CID officers making surprise examinations at selected post offices. This unit did 'valuable work out of all proportions to its numbers'.[62] The CID also engaged in propaganda. A News Bureau was created on 24 April 1922 to supply the press with authoritative reports and prevent misrepresentations.[63] It produced a curious bulletin that intermingled descriptions of IRA violence with English country cricket scores and quirky news stories from around the world: for example, under the headline 'Bobbed Hair Suicide', one edition contained a story describing how 'Ruth Evans a New York typist, the possessor of an exceptionally beautiful head of hair, became overcome with grief after bobbing it for the purpose of comfort during a heat wave, and committed suicide in her home on Thursday'.[64] The CID had an avowedly international reach. It carried out investigative activities in Britain and built up relationships with the imperial intelligence agencies in London – the Special Branch, MI5 and SIS. CID officers regarded themselves as equal members of this wider community of British intelligence professionals. Solly-Flood certainly had great ambitions for the CID, initially requesting an annual budget of £80,000, which would pay for 150 officers and clerks. Its peak establishment, reached in September 1922, was eventually sixty-four personnel, including seventeen women searchers.[65]

The CID had an unusually intimate relationship with the army Intelligence Branch in Northern Ireland. Indeed, the line between them was blurred. They shared the same building, Danesfort House, in Belfast and exchanged information freely. The military intelligence history is effusive in its praise of the CID:

> This organisation was composed almost entirely of men with military experience. They became the link connecting the regular police with the troops in Northern Ireland, besides organising and advising the police in Northern Ireland concerning modern military intelligence methods.
>
> The results of their advent were almost instantaneous. Liaison which before had been difficult was now a matter almost of routine; co-operation was made almost as perfect as possible; and in a very few months the power of the I.R.A. was broken and the disturbances in Northern Ireland abated.[66]

The military intelligence system, the CID and the province-wide network of Special Constabulary intelligence officers were able to collect very good intelligence on the IRA from May 1922 onwards. Some informers were recruited within the Catholic community, although covert penetration of the IRA proved difficult: the RUC told Scotland Yard that 'they had never been able to get within the inner circle in which the assassinations are worked out, that the members are very heavily oath-bound, and that in no circumstances is it ever possible to get them to drink.'[67] Most intelligence came from overt security measures. By far the best source of information was captured documents. In May a raid on a house in Belfast produced a full list of IRA officers in the city, as well as documents proving the involvement of southern IRA leaders in violence. Raids and arrests yielded further papers over the coming months. IRA officers had an irresistible habit of recording their activities on paper, perhaps in an attempt to demonstrate that they were part of a professional, legitimate army. In all, 162 CID raids turned up 'seditious documents' during this period.[68]

The improved flow of intelligence coincided with a fierce crack-down against the IRA. The legal underpinning for this action was provided by the Civil Authorities (Special Powers) Act, a draconian instrument authorising the Minister of Home Affairs to 'take all such steps and issue all such orders as may be necessary for preserving the peace and maintaining order'. On 22 May the IRA and related republican organisations were proscribed. Internment was introduced, and within a week 350 republican suspects were interned on a cramped, leaky prison ship in Belfast Lough, the *Argenta*. (In all, 700 people were interned before the measure was dropped in December 1924.)[69] Large numbers of Special Constables were mobilised to carry out 'saturation patrols', raids and house searches, assisted by a night curfew imposed across the province. Although Craig decided not to use the death penalty for those found in possession of arms, flogging was increasingly administered. This security response was directed by Major-General Solly-Flood, who was given 'supreme control of all the Constabulary Forces in Northern Ireland for all purposes' on 20 April 1922. The Belfast cabinet provided a 'written undertaking' that they would 'stand over any action taken' by him, even if it was not 'strictly covered from a legal point of view'.[70]

The security response crushed the IRA in Northern Ireland. Many IRA men were interned, while many others fled across the border. The support of the Catholic population, battered by two years of sectarian violence, waned. 'The Enemy are continually raiding and arresting', the commanding officer of the IRA 3rd Northern Division lamented. 'The heavy sentences and particularly the floggings make the civilians very loath to hide "wanted men" or arms.' By the end of June 1922 IRA attacks and inter-communal violence had petered out. This process was accelerated by the start of the Civil War in southern Ireland, as many of the most active IRA men went south to join the fray.[71] From July there was a complete change in the security situation in Northern Ireland. Peace had mostly broken out: the number of violent incidents declined to 487 in July, 309 in August and just 207 in September – the lowest figure since the start of 1922.[72] The IRA offensive had been a complete failure, destroying the republican organisation in the north, bringing further repression and suffering on the Catholic population, and securing the position of the Belfast government.

Institutional rivalry and reorganisation

T HE hybrid intelligence system assembled in the spring of 1922 had been successful in suppressing the IRA and establishing law and order in Northern Ireland. But this system was short lived: street fighting was soon replaced by bureaucratic in-fighting. The second half of 1922 witnessed a power struggle between Major-General Solly-Flood and the Inspector General of the RUC, Lieutenant-Colonel Charles Wickham. This reflected disagreements over the correct relationship between the RUC and the Special Constabulary, and the overall purpose of Northern Ireland security policy. Solly-Flood was the clear loser in this battle. It represented a reassertion of control by the Northern Ireland civil authorities over a security apparatus that became too militaristic, independent and expensive.

A Yorkshireman, Lieutenant-Colonel Charles Wickham came to Northern Ireland via Russia, where he had served with the army staff during Britain's ill-fated intervention in the Civil War.[73] He was appointed as RIC Divisional Commissioner, with responsibility for the northern six counties, in November 1920 and then became the first Inspector General of the RUC in May 1922. He initially made a poor impression on British security chiefs. He was 'an absolutely rotten man … and one of the type who is always trying to skrimshank from his regiment', General Macready wrote. 'The young man is simply out to feather his nest.' Even Lord Londonderry complained as late as August 1922 that he was 'not nearly a big enough man for the post'.[74] However, Wickham grew into his job, remaining as RUC Inspector General until 1945 and playing a crucial role in Anglo-Irish security. During the summer of 1922 he slowly built up the professional capabilities of the RUC. This included its intelligence and investigative functions: a Special Crimes Branch and an active detective department were created in Belfast; police officers began to collect information from the community in the course of their normal activities.[75] Wickham, supported by the Minister of Home Affairs, Richard Dawson Bates, argued that the RUC should assume control for security in Northern Ireland, with the Special Constabulary and Solly-Flood's staff playing a supporting role. Moderate unionists also advocated for the RUC to take charge, recognising that an undisciplined, militarised and partisan Special Constabulary was a danger to law and order.[76]

Solly-Flood had a very different conception of the security needs of Northern Ireland. Despite the success of the crack-down in May and June 1922, he was adamant that the government had not gone far enough. He warned that the threat of invasion from southern Ireland had not gone away: 'although enemy activities are considerably reduced for the moment', he reported, 'evidence is daily forthcoming of their importing arms and framing fresh plans for rendering law and order in Ulster impossible.'[77] Because he doubted whether the north could rely on the British government for assistance, he was intent on building up a strong, indigenous military force that could defend the province from external aggression. He recommended a further expansion of the C Specials into a heavily armed, mobile, territorial reserve of 15,000 men. He also urged the government to take extraordinary measures such as the complete closure of the border, application of the death penalty for those found carrying arms and the creation of special areas where 'disloyal' individuals would be forced to live – effectively concentration camps.[78] Solly-Flood had not grasped the changed security situation brought about by the destruction of the IRA in the north, the decision by the Free State government not to use force against the north and the new commitment in London to support Northern Ireland.

Solly-Flood's unrealistic schemes lost him the backing of the Northern Ireland government. The cabinet firmly stated that it did not need a military force to defend the province from external invasion because the British army could be relied on for that purpose. They also balked at his chaotic style of administration and the enormous costs of his proposed security scheme: Craig exasperatedly wrote that 'The one thing he does not understand is finance in any shape or form.' On 9 August 1922 Wickham was given full operational control of the Special Constabulary, and Solly-Flood was demoted to his original position as a pure adviser, assisted by a small staff.[79] He was deeply unhappy about this decision. 'I view the future with grave concern for Ulster', he informed Craig. 'However to be continually crying wolf becomes tiresome to oneself and to one's hearers.'[80] He remained in Belfast for another four months, preparing more grand schemes for the security of Northern Ireland, passing on titbits of CID intelligence to Sir James Craig and criticising the organisation of the RUC.[81] But almost all his recommendations were ignored, and he was increasingly marginalised: 'He has for many weeks now been a mere ornament', a British civil servant wrote in December. Fed up with the repeated snubs and the unfriendly attitude of key ministers, he finally resigned on 5 December 1922.[82] Solly-Flood may have been the right man for the crisis of the summer, but he was not the right person to develop a civil constabulary in a time of peace, as his assessments and recommendations became ever more divorced from reality.

The debates over security policy and the role of Solly-Flood had major impli-cations for the organisation of intelligence in Northern Ireland, and in particular for the future of the CID. The CID was subject to a sustained and ultimately successful bureaucratic attack by the RUC Inspector General and the officials of the Ministry of Home Affairs. It is a curious story that highlights the confused and hastily arranged nature of the intelligence system in the north. The outcome established the primacy of the RUC over internal intelligence and lessened the involvement of British personnel and organisations.

The CID was subject to four main criticisms in the second half of 1922. The first was that it was much too expensive. All treasuries are tight fisted as a rule, but the Northern Ireland Ministry of Finance had a particularly strong clench on the purse strings. They complained that the CID was spending too much on the salaries of senior staff: for example, thirteen CID officers were paid the same as RUC District Inspectors.[83] They also objected to the lack of transparency over what money was spent on. Moreover, together with the Minister of Home Affairs, they questioned the very concept of a Northern Ireland 'secret service':

> Experience has shown that the value of information or other results obtained from the expenditure of Secret Service bears no relation to the amount of money expended. The freedom from Departmental and Parlia-mentary criticism induces laxity in administration: senior officers entrust expenditure to juniors who have not the experience to know when or how much to pay, and make either entirely unnecessary or much too large pay-ments. The employment of regular agents brings a flow of useless infor-mation furnished to justify the continuance of payment. A regular system of propaganda tends to lack a spontaneity sufficiently obvious to defeat the purpose in view. In this province the police will number 1 in 25 of the whole population and constitute a local organization with such local knowledge as to considerably reduce, if not eliminate, the necessity for low grade Secret Service work.[84]

The second charge against the CID related to the type of informers and agents that it employed: it formed a shadowy alliance with criminal and ter-rorist elements within the Protestant community. One CID agent, R. Williams, planted letters in the homes of innocent Catholics, who were then arrested on suspicion of involvement in an IRA murder plot. It led to an RUC enquiry and a minor public scandal.[85] The RUC also arrested a number of undesirable characters in Belfast who had to be released when it turned out that they were CID officers or agents. These included Frederick Edwards, who, accompanied by two barmaids, demanded rooms at the Royal Avenue Hotel at the point of a revolver; and George Shaw, a well known criminal with a long list of convictions for housebreaking and larceny. The Minister of Home Affairs complained that 'The employment of men of the criminal class in such a way as to cloak the latter with authority, has brought the C.I.D. in a most unfortunate way before the public.'[86] Far more sinister was the CID's link with a vicious Protestant vigilante gang in East Belfast called the Ulster Protestant Association. According to a police report, this fifty-strong group, which carried out reprisal attacks on Catholics in the summer of 1922, attracted 'the lowest and least desirable of the Protestant hooligan element.' In an attempt to control it the CID took some of its members on as secret agents; Solly-Flood recruited others to the Special Constabulary. However, far from being restrained, the Ulster Protestant Association was responsible for a series of unprovoked murders in Belfast in September and October 1922 that threatened to renew the cycle of sectarian violence. Perhaps because the Ulster Protestant Association was shielded by its relationship with the CID, the northern authorities were very slow to take the sort of action against it that had been meted out to republicans: it was not until the murder of a Catholic woman on the Newtownards Road on 5 October 1922 that Ulster Protestant Association leaders were interned.[87] This episode confirmed that CID officers were willing to collude with Protestant extremists and criminals for intelligence purposes – they did not have the impartiality or respect for the law essential for police officers.

The third criticism of the CID was that its expensive and sometimes dubious methods were not effective. Although the British army and Solly-Flood had a very high opinion of the achievements of the CID, this opinion was not shared by the RUC and the Ministry of Home Affairs.[88] Wickham stated that local police officers could collect intelligence more easily, because the population was 'prepared to trust them with information, obtained, in most cases, gratis' that was 'unobtainable by the more costly methods of the C.I.D.'[89] RUC assessments of the security situation began to contradict those provided by Solly-Flood and the CID. Whereas the latter repeatedly warned of a coming IRA 'storm', the RUC produced measured and optimistic reports, noting that developments in the south greatly decreased the risks of attack: Wickham reassured the government that there was 'everywhere a greater feeling of security and confidence'.[90] The secretary of the northern cabinet concluded that 'inside Ulster we are getting far more reliable and detailed information through the R.U.C. and Special Constabulary than the C.I.D. are collecting through other sources.' The Minister of Home Affairs, Dawson Bates, was more blunt about the failings of the CID: 'It is little or no use to us at present. We rarely get any information of value from it.'[91]

The final charge against the CID was an objection to its ethos and independence. It was barely under the control of the civil authorities of Northern Ireland, and appeared to collaborate more closely with, and owe stronger allegiance to, the British army. Most of its officers were English imports. The attitude and conduct of individual officers also left something to be desired. Many came from Winter's old intelligence organisation, and they appear to have brought the same loose respect for the law that characterised that outfit. Wickham described it as 'an Organisation of temporary officials whose representatives in the Counties are young ex-Officers with little experience of the Country, less of investigating crime, and no knowledge of law or evidence'.[92] There were suspicions that CID officers were exaggerating the security threats facing Northern Ireland in order to justify and maintain their employment. These negative perceptions were shared by a senior British civil servant in Belfast: 'If one twentieth of what I have heard about the C.I.D. is true, the sooner it goes, the better', he wrote.[93]

These arguments led to 'deplorable friction' between the CID and the RUC between July and December 1922.[94] Northern Ireland officials observed that the CID and the RUC Special Crimes Branch were thoroughly 'at cross purposes', 'crabbing' at one another and leaking 'important secrets' in order to discredit the other branch.[95] The barrage of criticism against the CID took its toll on the agency. Its director, Colonel Haldane, went on three months' medical leave in September. He was temporarily replaced by one of the Military Adviser's staff, Lieutenant-Colonel B. H. Waters-Taylor. Other officers also departed. On 24 November the Northern Ireland government finally decided to put the CID under Wickham's control and amalgamate it with the RUC Special Crimes Branch. This was to come into effect on 8 December.[96]

However, there was one final twist to this story. When the RUC Commissioner for Belfast visited CID headquarters to take charge, CID officers refused to hand over files relating to 'military or imperial interests': they claimed that they owed 'allegiance' to what they described as 'higher authority', which they would not define.[97] They were supported by the British army, which intervened with Craig and the British cabinet to stop the reorganisation. British military concerns were due to lingering suspicions over the trustworthiness and competence of the newly formed RUC, conditioned by the army's experiences with the RIC over the past decade: military chiefs stated that CID intelligence files could not be 'handed over to persons not thoroughly trustworthy, as the lives of men are involved'.[98] CID files also contained secret 'imperial intelligence' from the Special Branch or SIS, in particular on a gunrunning case involving the ss *Wicklow Head*, which was too sensitive to fall into unionist hands.[99] Finally, it appears that CID records may have contained evidence that the military was sometimes working 'beyond, if not against, the interests' of the Northern Ireland government, for example by planning to implement an unfavourable Boundary Commission decision.[100] The feelings of the British army were so strong on this point that the War Office temporarily took over the running of the CID. Its files were divided between military intelligence (retained by the army) and criminal material (passed to the RUC).[101] The CID was then handed back to the Northern Ireland government at the end of the month. During 1923 it was gradually merged with the RUC Special Crimes Branch, which henceforth took the lead in intelligence and security matters.[102] This arrangement continued until 2007, when another British organisation, MI5, assumed responsibility for national security in Northern Ireland.

The confusion over intelligence policy and the severe friction between the RUC and CID in the autumn of 1922 may have contributed to the brief upsurge in sectarian violence at this time. However, the way in which this dispute was resolved reflects some credit on the Northern Ireland government. It had allowed the CID and the Special Constabulary under Solly-Flood to get out of control during the crisis of the IRA offensive – improvisation and expediency were the key features of this period. But once conditions settled and the RUC built up its capabilities the Belfast leaders reined in the dangerous activities of its intelligence officers. This indicates that the Northern Ireland government was serious about building up a professional security system, operating within the law and centred on the Royal Ulster Constabulary. The security system of the north would always be partisan and one-sided to an extent, as it was predicated on the defence of the state from the subversive threat of Irish republicanism. Its approach did little to remove the sense of alienation and despair felt by the minority Catholic community. But it was at least now a force for law and order, and capable of maintaining an uneasy peace, rather than a contributory factor in violence as it had been in the early months of 1922.

The shift in responsibility for security from British agencies to the indigenous police forces of Northern Ireland continued in 1923 and 1924. The British army's presence was scaled down: the number of battalions declined from a peak of twenty-three in July 1922 to fourteen in December 1922 and just five in April 1923 (a force of approximately 5,000 men).[103] The RUC had clear control over security matters, improved its criminal investigation and intelligence effectiveness, and soon proved to be more successful than the old, independent CID. In September 1923 the RUC managed to recruit a well-placed informer within the IRA for the first time. Though his identity is unclear, he was a senior figure with an excellent understanding of the state of the IRA organisation in the north. This informant provided very valuable reports at least until 1925. Local RUC officers also built good networks within the community and were able to pick up a steady supply of information in the course of their normal activities.[104]

The picture of the internal IRA threat that emerged from this intelligence was a reassuring one. After 1922 there were few political murders and the number of political 'outrages' dwindled dramatically.[105] The RUC's high-placed informant stated 'emphatically that the Republican party is almost finished in Northern Ireland'. The IRA was 'down and out' and would 'make no progress for years to come'.[106] In October 1925 Inspector General Wickham drew up a comprehensive intelligence memorandum that gave a similar assessment. The arrests and exclusions, and the apathy of the Catholic population, had 'discouraged and disorganised them to such an extent', he wrote, 'that at the present time no actual military organisation can be said to have any real existence in Northern Ireland although doubtless such may exist on paper'. It was doubtful whether the IRA could mobilise 300 men, and no arms dumps of importance had escaped discovery.[107] The British military came to an identical conclusion. After a tour of Northern Ireland a lieutenant-colonel from the War Office reported that

> matters were never quieter as far as civil and political crime are concerned. The general impression gained was that the intelligence organization of the R.U.C. and Special Constabulary could be considered as efficient and that sufficient warning could be counted on to take necessary measures for prevention of the situation, internally, of 1921.[108]

THE contribution of the British intelligence community to achieving peace and security in Northern Ireland was mixed. London initially refrained from building up its own military intelligence system in Northern Ireland, content to leave the matter to the local RIC and Special Constabulary. When violence intensified, it worked with the Northern Ireland authorities to develop a hybrid system: British personnel were drafted into a new Criminal Investigation Department, which was supported by an active army Intelligence Branch. Although this system helped to crush the IRA campaign in May and June 1922, it was also responsible for alarmist scaremongering and for dubious, extra-legal practices. The Northern Ireland government moved to establish civilian control and RUC primacy over internal security by the end of 1922, an arrangement that would persist for the next half century. Though unionist politicians had been more prone to alarmism than CID and military intelligence officers in the first half of 1922, this was reversed by the end of the year: the professional intelligence operatives were exaggerating the threats to Northern Ireland's security, possibly in an attempt to justify their continued employment.

British intelligence on Northern Ireland did not always adequately inform decision making in London. The impression remains that the British government never understood the dynamics of the political violence that rocked the six counties in 1921 and 1922. For political reasons it initially adopted a stance of neutral mediator between the conflicting unionist and nationalist camps; but it then threw its support behind the Belfast government in May 1922, ignoring accusations of sectarianism made against the unionist regime. London's overriding concern was to extricate itself from the affairs of Northern Ireland, while avoiding a break with the new government in Dublin. In the short term this was achieved. However, the imperfect settlement of the Irish question in 1921, and the bitterness engendered by the violence in 1922, meant that London could not completely ignore Northern Ireland. Most immediately, the Boundary Commission loomed in the background and would create an air of mild crisis in Anglo-Irish relations until the end of 1925. Internally, the regime's security policy, though maintaining a sort of peace, manufactured resentments within the Catholic community that were periodically expressed through violence in the 1920s, 1930s and 1940s. Partition also provided a long-lasting grievance for republican extremists and moderate nationalists in southern Ireland. And, of course, all the horrors of 1922 would be repeated after 1969 when the modern Troubles erupted. In many ways, Northern Ireland was the unfinished business of the Irish revolution.

PART II

The Restless Dominion, 1923–39

CHAPTER 5

British Images of Ireland

Britain's traumatic experience of the Irish revolution reinforced preconceptions about Ireland that would influence British policy decisions until the 1940s. Preconceptions are important to any understanding of intelligence and its role in policy-making. Policy-makers make decisions not on the basis of objective analysis of the facts, but by employing subjective cognitive premises and belief systems. They see what they want to see, select the information that fits their pre-existing hypotheses and biases, and ignore what is inconvenient. In his analysis of notable intelligence 'failures' of the twentieth century, Richard Betts concludes that 'the ultimate causes of error in most cases have been wishful thinking, cavalier disregard of professional analysts, and, above all, the premises and preconceptions of policy makers'. The role of preconceptions is especially powerful when information is incomplete, contradictory or ambiguous, or when the subject is inherently mysterious and unknowable. The most that an effective intelligence system can do is to educate and enlighten government leaders, shaping their cognitive premises and challenging obvious errors, so as to minimise distortions.[1]

This is the case today, even in those countries with sophisticated intelligence systems. Preconceptions had an even greater influence on British perceptions of Ireland in the 1920s and 1930s. At that time the British intelligence system was in a 'pre-modern' stage of evolution. There was no system for collating, assessing and synthesising the many different pieces of information flowing into the government. Professional intelligence agencies were neglected. Prejudices and assumptions distorted the British government's understanding of many other countries: for example, 'faulty expectations' and 'preconceptions' were at the heart of Britain's failure to accurately assess the German threat in the 1930s.[2] Preconceptions were especially important in relation to Irish affairs. Ireland was so closely connected to Britain, and had been an emotive political issue for so long, that most British leaders had strong opinions on its people, its problems and the right solutions. The informality of British intelligence on Ireland meant that these prejudices and assumptions were not systematically challenged.

There was no single British perception of Ireland in this period. Members of the British government continued to gravitate towards the two very different interpretations of the Irish situation that had first emerged following the signing of the Anglo-Irish Treaty in December 1921. On the one hand, the 'diehard unionist' camp maintained the deepest suspicion of the new Irish state, made dire predictions of its social development and political actions, and criticised any concessions made by London to Irish republicans. On the other hand, 'liberal imperialists' held out hopes that the Irish Free State would become stable and democratic, settle down within the empire as a loyal Dominion and perhaps one day succeed in wooing Northern Ireland into a united state.

The diehard unionist perspective was most prominent among five closely related groups. In Northern Ireland, unionists had a deeply prejudiced view of the Free State during the 1920s and 1930s.[3] Southern Irish loyalists, many of whom had resettled in Britain, shared the northern disdain for the new nationalist order, though this was often mixed with real affection for the 'common' Irish people.[4] In Britain these perceptions were most prevalent among the rightwing faction of the Conservative Party, which had opposed the grant of self-government to Ireland in the 1920s and campaigned against any weakening of imperial control (such as Indian Home Rule) in the 1930s.[5] There was also a significant strain of diehard unionism within the British military. The British army of the interwar period was a politically conservative, snobbish, anti-intellectual club, increasingly out of touch with British society: there was some truth in the pompous, reactionary, irascible Colonel Blimp character, created by the cartoonist David Low in London's *Evening Standard* in the 1930s.[6] These attitudes could also be found among the interwar intelligence services because they were recruited from the same circles.[7] Their most vocal trumpet was the *Morning Post*. Owned by aristocratic elders of the Tory Party until it was absorbed into the *Daily Telegraph* in 1937, it was notorious for its reactionary stance: it was quipped that no cause could be regarded as completely lost until the *Morning Post* took it up.[8] (Ironically, a future IRA Chief of Staff, Seán MacBride, worked as a 'spare night sub' at the newspaper in 1926; this would certainly have caused apoplexy among its owners had it been known.)[9]

The diehard unionist perspective was shaped by the experience of the Irish revolution between 1916 and 1923. The IRA insurgency and the loss of southern Ireland had a traumatic effect on the British imperial establishment. The legacy of this period would influence perceptions and policy over the next two decades, not least because many of the same individuals remained at the highest levels of government on the Irish and British sides. It has been said that nationalist Ireland created a myth history of this period that eulogised the separatist leaders and simplistically portrayed the events as a national struggle for freedom against a foreign oppressor. Yet there was a loyalist, imperial counter-revolutionary history that gave an antithetical version of what had happened in Ireland. It can be found in the internal histories of the Irish rebellion prepared by the British army and Colonel Winter's intelligence branch in 1922; in the memoirs of British military officers, British civil servants and Irish loyalists who had witnessed the revolutionary violence at first hand; and in books on history, social affairs and military strategy published in Britain in the 1920s and 1930s. As time passed and memories blurred, this alternative version of the Irish revolution evolved into a form of myth history for *these* communities.

At the core of this alternative history was a characterisation of the republican movement and its relationship with the Irish people. Sinn Féin's republican programme was dismissed as delusional, divisive and unwelcome to the majority of the country. Far from being a 'nation in arms', the IRA was an extremist and unrepresentative 'murder gang' that had hijacked the country. It was a combination of a small group of fanatical intellectuals and a larger number of 'farmers' sons and corner boys, who had no stake in the country and preferred earning a living by plunder and murder than by doing an honest day's work'.[10] A professor of history at King's College London recounted how 'the murder of constables became a lucrative profession', £60 to £100 per head being paid to 'successful assassins'.[11] When blood money and plunder were not a sufficient motivation, it was believed that unwilling men were terrorised into joining the IRA and fighting on its behalf: they were kept in 'slavery' by 'the bullies of the inner ring'.[12] Terror was also cited as the means by which the IRA imposed its will on the Irish population. The elections in 1918 and 1921 were dismissed as an exercise in intimidation: 'The elections represented the fear of the revolver rather than the free choice of the population.'[13] The gunmen were able to impose their will on the country because of the abject 'moral cowardice' and passivity of the Catholic Irish people. General Macready once complained that 'a couple of men with revolvers can cow a whole countryside of persons of so-called moderate views'.[14]

While dismissing the political legitimacy of the Sinn Féin movement, the diehard unionist camp was even more incensed by the way the Irish rebels fought. 'Many were of a degenerate type', the British army's record of the rebellion noted, 'and their methods of waging war were in most cases barbarous, influenced by hatred, and devoid of courage.'[15] Stories circulated about 'obscene mutilations carried out on dead British soldiers after an ambush or attack'.[16] Loyalists swapped tales of gruesome persecution during the Civil War: one Anglo-Irish man informed his readers how the country lay 'at the mercy of armed marauders who spare neither man, woman, nor child, who lay waste the country, burn and pillage the houses of the loyalists, rape their women, and shoot unarmed, defenceless men at sight.'[17] The British also objected to the military tactics used by the IRA against crown forces. IRA men were condemned as 'murderers' and 'cowards' for their habit of shooting policemen in the back, fighting out of uniform and conducting 'hit and run' ambushes before blending back into the civilian population. There was fury at the 'fiendish females who carried weapons concealed beneath their skirts to and from the scene of ambushes.'[18] British army officers had been brought up in a tradition of regulated, gentlemanly, even genteel, warfare, where a strict code of conduct regulated the more brutal aspects of killing one's fellow men. The Irish guerrillas were not fighting fair, not playing the game. There was moral outrage at this; but there was also palpable frustration at the difficulty of suppressing this sort of guerrilla campaign.

Although the diehard unionist history of the Irish rebellion was full of contempt for the IRA and the Irish people, it reserved the greatest opprobrium for the British government. Under this interpretation the Sinn Féin movement was a cancer that needed to be exterminated; the inert Irish people would tolerate, and probably welcome, this painful treatment.[19] London was criticised for flip-flopping between conciliation and coercion, hamstringing the security forces and never employing force to its maximum extent. 'The Irishman', Colonel Winter mused, 'without any insult being intended, somewhat resembles a dog, and understands firm treatment, but, like the dog, he cannot understand being cajoled with a piece of sugar in one hand whilst he received a beating from a stick in the other.'[20] Moreover, commentators claimed that even with its half-hearted counter-insurgency campaign the British state had been on the verge of defeating the IRA in the summer of 1921. As already described, there was a conviction that the Irish leaders, facing imminent defeat, had tricked the British government into agreeing a truce, thus giving the IRA an opportunity to rebuild its military capability.[21] The subsequent concession of Dominion status and the hurried British withdrawal, leaving southern loyalists at the mercy of the gunmen, was seen as a despicable surrender. In his *History of Ireland, 1798–1924* Sir James O'Connor, a former Lord Justice of Ireland, writes:

> The history of every country, England included, has its dark and shameful chapters. But I doubt if that of any civilized community in modern times can show anything which for cowardice, wickedness, stupidity and meanness can equal the handling by the British Government of the situation created for them by a couple of thousand Irish peasants and shop-boys.[22]

The notion that the British crown forces had brought the IRA to the point of collapse, only to be betrayed by cowardly politicians, would gain more and more ground as the campaign receded into the past – it helped explain away Britain's defeat at the hands of a ragtag irregular army.

The feelings of resentment and humiliation caused by the Irish revolution persisted within the British ruling establishment for the next two decades. For example, when one civil servant approached Prime Minister Stanley Baldwin in 1924 to discuss the Boundary Commission, he received a 'diehard reaction': the Conservative Party leader spoke hostilely about the Free State leaders, commenting that it was 'difficult to forgive assassination and to forget their behaviour in the war'.[23] One Home Office civil servant in 1936, when dealing with accusations of discrimination against Catholics in Northern Ireland, harked back to the 'campaign of murder and arson' waged by the IRA before 1922 and 'the mistaken and feeble of policy' of the British government in dealing with it.[24] This bitterness was particularly strong within the British army. It surfaced in 1929, when there was a suggestion that Irish army officers could join training establishments in Britain. The Chiefs of Staff objected, arguing that the Free State 'was born under conditions of ... blood and insensate hatred' and that among British officers who had served in Ireland before the treaty 'there still existed a feeling of intense bitterness' – placing them alongside Irish personnel would only lead to 'acrimony and recriminations'.[25]

The diehard unionist characterisation of the Irish revolution led to a deeply caustic and pessimistic attitude to the Irish Free State, which revolved around five recurring themes. The first was contempt for the new rulers and institutions of the Irish state: the memoirs of one former Dublin Castle civil servant condemned 'the bitter, cross-grained party which has governed the Twenty-Six Counties for nearly a generation ... That party has an odious past of murder and outrage and falsehood of which every decent Irishman is ashamed.'[26] The second was exaggeration of the persecution and discrimination faced by Protestant loyalists. This was placed in the context of a third factor: impending social and economic anarchy caused by misgovernment, the persistence of IRA banditry and a total lack of respect for the law. British army officers continued to attest to the 'pure moral cowardice' of the people and the inability to resist any extremist who shouted 'Down with England'.[27] Fourth, it was predicted that the Free State was on an unstoppable slide towards a fully independent republic, with the secret connivance of political parties that professed support for the treaty. Finally, there were dire predictions of the implications of a hostile southern Ireland for the security of the British empire, especially in time of war. The commander of the British army in Northern Ireland certainly expected the worst when devising a defence scheme for the province in 1924:

I consider that any scheme which takes the problem of defence seriously must regard the Irish Free State with its armed forces as certainly a possible and really a probable enemy. Even if a comparatively friendly government is in power in the Free State as at present, it is likely to be swept away in the excitement which the opportunity offered by a war between England and a foreign power would arouse amongst the republican party and in the Free State Army. I think, therefore, full consideration must be given to the chance of an oversea raid landing hostile troops in the Free State and joining the Free State forces in an attack on Northern Ireland.[28]

According to the diehard unionist interpretation, Ireland's present conditions and future development held out bleak prospects for the Irish people and the British empire.

What sort of policy did these diehard unionists advocate towards Ireland? There was agreement on some principles. The first was to hold on to what the United Kingdom had, which meant giving total support to Northern Ireland and maintaining the strategically important Treaty Ports in the south. The second was to mitigate the invidious position of southern Irish loyalists by providing financial compensation for losses and injuries suffered during the revolution and by pressing the Dublin regime to safeguard their rights. However, there was divergence in opinion over the correct British response to southern Ireland's trend towards independence. The more extreme unionists continued to wage a quixotic campaign for the restoration of the Union, if necessary by reconquest. Their shaky justification was that the Irish people would secretly welcome the return of a responsible British government capable of establishing law and order. 'The feeling towards England is very friendly', one British military officer wrote after a visit to Ireland in 1925, 'and I was assured by all classes that, in a secret ballot, 95% of the population would vote for the return of the British.'[29] A clear distinction was drawn between the opinions of the Irish majority and the extremist leadership. In contrast, by the 1930s other right-wing figures were keen for Britain to wash its hands of southern Ireland. They argued that the British government should stop trying to placate the ungrateful Anglophobes across the Irish Sea and allow them to destroy their country if they wished. This was based on an assumption that the vast majority of Gaelic Irish were virulently and irredeemably hostile to Britain. It reflected a persistent contradictory element within the diehard unionist perception of Ireland – they could never decide whether the Irish were naturally pro-British, but temporarily hijacked by a fanatical leadership, or all rabid republicans beyond British help.

Underpinning these images of Ireland were deeply engrained stereotypes of the Irish character. The Irish were seen as inherently opposed to government, law and civilization. According to a 1922 British military intelligence summary:

> the objection of the tribal Irish is not so much to the British Government as to any form of Government, either National or Local; a prejudice they share in common with the Boers of the BACKVELD, the Arabs of IRAQ, and other semi-wild races. The struggle of the Southern Irish in fact is a struggle not so much against the British Government, as against civilization; and so long as civilization endures, the struggle is likely to continue.[30]

Another observer asserted that the Irish possessed 'a certain latent savagery' that could only be satisfied by violence and bloodshed.[31] General Macready argued that 'a people characterized through past centuries by lack of discipline, intolerance of restraint, and with no common standard of public morality' could 'only be governed and held in check under the protection of a strong military garrison'.[32] Echoing colonial fascination with the 'Noble Savage', there were some positive representations of the Irish Celts – their rural primitivism, anti-materialism, artistic temperament, conversational brilliance. But this did not make them any more capable of self-government.[33] The British army's history of the rebellion concluded that the Irish were 'a difficult and unsatisfactory people. Their civilisation is different and in many ways lower than that of the English.'[34]

The most venomous and extraordinary denunciation of the Irish race was contained in a 1937 memoir by Hervey de Montmorency, a British intelligence officer who had served in Ireland under Colonel Winter. In his book he set out to expose 'the true Celtic Irish character' and 'its elements of vanity, treachery, poltroonery, and cruelty'. He claimed that every Irishman was 'inherently lawless', 'traditionally "agin" the Government' and 'a rebel at heart'. The clue to his rebellious character was 'extravagant vanity' and a search for 'notoriety'. An Irishman would 'prefer imprisonment, torture, nay, death, to obscurity', and the family 'whose son has died by the hangman's noose' was 'envied' – this was why murder was so prevalent in the country. Conditions were so unbearable that the talented and ambitious had all sought fortunes abroad, leaving 'only the third-class brain' at home:

> All that was best in Irish society must have fled with the 'Wild Geese' in the seventeenth century, how otherwise can be explained Ireland's heritage of an idle, thriftless population from which the criminal classes have too often been recruited? The gunmen in America are chiefly Irishmen and the records of our police courts are punctuated with Irish names. ... It is not nature, however, which is the Emerald Isle's bitterest enemy, but man:

the Irish are perverse, quarrelsome, vain, jealous, and easily influenced by degrading superstitions; they are garrulous, too, being even more readily intoxicated by their own verbosity than the Russians.[35]

The cause of these character flaws was sometimes given as the history of the island, in particular the fact that Ireland missed out on the civilising effects of Roman conquest.[36] However, Irish deficiencies were also explained by deeper genetic and racial factors.[37] Crude theories on the differences between races had emerged following the Darwinian revolution in the Victorian period and enjoyed a continuing fashion in the 1920s and 1930s. They often made use of a new classification, first proposed by a Harvard sociologist, that divided Europeans into three racial types: Teutonic or Nordic; Alpine; and Mediterranean or Iberian. Ireland was deemed to have a majority of Mediterraneans, whose inferiority was contrasted with the predominantly Nordic population of England. This theory formed the basis for a revival in the 1920s of a tendency, unseen since the 1880s, to characterise the Irish in derogatory racial terms. For example, in a history on Ireland, the former *Morning Post* correspondent Charles Bretherton described how the first inhabitants of Ireland had been 'a dark, dwarfish, long-headed race of troglodytes', whose Iberian latter-day descendant, 'a peasant savage with the slave mind', was 'quite incapable of rising above his position of semi-servitude, either individually or as a race'.[38]

Perhaps the most imaginative theory of Irish racial genealogy was provided by an ultra-nationalist political weekly *Plain English* and its controversial editor, Lord Alfred Douglas, the former lover of Oscar Wilde. He argued that the Irish were the direct descendants of the Attacotti, an obscure Eastern Mediterranean tribe of Roman auxiliaries briefly mentioned in ancient history. Under the name 'Firbolg', Douglas claimed, the tribe had come to Ireland around the time of Christ as the slaves of the Milesians or Celts, but had risen in revolt and massacred almost all of the latter. They had waged a war of extermination ever since against the 'fair-haired and clean-skinned' Celts and Anglo-Saxons. Contributors to *Plain English* expanded on this theory, imaginatively tracing the origins of the Attacotti to one of the lost tribes of Israel (which fitted with the anti-Semitism of the publication), to the apelike hominids whose bones were then being discovered in Africa, or, most incredibly, to the rumoured Yeti or Abominable Snowman of Tibet! These origins were used to explain the contemporary character of the Irish and the violent events of the 1916–21 period. 'Along with the beady eyes, low foreheads, dark, coarse, and often kinky hair, a strain of negro blood, and an abnormal fondness for destruction', the Irish had inherited the Attacotti's predilection for 'periodical outbursts of blood lust' directed against superior peoples at intervals of twenty to thirty years. The Irish War of Independence and the savage tactics of the IRA, therefore, were just the latest manifestations of ancient Attacotti barbarity.

At this time racial theorists began to change their views on the correct relationship between Britain and the backward Irish. In the early part of the century they had advocated the mixing of Anglo-Saxon and Celtic stocks. This miscegenationist solution to the Irish question was forthrightly advanced after the 1916 Easter Rising by the proprietor of the *Morning Post*, Lady Lilias Bathurst:

> The Irish race is, when undiluted with Anglo-Saxon blood, a weak, ignorant, lazy, emotional race, quite incapable of loyalty even to its own chiefs or leaders, and it has been so for centuries. ... Though the untravelled and pure-blooded Irishman is about the most unsatisfactory citizen of this great Empire, yet if he is half English, Scotch, or Canadian, or Australian, he becomes one of the finest people in the world ... Mix the races, import Irish into England, and *vice versa*. In the meantime even the pure Irish can be vastly improved by a course of Army training.[39]

However, after the separation of the Free State from the United Kingdom in 1921, racial doctrines tended to emphasise the incompatibility of the two races. An infusion of Irish genes was no longer regarded as a good thing; rather, it was argued that it would lead to the corruption and degeneration of the Anglo-Saxon racial stock. This led to widespread fears in England and Scotland about the 'cancerous' effect of increased Irish immigration in the 1920s and 1930s. One of the strongest proponents of this view was G. R. Gair, president of the Scottish Anthropological Society. In a series of articles in 1934 he pointed to the higher rates of disease, mental illness and criminality among Irish immigrants as evidence of their racial inferiority. He predicted that, because of immigration, intermarriage and the higher Irish birth rate, it was 'only a matter of time before an alien Mediterranean race supplants entirely the native Nordic peoples of this island'; the inevitable outcome would be 'the total collapse of Britain as a world and imperial power: and perhaps with it, who knows? civilisation'. Fears about the dilution of the indigenous racial stock were expressed by Scottish Members of Parliament in a parliamentary debate in 1932 and were taken up by the Eugenics Education Society, one of whose leading members (a Fellow of the Royal Society) called for the involuntary sterilisation of Irish immigrants. R. M. Douglas, who has extensively researched this subject, concludes that by the 1930s 'racial doctrines concerning the Irish had regained much of the ground they had lost since the late-nineteenth century'. (They did decrease somewhat in the late 1930s, because of growing public disquiet over racial doctrines, then unfavourably associated with Nazi Germany, and because of an improvement in Anglo-Irish relations.)

While many of the racial theories described here were exceptionally venomous and not part of the mainstream, they were not without influence. Racial Hibernophobia was common among Britain's academic, political, ecclesiastical and journalistic élite. Under the editorship of Lord Alfred Douglas, *Plain English* grew to a circulation that compared favourably with weeklies such as the *New Statesman*. The story of the Attacotti was, predictably, endorsed by the *Morning Post*. Many reports on Ireland circulating within the British establishment in the 1920s and 1930s were peppered by casual references to Irish racial difference and inferiority. These assumptions can also be found among the statements of leading British political figures of the day. The Prime Minister, Andrew Bonar Law, famously stated 'that the Irish were an inferior race'.[40] The Conservative Secretary of State for Dominion Affairs, Leo Amery, concluded that a 'curse' hung over Ireland. 'To unravel it would be like the tale of Atreidae', he wrote, 'but I fear the starting point is a fault in the blood, some element of ape-like savagery which has survived every successive flood of settlers.'[41] Even the architects of the treaty settlement and the strongest supporters of the Irish Free State indulged in this racial Hibernophobia. Winston Churchill wrote to his wife that there was a 'diabolical strain' in the Irish character, a 'treacherous, assassinating, conspiring trait which has ... prevented them from being a great responsible nation with stability and prosperity'.[42]

The racialisation of Irishness usually served a political purpose. Before 1918 it was used to justify Union between Ireland and Britain: the Irish needed the English to provide good government and to strengthen their genetic stock (through an infusion of superior Anglo-Saxon blood). During the War of Independence the characterisation of IRA violence as the product of a savage, racial trait served to delegitimise the republican cause and justify a ruthless British repression in the name of civilisation. After 1921, racial theories helped Britain come to terms with the loss of southern Ireland. This traumatic separation made necessary, to a significant degree, the reformulation and redefinition of concepts of British national identity. New theories of the incompatibility of the two races explained the failure of the Anglo-Saxon civilising mission in Ireland. It assuaged the humiliation of the British nation, whose identity the Irish had repudiated, by reconfiguring the now-truncated Union along ethnic lines and retrospectively representing the secession of the twenty-six counties as a symbolic expulsion.[43]

This racial characterisation of the Irish revolution had implications for British perceptions of independent Ireland. If Irish revolutionary violence was not due to political opposition to British rule, but was instead caused by a genetic dispo-sition to 'blood lust', then separation from Britain would not bring peace to the country; in fact, without Britain's moderating, civilising influence, things would only get worse. It helps explain the diehard unionist perception that southern Ireland was prone to political instability, social anarchy, republican violence and periodic aggression against the British race. This perception, in turn, influenced the production and interpretation of intelligence on Ireland.

The perceptions of Ireland described here were at the extreme end of the spectrum of British opinion. They were far from universal. There was another view of Ireland that was more optimistic about the contemporary Irish state and about future Anglo-Irish relations. Though sharing much of the disdain for the IRA's violent tactics before 1923, it recognised that many Irish grievances were legitimate, that Sinn Féin had considerable support for its political programme, and that a purely coercive response by Britain could not have worked. Though acknowledging some differences between the English and Celtic characters, it tended to emphasise the qualities of the Irish race. Moreover, it concentrated on all the ways in which the two peoples were connected – by language, culture, history, trade, migration and inter-marriage. This 'liberal imperialist' interpreta-tion praised the new Dublin government for establishing a peaceful, democratic state in difficult conditions. Above all, it expected the two countries to be drawn closer together rather than to drift apart. It was thought that after the animosi-ties of the revolutionary period had died down, the southern Irish would realise how closely aligned their interests were with Britain, settling down as a loyal, co-operative Dominion within the empire. The British government could accelerate this process by trusting the Irish government and making concessions to the fledgling state on finance, defence and constitutional matters. They should woo the Irish into friendship, rather than coerce them.

Some of these ideas could be found among the more thoughtful elements in the British army, which had concluded that Britain could not hold south-ern Ireland by force, given the opposition of the majority of the Irish people.[44] But these perceptions were most prevalent among the political architects of the Anglo-Irish Treaty and the civil servants of the Colonial and Dominions Offices, the men who had helped give birth to the Free State and were now responsible for managing its relationship with Britain. For example, when the Parliamentary Under-Secretary for the Colonies, William Ormsby Gore, visited Dublin in July 1923 he was struck by 'the impression of honesty, sincerity and determination on the part of the Government'. He had 'an entirely pleasant evening' with Free State Ministers during which 'His Majesty's health was duly drunk, not by any means as a mere formality, and the conversation, especially towards the end of the evening, was singularly free from any restraint or embarrassment'. He wrote to London:

> I feel bound to report that I have derived from my visit a conviction that the Free State, if she receives from us ready & generous co-operation, will in a very short time establish herself firmly as a loyal member of the British Empire.

The Earl of Birkenhead, one of the signatories to the Anglo-Irish Treaty, was very pleased with the Irish situation in 1926: 'When you recall the state of affairs which existed only four years ago', he wrote, 'I think you will agree that the Irish settlement is working better than in our most extravagant hopes we could have anticipated.'[45] The most optimistic believers in the commonwealth ideal even predicted that the Free State would draw closer to Britain as time went by. Lionel Curtis, who remained as special advisor on Ireland in the Colonial Office until 1924, was perhaps the most fervent advocate of this political philosophy. He wrote:

> Scarcely a day passes without reminding us how numerous and intimate are the threads which connect the social and economic life of these two Islands and (in spite of the recent divorce) their political life as well ... I do not myself believe that the Treaty will prove a final settlement of Anglo-Irish relations, and in time both Communities will find that the links which bind them are so close that some new political synthesis will have to be devised with the consent of both.[46]

This optimism resurfaced in the mid-1930s when certain British officials and politicians believed that a new agreement with the de Valera government would keep southern Ireland in the empire, improve Anglo-Irish relations and lead to the country's active participation in a world war.[47]

Politics, prejudices and preconceptions had such a strong influence on British policy-makers because intelligence on Ireland was so weak. The *ad hoc*, informal, and frequently contradictory nature of the intelligence meant that users could impose their own assumptions and pick out information that supported them. This was the case during the Irish revolution, when there was no good process for producing political intelligence. It was an even greater weakness after 1923. Although it remained within the empire, the Irish Free State was always a restless, reluctant Dominion. Britain did not receive the sort of co-operation on security matters that it expected. But neither could it treat southern Ireland as a foreign country and develop the type of intelligence mechanisms that it used in other parts of the world. A constitutional anomaly, the Irish Free State fell between the cracks of the imperial intelligence system.

Within this intelligence vacuum the diehard unionist and liberal imperialist preconceptions of Ireland battled for supremacy in the British government during the 1920s and 1930s. Their respective influence often depended on the state of Anglo-Irish relations. When relations were tranquil and the Irish Free State was behaving well, the British government was happy to believe that its neighbour was a loyal, stable Dominion. At times of crisis, the latent suspicion and hostility of the diehard unionist perspective could quickly come to the fore. In addition, aspects of these two interpretations could co-exist: both shared a pre-occupation with the threat of militant republicanism (and especially the IRA), although each came to different conclusions on how Britain should handle this threat. The importance of these preconceptions meant that a form of schizophrenia affected much of the British government's dealings with southern Ireland in the first two decades after the Anglo-Irish Treaty: on the one hand, there was a deep-rooted pessimism regarding the power of militant republicanism in Ireland; on the other, there was a blithe optimism that the Dublin government would return to the imperial fold. As we shall see in the following chapters, neither of these characterisations was entirely correct.

CHAPTER 6

The Cosgrave Years

T HE evolution of the Irish Free State after 1923 offered support to each of the conflicting British images of Ireland. On the one hand, the new state experienced eight years of remarkable political stability. The pro-Treaty party, Cumann na nGaedheal, remained in government throughout this period, under the leadership of William T. Cosgrave. It was cautious in its nation building, placing pragmatism before idealism, because its priority was to restore economic, financial and social order after a decade of revolutionary upheaval. Irish ministers avoided radical economic reform, incorporated existing institutions into the new state and accepted assistance from the British imperial authorities. Kevin O'Higgins famously remarked that 'we were probably the most conservative revolutionaries that ever put across a successful revolution'. Moreover, due to the bitterness engendered by the Civil War, they were implacably opposed to the republican movement and committed to working within the framework of the Anglo-Irish Treaty. Developments appeared to support the British liberal imperialist expectation that the Free State would settle down to a peaceful existence as a loyal, co-operative Dominion within the empire.[1]

Yet there were dissenting voices within the Free State. Although reeling from defeat in the Civil War, the republican movement maintained a latent strength. Its underground army had not gone away. The new IRA Chief of Staff, Frank Aiken, made this plain in his instructions to officers on 28 May 1923, five days after the cessation of hostilities:

> We joined the I.R.A. and enlisted men to firmly establish the Republic of Ireland. We fought for that, our comrades died for it. Until we reach that object it is our duty to push towards it, using at every moment the means at our disposal best suited to achieve our purpose ... The dumping of arms does not mean that the usefulness of the I.R.A. is past, or release any member of it from his duty to his country. On the contrary, a disciplined Volunteer force, ready for any emergency, will be a great source of strength to the nation in its march to Independence. It is clearly our duty to keep the Army Organisation intact.[2]

Anti-Treaty Sinn Féin, led by Éamon de Valera, represented the political wing of republicanism. Although it had little chance of gaining power and would soon split into two groups, it won 27.6 per cent of first-preference votes in an election held immediately after the Civil War. Throughout its term the Cosgrave government faced a minor subversive threat from armed militants, together with a more serious risk of losing the patriotic high ground to republican propagandists.

The existence of this republican constituency was one reason why the Cosgrave administration kept its distance from imperial institutions and pursued policies that disappointed London. Starting in 1923, Dublin pressed for the establishment of the Boundary Commission, in an attempt to reverse the partition of the country. For over two years Northern Ireland and the Free State engaged in an intense 'cold war', much to the exasperation of the British government. At the end of 1925 the border issue was shelved, allowing Anglo-Irish relations to settle into a more placid rhythm. But the Irish government was never a compliant imperial partner. Few in the Free State embraced the Anglo-Irish Treaty with any enthusiasm, or felt great allegiance to Dominion status or to the empire. To many, the treaty was merely a 'stepping stone' to greater independence. Consequently, the Cosgrave government assumed more and more sovereign powers, stretching the treaty to its limits. The Irish established diplomatic legations abroad against the wishes of London; they minimised the role of symbols of empire in domestic affairs; they refrained from the security and intelligence co-operation that Britain routinely received from the other Dominions. Irish ministers also set about changing what Dominion status meant; they played an active role in asserting the freedom and equality of the nations of the commonwealth, which culminated in the agreement of the Statute of Westminster in 1931.[3]

Britain never worked out how to integrate an uncooperative southern Ireland into its existing imperial or foreign intelligence systems. As a result, the British government's understanding of Irish affairs was poor. During the Boundary Commission crisis, the influence of biased, politicised intelligence caused the diehard unionist characterisation of Ireland to resurface at the highest levels of Whitehall: there were fears of a republican takeover in the Free State, or sectarian strife in the north, which might necessitate British military reintervention. These threats largely disappeared after 1925. Henceforth the British intelligence system was largely indifferent to Ireland, confining itself to the investigation of comparatively minor plots involving the IRA and foreign agents. But the British intelligence system failed to track the real threat to the treaty settlement – the rise of moderate, constitutional republicanism in the form of de Valera's political party, Fianna Fáil. It would be wholly unprepared to deal with the crisis that erupted when de Valera was elected to power in 1932.

The Irish cold war

On 17 October 1924 SIS circulated a secret report on Ireland that caused a brief panic in Whitehall. SIS reported that Irish purchasers had acquired 100,000 Mauser rifles in Europe. The weapons were to be smuggled from France on board the ss *Clonlee*, a ship owned by a Mr. T. Jack of Larne Harbour in Northern Ireland. This was a huge quantity of arms, which, in the wrong hands, could pose a major threat to the security of both parts of Ireland. On investigation, the report turned out to be unsubstantiated. Inspector General Wickham of the RUC was from the start 'pretty confident that the story was "moonshine"', and his scepticism was confirmed when it emerged that the 400-ton vessel would be hard pressed to carry such a large cargo. What is interesting is British speculation about the identities of the arms purchasers. Initially, it was assumed that the weapons were intended for the usual suspects, the IRA. But when it was discovered that the vessel was based at Larne Harbour and that the cargo consisted of Mauser rifles, suspicion turned to northern unionists – the Ulster Volunteer Force had smuggled Mausers into Larne Harbour during the Home Rule crisis in 1914. It was possible that Ulster unionists were arming themselves again, this time to resist any changes to the border between north and south.[4]

Throughout the 1920s and 1930s gunrunning scares provide an excellent barometer of British anxiety about the political situation in Ireland. The 1924 incident came at a time of a major crisis in Anglo-Irish relations, caused by the looming Boundary Commission. Article 12 of the Anglo-Irish Treaty had stipulated that a commission – consisting of representatives from the Belfast, Dublin and London governments – should 'determine, in accordance with the wishes of the inhabitants, so far as may be compatible with economic and geographic conditions, the boundaries between Northern Ireland and the rest of Ireland'. All parties came away with different interpretations of this article: to Sinn Féin, it meant the transfer to the Free State of large chunks of territory with Catholic majorities, including counties Tyrone and Fermanagh, thus making the continued existence of Northern Ireland untenable; to the British government it meant only minor rectification of the border, with give and take on both sides; the Northern Ireland government rejected the whole idea and refused to participate in the Boundary Commission – 'Not an Inch' entered the unionist lexicon. On hold during the Civil War, this issue came to the forefront of Anglo-Irish relations in the middle of 1923. Tensions were most intense between April and October 1924, when the Belfast administration refused to appoint a representative to the commission. After referring the matter to the Privy Council, the British government reluctantly introduced legislation in

Westminster allowing it to appoint a representative on Northern Ireland's behalf. A second crisis was sparked in November 1925, when the draft decision of the three-man commission was leaked to the press. This revealed that they intended to make only minor adjustments to the border, including the transfer of some Free State territory to the north, much to the outrage of the Dublin government. After a flurry of negotiations the report was buried, and an agreement was struck by the three governments on 3 December 1925, leaving the border unchanged.[5]

Until this point Ireland remained a serious concern for the British government; the 'Irish Question' had not been answered after all. As a result, intelligence on Ireland was still in demand. London needed to know whether violence – republican or unionist – would break out on the border in response to the Boundary Commission. It also had to judge the possible effect of the crisis in the Free State, which was only emerging from civil war. There were persistent rumours of a republican take-over in the south, especially if the border issue was not resolved to the Free State's advantage. The continuing importance of Irish intelligence is illustrated by arrangements made in the War Office in 1923. An officer was assigned in its Directorate of Military Operations & Intelligence to 'be responsible for military intelligence work in Southern Ireland'.[6] This position was first occupied by Lieutenant-Colonel Hill-Dillon and then by Colonel Brind, the two most senior army intelligence officers in Ireland during the War of Independence. They collated all available information and held weekly meetings with the Colonial Office and the Special Branch.[7] Under their guidance the War Office played the lead role on Irish intelligence from 1923 to early 1926.

The problem was that it was unclear how they should obtain intelligence from Ireland. Ever since the signing of the Anglo-Irish Treaty, British intelligence chiefs had skirted around a difficult question: what sort of intelligence relationship should Britain have with the newly formed Irish Free State? Senior MI5 officers finally sat down to debate this matter in June 1924. In a top-secret document they set out three options for gathering intelligence from southern Ireland. The most obvious course was to treat the Free State like any other Dominion and rely on co-operation with the Dublin government. This would require a good personal relationship with a trustworthy senior official on the Irish side, who could make investigations and take action on the advice of MI5. If that co-operation was not forthcoming, the second option was to use Northern Ireland as a base to collect intelligence on the south. The third option was for MI5 to develop its own clandestine network of agents in southern Ireland without the knowledge of the Dublin government: in effect, this meant treating the Free State like a foreign country. In the coming years the British government would try all these approaches. None were entirely satisfactory.[8]

MI5's strong preference was to develop a close, collaborative intelligence relationship with the Free State government. In this it was disappointed. Dublin was willing to co-operate, but only in two areas. The first was control of aliens and immigration. An effective passport control shield had been established around the United Kingdom during the First World War, based on a 'Black List' of Bolsheviks, spies and other subversives, who were denied entry or departure. This shield was put at risk by the Free State's insistence on adopting its own passport and visa-issuing powers. At first British security chiefs ruled out supplying the Free State with a copy of the Black List, as it was 'extremely secret' and contained 'a certain number of well known Irishmen'.[9] However, they soon concluded that their only option was to persuade the Irish to operate the system with them. To their surprise, the Free State government agreed. The Irish Minister for External Affairs travelled to London to discuss the matter with the head of the SIS Passport Control Department, and an Irish official spent a fortnight's training with her British counterparts before setting up an 'Irish Free State Passport Control Office' in New York.[10] The Home Office was satisfied with the Free State's control of immigrants and communist agitators, though MI5 would later complain that the Irish were too lenient towards suspected foreign spies and Indian subversives.[11]

Communism was the second area of intelligence collaboration between Dublin and London: the Home Office noted that 'fortunately the F.S. Govt. are as strongly anti-Communist as we are'.[12] Liaison with Britain was effected through the respective police forces. The principal figure on the Irish side was Colonel David Neligan. His extraordinary intelligence career had seen him act as an IRA mole within the DMP and the British secret service in 1920–1, and then join the new Irish police force (the Garda Síochana) after the treaty, rising to become head of the Garda Special Branch. He was in contact with Colonel John Carter, the Deputy Assistant Commissioner (second in command) of the Special Branch of the London Metropolitan Police, and the man responsible for Irish affairs. During the 1920s Neligan occasionally travelled to London to meet Carter, and the two men maintained a fitful correspondence. The Free State leaders, fully aligned with the British government in their vigorous opposition to Bolshevik ideology, were happy to share intelligence on this subject. In general, they got more than they gave, because the British had better information on the worldwide communist movement.

Apart from these two areas, there was little intelligence collaboration between the Free State and Britain. Crucially, it did not extend to the one subject for which

Britain had the greatest intelligence need – the Irish militant republican movement. As we have seen, the Free State authorities had been slow to co-operate
with London during the Civil War, and only did so because they were fighting
for their survival. Once the Civil War was over, this collaboration ended. This
was partly because the Irish government regarded republicanism as an internal
family matter, partly because there would be domestic political repercussions if
it was revealed that the Dublin government was co-operating with the British
to oppress Irish patriots. The reluctance of the Free State to share intelligence
is revealed by a conversation between Neligan and Carter in December 1924.
Neligan went to London to obtain intelligence on the communist movement,
but Carter 'turned the conversation onto other topics', pumping him for information on the republicans and the political situation. In a report written on his
return, Neligan described how he parried the Englishman's questioning:

> What were the Irregulars doing? De Valera, Stack and Dan Breen. I replied
> things were quiet … at present, and that the Irregulars were going in for
> constitutional methods. He next asked me how was the National Army:
> what were Mulcahy and Tobin doing? Had they joined hands?
>
> I told him the Army was well disciplined and that the persons men-
> tioned were not under notice as doing anything remarkable.
>
> To questions as to their political behaviour I answered that I was only
> a minor official and that I had no information as to recent developments
> except what I read in the Press. The same answer I gave to his query as to
> 'what do your people propose doing on the Boundary business?'
>
> He next questioned me as to whether I did political work, and what
> were my relations with the Director of Army Intelligence? I replied that I
> did police work and that the Director of Intelligence did army work.
>
> The next question was 'How was Mr Cosgrave?' I replied that I had no
> information.[13]

Neligan emerges from this account as an unobliging intelligence partner. The
Special Branch, MI5 and the British armed services all complained that the Irish
Free State gave little help on security matters after 1923.

Indeed, rather than serving as a partner, the Irish Free State conducted clandestine intelligence activities on United Kingdom territory. Between 1922 and
1926 Irish army intelligence operated a covert network of agents in Northern
Ireland, who reported on the northern security forces, on the economy and
on political organisations. They sometimes obtaining high value material: for
example, agent 'No. 76' regularly furnished the text of the RUC's monthly intelligence summaries.[14] One of the functions of this network was to provide material

for the Free State's propaganda campaign against the six counties. In October 1922 a North-Eastern Boundary Bureau was created under the directorship of Kevin O'Shiel, a solicitor from Omagh in Northern Ireland, to collect data for the Boundary Commission and to 'work up' stories on the persecution of the Catholic community.[15] The RUC became aware of the Free State's intelligence activities at the end of 1923, thanks to a senior informant within the northern IRA.[16] Inspector General Wickham confirmed that it was 'definitely known that the Free State authorities have a number of paid agents engaged in espionage work in Northern Ireland by whom reports are sent to Headquarters in Dublin from time to time'. By the beginning of 1926 the RUC believed that there were eight agents working in the north, although they admitted that they had only been able to identify five of the 'divils'.[17]

The RUC took some steps to stamp out this activity. Its most visible success came in November 1923, when it arrested and interned Colonel Seamus Woods, a former commanding officer of the IRA 3rd Northern Division. RUC files showed that he had been 'about the most dangerous man in Belfast' in 1922. Since then he had been the Free State's principal intelligence officer in Northern Ireland. His role was revealed to the RUC by a high-level republican informant and subsequently confirmed by an incriminating document found in a house raid. After being closely watched, he was arrested when crossing the border from the south. This spy case led to a dispute between Dublin, Belfast and London. Cosgrave disingenuously assured James Craig and the British government that neither Woods nor any agents of the Free State were engaged in espionage in Northern Ireland.[18] British officials, however, supported the actions of the northern government. Mark Sturgis wrote that it was 'hardly fair play' for the southern Irish to use a man who had been so active in 1922 as an intelligence officer and then use his position in the Free State army to argue for his release.[19] Woods was tried for the murder of the Unionist MP, W. J. Twaddell, but acquitted. He was put across the border and given an order restricting him from re-entering the province.

The discovery of covert Free State activities may have made Belfast and London more willing to pursue the second intelligence option laid out by MI5 in June 1924 – using Northern Ireland to collect intelligence on the south. Recently discovered documents reveal that the Northern Ireland government organised its own clandestine intelligence service in the Free State at this time. Its security forces had been collecting intelligence from across the border since the middle of 1922. Initially this was carried out by Solly-Flood's Criminal Investigation Department (CID). From May to July 1922 Solly-Flood passed to James Craig a series of 'Secret Notes on Southern Ireland', based on CID informants, which purported to reveal a conspiracy between the republican and pro-Treaty factions in the south.[20] This intelligence continued to be collected after the CID was amalgamated with the RUC.[21] In the middle of 1923, however, the Belfast authorities decided to intensify their intelligence activities. A more extensive network of agents was developed in the south, and their activities continued until at least 1926.

Few details about this police network are available. It appears to have been run by Captain 'Fatty' Woolley, a former British army officer who had served in British intelligence during the First World War and had friendly relations with MI5 and SIS. He later boasted that he had 'good lines' with people in the south who were 'very willing to work'.[22] Some of his informants were travellers between north and south; others were residents in southern Ireland, most likely casual observers within the southern loyalist community. However, the RUC also had at least one highly placed agent within the Free State security apparatus. This individual passed on material from Free State army intelligence reports and named undercover Free State army agents in Co. Donegal. He even saw copies of RUC reports procured by the Free State intelligence service in the north. This indicates that the RUC had a strategically placed source within the Irish army.[23]

The Northern Ireland government supplemented its covert network in the south with two other intelligence-gathering activities – one subtle, the other less so. First, a small unit within the RUC continued to operate a censorship on the postal, telegraph and telephone communications of suspected republicans, especially across the border. This produced a steady trickle of information on IRA activities, political opinion and military developments in the south.[24] Its value depended on the secrecy with which it was conducted; when word got out that letters were being intercepted, the quality of information waned. Second, the RUC and Special Constabulary used more direct methods to get information from Free State soldiers who returned to the north after fighting in the Civil War. For example, Sergeant Denis Monaghan was roused from his bed when on leave at his home in Kesh, Co. Fermanagh and taken to a police barracks for interrogation. The barrage of questions that he faced provides a good indication of the intelligence concerns in Northern Ireland at this time:

> Do you think would the Free State Government fight if it came to that on the border? Why are you so anxious to get in Tyrone and Fermanagh? I suppose you imagine because you were able to beat the British Government out of the 26 counties you could put them out of the six. Do you think the six counties will fight before they would give up Tyrone and Fermanagh?[25]

Much of the northern IRA had joined the Free State army in the middle of 1922. Their return a year later was a security threat, but it was also an opportunity for the northern security forces to gather intelligence on southern Ireland.

The interrogation of Sergeant Monaghan was jointly conducted by an RUC Special Constable and a British military intelligence officer. RUC intelligence activity against the Free State was in many ways an extension of the British army's intelligence system – the two organisations worked closely together. Headed by Lieutenant-Colonel R. T. Hammick, the Intelligence Branch of the British army in Northern Ireland remained in place until March 1926. With the abolition of General Headquarters in Dublin, its remit was extended to the whole of Ireland. It reached its maximum size in early 1923, when it consisted of five intelligence officers and six clerks at Northern Ireland District headquarters, two Area Intelligence Officers and six County Intelligence Officers. Thereafter it was gradually reduced. By April 1924 there were just two intelligence officers at headquarters and three Area Intelligence Officers. (The County Intelligence Officers had been abolished.) The final reduction occurred in September 1924, when the Area Intelligence Officers were removed; henceforth just two intelligence officers remained at headquarters.[26] The reductions were effected because the army was happy to shift more responsibility for internal security and intelligence collection to the RUC. Although relations were not as good as when Solly-Flood's Criminal Investigation Department had provided the interface in 1922, the army continued to collate and analyse the information provided by the RUC and the Special Constabulary, maintaining the extensive records on the IRA that had accrued since the rebellion began.[27]

The British army also directed some independent intelligence activities against the Free State. Ever since warnings of invasion in the first half of 1922 had led to ill-judged pressure for military action, the British army had determined to have an independent capacity for collecting intelligence on the border. The British did not feel they could trust the often paranoid northern security forces – they occasionally still received 'absurdly alarmist reports' from the Special Constabulary. As a result Lieutenant-Colonel Hammick and other British military officers were a frequent sight along the border, carrying out periodic tours and investigating reports of disturbances.[28] In addition the British army created a chain of informants in the Free State, living up to about twenty miles from the border, to provide advance warning of attacks. It was an intelligence network in only the loosest sense, consisting of loyalist residents on the southern side of the border who would communicate with the army if they discovered anything suspicious in their locality. Although its reports had to be sifted carefully, the army found it useful in dispelling some of the wilder claims about IRA manœuvres.[29]

The Northern Ireland District headquarters also had a more reliable source of intelligence from within the Free State – signals intelligence. During the Civil War they had easily broken the wireless ciphers of the Free State army. This activity continued long after: the internal history of the army Intelligence Branch contains great detail on how the codes were broken, as well as occasional examples of intercepted communications. It was carried out by a small cryptographic unit within the local Intelligence Branch in Northern Ireland; the help of the Government Code and Cypher School (GC&CS) was not required. (It was common practice for local British army commands to establish their own codebreaking operations.) Information from this source was crucial in updating the Order of Battle of the Free State army compiled by British intelligence officers.[30]

The activities of the British army and the RUC demonstrate one of the striking features of Britain's intelligence relationship with Ireland between 1923 and 1925 – the north was used as a base to spy on the south. Although this was against the spirit of the Anglo-Irish Treaty, the lack of alternative sources and the perceived seriousness of the threats associated with the Boundary Commission meant that this material was eagerly accepted by intelligence chiefs in London.[31]

Yet relying on the north had its dangers. Northern officials had a pessimistic and biased perception of the Irish Free State, which reflected the wider prejudices of the northern unionist community. Coverage in the three unionist papers in Belfast – the *Belfast News-Letter,* the *Northern Whig* and the *Belfast Telegraph* – focused on the inexorable march of the Free State towards a republic, the 'anarchy and lawlessness' caused by a rampant IRA, the persecution of the southern loyalist minority and the impending economic collapse of the country.[32] Obsessed by the threat of nationalism, the Protestant community demonised the new southern state. Unionist biases were reflected in the intelligence reports on southern Ireland emanating from the northern security apparatus. During the second half of 1922 Solly-Flood produced a series of dire warnings on the threat from the south. He had no doubt that a republic with Bolshevik tendencies would soon be established, with the most dangerous repercussions for Northern Ireland.[33] After Solly-Flood's departure, and the amalgamation of the CID with the RUC, some of the more fantastic predictions disappeared. But the RUC continued to stress the danger of IRA raids on the border in connection with the Boundary Commission.[34] RUC reports also echoed Solly-Flood's conviction that the republicans were poised to take over the government of southern Ireland. Throughout 1924 the RUC's senior informant within the northern IRA provided a series of alarming assessments of conditions in the south. He stated that the republicans were gaining public support and would sweep an election; that Cosgrave was on the point of resigning; and that, once a republic was declared, force would be used against Northern Ireland.[35] Although confident that the IRA within the six counties posed little threat, the RUC worried about attacks on Northern Ireland from the south.

This intelligence flowed into the British government through the RUC's liaison with the British army. But Northern Ireland political leaders also by-passed these official channels to impress their views directly on British ministers. These northern leaders were more biased than the RUC, and their opinions more closely reflected the doom-laden attitude of the unionist press. For example, Lord Londonderry wrote to Churchill:

> The Free State is an impossible proposition and no one can make a success of the idea embodied in that title, and it is merely a question of whether at some stage of the descent of Ireland to anarchy and chaos the British Government will step in ... If Ireland is to be left to its own devices, it is an ugly sore and in the end may poison the whole body of the Empire.[36]

Unionist politicians over-reacted to the 'army mutiny' of 1924, when Free State army officers who had served in the pre-Treaty IRA objected to imminent mass demobilisation (and the potential loss of their jobs).[37] Lord Londonderry wrote to the Home Secretary in London, warning that there had been 'a serious mutiny' and that the position of the Dublin government was 'distinctly precarious' – 'should Mr. Cosgrave's Government fall, there is no knowing what may happen in Southern Ireland'.[38] These personal approaches were backed by a public propaganda campaign designed to influence British and international public opinion. Through pamphlets, newspaper articles and the activities of an Ulster Association for Peace with Honour, the unionist government emphasised the stable, law-abiding nature of Northern Ireland in contrast to the anarchic, republican tendencies of the south.[39]

The British government was susceptible to northern characterisations of the political situation in the Free State because it was receiving similar warnings from other 'secret' sources. When MI5 officers met in June 1924 to discuss Britain's relationship with the Free State they had considered a third option for gathering intelligence: developing their own clandestine network in southern Ireland. Officials shied away from this radical step, because it would represent a clear breach of the Anglo-Irish Treaty. However, a curious alliance of southern Irish loyalists, diehard unionists in London and right-wing newspaper men came together to create their own informal, unofficial secret service in Ireland at this time. This initiative was led by two men: the editor of the *Morning Post*, Howell Arthur Gwynne, and the leader of the diehard Conservative faction in the House of Commons, Colonel John Gretton, MP.

Gwynne was a strong ally of James Craig and a bitter opponent of British policy towards Ireland who had close relations with senior figures within the London intelligence community. On 25 April 1923 he had written to Craig urging him to form a secret service:

> I do not know whether you are aware that our precious Colonial Office – no doubt inspired by the great genius, Lionel Curtis – have set their face against any of our Secret Service – police, military, naval or foreign – having any agents, or making inquiries, in the Free State.
>
> The consequence is – as you no doubt may know – that it is becoming more and more a happy hunting ground for every disaffected and dangerous Communist; and it is likely to become, on this account, and because of the inefficiency of the Irish police, a jumping-off ground for criminals.
>
> Some of my friends who are engaged in secret service work are very much alarmed at this, and it was suggested to me that perhaps Ulster might find it necessary, in view of her close proximity to the danger zone, to establish a Secret Service in the South, which might be found useful.
>
> It was urged on me that this Service would be a very cheap form of security, inasmuch as it might, when it became efficient, enable you to dispense with some of your defences.

Gwynne wrote that he was making this suggestion because 'one of the finest of our supervisors is at a loose end'. It is possible that he was referring to Sir Basil Thomson, the former head of the Special Branch.[40]

This letter encouraged the Northern Ireland administration to intensify its intelligence activities in the south. But Gwynne must have considered this insufficient, as he took steps to develop his own secret service, in collaboration with Colonel Gretton. Both men distributed a number of secret reports on southern Ireland between 1923 and 1925. Considered highly confidential, Gwynne asked that they be burned in the presence of a witness after they were read. (Thankfully, this injunction was not always followed.) They were sent to James Craig in Belfast, sometimes in special parcels from the Ulster Association branch in London.[41] As they appear to have been in wide circulation, they would also have been received by sympathetic intelligence chiefs, military commanders and British politicians.[42] The head of the Conservative Party's Policy Unit, Colonel Lancelot Storr, distributed similar material at this time.[43]

Surviving reports contain an extraordinary mixture of detailed fact, political invective and conspiracy theory, around some familiar themes. The first was the duplicity of the Free State government. It was claimed that Cosgrave and his ministers were extremists whose goal was to establish a republic and destroy Northern Ireland. They were using the Boundary Commission for tactical advantage, while secretly working with the anti-Treatyite faction: 'a great conspiracy is on foot against the North, and the whole Executive of the Free State are in it', one report from March 1925 warned. The second theme was the power of the IRA. Gretton described how the organisation had sent two intelligence officers to the north, along with 270 tons of stolen gelignite, in preparation for fighting. He warned that 'all the dumps of arms and ammunition have been filled up to war strength', and that when the Boundary Commission made its decision 'the I.R.A. will be summoned to deal with the situation' by the Dublin government. A third feature of the alleged republican conspiracy was the threat to southern loyalists. Apparently, both the Irish police force and the IRA were studying pro-British residents in Dublin and preparing to launch a 'vendetta' against them, in the hope that this would influence the north. Fourth, these reports stressed the threat from Bolshevik groups in southern Ireland: Colonel Gretton gravely transmitted 'very secret' information that 'Russian officers' were 'coming over to join the Free State Army'. (The other 'Bolshevist agents in Southern Ireland' were, apparently, all 'American Jews'.) Finally, reports provided by Gretton and Gwynne repeatedly emphasised the economic difficulties of the Free State and the financial incompetence of the Dublin authorities: 'always ... behind other questions and overshadowing them is the impending bankruptcy of the Free State, economic and financial', a report from November 1924 warned.[44] The analysis of Irish political events contained in these reports was extremely biased, the facts often erroneous. By the middle of 1925, even Northern Ireland officials were 'inclined to be sceptical' about the information furnished by Gwynne and Gretton.[45]

Where did this information come from? One source was probably the British intelligence community. Gwynne described how he had the support of 'friends ... engaged in secret service work' who were 'very much alarmed' at the situation in Ireland.[46] The Special Branch of the London Metropolitan Police produced similar reports in 1924, based on censored correspondence and informers in the Irish community in Britain.[47] It is likely that some of the information obtained by Gwynne and Gretton was leaked by intelligence officers in London. Another source was almost certainly the *Morning Post* correspondent in Dublin, Charles Bretherton. An Englishman who came to Ireland at the start of the First World War to work as an intelligence officer, he penned an almost daily series of venomous diatribes against the treaty policy and the new Irish state. The content of his *Morning Post* articles was not so different from that contained in the secret reports circulated by Gretton and Gwynne.[48]

The principal source, however, was probably the Anglo-Irish community in southern Ireland. Around the time of the Irish Civil War, a number of organisations appeared to represent the plight of southern loyalists to British policy-makers and to the British public. The Southern Irish Loyalists Relief Association, formed in July 1922, worked closely with the government's Irish Grants Committee to provide relief to Irish loyalists and to top up compensation offered by the Free State (a process that did not finish until 1929). A Truth About Ireland League, founded by Mrs Stewart-Menzies, held public meetings in London to draw attention to loyalist suffering. The London Branch of the Irish Unionist Alliance remained active throughout the 1920s (mutating into the Irish Loyalist Imperial Federation in 1933). Less influential groups included the Irish Compensation Claims Committee and the Irish Loyalists Association. These organisations possessed networks of correspondents in Ireland and means for transmitting documents to Britain, sometimes avoiding the regular mail. In other words, they functioned as rudimentary intelligence networks. Gwynne and Gretton were active in these associations and could easily have arranged to receive reports from Irish residents. Outside of these organisations, Gwynne and Gretton would have received information from southern loyalists through the web of family and politics that linked the Anglo-Irish class with British politicians, military officers, civil servants, business leaders and aristocrats.[49]

The loyalist community in southern Ireland occupied an invidious position. Although still economically privileged, loyalists lost their traditional political power during the Irish revolution and suffered a disproportionate amount of intimidation, violence and property destruction. It is estimated that up to 20,000 loyalists fled as refugees from southern Ireland in the spring of 1922.[50] After the Civil War came to an end, persecution of loyalists largely ceased, and some refugees returned. Yet the community experienced a slow decline: the number of Protestants in southern Ireland decreased from 10 per cent of the population in 1921 to less than 6 per cent in the 1940s. With some notable exceptions, most loyalists felt alienated from the increasingly Gaelic, Catholic state. The historian F. S. L. Lyons, who grew up in the Anglo-Irish community in the 1920s and 1930s, has remarked that 'now on the defensive, the minority became intensely aware of their isolation and withdrew into a kind of ghetto.'[51] There was considerable contempt for the new order in the Free State, especially for the education and brogues of the uncouth ex-gunmen who led it. The Irish revolution, the whole nationalist project, were deplored. The peculiar attitude of the Anglo-Irish class, as late as 1934, was evocatively described by the author Virginia Woolf on a visit to the country. Referring to her conversation with one couple, she wrote:

Yes I felt this is the animal that lives in the shell. These are the way they live – he hunting all day, & she bustling about in her old car, & everybody knowing everybody & laughing & talking & picnicking, & great poverty & some tradition of gentle birth, & all the sons going away to make their livings & the old people sitting there hating the Irish Free State & recalling Dublin & the Viceroy.[52]

Southern loyalists were not representative of the Irish population and could give a distorted picture of events in the Free State. Some were so bitter about the recent past that they countenanced the most negative conspiracy theories about the new nationalist regime and fantasised about a possible British return. The latter appear to have had the most input to the reports prepared by Gwynne and Gretton.

Southern Irish loyalists, Ulster unionists and diehard Tories came together in 1924 to wage a venomous campaign against the Free State, based on supposed access to special 'intelligence'. This reflected the deeply rooted preconceptions and prejudices of the diehard unionist interpretation of Irish affairs. It was also a political ploy motivated by the circumstances of that year. Ulster unionists were determined to use every trick to scupper the Boundary Commission and pre-serve their territory. By portraying the Free State as a dangerous, lawless place on a disastrous slide towards a republic, they could argue that it would be unjust to thrust any more loyalists under such an inhospitable regime.[53] They also exploited the security situation to persuade the British government to pay for the maintenance of a large Special Constabulary: 91 per cent of the £7,420,000 spent on the Special Constabulary between 1921 and 1925 was met by British grants.[54] Southern loyalists and diehard Tories pursued their fantasy that the Free State would inevitably collapse, thereby necessitating British reinterven-tion; they tried to help the process of disintegration by obstructing Irish efforts to raise a crucial financial loan in the City of London.[55] The Free State govern-ment recognised that it was under attack. Cosgrave complained bitterly to the Prime Minister about 'the campaign of hate against the Free State, its people and its Government, which had been carried out with renewed vigour for some time past by a group in England'. He claimed that there was 'on foot in England a very deliberate and a very malignant conspiracy to create once again a state of hostility between the two countries'.[56]

The diehard unionist campaign against the Free State should be seen in the context of the shadowy intersections between British politics and British intel-ligence in this period. In the early and mid-1920s right-wing Conservatives and intelligence officers shared an obsession with the 'Red Menace', believing that British society was under threat from labour militancy and international communism. In January 1924 Ramsay MacDonald led the Labour Party into government for the first time (in a shaky coalition with the Liberals). It was a moment that anti-Bolsheviks and Conservatives had been dreading for years. They launched unprecedented attacks against the inexperienced government, which collapsed after just ten months.[57] Close links existed between intelligence agencies and the opposition Conservative Party at this time. A number of figures in Conservative Central Office – including the former Director of Naval Intelligence, Admiral 'Blinker' Hall – had served in British intelligence during the First World War. The party leader, Stanley Baldwin, was made an honorary member of the 'IB Club', a secretive group of former or serving intelligence officers, which held dinners under the chairmanship of Sir Vernon Kell. Intelligence officers and Tory organisers also had close relationships with the editors of the *Morning Post* and the *Daily Mail*, leaking intelligence to these newspapers to advance their political goals. The most notorious incident occurred in October 1924, when a forged letter from Grigori Zinoviev (President of the Executive Committee of the Comintern) was leaked to the *Daily Mail* on the eve of the general election. This 'political bomb' was planted by serving intelligence officers, working with members of Conservative Central Office, in an effort to discredit the Labour Party. It played a part in securing a landslide election victory for the Conservatives, who returned to power in November 1924 under Stanley Baldwin. Just as they collaborated to undermine politicians regarded as 'soft on Bolshevism', it was natural that intelligence officers, Conservative power-brokers and newspaper proprietors – part of an interconnected élite – would work together to undermine the Free State.[58]

W HAT effect did the campaign against the Free State have on the British government? Did it shape perceptions and policy? As during the Civil War, there were two different extremes of perception within the government. On the one hand, some grasped these dark intelligence reports as confirming their worst fears about the Free State. It was assumed that the Free State regime could not be trusted, that a descent into republican anarchy was inevitable, and that the United Kingdom would come under further attack. This view was most prominent within the armed forces and the Conservative party. For example, Leo Amery, who later became Secretary of State for the Colonies, warned Stanley Baldwin on 3 August 1924 that the southern Irish would declare a republic within months: 'That means a bigger thing than anything we have taken on since the war – and we shall have to see it through. Well if it must come, it must come.' The future premier, Neville Chamberlain, was similarly despondent about 'this beastly Irish problem' and did not see how 'civil war could be averted'.[59]

On the other hand, liberal imperialists kept faith that a peaceful and prosperous Irish Free State would take its place as a loyal, co-operative member within the British family. This view was most evident within the Liberal and Labour parties and the civil service departments responsible for southern Ireland (first the Colonial Office, then, from June 1925, the newly created Dominions Office). For example, the Colonial Office sent one of its senior staff, G. Whiskard, to Dublin in August 1924, and he produced a sensible, wide-ranging report on the Irish situation. He reassured London that the republicans were weak, gunmen were emigrating in large numbers to the United States, and the government was getting stronger each month. He emphasised the sincerity of the Irish leaders: 'I do not think that the present Government', he wrote, 'will ever, in any circumstances, consent to any action which might reasonably be construed as the declaration of a Republic.' [60] The assessments of the Colonial Office appear to have convinced the Labour-Liberal government then in power. When Lord Londonderry came to London in August 1924 warning that the establishment of a southern republic and raids on the border were imminent, British ministers did their best to persuade the Ulsterman that his fears were 'greatly exaggerated'.[61]

However, if a Labour-Liberal government refused to accept the thesis that a dangerous southern republic was inevitable, there was a consensus among all parties in London that such an outcome was guaranteed if the Boundary Commission was not resolved in a way favourable to the Irish Free State. In 1924, when unionist opposition made the British government reluctant to proceed with the commission, the Colonial Office warned that this would be disastrous. Lionel Curtis, the chief adviser on Irish affairs, wrote:

> The political situation in the Free State is highly precarious and any false step on the part of His Majesty's Government may ruin the Free State Government and bring into power a Government which will declare a Republic. Apart from all the other serious consequences of such an event, it could hardly fail to result in hostilities between Northern and Southern Ireland in which this country must necessarily intervene. A conflict of this kind would paralyse the Empire as a factor for peace in the world.[62]

It was fear of the repercussions of not implementing the treaty that left the Labour-Liberal government with little option except to push through the legislation setting up the Boundary Commission. Once the commission was up and running, the same fears surrounded its final decision. If it only produced a minor rectification of the border, the Colonial Office feared that the consequences would be the same as if the commission had never been created: the fall of the Free State government and its replacement by a republican administration. This was clearly stated in an important memorandum by Curtis on 15 May 1924 – it was so sensitive that the drafts were burnt and only five copies distributed.[63] This assumption was also recorded in the letters and diaries of senior figures in the Conservative Party.[64] Therefore the Boundary Commission, whether constituted or not, appeared certain to provoke a major crisis in Anglo-Irish relations.

It was agreed on all sides that Britain could not stand by and allow the establishment of a republic in southern Ireland. Therefore in the summer of 1924 the War Office was once again asked to plan a military response. Lionel Curtis argued that armed reconquest was impractical, and instead advocated an economic blockade, with the British army manning the Northern Ireland border to prevent attack; the British could sit back and wait until the economic hardship returned to power a more reasonable government. The military General Staff, however, doubted his 'optimistic conclusions' and was afraid that the army would be sucked into a bigger commitment:

> Judging by the recent history of Ireland, it is very questionable whether the more sober elements in the south will be able to make their views effective: it is more likely that they will be terrorised by the lawless element, which will be the last to feel the effects of the blockade. The blockade may therefore either have to be prolonged indefinitely or some fresh line of action initiated; and in the event of the failure of the blockade to produce the required effect, no other course beyond re-conquest of S. Ireland seems possible ... the commitment for the army is unlimited, indefinite and fraught with serious dangers both for the army itself and for Imperial defence

As always, the principal concern of the War Office was to keep the army out of Irish affairs.[65] This led to consideration of an even weaker measure: a policy of British 'non-recognition' that would result in the Free State's loss of various benefits – foreign representation, mutual agreements, external loans and postal facilities. It was hoped that this would be such a blow to 'the vanity of the Irish' that they would recant.[66] It is doubtful whether this vague, toothless policy would have achieved very much. In the end, no contingency plans could be agreed. London simply awaited developments.

The possibility of conflict with a southern republic was not the only thing that agitated the British government in 1924 and 1925. The flipside of the Boundary Commission crisis was the risk of conflict with northern unionists. Despite Craig's public bluffing, London believed that the Northern Ireland government would acquiesce in minor rectifications of the border.[67] However, the situation would be different if the commission made substantial transfers to the south, as the Free State government demanded. In that case British officials believed that 'the danger of disorder in the North' would become 'acute': the commission was 'almost certain to meet with the armed resistance of the Protestant majority throughout Northern Ireland.'[68] According to the General Staff, the Belfast government would resign, rather than act against this resistance. The police were 'not impartial and would be useless' for restoring order. Therefore the British army would have to be deployed throughout the province to prevent sectarian violence and to force the transfer of territory to the south. This was the nightmare scenario for the General Staff. It would require at least three divisions and would be extremely unpopular with the troops, most of whom would have 'to act entirely contrary to their convictions.'[69] It was in this tense atmosphere that SIS reported that 100,000 Mauser rifles had been shipped from Cherbourg to Ireland. London was not sure whether they were intended for republican or unionist extremists.

The British government appeared to face impossible choices in 1925: either enforce a decision by the Boundary Commission to transfer large areas to the south and provoke an armed unionist revolt; or accept a minor rectification of the border and watch southern Ireland lurch towards a republic. Everything depended on the final decision of the Boundary Commission. The British authorities kept a scrupulous distance from the commission and did not know what the outcome would be. They were as surprised as anyone when the decision, leaked to the *Morning Post* on 7 November, turned out to be in line with their interpretation of Article 12 and a major disappointment for the Free State.[70]

The verdict of the Boundary Commission did not produce the terrible consequences that had been envisaged. In fact, the crisis was resolved surprisingly easily when British financial generosity allowed the three governments to come to an agreement that buried the commission's findings. The British agreed to waive the Free State's share of the United Kingdom national debt, replacing a liability calculated at £150 million with a one-off payment of £6 million.[71] Craig, determined to get a share of this handout, also successfully extracted financial concessions from London. Lord Birkenhead later commented how both sides 'developed a friendly and competitive enthusiasm in the task of plundering us.'[72] The belief in the republican threat in the south was a major factor behind London's willingness to make concessions. In a pattern that would be repeated many times over the next two decades, this was skilfully played on by Free State ministers. When the Boundary Commission's decision was leaked, they categorically stated that they could not accept it and remain in power: the Minister for Justice,

Kevin O'Higgins, warned, 'we have a crisis which may be the defeat of Cosgrave and lead, if not directly then eventually to a Republic'. They could only 'succeed in keeping the controversy off the physical plane of direct action' if they could point to some sort of concession. The British accepted their arguments.[73] The irony was that diehard reports of the power of republican extremism and the instability of the Free State actually strengthened the negotiating hand of the Dublin government – Cumann na nGaedheal leaders could present themselves as the only thing standing between Britain and the 'wild Irish'.

How justified were British concerns over the threat of a republican takeover in the Free State? The first three years after the end of the Civil War were, in fact, difficult ones for Irish republicans. The defeated IRA went into sharp decline. Many IRA men emigrated, and those who were left became disillusioned. The roll call of members dropped from 14,541 to 5,042 between 1924 and 1926.[74] If the military wing of republicanism was in bad shape, the political movement was even worse off. Although performing well in the 1923 election, Sinn Féin lost credibility as an opposition party when it refused to recognise the Free State or sit in its parliament. Éamon de Valera, interned between 1923 and 1924, reached the nadir of his political influence. On his release, he decided that republicans should drop their policy of abstention, and pursue reform using electoral, constitutional methods. However, his proposals split Sinn Féin at an Árd Fheis in March 1926, and he left to form a new party, Fianna Fáil. Divided, demoralised and defeated, the Irish republican movement was at a low ebb.[75] The British government, therefore, probably exaggerated the threat posed by the republican movement to the stability of the Free State.

The resolution of the Boundary Commission crisis illustrates two points about Britain's attitudes towards Ireland. First, it shows how desperate London was to remove the Irish question from British affairs and dispense with the dreaded prospect of military reintervention. The British were literally prepared to buy off the nationalists and unionists in order to put the 'dreary steeples' of Tyrone and Fermanagh behind them. Once this was done, once the issue of partition had been at last buried, they were determined to keep it there. Henceforth they adopted an attitude of benevolent indifference towards Northern Ireland, allowing the Unionist Party to run the province as it saw fit, despite periodic demands from Irish nationalists for official enquiries into discrimination against the Catholic minority. Second, the image of southern Ireland as a dangerous, unstable place at the mercy of militant gunmen persisted long after the end of revolutionary violence. It was sustained by a relentless campaign by northern unionists and diehard Conservatives, based on spurious 'secret' intelligence that tried to occupy the gap left by the failure to develop official sources of Irish intelligence.

Ironically, this may have had the opposite effect to what was intended, by making British policy-makers more likely to make concessions to the Free State. The Labour government pushed through the Boundary Commission legislation in the face of unionist resistance in 1924, and the Baldwin administration yielded to many Irish demands in the deal to bury the commission's finding in 1925. Irish ministers played on these fears to advance their policy goals. Subsequent Irish administrations would employ the same tactics with even greater effect.

Minor plots and major omissions

THE atmosphere of perpetual crisis and impending violence which had surrounded Anglo-Irish relations for over a decade finally lifted after 1925. True, the Free State remained a restless Dominion, asserting its independence whenever possible. But it did so in a cautious, non-confrontational way. Good personal relations developed between ministers and civil servants on both sides of the Irish Sea. The Irish Free State actively participated in the evolution of the commonwealth. Even relations between Dublin and Belfast attained a sort of strained stability. The period between 1926 and 1931 represents the high water mark of the treaty settlement.

However, the improvement in Anglo-Irish relations did nothing to increase the quality of intelligence available to London. Apart from sharing information on the movement of foreigners and international communism, the Free State authorities still refused to engage in the sort of intelligence and security co-operation that Britain received from other Dominions (and, indeed, from many foreign allies). The only link between the British and Irish security agencies was the occasional correspondence between Colonel David Neligan of the Garda Síochana and Colonel John Carter of the Special Branch. On the other hand, the few mechanisms that had existed since 1923 to collect and analyse intelligence on southern Ireland were dismantled. The RUC wound down its intelligence network in the Free State in early 1926 – Captain 'Fatty' Woolley lost his job. The Intelligence Branch of the British army in Northern Ireland was also closed down around the same time. Inspector General Sir Charles Wickham of the RUC (knighted in the mid-1920s) continued to share reports with the British army and the Special Branch of the London Metropolitan Police, but Northern Ireland was no longer used as a base for intelligence operations against southern Ireland. It appears that the informal, loyalist intelligence service created by Gwynne and Gretton was similarly abandoned. Correspondence from southern loyalists continued to reach Whitehall through the web of friends, family and business that connected the two islands, but not in an organised, systematic way.

Curiously, MI5 briefly toyed with the idea of starting its own clandestine intelligence service in southern Ireland at this time. This was prompted by the discovery that the RUC and the British army were curtailing their Free State intelligence activities. Captain 'Fatty' Woolley wrote to his old MI5 colleagues in February 1926, urging them to start a replacement service. 'Please don't think that I am an alarmist when I say that never, more than at present, was an efficient system needed over here', he wrote.[76] His advice was taken up by a senior MI5 officer, Major W. A. Phillips, who was 'not at all happy about the state of affairs from an M.I.5. point of view in Southern Ireland'. Phillips argued that, because London had been unable to forge the sort of link that existed in other Dominions, MI5 should build its own network of secret agents in southern Ireland. He proposed to form a small bureau, under the guidance of MI5, but separate from it, to work agents in Ireland, north and south. It could be run under the guise of a private detective agency or commercial venture, with an office and chief agent in a city such as Liverpool. The total cost would not be above £4,500–5,000 per year.[77] However, Sir Vernon Kell (MI5 Director-General) was wary of the political risks, and the idea was dropped.

The changes in 1926 had the advantage of ending the flow of biased, politicised intelligence on Irish affairs. But nothing took its place; the British government received very little intelligence from Ireland, of any kind, during the next five years. A principal reason was the lack of official British representation in southern Ireland. The British armed services maintained a small presence in the country, but it was not well suited to intelligence duties; moreover, there was no civil, diplomatic representative in Dublin to represent British interests.

The British army maintained garrisons at the three ports retained under the treaty – Cobh (formerly named Queenstown) in Co. Cork, Berehaven in Co. Kerry and Lough Swilly in Co. Donegal. The War Office initially hoped to utilise these garrisons to gather intelligence.[78] However, the commanding officer of these troops was reluctant: 'I am of opinion that the existence of an organized Intelligence system in the garrisons of South Ireland would be likely to compromise, and therefore endanger the troops', he wrote, 'as it would probably become known and naturally cause bad feeling and hostility.' Instead, there was a loose arrangement whereby officers sent occasional reports on local conditions and briefed the War Office when on leave.[79] At sea there were three destroyers stationed in Irish waters (two based at Cobh, one at Berehaven), controlled by the Commander-in-Chief at Devonport in Britain. After 1929 their number was reduced to two. They spent most of their time at the Treaty Ports, but also visited other parts of the coast. The commanding officer of each ship was obliged to return weekly surveys of his activities, which invariably became intelligence reports on the areas that he visited.[80]

The quality of intelligence provided by army and naval officers depended on their degree of integration with the local community. This was high at Cobh, where relations with the civil inhabitants during the 1920s were 'most friendly': 'the weekly dances given at the different forts by the other ranks are embarrass-ingly popular with the native female element', one officer recorded. However, it was much lower at the other two Treaty Ports: officers stationed at Lough Swilly complained that there was 'an insufficiency of female society', 'the "mountainy" men' were 'not the most attractive looking types', and the garrison suffered 'from an inevitable feeling of isolation'.[81] Overall the Treaty Port garrisons and the Royal Navy made only a minor contribution to London's understanding of the situation in Ireland.

The British armed services also collected intelligence in the Free State through visits by officers from Britain or Northern Ireland. Some went on official mis-sions. For example, in 1925 Lieutenant-Colonel H. D. G. Crerar, a member of the War Office staff, carried out a tour of the south Irish Treaty Ports and Northern Ireland. He was sent to investigate the port defences and the condition of the troops, but he also reported more generally on the political situation in the south. Similarly, staff officers from the British army in Northern Ireland took advantage of visits by military football and boxing teams to the Free State to 'pick up gen-eral news further south'.[82] Other officers went to the Free State for personal rea-sons, visiting friends and family, or taking holidays: in 1930 the Director of Naval Intelligence spent two weeks holidaying in Ireland.[83] The close links between the two countries made these casual visits a fruitful source of general information. However, they provided sporadic snapshots, rather than tracking developments over time. They also suffered from the same disadvantage as intelligence from the Treaty Port garrisons and the Royal Navy: British officers associated mostly with the Protestant and loyalist class, which could give a biased picture of the political situation.[84]

Britain's civil representation in the Free State was even more problematic. In the other Dominions Britain relied on the Governor-General and his staff to carry out official business, liaise with the local government and report on local conditions. However, in southern Ireland, the Governor-General never fulfilled this role – he was an Irish appointee who represented Irish interests. In addition, the political conditions made it impossible to appoint a British High Commis-sioner. Instead the British government had to make do with temporary, low-ranking officials. Between 1922 and 1924 a British official stationed in Dublin (first Alfred Cope and then N. G. Loughnane) acted as liaison to the Free State government. After this post was abolished, there was no British government representative in the Free State until a British Trade Commissioner was appointed in April 1929. For the first six years this post was ably filled by William Peters. Educated at Aberdeen University, Peters had served for six turbulent years in the British Commercial Mission to Russia, before spending a quieter year as Commercial Secretary for Sweden and Denmark.[85] He was highly regarded by the Foreign Office, which praised his 'marked talent' and 'pleasant manner', listing his strengths as 'a great capacity for intensive study, an excellent and ordered memory, and clarity in his methods of expression'.[86] Although appointed to Dublin with an economic brief by the Department of Overseas Trade, Peters quickly developed a wider role: the Dominions Office was anxious 'to utilise him, in the absence of a High Commissioner, as a source of information on political developments in the Irish Free State'.[87] Yet, although he quickly impressed his superiors as 'a man of great ability, tact and discretion', Peters was no substitute for a senior political representative. At the Irish end, he was not brought into the confidences of the government because of his 'lowly' status. For the same reason, his advice was often ignored by policy-makers in London. Peters, who felt he 'was rusting away through lack of opportunity', repeatedly asked for a change of post.[88] Eventually it was decided in 1935 that his 'ability and energy' could be better used elsewhere. The next Trade Commissioner was chosen on the basis that he was 'nearing the retiring age', which implies that the position was an easy sinecure. Peters' successors kept a low profile and did not attempt to go beyond the narrow remit of trade.[89]

The absence of a senior British representative in Dublin would have serious consequences for political intelligence on Ireland. The diplomatic service was the most important source of foreign information for the British government – much more valuable than secret intelligence.[90] It was the job of a diplomat to test a country's political temperature, to maintain contact with different political leaders and to digest the national press, synthesising all this into regular reports for home consumption. Because of the presence of an American Consul in Dublin (later upgraded to Minister), this sort of information can be found in the records of the State Department over 3,000 miles away. It is noticeably absent from files in London. Peters, well aware of the limitations of his position, frequently pressed London to appoint a proper diplomatic representative. In 1934 he told the Dominions Office:

> As a result of his five years in Ireland his own view was that it was more important than ever that the United Kingdom should have a political

representative in Dublin: it seemed to him absurd that Dublin was practically the only capital in the world in which the United Kingdom Government was not represented ... he personally felt very strongly that the right course was to appoint a political representative with status and credentials which would enable him to meet Ministers.[91]

However, because of Anglo-Irish political disputes, a UK political representative was not appointed until 1939. Thus, for most of the 1920s and 1930s southern Ireland was in the extraordinary position of being one of the few countries in the world without official British diplomatic representation. This was perhaps the greatest weakness in Britain's intelligence relationship with southern Ireland.

The limited intelligence-sharing by the Irish government and the absence of alternative official sources of information meant that British intelligence on Ireland was poor. This was magnified by an abdication of responsibility for Irish affairs within the British intelligence community in London. In early 1926 the War Office stopped assigning a military intelligence officer to Irish affairs. Henceforth, the only intelligence agency that devoted much time to Ireland was the Special Branch. Yet it too reduced its activities: in 1926 the section on Irish republicanism, which had appeared for many years, was dropped from its monthly reports on revolutionary organisations in the United Kingdom. MI5 and SIS took an occasional interest in Ireland, when specific security threats arose; but, generally, they outdid each other to shirk Irish duties, as they were seen as politically risky and outside the bounds of normal operations. The British intelligence community's engagement with Ireland after 1925 was sporadic, reluctant and half-hearted. No single agency took responsibility for Irish affairs.

Why was this? One reason was the overall state of the British intelligence community in the 1920s and 1930s. These were years of depression and retrenchment in which the intelligence services suffered heavily: the Secret Service Vote was cut from a high of £1,150,000 in 1918 to £180,000 by 1924, and remained at that level until 1936.[92] MI5, reduced to just ten officers by 1925 (excluding clerical staff), came close to being shut down completely. It struggled to keep pace with its core targets of communism, fascism and foreign espionage. SIS was similarly under-resourced. Its absorption of the Passport Control Office provided much-needed visa revenues that went towards covert operations, but it occasionally had to rely on the private income of its officers to fund activities. It focused its efforts on tracking the Bolshevik movement in Europe. The Government Code & Cypher School, established in 1919 by merging the remnants of the Admiralty and War Office cryptographic units, had only thirty codebreakers. The intelligence departments of the armed services also suffered, as they were the first to be sacrificed to defence budget cuts. At the War Office, intelligence was subsumed in the new Directorate of Military Operations and Intelligence; the Naval Intelligence Division had insufficient resources to deal with Britain's vast global commitments. Moreover, these departments were regarded as professional backwaters, attracting poor-quality officers, because intelligence work was given a low priority by the armed services. This reflected a persistent failure to appreciate the value of intelligence in peacetime, both among politicians and service chiefs. Thus, the deficiencies in Britain's intelligence on Ireland during this period reflected deeper flaws in the British intelligence system.[93]

Yet these problems were greatly magnified by southern Ireland's anomalous constitutional and political status. If southern Ireland had been a 'normal' loyal Dominion, MI5 would have formed a link with Irish security officials, the two police forces would have exchanged information, the British army and Royal Navy would have enjoyed close co-operation with Irish armed forces, and the government would have been politically represented by the Governor-General or a High Commissioner. On the other hand, if southern Ireland had been a foreign country, the British government would have been represented by an ambassador and a diplomatic mission, the armed services would have exchanged attachés, and SIS could have chosen to run covert intelligence operations on Irish territory. The southern Irish state was somewhere in the middle. The 1921 Anglo-Irish Treaty had placed a constitutional framework on southern Ireland that did not correspond to the attitudes of its people or its government. It also placed a straitjacket on Britain's intelligence engagement with the new state.

IRELAND was a low priority for the British intelligence system between 1926 and 1931. Only three security threats merited attention. The first was the continuing threat of IRA subversion, especially the possibility of attack on British targets in the Free State. The second related to attempts by foreign powers, such as the Soviet Union or Germany, to gain influence in Ireland. The third was the threat that foreign powers would use Ireland and Irish organisations for espionage against Britain. These were sporadic plots, which posed only minor risks to British interests. Yet they occasionally excited British intelligence officials eager to uncover hidden conspiracies. On the other hand, the British intelligence system failed to track the one major threat to Anglo-Irish relations that emerged towards the end of this period – the rise of a populist, republican, constitutional party under the leadership of Éamon de Valera.

During 1926 there were some figures within the British intelligence community who continued to fear a republican takeover in southern Ireland. For example, when Captain 'Fatty' Woolley, the controller of the RUC network in southern Ireland, faced demobilisation in early 1926, he wrote to MI5 with a very alarmist report on the Free State:

> The Republicans ... have strengthened their hand, and the I.R.A. are gradually absorbing into their ranks the worst of the hooligan element from amongst the 'unemployables' and for the Southern Government the future is full of very disagreeable possibilities ...
>
> It is believed that the 'Dump Arms Order' of 1923 will be repealed which will be tantamount to a declaration of a resumption of hostilities against the present constituted government and this time a good number of the F.S. Army will go over to the enemy – certain!!
>
> The Army is 'buzzing with discontent' and free fights occur nightly in Barrack rooms etc. between the rival factions. If only Gilbert and Sullivan had been alive they would have suffered no lack of copy for innumerable comic operas.[94]

This information prompted MI5 to consider starting its own intelligence network in Ireland, and was used *verbatim* in a major MI5 report that set out the dangers to British security emanating from the Free State. There was an engrained habit within some intelligence professionals to see secret conspiracies where they did not exist, and always to accept the worst-case scenario as the likely course of events. This was partly political bias, but it also served to justify the existence of intelligence agencies whose purpose was to uncover secret plots. This was Woolley's motivation: he ended his report with a request that he be placed in charge of a new clandestine intelligence organisation in Ireland.[95]

Others within the British intelligence community had developed a more balanced reading of the Irish situation. In response to MI5's suggestion that a clandestine network was needed, the War Office's Director of Military Operations and Intelligence wrote: 'I am not unhappy about the Irish Free State, nor in the least frightened of it, and I don't believe it wants to, or is in a position to do us any harm.'[96] The Special Branch began to produce reassuring reports from its informants in Britain on the republican movement in Ireland. It reported that the IRA was 'fast deteriorating' and could probably arm only 4,000 to 5,000 men (a sound analysis). It added that republicanism 'as a political creed' had 'lost ground very badly ... mainly owing to its stupid and intolerant propaganda and the narrowness and bitterness of outlook of its leaders.'[97] This was also the view of the Dominions Office. The liberal imperialist school of thought, which assumed that the Free State would settle down as a loyal Dominion, was the dominant perceptual framework in Whitehall.

Developments in Ireland supported this interpretation. The Irish militant republican movement noticeably weakened in the second half of the decade. On the political side, after de Valera departed to set up Fianna Fáil, a tiny group of Sinn Féin irreconcilables persisted in the claim that it was the legitimate government of the republic. 'It retreated into a republican ghetto', writes one historian of Sinn Féin, 'and throughout the following decades it became little more than a society of ageing and quarrelsome idealists.'[98] The IRA also drifted further away from political influence. In November 1925 it withdrew allegiance from the remnants of the Second Dáil, vested all authority in the IRA Army Council, and returned to its Fenian, secret society traditions – it became an 'army without a nation'.[99] Its strategy, such that existed, was to maintain its structure and wait until political conditions were more favourable for a republican takeover, whether through a *coup d'état* or elections. In the meantime, it was responsible for sporadic acts of violence. IRA members waged an 'anti-imperialist' campaign against British institutions, against premises flying the Union Jack and against poppy-sellers on Armistice Day – they even raided Baden Powell Boy Scout camps and destroyed their tents. The IRA also became involved in social agitation, attacking Jewish moneylenders and urging farmers to withhold payment of land annuities to Britain. These activities led to clashes with the Garda. Six murders between 1926 and 1930 can be traced to the IRA: the most notorious was the assassination of Kevin O'Higgins (the Vice-President and Minister for Justice) on 10 July 1927. Incidents such as this eroded public support for the militants. Overall, the underground army was in decline: membership dropped from 5,042 in November 1926 to a low of 1,833 in 1930.[100]

The only threat that continued to worry British officials was the risk of small-scale IRA attacks on British targets in southern Ireland. The most obvious and symbolic targets were the army garrisons at the Treaty Ports. On 21 March 1924 this target had been struck: Private H. Aspinall became the last British soldier to die at the hands of the IRA until 1971. He was among a party of soldiers on recreational leave, flush with their Friday pay, which landed at Cobh from the nearby British fort on Spike Island. As they were stepping onto the pier, four men opened fire with high-powered Lewis machine guns from a nearby Rolls Royce car. The attackers were from the Irregular 1st Cork Brigade, although they wore Free State army uniforms to give the impression that they were associated with the recent army mutiny. The shooting only lasted seconds, but it left Aspinall dead and a number injured, some so badly that their limbs required amputation. Among the twenty-three casualties were five civilians who had been crossing from Spike Island with the soldiers: they included two daughters of a military clerk and a butcher boy who had been delivering meat.[101] (There was a second incident an hour later when the commanding officer of a party of troops guarding the pier was shot in the right buttock. All involved on the British side claimed that this was another IRA attack, but it would appear that the officer was actually the victim of accidental firing by his own men.)[102]

The attack was forcefully condemned by the Cosgrave government, which agreed to pay £19,126 in compensation to the injured and to the family of Private Aspinall (quite a price for 20 seconds of shooting). The Irish response won the warm support of the British government and the House of Commons, and, if anything, the incident strengthened Anglo-Irish relations.[103] However, although it had little political impact, the Cobh outrage demonstrated the persistent danger of isolated IRA attacks on the port garrisons. This remained a constant feature of the British military's threat assessments in the 1920s. When the War Office sent Lieutenant-Colonel Crerar on his tour of the south Irish coast defences in 1925, he noted that the role of the garrisons was 'quite opposed to the normal' because their 'daily attentions' were 'still infinitely more concerned landwards than seawards'. Their primary role was defence against armed raids 'by hostile elements among the surrounding population'.[104] As a result, the garrisons were large compared to equivalent fortifications elsewhere. The War Office periodically looked for ways to reduce personnel for reasons of economy, but always came to the conclusion that this was unfeasible due to the continuing risks.[105] Concerns over the risk of attack on the Treaty Ports would play an important part in the eventual decision in 1938 to hand these facilities to the Irish state.

The threat of IRA attack also surrounded visits by high profile British figures to southern Ireland. The Irish government gave this as the reason why it could not allow Royal Navy ships to make official visits to Irish towns; after much grumbling over disloyalty and the navy's imperial rights, the Admiralty eventually accepted that this risk was real.[106] In 1928 there were worries over a visit by Lord Lascelles and Princess Mary (daughter of King George V) to their estates in southern Ireland. They considered cancelling their plans, although in the end decided against it, as it might make future visits to the Free State by members of the royal family difficult. Special Garda protection was arranged for them after the Special Branch liaised with Colonel David Neligan.[107] That these fears were not groundless was shown by the discovery of an IRA plot to abduct Earl Jellico – commander of the British Grand Fleet during the First World War and a former Governor-General of New Zealand – during a visit to Dublin in October 1930. The IRA planned to kidnap the earl, chain him inside a large box with only his head protruding and place him on a donkey cart. 'The donkey and cart were then to have been driven at a strategic moment into O'Connell Street, the sack hurriedly withdrawn and the distinguished personage within the case made an object of public ridicule', a Garda report dryly noted. 'There were to have been placards, such as "Earl Jellyfish", ready to place on the side of the box.' Practically every known IRA man in Dublin assembled in the city centre on the day of the earl's arrival, but due to police precautions the scheme was abandoned.[108]

Many of the IRA plots had an air of comic farce about them. A more insidious threat, with deeper strategic implications, surrounded attempts by Britain's foreign enemies to gain influence in newly independent southern Ireland. Most obviously, this was associated with the Soviet Union and the international communist movement. The 'Red Menace' was still a major preoccupation in Britain in the mid-1920s. The first Labour government gave *de jure* recognition to the Soviet regime in 1924, but relations remained tense, and they were broken off in 1927 following evidence of Soviet subversion in the British empire. Right-wing Conservatives continued to exaggerate communist influence in Ireland: for example, the 'secret' intelligence reports circulated by Gretton and Gwynne contained many references to 'Bolshevik agents'.[109] However, by the mid-1920s British intelligence professionals had developed a more balanced understanding of the global communist threat, which was reflected in their assessments of Ireland. The Special Branch wryly tracked the personal squabbles, innumerable splits, false starts and unmistakable failure of the extreme Left in the Irish Free State, paying particular attention to James Larkin, who made an aborted attempt to gain control of the Irish union movement after he returned to the country on 30 April 1923. In a comprehensive memorandum two years later, the Special Branch sanguinely concluded that communism posed little threat to the stability of the Free State:

> Ireland is not a fruitful soil for Communism and Larkin will find he is in for a very uphill fight. He is an attractive personality and may, for a time, command a limited following, but as a permanent leader he is almost certain to fail. In addition he is heavily handicapped by his many acrimonious disputes with the recognised leaders of labour in Ireland.[110]

The Special Branch's analysis is in keeping with the consensus among historians that 'the revolutionary Left had a thin time in the 1920s'.[111]

Surprisingly, when the British intelligence community considered the problem of 'alien penetration' of the Irish Free State, it was more concerned about German activity than Soviet subversion. The Cosgrave government was determined to assert its independence from Britain by forging links with countries such as Germany: it was the first state with which the Irish Free State signed a commercial treaty and exchanged diplomatic representatives. Moreover, nationalist Ireland, especially the revolutionary governing élite, had a friendly attitude towards Germany because of its support for the 1916 Rising. German nationals were recruited to senior positions in the new state: for example, Major-General Fritz Brase was appointed as bandmaster of the Irish army, Dr Adolf Mahr became Director of the National Museum. When the Irish government decided to build an ambitious hydro-electric plant at Ardnacrusha on the River Shannon, it awarded the contract to Siemens Schuckert, rather than a British bidder.[112]

This conspicuous Irish desire to develop closer economic, cultural and diplomatic ties with Britain's erstwhile foe was regarded as a sinister development by some British observers. In military and intelligence circles an emotional antipathy to the 'Boche' outlived the end of the First World War: there was a widespread feeling that the struggle with the Teutonic enemy was not over. There were a number of angry reports in the late 1920s from loyalist, unionist and intelligence sources on growing German penetration of Ireland. One of Colonel Gretton's secret documents warned that the Shannon scheme would be used as cover to import German military officers. The writer was not sure if the object was to 'teach the Free State Army all the latest German methods and how to get together a secret army', or to give assistance to the Irish army 'should the North prove troublesome'; but he had no doubt that there was something connected with this which was 'not quite genuine' and required 'looking after'.[113] These suspicions received some corroboration from Captain 'Fatty' Woolley in Belfast. In letters to MI5 in February 1926, he complained about an 'enormous … alien influx', estimating that 750 Germans had arrived in Limerick. He made a point to meet them and was shocked by their attitude:

> The Shannon Valley is absolutely 'stiff' with 'Bosche' and many of them with whom I have talked (as a perfectly good Irishman) evidently do <u>not</u> entertain the 'Locarno Spirit' towards Great Britain and are not backward in saying 'it's only a matter of time and then …'??[114]

Woolley presented the alien penetration of southern Ireland as a reason why MI5 or SIS should start a clandestine intelligence service in the country. This was also the motivation behind another approach to MI5 from a former intelligence officer, Captain Edward Twiss. He had served as a Brigade Intelligence Officer with the 2nd Munster Fusiliers in the west of Ireland until, 'after many adventures', the IRA 'ran [him] to earth in 1921'. He subsequently held administrative positions in Uganda and Hong Kong before returning to live in Dublin. In a rambling letter to MI5 he predicted that 'Russia with Germany's aid would sweep westward' and warned that both countries were conducting secret intrigues in the Free State:

Germany and Russia have their agents all over this country and it galls me when they approach me with their sinister schemes. I can only listen and draw my own deductions. ... A powerful German Syndicate I hear on very good authority has the capital ready to control a scheme which will make Blacksod Bay a trans-Atlantic port, and a strategic menace to England in the event of war. Not alone did I hear it but I have seen the plans. So I write to you to know if there might be a chance of obtaining a billet from the War Office again in the S.Service.

He went on to say that his war record was excellent; he was only thirty-two; he had no ties; and his connections were such as to allow him to carry out intelligence work successfully: 'I am acquainted with the people who count in the Free State', he added, 'and I hate them.' MI5 initially turned down Twiss's offer but a year later became interested in employing him. The Dominions Office intervened to prevent this, citing his poor record in Hong Kong and his obvious biases. 'This sort of man employed on secret service may be <u>most</u> dangerous', a Dominions Office civil servant warned, 'we had several agents of this type in Ireland in 1920–21.'[115]

The recent release of secret records shows that MI5 shared some of Twiss's concerns about foreign subversion in southern Ireland. The agency had received some worrying intelligence on this subject over the previous two years. In August 1924 SIS reported that the German government employed a number of secret service agents in Ireland and were kept informed about the Free State Army by Major-General Brase and his German bandmasters. Twiss's warning about German naval bases in Ireland received some corroboration at the end of 1925, when MI5 learnt that a German-American syndicate, introduced to the Irish government by an IRB contact, had offered the state £500,000 for exclusive fishing rights around the coast of Ireland. This was not what it seemed: special fishing trawlers would be introduced that could be quickly converted into fighting craft to seize Irish harbours 'in case of international trouble'. In a two-page dossier entitled 'Alien Penetration in Irish Free State' MI5 gave a number of examples of undesirable foreigners who had gained entry to the Free State. One was Joseph Marks, a German spy who had been convicted in a British court in 1915; he was prohibited from entering the United Kingdom, but had managed to secure a visa from Free State officials. Another was Baron Von Horst, who had likewise secured a Free State visa despite being well known to the British authorities for 'fomenting industrial and political troubles' in Britain and Ireland before 1914.[116] MI5 was not happy with the co-operation received from Dublin: 'the Southern Irish Government must have been fully aware of our feelings with regard to the activities of these men', Major W. A. Phillips sternly noted, 'yet they granted them permission to travel to Ireland.'[117]

The principal reason for British concern was the risk of espionage. 'We ... have to consider Southern Ireland from the point of view of it being utilised by foreign powers as a jumping off place for secret service agents working against this country', Phillips warned. He fretted that an enemy agent could land in the Free State, travel to Britain without any checks, collect secret information and then return to the Free State, where he could send his report to Europe by direct boat.[118] This was the third aspect of Irish security that troubled the British intelligence community in the second half of the 1920s. It was the most intensively investigated and also the most secret – only the recent release of MI5 records has brought it to light.

Britain had some grounds for concern, although the real threat came from the IRA organisation in Britain, not German agents in Ireland. Starting in 1925, the IRA conducted military espionage against Britain on behalf of the Soviet Union. With a tradition of sophisticated intelligence work and an underground organisation stretching across the British Isles, the IRA was a natural partner for a Soviet military intelligence apparatus eager to use local communist parties and affiliated organisations for espionage. The IRA accepted this role because it wished to strike a blow against Britain and hoped to secure Soviet military and financial assistance in return. The collaboration began in June 1925, when two IRA men (Seán Russell and Pa Murray) travelled to Moscow, met with Joseph Stalin and requested arms and the opportunity to train with the Soviet air force. The Russians were unwilling to provide such open support but did take up the Irish offer to provide military intelligence from Britain. Soon after, Russell and Murray met in London with a Soviet controller, 'Mr X', who had come from Berlin. Future meeting places, and methods for postal and hand communications, were fixed up. 'Mr X' furnished Murray with a detailed list of information required, which included drawings from the Patent Office of an optical instrument for directing aeroplanes, samples of a new gas mask and other military items. Apparently Murray was successful 'in supplying all his requirements' within weeks.[119]

It is likely that 'Mr X' was Walter Krivitsky, a senior officer within Soviet military intelligence (the Razvedupr or GRU), who ran its operations in Germany. Krivitsky defected to the United States of America in 1937 and published a best-selling exposé of the depredations of Soviet Russia, *In Stalin's Secret Service*. In 1941 he was found dead in a hotel room in Washington, DC, the victim, according to many, of assassination (although the police deemed it suicide). Before his death he was debriefed by Captain Guy Liddell of MI5, providing the British with their first detailed insight into the Soviet intelligence system. He recalled how, around 1926, he had personal contact with three IRA officers who asked for Soviet support and offered to undertake espionage. He worked with them for a time and 'got quite useful information out of them'.[120]

IRA involvement in espionage was discovered by the Special Branch in 1924 and repeatedly investigated over the next four years. (The Special Branch, not MI5, took the lead on this matter.)[121] In July 1924 the Special Branch reported that an IRA 'Intelligence Organisation' in Britain had been created and was 'getting into its stride'. A Chief Intelligence Officer named McGough had been appointed in London, and he controlled Area Intelligence Officers around the country. McGough and another IRA man were arrested, and pleaded guilty on 10 February 1925 to breaches of the Official Secrets Act, receiving relatively lenient sentences of fifteen and eighteen months imprisonment.[122] The arrests temporarily disrupted the IRA organisation, but the IRA leaders were not deterred for long. A month later, in March 1925, Scotland Yard received information 'from a fairly reliable source that a meeting had recently been held in DUBLIN in connection with a system of espionage in this country particularly with regard to Naval and Aircraft matters'.[123] Soon after, Cornelius 'Con' Neenan, a leading figure in the pre-Treaty and Civil War IRA in Co. Cork, was appointed as the new Intelligence Officer in Britain. The Special Branch warned that he was a 'smart intelligence man' who would 'liven things up'.[124]

Evidence of the IRA's willingness to engage in espionage against Britain also came from the SIS network in Germany. By 1927 SIS was convinced that Weimar Germany was working with the Soviet Union to spy on Britain. SIS drew together the facts on the IRA intelligence network in Britain and secret information from its agents in Germany to hypothesise that the IRA had offered its services to a joint 'German-Soviet espionage organisation'. The development of this Irish–German–Russian *ménage à trois* was sketched in a SIS memorandum produced on the instruction of 'C' in April 1927:

> After the Irish Treaty had become effective, the I.R.A. organisation in England tried for a while to continue creating trouble in Ireland. Finding no support, its leaders looked around for some method of employing the machine they had created, and incidentally of making money and doing harm to England. Already in touch with certain IIIrd International [*sic*] and German parties they, through these connections, offered their services as an espionage organisation, either to the International or the Germans or both. Having given proof that they possessed an organisation of couriers, collecting centres, fixed agents and so on, their services

were accepted following on a secret meeting in Glasgow as early as 1922, between representatives of the I.R.A. and one or two delegates representing the German espionage service.[125]

MI5 was inclined to dismiss the notion that Germany and the Soviet Union were co-operating for espionage purposes.[126] However, they had plenty of evidence that the IRA was working on behalf of the Soviet Union. German communists, if not the German government, were mixed up in this plot.

In 1927 and 1928 Irish republicans appeared on the fringes of a series of espionage cases that had grave implications for Anglo-Soviet relations. The Special Branch tracked an IRA man, Michael Cremin, who had been involved in gunrunning from Germany in 1921. He came to attention when he called at the offices of the Cambridge Instruments Company in London and enquired about the cost of sound ranging apparatus (used to locate enemy artillery). Cremin was associated with Irish republicans active within the Communist Party of Great Britain (CPGB) and its various front organisations.[127] One of these groups was the Workers' Defence Corps, a paramilitary wing of the CPGB created to defend workers' interests. It was led by Captain Jack White, a radical former British army officer from Co. Antrim who had trained Connolly's Irish Citizens' Army in 1913, and went on to fight with the anarchists in the Spanish Civil War.[128] MI5 concluded that the Workers' Defence Corps provided a link between the IRA and the director of the Soviet spy network in Britain, Jacob Kirchtenstein (who went by the alias 'Johnny Walker'). According to MI5, the 'Irish Republican Intelligence Service' was one of four sections in his network. IRA members were implicated in at least two high-profile cases related to Kirchtenstein that came to trial in 1927: that of Kate Gussfeldt (alias Ethel Childs), a communist spy who was deported to Germany; and that of George Hansen (alias Johnson), a native of Cologne who was sentenced to ten years penal servitude for receiving and transmitting information for Moscow. These cases were significant as they were evidence of what British intelligence chiefs identified as 'a recrudescence of espionage on behalf of Russia'. They precipitated a raid by British police on the Soviet trade company, Arcos Ltd, on 12 May 1927 and contributed to the government's decision to break off diplomatic relations with the Soviet Union later that year.[129]

The discovery of IRA involvement in Soviet espionage not only soured Anglo-Soviet relations but had an immediate impact on recruitment to the British armed forces in southern Ireland. Both loyalist and nationalist communities had long been an important source of officers and other ranks to the British army and navy. This came under threat when the British intelligence community learnt in March 1925 that 'a certain number of Irish rebels may possibly endeavour to join H.M. Navy' for the purpose of 'espionage, sabotage, or propaganda'. The Director of Naval Intelligence placed a 'virtual embargo' on recruitment from the Irish Free State, which remained in place for the next year. The army took similar action.

Recruitment only restarted when the British were able to put in place special procedures for screening applicants. The Free State government was unexpectedly helpful, allowing the British to quietly check with local Garda on the suitability of applicants (generally, whether the person was a known republican). In addition, the armed services built up a network of respectable loyalists in the Free State – such as clergy and ex-servicemen – to provide references. In practice, this meant that anyone who wished to apply to the British armed forces had to approach a loyalist referee.[130] (Some loyalists also took a more active role in encouraging recruitment: in 1930 the Irish Department of Justice launched an investigation into 'a number of persons of independent means' and 'holders of pronounced imperialistic views' in Dublin, who expounded the advantages of a military career to young Irishmen, gave potential recruits lodging and advanced their fare to recruiting stations in Belfast or Liverpool. This activity came to the angry attention of extreme nationalists, who viewed it as treasonable.)[131]

Attempts by the Soviet Union to use the IRA for espionage purposes ended in 1929. Walter Krivitsky later told his British debriefers that he decided to 'drop' his IRA contacts because he found that he was 'getting involved in the affairs of the organisation' and was being asked to give assistance for a 'terrorist plan'. The Soviets only wanted information and were not interested in helping the 'Irish cause', as it risked destabilising Anglo-Soviet relations too much. They were also concerned about the security of their highly secret networks and may have concluded that collaboration with the British IRA was too risky: for example, one of Krivitsky's colleagues, Ignace Reiss, was forced to close his Amsterdam station in 1928 after the Special Branch traced Irish contacts to him.[132] However, though the official collaboration with the IRA ceased, the Soviets continued to view Irish *individuals* as suitable spy material. Krivitsky recalled that if the Soviet intelligence agencies were looking for an agent or contact in any particular place, their first recruiting ground was the Communist Party, and if that failed they invariably tried to find an Irish person. This was 'purely on the basis that an Irishman was probably anti-British and would be more willing to work for them than an Englishman'.[133]

It is paradoxical that Soviet military intelligence decided to distance itself from the IRA at the end of the 1920s, as this was when the Irish republican movement edged closest to communism under the leadership of a new generation of left-wing radicals – men such as Peadar O'Donnell, Frank Ryan and George Gilmore. In 1927 the IRA Army Council pledged to support the Soviet Union in any war with Britain. At the invitation of the Comintern, twenty-one Irish revolutionaries received training at the Lenin School in Moscow between 1926 and 1935. They formed the Revolutionary Workers' Groups (or Party) in 1930, as a prelude to the re-establishment of an official Communist Party of Ireland in 1933.[134] Together with IRA leaders they also formed a new political party, Saor Éire, and seeded a plethora of other revolutionary organisations in 1930 and 1931: the Irish Labour Defence League, the Workers' Defence Corps, the Irish Working Farmers' Committee, the Friends of Soviet Russia, to name a few. This injection of left-wing ideas, together with economic depression and restrictions on emigration, led to a revival of the IRA: in October 1931 the Irish Special Branch estimated that membership had more than tripled to 4,800 over the past year. IRA members intervened more forcefully in labour and land disputes and continued to attack symbols of the imperial connection. The IRA also reacted violently to the state's attempts to suppress it. Juries and witnesses involved in republican trials were intimidated, and two suspected informers and a zealous Garda officer were killed.[135] The rise of socialist agitation and republican violence provoked a 'Red Scare' among Cumann na nGaedheal supporters and the Catholic church. In October 1931 the government passed a ferocious Public Safety Act, which allowed for trial without jury for subversive activities, and proscribed a long list of socialist and republican organisations, including the IRA. This was ostensibly a reaction to the socialist menace, but the government was also exploiting the issue to justify draconian measures that could be used to suppress republicans.[136]

Indications of these worrying developments reached the British government through the *ad hoc* channels that existed for gathering information on Ireland. The British Trade Commissioner, William Peters, did his best to bring the situation to the attention of British policy-makers. In an important memorandum of September 1931 he analysed the 'Red Scare' at length. He correctly realised that it 'rather suits the book of the Government to emphasize the danger of socialistic and anti-religious propaganda', but he also stated that it was impossible to ignore that there had been 'a good many unpleasant happenings recently', and that 'subversive forces' had been 'making much headway'. These forces had a decidedly red tinge:

> The extremists who are gaining ground in the country and who control the extensive illegal 'Irish Republican Army' are definitely more and more becoming permeated with what may be called Soviet ideals. The position

in some of the extremist organisations resembles the position in many of the organisations in the pre-Treaty days, in the sense that the organisations are being used as stalking horses.

He warned that, while there were 'very few' convinced believers in communism in Ireland, this 'did not mean that the few revolutionary leaders will be unable to control big forces'. There was 'engrained in the Irishman a sympathy with any action that is against the Government'; this, together with fear of IRA retribution, meant that it was impossible to persuade jury or witnesses to bring about convictions in cases of political violence. Illegal drilling was going on almost everywhere, and the IRA was well supplied with weapons, some of which had only recently been smuggled into the country. Peters qualified his warning, stating that 'it would be wrong to exaggerate the movement'. Nevertheless, his memorandum caused quite a stir in the Dominions Office, which made an unsuccessful attempt to have it circulated to the Prime Minister and the cabinet.[137]

There were also stirrings of concern within the British intelligence community. Through informers in the CPGB and agents in Europe, the British intelligence community received good information on the links between Ireland and the international communist movement: this revealed the despatch of organisers by the CPGB to Ireland, the transmission of regular funds by the Comintern and the presence of Irish revolutionaries at the Lenin School in Moscow.[138] However, British intelligence officers had a poor understanding of the Irish republican movement and the wider political situation. In October 1931 the Director of Military Operations and Intelligence raised the possibility of attacks on the Treaty Port garrisons, admitting that he was 'virtually in the dark as to what is going on there'. MI5 agreed that 'military intelligence regarding the I.F.S. is not as strong as it should be'. As a result they once again considered the different options for gaining information from the south. MI5 was still hesitant to run its own agents in Ireland: the MI5 Deputy Director, Lieutenant-Colonel Sir Eric Holt-Wilson, remarked that 'It would ruin our official work if it were discovered that we did such work direct from this office'. He considered passing the matter to SIS, because the Irish Free State was 'so nearly "foreign soil"'.[139] In the end, London turned again to Northern Ireland. Holt-Wilson travelled to Belfast in December 1931 and met with the RUC and staff officers from the British army. The RUC advised MI5 against forming a direct link with Colonel David Neligan in Dublin, as he would probably be removed if a new government came into power; MI5's papers and correspondence might therefore 'fall into unsympathetic hands'. Instead the RUC claimed that they were 'sufficiently informed of doings in the South' and could probably provide enough information to MI5 for its purposes.[140] This somewhat reassured the security chiefs in London.

Into this tense atmosphere came another report from SIS about supposed gunrunning to Irish revolutionaries. According to an SIS informant in the Soviet mercantile marine (the Sovtorgflot), on 12 October 1931 the steamship *Aleksei Rikov* had transhipped forty-two cases of arms and ammunition to the German-owned sailing vessel *Max* in the North Sea, while *en route* from Leningrad to London. The consignment was 'destined for a secret revolutionary committee in Ireland' and was said to be accompanied by a British communist named Johnson, a man of about 40 years of age, thick set and of average height, with reddish hair and a hook nose. SIS and MI5 made urgent enquiries into his identity and the location of the two named vessels. The report was also sent to the Irish government. Although the IRA did attempt to import weapons from Soviet and German sources in the mid-1920s, there is no evidence that any large shipment was brought in during 1931. Therefore, it can be assumed that this was yet another of the many spurious rumours of IRA gunrunning that SIS produced in the 1920s and 1930s. But it would only have reinforced fears in Dublin and London that subversive forces were gaining strength in the Free State – the prevalence of gunrunning reports is one of the best barometers of British anxiety over Irish republicanism.[141]

Despite these warnings, the rise of subversive forces in Ireland did not significantly impinge on the higher echelons of the British government. The papers of the Dominions Office contain few references to the escalating political violence in the Free State. It was never raised at cabinet level. British ministers were glad to be rid of the Irish problem, had largely ignored the country for the previous five years, and were determined to shut their eyes and ears to any signs of renewed trouble. Moreover, the British government and its intelligence system completely failed to spot the real threat gathering force in southern Ireland: this came not from communists, nor from the IRA, but from the electoral challenge of de Valera's Fianna Fáil. Famously described as 'a slightly constitutional party', its strategy was to gain election into government through peaceful means; once in power it would tear up the treaty, remove British influence, and dare Britain to do anything about it. This clarion call to nationalist sentiment was combined with a leftist economic program that entailed tariff protection, stimulation of Irish industry and ambitious public spending. It proved a heady concoction, winning support across class boundaries. Within a year of its foundation Fianna Fáil had established 1,307 branches nationwide, and it performed strongly in two 1927 general elections, winning 35.2 per cent of first-preference votes. In 1931 it was able to capitalise on popular discontent with the long-established Cumann na nGaedheal government to position itself for victory in the general elections scheduled for February 1932.[142] What is remarkable is that, despite previous obsessions about a republican takeover, this steady march was barely tracked by officials or ministers within the British government. Apart from a couple of insightful reports from William Peters, there are hardly any documents that assess the strength of Fianna Fáil and its likely policies. This was partly because of the low priority that Ireland had in British affairs and the deficiencies in British political intelligence. It was partly because of an unfounded hope that the Irish would see sense and return the Cosgrave government; in some ways the alternative was too horrible to contemplate, as it would necessitate a complete reformulation of the Anglo-Irish equation. The neglect of Irish affairs and the failure to understand the rise of Fianna Fáil in the months and years before the 1932 election meant that the British government was wholly unprepared to deal with the de Valera challenge when it came.

CHAPTER 7

The de Valera Challenge

I N August 1932 the Foreign Office received a curious letter from three British citizens employed at the Bray Printing Company in Co. Wicklow, just south of Dublin city. They described how their employer had received threatening letters from 'the local Fianna Fail and I.R.A.' demanding that they be dismissed from the firm because of their nationality. Following this, the printers were visited by two 'ardent IRA men' who bluntly stated that Fianna Fáil were determined to get them out of the country – 'hints were thrown of physical violence'. The IRA men added that this was 'only a beginning'; they intended to do the same to all offices where British nationals were employed. The printers wrote to the Manchester headquarters of the British Typographical Association, of which they were members, 'appealing for protection'. At the same time they prudently decided to enlist sturdier allies. 'As we are sure to incur the enmity of the militant section of the I.R.A.', they pleaded to the Foreign Office, 'we earnestly beg of you to render us assistance in some way through the powerful influences at your disposal, namely, the Intelligence and Secret Service Departments.' They took the precaution of having their letter posted in Britain in case it was intercepted by their Irish enemies: 'hence the English stamp', they helpfully explained.[1]

The way in which this letter was handled reveals a lot about how the British government perceived the political situation in southern Ireland in 1932. When the document was passed to the Dominions Office, two of its senior figures noted that if such a request had come from a foreign country, for example a South American republic (then a by-word for instability and corruption), they would appeal to the foreign government concerned and demand that protection be given to the British subjects. But in the case of the Irish Free State this was impossible:

> There is good reason to fear that any action taken vis-à-vis the present Government might only result in making the position of the individuals threatened worse rather than better. Apart from any question whether the present Irish Free State would or would not approve the policy of the I.R.A., there is every reason to fear that any such representations made to

them would be known to the I.R.A. and would no doubt make their treatment of the individuals worse.

Evidently Whitehall viewed the Fianna Fáil administration and IRA gunmen as closely linked. The standard of governance in the Free State had not even reached the level of the much-maligned countries of South America. As a result, the Dominions Office decided to make enquiries 'through other means'. Though unspecified, this probably included reference to the Secret Intelligence Service (SIS).[2] The appeal of the English printers for the protection of the 'Secret Service Departments' was not as ridiculous as it might first seem; just days before receiving this letter, the British government had decided to sanction clandestine intelligence operations on Irish territory for the first time since 1922.

The context for this incident was a major crisis in Anglo-Irish relations. Any complacency in London about the stability of the Anglo-Irish relationship was shattered by de Valera's coming to power on 9 March 1932 – the vanquished of the Civil War had now won control of the country. De Valera immediately issued a financial challenge to London by ceasing to hand over land annuities owed to Britain: the annuities consisted of payments by Irish farmers for acquisitions made under the land reform acts of the previous half century. De Valera also announced his intention to abolish the oath of allegiance to the British monarch. This was less tangible, but for both sides more important: to Fianna Fáil it was a symbol of the Free State's subjugation to the imperial power; to the British it was the common thread that bound the commonwealth together. The British government responded by slapping a crippling special duty on Irish imports, leading to a five-year 'Economic War'.[3]

This period was also marked by a recrudescence of political violence, as subversive undercurrents tugged at the moorings of the constitutional political system. De Valera had a very different attitude to the militant republican movement than his predecessor. Since 1926 Fianna Fáil leaders had maintained close relations with the IRA, and in the 1932 elections they had worked together to secure victory over Cumann na nGaedheal. One of de Valera's first acts on taking power was to lift the repression that had marked the final year of Cosgrave's administration: the Public Safety Act was suspended, the ban on the IRA rescinded and IRA prisoners released. De Valera tolerated the IRA, hoping to eventually wean it away from the gun by removing the imperial aspects of the constitution. Free to organise, recruit, drill and agitate, the organisation enjoyed a resurgence. IRA membership swelled to an estimated 10,000–12,000 by 1934. Weekly circulation of its newspaper, *An Phoblacht*, grew from 8,000 in January 1932 to a high of 27,700 two years later. Constrained by an uneasy truce with the state, IRA members turned their attentions to the Cumann na nGaedheal party, launching persistent attacks on its meetings: *An Phoblacht* proclaimed that 'free speech and the freedom of the press must be denied to traitors and treason mongers'. There were also sporadic attacks on symbols of the British connection: film reels depicting Armistice Day commemorations or the British royal family were seized from cinemas; bottles of Bass ale were smashed in Dublin pubs as part of a 'British Boycott' campaign. (One of the Bass directors was Colonel John Gretton, MP, arch-unionist and leader of the diehards in the House of Commons.) There were also further signs of the influence of communist ideas within the IRA. Social and economic topics were prominent in *An Phoblacht*, the IRA intervened more frequently in workers' strikes, and the most radical IRA leaders left in 1934 to form Republican Congress, a party that sought to establish not just a republic but a *workers'* republic along Soviet lines.[4]

These developments caused apoplexy among the leaders of Cumann na nGaedheal. They feared that de Valera would purge state institutions, turn the IRA rottweiler on his political opponents and – through his economic policies – allow communism to worm its insidious way into the Irish body politic. In 1932 they created a right-wing paramilitary organisation – the Army Comrades Association or 'Blueshirts' – that squared up against the IRA and protected Cumann na nGaedheal supporters from intimidation. In July 1933 it gained a new, flamboyant leader, the former Garda Commissioner General Eoin O'Duffy, who rechristened it the 'National Guard', adopted a vaguely corporatist constitution and began to adopt the sinister, straight-arm, fascist salute. The organisation grew to 50,000 members over the next year. De Valera moved to suppress it in August 1933 by using the military tribunals that had targeted the IRA two years before. In response, the three main opposition parties came together to form the United Ireland Party (or Fine Gael) under O'Duffy's leadership. Endemic violence between the Blueshirts and the IRA intensified in the winter of 1933–4. Blueshirts also began to clash with the police, as farmers reacted violently to the impact of the economic war.[5] Party politics was enveloped by mob violence and paramilitary posturing, as the Blueshirts, republicans and the Garda clashed throughout the state.[6]

De Valera's constitutional challenge and the unsettled conditions in southern Ireland came as a disturbing shock to the British government. It raised three major challenges for the British intelligence community, none of which drew an adequate response. The first was increasing the flow of intelligence from the Free State. There were attempts to deploy Britain's secret intelligence agencies on Irish matters, but the structural deficiencies in Britain's arrangements remained, and the information received in London continued to be *ad hoc*, incomplete and politically biased. The second challenge was assessing the intentions and trustworthiness of the new Irish government. How far would it go to damage British interests? Was it in league with militant republicans? What about the character and motivation of de Valera himself? The British government started from a position of ignorance and tended to demonise the Fianna Fáil leader and his ministers. Finally, a major task of the British intelligence system was assessing the power of the various subversive undercurrents that swirled beneath the political surface. Did the IRA have the power to launch a *coup d'état*? Did the emergence of the Blueshirts signal a descent towards another civil war, this time with an infusion of continental European ideologies of the Left and the Right? How great was the risk of attack on British nationals in the Free State and on the border with Northern Ireland? We shall see that British officials and politicians were preoccupied with the forces of subversion and the threat of political violence: the Free State was once more seen as an unstable and anarchic place. Exaggerations of the political instability of the Irish state and misconceptions around the nature of the de Valera government would both have an impact on the unfortunate and ineffective policy decisions taken by the British government in 1932 and 1933.

The intelligence target

Developments in early 1932 made the need for better intelligence on southern Ireland acute. British intelligence chiefs dusted off earlier discussion documents that had framed the three options for gathering this information: co-operation with the Dublin authorities, reliance on Northern Ireland, and independent clandestine operations. The first option was out of the question due to the change of Irish government. The limited collaboration between Dublin and London ceased; indeed, the chief liaison officer on the Irish side, Colonel David Neligan, was removed from his position as head of the Garda Special Branch because of his role in the Irish Civil War. The second option was utilised to some extent – the Northern Ireland authorities provided some information on conditions in the south – but it was not considered sufficient. As a result, the British government decided to pursue the third option. It sanctioned clandestine intelligence activities against the Irish Free State. This occurred in two ways; the decryption of Irish diplomatic communications and the creation of a network of secret informants in southern Ireland.

In 1932 the most powerful weapon in the British intelligence armoury was turned on Ireland: the Government Code & Cypher School (GC&CS) was tasked with breaking Irish diplomatic ciphers. Headed by Alistair Denniston, the highly secretive GC&CS was a small agency at this time, focusing most of its effort on the Soviet Union.[7] Its recently released files contain a number of decrypted telegrams to and from Ireland in 1932. These include messages between the Irish Department of External Affairs and its representatives in the United States, Canada, Berlin, Paris, Geneva and South Africa; between the Irish government and other Dominion governments; and between foreign missions in Dublin and their respective countries. These telegrams were obtained through a long-standing secret arrangement with British cable companies, and it is likely that the British cryptographers had little difficulty breaking the simple ciphers employed by the Irish authorities. The Irish operation must have been one of the codebreakers' most sensitive activities. Spying on enemies was expected; spying on friends tolerated; but it was another thing to spy on member's of one's imperial family.[8]

The decision to use GC&CS indicates how southern Ireland was increasingly viewed as a foreign country in intelligence terms. However, this initiative did not yield much. The number of Irish telegrams in the official records is trifling – just eighteen, all within a period between March and July 1932. It seems that GC&CS did not put much effort into this task. With a staff of just thirty, it was a 'physical impossibility' for the agency to tackle all the cipher traffic available from around the world; it was therefore forced to discriminate.[9] Moreover, the value of the Irish decrypts obtained by the agency was low; they say little about the Irish government's intended policies, partly because the most important Irish policy communications went by diplomatic bag, and partly because de Valera took personal control of foreign policy and did not keep his foreign representatives closely informed.

The low value of signals intelligence led to efforts to develop a human intelligence network within the Irish Free State. This was sparked by fears of IRA attack on the Treaty Ports at the height of the Anglo-Irish crisis in August 1932. A special cabinet Irish Situation Committee recommended that 'further investigation was required as to the possibility of obtaining information as to activities in the Irish Free State, both from the point of view of military intelligence, and also of political intelligence'. The Chief of the Imperial General Staff, Field-Marshal Sir George Milne, undertook to investigate the matter with the assistance of Sir Maurice Hankey, the Cabinet Secretary.[10] The outcome of this initiative was a mystery until the recent release of an internal history on MI5's wartime Irish activities. It described how SIS agreed to carry out the first clandestine British operation in independent Ireland:

> In 1932 when de Valera and the Fianna Fail Party came into power, the
> British Government realised that it would become increasingly difficult

to obtain reliable information about happenings in Eire [southern Ire-
land]. Sir Vernon Kell, then head of M.I.5., was asked if he would organise
a Secret Intelligence Service in Eire, but after consideration, declined to
do so. A similar request was then made to the head of S.I.S. who agreed
to provide, not an Intelligence Service, but a very restricted information
service.[11]

This service was run by Section V of SIS, a counter-espionage unit created in
1931 to provide a link with MI5. Its head was Major (later Colonel) Valentine
Vivian. The son of a well-known Victorian portrait painter, he had made an early
career in the Indian police. He was known to his colleagues as 'Vee-Vee' and possessed a glass eye, which he tried to shield from view by standing at a right angle
to those he met. One colleague, Kim Philby (later exposed as a Soviet agent),
described him as a timorous figure 'long past his best – if indeed he ever had
one'. Others found him lean, elegant, courteous and meticulous. Most agreed
that he had a 'reflective', even 'strangely romantic', temperament and was apt to
discourse widely and entertainingly on SIS history, politics and personalities.[12]
Vivian's chief duties were tracking the international communist movement, or
fascist and German organisations – his Irish work was something of a sideline.[13]
Yet he continued to lead SIS's Irish activities until the end of the Second World
War, and would play an important role in shaping the British intelligence community's relationship with the country. Vivian worked with Captain Guy Liddell,
the head of B Division, MI5's counter-espionage branch. The two agencies collaborated closely on Irish affairs during the 1930s, although SIS was the dominant partner for most of this period.

The 1930s SIS Irish network is shrouded in secrecy, and it is difficult to ascer-
tain the type of intelligence it produced, or the identity of its members. Having
been almost completely weeded from government files, only one example of its
reports remains, buried within Admiralty records. Dating from 24 November
1932, it describes a meeting of the county leaders of the Army Comrades Association (the forerunner of the Blueshirts).[14] It is possible to judge the frequency
of this material as each report was labelled 'QRS' and numbered sequentially:
twenty-eight reports were produced between August and November 1932 and
a total of 154 by November 1939 (when the next report surfaces in government
records).[15] Thus, the volume of intelligence was greatest during the tense early
years of the de Valera administration, thereafter trailing off. As for the identity
of the agents, MI5 later described it as a ' "static" network' and stated that 'at no
time did S.I.S. employ "trained agents" in the usual sense of this term'.[16] It seems
that the network was composed of loyalist residents in southern Ireland, the

type who had made up Admiral 'Blinker' Hall's secret coastwatching network in Ireland during the First World War, who formed an informal intelligence service for Gretton and Gwynne in the mid-1920s, and who provided discreet assistance for recruitment to the British armed services. SIS also received the assistance of the RUC, which may have reactivated some of its informants from 1925: Vivian visited Belfast in 1932 and entered into 'special relations' with the head of the RUC Criminal Investigation Department, Inspector E. Gilfillan.[17] In many ways the SIS network was simply a formalisation of the channels by which rumour and individual observation from the loyalist community in Ireland, often conditioned by political bias, had always reached British policy-makers. Its chief distinguishing feature was its secrecy. As MI5 later remarked, 'the reports furnished by this service did not do more than give a limited cross section of private opinion on current events of political or public interest in Eire'.[18] There is little evidence that the SIS operation helped the British government to understand the dynamics of Irish politics in this period; indeed, there are some indications that it fed alarmist and unfounded scares into the policy-making system.[19]

The hasty, half-hearted introduction of secret intelligence collection techniques in 1932 could not compensate for the structural deficiencies in Britain's intelligence relationship with the Irish Free State. The lack of a senior representative in Dublin was never more keenly felt – London did not receive the high quality political intelligence that would normally be supplied by an embassy or High Commission. Peters, the Trade Commissioner, did his best, but he lacked status in both capitals. The only other source of official information from southern Ireland was the Royal Navy. The commanding officers of the two British destroyers stationed in the south-west produced weekly reports on the political situation, which were circulated by the Admiralty to other government departments. However, the quality of this intelligence depended on the contacts that officers made onshore. There was a tendency for naval officers to associate with the loyalist class and to remain suspicious of anyone else: for example, when handing over his duties, one naval commander advised that 'it was safer to regard unknown persons as knaves until they themselves proved their honest intentions'.[20] The priority that naval officers assigned to intelligence work also varied considerably. Some made a conscious effort to cultivate people onshore and to analyse political developments in the country; others were more concerned with organising and recording the frequent sporting competitions (football, cricket, boxing, to name a few) in which the ships' crews were pitted against the army garrisons. The navy's intelligence capacity was further hampered by a change in deployment in 1933 due to fear of IRA attack. The families of officers were evacuated; henceforth, destroyers were restricted to short stays and mostly confined to the Treaty Ports. This made it difficult for commanding officers to build up relationships onshore or to get an accurate understanding of Irish politics.[21]

Instead of official reports, the British government was reliant on *ad hoc* sources of information. A range of well-connected Anglo-Irish individuals, who were not representative of Irish political opinion, queued up to give their advice on the Irish situation. These included a prominent earl, a political economist from Glasgow university, an Irish judge, a Harley Street doctor, a Church of Ireland minister and a retired British army officer living in Co. Kerry.[22] British officials also liaised with a new group within the Free State – the leaders of the Irish political opposition. British policy was designed in conjunction with, and in some cases at the behest of, Cumann na nGaedheal leaders. The danger was that their interests were not identical with British interests: their goal was not the settlement of the Anglo-Irish dispute, but their own return to power.[23] When the British did attempt to conduct 'secret diplomacy' with de Valera, they employed intermediaries who were sometimes of comic unsuitability: one of the more bizarre was the champion Irish jockey who met with the Secretary of State for Dominion Affairs at Gatwick racecourse, and later called him from a cabinet meeting at 10 Downing Street.[24] Southern Ireland still occupied an anomalous position in relation to the British intelligence and foreign relations systems.

High politics and subversive undercurrents

T HE deficiencies of British intelligence were manifested in the government's inability to comprehend the character, intentions and political strength of Éamon de Valera and his Fianna Fáil government; and a persistent exaggeration of the power of the subversive undercurrents that swirled through Irish politics. The British response was conditioned by many years of neglect and ignorance. There had been no steady flow of political intelligence into Whitehall before the 1932 election; Fianna Fáil's strategy and gradual rise to electoral dominance were barely recorded, let alone understood. Similarly, Éamon de Valera remained the chief bogeyman of 1922–3, the man who had rejected the treaty and caused the Civil War. This was always a simplistic analysis, and there was no recognition of the political journey de Valera had travelled over the subsequent decade. The MI5 file on de Valera, recently opened to the public, contains almost no material from after the revolutionary period: it presents an image frozen in 1923. As a result, when de Valera took power in 1932 he was no less than a demon figure to British observers: the words 'lunatic', 'visionary', 'dreamer', 'crank' were sprinkled in letters, diaries and minutes.[25] A Secretary of State for Dominion Affairs who later developed a good relationship with the Irish leader acknowledged that at this time he saw him 'as the arch-traitor among Irish rebels against the British Crown – an unscrupulously mischievous enemy of my country, my compatriots (including presumably myself) and everything else British.'[26]

It was assumed that de Valera was closely tied to militant republicans and the IRA, just as he had been a decade previously. His immediate relaxation of security measures appeared to confirm this, and it was given the most sinister interpretation. A journalist from the *Chicago Tribune*, who was interviewed by British ministers, returned from Dublin with 'weird prophecies', reporting that 'the gunmen were expecting to be set free and made Generals in the Free State Army.'[27] Major Ralph Glyn, Ramsay MacDonald's private parliamentary secretary and a director of an Irish railway company, travelled to Dublin and wrote on his return:

> The outstanding feature of the political situation is the influence of the Irish Republican Army. Nobody doubts that they have the Fianna Fail Government entirely in their power, and it is believed that President de Valera can neither move forward nor back and that he is under continued threats by the extremists of the I.R.A.[28]

The Prime Minister agreed that de Valera 'will do nothing except what is a step to an Irish Republic, and is undoubtedly a complete prisoner to the Irish Republican Army'. Behind it all, he claimed, was the romance of force and of arms – shooting, murdering and being murdered. 'It is a gay adventure of the fool put into a china shop in hob nail boots with liberty to smash.'[29] MI5 was also appalled by the decision to 'set at liberty a number of the most extreme Republicans' and found it 'impossible to say what the situation may be in a few months time'.[30] This image of de Valera as in league with the IRA led to the conclusion that he was an intractable fanatic, impervious to negotiation; London had no option but to work towards his downfall.

In the second half of 1932 there was a temporary shift in British perceptions of de Valera. Increased personal contact meant that his fiendish mask slipped. British representatives, though they still commented on his obstinacy and fanaticism, found the Irish leader friendly and sincere. They briefly saw him as a possible victim, rather than beneficiary, of IRA violence: there were suggestions that he might find himself the target of IRA assassination for not being radical enough.[31] Yet the Irish government's repression of the Blueshirt movement in 1933, which was regarded as a partisan, unjustified measure, reinforced all the earlier suspicions. The Secretary of State for Dominion Affairs, the former union leader Jimmy Thomas, gloomily informed his colleagues that 'there was no evidence to support the view that Mr. de Valera was leaning to the Right;

the evidence was the other way.' He added that the dismissal of the Garda Chief Commissioner, General Eoin O'Duffy, was 'clearly dictated by the I.R.A.' [32]

A belief in the extremist nature of the de Valera regime was accompanied by British concern over subversive forces in the Irish Free State. Ireland was once again regarded as a place of fanaticism, violence, intimidation and instability, where gunmen cast a long shadow. Initially there were persistent rumours that the IRA, unhappy with de Valera's moderate policies, might attempt a *coup d'état* against the government: the British cabinet was concerned by reports of an imminent IRA rising in June 1932.[33] Lord Granard (Anglo-Irish landowner, Master of the Horse at the royal court, and chairman of Arsenal Football Club from 1936 to 1939) told ministers that de Valera 'held office substantially at the will of the extremists'; 'the danger was that there might be a *coup d'état*, resulting in the removal of the present Government and the substitution of the Revolutionary Party.'[34] A year later Henry Hall, an Australian history student returning from Ireland, stated that the IRA was 'growing in power and numbers' and plotting a 'violent revolutionary move in the near future. ... He was told that in some parts of the West the noise of firing at night almost reminded one of the front in France.'[35]

Concern over the IRA was accompanied by a renewed preoccupation with the threat of communist subversion in southern Ireland. The British intelligence community, after a decade studying the gap between Bolshevik rhetoric and reality, did not exaggerate this threat to the same extent as in the early 1920s. One MI5 officer presciently identified the contradictions inherent in any co-operation between the communist party and the IRA. 'The aims of the two bodies differ so widely as to prevent any permanent basis of agreement', he wrote. 'It could only have been Irishmen that would seriously have thought that persons adhering to the policy of the Third International could work in peace and amity for any length of time with a fanatical Nationalist Catholic body.'[36] Yet, another MI5 officer, Brigadier 'Jasper' Harker, had 'no doubt that the extreme Irish Republican element' would be offered, and would accept, 'assistance from the C.P.G.B. and the Soviet Government, in their endeavours to embarrass the British Government.'[37] MI5 and Special Branch realised that their understanding of the role of communist ideas in domestic Irish politics was limited: 'we are entirely in the dark as to the progress that subversive influences have achieved in the Free State', one officer confessed in March 1932.[38] This information vacuum was eagerly filled by right-wing politicians and the *ad hoc* observers who provided information to the British government. A number of correspondents pointed to the risk of a communist takeover in the Free State. Like Michael Collins before him, de Valera was compared to a Kerensky figure, who might be displaced by the extreme forces that he had stirred up to obtain power.[39] Viscount Hailsham, the Secretary of State for War and the most diehard cabinet minister on Ireland, was certainly preoccupied with this notion: 'I think that there is a real danger of the Communists getting control', he wrote.[40]

In 1932 the British press was filled with alarmist tales about the growth of the IRA and communism in Ireland. This was common to newspapers of all political shades – the *New Statesman and Nation*, the *Daily Telegraph*, the *Observer*, *The Economist* and, of course, the *Morning Post*.[41] The most extraordinary story appeared in the *Evening Standard*. In October 1932 it ran a series of eight articles blessed with titles such as 'Secrets of the I.R.A.: The Power Behind the Scenes in Ireland', 'I Visit the Army's "Hush-Hush" Headquarters', and 'Leader Who Must Keep Forever on the Move: Twomey, the Mystery Man', complete with photographs of IRA leaders and parades. The articles were written by an unnamed 'special correspondent' who went to the Ireland 'to inquire into the strength and organisation of the Irish Republican Army':

> What I saw startled me. I think it will startle you. I saw a country threatened with civil war. Ireland is in the grip of the I.R.A. Mr. De Valera is the President of the Free State Executive, but the virtual rulers of the 26 counties are the chiefs of the I.R.A. ... In every village and town in the Free State the I.R.A. has its outposts ... 'It is the power of the Gun', the local people say.

Despite being 'warned off' on numerous occasions by men in trench coats whose pockets 'bulged significantly', the intrepid journalist discovered IRA units whose drilling 'would not have discredited a Guards regiment'. He eventually 'penetrated to the secret headquarters' of the IRA in Dublin and interviewed the IRA Chief of Staff, Maurice Twomey. He was told that the IRA boasted a strength of between 30,000 and 40,000 (although another informant claimed that they could put a force of well over 100,000 men into the field). In contrast, the national army was dismissed as small, of 'doubtful allegiance' and, in apparent contrast to the IRA, 'far from possessing the efficiency of the British Army'. The correspondent also reported that Russian-trained communists were infiltrating the IRA and 'under the pretence of a patriotic passion to free "ould Oireland" from tyranny ... inciting the more illiterate against England'. The articles ended with a sombre appeal: 'Ireland is a distracted, faction-ridden, intimidated country. Is it too late for some strong, wise men to deflect her from the path of fanaticism and into the path of ... safety?' [42]

To many British observers, the Blueshirts were these 'strong, wise men'. The emergence of the Army Comrades Association was viewed with considerable sympathy and regarded as an inevitable response to Valera's partisan government. The structural biases of British intelligence meant that loyalists and opposition elements kept London well informed about the development of the movement, casting it in a positive light. Major Ralph Glyn, the Prime Minister's parliamentary secretary, witnessed its usefulness at first hand during a Cumann na nGaedheal meeting in Trim, Co. Meath. He concluded that the 'White Army', which was 'recruited from a far better class of person', would deter the IRA from attempting a *coup d'état* should a Cosgrave administration be re-elected.[43] It is perhaps not a coincidence that the only surviving report from the Irish SIS network deals with this subject. It describes a secret meeting of the county leaders of the Army Comrades Association, which proposed that 'some secret arrangement might be entered into between the British Government and the Cosgrave Party in Ireland anterior to the general election'. Under this arrangement the British would agree to a total remission of the land annuities, the reopening of the boundary question and the return of the Treaty Ports, while the Cosgrave party would agree to maintain the oath and to introduce a bond to ensure that the arrangement would remain inviolate for at least forty years. In the meantime, SIS reported, the Army Comrades Association would organise mobile columns in each county, and 'become thoroughly acquainted with the personnel and arrangements of the I.R.A.' If Cumann na nGaedheal returned to power, 'these mobile columns would be directed to arrest and disarm every available member of the I.R.A.'[44] There is no evidence that London intervened to promote the growth of the Blueshirts (although the more paranoid Fianna Fáil leaders believed so), but the British did welcome the movement as a sign of popular discontent with de Valera's policies and as a force that could possibly bring down the government.

However, as factional violence increased during 1933, and the Blueshirts adopted the trappings of fascism, the movement was seen in a more negative light – as a force pushing the Free State towards outright civil war. This was an outcome that was frequently predicted in reports reaching Whitehall. London was perhaps unfortunate that the senior naval officer in Irish waters in the summer of 1933, Lieutenant-Commander W. N. T. Beckett of HMS *Amazon*, had strong biases about Ireland: he provided a number of warnings that civil strife would break out.[45] This thesis was also developed in a series of long, scholarly surveys by Professor W. R. Scott, a distinguished economist at Glasgow University. Writing from his home in Omagh, Co. Tyrone, Scott's analysis was that the Free State was economically 'living on its hump' and heading inexorably for a total collapse. The 'forces of disorder' would eventually topple de Valera, who would face 'the usual nemesis of the revolutionary: to pave the way for

Revolution, it is necessary to bring Government into contempt. Once people are educated in licence, especially the Irish, it is very difficult to establish respect for law.' Scott's partial interpretation of events in the Free State, replete with negative stereotypes of the native Irish, reflected his unionist background.[46] However, they were well received in London, where Scott had family links with Sir Edward Harding, the Permanent Under-Secretary at the Dominions Office. They were circulated to the Director of Military Intelligence and the Director of Naval Intelligence, to their obvious gratitude. (Other more sober appraisals around the same time did not go beyond the Dominions Office.)[47]

In 1933 the British press continued to tell their tall tales of Free State turmoil. Press interest peaked on a weekend in August when a planned Blueshirt march in Dublin was banned by the Irish government. The Dominions Office noted how 'the more sensational of the London papers did their best to work up a scare about an impending "rising" in the Free State', blaring headlines such as 'Threatened Coup d'Etat' and 'Armed Rising Imminent'.[48] Even the BBC felt that it should give the public an impartial survey of the facts in view of the 'wild stories' about Ireland appearing in the press. After consulting the Dominions Office, the BBC Director-General, Sir John Reith, arranged for a soothing talk to be given on an evening radio show on 11 August 1933.[49]

Once again gunrunning scares provide a good indicator of the level of British anxiety. There was a string of intelligence reports, press articles and rumours in 1932 and 1933 relating to the smuggling of weaponry to revolutionaries in Ireland. Recently released documents reveal that this began with a series of reports from SIS stations in continental Europe. On 26 May 1932, acting on information from a 'sure source', SIS reported that the motor vessel *Jeanette* had loaded 500 tons of munitions of Russian origin at 'a small Rhine port'. She had proceeded to Antwerp, where she had taken on a further 5,000 revolvers, 1,100 light carbines, 300 bombs and a large quantity of ammunition, before departing for Ireland. Two weeks later SIS reported that the weapons had been transferred at sea to smaller vessels: there were 'some eighteen small steamers cruising around the Irish coast loaded with special cargoes', as they dared not enter any port.[50] Similar stories surfaced three months later, when a 'notorious … arms supplier' named Herr Bruno Spiro was implicated in a plot to smuggle arms from Czechoslovakia to Ireland via Hamburg, disguised as cases of sugar. Spiro was an old hand at Irish gunrunning: he had provided the weapons that were landed by the Ulster Volunteers at Larne in 1914.[51]

Reports of gunrunning led to intense naval activity around the Irish coast. Following the first SIS warning, destroyers at British ports and at Cobh were 'scrambled' and ordered to patrol the seas. They searched at least one ship in

Irish waters, although no arms were discovered. London also informed de Valera of these gunrunning reports and put the ships of the Royal Navy at his disposal.[52] However, the Irish authorities 'felt sceptical as to the existence of the gun-runners' and protested when the British carried out searches in Irish waters. On 10 June de Valera went even further and asked that British destroyers stay out of Irish waters altogether.[53] The Admiralty angrily retorted that under these conditions its patrols were a waste of time and money. It withdrew the extra destroyers and instructed those stationed at the Irish Treaty Ports that they could not stop or search suspected ships, only shadow them.[54] This incident reflected the almost complete absence of any security or intelligence co-operation between the British and Irish states. To London it was a deeply unsatisfactory state of affairs, as it was by no means certain that the SIS intelligence had been incorrect. Although the Dominions Office came to share Dublin's scepticism about the reports, some British cabinet ministers had no doubt that gunrunning had 'been going on more or less the whole year'.[55]

Stories of rampant IRA gunrunning frequently appeared in the British press. The *Evening Standard* correspondent gave a typically graphic account in October 1932:

> There is more gun-running going on in Ireland today than at any time during the last ten years. The I.R.A. have dumps all over the country, with large stores of revolvers, rifles and ammunition. ... In hundreds of places along the West Coast no attempt is made to work in secret. It is possible many nights to hear the signal of a ship's siren calling its message to watchers on shore that another case of guns has been brought safely across the Atlantic and that a motor-boat is wanted to take it ashore.[56]

These stories peaked in the summer of 1933, at the time of the confrontation between the Blueshirts and the Irish government. On 30 June an unusually convincing story in the *Daily Herald* described how 3,000 rifles and a quarter of a million rounds of ammunition had been smuggled ashore by the IRA on the Cork coast. The paper contained an interview with an English 'master mariner', 'well-known in London mercantile marine circles', who claimed to have navigated the smugglers' ship. Apparently, he was approached by an Irishman in a quayside cafe in Antwerp, questioned about his knowledge of the Irish coastline and asked to take the cargo across. They steamed for four days, rendezvoused with three Irish trawlers at night, and transferred their load. After opening a case of whiskey to celebrate, they returned whence they came. 'I was paid what I was bargained for', the English mariner said, 'and there, as far as I was concerned, the matter ended.'[57]

Around the same time, in July 1933, the intelligence services produced an extraordinary report of IRA–Soviet co-operation, involving massive shipments of arms. This report claimed that the IRA had signed two separate agreements with the Executive Committee of the Comintern in April 1933. The political agreement, negotiated in New York, contained the following text:

The Political Secretariat of the Executive Committee of the Communist International recognises the Irish Republican Party as a fighting detachment of the nationalist revolutionary forces which is fighting against British imperialism and the government of the Irish capitalists; taking this fact into consideration the Political Secretariat thinks it necessary to render the Irish Republican Party every possible assistance and to support it politically.

The military convention was signed in Bergen by the Military Section of the Executive Committee of the Communist International, with the assistance of Soviet military intelligence (Razvedupr or GRU). It required the Soviets to secure arms, ammunition and explosives for the IRA. Under these arrangements, 6,000 rifles, 60 bomb-throwers and 120 heavy and light machine-guns had already been landed in Ireland in May 1933; a total of 80,000 rifles, together with a considerable number of machine guns, would be smuggled into the country by the end of the summer. These were huge numbers, and would have made the IRA better armed than the Irish National Army.

This report reached the British intelligence services through convoluted channels. It originated with one Goutchkoff, a former minister in the Kerensky government then living in Paris, who passed it to Anatole Baikaloff, a leading Russian émigré in London. They were part of an informal network of White Russian exiles who had settled in western Europe and were actively working to topple the Bolshevik regime. Baikaloff gave it to the Duchess of Atholl, a Conservative MP and a tireless campaigner against the Soviet regime (as well as female circumcision in Africa). She passed it to Viscount Hailsham, the Secretary of State for War, who then provided it to SIS and MI5. This is a good example of how informal connections between White Russians and the British élite were used to feed information into the British intelligence system (which was not dissimilar to interactions between southern Irish loyalists and the British establishment). Years later MI5 came to the opinion that Baikaloff was 'a highly unreliable informant'. But at the time this report was taken seriously: it struck Major Vivian as 'not by any means impossible, or even improbable, information'.[58]

Another possible channel for arms smuggling consisted of Spanish fishing trawlers. In the early 1930s Spanish vessels became a frequent sight on the southern Irish coast, where they called for coal, water and other supplies while fishing off the island. That seafood might not be their only cargo was first imputed in June 1932. The captains of two Welsh trawlers informed the Ministry of Agriculture and Fisheries that they had observed Spanish ships entering 'small secluded coves' where they would certainly not have gone for the purposes of fishing. They suspected the Spanish of smuggling arms. This accusation was taken seriously in London. Senior officials were summoned to an emergency meeting on a Sunday, following which a member of the Dominions Office was sent to Sir Vernon Kell's house in Kensington. (MI5 had taken over responsibility for tracking illicit arms traffic from the Special Branch in 1931.) Kell immediately despatched an MI5 officer by the five o'clock train to Swansea to interview the two Welsh skippers. The results were disappointing. The MI5 officer discovered that Spanish trawlers visited Irish bays to sell their catch; the real complaint of the Welsh skippers was that the Spanish undercut them and stole their market. There was no evidence of gunrunning. Kell admitted that 'this was a complete wash-out'.[59]

Accusations that the Spanish trawlers were engaged in more sinister activities resurfaced a year later thanks to the army garrison and naval officers at Berehaven. In 1933 Spanish trawlers began calling for supplies at Bere Island, close to the British forts. Their presence irritated the British army commander, Major R. A. Woods. He worried about infectious diseases carried by 'unvetted Southern European sailors', about the danger to the virtues of the local women who were 'pestered and insulted by Spanish crews' and, above all, about the opportunities for illicit gunrunning.[60] In June 1933 the senior naval officer, Lieutenant-Commander Beckett of HMS *Amazon*, received instructions from London 'for Spanish trawlers to be kept under particular observation in future'. Beckett, an energetic and ebullient character, threw himself into this detective work with great enthusiasm. When a Spanish trawler docked in Cobh for recoaling, an officer was sent in plain clothes 'to look them over and see if he could find out what they were doing'. Beckett also built up his own informal intelligence network onshore among 'right thinking people' to report on republican activity. He developed an intense suspicion of a successful farmer, businessman and local politician, the 'uncrowned king of Bere Island', Mr. Murphy. 'I am prepared to say', he informed the Admiralty, 'that there is no underhand work or illicit practice between Old Head of Kinsale and Kenmare River in which Mr. Murphy is not implicated, or of which he is not cognisant.'[61]

Beckett pestered the new local Garda Superintendent, Patrick Doyle, to take action against presumed arms smuggling by the Spanish trawlers. (He dismissed Doyle's explanation that the ships were calling at the island to purchase 'contraband liquor' on the basis that 'the Spaniards being a nation of wine and brandy drinkers, would hardly consider the idea of imbibing "potheen" '.) When Doyle proved less than energetic, Beckett came to the startling conclusion that the Free State authorities were deliberately allowing gunrunning to go ahead. He described Bere Island as 'a veritable "Tom Tiddler's Ground" ' where British powers were 'strictly limited' and Free State supervision could 'hardly be said to exist'. He claimed that the previous Superintendent, a 'hard man', had been replaced by the junior, compliant Doyle for a reason: Doyle had been instructed to adopt a passive attitude because the Free State government 'desired to have the Berehaven "bolt-hole" open' for arms smuggling. This was an extraordinary notion, which made little sense. It was a product of the naval officer's obsession with republican conspiracies. Yet Beckett was well respected at the Admiralty, and his accusations were accepted without much question by the Dominions Office. 'I think that you should see this odd story', a civil servant noted to a colleague. 'There seems little doubt that these Spanish trawlers are engaged in smuggling, possibly arms, and that the local police are conniving at the proceedings.'[62]

The rampant arms smuggling suspected by the British government would have strengthened the subversive, paramilitary forces in southern Ireland (whether the IRA or the Blueshirts) and made a *coup d'état* or civil war more likely. But a reinvigorated and well-armed IRA also created a threat of direct attack on British interests. One likely target was Northern Ireland. This was certainly a preoccupation of northern unionists. De Valera's election to government appeared to confirm their worst prophecies about the instability and danger of the Irish Free State. He was quickly branded as 'the puppet of the IRA'. Under headlines such as 'Wave of Republicanism Sweeps the Free State', 'Recruiting Campaign in Full Swing' and 'Mr Cosgrave in Grave Danger of His Life', the *Northern Whig* predicted that a rampant IRA would plunge the country into Bolshevism.[63] 1932 also saw an almost exact repeat of the IRA invasion scares of 1922. On 4 July 1932 James Craig (now Lord Craigavon) brought a deputation from Tyrone and Fermanagh to the War Office, where they were interviewed by Viscount Hailsham:

> The Deputation said that the B. Specials were incapable of dealing with armed forces such as the I.R.A. had available for making incursions across the border and that it was possible that a raid might be made on Enniskillen and great damage to property and loss of life occasioned. The situation was in their opinion worse than in 1925 and comparable to that which existed in 1922.

The only 'evidence' that the deputation could provide was that 'strange characters had recently come into Enniskillen, and also that arms had recently been landed in Ireland'. Nevertheless, they asked for a large increase in the size of the British army garrison in the province. Though unwilling to sanction this, the War Office instructed the local British commander to concert special plans with the Inspector General of the RUC.[64]

Another likely target of IRA attack consisted of the garrisons of the three Treaty Ports in southern Ireland. As Anglo-Irish relations deteriorated during the summer of 1932, the cabinet, the First Lord of the Admiralty and the Chief of the Imperial General Staff all expressed concern about 'the possibility of hostile action by revolutionary bodies (especially the Irish Republican Army) in the Irish Free State against the Coast Defence Stations'. This threat led to the decision to create the clandestine SIS network in the Free State in August 1932.[65] Measures were also taken to improve the defences of the army garrisons. Extra destroyers were discreetly sent to Irish waters.[66] Onshore, £6,000 was spent on improving the defences of Bere Island and Cobh against land attacks: barbed wire entanglements, concrete pill boxes and flood lights were erected at each fort.[67] Finally, sometime in 1932 or 1933, 'very secret plans' were drawn up 'for rapid reinforcement of the three reserved ports and Northern Ireland District in the event of trouble in the Irish Free State'.[68] It was agreed that British troops would take offensive action against any IRA units gathering for an attack without consulting the Free State authorities, as it was believed that 'any detailed communication to the Irish Free State Government … might possibly come to the knowledge of the revolutionary bodies concerned'.[69] Evidently London did not trust de Valera to keep any secrets from the IRA.

Anxiety about an IRA attack on the Treaty Ports reached a peak in June 1933. The source of this scare was London, not the local commanders, who were by then inclined to disbelieve rumours of IRA action. On the night of 24 June the senior naval officer in Irish waters received a cipher telegram from the Admiralty instructing him to take special precautions against an IRA attack, possibly involving 'armed boat raids'. The next morning an army officer hurriedly arrived from Britain with information that 'the Irish Free State were expected to declare a Republic at any time, in which case it was considered that the I.R.A. might get out of hand and attack the forts'. The military garrisons were instructed to institute extra patrols and to burn searchlights at night. A submarine was sent to the area. HMS *Westminster* took up a position in an outer anchorage by the forts, kept steam up at night and cleared away her guns for action. These precautions remained in place for some days, as the army authorities in Britain were 'still very uneasy about the situation over there'. They were only relaxed when the General Officer Commanding of Western Command visited Cobh personally on

9 July and 'came to the conclusion that the situation was not so serious as he had thought.'[70] This was a curious incident. The warning came from London, and the local commanders do not appear to have been unduly worried. The naval officers, in particular, reported that the situation was 'perfectly normal' and counselled against extraordinary protective measures, as they only excited local press comment.[71] The most likely source of this scare was the rudimentary SIS network in Ireland – after all, its chief purpose was to warn of planned attacks on the British garrisons. It shows both the deficiencies of its intelligence and the jitteriness of those in London handling it.

It is clear that in 1932 and 1933 the British government had the gravest suspicions of the de Valera government and attributed major importance to subversive forces in southern Ireland, in particular to the IRA. The diehard unionist perspective on Irish affairs held sway within British government circles. This had a significant influence on British policy. The assumption that de Valera was an intractable fanatic – in league with the IRA, incapable of good government and impervious to negotiation – led to the conclusion that Britain had no option but to work towards his downfall. It was a principal reason behind the decision to impose a crippling special duty on Irish imports in July 1932. Ostensibly, the purpose of this measure was to recoup the loss of the land annuities that the Irish government had withheld. But the main issue was political not financial – the oath of allegiance and not the annuities. In reality, London was attempting to use economic sanctions to topple de Valera administration. British ministers contemplated a 'purely temporary' tariff regime, 'a short and sharp campaign which would result in the election of a new Government in the I.F.S.'[72] Over the coming months, convinced that this would be successful, they adopted a sufficiently intransigent position to ensure that all negotiations with de Valera failed.[73] The basis for this sanguine opinion was a series of reports from opposition leaders and loyalists in southern Ireland. Indeed, the policy was devised in conjunction with Cumann na nGaedheal representatives, who saw in it the key to their own re-election. London felt that it could not be abandoned without letting down their Irish allies.[74]

British assessments of the power of Irish subversive organisations, on the Left and the Right, also influenced policy deliberations. First, gunrunning reports and rumours of an imminent IRA coup contributed to an unfounded expectation in autumn 1932 that de Valera would be forced to make a compromise settlement with Britain, as it was thought that only by doing this could he save himself from the republican gunmen. In November 1932 Thomas told his cabinet colleagues that 'Mr. de Valera had become seriously perturbed regarding the growth of Communist tendencies in the I.R.A., and was himself inclined to lean more towards the Right and genuinely to desire peace with this country'.[75] Yet this was not borne out. When de Valera took strong measures to crush the Blueshirts the following year, British ministers gave up any hope that he would seek compromise out of fear of the IRA. Instead they placed their hopes on subversive undercurrents bringing down the de Valera government. The premise of British policy was that the economic sanctions would eventually produce a 'breaking point', 'a civil rising against impossible conditions', which would sweep de Valera from power. They welcomed the emergence of the Blueshirts as a potential nucleus for such a rising. Thus, British policy-makers had an ambivalent attitude towards the rise in political violence in Ireland in 1933: on the one hand, they were appalled; on the other hand, they saw it as evidence that their policy of destabilising the Irish government was working. They accepted that things might have to get worse before they got better.[76]

A bankrupt policy

THE British policy of economic sanctions and political intransigence was a complete failure. This was demonstrated by political developments in the Irish Free State after 1932. The Fianna Fáil administration did not collapse in the face of electoral resistance or civil disorder. Indeed, far from suffering any damage, de Valera 'sounded the trumpet for the "fight against England"', to quote the British Trade Commissioner, and 'got immense political mileage out of the economic war'. Fianna Fáil swept to victory in a national election in January 1933, increasing its share of the vote from 44.5 to 49.7 per cent and winning an overall majority in the Dáil for the first time. This strengthened de Valera's position and gave him a mandate for more radical constitutional reform. Over the next four years he slowly and methodically stripped away the objectionable features of the Anglo-Irish Treaty: the right of Irish citizens to appeal to the Privy-Council in London, the position of the Governor-General as the British monarch's representative in Dublin, the role of the crown in Irish internal affairs. This culminated in the adoption of a new, essentially republican, constitution in 1937, although de Valera refrained from declaring a republic; he simultaneously passed legislation associating the country with the British crown for the purpose of external affairs, and thereby kept the state (now renamed 'Éire' or 'Ireland') in the commonwealth by a thread. By peaceful, constitutional means he had achieved the position that he had been prepared to fight for during the 1922–3 Civil War.[77]

Éamon de Valera was more than capable of containing the subversive forces that had been unleashed by the unsettled political conditions. His actions in crushing the Blueshirt threat have already been described. He also began to take similar steps against the IRA. The militant and constitutional wings of Irish republicanism were always destined for a break. IRA leaders were deeply unhappy with the slow pace of de Valera's reforms and police interference in their activities. For his part, De Valera was prepared to tolerate the existence of the IRA while he wrought his constitutional changes, but he would not tolerate violent acts. The security apparatus of the state was increasingly turned against republicans.

Matters came to a head after three IRA murders in 1935 and 1936. One victim was the son of a land agent embroiled in a dispute with the IRA, another was a suspected informer from Co. Wexford. The most notorious incident illustrates the dangers that southern loyalists faced when giving assistance to the British government. On 24 March 1936 a 73-year old retired naval officer, Vice-Admiral Henry Boyle Somerville, was gunned down on the doorstep of his home in Co. Cork. A popular man, active in the Cork Historical and Archaeological Society, Somerville came from a prominent local Anglo-Irish family with a long maritime tradition: his brother, Hugh, had served as Senior Naval Officer at Queenstown in 1922. He was part of the network of loyalist referees that the British armed services had set up to screen potential recruits after the IRA espionage scare in 1925. A card thrust through the letterbox stated that he had been killed by the IRA for assisting locals to join the Royal Navy.[78]

These murders forced de Valera to publicly break with the gunmen. The Garda began to suppress IRA activities, and dozens of IRA men were brought before the military tribunals. Raids in April and May 1936 led to the arrest and imprisonment of practically all the main leaders of the IRA, including the Chief of Staff, Maurice Twomey. The IRA was officially proscribed on 18 June 1936. The security crack-down was accompanied by other Fianna Fáil policies, such as the creation of a volunteer army reserve and the granting of pensions to veterans of the revolutionary war, which lured away many actual and potential IRA members. The organisation went into a rapid decline: its strength fell from 8,036 in September 1934, to 7,358 in late 1935, and to a mere 3,844 in November 1936 (of whom only 2,038 could be considered active). There was also dissension and turnover within the leadership: Seán MacBride, Tom Barry and Mick Fitzpatrick all acted as Chief of Staff in quick succession between 1936 and 1938.[79] Historians agree that after 1936 'the IRA was a spent force' and was 'no longer a formidable force on the domestic political scene'.[80]

These developments had two effects on British intelligence and British perceptions of Ireland. First, the overall level of British concern declined and Irish affairs received less and less attention at the ministerial level. Second, perceptions of the Irish situation began to bifurcate. Whereas before the middle of 1933 a pessimistic, diehard unionist perspective had gripped British policy-makers, afterwards this unanimity was not present. One group continued to exaggerate the vigour of the IRA, the possibility of civil war and the fanaticism of the de Valera government, while advocating the continuance of economic sanctions in an attempt to topple the regime. But another camp belittled the subversive dangers, commented on the calm and normality of mainstream Irish politics and believed that Britain should come to terms with de Valera. These conflicting interpretations were evident in the intelligence received in London, and in the opinions expressed by British policy-makers. It was a reappearance of the bipolar representation of southern Ireland that had been present in British thought since the early 1920s – the diehard unionists versus the liberal imperialists.

A dovish, liberal imperialist perspective began to appear in reports from individuals in southern Ireland by the end of 1933. Irish opposition leaders lost some of their hysterical antipathy to de Valera and changed their advice to London. For example, Frank MacDermot, a leader of the United Ireland Party, told British officials in June 1934 that de Valera was firmly in control and that the British should not expect the economic sanctions to produce a 'breaking point'.[81] Cosgrave agreed that they could not expect a collapse of the government and urged London to come to a settlement with de Valera.[82] Some of the naval commanders who assumed responsibility for the destroyers in Irish waters also produced more sober appraisals of the situation – certainly none matched the conspiratorial alarmism of Lieutenant-Commander Beckett. (This included a definitive conclusion that the crews of Spanish trawlers were not smuggling arms: they were 'a most uneducated crowd of ruffians and would hardly be capable of the crime', one naval commander wrote.)[83] The Trade Commissioner in Dublin, William Peters, who had opposed the sanctions policy from the start, also produced a number of important reports at this time, urging conciliation. He wrote in September 1934:

> De Valera ... holds the stage. He has again succeeded in splitting the opposition. His name stands as high as ever with the bulk of the people. ... My reading of the position is therefore that we should not waste time on a search for possible alternatives to a de Valera Government but should face the problem of how best to negotiate with de Valera.[84]

These moderate and conciliatory views found a receptive audience among the civil servants of the Dominions Office. They had always had reservations about the policy of using economic warfare to topple de Valera, but had been overruled by the hawkish Secretary of State, Jimmy Thomas. In November 1935 this minister was replaced by Malcolm MacDonald (whose father, Ramsay, had been Prime Minister until five months before). The new Secretary of State for Dominions Affairs saw it as his mission to restore harmony between the two countries, and he was not too bothered about the constitutional concessions that would be necessary to achieve this. He was an altogether more dynamic and persuasive operator than his predecessor, and more truly represented the views of the Dominions Office, which welcomed his arrival as 'a breath of fresh air'.[85]

However, this optimist interpretation of Irish affairs was counterbalanced by much darker assessments from hawkish diehards. For every sober and conciliatory report reaching Whitehall, there was alternative material that provided very different information. Some naval commanders continued to predict that the economic sanctions and the struggle between the IRA and Blueshirts would lead to a paroxysm.[86] At the end of 1934 Commander C. B. Turner of HMS *Versatile* presented a detailed, pessimistic analysis in which he predicted 'yet another of those convulsions which have disfigured [Irish] history from time immemorial and littered their fair country with ghastly reminders of the "troubles" of various ages'.[87] The economics professor in Co. Tyrone, W. R. Scott, still predicted that the Irish people would reach 'their breaking-point' and that 'an explosion' was likely: this might take the form 'either of an attack on Northern Ireland, or a relapse into some kind of Bolshevism'.[88] It was also a theme of a regular missive, *Notes from Ireland*, produced by the Irish Loyalist Imperial Foundation in London. In a 1935 issue it described the 'tragedy of Southern Ireland': a ruined economy, a parliament that was 'frequently reduced ... to the level of a bear-garden', a dwindling Protestant community facing constant 'intimidation'. These unionists still proffered the same quixotic solution:

> Most public men in England seem to shudder at the very mention of Southern Ireland. They just shut their eyes to the implications of what is happening there. Sooner or later the problem of the future government of the country will have to be faced afresh. The longer it is postponed the more difficult it will be, as new vested interests arise and the loyal become submerged. The experience of fourteen years has proved conclusively that there is only one possible policy in the interests of the British Isles as a whole and the security of the Realm, and that is the policy of William Pitt, which was abandoned through fear in 1921.[89]

These views were shared by Conservative politicians such as Viscount Hailsham, the Secretary of State for War, who advocated continuing economic pressure on Ireland and refused to accommodate de Valera's constitutional reforms.[90]

Because of the composition of the British government, these hawkish assessments had much influence on British policy towards Ireland. From 1931 until 1935 Britain was ruled by a coalition National Government, led by Ramsay MacDonald, in which real power was held by the Conservatives. In June 1935 MacDonald was replaced as Prime Minister by the Conservative Party leader, Stanley Baldwin. Conservative ministers tended towards the diehard unionist interpretation of Irish affairs. They refused to accept de Valera's constitutional amendments, wishfully hoping that economic pressure would lead to his replacement by a more compliant administration that would turn back to the clock to the 1921 treaty. This was not politics as the art of the possible, because by this stage the Irish opposition parties had promised that they would not reverse de Valera's reforms if elected to power. Yet, due to the system of cabinet collective responsibility, Tory ministers exercised a veto on policy towards Ireland. They blocked attempts by the Dominions Office to develop a more imaginative approach. As a result, though there was a gradual thaw in Anglo-Irish relations after 1933, there was no substantial change in the British position until 1937. A static, bankrupt policy persisted for five years.[91] One Anglo-Irish resident, Lord Granard, bemoaned the short-sightedness of British policy during this period:

> What a strange fatality has ever seemed to dog the footsteps of British Statesmen in their efforts to solve the Irish Problem. Successful, indeed signally successful, everywhere else they have ever failed here. The only conclusion that one can draw is that their intellects never got a fair chance; they were shackled either by personal prejudice, or by the urgings of those foolish people who could never see any good in Ireland. Else they could not have seemed ever unable to grasp the truth patent to all outsiders that it would be infinitely better for Great Britain – even at the worst – to have Ireland completely separated but friendly, rather than forcibly held but unfriendly, and ever waiting the opportunity to strike.[92]

F ROM 1932 until 1936 the threat to British security from Irish militant republicanism was ever present in British policy deliberations. Until the middle of 1933 there was unanimous concern over the fanaticism of the de Valera regime and the power of subversive organisations. Thereafter, this diehard unionist perspective of Irish affairs persisted among the political right and was sufficiently influential to affect policy decisions. But how accurate were these perceptions of southern Ireland? Most Irish historians have been keen to stress the peaceful, stable evolution of the Irish state. The formation of a Fianna Fáil administration is regarded as the ultimate sign of the maturity of Irish democracy. There has been a tendency to ridicule the subversive undercurrents of this time: the

Blueshirts were only playing at being fascists; the communists had no chance of acceptance in conservative Catholic Ireland; the violence between rival political factions across the country was harmless exuberance, or a last gasp of Civil War animosity. The state was never seriously threatened.[93] However, the prominence of a darker image of Irish affairs within Britain, initially shared across the political spectrum, indicates that these security threats were real. There were armed groups hostile to the state; low-level political violence was endemic; the government was compelled to use extraordinary security measures; individuals died at the hands of the IRA and the Irish security forces. This was not on the same scale as the turmoil in other European countries during the 1930s, but it was different from politics in Britain. With hindsight we can see how these forces fizzled out, but it is perhaps understandable that contemporary observers were less sure about the future of the youthful Irish democracy.[94]

Having said this, we must still conclude that the British government had a poor understanding of the Irish situation, especially in 1932 and 1933. London exaggerated the power of the subversive undercurrents that swirled beneath the political surface. The IRA never had the capacity to launch a successful *coup d'état* against the Irish government, or to seriously attack British interests; it lacked the will, the personnel and the weaponry. Its flirtation with communist ideas was brief. Shocked by the virulence of the domestic 'Red Scare', it frantically distanced itself from the Soviet Union after 1932, prohibiting its members from joining the Communist Party of Ireland.[95] In addition, the many reports of IRA gunrunning that gripped London in 1932 and 1933 appear to have been thoroughly bogus. The chief historian of the 1930s IRA states that smuggling operations at this time were 'small scale' and concentrated on the United States – stories of huge shipments of Russian weapons sailing from Europe were fantastic.[96] Similarly, the Blueshirts disintegrated at the end of 1934, and O'Duffy was pushed to the margins by Cosgrave and other moderate opposition leaders – Ireland would not follow the route of Italy, Spain or Germany. Above all, the British government had a number of misconceptions about de Valera. He was not a republican fanatic 'in the hands of the IRA'; neither did he have to give in to British demands to maintain his position. De Valera was capable of containing the militants, riding the wave of nationalism unleashed by the economic war and manipulating the situation to strengthen his position. A major cause of these misperceptions was the lack of good intelligence from Ireland, which meant that the preconceptions and biases of policy-makers in London were not adequately challenged. The result was a period of spectacularly unsuccessful policy. It only ended when the deteriorating international situation and the approach of war compelled British policy-makers to rethink old principles and prejudices.

CHAPTER 8

England's Back Door

F OR centuries the defence of the realm against foreign attack had been a
major consideration when British statesmen dealt with Ireland. It drove the
conquest and plantation of Ireland in the sixteenth and seventeenth centuries,
the passing of the Act of Union in 1801, and opposition to Irish Home Rule in
the later nineteenth and early twentieth centuries. Although it fell into abey-
ance during the 1920s and early 1930s, the deteriorating international situation
made it of dominant importance after 1936. In that year Adolf Hitler remilita-
rised the Rhineland and accelerated a massive armaments programme, while
Mussolini's Italy and an expansionist Japan threatened Britain's position in the
Mediterranean and the Far East. In response to these challenges the British government belatedly rearmed, sought alliances with friendly states and attempted
to avoid conflict by acceding to the demands of the fascist dictators. The policy
of appeasement was taken to its furthest extent by Neville Chamberlain, who
became Prime Minister on 28 May 1937. Yet he could do little to arrest the world's
slide towards armed conflict. Because of its position as England's 'back door', Ireland would have a vital strategic role in this struggle. Consequently, from 1936
defence became the most powerful factor in Anglo-Irish relations, trumping
the long-held principles and preconceptions that shaped British policy towards
Ireland.

The menacing international situation and the increasing importance of
defence made intelligence on Irish security threats more vital than ever. The
fundamental question for the British government was to what extent southern
Ireland would assist in the defence of the British empire if war came. Would it
be a hostile presence on Britain's flank? Would it participate in the war alongside Britain? Or would it adopt a stance somewhere in between – neutral but
co-operative? An assessment of the likelihood of these outcomes was necessary to inform British policy-makers as they sought to negotiate a settlement
with de Valera in 1938. The British government also faced real security threats
during this period, in the form of German propaganda and espionage activities in Ireland, and an IRA bombing campaign on English soil. In response the
British intelligence community increased its engagement with Ireland and took
advantage of a new willingness on the part of the Irish authorities to co-operate

on security matters. However, Anglo-Irish intelligence co-operation was never complete, and independent British intelligence sources remained imperfect. As a result, there was considerable unease and uncertainty about Ireland's role as war approached – to many, southern Ireland was a dangerous chink in the imperial armour.

Defence and appeasement

THREE strategic imperatives governed Britain's defence relationship with southern Ireland. The first was securing Britain from invasion or physical attack from Irish territory. Such an attack might be carried out by indigenous Irish forces, by a foreign enemy using Irish bases at the invitation of the Irish government or by a foreign enemy seizing Irish territory from the Irish state.[1] The second imperative was gaining access to Irish naval and air bases in order to protect Britain's sea communications, the 'umbilical cords' that brought the trade crucial to the country's survival. In 1933 the Director of Naval Intelligence bemoaned that policy-makers frequently ignored this aspect of Anglo-Irish relations:

> I am always struck by the fact that amidst all the views put forward on the Irish situation by authoritative people … the strategical aspect is almost never mentioned. However important the political and economic aspects may be they become of secondary interest to the strategic problem when the welfare of Great Britain and, indeed, the Empire, are concerned. One can't get over the geographical fact that Ireland is our front line trench. It is not enough that Ireland should not be in hostile hands. Unless the Navy can freely use <u>all</u> Irish waters and harbours in war (and that means their use to a certain extent in peace), it would be unable in certain wars to protect the Western Approaches and that of course would be disastrous.[2]

Britain's third strategic imperative was gaining the security and intelligence co-operation of the Irish state. It was necessary to have intelligence on the movements of enemy ships, submarines and aircraft around the island. It was also necessary to prevent enemy espionage, sabotage and propaganda on Irish soil. The holy grail of British military planners, through which all these strategic imperatives would be satisfied, was a defensive-offensive alliance under which Britain would 'guarantee the safety of the territory and communications of the Irish Free State', while the Irish state would 'guarantee every facility required by the forces of Great Britain in war.[3] In effect, it was hoped to integrate Ireland into the system of imperial defence, like the other Dominions.

However, as in so many other areas, southern Ireland was an anomaly in defence matters. None of Britain's three strategic imperatives had been addressed by 1936. A year earlier, de Valera had pledged that he would not allow Ireland to become a base for attack on its neighbour; but the failure of the Irish state to build up its defence forces, together with its unwillingness to collaborate with the British armed services, made it an easy target for foreign aggression – Britain's 'back door' was barely locked. In addition, Britain's retention of three naval bases under the 1921 Anglo-Irish Treaty was under attack. The Cosgrave government half-heartedly suggested the return of the ports in 1927; de Valera renewed this request in October 1935 with greater vigour. It became a prerequisite for an overall settlement with Britain, as de Valera realised that without their return his country would be unable to stay neutral in the coming war.[4] Finally, there was a complete absence of Anglo-Irish security and intelligence co-operation. The British government had tried on many occasions since the 1920s to secure Irish help on important security issues (such as wartime coastwatching and censorship), but they had been rebuffed.[5] Thus, when British military planners drew up an official 'War Book' in January 1936, the Free State was omitted. A special addendum euphemistically drew attention to the quandary it posed:

> With regard to the Irish Free State, it has not so far been possible to make such progress in respect of previously concerted arrangements as has been made in the case of the other Dominions, and the position generally with regard to co-operation with or by the Irish Free State … is uncertain.[6]

The implications of the Anglo-Irish stalemate for Britain's defence made the British government desperate to improve relations with the Irish government. This was illustrated by Britain's response to the new, quasi-republican Irish constitution in 1937. It was incompatible with commonwealth membership, and should have led to Ireland's expulsion; instead, London reacted with grudging acquiescence (thus radically redefined the nature of the commonwealth) because it wanted to keep Ireland 'firmly inside the Empire' for security reasons.[7] Over the following months, the new Prime Minister, Neville Chamberlain, (strongly supported by the Secretary of State for Dominion Affairs, Malcolm MacDonald) made a determined effort to find a basis for a settlement with de Valera. Defence was the primary motivation: Chamberlain admitted that he 'was very anxious to see a defence agreement with the Free State put into effect. Even an agreement which fell short of being completely satisfactory would be better than the insecurity of the present situation.'[8] Negotiations between the two governments began on 17 January 1938 and, after three months of difficult wrangling, a new Anglo-Irish Agreement was signed on 25 April 1938.

Even though defence considerations had driven the British negotiators, the agreement appeared to diminish, rather than strengthen, Britain's security: it transferred the Treaty Ports to Irish control without any guarantee that they would be available to the Royal Navy in time of war. Some Irish historians have seen nothing surprising in this, claiming that the ports were 'not strategically vital'.[9] This was not the case. Denial of the ports handicapped Britain in the Second World War: an historian of the geopolitics of Anglo-Irish relations states emphatically that it was an 'astonishing decision' by the government, and that 'the price to be paid was a heavy one'.[10] It is even more astonishing when it is realised that Britain's pivotal concession on defence was not compensated by gains elsewhere: for example, on finance, trade or relations with Northern Ireland. As the American Minister in Dublin reported, the 1938 agreement was 'a complete triumph for De Valera'.[11] The weaknesses of British intelligence played some part in bringing this about. British negotiators did not have a good understanding of the political situation in Ireland, nor of the likely risks and benefits to British security of different negotiating outcomes. This allowed de Valera to manipulate his British listeners in pursuit of his goals.

An analysis of British deliberations in 1937 and 1938 reveals some surprising views of Ireland. The British made such sweeping concessions because they feared the consequences should the *status quo* continue. Though the Admiralty insisted that the Treaty Ports were strategically important for naval operations, the War Office warned that it would require a serious military commitment to make them usable during war. If Ireland adopted a 'hostile attitude', the British would be forced to occupy the hinterland to secure the bases, which would require at least an army division, with anti-aircraft defences, at each location: it would 'involve a most formidable military commitment, and might, even so, be impossible'. The Chiefs of Staff expected raids on the ports by the IRA – a constant feature of all plans drawn up in the 1920s and 1930s. However, the perceived threat also took on a much more serious dimension. The Chiefs of Staff envisaged large-scale attack by the regular armed forces of the Irish state. They feared that initial clashes between the IRA and British troops would radicalise the population and produce a hostile government in Dublin. This more serious threat would require the deployment of large forces at each port.[12] If this was true', the Minister for Co-ordination of Defence, Sir Thomas Inskip, asked, 'was it any use our continuing to hold them?' The answer arrived at was 'no'. The British government concluded that the ports would be practically unusable if retained; therefore, it would be no worse off from a purely military point of view if the ports were surrendered to Irish control.[13]

The prospect of a 'hostile Ireland' also led to consideration of even more threatening contingencies. Not only might the Irish state authorise attacks on the British garrisons at the ports, but it might actively co-operate with Britain's enemies by granting them bases for operations. On the eve of negotiations, when asked by the cabinet to examine the consequences of an unfriendly Ireland, the Chiefs of Staff strongly stated that they 'would be confronted with an almost intolerable situation if Ireland were hostile'. It had 'even more serious implications' than the possible denial to Britain of the use of the ports, as Ireland could be used as 'a base for hostile action' by submarines, aircraft and land forces against Britain, Northern Ireland or the imperial sea trade.[14] In many ways this was simply a worst-case scenario and an unlikely one at that. Yet Malcolm MacDonald later recalled having 'a vague impression that Ireland might become an enemy' in a war. A former Labour Home Secretary concluded a gloomy discussion of the Irish dispute in his 1937 memoirs with the words: 'There are those who say, even now, that unless the Irish problem can be settled permanently and justly very soon, Ireland, in view of her immense strategic importance in any aerial war in which Britain may later be engaged, might yet become the cockpit of Europe.'[15] Even if a worst-case scenario, it was sufficiently real to act as a spur to compromise with de Valera.

The chief emotion shaping British policy towards Ireland was fear – fear of the situation that would develop if there was no settlement and the *status quo* persisted until the outbreak of war. On the other hand, the dark courses that beckoned should the British government fail to achieve a settlement were counterbalanced by the glorious benefits that would flow from success. The prize that awaited was Irish 'good will'. This was explained by Neville Chamberlain in a meeting with British ministers:

> The Prime Minister felt certain that we ought to hand the treaty ports over now. If we did it with a good grace we should have gone very far to secure that when war came we should enjoy the good will of the people of Eire. No more would be heard of the old cry 'England's difficulty Ireland's opportunity'. ... The most valuable part of our agreements with Eire would not be found in black and white. It would consist in what was written between the lines. The great gain would be that the attitude and atmosphere in Eire would be altered. Our trust would be justified by results.[16]

It was hoped that this improved atmosphere would yield tangible rewards in the three areas that affected British security: it would confirm de Valera's commitment not to allow Ireland to become a base for attack on its neighbour; it would bring about active co-operation between the defence forces of the two countries; above all, it would lead to Ireland's active participation in Britain's wars.

The last point was never clearly stated, but there was a tendency towards wilful ambiguity and wishful thinking among British policy-makers. It was hoped that by the time war began, Anglo-Irish rapprochement would have produced such good political feeling that Dublin would return to the imperial fold and fight alongside the other Dominions. At the very least, this issue was clouded with remarkable vagueness. For example, the Prime Minister wrote after one briefing, 'I think [Malcolm MacDonald] said that De V. expressed the view that we should have the use of the ports in war, though I am not quite certain about this.' [17] Many policy-makers were left with the vague feeling, a product of hope as much as anything, that Britain would get use of Irish facilities even without a prior guarantee. Thus, in the final analysis, London surrendered ports that it considered unusable in the hope of eventually getting them back.

British policy was guided by two main premises about the political situation in southern Ireland: one related to the dire consequences that would result from a failure to agree a settlement, the other to the benefits that would accrue to Britain following an amicable Anglo-Irish agreement. It reveals the schizophrenia that affected so much of the British government's dealings with Dublin in the first two decades of independence: on the one hand, a deep-rooted fear of the power of militant republicanism; on the other, a blithe optimism that the Dublin government would return to the imperial fold. Each view can be traced back to the competing strains of diehard unionism and liberal imperialism that had shaped British thinking on Ireland for almost two decades. It could be argued that both were misplaced. Certainly, any optimism that Ireland would join Britain's wars would be punctured by subsequent events. Yet this had been no more than tentative, a hope rather than a prediction; it was the fear of the negative consequences of the Anglo-Irish stalemate that had a more powerful influence on British thinking. Here the misperceptions are even more striking. The concept of a 'hostile Ireland' launching attacks on the Treaty Ports was initially stated as a conditional, a worst-case scenario ('*if* Ireland was hostile'); but it gradually metamorphosed into a prediction of what *would* occur in wartime. Although it is impossible to say what might have been, our knowledge of the strength of militant republicanism in Ireland and the conservatism of the de Valera administration indicates that these concerns were exaggerated. Perhaps a more likely outcome than violent hostility was a sullenly neutral, but acquiescent, Ireland, a context within which the British might have been able to utilise the Treaty Ports as 'mini-Gibraltars'. At least this hypothesis should have been examined. The handling of this issue, both by the cabinet and the Chiefs of Staff, does not demonstrate any great understanding of Irish affairs.

To some extent, British misperceptions reflect the deep-rooted preconceptions about Ireland that were such a feature of British policy in the 1920s and 1930s. However, they were also influenced by the statements of Irish leaders and civil servants. From the beginning of his conversations with British representatives, de Valera constantly played the 'IRA card', terrifying his listeners with warnings of what would happen if the British did not concede his demands. In a long discussion before the 1938 negotiations, he explained how initial IRA raids could escalate into full-scale Anglo-Irish war. MacDonald recounted the gist of this conversation to his colleagues:

> If we stayed in the ports, our occupation of them would remain a point of serious friction between the people of the Irish Free State and the people of Britain. The Irish regarded our occupation as an infringement of their national sovereignty. If in those circumstances we were to become engaged in war, [de Valera] was afraid that feeling in Ireland would be so strong that there would be land attacks on the ports by irresponsible but considerable Irish forces. We would, of course, have to defend them against those attacks. Military action between our forces and Irish forces on Irish soil would arouse further the hostility of the Irish people. Any possibility of their coming into the war on our side would be at the least gravely prejudiced. We might find that we were involved in the reconquest of Ireland.[18]

On the other hand, the tone of the Irish negotiators changed entirely when they spoke of the great benefits that would flow from a just Anglo-Irish settlement. During secret discussions on the eve of the negotiations, one Irish official – the Secretary of the Department of Foreign Affairs, Joseph Walshe – gave the impression that Britain would get use of the ports in wartime: 'Mr. Walshe said at once that Mr. de Valera had never said publicly that Ireland would declare its neutrality', a member of the Dominions Office recorded. 'He (Mr. Walshe) thought that Mr. de Valera would never do so, and indeed that no Government of Ireland would be in a position to do so.'[19] Though de Valera himself never gave any commitment that the ports would be made available, he left the matter vague. A few months before the negotiations, he tantalisingly held out the prospect of Irish participation in a war in a statement to Malcolm MacDonald that perfectly sums up the actual calculations behind British policy:

> We had to choose between, on the one hand, continuing our occupation of the ports, incurring the further ill-will of the Irish, risking an Irish rebellion against our occupation if we became engaged in war, and so prejudicing the whole chance of the Irish nation coming in on our side; and on the

other hand, abandoning the occupation of the ports, gaining the greater goodwill of the Irish, ushering in a period of co-operation in matters of defence, and securing at least the benevolent neutrality of the Irish and perhaps their positive military assistance in case of war.[20]

It is impossible to escape the conclusion that Irish leaders and officials were deliberately manipulating the British government, especially by playing up the threat of militant republicans. Some years earlier the leader of Clan na Gael in the United States had urged de Valera to make use of the IRA when dealing with Britain: he stated that it was 'the extreme, the fanatical thing' that frightened the English and caused 'them to seek for peace'. This had some validity: the militant republican movement was of great use to de Valera when handling the British government.[21] De Valera was only able to play the IRA card with such triumphant effect because he exploited latent fears about militant republicanism and the instability of the Irish state that were deeply engrained in British governmental perceptions. Similarly, his assertions were never challenged because of the continuing inadequacy of British political intelligence. Due to the absence of a diplomatic representative in Dublin, Whitehall had only the vaguest notion about political conditions in Ireland and the possible effects should the negotiations fail. This was recognised by Britain's wartime Representative in Dublin when he looked back at this period from the vantage point of 1945:

> The history of the negotiations in 1938 is illuminating. If there had been a British Representative in Dublin at that time the ports would not have been handed over. In a sense, Mr. Dulanty [the Irish High Commissioner in London] was the adviser of both Governments. The fact is that Mr. de Valera, in 1938, was at the end of his tether. Economically the country was on the rocks as the result of the economic war. He had to get a settlement at all costs. The farmers were in revolt. If he had come back to Dublin without a settlement he and the Fianna Fail Party would have fallen. But he saw his tactical advantage in London and he scored the Grand Slam.[22]

The giving of tangible concessions in the hope of receiving intangible rewards of goodwill – British policy towards Ireland – is the definition of the contemporary policy of appeasement. The link was often explicitly made at the time. On a number of occasions British ministers compared de Valera's unilateral constitutional reforms with Hitler's actions. Chamberlain justified the concessions by warning that, in view of a recent Anglo-Italian agreement, 'no ground must be given for the allegation that we had treated Italy better than Eire'.[23]

It is no coincidence that Winston Churchill, the main opponent of Chamberlain's appeasement of Germany, also condemned the Anglo-Irish Agreement. 'You are casting away real and important means of security for vain shadows and ease', he warned the House of Commons on 5 May 1938.[24] The role that British intelligence played in the appeasement of Germany has received detailed study, and it is possible to see parallels with London's handling of the Irish problem. In both cases there was an absence of good intelligence on the intentions of the opposing governments. In both cases there was a reversion to worst-case scenarios that magnified threats, highlighted British vulnerability and led to major concessions. And in both cases the results would ultimately disappoint.

The failure of the 1938 agreement to produce a full Anglo-Irish reconciliation was not immediately obvious. For the remainder of the year, British officials were delighted to witness the first substantive military and intelligence cooperation between the two countries since the end of the Irish Civil War. This had begun during the negotiations on 4 February 1938, when Joseph Walshe attended a meeting of Britain's Joint Planning Sub-Committee and asked for advice on how to strengthen Ireland's defences.[25] Over the coming months the Irish requested British military supplies, received 'a cartload of promiscuous documents' on defence matters and worked with the British armed services to improve the fortifications of the former Treaty Ports.[26] London's willingness to help was rewarded by Irish collaboration on security and intelligence matters. After accepting the need for a rigorous censorship, the Irish authorities accepted details of the British scheme, sent Post Office representatives to London to receive training and worked out a plan that would be implemented when war broke out.[27] They agreed to British demands to prevent their public radio transmitters from being used as navigational beacons for German planes by creating 'spoiler stations' in Britain, which simultaneously transmitted Irish radio programmes sent by landline from Dublin.[28] Most importantly, MI5 forged a counter-espionage link with Irish military intelligence (G2) that would assume enormous significance during the Second World War. (This is discussed below.) In October 1938 the Dominions Office commended de Valera for the 'extremely courteous and considerate way in which he had consulted [them] about his plans for defence'. They noted that 'in his attitude to us on questions such as defence, Mr. de Valera had always been better than his word and that we very much better friends than might appear to the outside world'.[29]

Yet defence and security co-operation never met British expectations. It was pursued by the Irish government for Irish interests, but that was all. It did not go beyond the intended policy of neutrality, or the commitment that Ireland would not become a base for attack on Britain. Indeed, a strengthened defence force, censorship and counter-espionage were just as capable of being used *against* Britain should it interfere with Irish neutrality.[30] When London sought to obtain collaboration that was inconsistent with neutrality, when British and Irish interests diverged, Dublin was prepared to go its own way. Consequently, British military chiefs experienced a series of disappointments towards the end of 1938. The Irish authorities refused to engage in joint military planning. Apart from contact on technical issues, there was little liaison between the Irish general staff and their British counterparts: the Anglo-Irish defence relationship was mediated by a diplomat, Joseph Walshe, who was closely controlled by de Valera.[31] When de Valera decided that his country needed professional military expertise he turned not to Britain, or to the commonwealth, but to the French – he intended to appoint a Gallic military adviser. Although this never materialised, the decision caused consternation in Whitehall. It was regarded as 'a breach of trust', because Dublin had been provided with highly secretive information on counter-espionage techniques and military technology. At this time London did not trust the French: Inskip stated that they were a potential enemy and 'not in any case very good at keeping secrets'. The Chiefs of Staff fulminated that de Valera 'was using this matter of a defence adviser as part of a deep political game'.[32]

The incompleteness of Anglo-Irish intelligence co-operation was epitomised by the failure to come to an agreement on wartime coastwatching. During the First World War the Admiralty had operated an extensive coastal intelligence service of 793 officers and men, who provided information on sightings of U-boats and other enemy craft. The British government urged Dublin to establish an efficient service on these lines and to share its information with London. There was some justification in this demand, as the Irish state was unable to prevent vessels from encroaching into its territorial waters. From 1938 the British repeatedly raised this matter with the Irish government as 'a matter of considerable urgency'. They offered technical assistance, suggesting Admiralty officers who could secretly travel to Dublin to advise. They even supplied a list of potential recruits for an Irish coastwatching service, drawn from retired naval personnel (although it was remarked that many were 'rather too old to be efficient for the purpose'). In July 1939 Percivale Liesching, an Assistant Under-Secretary at the Dominions Office (and future High Commissioner to South Africa), was sent to Dublin by the Director of Naval Intelligence to go into this question. Despite assurances from Irish officials, little progress was made: Liesching complained of 'the failure of the Eire authorities to respond at all to the proposals for full co-operation in Coastwatching & Intelligence Services'. It drove the Director of Naval Intelligence to consider creating his own clandestine coastwatching service in Ireland, using local personnel who remained from the First World War.[33]

This proposal would be revived in October 1939 when naval intelligence became a priority.

The lack of intelligence co-operation was accompanied by a public souring of relations between the two countries. The cause was partition. This was a personal obsession for Éamon de Valera. Like many nationalists, he conveniently ignored the distinctive identity of Ulster unionists, and blamed British statesmen for causing and perpetuating the division of the Irish nation. Consequently he warned that there could be 'no final settlement of the relations between the two countries' until Britain undid this crime.[34] Before and during the 1938 negotiations, partition was explicitly given as the only reason why de Valera could not guarantee Britain use of Irish facilities in war, nor sign a defence agreement: MacDonald concluded that 'The discussions of the last two months have revealed that the difficulty between North and South still lies at the root of the Anglo-Irish problem.'[35] When he was unable to secure any progress through negotiation, de Valera embarked on a large-scale propaganda campaign. During 1938 he founded an Anti-Partition League in southern Ireland and made a number of public speeches condemning the treatment of the Catholic minority in Northern Ireland. This culminated in an interview with the *Evening Standard* of 17 October 1938, in which he put forward a proposal for a united Ireland.[36] This caused consternation among the Belfast government, which responded by creating its own propaganda machine, opening an Ulster Office in London and distributing weekly bulletins to the press and influential institutions in Britain.[37] 1938 saw a return to the 'cold war' conditions that had existed between northern and southern Ireland in the early 1920s. A combination of British apathy and powerful support for northern unionism among the Conservative Party meant that Northern Ireland retained its autonomy – the British government was determined not to get dragged into the affairs of the six counties. But the price paid was a deterioration in Anglo-Irish relations. The Dominions Office concluded with disappointment in February 1939 that 'broadly speaking, the political effect of the 1938 Agreements has not been so satisfactory as was hoped at the time. The removal of other causes of friction has resulted in concentration by Eire on the Partition question, with unpleasant results.'[38]

Underlying the partial improvement and ultimate disappointment of Anglo-Irish rapprochement was one fundamental question: would Ireland join the war or remain neutral? With the benefit of hindsight, it is clear that the Irish government had only one intention, and that was to stay neutral. This had been official policy ever since the establishment of the Free State. De Valera clearly expressed it after he took office, both in the Dáil and at the League of Nations.[39] Percivale Liesching, one of the few British officials to visit Dublin and sample a wide range of opinion, held out little hope for Irish co-operation. Similarly, the Admiralty, with a considerable interest in Ireland because of the ports and coastwatching, was also by the summer of 1939 preparing itself for Irish neutrality.[40] MI5, in its post-war internal history, claimed that 'De Valera had never disguised his intention to remain neutral' and that 'Eire's neutrality can hardly have come as a surprise to those connected with Irish affairs.'

However, the MI5 history adds that 'The British public and even certain official and political circles may have cherished the illusion that in the event of war with Germany, Britain would be allowed to use the Eire ports which had been given up in 1938.'[41] The argument was that, while Ireland may declare its neutrality at first, German attacks on seaborne trade would soon demonstrate that Irish and British interests were identical, and lead the country into full participation in the war – just like the United States of America. This view was prevalent in the Dominions Office. One official stated in May 1938 that 'it was very unlikely that Eire would stand out, at least so long as its present Government was in power'. Malcolm MacDonald retained similar hopes.[42] The future Secretary of State for Dominion Affairs, Sir Thomas Inskip, assured the Chiefs of Staff that 'although [de Valera] would give no pledge in advance of an emergency, there was little question that he would be prepared to place the harbours of Eire at our disposal in time of war'. This view also pervaded the War Office, which apparently thought that Ireland would join the fight within a month.[43]

The misunderstanding of Irish intentions reveals the continuing inadequacy of political intelligence on Ireland. It is striking that the question of whether Ireland would remain neutral was rarely examined in any great depth. This facilitated the fuzzy thinking and uncritical optimism that was a persistent feature of British policy towards Ireland. There was a conceptual failure here, an unwillingness to accept that the state was effectively independent, that it had fled the nests of union and empire, never to return. Instead, officials took refuge in what a wartime Director of Naval Intelligence defined as 'wishfulness': 'the habit of "discounting what one does not wish to hear", of taking the word for the deed and believing that obstacles can be overcome by being overlooked.'[44] These misconceptions were even more prevalent among the British public, which presumed that a secret defence pact lay behind the unsatisfactory 1938 agreement. It meant that when Ireland declared its neutrality on the outbreak of war, there was a feeling of shock and betrayal among the public and sections of government.

Whether Ireland would stay neutral or join the war was the big question that troubled the British intelligence system in 1938 and 1939. However, Britain was also faced with subversive threats unconnected with this political decision. First, evidence emerged that Nazi Germany was conducting propaganda and espionage operations in southern Ireland and seeking an alliance with the IRA. Second, the IRA became a domestic terrorist threat when it launched a bombing campaign on English soil. The co-operation of the Irish authorities would be essential to investigate and suppress these subversive activities. Unfortunately for Britain, this was only partially forthcoming.

Nazi intrigues

B RITISH concern about German penetration of the Irish Free State, which had first arisen in the mid-1920s, was sustained by further examples of Irish–German collaboration during the de Valera era. The Irish government signed trade agreements under which its agricultural products were exchanged for German goods. Germans with necessary technical skills were appointed to civil service positions.[45] By 1939 there were 194 Germans resident in southern Ireland, alongside 54 Austrians (who became citizens of the Reich after the Anschluss). The loyalist community in southern Ireland was particularly concerned about this dalliance with Berlin. In a paragraph entitled 'German Penetration', a pamphlet from the Irish Loyalist Imperial Federation described how in terms of appointments and contracts 'officially Germany is favoured to the exclusion of Great Britain'. When a delegation of loyalists led by Colonel John Gretton MP met the Prime Minister in 1937, they warned that increasing German penetration of the country posed a strategic threat to Britain.[46]

This matter also came to the attention of the British intelligence community. From 1936 the main focus of British intelligence shifted from communism and the Soviet Union to fascism and Hitler's Germany. MI5 began to investigate a range of Nazi propaganda and espionage networks, active in Britain and other parts of the empire. Ireland was pulled into this investigation on 18 May 1937, when a German automobile merchant named Udo Olsen landed at a British aerodrome *en route* to Dublin. British immigration officials became suspicious when they discovered that his passport had been issued by a Berlin police station that had provided a passport to a previous German intelligence agent. Olsen was also in possession of a number of documents on Irish–German relations that made uncomfortable reading. One paper pointed out that, because of 'the geographical position of the land', Ireland was 'the key to England's world power and to her domination of the sea'. It recommended that Germany cultivate 'silently' the favourable relations between the two countries that already existed in the cultural and economic spheres. After an extended interrogation, MI5 had 'little doubt in saying that Olsen was a Gestapo agent ... on his way to Ireland to establish certain contacts there'.

Olsen's journey was given added significance by an extraordinary report emanating from SIS sources in Germany on 8 June 1937. It quoted sinister remarks made by a senior Nazi official during a private conversation:

(ii) The close proximity of the Irish Free State to important English ports and industrial centres was a weak spot in British defences, which might prove of considerable value to an enemy in the preparation of a surprise air attack.

(iii) In certain Nazi quarters it was believed that the Irish Free State remained fanatically antagonistic to the British Empire and would seize any opportunity to create an independent Irish Republic covering the whole of Ireland. In order to reach their goal, it was believed, the Irish would accept outside help.

(iv) In these Nazi quarters it was being urged that a closer liaison should be established between Germany and the Free State and that an arrangement should be arrived at which would provide air bases for German aircraft in the Free State. Recent experience in Spain had shown that aircraft could be transferred from one country to another in considerable number without attracting attention. In this particular case of the Irish Free State the previous establishment of a Fascist, pro-German and anti-British régime in Spain would be of military importance. Bombers could be flown at a high altitude from Spain to the Irish Free State without crossing land.

(v) Another argument advanced in these Nazi circles in favour of co-operation with the Irish Free State was a reputed growth of Fascist feeling in the latter country.

In a letter to Sir Robert Vansittart (Permanent Under-Secretary at the Foreign Office), Sir Vernon Kell warned that this SIS intelligence, together with the Olsen case, showed that 'the Germans have exactly the same ideas as they had in 1914 about the uses to which Ireland could be put in the event of war. Quite clearly their intention is to build up their contacts there on similar lines and for a similar purpose.'[47] It is unlikely that anyone in Whitehall believed that the Dublin government would be amenable to German approaches, but this secret intelligence must have contributed to anxiety about the likely behaviour of Ireland in a major war; it may explain why this was such an important consideration during the Anglo-Irish negotiations six months later.

From this time MI5 began to take a far more active interest in Irish affairs. It used the limited sources available to investigate suspected German intrigues.

The most important source remained the use of Home Office Warrants to examine letters in the Royal Mail. This was used on correspondence between Irish residents and German agents in Britain, and between Ireland and European addresses associated with the German intelligence services. The rudimentary, clandestine SIS network in southern Ireland, active since 1932, was another occasional source of intelligence, which tallies with the more open loyalist concern about German penetration. The RUC provided information on Germans in Northern Ireland and very occasionally about those in the south; but this was very limited, as the RUC largely ignored the threat of foreign espionage and had very little knowledge of German intelligence methods. Supervision of the movement of persons between Britain and Ireland sometimes yielded information – as the Olsen case indicates. However, MI5 complained that the opportunities were 'very slight', because of the lack of control over travel between the two islands. Referring to British security, MI5 concluded that 'though the front door on the English Channel and North Sea ports was reasonably secure, the back door on the Irish Channel was at least comfortably ajar to travellers in either direction.'[48]

The most significant development of this period was the beginning of collaboration between MI5 and Irish military intelligence (G2). This was a function of the 1938 Anglo-Irish Agreement and de Valera's commitment not to allow Ireland to be used as a base for attack on its neighbour: to Britain's great benefit this was stretched to encompass counter-espionage and security matters, not just military invasion. Until 1938 southern Ireland had no counter-espionage service, and, apart from the communist movement, the Garda paid little attention to uncovering the covert activities of foreign powers. This was a significant intelligence failure. Steps were taken to remedy this defect only in spring 1938, after the British government warned that German espionage activities extended to Irish territory. This, combined with other evidence of German intrigues, caused alarm in Dublin. It led to the establishment of a new 'defence security intelligence section' within G2, which gradually constructed an extensive security apparatus. As part of this, a special unit in the Garda Aliens Office under Sergeant Wymes was tasked with carrying out investigations, and the Post Office arranged for postal and telephone supervision. G2 slowly began to build up intelligence on the German and Italian communities in Ireland.[49]

From the outset, this counter-espionage function was developed in conjunction with the British authorities. The key figure on the British side was Captain Guy Liddell of MI5. He has been described as the 'pre-eminent counter-intelligence officer of his generation'. After serving in the Royal Artillery in the First World War (and winning the Military Cross) he joined Basil Thomson's Scotland

Yard in 1919 and became a leading expert on the communist movement. In 1931 he was transferred along with other Special Branch officers to MI5, becoming deputy director of the counter-espionage B Division. Liddell had strong links with Ireland. He had spent many summers with Irish relatives in his youth and was married to Calypso Baring, the daughter of the Irish peer Lord Revelstoke, whose home was on Lambay Island off the Dublin coast – at parties hosted by Calypso in London, he sometimes volunteered to teach an Irish jig. Following separation from his wife, he lived alone in a flat off Sloane Street and became increasingly absorbed in his work, one of his few diversions being the cello. Although an increasingly influential figure in British domestic intelligence, Liddell was happy to remain in the shadows.[50] A rare portrait – penned by W. Somerset Maughan in a wartime book without disclosing Liddell's name – described how in appearance he did not 'at all resemble the secret agents of fiction':

> [He] was a plump man with grey hair and a grey moon face, in rather shabby grey clothes. He had an ingratiating way with him, a pleasant laugh and a soft voice. I do not know what you would have taken him for … if you had found him standing in a doorway where you had sought refuge from a sudden shower – a motor salesman perhaps, or a retired tea planter.[51]

For over a decade Liddell did more than anyone else to nurture the Anglo-Irish intelligence relationship.

The start of this relationship can be dated to 31 August 1938, when the Secretary of the Department of External Affairs, Joseph Walshe, travelled to London and asked the Dominions Office to put him in touch with 'the British counter-espionage Department'. He believed that the Germans were conducting activities in southern Ireland that 'virtually infringed their sovereign rights'. The Dominions Office immediately phoned Captain Guy Liddell and asked him to join an informal conference. Walshe explained to Liddell that the Irish government wished to set up its own counter-espionage agency and asked whether MI5 could give any 'advice and assistance'. Liddell was happy to oblige. Within days he had drawn up a simple memorandum that made 'tentative suggestions' for an Irish organisation. He also handed over a recent British intelligence assessment of German foreign activities. Over the next two weeks the Irish High Commissioner in London, John Dulanty, kept up the liaison, meeting with Liddell and lunching with Sir Vernon Kell. Finally the head of G2, Colonel Archer, travelled to London on 14 October 1938 for discussions with Captain Liddell and another MI5 officer. Archer provided information on suspicious German activities in Ireland, and asked for advice on intelligence-gathering methods such as phone tapping – he revealed that he was 'starting up an M.I.5 show from scratch'. The three men had an in-depth discussion which continued for a further three hours over dinner. By the middle of 1939 the two services were regularly corresponding by means of the Irish High Commissioner's diplomatic bag. The contemporary MI5 documents reveal palpable excitement over these developments. For fifteen years the agency had tried to establish liaison with the Irish government; when this never materialised, it had periodically flirted with the idea of starting its own clandestine service in Ireland; now the Irish had finally come to them. Thus began a fruitful partnership, known by MI5 as the 'Dublin link'.[52]

The secret liaison between MI5 and G2 would have enormous benefits for Anglo-Irish relations during the Second World War. However, as will be shown, G2 did not immediately fill MI5's needs: it would be well into the war before the two organisations developed a fully collaborative and trusting relationship. This, combined with MI5's own weaknesses and lack of experience with Ireland, meant that the British intelligence system had only partial success in uncovering German intrigue in Ireland.

The first German activity to come to MI5's attention involved propaganda. The principal aim of Nazi propaganda was to develop friendly opinion towards Germany so that the Irish state would adopt a helpful attitude in any war. A secondary aim was to cultivate Irish individuals who would be prepared to carry out active espionage and sabotage against Britain. The most important organisation for this purpose was the Auslandsorganisation, the foreign arm of the Nazi party, which sought to weld together all Germans abroad 'into one great block'.[53] Thirty German and Austrian residents in Ireland were members in 1939. It was led until July 1939 by the Director of the National Museum, Dr Adolf Mahr; his successor, Heinz Mecking, was Chief Advisor to the Turf Development Board. The Nazi party members were far from discreet about their political affiliation, organising social events in the Red Bank restaurant in d'Olier Street and the Gresham Hotel, at which Hitler was saluted and the Nazi party anthem passionately sung. A second and more subtle propaganda organisation was the German Academic Exchange Service, which played on the Irish nationalist desire for cultural and linguistic independence from Britain by organising visits by German students and lecturers to Ireland (and *vice versa*). It had fairly innocent beginnings but 'became an organ of Nazi propaganda and penetration in foreign countries' after Hitler came to power. It was directed by Helmut Clissman, a German who had come to study at Trinity College in 1933. A third organisation with a presence in Ireland was the Deutsche Nachrichten Buro, the German press agency, which in early 1939 appointed an official representative to Ireland (Dr Carlheinz Petersen). His functions were to disseminate German propaganda and to provide suitable news stories about Ireland for publication in the German press. The fourth German propaganda organisation active in Ireland was the Deutsche Fichte Bund. From its headquarters in Hamburg it maintained a system of correspondents around the world, recruited through newspaper advertisements in foreign countries or through German business contacts. They were sent pro-Nazi literature and asked to pass the material to acquaintances, thus widening the circle. Oskar Pfaus was the head of the department for the United States, Canada and Ireland. His most important contact in Ireland was Liam D. Walsh, an employee of the Italian legation. G2 described him as a person 'of poor calibre who would do anything for money': he had been dismissed for embezzlement from positions in the IRA Dublin Brigade (in 1921), the Blueshirts (in 1933) and, most recently, the crossword section of the *Irish Independent*.[54]

MI5 developed some good intelligence on the activities of the first three German propaganda organisations through censorship of correspondence from Ireland and co-operation with G2. In the case of the Auslandsorganisation it was helped by the fact that the Irish branch reported to London (just like the Communist Party of Ireland).[55] It also discovered the activities of Liam D. Walsh in July 1939 after intercepting his letters to Pfaus and receiving a report from an undercover agent in the United States who had joined the Fichte Bund.[56] However, MI5 later admitted that it 'knew little more than the fact that the Fichte Bund was disseminating propaganda in Eire and was not in a position to know the extent to which this was being done or the names of the recipients in Ireland'.[57] This was a fair summary of British intelligence on all German propaganda activity in Ireland before the war. They knew the Germans were conducting propaganda, they were fortunate to discover certain instances (mainly through postal censorship), but they did not have anything like detailed knowledge.

If this was the case with such an open activity, then it applied to an even greater extent to a more clandestine form of German intrigue – espionage. The organisation with responsibility for German foreign intelligence collection (as well as domestic counter-espionage) was the Abwehr, a part of the German military that reported directly to the High Command. Its chief since 1935 was Admiral Wilhelm Canaris. A complex figure, who has been described as 'the Hamlet of conservative Germany', he opposed the Nazi regime and was eventually executed in July 1944 for his part in The Black Orchestra, a plot to overthrow Hitler.[58] However, before 1939 he followed Hitler's instructions to build up an extensive secret espionage organisation throughout Europe in preparation for conflict. The official history of MI5 makes clear that the British intelligence community was very much 'in the dark' about these activities. Although

MI5 stumbled across some German agents, it could find out very little about the organisation behind them; similarly, SIS had little success in penetrating the Abwehr in Europe. As a result, the British intelligence community 'had no practical working knowledge of the Abwher before 1941.'[59]

The British government's uncertainty around the extent of German covert operations was evident in its dealings with Ireland. The key early figures in Abwehr operations in Ireland – Helmut Clissmann and Jupp Hoven – were connected with the German Academic Exchange Service. Both men visited Ireland, maintained a wide range of contacts, provided intelligence reports for Berlin and went on to assist Abwehr operations during the war. British intelligence agencies kept tabs on Clissmann and received a detailed report from the RUC on Hoven (who supposedly visited Northern Ireland in 1939 'to see the beauties of the Glens of Antrim').[60] The two men were 'suspected', MI5 later admitted, 'but at that time the true nature of their activities was not known, nor was it known that Jupp Hoven had been visiting Eire fairly regularly since 1931.' MI5 was also completely unaware of at least one other Abwehr agent, a Breton nationalist named Leon Mill-Arden who ran a seed potato importation business in Dublin. The MI5 history concluded that

> ... the Security Service had, before the war, a fairly complete, though not
> very detailed picture of the various forms of the German penetration of
> Eire. But, while it was realised that any of these might be used for pur-
> poses of espionage, there was ... little, if any evidence of this.[61]

A handful of Abwehr espionage operations in Ireland did come to the attention of MI5. Perhaps the most serious was the case of a German woman living in Dublin who acted as a 'post-box' for the Abwehr. She received 'accurate, and therefore dangerous, espionage reports' from a traitor in the French navy, which she then passed to Germany. The operation was uncovered, and the French officer was executed in November 1938.[62] A less satisfactory case involved an unstable Irishman named Charles Bernard Compton Phillips. He drew the attention of Special Branch officers while passing through Holyhead wearing a large badge of Swastika design, expressing his ardent support for the Nazi Party and carrying a passport revealing frequent visits to Germany. Phillips had been working for the Abwehr since late 1937 (although his contribution was poor). Though evidence linking him with payments from the Abwehr existed in the MI5 registry, the connection was not made, and he was allowed to go free. It was not until 1942 that his previous activities were uncovered.[63]

The final and most interesting case involved an Irish bicycle salesman, whose identity remains a mystery, and a German agent named Kurt Wheeler Hill. The latter arrived in Dublin in early 1937, advertised for language exchanges in an Irish newspaper and attempted to recruit espionage agents from the respondents. The mysterious Irish bicycle salesman took up this offer and visited the Abwehr in Hamburg, where he was asked to cultivate men in the British armed forces and to construct a secret radio link with Germany. Instead, he approached the War Office in London and provided full details of his adventure. At this point MI5 began a double-cross operation. It attempted to infiltrate one of its own officers, posing as 'a Fascist-minded young journalist', into the German network. He travelled to Dublin, obtained an introduction to Hill from his Irish informant and offered to provide secrets on the British armed forces. The Abwehr station in Hamburg expressed interest and the undercover officer returned to Dublin for a second time with information on British tanks. In September 1938 MI5 passed an account of this case to G2 and both services agreed to work together on it. However, at this point the trail went cold, as the Abwehr did not respond, for reasons that are still unknown. Although MI5 was proud that it succeeded 'in introducing an officer, under cover, into German circles in Dublin', it regretted that it could not fully exploit the case because the development of the 'Dublin link' precluded covert operations on Irish soil. It regarded it as a missed opportunity, because the case left the impression that the Abwehr had recruited other agents in Ireland.[64]

The most dangerous threat to both British and Irish security, however, came not from espionage, or from propaganda, but from the burgeoning alliance between the IRA and Nazi Germany. Long shrouded by republican reticence, and notwithstanding a few remaining uncertainties, a fairly complete picture of the relationship between this odd couple can now be given. It is actually not as remarkable as it might appear that the IRA – one-time allies of the Soviet Union, advocates of left-wing ideals for the past decade, bitter opponents of the proto-fascist Blueshirts – should find themselves in alliance with Hitler's Germany. For centuries Irish revolutionaries had been ecumenical in their approach towards Britain's enemies. Now weakened and marginalised, the IRA was even more willing to ignore any ideological inconsistencies. De Valera, when explaining the republican position to the American Minister in Dublin, referred to the analogy of 'a mouse being shaken by a cat ... who regarded as a friend the terrier which chased the cat away'.[65] For its part, the Nazi terrier was willing to use the IRA for sabotage and espionage, as it did other militant nationalist groups.

It is perhaps fitting that the first approach by the IRA to Germany occurred in the United States, where two decades earlier Clan na Gael leaders had obtained German assistance for the Easter Rising. It was made by two men who represented the republican physical force tradition on either side of the Atlantic:

Joseph McGarrity, leader of Clan na Gael since 1920; and Seán Russell, IRA Quartermaster and a future IRA Chief of Staff. While visiting the United States in October 1936 Russell, with McGarrity's assistance, presented a document to the German ambassador in Washington on behalf of the IRA. It harked back to the events of 1916:

> The Government of the Republic and the people of Ireland are, and will continue to be, mindful of the debt they owe to the German people and their government for assistance in a fight calculated to rid our country of the foreign rule that now uses the 'Free State' as its domestic agent. ... Ireland as a nation is disposed to, and shall be glad of the arrival of the time when she may, make returns to her friends in Germany for their valued assistance in the early days of the present phase of our fight.[66]

The Germans responded in early 1937. Tom Barry, the IRA Chief of Staff, was brought by Jupp Hoven to Germany, where he was 'treated as a distinguished visitor' and asked about the possibility of IRA sabotage against Britain in wartime. Barry, along with the former IRA Chief of Staff, Moss Twomey, remained in close contact with Hoven and Clissmann until early 1939. The German–IRA link was then handed to the IRA Director of Intelligence, Seán MacBride, who was a frequent visitor to the house of the German Minister: according to G2 he was 'working for the Germans even more than for the IRA.'[67]

Because Hitler still hoped to maintain good relations with Britain, there were few concrete results from these contacts. However, the courtship between Germany and the IRA accelerated in 1939. In February the most significant German representative arrived in Ireland: the Fichte Bund official Oskar P. Pfaus. He was brought to a meeting with several IRA leaders, including Seán Russell and Moss Twomey. There was some wariness on both sides, and Pfaus was not authorised to enter into detailed discussions, but he did lay the basis for a more substantive liaison. The IRA men tore up a one pound note and handed one half to Pfaus, so that it could be used to identify their representative at a further meeting. This was quickly arranged. It was decided to send James O'Donovan, who spoke some German, as the republican envoy to the Abwehr. He made three trips to Germany in 1939. In the first, at the end of February, he made contact with an Abwehr officer and gave details of the arms and ammunition needed by the IRA. The Germans refused to supply immediate help but were interested in arming the IRA and using it against targets in the United Kingdom once war broke out. In a second visit between 26 April and 15 May O'Donovan discussed the establishment of a radio link with Germany, a courier route for messages and armaments, and a safe house in London. A final series of meetings occurred in

August 1939, just days before Germany invaded Poland. O'Donovan was accompanied by Joseph McGarrity, who also met with the Abwehr and other German officials. They were told, 'There is to be war. Probably in one week.'[68]

The British intelligence community did not receive any proof of the contacts between Nazi Germany and the IRA until early July 1939. The first evidence came from SIS intelligence activities in Germany, rather than Irish sources. SIS provided a report that 'on the 20th and 25th June a conference had taken place in Berlin between Admiral Canaris, head of the Abwehr, a representative of the German War Office, and a responsible member of the I.R.A. ... Canaris was reported to have undertaken to supply him with arms and funds.' Though mistaken as to the date, the place of the meeting and the presence of Canaris, this report referred to Jim O'Donovan's mission (although he was not identified by name). F. H. Hinsley writes in his *British intelligence in the Second World War* that 'it was understandably accepted by MI5 as confirming its belief that Germany had made definite plans for using the IRA against the United Kingdom.'[69] Other sources indicate that MI5 was 'inclined to regard the danger of Germany organising sabotage with the assistance of I.R.A. terrorists as a very serious one.'[70]

British knowledge of Nazi intrigues in Ireland was incomplete. Yet enough evidence emerged to generate major concerns about the uses that Germany could make of Ireland when war came: England's 'back door' appeared to offer an easy entrance for German agents. The 'Dublin link' was obviously inadequate when it came to dealing with this threat. One reason was the lack of intelligence in the possession of G2. It was starting from scratch, with limited personnel and funds, and it took some time to get to grips with the problem. The greatest gap in Dublin's knowledge was in relation to German involvement with the IRA: in the first half of 1939 de Valera and his ministers repeatedly denied that there was any connection. This was a significant Irish intelligence failure, as the German-IRA relationship posed a huge threat to Irish domestic security and Irish wartime neutrality.[71] On the other hand, even when the Irish did possess intelligence, they were sometimes reluctant to share it with London. The MI5 history records that G2 was 'subject to strict political control and could only be relied on as a source of information or security co-operation to the extent to which it suited Eire policy.' Colonel Dan Bryan, G2's deputy chief, admitted that 'at this time, all queries from London, were treated with considerable caution' and 'reticence', on the instructions of the Anglophobic Minister for Defence, Frank Aiken. Again, this particularly affected the subject of the IRA's links with Germany. The MI5 history states that liaison was confined to the activities of German nationals in Ireland: 'Before the war and for some time after, it was not considered advisable to make enquiries about Eire nationals'.[72] The Irish government was willing to act as Britain's policeman in espionage matters, but it was unwilling to extend this service to the Irish republican movement, which was still regarded as an internal family affair.

The inadequacy of the 'Dublin link' was demonstrated by the handling of a final intelligence report on the contacts between the IRA and Germany in the summer of 1939. On 20 July the Czech Consul in Dublin informed the British Foreign Office that the German Minister, Dr Eduard Hempel, and three members of the Nazi Party had travelled to Co. Donegal for a meeting with the leaders of the IRA. A month later the same source reported that Dr Hempel was in touch with leading republicans in an attempt to organise an Irish legion to fight for Hitler. Neither of these reports had any substance, and MI5 was rightly inclined to dismiss them. What is interesting is the reaction they caused when passed to the Dublin authorities. In order to protect its source, MI5 claimed that the information came from a Czech servant in the German legation. When Joseph Walshe learnt of this, he immediately informed the German Minister, who sacked the unfortunate servant. Thus, far from protecting a supposed intelligence source, or working with the British to exploit it, the Irish government moved to silence it. MI5 concluded that 'Joe Walshe feared that the Czech informant in the German legation might prove embarrassing to the Eire Government' by passing on details of secret Irish–German discussions. Irish interests were not identical with British interests in these security matters. An MI5 internal history concluded that 'this report and the enquiries which followed show how difficult it was, even with the assistance of the "Dublin link", to obtain any definite information about the activities of the Germans in Ireland'.[73]

The IRA bombing campaign

THE limitations of Anglo-Irish intelligence co-operation would be more strongly confirmed by the bombing campaign conducted by the IRA in England in 1939. This was the most serious domestic terrorist threat faced by Britain from the time of the Fenian movement in the 1880s until the activities of the Provisional IRA in the 1970s. It was a surprising development, considering the weak state of the republican movement in Britain over the previous fifteen years. The return of the 114 deportees from Ireland in 1923 had been followed by recriminations, splits and decline. Art O'Brien (leader of the Irish Self-Determination League) was discredited when a criminal trial revealed that he had embezzled Sinn Féin funds. Those who had avoided deportation were jealous of the compensation received by their comrades, demanding that it be handed over to the republican cause. 'Whatever else may be said of the Government's action in deporting these people, the payment to them of compensation has had a most demoralising effect', the Special Branch noted with satisfaction. 'They have been fighting like Kilkenny cats ever since.'[74] Attempts to revive a nationwide republican organisation in Britain failed; instead a few Republican or Sinn Féin Clubs emerged, although they were more concerned with organising social events for their members than agitating for the destruction of the Free Sate. On the military side, the IRA kept its organisation intact for longer, showing signs of renewed activity in 1924 and branching into espionage work on behalf of the Soviet Union in 1925.[75] Yet it too was soon wracked by feuds. 'The Irish Republican Army in Great Britain', the Special Branch concluded in August 1925, 'is a negligible quantity, owing to rows and bothers amongst its leaders.'[76] Its numbers fell from 344 in August 1924 to just 189 by late 1926. Over the following decade its chief function was social – dancing proved more popular than drilling. Even the Anglo-Irish dispute and IRA revival in Ireland during 1932 and 1933 had little positive impact on the republican movement in Britain.[77] According to a Special Branch report, 'the only ones left to keep the Republican Flag flying' in Britain were 'a few unimportant men and spitfire women of the school teacher type'; their followers were 'mainly young men and women more interested in sport and amusement than anything else.'[78]

The Special Branch had traditionally been responsible for monitoring Irish republican activities in Britain. This arrangement survived a major reorganisation of the British domestic security system in September 1931, when MI5 was given responsibility for almost all domestic subversive movements, including communism. With this came many of Scotland Yard's leading experts on subversion, such as Captain Guy Liddell. Kell noted exultantly, 'we took over Scotland Yard intelligence'. (As a sign of its increased stature, MI5 began to adopt the name the 'Security Service'.)[79] There was one important exception to this transfer of powers: the Special Branch retained responsibility for 'Irish and anarchist matters.'[80] This decision shows how closely identified the Branch was with Ireland, from its original inception to fight the Fenian dynamiters in the 1880s, through Basil Thomson's involvement in covert intelligence operations in 1920 and its lead role in investigating IRA espionage in the mid-1920s.

The Special Branch kept a watching brief on Irish republican organisations in Britain in the 1930s: for example, in August 1936 it reported on a meeting of the London branch of Irish Republican Congress (a new group set up by left-wing IRA members).[81] Yet it was a distant watch. This was partly because the Special Branch had a police, not an intelligence, mindset. Recruited from police detectives, its *modus operandi* was the prevention of crime, not the collection of intelligence *per se*. It inevitably relaxed its grip on Irish organisations when they were not manifestly breaking the law. The limitations of the Special Branch approach were remarked on by Captain Guy Liddell in 1942:

> In peace time Sir Vernon Kell disclaimed all responsibility for I.R.A. activities, which were always regarded as the province of the police. The consequence is that the I.R.A. has never really been studied properly as a Movement. The police have always dealt with it on the basis of a number of individuals who might at any time transgress the law by committing acts of violence. Certainly when I was at the Yard little attempt was made to acquire any real understanding of the organisation and the aims and objectives of those behind it.[82]

These limitations were exposed in 1939, when the IRA leadership decided to make England the target of its long-awaited physical force campaign. The chief figure behind this campaign was Seán Russell. A key figure behind the Bloody Sunday attacks in 1920, he had served as the IRA's Director of Munitions in the revolutionary period and remained a dedicated IRA activist through the vicissitudes of subsequent years: according to one historian, he was 'anti-political', 'a pure physical force man' and 'a revolutionary of an intensity, commitment, and endurance unusual even within the republican movement'.[83] A British newspaper described him as 'grim, silent and ruthless' with a 'fanatical face', a 'non-smoker like Hitler', who loved 'to drive at desperate speeds' like Mussolini. (Apparently, he also had a softer side: he took parties of children for picnics outside Dublin in his red sports car and grew lettuces and tomatoes in a market garden north of the city.)[84] The IRA had been decimated by the Dublin government's crack-down, retreating to its former status as a small, underground, extremist movement, constantly harried by the authorities. Russell believed that the only way to revive the organisation was to use force to end partition. He advocated a bombing campaign on English soil, arguing that the IRA could inflict such destruction that the British government would decide to pull out of Northern Ireland. This plan had the advantage of avoiding sectarian violence and loss of life in Ireland. Russell was opposed by the then IRA Chief of Staff, Tom Barry, who instead argued that the IRA should raid across the border and wage a guerrilla campaign in Northern Ireland. As a result of this dispute, in 1937 the ruling Army Council temporarily expelled Russell from the movement. However, after collecting supporters tired of the inertia of the ruling clique, the Russell faction triumphed at an IRA convention in April 1938. Russell became Chief of Staff, his allies formed the new IRA Executive, and his scheme for an English campaign was authorised. In yet another of the innumerable IRA splits, Tom Barry and other senior leaders subsequently left the movement.[85]

Russell turned to James O'Donovan (who would later represent the IRA in Germany) to formulate a detailed plan for the bombing campaign – the 'S-Plan.' O'Donovan, the holder of a degree in chemistry from University College Dublin, had been the IRA's director of chemicals in 1921 and therefore its chief bombmaker: he bore his credentials for all to see, as a faulty experiment had left him missing two fingers. He had been a peripheral figure in the movement since 1924, taking up a comfortable position in the state-run Electricity Supply Board (ESB), but he was sufficiently enthused by Russell's vision of a bombing campaign in England to come out of retirement.

O'Donovan's S-Plan described in detail how a well-organised group could wage an effective terrorist campaign in an industrialised, democratic state. The IRA's weapon would be sabotage, and its field of action would be England. (Scotland and Wales escaped because they were fellow Celtic nations.) Because the most effective targets – factories crucial to British rearmament – would be too heavily guarded, the IRA would concentrate its efforts on England's public services. The prime target would be the electric grid. Apart from the dislocation of industry and business, O'Donovan believed that 'the moral and panic effects of extensive black-outs' would be 'very great.' Of equal potential was disruption of the public transport network, as this 'would have a paralyzing effect on every branch of industrial and commercial life.' O'Donovan admitted that 'major operations' against key public services or buildings could only be carried out at the beginning of the campaign; the bombers would be forced to select 'softer' targets once the security response intensified. He described how post offices and pillar boxes were susceptible to mail bombs. Government departments in Whitehall were equally vulnerable, because 'nothing would be simpler' than for a sympathetic employee to deposit an incendiary unit before locking up on a Saturday afternoon. One of O'Donovan's more ingenious schemes targeted the sewage system: IRA men would load two tons of quick-setting cement into a lorry, pull up to a manhole at a main sewage conduit and, posing as workmen, empty bag after bag of cement down the hole. The S-Plan listed an even wider range of targets among the commercial and industrial sectors: 'commerce, banking and shipping; ordinary industries; cotton mills etc, grain, tobacco and spirit stores, motor car tyre stores, timber yards, etc.' Two general principles would govern the IRA campaign. First, it should entail no loss of life, as this would be politically counterproductive. Second, the IRA was so outnumbered by 'the enemy' that operations must be 'so foolproof and so certain in action as to afford a 10,000:1 margin of safety, i.e. freedom from detection or capture.' Neither of these caveats would survive the test of reality.[86]

Inspired by the S-Plan, the IRA made preparations for the campaign during 1938. The first requirement was to secure bomb-making materials. Gelignite was stolen from quarries. At considerable risk to themselves and those around them, IRA members prepared a home-made explosive (known as 'Paxo') from chemicals available on the open market: chlorate of potash mixed with a carbonaceous substance (such as sugar or charcoal) or with a metallic substance (such as oxide of iron or aluminium powder).[87] Material acquired in Ireland was smuggled across to Britain, or purchased there by men despatched from Ireland with funds. IRA documents later captured by the British police showed that:

> two tons of potassium chlorate, a ton of magnetic iron oxide, 450 pounds of aluminium powder and eight gallons of sulphuric acid had been bought and distributed to various centres in England. In addition ... quantities of gelignite and detonators had been stolen from coal mines and quarries over a period of a year or more. Necessary accessories, such as implements for mixing explosives, dry batteries, alarm clocks for time bombs, etc., had also been acquired.[88]

The second requirement was a cadre of trained personnel who could make and plant the bombs. Some were drawn from the rudimentary IRA organisation in Britain, but most were sent from Ireland. Groups were taken for training to places such as Killiney Castle in south Dublin, which became a hive of activity and strange odours at the end of 1938. Twelve handpicked volunteers crossed over to Britain during Christmas week to direct operations. The bombers were assisted by a more diffuse network of friends and sympathisers among the Irish immigrant community, many of whom gave help unknowingly.[89]

Alongside these 'military' activities, the IRA prepared the political ground for the bombing campaign. The S-Plan pointed out that 'Propaganda' was as 'vitally necessary' as 'Action'. 'The misinterpretation, the ridicule, the false propaganda or counter-propaganda that will be broadcast a thousandfold more effectively than we can possibly aspire to, may have a shattering effect on otherwise moderately effective military action', O'Donovan wrote. 'It may make all the difference between sympathy and hostility at home.' [90] (This was apposite, considering later developments.) Russell's first step was to persuade the remnant of the 1922 Second Dáil, which still claimed to be the legitimate government of the Irish Republic, to transfer its notional authority to the IRA Army Council. This enabled the IRA, as the representative of a 'state', to send an ultimatum to the British government on 12 January threatening war if it did not signal its intention to withdraw from Northern Ireland within four days. When there was no response, the IRA issued a second notice on 16 January, signed by the seven-member Army Council and pasted up in streets in both parts of Ireland. It was a formal declaration of war and a signal for the bombing campaign to commence.[91]

In the early hours of 16 January 1939 three explosions occurred in the London suburbs, three in Manchester city and ten others in the Midlands, Lancashire and Northumberland. All were directed against power stations or the infrastructure of the electrical grid, and one resulted in a black-out in north London that affected 25,000 consumers. A cardinal principle of the S-Plan was immediately broken: a 27-year old fish porter named Albert Ross was killed by a blast in Manchester after he stepped off a bus while on the way to work.[92] Countless explosions and six more deaths would follow before the IRA campaign came to an end.

Had the IRA succeeded in taking the British authorities 'completely by surprise', as Seán Russell boasted a week after the campaign began?[93] The Special Branch had some indication that IRA action was being planned. Sir Norman Kendal, Assistant Commissioner of the Metropolitan Police and head of the Special Branch since 1928, wrote that 'during 1937 and 1938 informants within the Irish Republican Army gave warning that the movement was being revivified and reorganised in preparation for an attack on Britain, aiming at forcing the fusion of Northern Ireland with Eire, and of the complete separation of the latter from the Empire'. Further information was received from 'several independent sources' at the time of the Munich crisis in September 1938.[94] However, these signals were vague and did not provoke any police response. All the indications are that the IRA campaign took Whitehall completely unawares. Three days after the explosions began, the Dominions Office admitted that they 'knew no more than what has appeared in the Press'. The Home Office was equally baffled.[95]

This points to lapses in the British intelligence system. There is evidence that the IRA campaign was common knowledge in Irish immigrant circles: the Irish High Commissioner had certainly learnt that something was planned.[96] The IRA's American wing, Clan na Gael, had mistakenly released the IRA proclamation of war to the media six weeks early – its significance did not register with the Foreign Office.[97] Similarly, when the IRA ultimatum was received in Whitehall it did not excite any concern and was not passed to the Special Branch until 16 January – after the campaign started. The Branch was hardly blameless itself: it had arrested two known IRA men in October 1938 with a van-load of potassium chlorate without recognising the significance of the find. This indicates that the Special Branch had grown complacent during the 1930s and had relaxed their surveillance of Irish militant republicans.[98] Of course, it was not helped by the absence of intelligence from southern Ireland, the base from which the campaign was planned and directed.

If the Special Branch was slow to predict the IRA campaign, it was quick to react. A round-up of republican suspects began at dawn on 18 January: over the next month forty-six people were arrested in London, Manchester, Liverpool, Birmingham and Cardiff. Thirty-three of this group were eventually convicted. A large quantity of explosives and weapons was uncovered: for example, 500 pounds of explosives and 40 sticks of gelignite were found in a chip shop and two other buildings in Manchester. The Special Branch and local police forces must have had some knowledge of the republican movement, as they picked up many of the right people at short notice: the IRA 'Officer Commanding, Britain', Michael Mason, was captured in this initial sweep. These raids also yielded a crop of incriminating documents, the most important of which was a copy of the S-Plan, discovered in the possession of Michael O'Shea in London in early February.[99] A senior Special Branch officer commented that 'The work of the authorities in tracking down the terrorists was considerably facilitated by the carelessness which the latter displayed in the custody of secret documents.' He cited the example of how 'in one instance a coded message and the cypher key were left in the same drawer'.[100] With these documents, the same cycle that led to the breaking up of gunrunning networks in 1922–3 came into play: initial arrests yielded papers that led to other suspects; they were then placed under physical and postal surveillance until enough evidence was collected for their arrest; further documents would inevitably be found, allowing the police to unravel another piece of the web. Although local police forces played an active part in tackling the IRA organisation, the Special Branch co-ordinated all information and provided specialist assistance nationwide, as well as dealing with the London metropolitan region. By early May the strength of the Branch had been considerably increased by the transfer of CID officers.[101]

The IRA explosions led police to institute a range of passive preventative measures. Special protection was given to politicians, government buildings and public services: on a single day (21 February) seventy-nine extra police officers were assigned to these duties in London.[102] Chief Constables around the country adopted special measures to protect explosive stores and to guard elevated canals – the S-Plan indicated that the latter were a special target for attack.[103] The Special Branch also appointed security officers to Holyhead and Fishguard to screen passengers from Ireland.[104] For example, when three IRA men from Tralee, Co. Kerry, joined up with a rugby excursion to London in February 1939, their train was met by a line of police at Paddington station. On their return, 'the plain clothes police ... were thick on the ground' at Fishguard port, and two detectives sat with them in the ship's bar during the sea voyage. (The IRA men boasted that they still accomplished their mission, but it was 'a near thing.')[105] Many of these measures stayed in place until the outbreak of war, when they were adopted on a permanent basis as part of the country's wartime anti-sabotage scheme.

The risk of sabotage was greatest in facilities connected with Britain's rearmament programme. Many factories employed Irish people due to a recent wave of immigration. These workers immediately fell under suspicion. This was one area where MI5 – keen to distance itself from responsibility for the general IRA problem – pressed for action. Its Director, Sir Vernon Kell, wrote to Chief Constables around the country asking to be supplied with a list of IRA sympathisers employed in government establishments, armament firms or other 'vulnerable points'.[106] The initial plan was to wait until war started before dismissing these workers from service (as was the policy for foreign nationals); but in June 1939 Kell was given authority to instruct factory owners to discharge individuals immediately, so long as he consulted with the local Chief Constable and was convinced they were active members of the IRA.[107] Men lost their jobs on the flimsiest evidence. One worker in a Stockport aircraft factory, George Spain, was fired after being denounced by a fellow Irishman who remembered him professing IRA sympathies six years earlier. (This case caused some problem for the Home Office because Spain was a friend of a Member of Parliament.)[108]

Despite the security crack-down, IRA outrages continued in 1939: there were forty incidents in March, thirty in May and seventy-two in June.[109] The bombers undertook a handful of major operations. An attempt was made to destroy the aqueduct carrying the Grand Junction Canal over the North Circular Road in Harlesden, London. On the eve of the Oxford–Cambridge Boat Race on 29 March, there were two large explosions at Hammersmith Bridge, which led to a major police operation on the river the next day; newspaper reports claimed that a Chiswick hairdresser 'saved the bridge' by throwing one of the bombs into the water, after he heard sizzling noises coming from a package on the footway. However, as operations became progressively more difficult, the IRA gravitated towards the 'softer' targets featured in the S-Plan. Of the seventy-two incidents recorded in June, sixty-five were minor attacks designed to cause alarm: there was not one serious attempt to dislocate public services. Explosive or incendiary devices went off in railway station cloakrooms, two carriages on the Euston to Wolverhampton express, post offices, high street stores, a London tailor's, a motor showroom, at least one newspaper office (the *News Chronicle*), eight seaside hotels, five London banks, letter boxes, telephone kiosks, public lavatories and litter bins in busy shopping streets. In a chilling portent of twentieth-first century terrorist attacks, the IRA exploded bombs in two London tube stations, and a smoking attaché case filled with explosives was found under a seat on a bus in Warwickshire. In some of the softest attacks, members of Cumann na mBan let off tear gas canisters in cinemas. These types of attack were very difficult to guard against: a Special Branch officer complained that 'the worst of it was that you could never tell where they were likely to plant their bombs'.[110] Moreover, the decline in the quality of the campaign was accompanied by increased bloodiness, as the targeting of crowded areas inevitably led to casualties. On 25 July 1939 a Scottish university lecturer lost both his legs in an explosion at King's Cross station. He died soon after. In the worst incident, five were killed and fifty-one injured by an explosion in a busy high street in Coventry on 25 August 1939.

The British security effort against the IRA bombing campaign was severely hampered by the unwillingness of the Irish authorities to co-operate. Some historians have claimed that de Valera did everything he could to prevent the IRA attacks and that the British government was satisfied with his response.[111] This was not the case. Special Branch officers were rebuffed when they requested information on IRA suspects arrested in Britain in January 1939. The Irish High Commissioner in London, Dulanty, explained that these were 'political crimes' and 'that Mr. de Valera would be incurring very great political danger if it transpired that an Irishman was sent to gaol in England partly as a result of information obtained by the police authorities in Eire'. Dulanty assured British officials that 'their police would communicate any information they received with a view to preventing any further outrages'. Yet, with the exception of a Garda warning at the time of the international rugby match in London, even this information was not forthcoming.[112] The new Secretary of State for Dominion Affairs, Sir Thomas Inskip, concluded that 'the police authorities in Dublin were not willing to place all their information at the disposal of Scotland Yard in order to prevent these outrages', let alone 'to convict and punish the persons responsible for them'.[113] This had a major impact on British security, as new IRA operatives were being sent over from Ireland to carry out missions. In July 1939 Percivale Liesching of the Dominions Office was sent to Dublin to make a final effort to secure intelligence co-operation. He met Joseph Walshe and 'impressed on him very insistently the difficulties confronting the Police in Great Britain in dealing with this campaign of violence':

> I told him that, apart from a message received by Scotland Yard on the occasion of the International Rugby Football Match earlier this year, which had enabled our Police to act, there had been no response whatever to our requests for Police co-operation. The difficulties were thus

enormous, and, although we had succeeded in dealing with a number of the I.R.A. after they had committed dangerous acts of violence, it was proving impossible in the absence of information from Eire to take measures for preventing crime which were necessary if the safety of the public was to be safeguarded.[114]

In the summer of 1939 the Irish authorities finally took steps to tackle the IRA. A draconian Offences Against the State Act was passed on 14 June, and nine days later this Act was used to officially proscribe the organisation (whose earlier proscription had lapsed when the new constitution came into force). A number of IRA leaders were arrested, a Special Criminal Court was established to try IRA offences, and internment provisions became effective. However, the nature of these measures should not be misunderstood. The government took action against the IRA members in so far as they broke domestic Irish law, not because of their extra-territorial terrorist campaign. De Valera insisted that 'he did not propose to prosecute those guilty of disorder and terrorism in England ... but when it came to a defiance of Irish law, an open challenge to the present Irish Government ... there would be no temporising'.[115] Dublin's subsequent refusal to extradite IRA bomb suspects to Britain was entirely consistent with this. Ireland, therefore, remained a safe, if precarious, haven from British justice.[116] Second, the full force of the new security measures was only turned on the IRA after war broke out. This was done to safeguard Irish neutrality, not British interests. Finally, this crack-down did not make the Irish authorities any more willing to share intelligence on republicans. For example, when the Southport police found shirt collars marked with an IRA suspect's name after an arson attack, and sent them to the Garda with a request to trace this man, not only did the Garda refuse to help, but the collars disappeared while in their possession, thus depriving the British police of an important piece of evidence.[117] Liesching left Dublin with the conclusion that 'fundamentally there remains the profound reluctance to give any information about any Irishman to any Englishman in a matter of this kind'.[118]

Ireland was not the only source of support for the IRA bombing campaign: as before, the militant republican movement was an international conspiracy. The most important help came from the United States of America. Clan na Gael had been in a steady decline since the end of the Irish Civil War. Its leader, Joseph McGarrity, was determined to arrest it by convincing the IRA to return to military action. There is evidence that McGarrity first suggested the idea of an English bombing campaign to Russell during the latter's visit to the United States in 1936: Russell wrote to the Clan leader on his return, 'we have been working very hard on your suggestion regarding operations in England.'[119] American money was crucial for purchasing the supplies and meeting the living expenses of IRA operatives. Irish military intelligence later estimated that a total of £80,000 (or approximately $370,000) was raised in the United States for this purpose.[120] Ammunition, explosive powder and a radio transmitter were also smuggled across the Atlantic. The extent of American involvement in the bombing campaign was common knowledge. In February 1939 a new organisation named the Irish Republican Alliance, a front for Clan na Gael, assumed responsibility for the campaign in a press conference in New York, pledging 'moral and financial support' to the Irish Republican Army 'in its new offensive against the British Empire.'[121] In its *Irish Bulletin* the IRA publicly thanked Clan na Gael 'for the signal help they have given us both in money and material. It is hardly too much to say that without the fund they have transferred to us we should hardly have been able to embark upon our present policy and certainly should not have been able to sustain it.'[122] The head of the Special Branch, Norman Kendal, confirmed in April 1939 that all his intelligence pointed to the fact that 'a good deal of money' was received by the IRA 'from Irishmen and persons of Irish descent domiciled in the United States of America', just as in the 'pre-Treaty days.'[123] Because British intelligence on Irish-American organisations was weak and the American authorities were reluctant to take action, Britain could do little to stop this assistance reaching the IRA.

Did Nazi Germany also assist the IRA? Rumours of German involvement in the IRA bombing campaign were widespread on both sides of the Irish Sea. The *Sunday Express* wrote in January 1939 that the 'theory openly held in Dublin now is that the conspiracy is being financed and to some extent directed by secret agents of a foreign Power', an obvious reference to the Third Reich.[124] An examination of seven Sunday newspapers in the first week of July revealed 'complete unanimity in attributing to German gold and German agitators blame for I.R.A. activities in England'. However, the IRA hotly denied these allegations, stating that they were part of a British 'campaign of lies and deception and, above all, self-deception'. Éamon de Valera also adamantly denied that the IRA received any financing from Berlin.[125] British intelligence officers, though uncertain, tended to side with this view. MI5 concluded in June 1939 'that they had no evidence that German agents had been responsible for the I.R.A. bombing campaign.'[126] In fact, it appears that the Nazi regime did financially assist the IRA bombing campaign in England, although through Clan na Gael and therefore indirectly. In 1943 Tom Barry stated that Clan na Gael was acting on behalf of German agents, and that much of the financial aid came from that quarter.[127] G2 later concluded that the IRA 'had obtained considerable financial aid from the Germans ... handled entirely by Joe McGarrity' in the United States.[128] This was the one instance where British intelligence officers underestimated the scale of the militant republican plot.

By April 1939 the British authorities were dissatisfied with the progress of the anti-terrorist campaign. This frustration was expressed at a conference attended by the Home Office, MI5, the Special Branch and police Chief Constables:

> The unanimous view of the police representatives was that the I.R.A. is a growing menace which cannot be dealt with effectively under existing powers, that a large amount of public money is being spent on guarding vulnerable places, and that very much more drastic measures must be sanctioned if effective action is to be taken. They explained that the damage done might easily have been far more serious and it was due to good fortune as much as any other factor that they had been able to effect a number of arrests.

The police faced two main challenges. The first was collecting good intelligence. The police described how the IRA took active measures to prevent infiltration and had an 'effective system of testing the loyalty of members': the individual was told of an invented plan for an outrage and the IRA leaders then watched the place to see if the police took action. As a result, the police were 'in a dilemma' when they received information, as if they acted they might lose the services of the informer. One of the great differences from the 1920s was that 'little information' was obtained through censorship of the mails, because the IRA sent messages by word of mouth or by female couriers. In addition, normal members of the Irish community were afraid to give information, and often turned a blind eye to IRA activities. As a result, police chiefs admitted that they had 'no complete knowledge of the organisation in this country or of the plans being made by it.' The second major problem was the difficulty of working under the 1883 Explosive Substances Act (which had been introduced in response to the Fenian dynamite campaign). Membership of the IRA was not an offence, and it was difficult to secure a conviction unless someone was found in actual possession of explosives. Security chiefs wanted new legislation to make membership of the IRA an indictable offence, to allow the government to deport suspects to Ireland and to give police extra powers of search.[129]

The Home Office initially resisted these calls. It was reluctant to tamper with the established judicial system and afraid that deportation powers might set a bad precedent of 'exclusion' that could be used against other citizens of the empire – unfortunate victims might include 'Cypriots, coloured persons or persons of criminal record.'[130] Action was not taken until July 1939. What tipped the balance was evidence that the IRA was turning towards bloodier tactics. On the evening of 24 June incendiary devices went off at Piccadilly as people were emerging from West End theatres. An additional parcel containing ten sticks of gelignite was found in a nearby gutter: 'had this exploded, there would inevitably have been a heavy loss of life', a British official noted. Moreover, in the course of police searches, loaded weapons were found in the baggage of persons who had hitherto not been in possession of firearms. The authorities feared that 'the I.R.A. might be turning at any moment to deliberate attempts on human life as part of their campaign', perhaps even assassination of political leaders.[131] A revival of the old habit of sending anonymous threatening letters created further unease. Winston Churchill received a grim example at this time, signed 'Seán O'Brendhay, Secretary, Northern Divisional Area, IRA':

> As you are the greatest enemy to our National Freedom that exists in the world to-day, we are going to get you even if it is the last thing that we do. Ever since the days of the Coalition Government when you sent your murderous Black-and-Tans to this country to outrage the consience [sic] of civilised man you have not hesitated to blackguard our people in every way possible. Now however, we are going to give you a taste of your own medicine. If we do not get you in your talking sanctuary at Westminster we will get you at your private residence. No matter how many bodyguard [sic] you may choose to surround yourself with we are going to riddle your fat carcass with bullets.[132]

In response, the government passed the Prevention of Violence (Temporary Provisions) Bill in an emergency sitting of the House of Commons on 24 July 1939. The bill became law four days later. It gave the police sweeping powers: officers not below the rank of superintendent could issue search warrants, and suspects could be held for five days without charge. It also gave the Home Secretary powers to issue expulsion orders against IRA suspects living in Britain and to issue prohibition orders against those trying to enter the country. The new legislation helped to turn the tide against the IRA. During 1939 and 1940, 156 persons were deported to Ireland. Many more suspects on the deportation lists left on their own initiative when the legislation was unveiled: the boats to Ireland were crammed with returning republicans in the last days of July 1939. The additional powers of search and arrest enabled the police to achieve a further thirty convictions over the coming months.[133] There is also evidence that the police began to receive better intelligence from within republican circles: a plot to blow up the Bank of England was foiled thanks to an informant.[134] The Special Branch was confident that now 'the I.R.A. were getting the worst of the struggle.

Their front-line assassins were being caught; and their back-room planners were running out of funds.'[135] By the outbreak of the war the bombing campaign had been effectively crushed by these sweeping security measures. There were no incidents in September 1939. Although IRA explosions recurred later in the year and spluttered on until March 1940, they were spasmodic and little more than an irritant.[136]

The bombing campaign was an unmitigated disaster for the IRA. In Britain its organisation was completely destroyed. Over the course of the campaign 128 members were arrested, of whom 96 were convicted, 156 were deported to Ireland, and many more fled on their own initiative; most of those remaining were interned on the outbreak of the war.[137] In Northern Ireland the organisation was crippled by the internment of leading members and intensified security measures. In the south the campaign lost the IRA its remaining public support and allowed the government to sharpen its weapons of coercion, ready to strike once war began. There were two reasons for the failure of the campaign. First, its execution left much to be desired: operatives were poorly trained in the use of explosives; safe houses and storage facilities were not adequately prepared; IRA members exhibited lax security, especially by producing incriminating written communications. James O'Donovan later condemned the IRA operation as 'hastily conceived, scheduled to a premature start, with ill-equipped and inadequately trained personnel, too few men and too little money ... unable to sustain the vital spark of what must be confessed to have fizzled out like a damp and inglorious squib.'[138] However, the most perfect execution of the S-Plan would not have compensated for its greatest failing – the absence of any realistic strategy. Russell and O'Donovan had some vague notion that a campaign of terror and destruction would compel the British government to withdraw from Northern Ireland. In fact, it only strengthened British support for Ulster unionism, caused renewed sectarian bitterness in Northern Ireland and further marginalised the militant republican movement in southern Ireland.

The ghost of John Redmond

THE British security apparatus had been able to crush the IRA terrorist campaign on the eve of the Second World War with the aid of extraordinary security legislation and considerable police resources. Yet it raised worrying questions about the threat posed by militant republicans in the United States and Ireland. The British government became concerned that Irish-American agitators would once again use the Irish question to poison American attitudes towards Britain. The actions of the IRA, together with de Valera's heated anti-partition campaign, also implied that there was a sizable anti-British, republican constituency in southern Ireland, which might once again view England's danger as Ireland's opportunity. London feared that de Valera might be swept away by radical forces to his left – just like John Redmond, the leader of the Irish Parliamentary Party, in the First World War. Together with evidence of German intrigues, it created fears that Ireland would be a source of insecurity for Britain if war broke out.

During the 1930s the United States became of increasing importance both to Irish nationalist leaders and their British opponents. Immediately after his election to power in 1932 de Valera tried to mobilise Irish-America in support of his struggle against Britain. The American Association for the Recognition of the Irish Republic (AARIR) was revived at a convention in New York on 12 August 1932. It produced a steady stream of anti-British propaganda over the next seven years: Jimmy Thomas, the Secretary of State for Dominion Affairs, complained that 'there was plenty of evidence to show that every opportunity was taken in the U.S.A. ... to give a totally misleading impression of the facts, and to put the United Kingdom in the wrong'.[139] During the 1938 negotiations de Valera pointed to the anti-British bias of Irish-Americans as a reason why London should offer a generous settlement. After the agreement was reached, de Valera made the United States the main front in his public campaign against partition, urging the AARIR to increase its agitation.[140] The AARIR issued strident circulars, advising Irish-Americans to block British attempts to forge an alliance with Washington. In 1939 de Valera planned to visit the United States to open the Irish pavilion at the World's Fair; he would combine this with a public speaking tour on the iniquity of partition. Malcolm MacDonald 'supposed Mr. de Valera would make some frightful speeches' – he was relieved when the Irish leader cancelled the trip because of the international crisis.[141]

Seán Russell also recognised the importance of the United States to the Irish cause. In May 1939, at the height of the bombing campaign, he made a sensational visit across the Atlantic. He attended the Clan na Gael annual convention, toured the country and gave interviews to the press and radio stations. 'You know those bombings in England you've been reading about?' he boasted to the *Los Angeles Examiner*. 'I ordered those ... and they'll keep on with systematic regularity until the British troops are taken out of Ireland and my men are released from jail.'[142] Russell's trip coincided with a tour by the King and Queen to Canada and the United States. The British Consul learnt from an informant (albeit of 'doubtful reliability') that Russell was in touch with local German-American leaders with a view to arranging an 'attempt on the King in New York'.[143] The New York Police Department also received a report that explosives were stored in a building in

Newark for the purpose of blowing up the royal train.[144] Although these reports were unconvincing, the British government feared that Russell would organise 'hostile demonstrations' against the royals during a visit to Detroit. At its request, US immigration officials arrested Russell on 5 June on the charge of illegally entering the country, and held him until the dignitaries left the country.[145] The reaction of the Irish-American lobby revealed the American government's difficulties in dealing with Irish-American revolutionary activity. McGarrity's political allies led questions in Congress, appeals were directed to President Roosevelt, and the whole affair received a great deal of press coverage. As far as Clan na Gael was concerned, it was the best thing that could have happened: McGarrity commented that 'the rumpus raised about it in Washington has done our cause a great service, thank God for that'.[146] It demonstrated the capacity of Irish-America to flex its political muscles and the danger to the US administration of appearing to act as Britain's policeman. The result was that Russell went free, the deportation case against him collapsed, and his passport was returned to him some weeks later.

The attempts by de Valera and Russell to drum up American support threatened British interests. Britain's strategy for confronting the Axis powers relied on extracting maximum co-operation from the United States and, ideally, bringing the country into the war on its side. But Britain was opposed by a strong isolationist movement in the United States that was determined to keep the country out of European entanglements. Irish-Americans leaders were prominent in this movement and opinion polls showed that it had considerable support among the Irish-American community. Moreover, Irish-American republican organisations began to adopt explicitly isolationist stances as part of their anti-British propaganda. AARIR circulars at this time devoted more space to Britain's attempts to inveigle the United States into an alliance than to its treatment of Ireland.[147] Clan na Gael organised mass rallies in Philadelphia in February and April 1939 on the twin themes of support for Ireland and opposition to any American support for Britain. In May 1939 the Clan convention departed from its usual concentration on Irish matters to pass a resolution demanding that Britain and France repay the First World War debts owing to the United States – a key demand of the isolationist movement.[148] The British government did not exaggerate this threat: the Irish-American lobby was nowhere near as powerful has it had been between 1916 and 1921. Yet London constantly looked at the American dimension when formulating its Irish policy. For example, it was one of the main reasons why it decided not to extend conscription to Northern Ireland. 'It is of course most desirable to avoid a position which will result in Mr. de Valera stirring up formidable opposition to this country in the United States.'

British cabinet ministers warned. 'The American reaction to the contention that Great Britain is exercising a tyrannical coercion over Irishmen is a greater danger than the reaction in Eire itself.'[149]

IRA violence and the public campaign against partition also influenced British perceptions of political conditions in southern Ireland. As we have seen, British concerns about militant republicanism and de Valera's 'Left Wing' had played a major role in the decision to make generous concessions as part of the 1938 agreement. De Valera had skilfully manipulated these fears to his advantage. He now tried to use exactly the same arguments to convince the British government that the continuation of partition would be a cause of great insecurity in time of war. He told Malcolm MacDonald that:

> Just as one of his chief fears about our occupation of the ports was that if we were involved in war there would be an Irish attack on the ports and there would be hostility instead of friendship between our two people, so also if partition were still in being when the next war came he was afraid that it would be a powerful element influencing people in Southern Ireland to oppose us. He feared that there would be serious trouble on the border, which would be extremely embarrassing to him and an additional centre of trouble for us.[150]

He warned that if partition remained 'it was inevitable that in the course of time he and his Party would be superseded by something to the Left of them who would not be as patient and law-abiding as he had been.'[151] However, as with the ports, de Valera held out the prospect of complete defence collaboration and Irish participation in any war should partition be removed.

As war approached, de Valera hammered at British insecurities with increasing intensity. This was particularly evident at the time of the Munich Crisis in Autumn 1938, when he met the Prime Minister and other British representatives. De Valera not only supported Chamberlain's appeasement of Hitler but drew an explicit parallel between the Sudeten question and the position of the Catholic minority in Northern Ireland, asking that the British extend their generous policy to the latter.[152] More ominously, de Valera flirted with the notion that he too might sanction the use of force to resolve a minority problem. He stated that 'there was a time when if he had felt strong enough he would have moved his troops up to the line to which he thought he was justly entitled, just as Hitler was doing.'[153] De Valera generally qualified these threats with the assurance that 'he would not now adopt that solution', but it certainly caused doubts in London about Ireland's behaviour in a future war. Furthermore, the Dominions Office was concerned that while they knew of the friendly relations and co-operation

between the two governments, 'the world in general, and Herr Hitler in particular, knew none of these things'. This was pointed out by the Parliamentary Under-
Secretary for Dominion Affairs in October 1938:

> I thought it almost inevitable that the effect of Mr. de Valera's statement
> upon Herr Hitler would be to produce in his mind a certainty that in the
> event of war between England and Germany he could rely upon our hav-
> ing serious trouble in Ireland ... Herr Hitler might easily suppose that he
> [de Valera] was reorganising his Army in order that it might march upon
> Ulster: the language was Hitlerian and Hitler might well suppose that his
> pupil would copy his actions as well.[154]

When de Valera made similar noises to the American envoy in Dublin, it had
exactly this result. The Americans at first refused to supply an Irish arms purchasing mission when it visited Washington, believing that the weapons would
be used by Dublin in an attack on the north.[155]

The IRA bombing campaign in England provided further fuel for de Valera's
arguments about the precariousness of the political situation in southern Ireland. Far from being embarrassed, as some historians suggest, de Valera subtly exploited IRA actions to advance his case. This peaked as Britain's policy of
appeasement reached its nadir with Hitler's occupation of the rest of Czechoslovakia in March 1939. De Valera visited Chequers and, after expressing a hope
that 'what had happened would not deflect [Chamberlain] from the policy of
appeasement', he pointed out the dangers of partition.

> He said that he was very anxious about the bad feeling which was, he
> thought, growing in Ireland in consequence of the situation between
> North and South ... England was being blamed because she stood in the
> way and covered Northern Ireland with her protection, without which
> Eire would make short work of her. He himself strongly deprecated the
> use of force, but there were many in Ireland who would like to try out the
> issue in that way and he feared that, in the event of our being engaged in
> a European war, his position might rapidly come to resemble that of Mr.
> Redmond in the Great War when the latter lost the support of the major-
> ity in Ireland through his loyalty to the Empire.[156]

These are remarkable prophesies. Were they based on reality? According to
current historiography, certainly not: there is a consensus that militant republicanism was a spent force by this time, easily contained by the state. Moreover,
future events do not bear out de Valera's grave prognostications: war came, partition remained, yet the IRA did not launch any major attacks on the north, and

the stability of the south was barely affected. There is evidence that senior Irish officials did not share de Valera's concerns; indeed, they directly contradicted them. This was noted by the American ambassador in Dublin, John Cudahy. He reported how in August 1939 the Minister for Justice 'deprecated the sensationalism of the press, especially foreign newspapers, in dealing with the activities of the I.R.A', dismissing them as 'a group of young irresponsible hot-heads' numbering no more than 1,000. Similar analyses were provided to Cudahy by Joseph Walshe and the President of the High Court of Ireland. (On the other hand, de Valera gave the same sort of alarming assessments to Cudahy that he provided to British ministers – he was at least consistent in his statements.)[157] It is not clear whether de Valera sincerely believed that the threat was real, or was playing up the IRA threat for all it was worth to squeeze concessions from the British government, as he had successfully done during the negotiations in 1938.

De Valera's warnings did not change British policy on partition, but they generated concern in London about the power of militant republicanism in southern Ireland and the political stability of the state. In April 1939 the new Secretary of State for Dominion Affairs, Sir Thomas Inskip, warned that de Valera was 'doubtless faced with the unpleasant prospect of finding himself displaced by people more extreme than himself, and altogether unfriendly in their personal attitude to ... the United Kingdom Government'. He added that this was 'not a new experience for Irish leaders' – the ghost of John Redmond stalked British memory.[158] This image of Ireland as an unstable, violent place, menaced by republican wild men, had periodically resurfaced in British thinking throughout the 1920s and 1920s, usually at times of crisis. It reflected British stereotypes about the Irish that had much deeper roots.

O N the eve of the Second World War the British government looked nervously at its Irish 'back door'. First, there was no guarantee that British armed forces would be able use Irish naval and air bases to protect the vital Atlantic trade. Although some observers held out hopes that southern Ireland would return to the imperial fold once war broke out, neutrality appeared more and more likely. Second, there was evidence to suggest that Nazi Germany was carrying out propaganda and espionage in and through Ireland, and would try to use the IRA to conduct sabotage in the United Kingdom – the IRA's bombing campaign indicated that it was a willing partner. Third, there was a growing perception that a powerful republican 'Left Wing' threatened the survival of the de Valera government and the stability of the Irish state. The implications of these threats would largely depend on the attitude of the southern Irish government. The 1938 Anglo-Irish Agreement had produced an improvement in relations and intelligence co-operation on German subversion (in the form of the 'Dublin link'). Yet Dublin kept a distance compatible with neutrality, and refrained from full co-operation on intelligence and security matters, most notably with regard to the IRA. Because of the inadequacies of the British intelligence system's engagement with Ireland (for example, the lack of diplomatic representation), this meant that British knowledge of these threats was limited. Enough intelligence was collected to indicate that the threats were serious, but not enough to map their boundaries. British officials assumed that what they knew about German and IRA activities was the tip of a vaster and more dangerous conspiracy. This laid the basis for the emergence of the Irish 'fifth column' as a powerful influence on British policy after war was declared on 3 September 1939.

PART III

War and Neutrality, 1939–45

CHAPTER 9

The Irish Fifth Column

O N 1 September 1939 Hitler's troops invaded Poland. Two days later Britain and France declared war on Germany. The deadliest conflict in human history had begun. Éamon de Valera immediately declared that the Irish state, unlike the other Dominions, would remain neutral. Although hardly unexpected, this was the outcome that had haunted British military theorists ever since the Anglo-Irish Treaty was signed in 1921. Irish neutrality held many strategic dangers for the British war effort. First, Ireland presented opportunities for German covert operations against the United Kingdom: its waters and coasts, stretched across vital British trade routes, could be used for the clandestine shelter and supply of U-boats; it was an ideal base for espionage and sabotage; it was fertile ground for German propaganda and agitation. Second, there was a risk that Germany would seize Irish territory, using it as a base for attacks on British cities and shipping, or as a 'back door' for invasion of the United Kingdom. The third threat consisted of what Irish neutrality denied to Britain – the use of Irish naval and air bases by British forces. Exclusion from southern Ireland would greatly handicap Britain's ability to protect its Atlantic trade from German attack in the first two years of the war.

These three factors pulled British policy in different directions. Preventing German covert operations and deterring a German invasion required the goodwill and co-operation of the Irish government; on the other hand, access to Irish ports and air bases could only be achieved through pressure on the Irish state. British policy towards Ireland veered between accommodation and confrontation, depending on the fluctuating perceptions of these strategic dangers. Aware that British attitudes were finely poised, Éamon de Valera was prepared to make concessions to ensure that the balance was tipped in his favour. Neutral Ireland showed a 'certain consideration' for British needs. The Irish provided Britain with operational intelligence (such as sightings of enemy U-boats and meteorological reports), assisted the repatriation of British airmen who landed on Irish soil, and cracked down on Axis espionage, sabotage and propaganda activities. De Valera summed up this attitude in September 1939, when he assured London that he did 'not want Irish freedom to become a source of British insecurity.'[1] Rather than a moral stance, this was a finely judged policy to protect Irish neutrality. De Valera gave enough concessions to dissuade Britain from using force to seize Irish territory; he ensured that, from the British point of view, the benefits of co-operation would always (just) outweigh those of coercion.

The start of the Second World War brought some changes to Britain's intelligence arrangements *vis-à-vis* Ireland. The most important development was the establishment of a political representative in Dublin: in October 1939 Sir John Loader Maffey took up the position of 'United Kingdom Representative to Eire'. Educated at Rugby School, Maffey had served in the Indian civil service for more than two decades, before becoming Governor-General of the Sudan in 1926 and then Permanent Under-Secretary of State for the Colonies.[2] His new role in Dublin was intimately connected to intelligence. First and foremost, he provided crucial political intelligence from Ireland, something that had been sorely lacking since the establishment of the Irish state. For this purpose, he was a wise choice, as he quickly showed a real understanding of Irish political culture and began providing accurate, thoughtful reports to London. The creation of Maffey's position also made possible the appointment of British attachés and other officials in Dublin – Britain gradually built up all the accoutrements of formal diplomatic representation in southern Ireland. At the same time MI5, SIS and the intelligence departments of the Admiralty, the War Office and the Air Ministry all began to increase their engagement with Irish affairs.

Yet these developments did not make up for the long-standing deficiencies in Britain's Irish intelligence. Due to years of neglect, the British intelligence community started from a position of ignorance. The Director of Naval Intelligence, Rear-Admiral John H. Godfrey, later admitted that 'in 1939, we knew very little about Ireland or the Irish; had we known more we might have tackled the problem more effectively from the start'. Guy Liddell concurred that MI5 was largely 'in the dark as regards activities in Eire' in September 1939. It would take time for new agencies and personnel to build up an understanding of the situation in southern Ireland. In addition, there was persistent confusion over whether to rely on covert intelligence operations or co-operation with the Irish authorities to protect British security. Britain half-heartedly pursued both approaches in the early months of the war, but neither was entirely satisfactory.

Ireland continued to pose a unique conundrum for the British intelligence community: it was neither loyal Dominion, nor foreign state; neither entirely co-operative, nor entirely apart; neutral, but benevolently so. Rear-Admiral Godfrey described it as a 'political anomaly':

> The problem of intelligence in Eire was altogether different from that in any part of the world. Eire is a part of the British Commonwealth, and yet

a neutral republic. So close, that its defence is vital to that of Great Britain and Northern Ireland, but so politically cut-off that the elements of co-operative defence can only be arranged surreptitiously. Sentimentally united, but full of hatred and grudges against the English. A determined neutral with an enemy legation in its capital, it had a practically open frontier with Ulster. …

From the intelligence point of view Eire presented us with a lively paradox, and a continually developing and changing background, against which appearance and reality never reached a reasonable, much less a final, conclusion.[3]

The later achievements of wartime British intelligence can obscure its early problems. British intelligence on Ireland was highly deficient in the first year of the war. This was most evident in London's obsession with the Irish 'fifth column'. This term was first coined during the Spanish Civil War: when Franco converged on Madrid with four military columns, it was claimed that he had a 'fifth column' of supporters inside the city, ready to rise up against the Republican government.[4] Many believed that the fascist and communist powers had organised their ideological allies into similar fifth columns all across Europe. Because of its neutrality and the existence of powerful Anglophobic tendencies, Ireland was seen as prime fifth column territory. In the early months of the war the British intelligence system became increasingly worried about the activities of German U-boats, undercover spies and IRA gunmen. When magnified by emerging fears of a German invasion, this turned into full-scale hysteria during the summer of 1940. Exaggerated fears about the Irish fifth column would drive British policy and have a major, almost calamitous, impact on Anglo-Irish relations.

The war of nerves

THE outbreak of war was followed by seven months of uneasy, unreal calm. Apart from Finland's defence against Soviet invasion and naval skirmishes in the Atlantic Ocean, there was no serious fighting between the major powers. Germany carved up Poland, while preparing for a western campaign in the spring of 1940. Trusting in the defences of the Maginot Line, Britain and France were reluctant to go on the offensive, and took a leisurely approach to cranking up their war machines. This period came to be known as the 'Phoney War', the 'War of Nerves' or the *Sitzkrieg* (the 'sitting war').

During this period some members of the British government, led by the new First Lord of the Admiralty, Winston Churchill, refused to accept the constitutional legitimacy of the Irish policy of neutrality. Following a deterioration in the shipping situation in October 1939, Churchill urged his cabinet colleagues to make clear to the Irish government that they 'must have the use of these harbours, and intended in any case to use them'. He menacingly asserted that they should 'take stock of the weapons of coercion'.[5] His attitude was informed by deep animosity towards de Valera and profound disappointment at the evolution of the Irish Free State. As one of the original signatories to the Anglo-Irish Treaty, he viewed de Valera's constitutional revolution as a personal affront and a political humiliation. Since 1932 he had pressed the British cabinet to adopt the hardest possible line against the Irish leader. He had gravitated towards the diehard Conservative faction in parliament, making alliance with Colonel John Gretton and Howell Arthur Gwynne, the men who had bitterly condemned his actions in 1921 and 1922.[6] His wrath towards Irish behaviour was recorded by the new American Minister to Dublin when they discussed Irish neutrality: 'Churchill roared for a time, said he was sick of them (the Irish) that the English had given them a generous settlement and that immediately they began to break their engagements and were now stabbing England in the back'.[7]

However, Churchill was not representative of the entire British government. His sabre-rattling was successfully resisted by more moderate forces in the cabinet led by the Prime Minister, Neville Chamberlain, and the new Secretary of State for Dominion Affairs, Anthony Eden. They refused to countenance any seizure of the ports, recognised that, as a Dominion, Ireland had a right to declare neutrality and argued that neutrality had the support of the vast majority of Irish people.[8] They decided that the best policy was to co-operate with the Irish government in order to obtain the most benevolent neutrality possible. During the Phoney War the accommodating strain in Britain's Irish policy was in the ascendancy; consequently, Anglo-Irish relations remained fairly placid.[9]

With little risk of German invasion, and having accepted the non-availability of Irish bases, the focus of the British intelligence community was uncovering German covert operations and other subversive activities in Ireland. The first challenge was coastwatching, in particular the investigation of reports that U-boats were being 'succoured' on the Irish coast. The second was counter-intelligence: the prevention of German espionage and leakage of sensitive information. A third was assessing the IRA threat in Britain, Northern Ireland and, most of all, southern Ireland. The British response was to pursue co-operation with the Irish authorities, while engaging in limited clandestine intelligence activities. Neither approach yielded an adequate supply of intelligence; moreover, it would take time to build up a good understanding of Irish affairs. Consequently, British intelligence officers gave too much credence to the many rumours of nefarious German and IRA plots that flowed into Whitehall. They became increasingly concerned about the internal security of southern Ireland.

In the First World War there had been persistent rumours that German U-boats were sheltering along the craggy Irish coastline and receiving supplies of fuel, water and food. Identical rumours swept Whitehall in the autumn of 1939. Predictably, they received close attention from a belligerent Winston Churchill. Within two days of taking office as First Lord of the Admiralty, he asked:

> What does Intelligence say about possible succouring of U-boats by Irish malcontents in west of Ireland inlets? If they throw bombs in London, why should they not supply petrol to U-boats? Extreme vigilance should be practised.

On 24 September he noted that 'there seems to be a good deal of evidence, or at any rate suspicion, that the U-boats are being succoured from West of Ireland ports by the malignant section with whom De Valera dare not interfere'.[10]

Unlike in the First World War, the Royal Navy did not have its own coast-watching service in Ireland to investigate this threat; instead, it had to rely on the Irish authorities, which was a cause of deep dissatisfaction. Dublin had been slow to create a coastwatching organisation, declining repeated offers of British assistance since the start of 1939. A future head of G2 admitted that there was 'much confusion and some growing pains in the early days' of the service.[11] Most seriously, by the time war broke out, there was no system for communicating its reports to Britain. Sir John Maffey made some progress on this issue immediately after his appointment, persuading the Irish authorities to broadcast reports by radio *en clair*, so that they could be picked up by British listeners. However, the Admiralty did not have much faith in the competence of the Irish service or its willingness to transmit information.[12]

Rumours of U-boat activity around the Irish coast were taken seriously by the Naval Intelligence Division (NID). Its Director since early 1939 was Rear-Admiral John Godfrey. Regarded as an 'intellectual', Godfrey built NID into a large department and became an influential figure in British intelligence.[13] He also took the lead on Irish intelligence matters during the Phoney War. On 21 November 1939 he drew up a strongly worded memorandum for the War Cabinet, stating that there was no doubt that U-boats were using Irish territorial waters for the purpose of shelter and rest. In addition, he claimed that there was 'considerable' information that U-boat crews were obtaining provisions on land, as well as reports that certain individuals in the south-west were importing large quantities of fuel oil, which made the existence of U-boat 'refuelling bases' a real possibility. None of these incidents had been reported by the Irish coast-watching service. According to Godfrey, it could not be relied on, because the personnel did not report sightings 'to save themselves embarrassment' or were 'restrained by fear of the malignant anti-British elements in Eire'. He warned the cabinet:

(a) Eire is a dangerous open field for enemy activity.

(b) At present there is in regard to Eire a wide and lamentable gap in our Intelligence organisation.

(c) The gap cannot and will not be filled by relying on the Government of Eire to supply information.[14]

Godfrey concluded that this gap could only be filled by covert British intelligence activity. NID initiated a number of schemes of this sort in the early months of the war. First, in a conscious echo of the cruise of the *Sayanora* in the First World War (when Admiral Reginald 'Blinker' Hall had crewed a yacht with bogus Irish-Americans and sent it to Ireland to root out German intrigues) the Admiralty despatched undercover ships, or 'Q-ships', to Irish territorial waters.[15] This time they took the more prosaic cover of fishing trawlers working out of Milford Haven. From October 1939 the HMS *Tamura*, manned by Royal Navy personnel under Lieutenant Commander W. R. Fell, nosed around the bays and harbours of the west coast, ostensibly engaged in fishing, but actually on the hunt for German U-boats. None were ever discovered; instead, Lieutenant Commander Fell diverted his attention to suspicious activities on land, investigating cases of light signalling and reporting on dissolute natives who were 'perfectly capable of anything'.[16] A second form of intelligence-gathering authorised by the Admiralty was aerial reconnaissance: the maverick businessman and pioneer of aerial photography, Sidney Cotton, carried out a survey of the Irish west coast in an aircraft.[17] Finally, the Naval Intelligence Division asked serving and retired naval officers travelling to Ireland on their own business to investigate reports of U-boat activity.[18]

The Admiralty also pressed SIS to create a clandestine intelligence service among Irish residents on the coast – in effect, a duplicate of the official Irish coastwatching service. Churchill, with his love of secret service, had been quick to advocate this approach, minuting in the first week of the war:

Ask 'C' [head of SIS] what is the position on the west coast of Ireland. Are there any signs of succouring U-boats in Irish creeks or inlets? It would seem that money should be spent to secure a trustworthy body of Irish agents to keep most vigilant watch. Has this been done? Please report.[19]

Noting that 'in no civilised part of the world is Great Britain less able to obtain vital information than in Eire', Rear-Admiral Godfrey agreed that they could only deal with the 'dangerous gap' in their intelligence through 'the institution of S.I.S. organisation in Eire'.[20] Under Colonel Valentine Vivian SIS had operated a rudimentary 'information service' since 1932, based on a network of agents drawn from the Anglo-Irish loyalist community. However, Vivian resisted the Admiralty proposals in 1939, pointing out that an effective coastwatching service would require 1,000 agents, equipped with wireless transmitters, which would definitely come to the attention of the Irish authorities – this might imperil MI5's important relationship with G2 (the 'Dublin link'). Instead, Vivian agreed to extend his existing organisation in Ireland 'in a very small way without running any great risk of detection'. This compromise was accepted at a meeting with Godfrey on 27 November 1939.[21]

SIS began expanding its covert Irish network in the final weeks of 1939. Vivian appointed three or four 'head agents' in Ireland, dividing the south, west and north-west coastline between them. One head agent made a number of tours of the Kerry coast posing 'as a student of the habits and migrations of sea birds'. Another used old contacts in the boating community as 'unconscious informants'. They also recruited paid sub-agents among trustworthy friends. Progress was slow – by May 1940 they were still looking for 'local representatives' in Galway, Mayo, and Donegal – but the situation improved with the opening of the tourist season, as it facilitated access to a number of remote bays that agents had previously been somewhat 'chary' of visiting. By then SIS had a loose network, mostly drawn from ex-servicemen and Anglo-Irish loyalists, strung along the Irish coast. Coastwatching information was distributed in special 'QCW' reports (whereas reports from the pre-existing SIS information service were marked 'QRS'). In the Admiralty they were circulated under the codename 'Potatoes'.[22]

Although the new SIS network would remain undetected for some months, the poorly disguised NID activities came to the attention of the Irish authorities. For example, Godfrey described how Lieutenant Commander Fell was 'not only adventurous but credulous, went ashore at night on some wildgoose chase after an alleged spy, and was arrested by the Eire police'. Luckily he was courteously released the next day on a personal assurance from Godfrey, passed through Sir John Maffey, that 'he meant no harm'.[23] Two other retired officers, Lieutenant Michael Henry Mason and Captain Stuart Pearson, came to the attention of G2 in October 1939 when they boasted of collecting intelligence on behalf of the Admiralty. There is evidence that both men had some connection with NID, but they exceeded their mandates and were a source of great embarrassment to London. The political repercussions of these cases reinforced the reluctance of MI5 and SIS to engage in large-scale covert operations on Irish territory.[24]

Instead, the British government made further efforts to forge a satisfactory liaison with the Irish coastwatching service. Crucial to this was the appointment of Captain Alexander Boyd Greig as naval attaché in Dublin on 2 November 1939. Prompted by their discovery of British intelligence agents, the Irish authorities were determined to prove the efficiency of their coastwatching organisation. They encouraged Greig's appointment and allowed him to personally inspect the coastal network. The report that he made on 4 December 1939 'was unexpectedly favourable', while the Admiralty found his success in establishing good relations with Irish officials 'very heartening'. (At the same time, the naval attaché wrote that attempts at amateur espionage 'tend to cloud the co-operation between us and the [Irish] … officials'.) Following Greig's recommendation, the British agreed to supply wireless transmitters to the Irish service, thereby allowing outposts to communicate rapidly with headquarters. There was now a satisfactory arrangement for the transmission of reports of U-boat sightings to the Admiralty.[25]

The development of closer co-operation with the Irish coastwatching service led to a partial decline in Admiralty concern about the 'succouring' of U-boats on the Irish coast in the early months of 1940.[26] However, alarming rumours on this subject continued to reach London from private individuals and the SIS network. For example, on 18 January 1940 SIS circulated a 'disquieting report' that a submarine base, near the mouth of the Doonbeg river in Co. Clare, was visited three times per week by a German submarine camouflaged by a canvas screen. This went unreported because the head of the nearby Irish coastwatching station was an IRA member, recently deported from Britain, and the local Garda were 'terrorised' into silence.[27] NID lacked the confidence to give these unsubstantiated rumours the short shrift they deserved. Ironically, the absence of U-boat activity around the Irish coast may have contributed to British unease. Between October 1939 and May 1940 the Irish state's coastwatching system produced only four sightings of U-boats.[28] Godfrey later learnt that this was because 'Germany was, for the time being at any rate, being careful not to infringe Irish neutrality.'[29] But this was not realised at the time. Instead the absence of reports created further doubts about the ability of the Irish coastwatching service. It was assumed that German vessels *must* be exploiting Irish territorial waters. After the German military advance in the summer of 1940, 'all the old fears were revived.' Whitehall was inundated with reports of German U-boats calling on

Irish shores, and the Irish coastwatching service was again condemned as 'inefficient'.[30] It was not until the end of 1940 that this bogey was laid to rest.

It would take even longer for the British government to put a second threat in perspective: that of German espionage. For the first year of the war the British intelligence community laboured under the illusion that there was a German spy network operating in the United Kingdom. It was convinced that information on RAF sorties, naval movements and British operations in Norway had leaked to the enemy. This was not the case. The number of German agents was small, MI5 successfully detected all of them, and there was no evidence pointing to the existence of any others. Yet, because of organisational deficiencies and ignorance of Abwehr methods, 'MI5 and SIS were inclined to attribute the paucity of their evidence to the inadequacy of their sources of information.'[31] They worked on the worst-case assumption that their discoveries were no more than the tip of an iceberg. 'The Security Service was ... in the position of searching in the dark for something which did not exist', MI5's official history admits.[32]

Neutral Ireland was automatically implicated in these scares because it appeared to offer an ideal base for German espionage activity. The most obvious consequence of neutrality was the continuing presence of the German legation in Dublin. Although its diplomatic bag was suspended when war began, it was able to communicate with Berlin via telegram, subject only to a ninety-six-hour delay in London. Because the German diplomatic cipher was not broken until 1943, the British did not know what sort of information the Germans were sending. In addition, there was the prospect that the Abwehr had recruited agents in Ireland, unbeknownst to G2 and MI5. The small German and Austrian community was a likely pool of agents. Some of the more dangerous members were attending a Nazi conference in Nuremberg at the time war broke out; fifty others elected to return to Germany, and were shepherded through Britain under police escort; but many more remained.[33] The dangers were magnified by the decision to exempt Ireland from the elaborate wartime system of censorship and travel controls that separated the United Kingdom from the rest of the world. MI5 complained in November 1939 that 'the present situation in Eire may be considered as virtually neutralising the value of the rest of our security measures in the United Kingdom'.[34]

This threat caused varying reactions in Whitehall. The armed services and the intelligence agencies exhibited great concern. As early as 16 September 1939 the Chiefs of Staff discussed 'the necessity for taking steps to counter enemy activities' and 'spies' in Ireland. On the same day, the censorship department discovered that an illicit IRA radio station was broadcasting propaganda programmes across Ireland.[35] Once again the Admiralty took the lead on this Irish matter.

When it was proposed to move the main fleet to the Clyde in Scotland, Churchill warned that its whereabouts would soon become known to the enemy:

> There are plenty of Irish traitors in the Glasgow area; telephone communication with Ireland is, I believe, unrestricted; there is a German ambassador in Dublin. I should expect that within a few hours of the arrival of these ships it would be known in Berlin that the British heavy ships were definitely out of the North Sea, and could not return for more than sixty hours.[36]

This prompted Rear-Admiral Godfrey, with the support of MI5, to draw up a memorandum describing the 'large hole' in British censorship arrangements created by Irish neutrality.[37] Armed with these facts, Churchill persuaded the War Cabinet to set up a Leakage of Information Committee under Lord Hankey to recommend on tightening security.[38] However, Lord Hankey and the civil departments were less concerned about the danger of enemy espionage in Ireland than the intelligence chiefs: they concluded 'that on the evidence so far available, there was no justification for going beyond the statement that Eire might be presumed to be one of several sources of leakage of information to Germany.'[39] They acceded to Godfrey's demand that all telephones calls between the two countries should be monitored, but they shied away from imposing similar measures on telegrams and mails, because of the resources required and the possible political repercussions.

Instead the Leakage of Information Committee recommended an increased effort to obtain the co-operation of the Irish authorities. This touched a number of areas. First, the Irish government was persuaded to route all its foreign outgoing and incoming telegrams via London, which brought them under British censorship. Second, the Irish censorship department was encouraged to prevent sensitive military information being published in the press: it was 'extremely benevolent in its attitude', according to British officials. Third, the Irish and British authorities worked together to track down the illicit IRA broadcasting station. On 16 November two Irish officers visited the wireless detection organisation in the War Office to study its equipment and techniques. Using this knowledge, the IRA station was located, raided and put off the air on 29 December 1939.[40]

MI5 also sought to increase co-operation with Irish military intelligence (G2). On the outbreak of war MI5 set up a new Irish section, B9 (later B1H), within its counter-espionage branch. Captain Guy Liddell, second in command of B Division on the outbreak of war and its highly successful director after 1940, brought in his brother, Cecil, to run the Irish section. Educated at the University of Angers in France, Cecil had served alongside his brother in the Royal Artillery during the First World War (also winning the Military Cross). He studied law, but never practised, instead working in advertising. Because of family connections, he knew Ireland well and had spent many summers there in his youth.[41] Under the supervision of his brother he would manage MI5's Irish activities until the end of the war.

The Liddell brothers' chief task was developing the liaison with G2's director, Colonel Liam Archer. This 'Dublin link' had begun in 1938, and the two organisations were in regular correspondence by means of the Irish High Commissioner's diplomatic pouch and the Department of External Affairs in Dublin.[42] Yet, although co-operation increased during the Phoney War, the relationship was not as close as MI5 wished – and far less intimate than it would become. Colonel Archer declined to meet with MI5 officials during the first eight months of the war, despite repeated requests for a conference.[43] The first meeting between Cecil Liddell and his Irish counterpart did not take place until 15 May 1940. This had the effect of limiting British confidence in G2's abilities; the development of the 'Dublin link' after 1940 would demonstrate that personal contact was essential to good collaboration. G2 responded to specific MI5 requests on individual German suspects but it did not go out of its way to explain the overall security situation to the British. The deputy chief of G2, Dan Bryan, admitted that 'at this time, all queries from London, were treated with considerable caution', and 'the people in London … evidently felt that they were getting no background or general comments from us'.[44]

Neither G2's co-operation with MI5 nor the measures ordered by the Leakage of Information Committee were enough to overturn the conviction that German spies were rampant in Ireland. In the spring of 1940 there was a concerted campaign on this issue in the British press. On 31 March 1940 the Marquess of Donegall demonstrated to readers of the *Sunday Dispatch* how an individual could freely travel to Northern Ireland 'with plans of everything that every German spy has been able to collect', then take a train to Dublin and hand them over to the German Minister. The efforts of the Marquess in Belfast were matched by that of another amateur spycatcher in Dublin, Charles Graves of the *Daily Mail*, who found a viperous nest of enemy espionage and propaganda. Similar pieces occurred in the *Evening Standard* and the *Daily Mirror*, culminating in a long survey in the *News Review* on 2 May which described how, since the appointment of the German Minister in Dublin, 'strange men with square heads began striding self-importantly in and out of the red-brick Legation', part of an 'army' of commercial attachés sent to Ireland to spy on Britain.[45] The writers of these articles were the first of many journalists who went 'spy-hunting' in Eire during the war, determined to countenance any rumour of German intrigue.[46]

This press campaign evoked a storm of protest from the Irish government, which was confident that Germany was not receiving any valuable information via the country.[47]

Although the Dominions Office and Sir John Maffey were inclined to agree with the Irish government, the armed services and the intelligence agencies did not share this complacency. The War Office and the Admiralty had vetted the article by Charles Graves before it appeared: they not only raised no objection to it, but were 'anxious that it should be published'.[48] This was because British military and intelligence chiefs had come to the same conclusions as the British press. On 15 February 1940 they had detected a second illicit wireless transmitter just south of Dublin, which used the German diplomatic code – this suggested that the German legation might possess its own transmitter.[49] SIS sources also (erroneously) reported that the Germans had two more transmitters in the west of the country, sending regular meteorological information. On 2 May 1940 MI5 drew up an important memorandum listing all the advantages that southern Ireland possessed for German espionage.[50] Indeed, at this time MI5 believed that 'all the German system for transmitting information' from Britain to Germany was 'centered in Eire'. Thus, Eire was not just *a* source of information but *the* centre of the whole German espionage system.[51] This was an exaggeration. German intelligence activities in Ireland were limited; little, if any, valuable information leaked from Ireland to Germany in this period.

In its memorandum describing Ireland's suitability for German espionage, MI5 had pointed to the existence of 'subversive anti-British movements in Ireland' willing to work for the 'German Secret Service'.[52] Primarily, this meant the militant republican movement and its armed wing, the IRA. This was the third, and most serious, threat to exercise the concern of the British intelligence community during the Phoney War.

The IRA was most directly an internal security problem of the United Kingdom. The 1939 bombing campaign spluttered on into the war, albeit at a much-reduced level. Although there were no explosions in September, there were eight in October, forty in November, one in December, and a handful more in the coming months. The last incident was on 17 March 1940, St Patrick's Day. Attacks were confined to soft targets – such as mail boxes, public lavatories, phone boxes and shops – and were of little consequence to the war effort. Furthermore, the timing of the bombing campaign had been a boon to the British authorities as it had allowed them to crush the IRA organisation before the war began. This crack-down continued into the war: of the forty British subjects selected for internment under wartime Defence Regulation 18B in September, eighteen were members of the IRA.[53] Many more were pressured to leave the country, while others were convicted by the normal courts and imprisoned. (The best known was the future writer Brendan Behan, who was sentenced to three years detention in a borstal by a Liverpool court.) The Special Branch orchestrated this security effort, maintained a close surveillance on suspects, and had good intelligence on what was left of the republican movement. It concluded on 2 February 1940 that the IRA had 'ceased to exist as an organised body' in Britain.[54]

However, because of widespread unease about fifth columns, it was inevitable that there would be some concern over the threat of IRA attacks on military installations and war industries. Guy Liddell complained that although communists and fascists were extensively vetted before receiving employment, there was 'no check on the IRA', even though the latter were 'by far the most dangerous from a security point of view'.[55] Due to a discrepancy between the amount of explosives accounted for by the police and the quantity indicated in captured IRA documents, the Special Branch was concerned that there might be undiscovered IRA explosives dumps in the country.[56] As a result, the Home Office kept a tight control over Irish seasonal farm labour, and Irish workers were removed if suspected of republican sympathies: for example, an Irishman was moved from the naval fuel storage tanks at Scapa Flow, as he was 'accustomed, when in drink, to express I.R.A. sentiments of considerable violence'. British security chiefs thought it possible that the Germans had prepared a sabotage campaign; if this was the case, it was assumed that the IRA would be mixed up in it.[57]

The 'enemy within' had an even stronger resonance in Northern Ireland, where the term was sometimes applied to over one-third of the population – the Catholic minority, which was sullenly opposed to the unionist regime, blameful of the Westminster government for creating partition and potentially sympathetic to the Germans (who promised a united Ireland in the event of victory). One British official described their role as 'that of a neglected Achilles heel'.[58] Various forms of civil disobedience appeared in Belfast: the black-out was flouted in Catholic areas, gas masks burnt, two soldiers stripped of their uniforms, police patrols stoned, and a reservist shot in the abdomen. Republican slogans began appearing on walls:

> Damn your concessions England, we want our country.
> Join the IRA and serve Ireland.
> Remember 1916.
> England's difficulty is Ireland's opportunity.[59]

A long-planned security response was activated by the civil and military authorities under the auspices of the draconian Special Powers Act. Underpinning this response was internment: a large camp was constructed at Ballykinlar to receive IRA suspects. As in Britain, the task had already begun during the bombing campaign, and the wartime period simply saw an intensification of the crackdown.

The British army in Northern Ireland worked closely with the RUC to monitor the IRA threat. The commanding officer of Northern Ireland District, Major General R. V. Pollock, admitted that his forces were located there 'entirely with a view to internal security'. In a memorandum for his officers he wrote:

> The internal situation at the moment (owing to the unrest in EIRE) may be described as serious, but not alarming. The enemy within the gates when he strikes, strikes unexpectedly and where least anticipated. All ranks must be made to realise the situation; keep their eyes and ears open and their mouths shut.[60]

Because he 'felt himself very much in the dark about Irish affairs', Pollock called Colonel S. Hill-Dillon – a leading military intelligence officer in Ireland in 1921 – out of retirement and appointed him to his staff.[61] Pollock's warnings were somewhat vindicated by events on the night of 10 February 1940, when the IRA successfully raided a Royal Irish Fusiliers store at Ballykinlar, escaping with forty-three rifles.[62] However, although army chiefs devoted much thought to the security problems of Northern Ireland, they did not envisage any serious revolt. They were generally confident of their ability, and that of the RUC, to deal with the subversive threat.[63]

IRA activity in southern Ireland posed the greatest challenge for British intelligence. As the IRA's home base, events in southern Ireland determined the ability of the organisation to inflict damage in the United Kingdom. But the IRA also posed a threat to the political stability of the southern state that might have a more fundamental impact on Anglo-Irish relations. The crucial factor was whether the Irish authorities would be willing and able to crush the organisation. Initially, it looked as if they would. De Valera was committed to strong action against militant republicans, because their attacks on the United Kingdom and their flirtation with Germany threatened Ireland's neutrality. On the outbreak of the war he bolstered the special legal and security measures introduced in response to the IRA bombing campaign with a new Emergency Powers Act, which granted the government sweeping powers to intervene in every aspect of national life. The uncompromising Gerald Boland was made Minister for Justice, and immediate steps were taken against the republican movement. Warrants were issued for the internment of seventy IRA men on 15 September; fifty-five men had been apprehended by December; there was a concerted police effort to cut off IRA funding and to unearth arms dumps. This dislocated the organisation and prevented any major activity in the first months of the war.[64]

However, this quiescence did not last, as the IRA enjoyed a series of propaganda coups. It began with a high profile hunger strike by three men arrested at the start of the war. De Valera gave in to republican pressure and released the men, a decision he later regarded as 'one of the biggest mistakes' of his life. In any case, the hunger strikes proved unnecessary, as on 1 December an Irish judge ruled that internment without trial was in conflict with the constitution; all fifty-five IRA internees were released the following day.[65] Soon after, the IRA received another boost from the pending execution of two of its members (Peter Barnes and James McCormack) for their part in the 1939 Coventry explosion. A broad range of Irish organisations mounted a campaign for clemency, because, although both men had helped to prepare the bomb, they had not been responsible for placing it in the busy shopping street. When this failed – the men were executed on 7 February 1940 – there was a brief outburst of anti-British sentiment: protest marches were staged in Dublin, flags were flown at half-mast, and cinemas and theatres closed. De Valera responded to the executions with a bitter public attack on the British government. In England IRA bombs exploded on the eve of the executions and again two weeks later – seven people were seriously injured.[66]

The IRA was also responsible for some audacious paramilitary operations in southern Ireland. On 23 December 1939 IRA men raided the Magazine Fort in Phoenix Park, the repository for the bulk of the Irish army's ammunition, and stole over a million rounds of ammunition. Although 90 per cent was soon recovered, the raid generated huge publicity – a future chief of G2, Colonel Dan Bryan, later referred to it as 'our Pearl Harbor'.[67] Soon after, a Garda detective was shot dead by an IRA man in Cork city. This was followed by three major IRA attacks in April and May 1940: on one occasion, a gang armed with machine guns attacked police guarding the state mails in a failed attempt to seize Maffey's diplomatic pouch. The government's response was to rush an Emergency Powers (Amendment) Bill through the Dáil, granting it new powers of internment.[68] The Irish army was also put on high alert, as it was believed that the IRA was planning attacks on the border and on army barracks in the south.[69] This time, when republican prisoners went on hunger strike the government stood firm: two men were allowed to die, and the hunger strike collapsed. De Valera made a special radio broadcast on 8 May 1940, stating that the policy of patience towards the IRA was over, which was a prelude to the unleashing of the full force of the state in the coming weeks.[70]

Throughout the Phoney War the IRA laid its plans in conjunction with Nazi Germany. In early September a Breton nationalist, Paul Moyse, carried an Abwehr keyword for enciphered radio communications to an IRA contact in London. From 29 October the IRA broadcasting station in Dublin was used to exchange messages with the Abwehr. After it was located by the Irish authorities two months later, the IRA employed an Irish writer with an impeccable republican pedigree, Francis Stuart, to restore the Abwehr link. Stuart had been impressed by Nazi Germany when he had carried out a lecture tour at the invitation of the German Academic Exchange Service shortly before the war. He accepted an offer of a lectureship from Berlin University and set off for Germany in January 1940, carrying a message from the IRA Chief of Staff.[71]

The Abwehr, impressed by the Magazine Fort raid, was also keen to restore communication with the IRA. It decided to infiltrate an agent named Ernst Weber-Drohl into Ireland to hand over money, instructions and a replacement transmitter. In a colourful profession, the sixty-one year old Weber-Drohl must go down as one of the most unusual agents to be employed by any intelligence service during the war. Born in Austria, he had worked as a professional wrestler and circus strong-man in America and Ireland, before purchasing the title of Doctor of Chiropractic in New York and finally settling in Germany. He attracted the attention of the Abwehr because he spoke passable English and because his sojourn in Ireland had produced two illegitimate children. He was landed by U-boat at Killala Bay on the west coast of Ireland on the night of 8 February 1940. Despite losing his radio when his rubber dinghy capsized, he succeeded in travelling to the house of James O'Donovan in Shankill, Co. Dublin, where he handed over a large sum of money ($14,450). He also passed on instructions that urged the IRA leaders to concentrate on military rather than civilian targets in its sabotage campaign, and asked them to send a liaison officer to Berlin who could accompany a shipment of arms to Ireland. After some weeks at liberty, Weber-Drohl was arrested by the Irish police, but his cover story that he was looking for his long-lost children fooled a judge. Despite the efforts of G2, who suspected that he was an intelligence agent, it proved impossible to keep him in detention.[72]

It was now the turn of the IRA to respond. Stephen Carroll Held, the son of a German immigrant and a close associate of the IRA, visited Hamburg between 20 and 23 April 1940. He passed on messages from the IRA Chief of Staff, Stephen Hayes, requesting German assistance. He also carried with him a plan for the invasion of Ireland, 'Plan Kathleen', which envisaged a German invasion of Ulster, combined with an IRA offensive across the border. Although the Germans were sceptical of this plan, Held returned home satisfied, as the

Abwehr promised to send a German liaison officer to Ireland to work out joint plans in more detail.[73]

With this last initiative, the IRA was not merely requesting German funds or arms but conspiring with Germany to organise an invasion of Ireland. What did the British government know of this serious threat? All the evidence indicates that the British had little intelligence on the real links between the IRA and Germany at this time. Francis Stuart and Stephen Held were able to pass through Britain on their way to the continent without hindrance; London did not intercept the messages sent via the IRA transmitter to the Abwehr; MI5, despite harbouring suspicions, was unaware of Weber-Drohl's Abwehr credentials until much later in the war.[74] British intelligence's failure to detect these contacts was partly due to a similar ignorance on the part of the Irish security agencies.[75]

Yet if London lacked real evidence of contact between Germany and the IRA, this was more than made up for by a flow of false reports on the subject. These reports came from the most unlikely places. In December 1939 the British naval attaché in Lisbon warned that German merchant ships in Vigo were loaded with arms and ammunition destined for Ireland. He added that some of these ships had already slipped through British patrols to land their cargoes. Similar information came from the British embassy in Madrid, which reported that a Spanish vessel, the SS *Castillo Monforte*, had sailed from Cadiz for Galway Bay loaded with 3,000 cases of artillery shells and small arms.[76] These unfounded reports joined the long list of gunrunning scares that had periodically surfaced at times of crisis over the previous two decades. An equally unreliable story came from a British naval attaché even further afield – in Buenes Aires. It was based on a conversation with a sailor from the *Graf Spee* who had spent two years attached to the German legation in Dublin. He claimed that IRA leaders were 'in close touch' with the German legation, that the IRA received funds from the German embassy in Washington, and that 1,000 IRA members 'had been instructed in explosive [*sic*] by German experts'. The sailor added that he had visited Cobh before the war and made arrangements for submarines to get food supplies.[77] This was probably invention on the part of a mischievous German sailor, if not a deliberate plant by German intelligence.

The Naval Intelligence Division was not the only source of reports of this nature. In the same month, January 1940, the Director of Military Intelligence circulated a report that was one of the most fantastic of the whole war. Its author was a southern Irish loyalist, then living in London, who had done most of his 'soldiering' in the Leinster Regiment before 1922. His information came from former regimental comrades, with whom he was still in touch. The report warned that everybody in the south was 'talking in dread of another rebellion which will take the form of a definite attack on Ulster' synchronized with a 'big German offensive'. American money was 'pouring into the South', together with arms from Germany, as 'every southern and western cove may harbour German submarines':

> To underestimate the republicans would be a mistake: they show a remarkable cleverness and an extraordinary cunning organisation in their bombing outrages in London and elsewhere. The fanatical spirit and determination of these people is not realised: they will stop at nothing, so strong is their misguided patriotism and their readiness to fight desperately, however, treacherously.

The writer asserted that 'the wretched, ill-disciplined and badly officered' Irish army would make little attempt to resist this German-IRA plot: 'One need only appeal to their hatred of Ulster and the Union Jack to get them to mutiny.' Moreover, once the attack was launched, de Valera would 'change over and be made (either through his own wish or at point of pistol) the leader of a new republic ... De Valera is anti-England to the hilt and will prove a traitor.' Referring to his previous service in India, the retired officer ended with the priceless exhortation:

> This is no cry of 'wolf', and I might add that I was the first to warn General Sir William Marshall in Malaber in 1920 re the pending outbreak of the Moplah Rebellion, having on shikari seen Moplahs sharpening knives, pikes and sickles, in outlying forges in the Jungle.[78]

This exotic report might have been dismissed had it not been in line with similar information provided by the clandestine network operated by SIS in southern Ireland. After the start of the war SIS produced very alarming reports on the power of militant republicans and the extent of German subversion in Ireland. One example from 28 November 1939 warned of an imminent IRA attack on Northern Ireland that would have the support of 90 per cent of the Irish army.[79] Guy Liddell noted in his diary that 'very gloomy' SIS reports for February and March indicated that 'revolutionary action' in Ireland was 'almost inevitable'.[80] Three reports for April and May provide some of the most startling information. They described worsening economic conditions, rising unemployment, numerous strikes and a dramatic decline in support for the de Valera government, all exploited by the IRA. The government's efforts at suppressing the IRA were not 'bearing fruit' and would 'hardly prove sufficient to check any possible insurrection'. Germany had provided money through the United States of America and had landed large cargoes of rifles by submarine: a man named Rickett was cited as an IRA representative who was in frequent communication with German

U-boats. Again, one of the greatest dangers was the attitude of the Irish army. The SIS report claimed that 'great efforts' had been made by the extremists 'to seduce soldiers from their allegiance' and 'some untoward event might lead to a considerable proportion of the Defence Forces throwing in their lot with the I.R.A.' In addition, there was a risk that republicans in Fianna Fáil would split from de Valera and set up a rival party. 'According to a credible source', SIS warned, 'the leaders of the extremist organisations are awaiting a favourable opportunity for effecting a *coup d'état* in Eire and then marching on Northern Ireland.'[81]

These were extraordinary warnings. Were they taken seriously? Some sections of the British government were inclined to be sceptical because the bleak intelligence on Irish affairs was counterbalanced by information from the United Kingdom Representative in Dublin, Sir John Maffey. In his regular reports to the Dominions Office, he concluded that the Irish government had the militant republican movement 'well under control.'[82] De Valera's violent reaction to the Coventry executions in February did briefly jolt Maffey, who pondered whether the Fianna Fáil party was 'to find common ground with their old and bitter enemy the IRA.'[83] Yet these doubts were temporary, his despondency possibly due to his being in bed with fever at that time. Maffey quickly reverted to a much more benign interpretation of the situation. This can be seen in his reaction when the Dominions Office paraphrased the alarming SIS reports and sent them to him for comment. On both occasions Maffey sent long and considered replies in which he refuted each SIS claim. He branded the reports as mere 'rumour' – 'I do not attach special significance to any of them' – and said that there was 'no indication of a storm brewing'. He wrote: 'You can discount all the rumours of extensive drillings, receipt of arms from German submarines, plans for attacking the Northern Border, etc.' He was convinced that the government had the measure of the IRA and had definitely 'put their foot down':

> There is no sympathy in the country with the activities of the 'new IRA' ...
> Now that the de Valera Government have at long last taken their measure
> the dangers inherent in the movement are definitely lessened, though no
> doubt there will be a flare up from time to time.

He dismissed suggestions that the morale of the Irish army was bad: 'Eire to-day is 90 per cent pro-Ally.'[84] This analysis was broadly accepted by the civil servants of the Dominions Office.

As in 1922 there was a clash of opinion between the British government's civil representative in Dublin and its intelligence chiefs. This was brought into the open when Maffey was summoned to London on 17 May 1940 for a meeting with Guy Liddell of MI5 and Colonel Vivian of SIS. Maffey dismissed the alarmist SIS reports then in circulation, stating that they 'were similar to hundreds of others that were going round Eire which had little or on foundation'. However, Vivian 'hotly contested this and told Maffey that he thought he was under-rating the position'; both MI5 and SIS were convinced of the power of the IRA and the threat of German subversion in Ireland. Thus, the civil departments and the intelligence agencies had diametrically opposed views of the situation in Ireland.[85]

The problem was that British policy-makers had no way to choose between the reassuring despatches from Maffey and the alarming reports circulated by the intelligence agencies. Intelligence was circulated in the 'raw', without any assessment of its worth. Reliable information and unfounded rumour floated around Whitehall with equal status, and it was left to the policy-maker to choose between them. Those without the benefit of the Dominions Office's knowledge of Irish affairs did not always choose wisely. There is evidence that many British cabinet ministers leaned towards the alarmist interpretation of Irish affairs peddled by the armed services, MI5 and SIS in the first half of 1940. The intense debates over whether the British government should offer a reprieve to the IRA men under sentence of death for the Coventry bombing indicate a widespread belief that the executions would prompt further IRA violence, weaken de Valera and possibly create a situation not unlike 1916: 'We could not hope to get through the war without trouble from the Irish', one Foreign Office civil servant gloomily noted on 12 February 1940.[86] This preoccupation with Irish rebels, together with reports of U-boats being succoured on the Irish coast and rampant German spying, created a perception in London that Ireland was a major threat to British security. This was an exaggeration.

The deficiencies in Britain's Irish intelligence during the Phoney War should be understood in the context of the performance of the overall British intelligence system at this time. As the official historian of British intelligence, Sir Harry Hinsley, points out, 'the early short-comings' of British wartime intelligence 'were as marked as the later successes'.[87] A flood of security work and rapid organisational expansion caused early confusion in MI5, which started off with just thirty-six officers. MI5 also began the war with a limited understanding of the German intelligence service, the Abwehr.[88] It was the job of SIS, and in particular Section V, to provide this sort of information, but it was unable to do so. Counter-intelligence work did not have a high priority in SIS: Section V had just one other officer and three secretaries in 1939, and even a year later it had only grown to eight officers.[89] This was in keeping with the poor performance of SIS during the Phoney War. It was not only unable to provide reliable intelligence on German intentions, but was itself penetrated by the German intelligence services in the Netherlands. The Government Code & Cypher School (GC&CS), which came under SIS control, had only marginally more success. It was not until May 1940, after assistance from Polish codebreakers, that it finally cracked the first version of the German Enigma code machine – that used by the Luftwaffe.[90] The service intelligence departments were perhaps the least prepared for war. They were the 'Cinderellas' of the intelligence world, neglected and abused during peacetime, and then expected to blossom into princesses on the outbreak of war. It took time to recruit the right people and to build up expertise.[91]

Perhaps the greatest failing of the British intelligence system was the way in which it used information: 'The most serious and continuous intelligence problem during the six months of Phoney War', the historian Christopher Andrew writes, 'was the problem of intelligence assessment.' Good intelligence was accompanied by a flood of contradictory, erroneous information from private individuals, the diplomatic service and secret sources. British officials and policy-makers had the greatest difficulty in distinguishing between them; instead, rumour and preconception drove decisions. What was required was a system that would collate information from all departments, scrutinise it and come to unified, authoritative appreciations. The Joint Intelligence Sub-Committee (JIC) had been created in 1936 to do just that, but it had been ignored by the Foreign Office, the Chiefs of Staff and the intelligence chiefs, unwilling to give up their departmental powers. It would be eighteen months before it would take its rightful place as the central body for the assessment and co-ordination of intelligence.[92] These weaknesses would be brutally exposed when the 'real' war started in the spring of 1940.

Fifth column panic

T HE unreal spell cast by the Phoney War was comprehensively shattered by the launch of German offensives across Europe. Germany invaded Denmark and Norway on 9 April. The Danes gave little resistance, but Norway fought back and was joined by military forces from Britain and France. However, the Allies could not stop the German advance, and in late June the Norwegians surrendered. By then, events in Scandinavia had been eclipsed by the German offensive in the west. On 10 May Germany began its invasion of Luxembourg, Belgium, the Netherlands and France, using devastating *Blitzkrieg* tactics to split the Allies in two and race towards the Channel coast. The British Expeditionary Force was pushed back to Dunkirk, from where over 300,000 British and French soldiers were hastily evacuated by sea between 26 May and 4 June. Meanwhile, German divisions advanced inexorably towards Paris. France surrendered on 22

June, leaving Britain as the only major power in the fight against Hitler. These startling military reverses caused panic in London and led to the fall of Neville Chamberlain's administration. On 10 May the bellicose, steadfast, inspiring Winston Churchill was appointed as the new Prime Minister.

The catastrophic Allied defeats produced a dislocating effect on British psychology, and generated two hysterias in the summer of 1940: first, fear of imminent invasion and, second, a 'fifth column panic'.[93] For centuries the cornerstones of Britain's security against invasion had been denial of the Channel ports to a potential invader and the strength of the Royal Navy. By May 1940 German divisions lay within sight of Dover. In addition, Germany had made novel use of parachutists, gliders and other forms of aerial transport in its European campaign, which raised the possibility that it could mount an airborne invasion of the United Kingdom, thus leap-frogging the Royal Navy.[94] In fact, Hitler had no wish to invade Britain at this stage, hoping instead to come to a negotiated peace. Preparations for a German landing only began on 2 July; the operation was never envisaged to start before September. However, the British intelligence community was ignorant of German intentions. There were no reliable SIS sources, signals intelligence was limited, and aerial reconnaissance was in its infancy. Instead, driven by erroneous assumptions, military and intelligence chiefs latched onto a stream of unfounded invasion warnings from representatives abroad. From the middle of May even as the German army still fought the French, the British government became convinced that a German invasion of Britain was 'imminent'.[95]

Fear of the enemy without was accompanied by even more hysterical fears of the enemy within – the 'fifth column'. This was partly caused by a failure to comprehend the reason for Germany's military victories in Europe. German success came from surprise, strength and the use of new military tactics, in particular the exploitation of armour and airpower in ground operations. However, British diplomats and journalists produced sensationalist accounts of how foreign agents and local sympathisers had given crucial assistance to the invaders by sabotaging military installations, guiding parachutists to their targets, issuing false orders and spreading defeatism. The British intelligence system, looking for a 'secret weapon' that would explain the incomprehensible, concluded that fifth columns had been instrumental to German conquests.[96] This failure of foreign intelligence had an enormous impact on British domestic security. It was reasoned that if Germany had assiduously cultivated fifth columns before attacking its European neighbours, and if the United Kingdom was the next target of invasion, then surely a similar fifth column must exist there as well. From May 1940 the press and public took this as a certainty. The idea of an indigenous 'fifth column' captured the darker recesses of the popular imagination, just as it had in 1914. 'Rumours grew and changed their shapes like the more incredible kinds of cactus', one woman recorded. 'From every part of the country there came the story of the Sister of Mercy with hob-nailed boots and tattooed wrists whom somebody's brother's sister-in-law's cousin had seen in the train.'[97] The Ministry of Information, which was responsible for monitoring opinion, noted that 'Fifth Column hysteria is reaching dangerous proportions.'[98]

The British government and its intelligence agencies were equally gripped by this hysteria. From Churchill to the Joint Intelligence Committee to the Commander-in-Chief of the Home Forces, it was taken as axiomatic that there was a powerful fifth column in Britain waiting to assist a German invasion. The inter-service Joint Planning Staff stated on 5 May:

> Bearing in mind the important part that the German 'Fifth Column' has played in their war plans and the extent to which freedom of action is given to the great numbers of enemy aliens in this country, there is no doubt that 'Fifth Column' activities will play a very dangerous and important part in any operation the enemy may undertake against this country, unless adequate steps are taken to deal with them.[99]

The Ministry of Information was even more blunt. 'There is a fifth column in Britain', it warned the public. 'Anyone who thinks there isn't, that it can't happen here, has simply fallen into the trap laid by the fifth column itself. For the first job of the fifth column is to make people think that it doesn't exist.'[100] This led to a dramatic tightening of domestic security. The service departments and MI5 persuaded the cabinet to introduce mass internment: by the end of June 27,000 enemy aliens and 1,335 British citizens, mostly fascists, had been detained.[101] In addition, a powerful, inter-departmental Home Defence (Security) Executive was set up under Lord Swinton 'to consider all questions relating to defence against the Fifth Column.'[102]

Whereas Britain did come under a very real threat of invasion (although not until later) the hysterical reaction to the 'enemy within' was unfounded. There were no enemy agents at large at the time; no instance of enemy sabotage ever occurred; there was no fifth column. How could the British intelligence community have been taken in by such an illusory threat? A principal reason was the deepening chaos within MI5. Public hysteria generated a flood of reports about suspected fifth column activity with which the organisation was unable to cope: the official historians of British wartime intelligence conclude that 'MI5 was near to breaking down completely by the spring of 1940.' Churchill sacked Sir Vernon Kell on 11 June 1940, ironically for not doing enough to uncover the fifth column. This heralded a period of greater confusion and plummeting morale, which only ended when Sir David Petrie, another former Indian intelligence officer, took over as Director-General in the winter.[103] In the meantime, MI5 officers threw themselves into investigating the limitless reports of fifth column activity. They were unable to find any real evidence, for the simple reason that no evidence existed, but this was put down to the inadequacies of their methods or the sophistication of the enemy. It never shook the belief that there was a powerful German fifth column in the country: the Home Defence (Security) Executive insisted that, although they had 'no precise knowledge of the organisation they were fighting ... they were convinced of its existence'.[104] In such a distinctly unempirical atmosphere, it was difficult to disprove the fifth column thesis.

The conceptual chaos in London in the summer of 1940 made it likely that the fifth column theory would be applied to Ireland no matter what. Yet evidence of Germany covert operations in Ireland magnified the effect. In the early hours of 5 May a German intelligence officer, Hermann Görtz, landed by parachute in Co. Meath. A failed lawyer, he had spied for the Abwehr in Britain in 1935, before being arrested and sentenced to four years imprisonment. Following his return to Germany, he was selected by the Abwehr as a liaison officer to the IRA. The aims of his mission were to establish a radio link between the IRA and Germany; to promote reconciliation between the IRA and the Irish state; to channel the efforts of the IRA towards attacks on military targets in Northern Ireland; and to report information of military importance. Although Görtz's landing went awry (he was dropped in the wrong place and lost his radio transmitter), he found his way to the house of Iseult Stuart (the estranged wife of Francis Stuart) and made contact with the IRA leadership. After handing over a considerable sum of money, he was shown a copy of Plan Kathleen and briefed on the strength of the IRA. He was then moved to the house of Stephen Held, but word of his presence leaked to the Garda and a raid was carried out on 24 May. Görtz narrowly evaded capture, but the Garda discovered a large quantity of incriminating material: this included his Luftwaffe cap, his parachute, $20,000 in cash, coded messages for transmission to Germany and a document referring to 'Plan Kathleen'. Stephen Held and Iseult Stuart were brought to trial. The Irish government allowed the affair to receive maximum publicity, as it wished to waken the country from its complacency and discredit the IRA.[105]

Undaunted, the Abwehr despatched five other agents to Ireland during the summer. The first, Walter Simon (alias Karl Anderson), was landed by U-boat in Dingle Bay on the night of 12 June. Like Görtz, he had engaged in pre-war spying missions in Britain and had been arrested, interrogated by MI5 and imprisoned. His primary mission in Ireland was to transmit weather reports by radio – the country's geographical position made this data vital to accurate forecasting. He was also to send information on the movements of escort vessels off the coast of Northern Ireland. However, on the morning of his arrival, he overindulged in Irish whiskey, boasted that things would change in Ireland 'when Hitler comes to this country' and began asking those around him whether they were members of the IRA. By the afternoon he was in Garda custody – he was sentenced to three years in prison for illegally entering the country. Simon was quickly followed by a second Abwehr agent, Wilhelm Preetz. Married to an Irishwoman, he spoke excellent English and had been in Ireland for much of 1939. He was landed at the end of June, most likely by U-boat on the Dingle peninsula. Like Simon, his mission was to send weather reports and to observe shipping traffic around the Irish coast. Because of his family connections he was able to avoid detection and set himself up in a Dublin flat, from where he used his radio transceiver to send messages to Berlin. However, he had little to report, as he 'spent a great deal of time in dissipation', lavishing his Abwehr funds on cars, women and entertainment. His transmitter was located by G2, and he was arrested on 26 August. Finally, the Abwehr landed a party of three men by boat in Co. Cork, from where they were expected to travel to Britain to carry out sabotage. Two of the men, Herbert Tributh and Dieter Gärtner, were from German South West Africa (now Namibia) and did not speak English, while the third, Henry Obed, was Indian. The conspicuous troika immediately aroused the suspicion of locals around Skibbereen. They were quickly arrested and their sabotage equipment discovered.[106] These unfortunate men were a prelude to a wave of twenty-one pre-invasion agents directly despatched to the United Kingdom between September and November 1940. In common with those sent to Ireland, almost all were ill-suited, badly trained and quickly apprehended by the security forces.[107]

At the same time as German agents were being infiltrated into Ireland, two IRA leaders, Seán Russell and Frank Ryan, made their way to Berlin. After a storm of controversy during his pre-war tour, Russell had gone to ground in America during the summer of 1939. Once war began, he approached the Abwehr, which smuggled him to Genoa on board a transatlantic liner and brought him to Berlin in early May 1940. Two months later he was joined by Frank Ryan, an IRA leader and committed socialist who had followed a very different path: he had been captured while fighting with the International Brigade in the Spanish Civil War and had languished in Burgos prison for two years, awaiting execution. In 1940 the Irish minister in Madrid, Leopold Kerney, turned to a Spanish lawyer with links to the Abwehr to secure his release. The matter was brought to the attention of Admiral Canaris, who used his influence with General Franco (an old colleague from the First World War) to arrange Ryan's 'escape'. On 14

July Ryan was met by Abwehr representatives on the French border, wined and dined in Paris and taken to join Russell in Berlin. There, both men were placed in the hands of Dr Edmund Veesenmayer, a senior SS officer who went on to become the German Foreign Ministry's *coup d'état* specialist, engineering the overthrow of hostile regimes in the Balkans. He decided to send Russell and Ryan to Ireland to prepare the IRA to assist a German invasion of the United Kingdom: a senior Abwehr officer later referred to it as 'a new version of the Casement operation'. Like the Casement mission, it was a failure. The two IRA men departed from Wilhelmshaven by U-boat on 8 August, but Russell died from a burst gastric ulcer just 100 miles away from the Galway coast. Because he had not been briefed on the object of the mission, Ryan elected to return to Germany.[108]

Outside of the IRA, other Irish groups emerged in the summer of 1940 to voice active support for the Nazi cause. Fascist ideas, first introduced to Ireland by the Blueshirts in the early 1930s, had a small group of adherents on the outer fringes of Irish politics. After German military successes in Europe, they became bolder. April 1940 saw the congregation of a new group called The Irish Friends of Germany around Eoin O'Duffy, Liam D. Walsh, Maurice O'Connor and J. J. Walsh. They also formed a party, Cumann Náisiúnta, which propounded the virtues of National Socialism. The Irish government later wrote that they were 'concerned at this time with securing that the Germans, if they invaded this country, would know that the members of Cumann Náisiúnta were their friends'. In August 1940 some of its members founded a second organisation with a similar ideology – the Peoples National Party. Its paper, *Penapa*, was virulently anti-semitic and expounded National Socialist policies. Apart from these small groups of quasi-intellectuals, there were larger sections of the Irish population, especially in the south-west, that were mildly sympathetic to Germany because of a traditional hostility towards Britain. Irish military intelligence concluded that many of these people might assist or tolerate a German invasion.[109]

These developments show that Ireland, unlike Britain, did possess a fifth column ready to assist a German invasion. But how serious was this threat? The Irish government was certainly not taking any chances, and introduced sweeping new security measures, such as internment, trial by military court with conviction to be followed by sentence of death, and the raising of a Local Security Force for the purpose of guarding against the 'danger of invasion' and 'subversive activities'.[110] The Held case provided de Valera with the political opportunity to unleash this security scheme on the IRA. On 3 June warrants were issued against 400 persons, and within days over 300 were interned in a special camp at the Curragh military base. The summer of 1940 was one of the quietest periods for

IRA violence. One of the few incidents occurred on 16 August, when Patrick McGrath and Francis Hart opened fire on a Garda raiding party, killing two detectives. The two IRA men were tried by the new military court and executed on 6 September, a clear signal of the government's uncompromising attitude.[111] The Irish authorities also took steps to control the pro-Nazi groups that sprung up in Dublin. *Penapa* was suppressed after one issue, fascist circles were heavily penetrated by Garda and G2 informers, and some of the leading figures (such as Liam D. Walsh) interned.[112]

It is impossible to say what would have happened if the Germans had invaded Ireland during the summer of 1940. The existence of willing IRA and fascist collaborators, and the ambivalent state of Irish opinion, meant that a German incursion could have produced some surprises. However, this should not be exaggerated. The vast majority of the Irish population was united behind neutrality, horrified by German aggression in Europe and prepared to resist a German invasion. The fascist groups that emerged in Dublin had miniscule support: one historian writes that 'Nazi Germany's Irish friends were insignificant figures', mostly 'psychologically flawed malcontents' or 'cranks, motivated by vanity or grievance'.[113] Whatever the actual power of the IRA organisation in May 1940, there is no doubt that it was neutralised by the government crack-down. The IRA Chief of Staff later confirmed that the events of this period finally killed the IRA as a political or paramilitary force in Ireland.[114] This was gradually realised by the Abwehr. After concluding that the IRA 'was rotten at its roots', Görtz sought to return to Germany so as 'to advise his authorities of the actual position in Ireland – about which there seemed to exist definite misconceptions'.[115] All the Abwehr operations in Ireland were comically disastrous. When interrogated by MI5 after the war, senior Abwehr officers observed with some disappointment that they never gained any significant results from Ireland or the Irish.[116]

Moreover, it is now clear that there was little threat of a German invasion of Ireland. Although an invasion plan (*Fall Grün*) was prepared, the German military staffs concluded that such an operation was unfeasible. They did not have naval supremacy; surprise would be almost impossible; the terrain afforded no protection; unpredictable weather made air support difficult; Ireland's position posed insurmountable supply problems.[117] Furthermore, it made no strategic sense to dilute the invasion of Britain by dispersing forces to Ireland, which was not vitally important. Thus, whatever Hitler's plans for invading the British Isles during the summer of 1940, they did not include Ireland. Rear-Admiral John Godfrey acknowledged this after the war: 'It is known now', he wrote in 1948, 'that Germany never seriously considered invading Ireland.'[118]

T HIS generally reassuring state of affairs was not evident to the British
government in the summer of 1940. Military developments on the European
continent wrenched Ireland from its sheltered position and thrust it onto centre
stage of the theatre of war. It was now a likely target of invasion, perhaps the next
neutral domino to fall. Invasion and fifth column hysteria ensured that evidence
of German intrigue would be magnified out of all proportion. Most immediately, this affected perceptions of the large Irish community living in Britain, as
it was thought to nurture fifth column elements. It would have an even greater
effect on perceptions of the militant republican movement in Ireland, as it was
thought that the IRA constituted a powerful fifth column capable of challenging the Dublin government and assisting a German invader. Ireland became an
issue of dominating importance during this period, as fantastic scares shunted
the more mundane realities aside.

Because of the IRA bombing campaign, it was inevitable that Irish citizens
in Britain would feel the effects of the paranoid, xenophobic and hyper-vigilant
atmosphere of the summer of 1940. The institution of a trial censorship on post
to Ireland in May contributed to this, as it revealed worrying attitudes among
the Irish community in Britain. The Postal & Telegraph Censorship Department warned that 'numerous letters' were 'passing from Irish Soldiers disclosing
arrangements to desert', while others disclosed 'the presence of I.R.A. or German sympathisers in this country'. Many Irish immigrants were 'so anti-British
in sentiment' as to make it questionable whether their presence in Britain was
'desirable'.[119]

The chief threat was, as always, the IRA. The Joint Intelligence Committee
(JIC) issued a major report on this subject on 2 May 1940. It listed four possible fifth column groups in the United Kingdom: enemy and non-enemy aliens,
the British Union of Fascists, the Communist Party of Great Britain and the
Irish Republican Army (whose strength, unlike the other groups, was listed as
'unknown').[120] A representative from the Home Office did his best to argue 'that
the IRA Organisation in this country had been almost entirely suppressed', but
the other JIC members disagreed. This fitted a pattern whereby the intelligence
agencies and armed services rejected the opinion of the Home Office on security
matters, deeming it overly complacent. The representative of the Air Ministry
could not be accused of this. Brigadier Hawes told the meeting that he was afraid
of aerodromes in Eastern Command being sabotaged by 'a few determined men
with automatic weapons ... just when the first major air attack was timed to
arrive' on the country:

There were large numbers of workmen on the aerodromes among which

might be IRA men or other enemy agents. The fact that there had been little if any sabotage up to date did not necessarily mean that the enemy had
not an organization prepared to carry it out at a critical moment. Speaking from the point of view of Headquarters Eastern Command, he would
like to see all aliens and Irish cleared out of the eastern part of the country
in which the fighter aerodromes were located.

A fortnight later the Director of Military Intelligence called for 'the measures in
force to ensure precautions against IRA action' to be 'increased'.[121]

On 8 June 1940 the discovery of a letter on a railway line near Manchester
produced a major scare. The document indicated that the Germans were planning a landing on the west coast of Britain in conjunction with the IRA, which
had established wireless communication between Arklow and the Pennines, and
had concealed arms and gunmen in caravans moving around the country. Guy
Liddell asserted that the contents of this letter rang 'fairly true' – he believed that
the IRA was more likely to be involved in a hidden German sabotage organisation 'than any other body'. It led to a special search of caravans throughout
Britain.[122] It also led the Prime Minister's intelligence adviser, Major Desmond
Morton, to conclude that Ireland was the 'power house' for the entire German
fifth column organisation in Britain.[123] There was little hard evidence of IRA
activity in Britain, but according to fifth column theory this was not a refutation;
indeed, it was even a perverse kind of proof.

A number of steps were taken to deal with this threat. Special checks were
imposed on Irish workers in critical factories and military facilities.[124] There
were strict controls on the movement of people between Ireland and Britain,
and Irishmen were prevented from travelling to Germany.[125] There was also an
intensification of the internment and deportation of IRA suspects (which had
been ongoing since the start of the war). For the first time the Irish authorities
provided information that led to the arrest of individuals in Britain, and asked
the British to share intelligence on those deported back to Ireland. Up to that
time they had been 'unwilling for political reasons to appear to be collaborating with the British Government'. The rate of deportation of 'I.R.A. undesirables'
became so great in May 1940 that the Irish government became 'rather concerned', as they could not keep track of them once they landed in Ireland. This
caused a change in British policy: from 1 June suspects were no longer deported,
but interned in Britain under Defence Regulation 18B.[126]

The decision to intern rather than deport was driven by the conclusion that it
was too dangerous to set such men loose in Ireland. The real importance of the
fifth column to Anglo-Irish relations lay not in suspicions of the Irish community

in Britain but in the belief that there was a rampant IRA fifth column in southern Ireland ready to assist a German invasion of that country.

Information to this effect poured into the British governmental machinery from unofficial sources – which mirrored the way in which the press and the public fuelled the wider fifth column panic in Britain. The British press had started a campaign on Ireland as a centre for German espionage in March and April 1940. This mutated into a full-blown fifth column scare following German successes in Scandinavia. One paper warned of 'the existence of a widespread movement in Eire to lend assistance to Nazi air and sea invaders'. It claimed that German paratroopers captured in Holland had declared that 2,000 members of their corps had been receiving 'lessons in Erse' for months. It added that Seán Russell, together with a 'well-known Irish novelist', a Dublin engineer and five IRA leaders from Britain, were all in Berlin assisting the Nazi General Staff.[127] Three days later the *Daily Mail* correspondent described how he had spent a week around the remote bays of the Kerry coast and had 'heard enough stories of "fraternisation" with U-boat crews to make any Briton's hair stand on end'. In Dingle he was shown a pub 'where Nazi sailors had toasted the downfall of "John Bull"'. He was told of a U-boat commander who regularly called at one of the islands for fresh vegetables: his usual 'hail' on pulling up to the tiny fishing jetty was 'Come on, Maggie, hurry up with those cabbages.'[128]

Whitehall received similar reports from private individuals. These came from sources as diverse as an Australian academic at Birmingham University, the Colonel Commandant of the Gloucestershire Special Constabulary, and a baron who served as an Inspector at the Ministry of Pensions.[129] Some of the most alarming tales came from Anglo-Irish residents in southern Ireland. A good example of how they used their connections to feed alarmist rumour into the governmental machinery was provided by Lady Dunalley, who lived on an estate at Kilboy, near Nenagh in Co. Tipperary. In a breathless report, she described how the Coventry executions had created 'a very hostile anti-British feeling all over Eire' with many expressing their hope that Germany would be victorious. She had been told that Germans had been 'pouring in lately into Eire' on neutral Dutch and Belgian boats. She had herself seen three specimens in Dublin – 'one a quite young man with scars on his cheek' – as well as 'a beautiful big silver car (an unusual sight in Eire) down at the Shannon driven by a foreigner – an unmistakeable Hun – with a frilly beard'. The IRA, 'run by very efficient men', was entirely financed and controlled by the Nazis:

> All this is Nazi work, and so are all I.R.A. activities. They have had a very
> easy time in Eire, and this neutrality has been a grand cloak. The fatuous

and pigheaded and shortsighted de Valera and his equally foolish party are easy tools, and the '5th Column' is getting it all its own way in Eire and <u>nothing to stop it</u>.

Lady Dunalley visited England in May and handed her report to Henry Morris-Jones, an MP who had distinguished himself in the hunt for the fifth column in Britain. He passed it on to Churchill, noting that 'even a layman can visualize the danger to our Western ports and shipping of anything like a firm occupation of Eire by the Bosch'.[130]

The press and private individuals provided many tales about the Irish fifth column. However, even more fantastic material came from within the British intelligence system. The government's obsession with the Irish threat was triggered by a discovery in Holland in the opening stages of the German *Blitzkrieg*. A German SS officer captured by the Dutch was found to be carrying plans for an invasion of Britain. A key part contained provisions for 'the simultaneous, or prior, occupation of Eire by air-borne troops, which would be landed with the assistance of the IRA'.[131] (It appears that these papers were lost soon after.)[132] This caused panic in Whitehall, as it was regarded as definite proof of German intentions. Over the coming months it was followed by a constant stream of reports that warned of a German invasion of Ireland. Many came from diplomatic missions abroad. Others emanated from SIS sources, which for two decades had furnished unreliable information on the IRA's foreign intrigues. The credence given to these reports was in keeping with London's general ignorance of German intentions and inability to filter unfounded invasion scares.[133] There is evidence that Germany conducted a campaign of deception in the summer of 1940 to convince Britain that an invasion of Ireland was imminent and thereby provoke a dispersion of forces from the main target – Britain.[134] It is even possible that the plans discovered in Holland were planted. Whether deliberate deception or not, British intelligence was well and truly deceived.

If the belief in an imminent German invasion can be traced to Britain's foreign intelligence, the fifth column obsession was the product of Britain's Irish intelligence. Spurious information was produced by many branches of the expanding British intelligence system. One of the most prolific sources was the postal censorship, which after 20 May 1940 was gradually extended to all incoming and outgoing Irish mails. This had primarily a counter-intelligence function, designed to prevent leakage of information to Germany. However, it also became a copious source of information on suspected IRA and German activities in Ireland: for example, on 19 July 1940 the War Office was studying a letter which indicated that eleven German parachutists had secretly landed near

Ballacolla in Co. Laois.[135] These letters contained little more than 'wild rumours', but they were given remarkable credence by the censors and by the intelligence departments to which they were circulated.[136]

Alongside the advent of full postal censorship, London despatched a number of individuals on covert and semi-official intelligence missions. The reports that survive indicate that these amateur spies did not have a good understanding of Irish conditions and frequently magnified the fifth column threat. For example, the Ministry of Information sent five representatives to Ireland between June and September 1940. One, a Miss Maxwell, gave a most alarming report. 'On all sides' she heard that the Irish army was 'riddled with graft', that it was 'a hot-bed of the I.R.A', and that British troops would find themselves fighting against Irish soldiers if the German invaded. 'The I.R.A', she warned, 'remain at the back of Irish politics, and have done for as long as I can remember, as a sort of perpetual bogey-man, who is always there, but is only spoken about in hushed whispers.'[137] Similar material was produced by the Naval Intelligence Division, which continued to conduct clandestine operations in southern Ireland. On 24 May Rear-Admiral Godfrey circulated a report from an informant who had contacts with the lower ranks of the IRA. He asserted that Germans were buying up properties on the Irish west coast at 'fabulous prices' in preparation for an invasion; that the IRA had assigned men to shoot leading politicians and army officers who would not fall in with its plans; and that 'the key of the German 5th column movement' consisted of thirty-five engineers in Dublin Corporation known as 'The Secret Brotherhood'.[138] It can be presumed that the intelligence branches of the War Office and Air Ministry, who also despatched officers to Ireland on amateur spy missions, produced the same sort of information.

However, when it came to the production of alarmist intelligence, no department could compete with the Secret Intelligence Service – it did more than any other organisation to foster the panic about an Irish fifth column. The chief culprit was the SIS man in Ireland, Sir Charles Tegart. A former Chief of the Bombay Police who had led a successful campaign against nationalist revolutionaries, he was probably the most famous of all the officers of the Indian Police.[139] In the 1930s he was posted from the Subcontinent to the British Mandate of Palestine, directing the construction of the infamous 'Tegart wall' – an eighteen-foot wide barbed wire entanglement erected on the border with Syria to exclude Arab rebels. As we have seen, he had been contracted to examine the Irish intelligence machinery at the height of IRA rebellion in 1920, but quit when he became disillusioned with his boss, Colonel Winter. He had kept up his links with Ireland in subsequent years, attending events of the Trinity College Dining Club and receiving an honorary doctorate from the university in 1933.[140] In the spring of 1940, when British intelligence in Ireland was again severely lacking, he was called back to the colours. Historians have tended to dismiss Tegart as an amateur busybody who was not taken seriously by the British government. This was not the case. Colonel Vivian (himself a former Indian policeman) asked him to 'keep an eye on events in Eire' – Tegart was therefore working for SIS. He made frequent trips to Dublin in the spring and summer of 1940 and produced reports that had considerable influence on the London government. His activities were in keeping with the rudimentary, informal nature of the SIS network already in place.[141]

SIS was the most powerful intelligence organisation in Irish affairs at this time. It took the lead over MI5, which was wracked by organisational problems. At meetings of the Home Defence (Security) Executive it was Colonel Vivian who quoted reports on IRA activity and passed on details of German agents captured by the Irish authorities.[142] When it was decided to draw up a 'Black List' of suspected fifth columnists in Ireland in August 1940, it was discovered that MI5's information was restricted to German nationals, that the Special Branch had information on just 200 Irish residents, 'all being members of the IRA', whereas SIS had a list of 700 'Irish suspects', both republicans and foreigners. Consequently, Vivian took charge of the project.[143] SIS's dominant role in 1940 indicates that the balance of Britain's intelligence relationship with Ireland was tilted towards covert operations rather than co-operation with the Dublin authorities.

SIS had been responsible for a steady stream of exaggerated reports on IRA activities and German intrigues since the start of the war. Unfortunately, few SIS reports are available from the summer of 1940. However, the type of intelligence that SIS was producing is indicated by a report that Major Desmond Morton, Churchill's intelligence adviser, wrote after a one-hour conversation with Tegart on 8 June. With references to Irish Gauleiters (regional leaders of the Nazi Party) and Quislings (derived from the name of a pro-fascist Norwegian politician who collaborated with Germany), nothing else in this period contained such a exaggerated tale of fifth column activity in Ireland:

> Did you know that the German Gauleiters of Eire are already there, known by name and functioning in a certain way? The local Quisling is Seán Russell, who has been landed in Eire by a German U-Boat. The whole of his shadow Government has been formed as the Apostolic Successor of the 1916 Revolutionary Government, and exactly parallel to Quisling's effort, this Government is awaiting the signal to declare a revolution at the moment that German troops land.

Tegart gave a graphic description of German penetration of the country. This contained some fact: he referred to the activities of Adolf Mahr and Klissmann [*sic*] since 1936. But it had far more fantasy: Tegart claimed that 'up to 2,000 leaders have been landed in Eire from German U-Boats and by other methods since the outbreak of war', and that 'local Irishmen accept the visits of U-Boats with as common place an air as they accept sun rise on a fine day'. After estimating that the staff of the German legation had grown to almost 300, he warned:

> They and other Germans in Eire have for the last year been buying up estates on the West and South coasts, rooting up hedges, levelling suitable fields for landing grounds, and ... they are now ready for most things ... there is no secret about this at all locally.[144]

Colonel Vivian read out similar reports to the Home Defence (Security) Executive on 29 May; his information – a hotchpotch of rumours about U-boats, German agents and IRA preparations for rebellion – was passed to the Irish government three days later.[145]

The British intelligence system, in particular the SIS network, became a vast machine for collecting every piece of rumour and gossip circulating in Ireland. This is the only explanation for the sort of material transmitted back to London. Sir John Maffey observed that Ireland was 'full of the wildest rumours and false intelligence reports' in the first year of the war.[146] It appears that Tegart and other British representatives swallowed these whole. This may have been accentuated by the social circles in which they moved. Most were closely linked to the loyalist community: for example, Tegart, did not have 'any sort of secret service' as such, but instead relied on his many Anglo-Irish acquaintances for information.[147] As the case of Lady Dunalley illustrates, southern loyalists were often prone to bias and unfounded scares, especially related to the IRA.

The alarming reports flooding into London had a major influence on the British government and its most senior military and intelligence committees. From May 1940 there was a growing consensus that a German invasion of Ireland was a certainty. This would not simply be a minor diversion before an invasion of Britain, but a major, independent operation that would seize Irish bases to enable attacks on Britain's ports and Atlantic shipping. The Chiefs of Staff set the Joint Intelligence Committee (JIC) and the Joint Planning Sub-Committee to investigate this on 20 May. Three days later they both came to the same conclusion: it was 'highly probable' that Germany would attempt 'the establishment of bases [in Ireland] from which to make war against the United Kingdom'.[148] Subsequently there was some dissent from this opinion. Surprisingly, given his earlier preoccupation with the Irish threat, this came from Winston Churchill, who questioned whether Germany would gain any advantage from such an operation.[149] He received some support from the JIC, which, in a reversal of its earlier assessment, stated that any German operation against Ireland would only be a diversion with the aim of drawing British forces away from the main threat. However, the military chiefs and planners dismissed these arguments, refusing to alter their conviction that the Germans intended a major invasion of Ireland. The JIC was compelled to submit a revised version of its report in line with this assumption.[150] A Joint Planning Sub-Committee memorandum was more to the taste of the Chiefs of Staff:

> In our view it is almost a forgone conclusion that, simultaneously with air attack, and perhaps seaborne invasion on our East and South Coasts, we shall be faced with a Nazi descent upon Eire. We know there are very large numbers of Germans in Spain, and accumulations of shipping in Vigo and other ports. There are indications of an expedition being assembled in Norwegian ports. There is reason to think that German aircraft have been to Eire within the last few days. It would be clearly folly to ignore the very real possibility of a simultaneous descent from the North and South simultaneously, combined with the landing of airborne troops and a rebellion by the I.R.A.[151]

After the French Atlantic ports fell into German hands at the end of June, the possible scale of attack was dramatically increased: the JIC now estimated that the Germans could employ five divisions of seaborne troops, alongside a sizable airborne contingent, against Ireland.[152]

British military and intelligence chiefs assumed that the IRA fifth column would provide crucial assistance to a German landing by seizing ports and aerodromes, preparing stocks of fuel, destroying communications and launching guerrilla attacks on the Irish army.[153] On 23 May the JIC estimated that 'the nucleus of the I.R.A.' was between 2,000 and 3,000, which 'might be expanded in the event of a successful invasion to about 15,000 to 20,000'. It was known that 'secret sources of arms' were in their possession, and it was possible that bombs and supplies for German aircraft had already been shipped to Ireland 'by clandestine means'.[154] It was also believed that an organisation of German agents in Ireland had prepared the ground for invasion.[155] There was particular concern about Rineanna aerodrome in Co. Clare (now Shannon airport) because German involvement in the construction of the nearby hydroelectric plant was believed to have produced a nest of fifth columnists – the RAF feared that the local German colony would act in conjunction with the IRA to seize the aerodrome, allowing German troops to fly in.[156] According to the British assessment, this extensive Irish fifth column would compensate for the difficulties of landing and supplying a German force, thus making a German invasion feasible.

However, the British assessment of the IRA threat went beyond this, into the realms of complete fiction. A second theory emerged, in distinction to that of a German invasion assisted by republican dissidents. It held that the IRA was capable of effecting a 'successful revolution' against the de Valera government with no more than minor German assistance.[157] This idea was born in a War Office memorandum in the middle of May 1940. It claimed that 'the main German effort' would be directed not towards seizing bases but towards 'the support and stiffening of the I.R.A. with leaders, teachers and equipment', so that the IRA would be able 'to conquer the Eire army, depose the Government and control the country'. This would necessitate the diversion of aircraft and troops from British defences. A later War Office memo estimated IRA strength as 15,000 to 20,000 men, which was contrasted with an Irish army of 8,000 poorly equipped regulars, 6,000 reserves and 16,000 Volunteers, whose loyalty could not always be presumed:

> Although it is not easy to assess the relative powers of the I.R.A. and the Eire Army, it may be assumed with some certainty that German organization and leadership, a supply of military equipment and some up-to-date bombing aircraft to the former, might well enable them to defeat the latter.[158]

This view was not restricted to the military. Neville Chamberlain, who became Lord President of the Council and retained a seat in the War Cabinet, told his colleagues on 30 May that 'the IRA were by themselves almost strong enough to overrun the weak Eire Forces'.[159] Any shortfall in the IRA's abilities would be compensated by the arrival of airborne German troops, who could easily avoid British air patrols and land under cover of darkness.[160]

The threat in Ireland was thus seen as taking two forms – a German invasion assisted by the IRA, or an IRA revolt assisted by the Germans. German intervention in Ireland was seen as not just likely but imminent. From May 1940 the British government was gripped by a succession of Irish invasion scares. As early as 15 May the JIC remarked that 'information has been received pointing to a probable German attempt to land parachutists in Ireland'. Ten days later there were indications of a seaborne expedition from Norway or Spain. On 29 May Major General Sir Hastings Ismay (secretary to the War Cabinet) informed Churchill that 'information from secret sources' pointed to the fact that the Germans had 'concerted detailed plans with the I.R.A.' and were 'ready for an immediate descent upon the country'.[161] During June Royal Navy destroyers were instructed to intercept two merchant ships off Iceland suspected of carrying troops for a landing in Ireland.[162] The invasion scares culminated in the first half of July: 'If anything is certain', the War Office recorded, 'it's a German attack on Eire in the *very near* future.'[163] The date for the invasion was initially given as the night of 7 July. Then on 14 July Maffey gravely informed the Irish government that it would come the next day.[164] Maffey's office was put on a 'war footing', with staff sleeping on the premises. Air and sea patrols were instituted off the Irish coasts, and submarines patrolled off Dingle Bay, to detect any German expedition from the south.[165]

High politics and low intelligence

THE British obsession with an imminent German invasion and a rampant Irish fifth column had a major impact on Anglo-Irish relations. Although it led to increased co-operation in the intelligence and military spheres, the measures taken by the Irish government did not go as far as the British demanded. As a result, there were major worries in London about the ability and willingness of neutral Ireland to defend itself from external invasion and internal subversion. In desperation the British government explored ways to push southern Ireland out of its neutral position, which almost led to a complete rupture in relations.

From May 1940 London put intense pressure on the Irish government to improve its internal security and external defences. At the intelligence level this led to intensified co-operation between G2 and MI5. On 15 May Colonel Archer flew to Droitwich airport and met with Guy and Cecil Liddell to discuss German subversion. Ten days later Archer transmitted copies of the documents found in the Held household.[166] He also provided the fingerprints of Walter Simon, who stuck to an alias during G2 interrogation. MI5 matched them with those of the spy who had been deported one year before from Britain, thus allowing Simon's identification – this was one of the most effective examples of the working of the 'Dublin link'. MI5 and G2 later swapped information about Wilhelm Preetz's radio transmissions from Dublin and the three saboteurs who were captured in Co. Cork.[167]

This period also saw the beginning of secret Anglo-Irish military collaboration at the highest level. On 23 May Joseph Walshe and Colonel Liam Archer met with representatives of the armed service departments and the Dominions Office in London to discuss the developing crisis. Two days later Colonel Clarke of the War Office travelled to Dublin, accompanied by two members of the army headquarters staff in Northern Ireland. They met Walshe, Archer, and General McKenna (Irish Chief of Staff). The British emphasised that a German invasion was imminent and urged Dublin to forestall this by obstructing all possible land-ing grounds. They also stressed the danger of fifth column activities, expressing considerable 'anxiety ... in regard to the activities of the I.R.A' – it was 'thought that the Germans might well decide to land a few troops to exploit' them. The Irish government gave a commitment that it would resist a German invasion and call on Britain for assistance. Under a hastily devised plan (codenamed the 'W-Plan') British troops in Northern Ireland prepared to move across the border to repel the invaders. The Irish military authorities agreed to the appointment of British military and air attachés in Dublin to facilitate liaison. Finally, the Irish government began the whole-scale arrest of IRA members and increased its sur-veillance of the German community. London initially regarded these results as 'most encouraging'.[168]

However, the Irish government also resisted the wilder British exhortations. First, it stressed that the IRA and other fifth column elements did not pose a major threat. On 23 May De Valera sent a message through Maffey 'that he did not feel any danger on the internal side from local fifth columnists, etc. All sus-pects in Eire were under watch and he was satisfied that the Eire authorities had full control of these.' [169] After his meetings with the Irish army, Colonel Clarke described how he had done everything to 'emphasise to them the very real dan-ger of the exploitation of the IRA by the Germans, but they remained unshaken' in their conviction that 'the threat of a successful revolution was "remote"'.[170] Second, the Irish challenged the British assessment of the likelihood of Ger-man invasion: de Valera stated that 'Hitler would leave Eire out of the picture' because it would be too 'difficult for him to reach and subdue'.[171] Finally, the Irish asserted that if the Germans did land they might not need British help: Colonel Archer told the new military attaché that 'Eire might be able to "handle it them-selves" and might not have to call for assistance'. In particular, they believed that they could mop up a small-scale German airborne expedition designed to aid an IRA revolt. This was why they insisted that, in the event of a German invasion, British forces could not enter their territory until after a formal invitation, which might be delayed for up to forty-eight hours.[172] They did not want Britain using an ill-judged, minor German landing as a pretext to occupy the country, as they suspected that the British might never leave.

These attitudes caused considerable anguish in London, as they were regarded as dangerously complacent. In its weekly intelligence reports in July, the Admiralty became increasingly critical of the policy of the Irish authori-ties: it caustically remarked that it was 'a hard task to rouse the Irish from their apathy and indifference' and that de Valera was 'determined to shut his eyes to reality'.[173] Military chiefs warned that the Irish authorities were 'too confident in their ability to deal with internal subversive activities, urging de Valera to intern all enemy aliens and to restrict the activities of the German legation.[174] Furthermore, the British were appalled by the Irish government's confidence in its ability to handle a German landing. A consistent theme in all British reports was that the Irish army was a weak, divided force, wholly incapable of tackling a German expedition and barely able to contain internal unrest.[175] As a result, the British government was convinced that 'the present plan was not enough'. Ireland could be overrun by German invaders before British assistance arrived. The only measure that would forestall German success was the prior occupation by British forces of strategic bases in southern Ireland. This was what British policy led up to in the summer of 1940. The argument made to Irish representatives in ever more desperate tones was that if southern Ireland stayed neutral she would become a scene of fighting for sure, whereas if she abandoned neutrality, and invited British forces in, she might deter German invasion.[176]

Misperceptions about the invasion threat and the Irish fifth column drove the British government to make an historic, if desperate, offer to de Valera: Ireland would be unified, if the south entered the war and allowed British forces to occupy key bases. Many subsequent commentators, and perhaps the Irish government at the time, regarded this initiative as simply an attempt to gain the Irish ports in order to safeguard British shipping. In fact the chief British motivation was to forestall a German invasion of Ireland by placing British forces in the country – the initiative was driven by invasion fears, not the Battle of the Atlantic. The proposal developed in direct response to the alarmist intelligence reports circulating at this time. Indeed, it was kick-started by none other than Colonel Vivian. In his diaries Guy Liddell describes how at a meeting of the Home Defence (Security) Executive on 29 May, Vivian 'made a very courageous bid for some statesmanlike move to bring the north and south together in the present crisis'. Although beyond the purview of the committee, this idea found its way to Churchill, who asked Major Desmond Morton and Neville Chamberlain to push ahead with it. They decided to take action after being presented with the fantastic reports of the SIS representative, Sir Charles Tegart. On 12 June Chamberlain wrote to de Valera and Lord Craigavon claiming to have 'fresh information' pointing to an IRA-assisted German invasion. When the Irish leaders declined to come to a conference in London, it was decided to send Malcolm MacDonald (now Minister of Health) with the momentous Irish unity proposals.[177] In later years MacDonald made clear that he was sent to Dublin because the British government thought that Ireland was 'in imminent danger of invasion by Germany'. Close reading of his discussions with de Valera confirms that this was the chief impetus for the initiative.[178] Thus, the threat posed by a largely imaginary fifth column and an imminent German invasion of Ireland prompted the offer of Irish unity.

The refusal of the Irish authorities to accept this offer led the British to suspect their intentions. This was particularly directed against the Irish army. It had grown out of the IRA in 1922, its senior officers had distinguished themselves in the War of Independence, and for two decades Whitehall had believed that it harboured strong anti-British, republican sentiments. In July 1940 senior RAF officers remarked that if the British had to repel an invasion of southern Ireland they 'should have to fight a large proportion of the Irish as well as the Germans'.[179] As a result, the RAF was reluctant to share any codes with the Irish Air Corps – 'They'll give it to [the] Boche.'[180] The civil departments also expressed similar views. The Foreign Office stopped the Americans from supplying Ireland with weapons, as they understood that 'a large proportion of the Eire Army' had 'I.R.A. tendencies' and there was 'a risk that these weapons may be used against us'.[181] It was feared that if the Germans did invade, a defeatist Irish government might offer no real resistance. An officer on the Air Staff pondered 'the uncertainty as to which way the Irish cat will jump, especially if the Germans lay the blame for invasion at England's door.' The Director of Plans at the Air Ministry was more forthright: 'I do not trust these bastards.'[182]

As a result the British flirted with the idea of invading southern Ireland themselves. On 18 June 1940 the Inter-Service Planning Staffs were instructed to carry out a tactical examination of the occupation of the Shannon Estuary, Cobh and Berehaven – 'in this examination Irish hostility was to be assumed'.[183] Major-General Bernard Montgomery, the veteran of the Irish War of Independence who would become the hero of El Alamein, was also 'told to prepare plans for the seizure of Cork and Queenstown in Southern Ireland'. He commanded the 3rd Division, one of the few British divisions ready for active operations after the evacuation of Dunkirk.[184] The Air Ministry was the most belligerent of the three services. On 7 July 1940 its Director of Plans asked the Joint Planning Sub-Committee:

> to consider at once whether we should not take off the old school tie and put the Canadian Division into EIRE now ... we should certainly put a spoke in the wheel of the Boche who probably counts on our doing nothing till he himself is ready.[185]

In the end, the operation was scotched at the planning stage, because it would involve too onerous a military commitment.

Nonetheless, in early July Dublin became convinced that a British invasion of Ireland was imminent. One cause was the degree of pressure placed on the

Dublin government to take appropriate countermeasures against what the Irish knew was a largely imaginary threat. For two months London had made a deliberate attempt to 'work upon the fears' of the Irish leaders by providing them with a continuous stream of intelligence on the threat of German invasion.[186] Yet the Irish were convinced from their own diplomatic sources that Germany would not invade. Therefore they suspected the British of inventing this bogey to bundle them into the war. Similarly, it was suspected that there was a hidden agenda behind the British preoccupation with the fifth column and the patently ridiculous information on which it was based: the British might be inventing a pretext to justify invasion. The MacDonald offer of Irish unity was regarded as a trap: if accepted, it would allow Britain to take possession of the ports; if rejected, it would lay the political ground for British invasion.[187]

The second reason why Irish leaders feared a British invasion was a renewed campaign in the British press in July about the dangers of Irish neutrality. The Irish government was right to suspect that British officials had inspired this press campaign; the stories were fostered by the Ministry of Information in order to pressure the Irish government into abandoning neutrality. Needless to say, it had the opposite effect.[188] The final cause of Irish jitters was the activity of covert British intelligence agents in Ireland in the first two weeks of July. Sir Charles Tegart approached leading political figures in Dublin (including some Fianna Fáil ministers), provided them with evidence of German subversive activity and attempted to turn them against the government's policy of neutrality. His activities came to the attention of G2, 'the mission was "blown"', and it was the subject of a strong protest from the Irish government.[189] At this time the Irish police also made their first discovery of the SIS network in the south-west of the country.[190] This was quickly followed by the arrest on 12 July of Major Byas of the military staff in Northern Ireland, while on an intelligence-gathering mission across the border. The new British military attaché recorded the impact this had in Dublin: 'the atmosphere ... was pretty bad owing to Tegart's activities but this has just put the lid on it.'[191] Covert intelligence operations could be risky, especially at periods of diplomatic sensitivity.

The Irish authorities regarded this covert action as not only a breach of trust but as British preparation for military intervention. A note by Joseph Walshe on 15 July stated that an 'early occupation by the British Army' would follow 'as soon as British political intrigues prove unsuccessful'. When reports were received of unusual military movements in Northern Ireland, it was immediately assumed that these were preparations for a move across the border.[192] Maffey warned that there had been 'an alarming change of attitude' and that Britain was now seen as the likely 'aggressor', while the Ministry of Information received reports that in all Irish quarters 'a British landing' was 'felt to be a more immediate peril than a German landing.'[193] Thus, at a time when Britain most needed Irish co-operation in order to meet an expected German invasion, the Irish government was preoccupied with the threat of British aggression.

I T is clear from the above that British policy was brought into dangerous courses by some startling conceptions of Ireland in the summer of 1940. This began with the belief that a German invasion of Ireland was certain and imminent. Even more striking are the perceptions of conditions within Ireland. It was believed that there was a powerful IRA and German fifth column ready to assist this invasion. Moreover, at times it was judged that the IRA, acting alone or with minor German assistance, could launch a successful revolution and overthrow the de Valera government. This was because the Irish army was suspected of being honeycombed with anti-British elements; in July there were even doubts about whether de Valera himself would resist a German incursion. It is clear now that these were exaggerations, scares, mistruths – a dramatic failure of the British intelligence system. How did this come about?

One reason was the nature of the Anglo-Irish intelligence relationship. Problems with the 'Dublin link' meant that it did not satisfy all Britain's security needs. G2 did not have a full understanding of German intrigues, especially related to the IRA. Moreover, G2 co-operation was still mostly confined to the exchange of information on foreign nationals and suspected German agents. G2 was reluctant to share information on the IRA or other indigenous subversive groups; it also shielded the German legation, because it did not want to give Britain grounds to demand its expulsion.[194] Intelligence sharing increased after Colonel Archer met with Cecil Liddell in May 1940, but it took time for British officials to develop confidence in the ability and intentions of their Irish counterparts. Rear-Admiral Godfrey later recalled how they did not 'feel then that the Eire Government could be trusted to counter German penetration.'[195]

On the other hand, there were many other deficiencies in the engagement of the British intelligence system with Ireland. Departments started from a position of ignorance of Irish affairs, because of many years of neglect before 1939 and only minor improvement during the Phoney War. With the sudden threat of invasion, the British intelligence community flung itself at the problem, devoting attention to the country on a scale not seen since 1921. However, it did not know how to handle the material that became available. Wild rumours from the press, individual correspondents and the postal censorship were accepted at face value. Moreover, British intelligence operatives generated and circulated identical rumours themselves. The SIS network was the chief culprit, and did more than any other source to foster the fifth column panic.

These reports were not subject to proper scrutiny in London. This was a task for MI5, but it was unable to puncture the fifth column myth. The MI5 Irish Section was overwhelmed: Cecil Liddell wrote that 'the flood of reports and enquiries was increased, partly by the products of controls, such as the censorship of Irish mail, but also by the wave of rumours and reports about the activities of supposed fifth columnists, which spread through the country after the invasion of Holland.' He admitted that 'it was difficult, if not impossible, to avoid the fatal and futile search for spies in the "in tray", instead of visualizing the situation as a whole, and this happened in the Irish Section.' [196] It is perhaps more surprising that the civil departments, and especially the Dominions Office, did not do more to overturn the misconceptions. Yet Neville Chamberlain and the new Secretary of State for Dominion Affairs, Viscount Caldecote, were 'all agreed' that the picture presented by SIS was 'a true one.'[197] In any case, the armed services and the intelligence agencies drove government policy during the fevered atmosphere of the summer of 1940, sidelining civilian officials.

Ultimately, British assessments of Ireland were shaped by biased assumptions. The first was the general assumption that a German fifth column must exist, in both Ireland and Britain. This places British fears of the Irish fifth column squarely in the context of the wider invasion and fifth column hysteria that gripped Britain in this period. Yet British assessments were also driven by assumptions that were peculiar to the Anglo-Irish context. Concern about the Irish fifth column was shaped by deep-rooted, cultural stereotypes of Ireland and the Irish. These included the notion that the Irish were violent and lawless; that the southern Irish state was fatally unstable; that the people were moral cowards easily intimidated by gunmen; that the country could be whipped into an Anglophobic frenzy by a republican minority; that de Valera and his former Sinn Féin colleagues could not be trusted. Underlying all these concepts was the idea of the Irish 'back door', the soft underbelly of the British lion that was vulnerable to exploitation by its enemies. These stereotypes were ancient, justifying the English conquest in the seventeenth century and unionism in the nineteenth. They found virulent expression during the Sinn Féin rebellion after the First World War and became the credo for those determined to crush it. In the two decades since the establishment of the Irish state such ideas, while not universal, were cherished by a right-wing, diehard element in British society and politics. They surfaced and occasionally took a wider hold at times of crisis in Anglo-Irish relations. There could be no greater crisis than that facing Britain in the summer of 1940, and it acted as a catalyst for the emergence of these ancient fears. They shaped not only the analysis of Irish intelligence but the type of information produced by private citizens, intelligence agents and the British press. In the end, to understand British intelligence on Ireland we must understand the place of Ireland in British culture and psychology; the British intelligence community simply reflected the politics, prejudices and perturbations of the British nation. The point, of course, is that an intelligence system should do far more.

CHAPTER 10

Operational Intelligence

T HE British intelligence community's handling of Ireland reached a nadir in the summer of 1940. Yet it was followed by a gradual, continuous improvement. British intelligence agencies greatly intensified their involvement with the country. They did this in two ways: first, stepping up covert intelligence operations; second, establishing ever-closer co-operation with the Irish authorities. British intelligence continued to move along these twin tracks of covert activity and official collaboration until late in the war, although there was a gradual shift in emphasis towards the latter as the Anglo-Irish intelligence relationship deepened. In addition, the increased flow of intelligence was accompanied by its better use in London, where it was subject to more sophisticated analysis and dissemination. As a result, the scares and alarms that were such a feature of the first year of the war were gradually debunked, gaps in knowledge were filled, preconceptions challenged. Eventually, and not without stutters, Britain developed a sophisticated intelligence system, which provided a foundation for wiser policy-making and allowed the British government to extract the maximum benefits from Irish neutrality.

This improvement can be seen in the four main tasks that faced the British intelligence community after the summer of 1940. One was investigating the Irish fifth column – republicans, fascist sympathisers, German agents – and taking appropriate counter-measures. The strength of the fifth column depended on Irish attitudes towards the war, so a second task for the British intelligence community was monitoring public opinion, gauging the influence of Axis propaganda and organising an Allied propaganda response. The third task, which retained its importance the longest, was preventing German espionage and leakage of information through neutral Ireland. The response of the British intelligence community to these challenges will be explored in the next three chapters. But the most urgent task in the summer of 1940, which we will look at here, was gathering the sort of intelligence that British forces would need to conduct military operations in southern Ireland. This would remain a priority so long as it was possible that British forces would have to intervene in the south – either to repel a German invasion or to seize Irish bases.

British officials deemed a German invasion of Ireland likely well into 1941, although there was greater difference of opinion on this matter than before. In August and September 1940, as part of Operation Sealion, the Germans made real preparations for a cross-Channel invasion of Britain. Winston Churchill and the Joint Intelligence Committee were rightly sceptical about the threat to Ireland, arguing that a German attack on the country made no strategic sense and had little chance of success.[1] In contrast, during the autumn 1940 the chiefs and planning staffs of the armed services continued to believe that a German move would be accompanied or preceded by a major expedition against Ireland.[2] Following the defeat of the Luftwaffe in the Battle of Britain and the arrival of hazardous winter conditions, Operation Sealion was called off – Hitler had missed his chance. Yet some senior military figures concluded that an invasion of Ireland was now *more* likely, relative to an attack on Britain, as the winter weather and longer nights meant that German ships in the Atlantic could more easily slip through Royal Navy patrols.[3] In early 1941, after German military successes in the Balkans and North Africa, the threat of invasion re-emerged. British officials still believed that Ireland could be a target: in January the War Office called for a reinforcement of troops in Northern Ireland because of 'a number of rumours … that Germany intends to invade Eire as a prelude to invasion of the United Kingdom'.[4] The army and naval staffs produced papers in February and March 1941 suggesting that the Germans might launch a major invasion of Ireland, not simply as a diversion before an attack on Britain, but as a stand-alone operation with the aim of obtaining a base for attack on British shipping and cities.[5] Hitler's surprise invasion of the Soviet Union on 22 June 1941 diverted the pressure, but his armies initially made alarming progress towards Moscow, and there was a chance that he would gain a rapid victory and turn his military might back towards the British Isles. Britain still could not predict Hitler's next move with any certainty.

The threat of a German invasion of Ireland was equalled and at times surpassed by a second strategic imperative behind British policy – the need for Irish ports and air bases to fight the Battle of Atlantic. By October 1940 the shipping situation had severely deteriorated. After the fall of France, German surface raiders and U-boats operated out of Atlantic ports, which, together with the introduction of enhanced Type VII U-boats, greatly increased their range of attack. U-boats inflicted very heavy losses on British shipping in the Atlantic, especially around the north-west coast of Ireland. Between July and October 1940, the Germans sunk 282 ships (1,489,795 tons) in this area – U-boat commanders called this 'happy-time'.[6] Denial of Irish bases handicapped Britain's ability to meet this threat. Use of the port facilities at Lough Swilly in Co. Donegal would have increased the range of British destroyers; in addition, the

Royal Navy wished to position its main battlefleet at Shannon in order to intercept German capital ships sailing out of France. 'It is impossible to exaggerate the importance of this matter', one naval planner wrote on 5 October 1940.[7] In recent years there has been a cosy Irish consensus that neutrality had no negative consequences for the Allied war effort, and that southern Ireland, through its secret co-operation on security and other matters, actually did its bit in the fight against Nazi tyranny. This is not true. In 1940 and the first half of 1941, Irish neutrality seriously hampered Allied forces in the Battle of the Atlantic – British, Canadian and American sailors and airmen died as a result.[8]

Because of the threat of German invasion and the need for Irish ports, the British armed services prepared to fight on Irish soil. Most obviously, they planned to move south in order to repel a German expeditionary force: this 'W-Plan' was worked out in collaboration with Irish military chiefs. However, the British services also secretly planned to seize Irish ports and air bases, which would mean fighting *against* the Irish army. This option was seriously considered in October and November 1940. The War Cabinet decided on 31 October that although 'the seizure and maintenance of naval and air bases in Eire ... would involve a very grave military commitment ... it might have to be done if the threat on our Western Approaches became mortal'.[9] In November Churchill instructed the commander of British Troops in Northern Ireland (BTNI) to draw up plans for the operation. He also sent reinforcements to the province and halted a promised delivery of weapons to the Irish army.[10] Although it was decided that the military risks outweighed the naval advantages, the plans were kept up to date, and it was broadly agreed that they would be put into effect if the shipping situation made it necessary – Britain would invade southern Ireland if its survival depended on it. The W-Plan, therefore, was very much a double-edged sword: on the one side, a sword of liberation to drive out German invaders; on the other, a sword of conquest that would seize Irish bases if British interests demanded.

The likelihood that British troops would have to fight in southern Ireland made operational intelligence vital. The British needed intelligence on Irish topography and defences: for example, information on roads, railways, ports, aerodromes, natural features, urban areas, water supplies, the electricity grid, petrol stores, forts and military positions. Having neglected the country for almost two decades, this basic information was lacking: when in August 1940 the Joint Planning Staff drew up a 'priority list' of places about which topographical information was required, southern Ireland was placed in 'Category I. Immediate Urgency'.[11] The British needed intelligence on the Irish armed forces: their strength, location, training, equipment and attitudes. Depending on the reason for British intervention, they would either be the forces that the British fought alongside, or those they fought against.[12] Finally, the British needed accurate, timely intelligence on any German landing in Ireland, so that their forces could react quickly and mount an effective defence. The intelligence community initially responded to these needs by launching independent, clandestine operations, but its emphasis quickly shifted to co-operating with the Irish authorities, who proved more than willing to help. By 1941 the British and Irish armed forces enjoyed an extremely close and productive relationship.

M ANY branches of the British intelligence community launched covert intelligence operations in southern Ireland in the summer of 1940. The intelligence departments of the British army, navy and air force were at the forefront. They were not prepared to leave Ireland to MI5 or SIS. The Director of Intelligence at the Air Ministry, Air Commodore Archibald Boyle, was not 'happy about the system of reporting' provided by the two agencies.[13] The Director of Naval Intelligence, Rear-Admiral Godfrey, was also of the opinion that 'the rudimentary S.I.S.–MI5 organisation had not proved successful'. He wrote that 'certain of its leading members had been compromised and the supply of intelligence through this channel was meagre and unimpressive … we never got much out of them'.[14] As a result, the service intelligence departments, turning their full attention to Irish affairs for the first time since 1922, tried to build up their own sources of information.

A range of crudely disguised, amateur spies flooded into southern Ireland at this time. In July 1940 Air Commodore Boyle sent two RAF officers 'in the guise of tourists' on a fishing holiday with the task of locating suitable sites for new RAF aerodromes.[15] RAF officers in Britain were encouraged to spend their holidays in Ireland beside sea bases and airports and to make 'mental pictures' of all they saw.[16] The headquarters of British Troops in Northern Ireland (BTNI) regularly sent its officers across the border in the guise of tourists. Major Parks, a staff intelligence officer, travelled south each week, often as the guest of Lady Cole, the daughter of the Earl of Enniskillen.[17] As noted, Major Edward Byas and his wife were arrested by the Garda, armed with maps and incriminating instructions, while reconnoitring roads south of the border.[18] Because the army transport corps had little up-to-date information about the southern Irish railway system, their officers 'frequently became apparently respectable citizens and would disappear for days at a time to return with bleary smut filled eyes but happily carrying in their heads much vital information'.[19] In the middle of 1941 SIS tried to persuade the army to stop these activities, offering to obtain this sort of information from its network instead, but British officers continued to take holidays in the south as cover for reconnaissance missions.[20]

Of the three armed services, the Naval Intelligence Division (NID) was most heavily involved in intelligence operations in Ireland. Rear-Admiral Godfrey regularly sent a selected man, Angus MacDonnell, to investigate reports of U-boats sheltering on the Irish coast. A businessman, a fisherman and 'a very good mixer', MacDonnell 'knew the West Coast of Ireland well'. Rear-Admiral Godfrey later wrote:

> When a report was received of a U-boat appearing off the coast, or using an out of the way harbour, I sent Angus MacDonnell to investigate – he could travel without difficulty ostensibly to fish, could establish quickly good relations with all classes and very soon get to the bottom of the rumour which was invariably false.[21]

Godfrey's other initiative was to use Northern Ireland as a base to spy on the south. After a visit to Belfast, Derry and Dublin, he concluded that 'much might be achieved by straightforward penetration of Eire from N. Ireland'.[22] In November 1940 he transferred the NID expert on Irish affairs, Commander George Penkivil Slade, to the province. Educated at Eton and Oxford, Slade had been a barrister before joining NID. His job, on arriving in Belfast, was 'to get information on all questions affecting Eire which may concern the Admiralty'. He extended his 'intelligence contacts not by "underground" organisation', but by developing contacts among those who travelled regularly between north and south Ireland, and by liaising closely with the RUC, the naval attaché in Dublin and local military intelligence officers. He also made occasional forays across the border himself.[23] His chief task was to investigate of rumours that U-boats were receiving supplies from the Irish shore.

The service departments also attempted to access useful information held in Britain. An Inter Services Topographical Department was set up under the control of the Naval Intelligence Division in May 1940, staffed by the best brains from the university, advertising and publishing worlds. It worked on the basis that more information could be got from open sources than from the work of spies, and that somewhere in Britain there was an expert on any subject or place. Intelligence officers such as Ian Fleming (who later created James Bond) established links with businesses, banks, travel agencies, newspapers, technical journals, photographic agencies, explorers and travellers. One of the department's first tasks was to deliver information on 'the hydrography and topography of the Irish locks', as it was feared that German seaplanes might try to land on them – photographs were supplied by a friend of one naval officer, while further details came from a firm that sold fishing tackle.[24] Other organisations approached included the Automobile Association, which was tapped for information on

Irish roads, and the oil companies, which provided data on Ireland's fuel stores.[25] Centuries of British rule in Ireland also came to the assistance of the service departments. Because most Irish military establishments had been taken over from the British in 1922 (or, in the case of the Treaty Ports, 1938), copious plans existed in military archives in London. Some of the best information was found in a 'Report on the Defence of Ireland' from 1909.[26]

If a German invasion of Ireland occurred, it was essential for Britain to have timely warning and good intelligence on military developments in southern Ireland. The British armed services hoped to use the SIS network in southern Ireland for this purpose, suggesting that 'well disposed Anglo-Irish' along the coast could be supplied with transmitters. This was not considered practical; instead, SIS agents were told to communicate urgent information by telephone or telegram to Dublin. In June 1940 SIS agreed to establish a covert transmitter and two trained operators 'in a friendly house in or near Dublin' so that this information could be rapidly sent to Northern Ireland and Britain.[27] Once a German invasion occurred, the British hoped to use the SIS network as a 'stay-behind' group to provide intelligence on the movements of German forces. In March 1941 a German-speaking military officer, Captain Caroe, was appointed as a joint MI5–SIS liaison to the BTNI command. In the event of military operations in southern Ireland, he would take control of MI5 and SIS records in the field and maintain contact with members of the SIS organisation. At this time the British army again raised the possibility of distributing radio transmitters to SIS agents in advance of a German attack, but this was turned down by SIS and MI5, because it would come to the attention of the Irish authorities and might imperil the link with G2.[28]

Another secretive agency to become involved in Ireland was MI9. It was set up in December 1940 to assist the escape of downed Allied airmen and Allied prisoners of war from enemy territory. It also plotted the escape of British airmen from neutral Ireland. In the early months of the war (and after 1942), the Irish government allowed Allied airmen landing on its territory to return to Northern Ireland, conspiring in the fiction that these men were on 'non-operational flights'. But in 1941 and 1942 Allied aviators were treated like their German counterparts and interned in a special camp at the Curragh in Co. Kildare. Approximately forty Allied airmen (including British, Canadians, Americans and a New Zealander) were interned in this way. Although this was a fairly congenial experience – the men were allowed to spend evenings in Dublin on parole – it was their duty to escape. They were assisted by MI9, which recruited a network of 'helpers' and 'safe houses' in Co. Kildare and Dublin, generally among Anglo-Irish loyalists and ex-servicemen. (In addition, one senior officer at MI9's

London headquarters happened to own a house near Dublin.) The MI9 operation culminated in a successful mass escape on 25 June 1941, the day the Irish Derby was held at the nearby racecourse. Nine men broke out through the main gate at dusk, after an internee returning from parole diverted the guard's attention by feigning drunkenness. Two escapees were immediately recaptured, but the other seven were whisked in waiting cars to Dublin, blending in with the large number of returning race-goers. They were given false papers by an MI9 source and took the train to Belfast, where they enjoyed 'a hell of a binge' before rejoining their flying units. (One escapee was Group Captain Hugh Verity, who later became renowned for his dare-devil flights on behalf of the Special Operations Executive into occupied France.) After this incident the Irish government delivered a protest so sharp that MI9 refrained from organising any more mass escapes, but it did smuggle equipment such as collapsible ladders and smoke bombs to internees, who continued to make occasional attempts.[29] MI9 also maintained its secret organisation of 'helpers', some of whom were investigated by the Irish authorities: one man, Norman Pearson, was interned after he drove an escaped internee to Northern Ireland in August 1942.[30]

The Irish response to MI9 activities illustrated the risks of undertaking clandestine operations in Ireland. In fact, the covert intrigues of MI9 and the armed services made only a limited contribution to British operational intelligence. Instead, the most important source was co-operation with the Irish authorities. From 1924 until 1938 there had been almost no contact between the British and Irish armed forces; in 1938 and 1939 there were limited exchanges of technical information; but after May 1940 officers from each country worked side by side to prepare for a German invasion. As part of this collaboration the Irish authorities supplied operational intelligence unreservedly. This shift in Irish policy was brought about by the changing strategic situation. The Irish realised that they would need British assistance to repel a major German attack; therefore, it was in their interests that the British were prepared. They also hoped that full collaboration would deter the British from attempting a pre-emptive occupation of Irish territory.

Three British service attachés in Dublin played a key role in the development of the Anglo-Irish military relationship. The naval attaché, Captain Greig, had been appointed in November 1939 and continued to work closely with the Irish coastwatching service. In June 1940 he was joined by new military and air attachés, appointed with the blessing of the Irish government under the greatest secrecy. The military attaché, Major M. H. ap Rhys-Pryce, was told that 'under existing conditions' it was essential that his true status and connection with the British army 'should be concealed from all persons'. He was not to wear uniform, or use the title of his rank, and would be simply described as a 'Civil Attaché to the United Kingdom Representative'.[31] Wing Commander R. Lywood was introduced to members of the Irish Air Corps as a civilian from the Air Ministry attached to Maffey's office to assist with the supply of aircraft parts.[32] Both men took up lodgings in the Shelbourne Hotel in the first week of June, but were asked to move to the less conspicuous location of Dún Laoghaire, where Maffey had his residence. The Irish government also 'frankly expressed disappointment' that Pryce was not 'pinker and plumper' and of a less military disposition – his 'incognito' was wearing pretty thin in social circles by October 1940. The men were eventually accredited as armed service attachés at the end of 1941.[33]

The primary function of the attachés was to liaise with their counterparts in the Irish forces. For Lywood, this meant the head of the Irish Air Corps, Colonel Pat Mulcahy. The two men spent many hours together, on land and in the air, developing a warm friendship.[34] Major Pryce's contact was Colonel Archer, which meant that Pryce, by good fortune, had direct access to the man who knew most about Irish intelligence matters. They met on 8 June, two days after Pryce's arrival, and over the coming weeks they held clandestine meetings in Archer's car almost every evening, sometimes until well past midnight.[35] Pryce found this 'Cloak & Dagger business of meeting people at street corners and being whisked off in a car to talk under a tree somewhere' a little trying. However, after July, their meetings became more open, with Pryce a frequent visitor to Archer's house.[36] The two men developed a good personal relationship, and in January 1941 Pryce penned an affectionate portrait of the pugnacious Irish officer:

> I have seen a fair amount of Col. Archer lately and I, personally, have found him very helpful and courteous; an earnest Roman Catholic; extremely patriotic; considerably anti-Ascendancy class whom he describes as a small class which lives in the country, does nothing for it, and waits for the Union Jack once more, and which 'cuts no ice' in the country; not entirely unforgetting of treatment meted to Irishmen to England and by British Forces in the past; hardworking and keen on his profession; somewhat foul-mouthed when heated, "f" is frequently used. ... I like him to deal with and I feel that he does all he can to help.[37]

The British attachés received voluminous information on Irish topography and defences from their Irish counterparts. Colonel Archer told Pryce that he 'took exception to uninvited road reconnaissance by officers from Northern Ireland' because 'they caused the population to think that they were designed against Eire' – the government could not admit that they were being undertaken 'with connivance'. 'There's a lot of tinder lying about on each side of the border', he warned Pryce. 'Your job and mine is to prevent it being lit.' Instead, he offered to supply the British with all the information they required.[38] Within days of arriving in Dublin, Pryce handed Archer long questionnaires on Irish defences, topography, communications and security, sent by the British military headquarters in Northern Ireland. At the end of June 1940 Archer began handing over detailed replies on all these subjects, including a full Order of Battle of the Irish army.[39] Wing Commander Lywood was the beneficiary of similar treatment. Two days after his arrival, Colonel Mulcahy brought him to Baldonnel aerodrome, allowed him to inspect its aircraft and took him on a reconnaissance flight from Dublin to Limerick, helpfully pointing out aerodromes and possible landing sites along the way. Mulcahy also gave permission for the RAF to carry out aerial photographic reconnaissance of beaches around Dundalk.[40]

As well as handing over reams of information, the Irish authorities allowed the attachés to carry out their own reconnaissance around the country. Wing Commander Lywood spent much of the summer driving around Ireland, identifying possible German landing sites and fields that could be converted into RAF airstrips. He was outdone by Major Pryce, who was engaged in almost daily road reconnaissance: he boasted of one mammoth 230-mile journey in a single day, and averaged about 1,000 miles per month. His chief objective was to pick routes that could be taken by the British army when operating in Ireland, although he also looked out for suitable billets for British troops – he recommended walled country estates over villages, as they had a regular water supply, provided better cover and were more secure.[41]

Both Lywood and Pryce cultivated a wide network in Irish society. For example, Lywood received information on German activities from his estate agent, Jellett, while associating with loyalists who were suspected of involvement with the covert SIS network.[42] (Indeed, Lywood's activities annoyed the Irish authorities so much that de Valera demanded his replacement when the attachés were officially accredited in 1941.)[43] Similarly, as the War Office made more requests for intelligence, Pryce 'gradually got drawn into a certain circle' that included figures close to the Irish army command. One was Captain MacManus, a Free State army Civil War veteran, who, although no longer serving, maintained close contact with senior Irish officers. He introduced Pryce to a serving Irish officer, Colonel J. J. 'Ginger' O'Connell, who had been involved in the training of Irish troops since 1922. The three men dined together on more than one occasion. Although Maffey was briefly concerned about the 'extremely delicate' situation created by these meetings, Pryce never strayed into clandestine intelligence activity.[44] In his cultivation of well-informed individuals, he was simply following the normal practice of the attaché system, which has been described as 'a time-honoured assemblage of conventions for gentle, non-provocative espionage against friendly countries'.[45]

The service attachés were at the heart of British efforts to set up a reliable system of communication in the event of a German invasion. Irish and British representatives met on 23 May 1940 and agreed that a first-class system of communication between Ireland and Britain was needed.[46] Three weeks later an RAF officer handed Irish authorities a wireless set designed to broadcast to the Air Ministry and Aldergrove aerodrome in Northern Ireland. Other radio transmitters were placed in the home of Wing Commander Lywood in Castleknock and in the office of the United Kingdom Representative on Mount Street. Five RAF officers were sent to Dublin to operate this equipment: they lived undercover, ready in the event of a German invasion to don uniforms stored at Maffey's office.[47] Radio communication was backed up by a 'hush hush' carrier pigeon system known as the 'Mago' scheme. Although pigeons sit somewhat incongruously alongside the technological advances of the Second World War, they were frequently employed by British forces. An RAF 'pigeon expert', Squadron Leader Raynor, visited the United Kingdom Representative's office in Dublin on 9 July and handed over birds trained to fly to Belfast and Britain. Because the birds had to be changed frequently, the military and air attachés travelled approximately every ten days to and from Northern Ireland with suitcases full of pigeons hidden in their cars.[48] The purpose of these systems was to transmit the Irish request for British military assistance after a German invasion. A number of codewords were devised to assist clear communication: de Valera was 'Wolf', the enemy 'Weasel', and the IRA 'Stoat'; a landing by German parachutists would be designated by the term 'Parasols'; 'Jackal' translated as 'IRA are co-operating with enemy'; the codeword instructing British troops to occupy battle stations was an unfortunate choice in the Irish context – 'Cromwell'.[49]

The Anglo-Irish military relationship was initially mediated by the British attachés in Dublin, despite efforts by the BTNI command to forge direct links with southern Irish officers. In July 1940, the British army created a special 'Military Mission No. 18' under Major General 'Jimmy' M. R. Harrison to work out a joint military plan with the southern authorities and to act as the liaison between British and Irish forces in the event of a German invasion.[50] However, the Dublin government was slow to sanction full co-operation with this unit. For example, when Harrison visited Dublin in August and September, he met only with de Valera, ministers and civil officials – no senior army officers.[51] Although the Irish had been generous with intelligence, there was still little substantive planning between the two armies on how they would respond to a German invasion.

As a result, the early version of the British W-Plan did not assume the co-operation of the Irish army and was designed to work without it.[52]

On 16 October 1940 this began to change. Major General Harrison finally met General McKenna, the Chief of Staff of the Irish army, and in the same week the RAF commander in Northern Ireland visited Colonel Mulcahy in Dublin.[53] Following this, members of Military Mission 18 travelled south to meet senior Irish officers on an almost weekly basis – they were allowed to keep cars on the other side of the border, which they picked up after crossing the frontier by train. Officials from the armed service departments in London were also invited to Dublin: the Director of Naval Intelligence, Rear-Admiral Godfrey, visited in August 1941.[54] By this time dozens of British officers were conducting extensive tours of the country with the permission of the Irish authorities: so long as the visitors did not flaunt cameras and maps, or excite local suspicion, they were given free reign.[55] Irish military officers also made trips to Northern Ireland to view British troop manœuvres. Co-operation was cemented by close personal relationships. For example, General McKenna became firm friends with the new BTNI commander, General Franklin: on one occasion, the two men brought their wives on a tour of southern Ireland that was more akin to a motoring holiday than military reconnaissance.[56] This was unprecedented co-operation, the sort that usually occurred between long-standing military allies. It was only constrained by the need to keep it secret from the Irish public and the German legation.

The Irish military authorities provided all the operational intelligence that the British needed – nothing was held back. 'The Eire Army Authorities have been most helpful', the Chief of the Imperial General Staff remarked on 7 May 1941, 'in answer to requests for detailed and technical information that would assist us in the event of operations in Eire.'[57] The armed service departments quickly concluded that their intelligence needs could best be met by collaboration with their Irish counterparts. For example, when in February 1941 the Air Ministry sought further information on possible sites for aerodromes in Ireland, it rejected the idea of sending officers disguised as tourists, instead deciding to obtain the information from Lywood and Irish officials.[58]

The shift in emphasis from covert activity to official collaboration is illustrated by the proposed involvement in Ireland of one of Britain's most secret wartime services – the Special Operations Executive (SOE). SOE was founded in July 1940 on a misapprehension: that fifth columns had been instrumental to German military victories in Europe. Its purpose was to turn the tables by promoting subversive warfare in German-occupied territory: in Churchill's evocative words, to 'set Europe ablaze'.[59] The creation of SOE was also part inspired by British experiences in Ireland between 1919 and 1921. Many of its founding officers had fought against, or studied, the Irish rebellion, and they argued that Britain should embrace the IRA tactics of sabotage, assassination, hit and run ambushes, and non-uniformed combat: a seminal paper by Colonel Lawrence Grand predicted that a 'combination of guerrilla and IRA tactics' would make 'German occupied areas' ripe for collapse. Thus, the British decided to adopt the 'ungentlemanly' style of IRA warfare that had so appalled them two decades before.[60]

While chiefly concerned with occupied territories, the SOE also created 'stay-behind' networks in those countries threatened by German aggression. In the early months of 1941, following a request from the Chiefs of Staff, SOE proposed to create such an organisation in southern Ireland. Its plan was to place secret dumps of sabotage material in Ireland and to train pro-British residents to carry out operations in the event of a German invasion. However, the scheme met immediate resistance. The headquarters of BTNI was adamant that SOE could not attempt a clandestine operation, and must instead work with the commanders of the Irish army. MI5 opposed the scheme because it would damage its liaison with G2. SIS objected because it would jeopardise its existing secret intelligence network. As a result, SOE was forced to completely reformulate its ideas. Rather than create a clandestine British organisation, SOE recommended that they should consult the Irish army and assist the Irish to develop their own stay-behind network by providing equipment and training – they could only proceed 'by taking the Irish into our complete confidence'. In the end this scheme was dropped, but the deliberations surrounding it show how the British mindset had changed. Collaboration with the Irish armed forces was now the first principle of British military strategy.[61]

The development of intense Anglo-Irish military collaboration, together with, to a lesser extent, independent British intelligence activities, transformed southern Ireland from *terra incognito* into one of the most heavily reconnoitred parts of the world – Eire was downgraded to Category II in the list of priorities for topographical intelligence in December 1940.[62] A good example of the quantity of intelligence flowing into London was a densely packed, eighty-page book entitled 'Ireland: Air Intelligence Notes', compiled by the Air Ministry in November 1940. Perhaps its most impressive feature was the detailed survey of dozens of sites suitable for aircraft. One example – describing the gardens of Roche Castle, Limerick – indicates the level of information available:

> Close cropped grass … Situated on the estate of Roche Castle 2 miles S.E. of Limerick. Ground slopes gently to S.E. Suitable for extensions to give

a landing area 900 x 900 yards. Accommodation and garage available in neighbourhood. Detailed information and plan available.[63]

In addition, the British now had an excellent understanding of the strength, plans and morale of the Irish armed forces. This brought about a complete change in British attitudes. Whereas in the summer of 1940 the Irish army had been regarded as incompetent, undisciplined and riddled with IRA supporters, the increasingly intimate liaison created a very positive impression of the ability and loyalty of the Irish forces. Moreover, British intelligence reports now contained remarkably warm appreciations of senior Irish officers, who were reclassified as definitely pro-Allied.[64] There was no longer any doubt that the Irish army would fight alongside the British in the event of a German invasion. As a result, by the middle of 1941 the Irish army was an integral part of the British W-Plan: Major Pryce told the American military attaché in Dublin that 'the problem was very complete and was worked out in great detail … the co-operation of the General Staff of the Eire Army is all that can be desired.'[65]

The depth of Anglo-Irish military co-operation is remarkable given the state of Anglo-Irish political relations at this time. After the nadir of July 1940, relations had temporarily improved, as the Dominions Office placed a steadier hand on the tiller of British policy.[66] But mounting shipping losses in the Atlantic provoked a new diplomatic crisis in October 1940. Churchill condemned Irish neutrality on the radio, refused to provide weapons to the Irish army and stoked up a press campaign against the Irish government. He toyed with using military, diplomatic and economic pressure to force Dublin to hand over ports and air bases. By December 1940 Irish leaders once more feared a British invasion: they rushed troops to the border to meet a rumoured incursion and made secret approaches to the German legation to obtain a promise of assistance in the event of a British attack.[67] Relations between the British and Irish governments remained fractious for most of 1941, as Maffey openly admitted to de Valera that Britain would seize Irish bases if they became critical to its survival.[68] Given this, it may seem puzzling that the Irish government allowed its army to provide such assistance to British forces, especially as it would have greatly helped the British if they had decided to invade. Yet the Irish calculated that it was a risk worth taking because they needed British help against a graver threat – German invasion. In addition, by showing what could be gained through co-operation, they gave the British a reason not to coerce southern Ireland too much. Finally there was an element of deterrence: by demonstrating that the country was united behind the government and possessed a loyal, well-trained (albeit poorly equipped) army, they hoped to convince the British that they would face formidable resistance if they attempted to seize Irish territory. So, although diplomatic relations were often strained and hostile, a productive and cordial liaison developed between military and intelligence officers.

The contradictions and paradoxes in the Anglo-Irish relationship occurred because Britain's strategic imperatives pulled its policy in different directions: preparing for a German invasion required the goodwill and collaboration of the Irish authorities; the need for use of Irish sea and air bases demanded coercion of the Irish state. Towards the end of 1941 the importance of both these factors diminished. The threat of German invasion faded, as Hitler's armies became bogged down in the Soviet winter. Equally, Irish ports and air bases were now less vital to Britain. The development of Derry as a base for escort vessels provided a substitute for ports in the south; the establishment of bases in Iceland, together with greater assistance from the United States, allowed the Royal Navy to extend convoy protection right across the Atlantic; the shipping situation improved.[69] Finally, the strategic situation was completely realigned with the entry of the United States into the war following the Japanese attack on Pearl Harbor on 7 December 1941. Although the tide did not turn against the Axis for almost a year, American belligerency, together with Soviet resistance, made British defeat impossible and the Atlantic Ocean secure. As a result, there was no longer much chance of British military intervention in southern Ireland. The W-Plan, the liaison with the Irish army and the constant reconnaissance missions all became rather academic.[70] BTNI headquarters and Military Mission 18 were maintained for a while to assist the thousands of American troops who began flooding into Northern Ireland. But the organisations dwindled in size, and were finally dissolved in April 1943.[71] Operational intelligence in southern Ireland was no longer a priority for the British armed services.

L ARGELY thanks to Irish co-operation, the British armed services had developed excellent operational intelligence on southern Ireland during the critical months of 1940. They produced hundreds of pages on every aspect of Irish topography, society and defence. The other tasks facing the British intelligence community in its dealings with Ireland – tackling the Irish fifth column, uncovering and countering Axis propaganda, preventing leakage of information – would provide a stiffer challenge. The threats posed by indigenous subversives and foreign agents were hidden, evolving, clouded by rumour: it was harder to assess Ireland's internal security problems and political mood than the condition of its armed forces and roads. Although the quality of British intelligence improved after the summer of 1940, it was not until 1942 that these security threats were put into proper perspective. As with operational intelligence, this was achieved through a combination of collaboration with Irish officials and covert activity in southern Ireland. In contrast to the mechanisms for collecting operational intelligence, however, Britain maintained an elaborate, clandestine network to investigate Irish security threats almost until the end of the war.

CHAPTER 11

Debunking the Fifth Column

T HE assumed existence of an extensive Irish fifth column had exerted a powerful effect on British policy towards Ireland during the summer of 1940. Fifth columnists would remain a serious threat so long as British military intervention in southern Ireland was a possibility: in the event of a German invasion they could provide crucial support to the invaders, divide Irish opinion and weaken resistance; if Britain sought bases in the south, they were a likely source of political opposition and violent attack. In addition, pro-Axis elements in Ireland constituted a pool of agents for German espionage, sabotage and propaganda operations against the United Kingdom – this threat persisted long after 1941. The British intelligence community set about investigating a wide range of individuals who might aid the enemy: the colourful cast of suspects included militant republicans, aspiring fascists, government officials, German diplomats and Abwehr agents. It took some time for British officials to get to grips with this threat. Although the wildest fears about the Irish fifth column and the IRA disappeared in late 1940, British intelligence officers continued to fret about Irish Quislings and the activities of the German legation. By 1942, however, the British intelligence community was less worried about Axis subversion and the activities of pro-Axis elements in Ireland. This was partly caused by reassuring developments in Ireland, partly by better British intelligence. Some of this intelligence came from an extensive covert network built up by SIS in southern Ireland. More came from the Irish authorities, either through the link between MI5 and G2 or from co-operation between the RUC and the Garda. After some problems in the middle of 1941, the Anglo-Irish intelligence relationship deepened considerably. For the rest of the war, Irish and British officials worked closely together to monitor and suppress any remaining threats to Allied security.

The dual intelligence approach

W E have seen how the need for operational intelligence caused British intelligence agencies to undertake clandestine missions in southern Ireland in the summer of 1940. The panic about the Irish fifth column generated an even greater response. The British government decided to collect its own information from southern Ireland, rather than rely on Irish officials, because the latter were suspected of, at best, myopia, and, at worst, being part of the fifth column themselves. The agency responsible for the most extensive covert intelligence operation in Ireland during the Second World War was SIS. It expanded its Irish operation after the middle of 1940, developing a presence on a par with its activities in other countries.[1] It is probable that the new Prime Minister, Winston Churchill, who was much more enthusiastic about secret service than his predecessor, had some hand in this. Unfortunately for the historian, SIS activity is one aspect of the British intelligence community's wartime involvement in Ireland that is only partially revealed in the available British records. Instead, we must turn to the archives of the Irish organisation that successfully uncovered the British network: Irish military intelligence (G2).

The crucial step in the expansion of the SIS operation was the creation of a British Permit Office at 30 Merrion Square in Dublin on 7 June 1940. It was under the control of a reserve officer in the Royal Engineers, Captain Charles Sydenham Collinson – he was described by Irish observers as 'a neat, severe, dapper little Englishman, about 50, with a small grey moustache.'[2] Ostensibly, his appointment was made to operate the stringent controls that were imposed on travel from Ireland. Yet Collinson's position of Passport Control Officer had been the cover for SIS officers throughout the world for two decades. This was no exception – SIS now had a base within southern Ireland. Collinson's staff, which grew over the coming months, were also implicated in his intelligence network. For example, in July 1940 agents wishing to make reports communicated with Miss Southam over lunch or tea. By October 1944, and possibly far earlier, she had been replaced by a Miss Houston. The Assistant Trade Commissioner, Lieutenant Commander Clarke, was also heavily involved, acting as 'contact man and paymaster for … some of the country groups'.[3]

Initially SIS maintained a separation between the coastwatching network set up at the behest of the Naval Intelligence Division (NID) at the end of 1939 and the broader 'information service' that had existed since 1932. There were still two distinct series of SIS reports ('QCW' and 'QRS') at this time. G2's knowledge was initially confined to the coastwatching branch of the SIS operation. Starting in the summer of 1940, the Irish authorities uncovered a number of British agents in the south and west of the country. For example, there were three agents in Co. Cork. One was James Flynn, a Catholic from a staunch loyalist family, whose mother was the proprietor of Roche's Hotel in Glengariff: she had been legendary for her 'unavailing kindness and hospitality' towards Royal Navy officers while they were stationed in Cobh and Berehaven.[4] The other two agents were Protestants residing at Bantry: one, Captain Hutchins, was a retired British army officer. These men received £65 per month for their work, a respectable sum. Other active individuals included a retired Royal Navy officer named Commander Gosnell, a local fisherman and a 'thorough rogue' named David Dudley, two lighthouse keepers, and relatives and friends of the late Vice-Admiral Somerville, who had been murdered by the IRA in 1936. In the west of Ireland the 'principal Agent' was Michael Fitzgerald. He collected information from his sub-agents and brought it by hand to a member of the British Permit Office. As an alternative means of communication for 'emergency reports', the cable station at Waterville was used: on one occasion, details were sent to London of a suspected landing of German parachutists.[5] It is not clear whether radio transmitters were distributed to SIS agents along the coast: Irish officials believed that this was briefly attempted, but British records indicate that SIS decided against it.[6]

G2 surmised that this organisation was set up 'largely due to the wild rumours and suspicions' about German U-boats generated by the 'Press campaign' in 1940. Its purpose was 'to collect information regarding the possibilities of German submarines obtaining shelter and supplies around our coasts, particularly in the south-west'. There was no suggestion that the agents should concern themselves with 'other internal matters'. However, in 1941 G2 learnt that the 'earlier naval organisation' on the south-west coast had been taken over by new handlers. Its remit had been broadened to the investigation of any individuals inimical to the British war effort, whether German intelligence agents, IRA members, suspect enemy aliens, fascist sympathisers or British renegades. 'Counter-Espionage & Security Activities' became the mainstay of this organisation.[7]

What G2 had discovered was a move to integrate the coastwatching service with the rest of the SIS network and to expand the entire operation. In the south-west, where the 'fragile coastwatching service' had been concentrated, a number of new agents were added.[8] G2 learnt that the British 'Ace', Collinson's 'best man' in the whole country, was 'an ex-officer of the British Army, a well known Mason and a popular social figure'. He was identified as Captain W. M. Reidy, secretary of Doyles Golf Club, who was 'exceptionally well placed for work of this kind with a wide circle, including public men and some serving army officers'.[9] Collinson also cultivated a wide network of agents in Dublin. They included a retired British army officer, a bookmaker, an employee of the Hibernian Hotel, a Thomas Cook's travel agent and a director of the firm of Knight & Petch who 'knew nearly all the members of the Government of Eire'.[10] The SIS network expanded across the whole country until there were representatives in every county. The last piece of the jigsaw fell into place in November 1941, when Colonel Les O'Callaghan and two others were appointed in Ennis, Co. Clare: at this point

Collinson expressed his confidence that he had 'the country covered'.[11] Finally, it appears that SIS had sources among Irish state officials. Collinson claimed to have under his control 'a number of policemen who were very reliable'. He also had a 'good man' in the Revenue Commissioners and an 'indirect contact' with a civil servant who was 'third from the top' in the Department of Justice.[12] By then the SIS network was an extensive organisation with tentacles spreading into all parts of the state.

As well as creating a network of agents, Collinson's turned to a private firm in Dublin to carry out targeted investigations. Stubbs Ltd. offered a commercial inquiry and debt recovery service from its offices on College Street. It was part of a British firm that had been used by British spies in the past – after the First World War intelligence chiefs briefly considered using it as a cover for 'secret service operations worldwide'. Its Dublin branch offered a ready-made detective service, as it held files on many Irish businesses and had the expertise and contacts to acquire information on almost any individual. Starting in 1941, Collinson employed the company to study persons or groups that aroused SIS suspicion, passing on short handwritten enquiries containing names, addresses and other available details. By April 1945 Stubbs had handled 1,882 of these enquiries, which illustrates the scale of its activity. The agency evolved into the most important component of the SIS network in Ireland, its investigative shock troops. The company manager, William A. Podesta, was taken fully into Collinson's confidence, and his deputy, Moore, who had many contacts in the Garda, did much of the investigative work.[13]

MI5 recorded that 'the S.I.S. service retained, generally speaking, its static characteristics'. It was composed of local residents and 'at no time did S.I.S. employ "trained agents" in the usual sense of this term'.[14] The evidence suggests that the majority of SIS agents were drawn from the loyalist class, those who had wanted to remain part of the United Kingdom in 1921 and were now fervently pro-British in the war. Most but not all were Protestants; many were ex-servicemen or had sons serving in the British armed forces; there was a disproportionate number of Freemasons. They were a perfect recruiting ground for British intelligence. Describing the agents in Co. Cork in July 1940, a Garda superintendent wrote:

> All are undoubtedly pro-British. It is well known that people of the Southern Loyalist type see only one enemy as far as this or any country is concerned. In other words they would fight against anything and everything except England. People of this mentality would, I have no doubt, supply information to England.[15]

This was the other fifth column in Ireland, the counterbalance to pro-Axis militant republicans – *Britain's* fifth column.

The SIS network in Ireland was controlled by Section V of SIS (the counter-intelligence branch) under Colonel Valentine Vivian. In January 1941 Vivian was replaced by Felix Cowgill and promoted to deputy chief of SIS, but he retained overall responsibility for counter-intelligence matters and retained personal control of the Irish operations. At some point a special 'Irish Section' was set up within Section V. It had the unusual distinction of being run by a woman, Jane Archer (née Sissmore). A trained barrister, Archer had worked in MI5's B Division as an expert on Soviet and communist affairs for over twenty years. The Soviet double agent Kim Philby described her as, apart from Guy Liddell, 'perhaps the ablest professional intelligence officer ever employed by MI5'. He added that she was 'tough-minded' and 'rough-tongued', and always spoke her mind. She had been affectionately tolerated by the old MI5 regime as a sort of 'court jester', but during the period of turmoil in the organisation at the end of 1940 she went too far, and on 18 November was sacked for insubordination. She moved to Section V of SIS, taking over responsibility for its Irish operation sometime in 1941.[16] At interdepartmental meetings on Ireland, SIS was henceforth represented by Archer accompanied by Colonel Vivian. She also collated and assessed the raw intelligence coming from Collinson's network and transformed it into two series of reports for circulation to other departments. The first, QK reports, were irregular and numerous, and dealt with 'information about suspects and aliens'. The second, bi-monthly QRS reports, provided a survey of Irish political opinion, as well as details about the activities of German intelligence agents, the Axis legations, pro-Axis Irish groups and the IRA.[17]

The expansion of the SIS network was accompanied by an improvement in the quality of its intelligence. Fantastic stories about a rampant fifth column gradually disappeared. By the beginning of 1941 SIS was reporting that there was 'little outward sign of illegal activities' by the IRA, and that the police had the situation was 'well in hand'.[18] SIS was also more sceptical about rumours of U-boats receiving supplies on the Irish coasts.[19] Although still liable to exaggerate the activities of German spies and diplomats, the SIS network no longer produced the wild scares that had been such a feature of the first year of the war.

At the end of the war MI5 concluded that the SIS operation was 'valuable' in two ways: first, 'as a source of original information'; second, 'as a check on reports received from other sources'.[20] The importance of its 'original information' was probably limited. SIS built up great detail on prospective anti-British elements in southern Ireland, but it rarely discovered any security threats that were not already being dealt with by the Irish authorities in conjunction with

MI5. G2 did not hold a high opinion of the organisation, claiming that 'they have rarely if ever got on to anything of importance.'[21] Instead the major contribution of the SIS network was to provide a 'check on reports received from other sources'. On the one hand, by independently investigating cases that were being dealt with via the 'Dublin link', SIS was able to confirm the *bona fides* of the Irish authorities. On the other, the SIS service was a channel by which the innumerable scares still being entertained in London, often by SIS headquarters, could be investigated and refuted, without being handed to the Irish authorities. In this regard the Stubbs agency had a pivotal role. It investigated hundreds of suspect individuals and organisations, usually showing that they were harmless.

However, there was one way in which SIS failed miserably: it allowed its network to be thoroughly penetrated by the Irish security organisations. The Irish had initially shown an 'innocence ... of the ramifications of the British Intelligence machine.'[22] The first indication of the existence of the SIS organisation came from a Garda Superintendent in Co. Cork on 2 July 1940. G2 then took the lead in uncovering the network.[23] It could call on the assistance of a special resource in the south-west of the country: the Supplementary Intelligence Service created by Florence O'Donoghue, which was essentially a resurrection of the IRA intelligence system that had been so successful in 1920–1. O'Donoghue uncovered many of the British agents in the south-west and succeeded in 'turning' James Flynn, who provided full information on the role of the British Permit Office.[24] G2's greatest coup came in Dublin in the middle of 1941, when it persuaded Podesta's deputy in the Stubbs agency, Moore, to work for it. Moore saw all the queries sent out by Collinson, was in charge of most of the investigations, and was briefed by Podesta on his conversations with Collinson. He obediently passed all this information to G2.

Collinson never suspected that there was a mole at the very heart of his operation. When he was withdrawn from Ireland in October 1944, he passed control of the remaining network to Podesta, with Moore as his loyal assistant. (Ironically, before leaving, Collinson complimented Podesta and his staff 'for the careful way things had been handled, especially their having avoided police contact'.)[25] This ranks as one of the greatest of G2's many successes during the war. It was partly due to the effectiveness of the Irish security apparatus: Rear-Admiral Godfrey later commented that 'having only recently emerged from a state of civil war the Irish police were particularly adept in detecting underground activities.'[26] It was partly due to lax SIS security. The Permit Office was not kept sufficiently distant from the agent network, and Collinson was far too expansive in his discussions with Podesta and Moore. Some of the SIS agents were distinctly unreliable, mainly due to their fondness for alcohol: for example, at the end of

1944 Podesta reported that one of his employees was 'drinking, helping himself to cash, and staying away from work', but could not be sacked, as he threatened to reveal everything to the Irish police.[27] In the early part of the Second World War SIS missions in Europe were notable for their poor security and easy penetration by domestic counter-intelligence agencies. Ireland was no exception.

Both SIS and MI5 were anxious to keep the agent network from the knowledge of the Irish authorities:

> It will be realised that this organisation had to be kept secret, not only from the enemy in Eire, but also from the Eire authorities. Had it come to the knowledge of the latter, the effect on our political relations with Eire would have been very serious and irreparable harm would have been done to the general security co-operation which had been built up with the Eire Government.[28]

These fears were not borne out. Although G2 thoroughly penetrated the SIS operation, the Irish government took no action. There were a number of reasons for this. First, G2 considered that if the network was suppressed, it might be replaced by another operation that the Irish would be unable to discover. Second, G2 concluded that the information supplied by the SIS network did little harm and in many cases some good by refuting the scares circulating around Whitehall. (This proves that, at least by the middle of 1941, the material produced by SIS was relatively sound.) Finally, the Irish government's attitude should be understood in the context of its handling of security throughout the war. It cracked down on any German intelligence activities, because these were necessarily directed against the United Kingdom, but it tolerated British covert operations, because they had a primarily defensive function. It accepted a principle frequently reiterated by Maffey: that 'a German in Eire is a menace to England, while an Englishman in Eire is no menace to Germany'.[29] This was part of the Irish government's wider effort to demonstrate that its territory was not being used as a base for attack on the United Kingdom.

In the end, far from destroying Anglo-Irish security co-operation, discovery of British covert activity spurred the Irish government into even greater co-operation. This, and not covert activity, would be the key to the British intelligence community's successful handling of Ireland, because the Irish authorities had a knowledge of the internal security situation that the British could not hope to achieve independently. The period between 1924 and 1938 had been remarkable for the almost complete lack of co-operation between the two countries on security matters. Although steps had been taken to remedy this after 1938, the exchanges were sporadic and generally limited to the activities of German nationals in Ireland. During the summer of 1940 this began to change. The Irish government showed a greater willingness to share its intelligence. Concerned by British perceptions of the Irish fifth column, de Valera threw open the doors of his security apparatus to prove that no serious threat to Britain existed. The British government began to realise that the Irish police and military intelligence had the ability to uncover Axis and IRA intrigues. The British also began to trust in the good faith of their Irish counterparts, accepting their commitment that they did not want neutral Ireland to be a source of insecurity for Britain. Anglo-Irish collaboration developed slowly, stuttering at times during 1940 and 1941, but an unprecedented intelligence relationship eventually emerged, albeit well hidden from public view.

The security co-operation that developed in the summer of 1940 functioned on three separate levels. The first was the liaison between the British attachés in Dublin, especially Major Pryce and Wing Commander Lywood, and their counterparts in the Irish armed services, in particular the G2 head, Colonel Archer. The primary mission of the attachés was to gather operational intelligence and prepare for a possible German invasion of Ireland. Yet they were also a conduit by which fifth column rumours could be passed from London to Dublin for investigation. These included Tegart's information regarding the clearing of fields in the south-west for a German landing, innumerable scares about the landing of German aircraft and parachutists, and a grave warning that foreign-looking men wearing yellow jumpers had been spotted in Dublin, Mullingar and Athlone – this was given a sinister interpretation because of reports that fifth columnists had used yellow handkerchiefs to identify themselves to German troops in Poland and Luxembourg.[30] Colonel Archer was able to refute these absurd stories and to demonstrate that the supposed fifth column posed little threat: he told Major Pryce that the IRA was 'practically dead' and that the authorities had 'the whole situation taped'.[31]

In addition, the attachés used their positions to investigate the supposed Irish fifth column themselves. 'I keep on asking all sorts of people about I.R.A. activities and pro-Germanism', Pryce wrote on 22 August 1940.[32] After developing a better understanding of Irish conditions, they were soon able to reject out of hand the rumours circulating in London. For example, when Pryce received a British postal censorship survey, he condemned it as containing the most 'fantastic' rumours of German activity in Ireland without any attempt to weigh either 'the reliability of the writers nor the accuracy of their statements'. 'What I do not understand is the point of re-publishing such statements in such a document', he wrote. 'It reads almost super 5th Column.' Pryce repeatedly assured London that the Irish would fight whoever invaded them first.[33] The opinions of the attachés were so important because they went directly to the armed service departments, which were often sceptical of the reassuring tones of the civil departments.

The second form of security co-operation was the relationship between MI5 and G2 – the 'Dublin link'. On 15 May 1940 Cecil Liddell, the head of MI5's Irish section, met with Colonel Archer for the first time. (This meeting paved the way for the pivotal defence talks involving Archer, Walshe and senior British military officers eight days later.)[34] Over the summer the two organisations worked closely together, mainly in connection with the Abwehr agents sent to Ireland, although MI5 also passed on other reports of fifth column and espionage plots so they could be checked by G2. Most communication was by correspondence, but Cecil Liddell visited Dublin in October 1940, and he was joined by his brother, Captain Guy Liddell, on a second visit to Dublin in May 1941.[35] At this time, the relationship was not as open or productive as MI5 wished. 'Information is probably withheld', Cecil Liddell wrote, 'which would provide us with a handle for saying that the Germans in Eire must all be interned or kicked out, or which would strengthen our hand in asking for the use of the Eire ports as bases.'[36] As we shall see, there was a serious strain in the 'Dublin link' in the middle of 1941, and for some months all contact ceased.[37] However, communication soon restarted, and the relationship quickly reached a new level of intimacy. The 'Dublin link' would be the key to Britain's handling of Irish security threats during the Second World War.

MI5's Irish section – then known as B9, but soon renamed B1H – expanded during this period. In May 1940 Cecil Liddell received his first additional staff, the barrister Joe Stephenson. His family had an unfortunate connection with Ireland: his great-uncle, Lord Frederick Cavendish, had been murdered by the Invincibles in 1882. Stephenson spent much of his time reviewing travel controls and material from censored post.[38] By July 1941 the Irish section had grown to six officers and eight secretaries, a figure that was maintained until March 1943. The unit then contracted: when the war ended, only Cecil Liddell, one other officer and two secretaries remained. This is a good barometer of the attention that Irish security matters received in London.[39] While the Irish section was only ever a small component of the MI5 machinery, the organisation's new Director-General, Sir David Petrie, paid close attention to its work: when handed the internal B1H history written by Cecil Liddell in 1946, Petrie remarked that he had 'been kept in pretty close touch all along' with Irish matters.[40]

Despite their very different methods, B1H worked hand in hand with Section V of SIS when dealing with Ireland. Guy Liddell got on very well with Colonel Vivian, even recommending the SIS officer for the vacant position of MI5 Director-General at the end of 1940.[41] Moreover, Jane Archer had worked in

MI5 for two decades and remained firm friends with both Guy and Cecil Liddell after she became head of the SIS Irish section. The two organisations exchanged all reports and correspondence, and no important step was taken without previous consultation. Writing after the war, the MI5 in-house historian, Jack Curry, wrote that 'one of the happiest features of the work of [B1H] was its relationship with its opposite number in S.I.S. and the completely harmonious way in which they all combined to secure results'.[42] This was worthy of comment because relations between MI5 and SIS, especially on matters of counter-intelligence, were often strained.[43]

In 1940 the MI5–G2 link dealt mostly with the activities of German agents and residents in Ireland. The most useful intelligence on the militant republican movement came from another channel – co-operation between the Garda and the RUC. Despite north–south political animosity, there had been collaboration at a local level between the two police forces for many years. However, communication between Garda and RUC headquarters only began after the southern crack-down against the IRA in the summer of 1940. On 23 June an RUC officer, Captain J. Roger Moore, travelled to Dublin to meet with 'officers of high rank of the Civic Guard'. The ostensible reason for his visit was to discuss the recent Stephen Held case. The Garda co-operated by sharing full details on Held, as well as files on other German nationals in southern Ireland. But when the subject turned to the IRA, the Garda were even more forthcoming. Moore later recorded how the interview 'opened up', there was no 'hedging', just 'plain speaking', as the officers found they were on 'common ground'. The Garda assessment of the IRA was encouraging:

> … my host spoke with tremendous confidence of his successes in 'knocking
> them out of action' by the recent arresting of nearly 500 I.R.A. leaders …
> He was confident that he had got the leaders, and that he had disorganised
> the organisation to such an extent as would paralyse them for some time
> to come. He said the old I.R.A. were very much against the New I.R.A.
> now, and were giving valuable information.

The substance of these talks was put into a detailed report that was brought before the Prime Minister in London.[44] For the rest of the war Captain Moore maintained a link with Superintendent P. Carroll, the head of C3, an élite Special Section of the Garda Detective Branch, which dealt with espionage and subversive activities.[45]

In 1940 structures were developed by which this sort of valuable information could be regularly fed into the British intelligence machinery. MI5 developed a much closer relationship with the RUC – what might be termed its 'Belfast link'. Cecil Liddell first visited Belfast in April 1940. He was followed by a high-level MI5 delegation at the end of August, which was 'most anxious to get the measure of the internal security problem' and eager for information on southern Ireland. The RUC Inspector General, Sir Charles Wickham, accompanied the MI5 delegation throughout its visit, producing a very good impression. 'In the personality and experience of Sir Charles Wickham', the MI5 officers concluded, 'the fighting Services have at their elbow a most valuable friend and counsellor, and the advisability of acting in the closest co-operation with him and the RUC cannot be too strongly emphasised.' This advice was taken to heart. For the rest of the war there was a regular interchange of information between MI5 and the RUC.[46]

In his talks with MI5 in August 1940 Wickham poured cold water on the wilder stories about the Irish fifth column, explaining that he had 'a very high opinion of the efficiency of the Civic Guard, at any rate in dealing with the I.R.A.'[47] He elaborated in a letter to MI5 the following month:

> It would be unwise to overestimate the I.R.A. as a German ally or the amount of assistance that they could give here in the North other than starting riots in Belfast. ... In the South the Government is just as anti-I.R.A. as in the North and should the troops enter Eire by request they would be wise to leave the I.R.A. to the Civic Guard, giving assistance if requested rather than to try to teach the Civil Guard a job at which they are quite expert.

In a subtle reference to the ill-fated 1922 Criminal Investigation Department, which had been staffed by English officers, he added a cautionary note: 'to deal with [the IRA] requires a considerable amount of experience in the country and our experience of strange intelligence officers is not a very happy one.'[48] The Northern Ireland administration had often been a source of alarming information on republican plots in the 1920s and 1930s, but now the RUC downplayed the threat, assuring MI5 officers that the indigenous Irish police forces could deal with it.

The armed service departments also began to realise Wickham's usefulness. The clearest statement of the value of the RUC – for intelligence on both northern and southern Ireland – was made by NID. After his appointment to Belfast, Commander Slade liaised closely with the RUC, and this source quickly overshadowed all others. 'The best source of intelligence as regards both Ulster and Eire is Sir Charles Wickham', Rear-Admiral Godfrey concluded in August 1941 after a visit to Ireland. 'His officers collaborate closely with the Civil Guard [*sic*] in Eire and he is thus able to keep close watch on German and I.R.A. activities on both sides of the Border.'[49] Godfrey was so impressed by the connection with Northern Ireland that he saw it as the key to all British intelligence needs in Ireland:

> Had we known in the spring of 1939, what we learnt by the autumn of 1940 about conditions in Eire, and the accessibility of Eire from Ulster, the fruitful liaison with the Royal Ulster Constabulary, and other Belfast activities could have been put into force on the outbreak of war instead of a year later.

He saw this as one of the 'first lessons' for NID in the post-war era.[50]

After the chaos of the summer of 1940 the British government diligently pursued a twin-track approach of deepening co-operation with the Irish authorities while increasing clandestine intelligence activities on Irish soil. This meant that by 1941 London had intelligence on Ireland on an unprecedented scale. Yet it still remained for it to be used correctly – this had hitherto been the principle failing of British intelligence. During the summer of 1940 it is possible to discern improvements in the dissemination and analysis of intelligence on Ireland. As for dissemination, all the major departments began distributing regular summaries of Irish intelligence. The SIS reports have already been described. MI5 is noted as 'producing periodical political reports' based on information from the Dublin government.[51] In June the War Office section dealing with Ireland started a weekly commentary on Irish affairs, while the Naval Intelligence Division issued regular 'Eire Situation Reports'.[52] These reports demonstrated a higher level of analysis, as rumours were scrutinised and placed in context.

Perhaps the most important development was the decision of the Dominions Office to play a more active role. In the second half of 1940 the Dominions Office reasserted its authority as the chief interpreter of Irish politics and the chief arbitrator of British policy towards Ireland. In doing so, it called upon its representative in Dublin, Sir John Maffey, who began to exert a stronger influence over British policy towards Ireland. Maffey had been strangely quiet on the subject of the Irish fifth column during May and June 1940, probably in deference to what he assumed was special intelligence available to London. But in July 1940, fearful that Anglo-Irish relations were sliding towards disaster, he made a forceful intervention. He wrote a series of strongly worded despatches and returned to London on 18 July to set matters right. He depreciated the chances of a German invasion of Ireland – 'if I were Hitler I should keep out' – and warned of the dangers of trying to scare Dublin into believing that it was imminent: 'these means to try and put the "wind-up" the Eire Govt in order to make them abandon neutrality, have little chance of success, and in fact do harm.'[53] He stated that the Irish authorities 'had tackled the fifth Column with vigour', sharing all their intelligence. He condemned the activities of Tegart and other amateur spies, and warned that recent events had led to a 'loss of confidence in our intentions' and a 'widespread belief' that Britain was about to invade southern Ireland. He urged that the British government damp down the press, go through his office for information, and declare that it had no intention of invading southern Ireland.[54] Much of this advice was heeded. Henceforth, the activities and outputs of British intelligence agencies would be subject to close scrutiny by the civilian department with responsibility for Irish affairs.

The maturing of the British intelligence community's engagement with Ireland should be seen in the context of remarkable improvements in the organisation and performance of the entire British intelligence system after the middle of 1940. By August 1940, even as the invasion threat intensified, senior MI5 officers had become sceptical about the existence of a fifth column in Britain.[55] Ironically, the arrival of the first genuine German agents in the United Kingdom in September 1940 accelerated this process. All but one were immediately captured, and their interrogation revealed that the Abwehr had no pre-existing network in Britain. This was confirmed by the breaking of the Abwehr hand cipher (codenamed ISOS) in December 1940.[56] Britain's foreign and military intelligence also began to improve. SIS began to recruit some valuable human agents in continental Europe. Most crucially, signals intelligence became available on a large scale: in spring 1941 the Enigma code of the German navy was broken, followed by that of the German army a year later. The cryptanalytic efforts of Bletchley Park would eventually provide Britain with an unprecedented knowledge of German intentions and capabilities.[57]

Perhaps as important were improvements in the analysis and co-ordination of intelligence. This occurred at a departmental level: Rear-Admiral Godfrey was at the forefront of a drive to ensure that intelligence departments scrutinised and graded their material before disseminating it.[58] But the most crucial development was at an interdepartmental level. On coming to power, Churchill had established the Joint Intelligence Committee as the central body for analysis and co-ordination of intelligence, but its opinions had often been rejected by senior military officers. It finally achieved sufficient authority in the spring of 1941 after the creation of the permanent Joint Intelligence Staff, which became the 'corporate memory' of the intelligence community. With it, the JIC became the authoritative, unified voice of British intelligence and the epistemological centre of the whole war effort. It made wide-ranging strategic assessments and managed the activities of the various intelligence services, transforming the latter into a proper 'community' for the first time.[59] The official history of British intelligence states that after the summer of 1941 'the conduct of operations and settlement of strategic decisions were rarely handicapped by the ignorance or the dangerously incomplete knowledge of the enemy from which they had suffered in the first two years of the war.' Britain was now winning the intelligence war.[60]

Changing perceptions

IMPROVEMENTS in British intelligence led to a gradual re-evaluation of the threats posed by the IRA and other Irish fifth columnists. This was first evident in a change in official attitudes towards the Irish community in Britain. The Special Branch had always played down the threat of IRA subversion in Britain. Towards the end of 1940 it expressed its views more forcefully. In a meeting with MI5, Special Branch officers asserted:

> 99% of these cases of Irishmen reported as having anti-British, I.R.A. sympathies are not genuine I.R.A. cases. Irishmen, who when they had a glass or in the heat of an argument say 'Up the I.R.A.' or 'Down with Britain', are not likely to be members of the I.R.A. The true I.R.A. do not drink and do not talk. They are religious fanatics.[61]

MI5 issued instructions to its regional security officers in December 1940 stating that the 'Special Branch, who have been watching the I.R.A. for nearly 20 years, have no positive evidence that the Germans have used it as a "Fifth Column".'[62] This reflected a general decline during the autumn of 1940 in fifth column hysteria among the public and officials.

The notion of a rampant fifth column in southern Ireland had stronger roots, but it was challenged by better material from the developing British intelligence system. Many of the wilder exaggerations about the Irish fifth column disappeared during the autumn of 1940. London was no longer gripped by stories of Germans buying up estates on the west coast of Ireland to prepare landing strips for German aircraft. Similarly, the idea that U-boats were accessing secret supply bases in Ireland was finally put to rest: by December 1940 NID had concluded that these reports, although 'constantly received', could 'usually be traced to idle gossip … no real evidence has been found that U-Boats use bases in Eire'.[63] As already noted, there was also a complete change in British attitudes towards the Irish army, which was now regarded as an effective, well-disciplined force, sympathetic to the Allies.[64] As a result, by August 1940 the IRA was no longer thought capable of launching a revolution in southern Ireland, even with the aid of small numbers of German troops.

The idea that the IRA could provide crucial military assistance to a full-scale German invasion of Ireland took longer to disappear. On 2 October 1940 the Joint Planning Staff stated that the Germans would effect 'the capture of ports and aerodromes, by means of parachute and airborne troops supported by "5th Column" activities. The German troops would be likely to act in conjunction with the IRA, the nucleus of which is believed to consist of some 2,000 to 3,000 men, all well armed.' The Joint Intelligence Committee (JIC) had given an identical estimate two weeks earlier.[65] London continued to exaggerate the strength, organisation and freedom of the IRA: the organisation was far from well armed, could not muster such a large force, and could not co-ordinate sophisticated plans with German invaders.[66] However, during the autumn and winter of 1940 these concerns dissolved. Neither the IRA nor the Irish fifth column was mentioned in the high-level policy papers that dealt with the threat of a German invasion of Ireland in early 1941. Concern about the IRA was confined to the British army in Northern Ireland, which feared that IRA sabotage might impede the move south in the event of a German invasion. There was particular anxiety over the security of the railway viaduct over the River Boyne at Drogheda, as the bulk of the army's equipment would be transported via this route: on 17 February 1941 General Harrison referred to a 'rumour' that the IRA intended to blow up the viaduct when German troops landed.[67] Yet, although this may indicate a continuing exaggeration of IRA capabilities, it is clear that the IRA was no longer seen as a major threat – it had declined from a strategic factor to a minor security problem.

The waning of the IRA as a military force and the debunking of the wildest fifth column stories did not remove all British concern about Axis subversion in southern Ireland. During 1941, with the threat of a German invasion still real, the expanding British intelligence system shifted its attention away from the IRA and investigated dozens of individuals, at all levels of Irish society, who were suspected of supporting the Axis cause. British intelligence officers, especially in SIS, were still too quick to see intrigues where they did not exist. This was evident in their preoccupation with Quislings, defined by SIS as 'public men who, in the event of an even partially successful German invasion, would probably be ready to collaborate with the Nazis and participate in any puppet government formed to assist their exploitation of the country'. Drawing up lists of Irish Quislings became a popular pastime for British intelligence agencies: MI5 circulated an internal report on this subject on 19 December 1940, and SIS produced a series of detailed 'sketches' on dangerous individuals one month later. Quislings were identified with three separate groups: militant republicans, right-wing admirers of fascism and anti-British elements associated with Fianna Fáil.

The Irish republican leader most cited in this regard was the barrister Seán MacBride – MI5 stated that he was 'one of the four Irishmen believed to be the destined Quislings of Eire'.[68] MacBride had fought with the IRA during the War of Independence and Civil War, briefly served as IRA Chief of Staff in the 1930s, and frequently defended militant republicans in the Irish courts. His family history made him well known to British intelligence. His father, Major John MacBride, had been executed for his part in the 1916 Easter Rising, while his mother, Maud Gonne, was a tireless campaigner for Sinn Féin and the anti-Treaty republicans. (She was also a famous beauty and muse to W. B. Yeats.) His half-sister, Iseult, sheltered Görtz when he parachuted into the country, and was married to Francis Stuart, who spent most of the war in Germany. During the Second World War MacBride acted as a link between the IRA and Germany, meeting frequently with the German Minister, Dr Eduard Hempel: indeed, G2 believed that he was 'working for the Germans even more than for the IRA'. This would become a sensitive matter, given MacBride's post-war political career. He became Irish Minister for External Affairs in 1948, international chairman of Amnesty International in 1961 and UN Commissioner for Namibia in 1973, receiving both the Nobel and Lenin Peace Prizes.[69]

The second group of potential Quislings consisted of right-wing admirers of German fascism, many associated with the old Blueshirt movement. An obvious candidate was the former Blueshirt leader Eoin O'Duffy, who was openly pro-Nazi. Although he was 'drinking heavily', 'unbelievably vain' and 'an exploded myth in Ireland', SIS believed that 'outstanding men' might 'use him' for their purposes. One such person was Ernest Blythe, a wealthy businessman and former Minister for Finance in the Cosgrave government who was '100% Nazi'. An SIS source reported that he was 'well-educated and cultured' and had 'lots of character, moral courage and determination', as well as 'outstanding mental qualities' – he was 'head and shoulders above any other pro-German in Ireland'. His close associate, J. J. Walsh, was also regarded as a potential supporter of a German invasion. Blythe and Walshe were respectively chairman and manager of the Clondalkin Paper Mill, which had drawn the attention of British observers in July 1940 when its chimney was noticed to be smoking 'in a queer fashion' – it was thought that it might be signalling to German aircraft.[70]

SIS also believed that it had uncovered a nest of potential Quislings within Fianna Fáil circles – this was the 'Left Wing' that de Valera had often drawn attention to before the war. One member of this faction was the famous old IRA leader from Co. Tipperary, Dan Breen, who was now a member of the Dáil (or 'TD'). According to SIS, he expressed strong anti-British and pro-German views, and it was 'better not to trust him in any way'. Perhaps the most sinister member of this group was Joe McGrath, Controller and part-owner of the Irish Hospital Sweepstakes. He had been a leading IRA gunman during the War of Independence and then a government minister in the 1920s, before taking a senior role at the Irish Sweepstakes and amassing great wealth. He also maintained 'a private army of a number of the worst thugs and gunmen produced by the I.R.A. in the troubled times' (the remnants of Collins's 'Squad') and had used his Sweepstakes organisation on behalf of the 'new I.R.A.' to move men, money and documents between Ireland, Britain and the United States of America. SIS described him as 'a typical self-made man of the gangster type, strong, forceful and extremely shrewd in judging character', who boasted 'in his cups' that he could 'buy, fool, or frighten 999 out of every 1,000 people' in the country. He went on 'periodical and extremely heavy drinking bouts' for up to six weeks at a time, followed by periods of abstinence, when he became very religious, went to Mass daily and supported charity. He was a close friend of Dan Breen and definitely anti-British.[71]

According to SIS, these anti-British and pro-German tendencies extended to the very heart of the Irish government. Two figures who aroused suspicion were Joseph Walshe (the Secretary of the Department of External Affairs) and Thomas Derrig (the Minister for Education). Yet by far the most dangerous was Frank Aiken, the Minister for the Co-ordination of Defence. He was top of the SIS list of potential Quislings in Ireland, and his name is peppered through British wartime intelligence records. A former IRA Chief of Staff, Aiken had been a bugbear for London in the early 1930s, when it was believed that he was in league with the IRA. In its 1941 report SIS described him as 'ambitious, dour and aloof', 'unpopular and with few real friends'. He had 'a very bad record of treachery', was in close contact with the IRA and was not only anti-British but 'definitely pro-German'. He had more influence with de Valera than anyone else, and would probably win control of Fianna Fáil if anything happened to de Valera. Nonetheless, he would have no hesitation in betraying his chief, as self-interest was his 'chief moral principle'. Should the Germans invade, he could not carry the Irish army with him in any 'treachery', but he might 'reduce them to chaos till it was too late'.[72]

SIS suspicions were confirmed when it learnt of a speech that Aiken gave in Lisbon when *en route* to the United States on an arms-purchasing mission: he informed a dinner gathering that Germany would win the war, and that this would be no bad thing, as it would lead to 'a more rational distribution of things'.[73] The British sabotaged Aiken's mission by sending J. Edgar Hoover (the FBI Director) a poisonous memorandum containing the SIS information. As a result, Aiken was treated as *persona non grata* in Washington: his visit reached a nadir when President Roosevelt terminated an acrimonious meeting in the White House by flinging his lunchtime crockery to the floor.[74]

As well as identifying potential Quislings, the British intelligence community monitored fringe Irish political parties that were avowedly pro-German and hostile to Britain. The Sinn Féin party had been reduced to a handful of irreconcilables clinging to Civil War politics; nonetheless, Captain Collinson sent agents to its public meetings and asked the Stubbs agency to provide the names and addresses of its executive committee so that they could be put under postal censorship.[75] Another group that came under scrutiny was Coras na Poblachta ('The Republican Plan'). A Catholic nativist party, it was set up in the autumn of 1940 with the goals of achieving a thirty-two county republic, restoring the Irish language and excluding non-Irish influences from Irish cultural and economic life. It criticised 'Free Masonry' and 'Jewry' and 'showed a characteristic anti-British bias'.[76] Captain Collinson sent agents to its meetings, and Jane Archer frequently referred to its activities in her bi-monthly reports on Irish affairs. Although there was some concern in September 1942 that the group might infiltrate the mainstream Labour Party, SIS later realised that it had no future in Irish politics: it noted with satisfaction that Coras na Poblachta 'made a particularly poor showing' in the 1943 general election.[77]

Groups such as Sinn Féin and Coras na Poblachta were obvious targets for British intelligence, but SIS also scrutinised the most respectable Irish institutions for signs of pro-Axis leanings. For example, it showed an interest in the secret fraternal organisation, the Knights of Columbanus, an ultra-conservative, Catholic equivalent to the Freemasons. It was suspected by some (including the American Minister) of having a sinister influence in Irish society. Collinson asked the Stubbs agency to uncover its officers and to report on the Supreme Knight, J. Stafford Johnson.[78] The organisation's pro-Axis news organ, *The Standard*, the biggest Catholic weekly with a circulation of 42,000, was an object of considerable suspicion: in May 1941 London received information from 'most secret reports' that the *Standard* and its editor were 'subsidized by the enemy'.[79] Another organisation accused of involvement in enemy propaganda was the Irish Red Cross: according to SIS, it 'was known to be exploited by extremist anti-British politicians'.[80]

The suspected source of all Axis subversion in Ireland was, of course, the German legation in Dublin. The SIS network devoted considerable energy to studying the activities of German diplomats. For example, a detailed report from April 1941 described a visit to Achill Island by the German Minister, Dr Eduard Hempel, listing the people he visited and quoting from a speech that he made at dinner.[81] Although Hempel was cautious and well respected, an SIS report in December 1940 gave an alarming picture of the activities of his staff. It described the Counsellor, Henning Thomsen, as anti-Semitic, a committed Nazi and a heavy drinker: he was 'a most objectionable individual, concerning whom never a good word has been heard'. The press attaché, Carlheinz Petersen (whose office at 58 Merrion Square was just a few doors down from the British Permit Office), also had an 'evil reputation' in Dublin: he had recently been taken into custody by the police after he became 'obstreperous' while drinking at the Palace Bar. These Nazi officials were not 'merely noisy' but were 'working with true German thoroughness' to advance a number of menacing objectives. These included espionage, propaganda and the financing of the IRA – Petersen lived with a woman who was part of a republican circle. The Germans were also organising a secret 'fifth column' in Dublin under the leadership of Mrs Erskine Childers, the widow of the Sinn Féin leader executed in 1922.[82]

Reports such as this perpetuated the image of Ireland as a hotbed of Axis intrigue. It meant that the British continued to worry about the danger of fifth columnists should the Germans invade; they could never be as confident about the security situation in neutral Ireland as they were about the situation in Britain. Towards the end of 1941, however, these lingering fears about the Irish fifth column began to dissolve. This was partly brought about by favourable developments in the security situation, in particular the Irish government's successful crack-down on IRA and Abwehr activities. But it was also due to the emergence of a much greater level of co-operation between MI5 and G2. The earlier restrictions on the relationship were removed, and the two agencies subsequently worked hand in hand to suppress any threats to Allied interests.

During 1941 the IRA was locked in an increasingly bitter struggle with the security forces of the Irish state. IRA leaders were arrested, arms dumps were found, and the numbers interned at the Curragh grew steadily: in all, over 1,000 IRA members were interned during the war. IRA members were responsible for occasional acts of violence in this period, but these were almost all *re*-actions to the relentless pressure exerted by the state. The English bombing campaign had proved a damp squib, and a German invasion had not materialised. A report by the Irish government makes plain that IRA members felt 'nothing but dissatisfaction at their position' by the middle of 1941.[83]

Failure, demoralisation and the success of the Irish police bred suspicion and paranoia within the IRA about possible informers. Amazingly, the gaze of suspicion fell on none other than the Chief of Staff, Stephen Hayes, an ineffectual leader and a chronic alcoholic, who had been singularly fortunate to avoid arrest. The leaders of the Northern Ireland branch of the IRA came to the conclusion that 'his luck was too good to be true' and that he was in fact a government agent. This was a preposterous claim: Hayes may have been inept, but he was no traitor. What his accusers wanted was a scapegoat for the failure of the IRA in recent years. Three Belfast IRA leaders abducted Hayes on 30 June 1941. He was kept in captivity for the two months, sentenced to death and forced to write a long 'confession' of his activities as a government agent – Irish officials called it 'one of the most amazing documents ever concocted'. Although Hayes escaped and turned himself into the Garda, the IRA Army Council decided to print and circulate his bogus confession in September 1941, thus ensuring that the whole affair generated maximum controversy.[84] The confession split the organisation. Some accepted it as a welcome excuse for previous failures, while others refused to believe its veracity. Many who were unsure left the organisation in despair: one man concluded that either 'Hayes was a traitor, in which case the IRA was a lousy organization for having such a man at the top, or else he was innocent, in which case the IRA was a double lousy organization to extract such a document from him'.[85] The affair led to a renewed security effort and the apprehension of the new leaders. All historians agree that after 1941 the IRA was 'smashed', and little more than a 'minor irritant'.[86]

The British government viewed these developments with satisfaction. When Rear-Admiral Godfrey visited Northern Ireland in August 1941, Wickham told him that the IRA was 'a spent force'.[87] The British intelligence community correctly interpreted the publication of the Hayes confession as signalling the complete implosion of the organisation. The weekly Admiralty intelligence report stated on 31 October 1941:

> The I.R.A. seem at present to be weak and disorganized, and the Stephen Hayes case gave an ugly impression of dissension within the party. The leaders have sought to cover it up by circulating a printed document alleging that Hayes was a Government spy. ... The allegations in this document have been publicly denied by the Government, and it appears to be generally regarded in Eire as a tissue of ingenious lies. When a Wexford man, Patrick Murphy, who had been arrested and charged with distributing I.R.A. documents, was asked whether he was a member of the organization, he replied: 'There is no organization now; it is all broken up.'[88]

Henceforth, the British army in Northern Ireland would be unconcerned about the IRA. A revised version of the W-Plan issued on 15 January 1942 made very little reference to the organisation.[89]

The crack-down against the IRA continued into 1942. In southern Ireland this led to some bloodshed: three Garda officers were shot dead during raids. However, by December 1942, of an estimated 1,553 active IRA members, 100 were serving terms of imprisonment and 508 were interned at the Curragh. Mass incarceration had improved the cohesiveness of the organisation before, but during the Second World War it had the opposite effect: the internee camp split into pro-Nazi, pro-Allied and neutral blocs. Many became disillusioned, signed undertakings for future good conduct and rejoined society to play no further role in the movement.

The state of the IRA was marginally better in Northern Ireland. When the leadership in the south collapsed, the Northern Command took control of the countrywide organisation. It decided to concentrate the IRA's remaining resources on a campaign of violence in the six counties. This desultory insurrection began in March 1942 and caused the deaths of five RUC officers (the first to be killed by the IRA since 1932). The centrepiece of the campaign was a march by the southern IRA on the north, scheduled for 2 September. However, only twenty members could be induced to take part, and they retreated across the border after a brief gun battle with the RUC – it was an ignominious outcome for a plan that had been in gestation ever since 1922. The short-lived northern campaign invited a renewed repression by the RUC. 320 men were rounded up and many interned; documents and weapons were captured; and three IRA members met their deaths – Thomas Williams was hanged, and two others were killed in gun battles in Belfast. After 1942 the IRA was almost as quiescent in the north as in the south. Most importantly, it lost its automatic support among northern Catholics, as German bombing and a sense of shared purpose brought the two communities closer together.[90]

The British intelligence community continued to monitor the IRA closely during 1942. The clandestine SIS network investigated suspected leaders such as Maurice Twomey: SIS agents learnt that he was 'the brains of the I.R.A.', that IRA plots were hatched in his house outside of Dublin, and that he possibly acted 'as liaison between the I.R.A. and the Axis'.[91] SIS also received indications that the IRA was still active in Co. Kerry, 'drilling, sheltering men on the run and obstructing recruiting to the defence forces'.[92] In general, the analysis given by British intelligence was that the IRA was in decline and that the Irish authorities had them well in hand, but this was still tempered with caution. Jane Archer wrote in July 1942:

> The Government continue to take energetic measures against the extremists and there has recently been comparatively little outward manifestation of I.R.A. activity. From the provinces reliable information tends to show that the extremists are losing ground even in such strongholds as Tralee in Co. Kerry. ... Reliable sources, however, agree that the main

structure of the I.R.A., although temporarily disorganised, is not seriously weakened by recent Government action. The organisation is still active and vacancies caused by arrests or retirement have been filled.[93]

The IRA raid on the border came as something of a shock, especially because G2 had been unable to supply any advanced warning; when the new G2 chief, Colonel Dan Bryan, visited London soon after, he was hauled before the MI5 Director-General and asked to explain this failure.[94]

Any lingering concerns evaporated during 1943. Both the RUC and the southern Irish government produced encouraging assessments of the state of the IRA in their respective jurisdictions. The regular SIS reports on 'Irish Affairs' all commented favourably on the 'lull in Extremist I.R.A. activity'.[95] Nothing occurred to change this analysis for the remainder of the war. In March 1944 Jane Archer wrote:

> The prevailing political apathy is making itself felt in the ranks of the extremist I.R.A., which continues to deteriorate in numbers and purpose. About half of the extremists interned at the Curragh have been released during the past year and the majority have shown no inclination to interest themselves further in I.R.A. affairs. The organisation lacks leadership and direction and there is still political disruption in its ranks. There have been no serious criminal activities by the extremists, nor has any attempt been made to reanimate the waning interest of sympathisers.[96]

When MI5 held a conference with G2 in May 1944 to discuss the security situation, it received a 'reassuring' report on 'the organisations … known to have pro-Axis leanings'. Cecil Liddell recorded how 'the most important of these, the I.R.A., was described as being at a very low ebb at the present time, and its members so divided among themselves that it could scarcely be described as an organisation'.[97]

Alongside its better understanding of the IRA, the British intelligence community also realised that the activities of German diplomats and agents posed little danger. The resolution of the Görtz case played an important part in this. Hermann Görtz was the one Abwehr agent landed in Ireland in the summer of 1940 who had managed to evade capture. A botched police raid on Stephen Held's house on 23 May 1940 had yielded some of Görtz's property but allowed the man to escape. He was henceforth sheltered by a network of IRA members and sympathisers around Dublin. He initially pursued the unrealistic goal of negotiating a truce between the IRA and the Irish government, which would allow the IRA to carry out military action in the north. But he grew suspicious of the IRA, and henceforth minimised his contacts with its leaders. Instead, he tried to create a rudimentary intelligence service among Irish sympathisers. He gathered some information from Northern Ireland, though he was never able to communicate this properly to Germany. From the autumn of 1940 Görtz also sought contact with a wide circle of Irish individuals – he later estimated that he had 'exhaustive discussions' with more than 500 people. Although there is still considerable mystery about their identity, one was certainly Major Niall MacNeill, an intelligence officer in the Northern Division and a Nazi sympathiser, and through him Görtz probably had contact with his cousin, Major-General Hugo MacNeill, the Assistant Chief of Staff.[98] These contacts, together with the failure to apprehend Görtz for eighteen months, have inevitably led to conspiracy theories: it has been claimed that the Irish government allowed Görtz to remain free in order to provide a channel of communication to the German High Command. Even Cecil Liddell harboured these suspicions because of the 'astonishing time-lag' before his capture.[99] This is not true. The inability to capture Görtz was due to the skill of the republican group that sheltered him and the man's extraordinary good luck.

Görtz's chief problem was that he had no means by which to communicate with Germany. He was largely shunned by the German legation (although it appears that he received financial support from the Japanese consulate). The Abwehr established contact with him only once, when Miss Mary P. Mains, an Irishwoman working as a governess in Madrid, travelled to Ireland in November 1941: she handed Görtz $10,000 in cash, a new supply of secret ink and a key word for radio transmissions. She returned to Spain with a situation report from the stranded German agent. In addition, Görtz made persistent attempts to obtain a wireless transmitter with the aid of his republican friends. In July 1941 an engineer employed at the Pye Radio store in Dublin, Michael Kinsella, finally managed to construct a set that could reach Germany. For some weeks an IRA man named Anthony Deery operated this set, sending messages to Abwehr headquarters. Of little intelligence value, they mostly concerned Görtz's attempts to escape from Ireland, as by now he was disillusioned with his mission and determined to return to Germany. He made a number of failed escape attempts in 1941. The most ambitious involved the purchase of a fishing boat, the *Venture*, at Fenit in Co. Kerry. On the eve of departure in February, the crew were arrested. Miraculously, Görtz managed to escape to Dublin, but he was increasingly bitter, and his reports became dominated by accusations of betrayal at those around him.[100]

Although Görtz's mission achieved little, his presence in Ireland was a serious threat to Irish neutrality and British security. It is startling that the Irish and

British intelligence agencies knew so little about him for so long. G2 did not receive any definite information about Görtz until the summer of 1941. Even then, it was not reliable. At one point G2 believed that there were two German intelligence agents in Ireland, both in close contact with the IRA and both travelling frequently to and from Germany, going out by submarine from Co. Kerry and returning by parachute.[101] As for British intelligence, it was even more ignorant of Görtz's activities. Although the evidence found in the Held raid in May 1940 suggested that a German agent had landed, the British were not able to draw any firm conclusions. For example, they did not know if the discovered German military uniform had been worn by a parachutist, or if it was being kept in readiness to be worn by Held or someone else when German armed forces invaded. 'I am unable to form any coherent story from the file', one baffled MI5 official admitted. 'Each time I resolve a series of incidents to make a coherent whole a discrepancy appears in a further note to make my story improbable.' All MI5 and SIS knew for sure was that the parachutist who landed in May 1940 had not been apprehended; therefore, they suspected that he might still be active in the country.[102]

The presence of Görtz in Ireland was finally confirmed in September 1941. Following the crack-down on the IRA after the Hayes confession, G2 learnt that a single German intelligence officer was at liberty and that his name was 'Dr Goertz'.[103] The way this information was handled illustrates the weakness of the 'Dublin link' at this time: Görtz's name was not passed by G2 to MI5; instead, the Garda passed the information to its contact in the RUC. The problems between MI5 and G2 in the middle of 1941 were caused by tense Anglo-Irish diplomatic relations, the reluctance of the Irish authorities to suppress the German legation's wireless transmitter, and Colonel Archer's replacement by his deputy, Colonel Dan Bryan – Guy Liddell initially regarded this change in leadership as a 'serious blow', as he did not think that Bryan was 'sufficiently strong to resist pressure from above'.[104] There was 'a certain coolness' in G2's dealings with MI5, and for some months all contact ceased.[105] The information about Görtz was eventually transmitted by the RUC to MI5, which recalled the German's prosecution for spying in Britain in 1936; it was also able to match the handwriting on documents from that trial with that found on papers in Held's house. The mysterious parachutist had finally been identified. This served as the catalyst for the restarting of the 'Dublin link'. Cecil Liddell wrote to Colonel Dan Bryan on 30 September 1941, enclosing photographs of Görtz and a summary of information from the MI5 file. Dan Bryan then visited London between 10 and 12 November to discuss the case – Guy Liddell remarked that his visit was 'very successful'.[106] The net closed inexorably on Görtz, and he was finally arrested in

Dublin on 27 November 1941, after being betrayed by one of his 'helpers', Joseph Andrews.[107]

The information provided by G2 to MI5 in the weeks after the Görtz arrest was meagre. 'So far the Irish tell us very little', Guy Liddell wrote on 6 January 1942. 'They probably fear that we should use this case as a pretext for pressing the Eire Govt. to forego its neutrality and turn the Germans out.'[108] Instead, the British turned to the clandestine SIS network for information; through his Garda contacts, Captain Collinson was able to provide some details on the Görtz case.[109] This was an example of how the two British approaches to Irish intelligence – clandestine operations and official collaboration – could complement each other. However, once Gortz was convicted, Anglo-Irish intelligence co-operation deepened significantly. Liddell provided a list of questions to be raised when Görtz was interrogated. On 9 January 1942 Bryan sent detailed reports on the outcome of the interrogation, which described the Held visit to Germany in April 1940 and Görtz's activities in Ireland over the preceding eighteen months. The exchange of information between G2 and MI5 continued in the aftermath of the Görtz arrest, when many of his former associates were tracked down. The most important development was the arrest of Anthony Deery in March 1942; in his house was found the radio transmitter that was used to send and receive messages from Germany. Over the coming weeks G2 and MI5 worked closely together, sharing information and testing hypotheses, to discover just what Görtz had been doing and who his contacts had been.[110]

This was the beginning of an intimate collaboration between MI5 and G2 that continued until the end of the war. G2 handed over hundreds of pages of documents on anyone who might conceivably pose a threat to Allied interests: the IRA, Catholic nativist parties, fascist sympathisers, Axis nationals living in Ireland, captured Abwehr agents and the staff of the Axis legations. Nothing was held back. Cecil Liddell soon came to see Colonel Bryan as an improvement on his predecessor:

> Colonel Archer, though at all times friendly and absolutely straight in his dealings, was a strong Irish Nationalist and inclined to limit his co-operation rather strictly. He was a conscientious, but not an enthusiastic Intelligence Officer. Colonel Bryan while just as mindful of his duty to his country, was wrapped up in Intelligence work for its own sake. Once personal relations and mutual confidence had been established, his enthusiasm for the work produced a degree of co-operation from the Irish side which increased steadily as the war went on.

The Liddells and Bryan developed a close friendship through a series of meetings in Dublin and Britain. (Bryan even sent the MI5 officers parcels of Irish meat, which was a welcome supplement to their basic food rations.) Looking back in 1946, Cecil Liddell concluded that 'the Dublin link has undoubtedly depended very much on good personal relations and especially on complete confidence between the Intelligence officers on either side.'[111]

As well as tackling the Görtz case, MI5 and G2 worked together to solve the other great mystery left over from 1940 – the fate of the IRA leaders Seán Russell and Frank Ryan. Although Russell had died on a U-boat off the Irish coast in August 1940, he was reported over the following months to be in places as diverse as Switzerland, Dublin, Lisbon, and Spain. British intelligence officers believed that he was still alive.[112] It was only in March 1942 that the Dublin government received the first conclusive evidence that he had died, and this was passed to MI5. The information came in a letter to the Irish minister in Madrid from Frank Ryan, who remained in Germany under the protection of the Abwehr until his death from natural causes in 1944.[113] His whereabouts were an equal mystery to British intelligence. In September 1940 intercepted correspondence from the International Brigade Association revealed that he had been released from prison in Spain. Over the following eighteen months, a close censorship of the letters of Ryan's family and friends revealed that he was alive and well, but there was no firm evidence as to his location: he was variously reported to have ended up in Berlin, Copenhagen, Lisbon and New York.[114] Ryan's true movements were finally revealed on 9 June 1942 by the double agent Springbok, the German aristocrat Hans von Kotze, who had been trained by the Abwehr for intelligence operations in Brazil before defecting to the British. During an interrogation in Canada, he told Guy Liddell that the IRA leader was in Germany trying to recruit a new 'Casement Brigade'.[115] Over the next two years MI5 and G2 were able to monitor Ryan from afar through censored correspondence and interrogation of captured Abwehr agents.

In the first half of 1942 many of the loose ends from the 1940 fifth column panic were tied up. This led to a change in British assessments of Axis subversion in southern Ireland. Although the Görtz case provided the first '100 per cent evidence' of the long-suspected collaboration between Germany and the IRA, the information revealed by the Görtz interrogation was very reassuring:

> Goertz himself states that he expected to find in the I.R.A. an organisation somewhat similar to the semi-military organisations in Germany such as the S.A. or S.S. He claims to have been very disappointed when he found that the I.R.A. in organisation, numbers and discipline was in no way similar to these bodies.[116]

The Görtz case also shone a light on the activities of the German legation: he had received little help from Hempel or his staff. By early 1942 the British intelligence community no longer believed that the legation was engaged in widespread subversive activities. The Director of Naval Intelligence concluded that its activities were 'on a limited scale' and that its 'capacity for assisting the Axis war effort' had been 'much exaggerated by popular rumour.'[117] SIS reports no longer contained lurid stories of Irish Quislings or rampant Axis subversion; instead, Jane Archer's bi-monthly surveys gave a largely positive picture of the internal Irish security situation. This reflected a shift in Irish opinion, as support swung behind the Allies after Americas' entry into the war.

I T had taken some time for the British intelligence community to put the threat of Axis subversion into proper perspective. London quickly retreated from the worst excesses of the fifth column panic after its Irish intelligence began to improve in the second half of 1940. However, British intelligence agencies continued to fret about Irish Quislings and Axis subversion until the end of 1941. SIS, with its 'secret sources', was still guilty of peddling alarmist rumours, which kept the idea of an Irish fifth column alive. On the other hand, Sir John Maffey, the service attachés in Dublin and the Dominions Office played down the internal security threats, and there is evidence that the MI5 Irish section shared this opinion at an early stage.[118] By the beginning of 1942 – following encouraging developments in Ireland, increased co-operation with Irish security agencies and improvements in the SIS operation – the British intelligence community reached a consensus that Axis subversion and pro-Axis groups posed little threat to Irish stability or Allied security. This equanimity was not troubled for the rest of the war.

CHAPTER 12

Opinion and Propaganda

T HE state of Irish opinion was a matter of some importance to British military and intelligence chiefs. It would determine the number of Irish people
willing to assist the Axis and the type of reaction the British would receive if they
were forced to intervene in southern Ireland. The study of opinion inevitably
led to the question of propaganda. The Second World War saw unprecedented
efforts by governments to assert control over information and public opinion.
They used 'white' propaganda techniques – the manipulation of news to extol
their cause; and 'black' propaganda – the use of deceit to sap the enemy's morale
(for example, by spreading false rumours). Joseph Goebbels was regarded as a
master of these arts. His Ministry of Popular Enlightenment and Propaganda
was credited with transforming Germany into a single-party Nazi state and
fatally weakening the resistance of neighbouring countries before Germany's
military conquests – it was thought that German propaganda begat the fifth
column.[1] As a result, the British intelligence system paid close attention to the
detection of enemy propaganda at home and abroad: it ranked just below sabotage and espionage as a priority for investigation.[2]

Within the British government the task of equalling Dr Goebbels fell to the
Ministry of Information. Created on the outbreak of the war, its duties were to
channel news to the press, to maintain morale at home and to publicise the Allied
cause in the empire and outside. The ministry's first year was not a happy one, as
it distinguished itself by its amateurism and muddle. The Prime Minister considered shutting it down after just two months. Its ministerial leaders changed with
alarming rapidity, and it was only when Brendan Bracken (an Irishman) took
over in July 1941 that it began to operate effectively.[3] One of his first steps was to
create the Political Warfare Executive, in conjunction with the Special Operations Executive (SOE), to carry out clandestine propaganda operations. Thereafter the British propaganda system became increasingly ambitious, employing
both white and black methods to weaken enemy morale, to foster resistance in
the occupied countries and to persuade neutral states to fight against the Axis.
Political warfare, or in American parlance 'psychological warfare', was one of the
key fronts on which the Second World War was fought.

The Ministry of Information, together with SIS and the Dominions Office, paid close attention to opinion and propaganda when dealing with Ireland. The state of Irish opinion would determine the strength of the fifth column in the event of a German invasion, the degree of resistance should Britain be compelled to seize Irish bases and the way in which the Irish government implemented the policy of neutrality. Irish opinion could, in turn, be influenced by propaganda. Thus, British intelligence set out to measure support for the Axis among the Irish populace and to discover whether Axis propaganda was propagating it. As with the fifth column, the influence of German intrigue was exaggerated, and it was some time before it was placed in a proper perspective. British officials also tried to devise a propaganda response. A number of schemes were suggested and some were implemented, although it was eventually concluded that aggressive British propaganda would be counter-productive. Ireland was one of the most difficult fields of operation for British propagandists during the Second World War. By 1942 this was less of a concern, because of clear signs that Irish opinion was swinging more decisively behind the Allies. However, observers still detected a deeply rooted strain of anti-British feeling that portended difficulties in post-war Anglo-Irish relations.

A propagandist's paradise

DURING the Phoney War the British government made an attempt to gauge Irish opinion towards the war and towards Britain. The Ministry of Information briefly assigned responsibility for Irish affairs to an official in its British Empire Division, Frank Pakenham, a lecturer and historian from a landed Anglo-Irish family (who later inherited the title Lord Longford and became well known as a campaigner for prisoners' rights). After a visit to Dublin in October 1939, he estimated that eight out of ten people supported neutrality and were 'mildly sympathetic' to the Allies.[4] This analysis was supported by Sir John Maffey and by the Prime Minister, Neville Chamberlain.[5] Although holding out little prospect of Irish entry into the war, it was broadly reassuring, as it indicated that the vast majority of the population favoured an Allied victory.

However, according to British observers, Irish opinion also had some worrying characteristics. One was a persistent strain of Anglophobia: in the words of Sir John Maffey, 'Anti-British feeling was the dynamic of Irish opinion, always there though often latent.'[6] He elaborated in early 1940:

> In this country if any agitation can be based on an anti-English motif that agitation, however unreasonable, is bound to succeed. ... I am surprised to find that hatred is a bigger factor here than it was 25 years ago. There

are fewer Englishmen here and individual Englishmen were and are popular, but England is now an abstraction. It has been a State industry to indoctrinate the younger generation with antagonism and the results are not surprising. The anti-Partition cry derives much of its force from the fact that it is a good anti-English cry. The emphasis rests strongly on the word 'English' for the root hatred lies in the old tribal blood feud.[7]

Moreover, the Irish were regarded as particularly susceptible to Axis propaganda because of defects in their character – racial and cultural stereotypes of the Irish still shaped British thinking. In 1940 one retired imperial civil servant wrote that 'the Irish people as a whole are probably more suggestible than the other peoples of these islands, with the possible exception of the Welsh. They will, in fact, accept anything they are told (within limits), provided they are told it in the right way, are told it often enough and do not hear too much of the other side of the case.'[8] The commander of British forces in Northern Ireland held a similar opinion:

> The Irish were like the Germans in one respect only; they lack civic pride and courage. The Irish are venal, they are fundamentally dishonest, they prefer to make money on the side line, to making on the straight [*sic*]. They are vulnerable to propaganda.[9]

A major SIS report on the subject concluded that 'Eire can be described as a propagandist's paradise'.[10]

The British intelligence community feared that the Axis powers were exploiting this favourable environment through organised propaganda. German radio broadcasts immediately came to notice. From December 1939 Germany transmitted directly to Ireland through a special radio service (the Irland-Redaktion), sometimes in the Irish language. The service was directed by German scholars with pre-war links to Ireland, and employed men such as John O'Reilly, a future German spy, and Francis Stuart, who lectured at Berlin University. Alongside standard German war news, they exhorted the Irish public to keep their neutrality by providing 'flashbacks' to British atrocities during the War of Independence, set to a background of traditional Irish music. (In addition, many Irish people listened to German broadcasts directed at Britain, especially to Lord Haw Haw (William Joyce), who had been raised in Co. Galway.)[11] In January 1940 the German service was brought to the attention of the British government by a retired official of the Malayan medical service living in southern Ireland. He claimed that the broadcasts had already produced a slight swing towards Germany. The use of Irish was a particularly insidious technique, as it appealed to schoolchildren studying the language and to the uneducated inhabitants of the west coast. He warned that the purpose of German propaganda was to foster anti-British sentiment, to encourage the IRA to carry out raids into Northern Ireland and to prepare the ground for German spies and the sheltering of U-boats. Maffey passed this letter to London, where it was received at a time of growing concern about the effect of German broadcasts in Britain.[12] The British government took special steps to investigate: the BBC monitoring service employed three Gaelic-speakers to listen to Berlin's Irish broadcasts; MI5 ordered a censorship on mails to and from Irish people on the continent in order to learn more about the radio presenters.[13]

British intelligence agencies also suspected the German legation in Dublin of organising and funding pro-Axis propaganda. This was the subject of a ten-page report by SIS in September 1940. SIS asserted that the German legation was 'extremely efficient in all questions of propaganda': it received information from German news services by wireless teleprinter and supplied this free to the Irish press; its staff cultivated individual members of the government and influenced the press censors to exclude newspaper stories that favoured Britain. Rear-Admiral Godfrey commented that this report made 'unpleasant reading', but a second report by SIS in December 1940 was even more alarming. It warned that German propaganda, previously subtle, had become more aggressive. The German Minister in Dublin, Dr Eduard Hempel, had received orders from Berlin to take a more active approach. He now travelled around the country, holidaying in Killarney and Connemara; he frequently attended the theatre and concerts, where he made a point of striking up conversations during the intervals; he received guests more frequently at his house, inviting Irishmen whose principles did not 'stand in the way of the temptation of a good dinner'. More sinisterly, this renewed social activity was accompanied by 'intensified intrigues in the realm of … propaganda' conducted by the Counsellor, Henning Thomsen, and the press attaché, Carlheinz Petersen. One of their schemes was 'to work up a vast system of verbal propaganda', whereby intermediaries would spread 'scare' stories about bad conditions in Britain and launch slogans favourable to Hitler. This material was introduced to Irish acquaintances at raucous drinking parties held at the Royal Hibernian Hotel on Dawson Street. (These parties may have disturbed the sleep of Cecil and Guy Liddell, as they normally stayed in the same hotel during their visits to Dublin.) The Germans were also using 'professional agents' to spread dissension among ship crews.[14]

The most important propaganda activity of the German legation was entirely overt: the dissemination of printed material. Carlheinz Petersen was responsible for producing and circulating a 'Weekly Review of the German News Agency' to people of influence: by April 1944 it had a circulation of 3,500. In addition, the legation occasionally printed and distributed other material, such as speeches by Hitler and Ribbentrop. The Italian legation produced a much smaller news-sheet, although the British believed that it was 'the more effective of the two, as emanating from a Catholic country'.[15] The SIS network devoted a great deal of time to investigating how these documents were produced and distributed.[16] When Sir John Maffey failed to persuade the Irish government to ban them, the British tried a number of stratagems to sabotage their production. They placed the Irish company that printed the German news-sheet on the commercial Black List; they considered cutting supplies to another Irish company that provided the paper; in 1943 decrypted German messages allowed London to prevent the transfer of money from Germany to Hempel via a Dublin bank account. Nonetheless, Hempel secured secret loans from the Irish government, in lieu of pre-war debts owed to Germany by Irish companies, and the German news bulletin continued to appear.[17]

There was some worrying evidence that Nazi propaganda was being reproduced by indigenous groups in Ireland. From October 1939 until its discovery by the police two months later, the IRA operated an illicit broadcasting station that transmitted programmes across Ireland. The IRA also printed a regular newsletter (under the titles *War News* or *Republican News*), and distributed posters and leaflets – despite the best efforts of the Irish police, these documents sporadically appeared until the end of the war.[18] Traditional republican messages became infused with pro-Nazi and anti-Semitic themes. For example, IRA broadcasts praised Nazi Germany and ranted against the 'Jewish War Minister' in London, Hore-Belisha, and Lord Beaverbrook, another Jew 'out for money'. A 1941 edition of *War News* condemned opponents of republicanism as 'Freemasons, Jews and ordinary traitors ... with their hands on their cash'.[19] The British Special Branch was convinced that the presence of these themes was due to German funding of the IRA via the United States.

MI5 was also concerned that members of the Blueshirt organisation around General Eoin O'Duffy were 'actively engaged in distributing German propaganda'.[20] One of their leaflets came into the possession of Sir John Maffey in early 1940 and he passed it to London for study. It left little doubt about the allegiance of the authors:

> WHO has for centuries trampled you in the dust? ... WHO let loose the scum of England – the Jew Greenwood's Black and Tans – to murder, burn and loot in our country? ... WHO has unceasingly endeavoured to represent us to all nations as a race of clowns and half wits? ... WHO is flooding Ireland

with Jewish-Masonic drivel and filth insulting to our national aspirations
and the Christian religion. ... THE ANSWER IS ENGLAND – IRELAND'S
ONLY ENEMY! WHO HAS NEVER CONCEALED ITS SYMPATHY WITH THE
IRISH PEOPLE AND THEIR CAUSE – THE GERMAN NATION. England's foes
and Ireland's friends – May they increase and multiply![21]

Between June and September 1940, at a time of panic over the Irish fifth
column and the expected German invasion, the Ministry of Information despatched five individuals on secret missions to Ireland to assess the influence
of Axis propaganda and the state of public opinion. Few details survive about
the first, Ian Morrow. The second was Arnold Lunn, a well-known writer for
the Catholic periodical, *The Tablet*. The third was Miss Maxwell, an Anglo-Irish
ministry employee whose family home was in Dublin. The final two representatives went on to achieve great literary distinction (and, befittingly, their reports
make unusually good reading). The future Poet Laureate and then member of
the Ministry of Information Films Division, John Betjeman, was sent to Ireland
in June 1940. But the most influential representative at this time was the Anglo-
Irish writer Elizabeth Bowen (who generally went by her married name, Mrs
Cameron). Wishing to travel to her home in Co. Cork to complete the writing of
a novel (*Bowen's Court*), she offered her services to the Ministry of Information
'as an entirely unofficial and unpaid correspondent, reporting on Irish opinion.'
She did this at the suggestion of the Irish High Commissioner in London, John
Dulanty, who wanted London to have a supply of information from a sympathetic, well-informed commentator to counterbalance the alarmist rumours
swirling around the city.[22] Bowen's role has sometimes been given an unwar-
ranted air of adventure. Her activities were fairly mundane: she split her time
between Co. Cork and Dublin, meeting friends and family and engaging in normal conversation. The only difference was that she recorded and analysed what
she heard and had a special channel of communication to London – Maffey's
diplomatic bag. Was she 'a kind of spy'? In a sense, yes, so long as it is recognised
that this is often what 'spying' meant.[23] Bowen provided a number of sober and
influential reports on conditions in Ireland that were circulated to Whitehall
departments and even to the Prime Minister. They were especially well received
in the Dominions Office, where they were regarded as 'sane and interesting' and
containing 'a shrewd appreciation of the position.'[24]

All the Ministry of Information representatives agreed that the majority of
the Irish people supported neutrality, hoped for an Allied victory and were prepared to resist any invader, whether German or British. Yet each representative
identified a pro-Axis, anti-British element in the country, albeit of uncertain

composition. Arnold Lunn concluded that 'about 5%' of educated Catholics were impressed by Hitler's success and disliked Britain so intensely that they might be regarded as 'Nazi propagandists'. Although he found it more difficult to guess at support for Germany 'among the uneducated majority', one thing was sure: 'demoralisation and muddle' would be widespread if the Nazis invaded Ireland.[25] John Betjeman estimated that at least 150,000 people were sympathetic to the Axis, and would 'not oppose the Germans if they invaded'. They comprised a small group of fascist pseudo-intellectuals in Dublin; the bulk of Counties Kerry and Donegal, who were driven by traditional enmity towards Britain; and an indeterminate number among the unemployed, who had a vague belief that National Socialism would improve their lot.[26] Elizabeth Bowen, while less alarmist than the others, identified two types of pro-Nazi feeling. The first, 'largely sentimental and not very dangerous', was found among young people interested in the German youth movements. The second, more dangerous type was the 'distinct Fascism' of the Catholic middle classes, who, like the Falangists in Spain, regarded the Axis powers as a barrier against Bolshevik Russia and a prop to the *status quo*. This was indulged by the Catholic church, which was officially 'opposed to progress, as not good for the people'.[27] Such opinions were not confined to Catholics. Miss Maxwell was startled to find a strain of pro-German sentiment among the Protestant Anglo-Irish class. An Irish barrister told her that 'a large section of the Irish Bar' was 'strongly anti-British if not pro-Nazi'. A member of her mother's bridge club 'turned out to be an ardent admirer of Hitler'.[28]

The extent of pro-German feeling in southern Ireland was never estimated at more than 10 per cent, usually closer to 5 per cent. Yet this was still a significant number – at least 150,000 people. Moreover, it was possible that others would drift into this camp not because of ideological support for the Nazis but because of a widespread assumption that Britain would lose the war. In 1940 all the Ministry of Information representatives commented on a worrying strain of 'defeatism' among the Irish population and within the political élite; Elizabeth Bowen even suggested that 'the worst defeatism' was to be found among the Protestant Anglo-Irish.[29] Defeatism was also prevalent in Irish letters intercepted by the postal censorship.[30] As late as May 1941, SIS warned that British military reverses in the Middle East were increasing pro-German feeling in Ireland, elevating the status of the German Minister in Dublin and making de Valera 'even more obstinate in his policy of leaving open channels for negotiations with either belligerent'.[31] So long as Germany looked like winning the war, it would always attract some support: as one SIS source put it, 'the popular side in Eire is the winning side'.[32]

British observers were also appalled at the moral neutrality, and even indifference, of the Irish public when it came to differentiating between the two sides in the war. This was largely caused by the Irish government's notoriously rigorous censorship policy. Dublin operated a more prohibitive form of media control than any neutral European state and most belligerents, Britain included. Although basic information about the war could be given, no comment or analysis favourable to either side was tolerated.[33] London initially believed that this worked to the 'British advantage', as pro-German opinion was suppressed, while the British perspective was propagated through British newspapers and the wide availability of the BBC.[34] However, because the censorship prohibited comment on the moral and political aspects of the war, it eventually worked to Britain's disadvantage. The British were convinced of the righteousness of their cause, yet the Irish press was forced to observe a strict neutrality between the two sides – moral equivalence was enforced. This was particularly noticeable in the later stages of the war, when details of the Holocaust and other German atrocities were meticulously excluded from the Irish press. The control of this policy by the 'notoriously pro-German' Frank Aiken did nothing to commend it to the Allies.[35]

The effect of this rigorous press censorship has often been noted. Together with restrictions on travel and the curtailment of trade, it isolated southern Ireland from the momentous changes being experienced in the rest of the world. In a famous image, the historian F. S. L. Lyons wrote:

> It was as if an entire people had been condemned to live in Plato's cave, with their backs to the fire of life and deriving their only knowledge of what went on outside from the flickering shadows thrown on the wall before their eyes by the men and women who passed to and fro behind them.[36]

Although the accuracy of this analysis has been challenged by recent historians, there is no doubt that British observers saw Ireland in this way. One visitor detected 'an increased introversion of the Irish mind. ... Ireland, always inclined to be a *malade imaginaire*, is now more than ever confined by the walls of her sickroom, and outside events are of little interest unless they seem likely to enter and disturb it.' Maffey ruefully told de Valera that Ireland was 'like a leaf in a backwater between rushing torrents'.[37] Ireland seemed detached from the real world, trapped within its insular boundaries, unable to see the wider dimensions of the war or the moral differences between the participants.

Counter-propaganda

I T was hoped that Allied propaganda could puncture the Irish veil of ignorance and counter German misinformation. Yet the Ministry of Information struggled to formulate a settled policy towards Ireland. As with intelligence, propaganda in Ireland was something of an anomaly. In a long survey, the
Ministry of Information later concluded:

> Propaganda in Eire presents a very complex problem. Eire regards herself
> as a neutral country 'whose neutrality in thought' is safeguarded by strict
> censorship, but is at the same time a member of the British Common-
> wealth of Nations. She is a neighbouring predominantly English-speaking
> country, whose psychological outlook is entirely different from our own
> and whose people inherit a profound and instinctive distrust of Britain.[38]

Of all the neutral European nations in the second world, southern Ireland proved
to be the most difficult for Britain to influence through propaganda.[39]

During the Phoney War the Ministry of Information had been reluctant to
conduct any activities in Ireland. After his visit to the country Frank Pakenham
judged that it would be wrong to start propaganda in the country: 'to achieve any
serious effect, it would have to be organized; the fact of its organization would
be straight away detected and resented.'[40] His recommendation for inaction was
accepted, and he left the Ministry of Information to join his regiment.[41] In the
early months of 1940 this policy came under pressure from the military and
intelligence services. The army commander in Northern Ireland was concerned
about German propaganda activities and by a burst of republican agitation at
the time of the Coventry executions. He urged London to launch its own propaganda, suggesting that they work through the French, the Americans and the
Catholic church.[42] At the same time, the Special Branch and MI5 drew attention to the increasingly anti-Semitic and pro-German tone in IRA propaganda.[43]
The Ministry of Information called an interdepartmental meeting to discuss this
issue in April 1940. It considered proposals to work through the French legation and the Papal Nuncio in Dublin, and to create a rival broadcasting service directed at Ireland, but all these schemes encountered obstacles. The only
action taken was in Northern Ireland, where a Ministry of Information regional
officer was appointed to conduct propaganda among the Protestant community.
In contrast, the Ministry of Information shied away from all initiatives involving
nationalist Ireland.[44]

This complacency was no longer acceptable after the German conquests in
western Europe. Ireland now became an important propaganda issue because

of its geographical position and the perceived imminence of a German invasion. There was a need for British propaganda to generate pro-Allied feeling among the Irish population, so that the German invaders would be strongly resisted and British troops welcomed. In later months, when the need for the ports increased and the British considered invading Ireland, propaganda and Irish public opinion were still of vital importance. Although it was never believed that British propaganda could eradicate popular support for neutrality, it was thought that it could minimise resistance to a British incursion. Thus, propaganda, like intelligence, was required to prepare Irish ground for possible British military operations.

As a result, the military authorities resumed their pressure on the Ministry of Information. One staff officer, Major Clive, wrote on 11 August 1940:

> We are again becoming rather exercised by the anti-British propaganda question in Eire and Northern Ireland. There seems to be little doubt that this, uncontradicted as it is, is having a certain amount of effect upon the people. Propaganda is being disseminated by wireless and leaflets and the press, and, of course, by rumours generally.
>
> All we want to do is to lay on some way of putting across the pro-British news and facts, as a makeweight to the I.R.A., etc. broadcasts. We have no wish to make things difficult for the Government of Eire, nor to try to push them off their neutral perch.[45]

The War Office complained that it was 'up against a blank wall'. 'The Ministry of Information is frankly frightened of burning its fingers over Irish propaganda', Major Clive wrote, 'and prefers to do nothing rather than to get itself into trouble.' It struck him 'that the M. of I. was singularly deficient of ideas or imagination' – an accusation that many aimed at the department in the troubled early phase of its existence.[46]

In response to this criticism the Ministry of Information asked the five representatives that it sent to Ireland in the summer of 1940 to investigate whether a propaganda campaign was feasible. All warned that aggressive methods, such as the publication of a news-sheet, would be counterproductive. However, they agreed that one form of propaganda would be effective – personal contact. Elizabeth Bowen recommended that 'very much could be done by unofficial diplomacy' – 'talk ... cuts more ice than anything else.' The idea of appointing a permanent British press attaché was mooted.[47] Because of the rigours of the Irish censorship, he would be unable to place pro-British material in the Irish press. Instead, his job would be to develop contacts within circles not frequented by existing British officials – the press, the arts, academia, the intelligentsia. 'This is rather different from the work normally expected from a Press Attaché', one

British official noted, 'though it doubtless corresponds more with the sort of work done by the Press Officer of the German Legation in so far as he is not entirely concerned with secret service activities.'[48] Despite initial resistance by the Dominions Office and Maffey, the decision was taken to appoint a press attaché in early November 1940.[49] After a long search for the right person for the job, the Ministry of Information eventually settled on the man who had originally put forward the proposal – John Betjeman.

While never entirely discreet or tactful, Betjeman was an inspired choice. He threw himself into his task with enthusiasm after arriving in Dublin in January 1941. Though quintessentially English, he immersed himself in Irish culture, beginning his reports with the salutation 'A Chara' and signing them 'Seán Ó Betjemán'. He was frequently to be seen in bohemian watering holes (including Carlheinz Petersen's favourite, the Palace Bar), where he cultivated an extraordinarily wide circle of friends. He described his principal duty as 'keeping in with Irish journalists ... drinking with them: having them to meals & to stay'.[50] He also 'kept in' with other 'influential Irishmen' in 'the religious, literary, art, theatrical & social worlds', as well as government officials dealing with censorship and foreign affairs.[51] Indeed, the most curious aspect of Betjeman's activity is that he went out of his way to cultivate the people who should have been most hostile to him, befriending Catholic conservatives, republican activists and leading communists.[52] This turned him into a hectic socialiser, the quintessential man-about-town. This was both an enjoyable way to spend the war and skilful propaganda work: Betjeman subtly put Britain's case forward and was able to win over some of the anti-British elements, by force of personality as much as argument. Tony Gray, an *Irish Times* journalist who met him at the Palace Bar during the war, remembered Betjeman as a popular figure who endeared himself to the Irish: 'He was very witty and very English and people loved him.'[53]

Apart from incessant socialising, Betjeman had many duties as press attaché. He arranged for prominent figures from the British arts to visit southern Ireland. For example, in April 1941 he carefully orchestrated a visit by the popular film actor Robert Donat (star of Hitchcock's *The 39 Steps* and an Oscar-winner for his role in *Goodbye, Mr Chips*). The actor gave a stage performance of *Mr Chips* that 'reeked of England' and charmed Irish officials and newspaper editors at an intimate dinner later that evening. The visit was regarded as a triumphant success by those involved. Perhaps Betjeman's greatest coup came when he persuaded Laurence Olivier to shoot his ultra-patriotic *Henry V* in Ireland. With its symbolism of a beleaguered England outnumbered by European enemies, the film acted as powerful wartime propaganda.[54] Betjeman also acted as 'nursemaid, mental & physical' to journalists visiting Ireland. Because so many came on the hunt for spies, Betjeman insisted that every journalist should see him first, so that he could brief them on the situation and warn them off certain types of stories. In addition, he assisted Irish journalists to make the journey in the other direction, obtaining permits so they could see conditions in Britain for themselves. Even the most anti-British and defeatist usually came back with a more favourable attitude.[55] Finally, he was responsible for the distribution of printed material. He sent Ministry of Information literature only to people who requested it, or to those he knew to be sympathetic to Britain. In addition, he arranged for Ministry of Information booklets, regarded as 'the most effective form of written propaganda which can be freely circulated in Eire', to go on sale in Irish bookshops.[56]

Betjeman's work attracted early praise from the Ministry of Information: it had 'ample first-hand evidence' that he had 'achieved a substantial measure of success in Dublin'.[57] However, his cultivation of anti-British elements had its dangers. When the editor of *The Standard* took a libel action against the *Daily Mail* for an article describing the paper as virulently pro-Axis, Betjeman was almost forced to testify in a London court. He had assiduously cultivated the editor of *The Standard* and refuted the *Daily Mail* allegations in a personal letter that the editor threatened to use in support of his action. The Dominions Office viewed the prospect with horror, as it would lead to an airing of the whole issue of Axis activities and censorship in Ireland. The proprietor of the *Daily Mail*, Lord Rothermere, was persuaded to settle the case out of court.[58] Although Betjeman remained in post until 1943, the matter did not reflect well on his judgment, and the Dominions Office never quite regained its earlier faith in him. They later criticised him for mixing largely with 'the more Bohemian type of Irish writer', who cut little 'ice' and were often implacable opponents of Britain, while neglecting to cultivate more traditional elements such as businessmen, clergy and professionals, who would be more easy to 'convert'. They felt he spent too much time in insalubrious pubs and not enough time in higher-class establishments.[59]

Because of his later fame as Poet Laureate and 'uncle to the nation', Betjeman's wartime activities have been the subject of media interest, and have led to recurring claims that he was a 'British spy', a 'successful secret agent'.[60] A television documentary contained the extraordinary story that the IRA plotted to kill Betjeman for this reason, but 'called the gunmen off because they liked his poetry'.[61] While the label 'spy' is too ill-defined and accusatory to be of much use, it is clear that the press attaché did engage in clandestine activity. He worked with Captain Collinson to investigate the source of German propaganda, and used the

SIS network to disseminate pro-British information by word of mouth.[62] In 1942, after obtaining a copy of a manifesto issued by an anti-fascist faction in the IRA internment camp, he suggested secretly printing this document and circulating it through Ireland in order to exploit divisions within the IRA – this was not the sort of activity normally associated with a press attaché.[63] Through his contacts Betjeman was able to provide useful intelligence to SIS about the republican and communist movements in Ireland – his information on the splits within the IRA internment camp appeared in a SIS report some weeks later.[64]

The clearest evidence of Betjeman's undercover work was his involvement with a highly secretive SOE 'whispering' campaign aimed at Axis, not Irish, opinion. Whispers (or 'sibs') were rumours started by the British government for the purpose of propaganda and deception. They were released into the world and allowed to work their way towards the enemy. Their content ranged from the subtle to the fantastic: for example, one whisper at the time of the threatened German invasion of Britain revealed that 200 man-eating sharks from Australia had been released into the English Channel. A complex machinery, overseen by the Inter Service Security Board and operated by SOE and the Political Warfare Executive, managed this activity. Ireland, with its enemy and neutral legations, was an ideal avenue for spreading whispers.[65] Moreover, the British received 'frequent evidence' that the German colony in Ireland had 'originated whispering campaigns' that were 'not altogether unsuccessful'.[66] For example, Hempel received careful instructions from Berlin in March 1942 for 'the persistent diffusion of rumours' prophesying the impending retirement of Mr Churchill and his replacement by the left-wing politician Sir Stafford Cripps.[67] It was only natural that the British would respond in kind.

SOE had first exploited Ireland for this purpose in March 1941. Roddy Keith, an advertising executive, was sent to Dublin, and whispers were passed to him via the British military attaché. One example of the rumours circulated by Keith survives from May 1941:

> The USA had just handed over to Britain, under Lease and Lend, one of three fortified floating islands equipped with electrical defence apparatus, which is to be used as a base for anti-U-boat aeroplanes in the Atlantic. It has already accounted for three submarines in the last ten days.[68]

Keith lost the confidence of his superiors and was recalled, but the matter was revived in February 1942 by the Political Warfare Executive, which was anxious to use the services of John Betjeman. SOE agreed: 'Dublin is an ideal whispering centre, and we are very keen to get started there again.' The chief of SIS gave his approval and offered to transmit the material to Dublin in his secret bag.[69] Betjeman identified three individuals through whom whispers could be disseminated, as well as someone in Dublin who could run the operation: this was the Director of the National Gallery, Dr George Furlong, an expert in tenth- and eleventh-century Anglo-Saxon manuscript illumination who had previously worked at the National Gallery in London. Betjeman then acted as the intermediary between Furlong and SOE in London.[70]

The SOE whispering scheme illustrates how Britain was prepared to undertake more ambitious and aggressive propaganda operations in 1941. Another operation targeted the Irish-American community in the United States, which was still an important factor in Anglo-Irish relations. For the first year of the Second World War the British had shied away from conducting propaganda among Irish-Americans. This was partly because of a Foreign Office assessment that this lobby had limited influence on Washington's foreign policy; partly because of a Ministry of Information policy of refraining from any propaganda in the United States.[71] All this changed in 1941. The United State of America had become the key to Britain's fate, as Churchill's entire war strategy depended on obtaining American assistance: first, in the form of Lend Lease supplies; eventually, through full participation in the conflict. Although the administration of President Franklin D. Roosevelt was sympathetic, it was opposed by a strong, domestic isolationist lobby that fought against foreign entanglements. Irish-Americans were prominent in this movement: one British diplomat noted how their more extreme publications were 'violently anti-Roosevelt, isolationist and quasi-Fascist'. In addition, the American dimension had become critical to Britain's hopes of securing Irish bases. The British hoped that the American government would apply diplomatic pressure on Dublin to hand over bases, or co-operate in a seizure of these facilities. However, Irish-Americans reacted by forming an advocacy group, the American Friends of Irish Neutrality, which condemned British threats against Dublin and pressed the Washington administration to respect Ireland's independence. With the stakes so high, the British were now prepared to use clandestine propaganda to counter the Irish-American isolationist movement and to break Irish-America's automatic support for neutral Ireland.[72]

In the middle of 1941 the Ministry of Information gave some thought to 'the tackling of Irish opinion in the United States', and concluded that they 'should not accept the timid policy of reluctance to grasp the nettle'.[73] They attempted to reach Irish-Americans through the Catholic church, distributing hundreds of copies of a British Catholic newsletter to clergy and newspaper editors.[74] A far more ambitious scheme was launched by Britain's secret service in America, which went under the name British Security Coordination (BSC). Headquartered in the Rockefeller Center in New York, BSC was set up by SIS in May 1940 to counter Nazi propaganda and to protect Allied convoys from sabotage.[75] Its internal history records how:

> BSC sponsored an Irish interventionist society in the autumn of 1941. Contact with it was maintained by a good cut-out, a man who followed directives from the BSC office and kept BSC posted on every move made. In return, BSC financed the society (after a few months it was self-supporting) and supplied it with propaganda material, much of which was culled from intercepted letters from Eire.

The name of the society was the 'American Irish Defence Association' (AIDA) and it was run by prominent Irish-Americans from academia, business and the church. They set up committees in New York, Washington, Boston and Chicago, conducted opinion polls, held public meetings, distributed literature and organised a visit by the Irish Senator Frank MacDermot, who made 'pro-British and interventionist' speeches and radio broadcasts.[76] Though BSC later claimed that the organisation had great influence on Irish-American opinion, the evidence suggests otherwise. Its leaders, who had played no part in the nationalist movement, were little known; it provoked great opposition from the established Irish-American organisations that supported Dublin's neutrality; and its murky origins were revealed when a US Senator publicly accused British intelligence operatives of creating it. The Dublin government remarked on its 'futility', claiming that Irish-America was solidly behind their policy of neutrality until December 1941.[77] The real change in Irish-American opinion came after the United States entered the war. Irish neutrality clearly impeded the Allied war effort and cost the lives of American sailors and airmen – under these circumstances, Irish-American patriotism trumped loyalty to the old country.

Back in London some British officials advocated starting a similar propaganda organisation in Ireland. In June 1941 the Commercial Relations Division of the Ministry of Information proposed to 'get hold of a group of Irishmen who would do propaganda work in Ireland by the Irish for the Irish and paid for by the Irish, to make them realize that Eire's future was inextricably bound up with the survival of the British Empire'.[78] It turned to Lieutenant-Colonel C. J. Newbold, the Managing Director of Arthur Guinness Sons & Co. in Britain, who put forward the names of three Irish individuals who might be prepared to start a new association: T. B. Case, the Managing Director of Guinness in Dublin; Sir John Keane, the Governor of the Bank of Ireland; and Judge Wylie, a member of the Royal Dublin Society.[79] The Commercial Relations Division believed that 'efficient and well-conducted publicity' could 'win through' in Ireland, although it recognised that 'each and every step must be "cast-iron" safe, and leave no possible chance for any charge of propaganda, or of linking up with Britain officially'.[80] However, this scheme fell foul of the Irish experts in the Ministry of Information. They objected on the grounds that it would be impossible to hide the British inspiration, and that the Anglo-Irish had no influence:

> It is abundantly clear from the numerous secret reports about Eire which we receive that the only Irish businessmen who would consider for a moment taking part in any form of propaganda designed to show that Eire's future was bound up with the survival of the British Empire would be members of the Anglo-Irish minority. Most of these, like Sir John Keane and Judge Wylie, are wise enough to realise that any action of this kind with which they might associate themselves would defeat its own object, and even if certain members of that minority were found who were prepared to take the risk, their work would be stultified by the fact that in these days the Anglo-Irish cut no ice whatever.[81]

The Dominions Office and Sir John Maffey were even stronger in their opposition, because of concern over the possible reaction of the Irish government.[82] Faced with this barrage of criticism, the idea of a Guinness-backed 'Ireland For Ever Association' was scrapped.

This was just one of a number of ambitious, covert propaganda schemes that emerged at the end of 1941, only to die at the planning stage. One idea was to bankrupt pro-Axis Irish newspapers and periodicals by persuading British companies to withdraw their advertising. The Ministry of Information set about discovering the distributors of a long list of products: Rhyno pig food, Dr Witts' catarrh cure, Bile Beans, California syrup of figs, Birds Jelly de Luxe, to name but a few. The proposal proved unworkable, partly because it needed the co-operation of Irish advertising agencies, partly because British companies such as Unilever refused to subject their advertising to this sort of political control. Another suggestion was to insert propaganda leaflets in goods supplied to Ireland, drawing attention to the fact that they had been carried in British ships protected by the Royal Navy. On examination, however, the Ministry of Information found that these leaflets would not find their way to the consumer, because goods were delivered in bulk and then packed locally.[83] Moreover, Maffey's office objected, warning that the Irish authorities would take exception to this sort of propaganda. As with so many other schemes, it came to nothing, much to the frustration of the Ministry of Information. 'At present, the situation is thoroughly unsatisfactory', Dr Nicholas Mansergh complained in reference to the attitude of Maffey's office, 'since every proposal put forward at this end is torpedoed on the ground of policy at the other.'[84] This served as an epitaph for so many of the proposals in 1941.

In the end the only new initiatives undertaken by the Ministry of Information involved very subtle propaganda. One was to increase the amount of BBC radio programming that targeted Irish audiences. The BBC had appointed Denis Johnston, an Irish playwright from a liberal Protestant background, as its correspondent in Dublin in 1940. His news pieces on Ireland were included in the BBC's Northern Ireland programming and in its overseas service, which broadcast to members of the armed forces abroad. In late 1941 the BBC started a specialist, half hour magazine show, the *Irish Half Hour*. Ostensibly designed for Irish people serving in the British armed forces, its real aim was to influence opinion back in Ireland. It took a humorous approach to wartime conditions in Ireland, running comedy sketches performed by well-known Irish actors, usually portraying roguish Paddies with a fondness for drink. It tried to show that Britain and southern Ireland were 'in it' together, suffering from the same war restrictions with equal stoicism and humour. These shows reached a large audience. There were approximately 180,000 licensed radio sets in southern Ireland during the war, as well as at least 25,000 unlicensed sets. However, the impact of BBC propaganda was gradually lessened by the dwindling supplies of the equipment – especially batteries – needed to run the radios. Despite Betjeman's urgent appeals to London for 'More Zinc for Éire', British supply needs took precedence, and many Irish radios fell silent.[85]

Ultimately, the Ministry of Information put the greatest effort into the form of propaganda that its representatives had first advocated in the summer of 1940: promoting personal contact between Irish and British people. 'I do not think', John Betjeman wrote, 'so far as British publicity in Eire is concerned, that the printed word counts for half so much as social contacts.'[86] Betjeman epitomised this approach, with his frenetic socialising in Dublin during the war. The Ministry of Information also arranged to send a wide range of visitors to Ireland to spread the right message by word of mouth. Commercial travellers were suited to this task: for example, employees of Rowntree's and the Aga Cooker company were specially briefed before visiting Ireland. Though the numbers involved were small, they proved of 'great assistance', especially because they reached provincial towns that were otherwise neglected.[87] More numerous were officers of the armed services, who were encouraged to holiday in southern Ireland.

The most sophisticated form of unofficial diplomacy was the sending of a steady stream of distinguished individuals 'to mould opinion ... in influential political, literary, academic and professional circles'. One good example was the visit of Christopher Hollis, an Air Ministry officer who was co-editor of the Catholic *The Tablet* and author of a book on Erasmus. He gave a lecture on Erasmus at Maynooth University in March 1942, stayed an extra week and met with the archbishop of Dublin, de Valera and many others. The visit was such a success that he was invited back later in the year. 'I have never known an English visitor more welcome in Ireland than you are,' Betjeman wrote to Hollis. 'The success you have scored with bishops, Maynooth and Government circles is enough to get you an Order from the Irish Government if it had one to give.' [88] Other visitors included British MPs, senior clergy, academics, writers, artists and actors, as well as representatives from Allied Belgium, Poland, Czechoslovakia, France and Holland. In all, the Ministry of Information supported visits by 100 people during 1942. It was the result of a conscious decision in that year 'to concentrate on Public Relations Work rather than propaganda'. Looking back, the Ministry of Information concluded that this shift in emphasis had 'clearly been justified by results'.[89]

This change in emphasis was facilitated by American entry into the war and the changing strategic situation. At the beginning of 1942 it was decided to leave the field of traditional, direct propaganda to the Americans – the ambitious schemes put forward by the Ministry of Information at the end of 1941 were dropped for good. This made sense; because of traditional sympathy with the United States, the Irish would be more amenable to American influence. The US legation agreed to encourage the circulation of American newspapers, periodicals and books. It soon began producing a weekly news-sheet, the 'Letter from America', a big, brash affair with a circulation of 20,000, to counteract the German bulletin. In addition, the changing strategic situation altered the purposes of Allied propaganda. There was no longer any need to prepare Irish ground for a possible German invasion or a British seizure of bases. Instead, the purpose of Allied propaganda was to foster goodwill towards the Allied cause. This would help secure maximum concessions from the Irish government while the war persisted and guarantee a friendly Ireland after the war finished.[90]

The perpetual bogeyman

DURING 1942 there was plenty of evidence that Irish goodwill was forthcoming. Following greater co-operation with the Irish security apparatus, British intelligence officers revised their earlier assessments of the influence of German propagandists, concluding that they had little impact.[91] After American entry into the war and German military defeats, reports from Ireland indicated that public opinion was shifting steadily towards the Allies: 'Erstwhile Nazi sympathisers', Jane Archer wrote, were 'hastily turning their coats.'[92] In a wide-ranging survey of Irish opinion and British propaganda in February 1943, the Ministry of Information concluded that pro-German feeling was insignificant:

> In general, German propaganda to Eire has been most successful amongst pseudo-intellectual circles in Dublin which are specially cultivated by Carl Petersen, the Nazi Press Attache (there has long been in Dublin an over-production of university graduates, and it is to this type that Nazi doctrines often appeal most readily); and amongst the depressed rural classes, particularly along the western seaboard. Here, especially in 1940–41 Nazi promises of work and high wages for all and a ready market for Irish agricultural exports found a receptive audience. In general, however, German propaganda has made little headway in Eire; and its influence is steadily declining.[93]

At the same time there was growing support for the Allies among the general Irish public. 'The most encouraging feature of the situation in Eire', the Ministry of Information stated, 'has been the fact that public opinion has become consistently more favourable to the cause of the United Nations in general, and of the United Kingdom in particular, over the past two years.' It estimated that 80 per cent of people were pro-Ally and anxious for an Allied victory. This did not mean that there was any questioning of neutrality, which had attained the status of a 'religion'. Yet the country did regard itself as neutral on the side of the United Nations, and there was an increasingly popular view that Ireland's 'benevolent neutrality' was of the same value to the cause as belligerency.[94] SIS detected similar developments in Ireland. It noted in January 1943 that 'a rapid allied victory is the hope of the overwhelming majority of the people' and pointed six months later to 'a wave of pro-British feeling throughout the country'. This was accompanied by 'a distinct improvement in the attitude of the Eire Government and some anxiety to show how Eire has helped the Allied war effort'.[95]

Nonetheless, despite these positive developments, London saw distant, dark clouds forming around post-war Anglo-Irish relations. For all its pro-Allied fervour, Irish opinion was still regarded as containing an Anglophobic, republican element that had the power to corrupt relations between the two countries. In February 1943, the Ministry of Information concluded that 20 per cent of the population were 'strongly anti-British' and sympathetic towards the IRA; even the 80 per cent who were pro-Allied were not necessarily friendly towards Britain. The ministry warned that 'the existence of latent anti-British feeling amongst the majority of the people must at no time be overlooked whatever superficial appearances may be'.[96] The same observation was frequently made by Sir John Maffey. At the end of the war, he wrote:

Eire is more than ever a foreign country. It is so dominated by the National Catholic Church as to be almost a theocratic State. Gaelic is enforced to show that Eire is not one of the English-speaking nations, 'foreign' games are frowned upon, the war censorship has been mis-applied for anti-British purposes, anti-British feeling is fostered in school and by Church and State by a system of 'hereditary enemy' indoctrination. There is probably more widespread anti-British sentiment in Eire to-day than ever before ... Young minds are moulded to hate an abstraction, England. Irish politics live on this racket, and Ireland endeavours to poison the ear of the world against us.[97]

While bred by history, the chief sustenance of this animus was partition. Like Churchill in 1918, when the British government looked to the future, it saw the dreary steeples of Tyrone and Fermanagh rising among the clouds. It was feared that the Irish government would start where it had left off in 1939 by raising a ferocious agitation on both sides of the Atlantic, in an attempt to have the border removed as part of an international peace settlement. De Valera signalled his intent to Maffey in April 1943, when he spoke at length of the intolerable position of nationalists in the north: Maffey noticed that 'this topic as usual created visible excitement in the speaker and revealed some of the fanaticism that made him the rebel of '16'.[98]

From 1943 the SIS network detected signs of a burgeoning anti-partition campaign in southern Ireland. It investigated new political groups such as The Green Front and the Anti-Partition League. Perhaps the most dangerous was a Catholic nativist political party named Ailtirí na hAiseírghe ('Architects of the Resurrection').[99] Led by Gerald O'Cunningham, and supported by the potential Quislings Ernest Blythe and J. J. Walshe, it had obvious fascist credentials: its object was to form an Irish Christian corporative state on authoritarian, Francoist lines, naturally with O'Cunningham as leader. It began an active campaign, holding outdoor meetings, producing large numbers of pamphlets and organising lectures on social and political subjects. Though its numbers and influence were small, it attracted adherents from diverse backgrounds, often young people with no marked political predilections who were open to new ideas.[100] For a time in 1943 and 1944, because it appeared to be taking deeper roots than the other pro-Axis organisations that sprouted during the war, it caused some anxiety within the British intelligence community. In November 1943 G2 recorded that known 'British Agents' were taking 'a keen interest in the activities of the organisation'.[101] Jane Archer warned that the 'party may yet prove a dangerous factor in the event of serious post war confusion and disillusionment'. It was being used as a 'breeding ground for the IRA' – membership of one might lead to membership of the other. Archer could not understand why the Irish authorities did not do more to suppress it, but this was part of a wider trend whereby the government tolerated anti-partition movements. 'The Government is taking no apparent action against subversive and pro-Fascist organisations which openly advocate the abolition of the Border by force', she complained.[102]

It was feared that an anti-partition campaign would raise political temperatures and lead to a revival of the IRA. Warnings to this effect came from Éamon de Valera. In a return to the arguments that he had used before the war, he frequently warned that his 'Left Wing' might get out of control. 'Mr. de Valera's main preoccupation is that with the war ending we are heading for bitter trouble over the Partition question', Maffey wrote after an interview with the Irish leader on 10 November 1944. Worryingly, Maffey supported this prediction. He warned that resentment at partition could result in a rising by Catholics in the north, or IRA attacks from the south, which might draw in the Dublin government – he was 'constantly reminded of the North-West frontier of India, with its fanaticism and vendettas'. He argued that something should be done about partition, suggesting the redrawing of the boundary or international arbitration. This 'depressing document' was received with concern in the Dominions Office, which recalled Maffey to London for consultation.[103]

Thus, as the war drew to a close the attention of the British intelligence community had returned to its traditional enemy, the 'perpetual bogeyman' – Irish republicanism. Despite the collapse of the IRA, the removal of foreign intrigues and the development of unprecedented security co-operation with the Dublin authorities, London was still haunted by the prospect of violence on the border and an upsurge of anti-British sentiment in the south. From 1943 onwards, Britain's policy towards Ireland was governed by how to nullify the threatened anti-partition agitation. As we shall see in the next chapter, London and Washington tried to exploit the war to remove Irish-America's traditional support for the Dublin government. In Ireland the British attempted further propaganda. Arguing that the continuation of its work in Ireland was 'as important or perhaps even more important', the Ministry of Information set out to counter anti-British sentiment in the country and to build up a store of sympathy in preparation for any post-war partition agitation. It noted that 'the time has come when the United Kingdom case can with advantage be put more firmly and more outspokenly than was considered expedient in the earlier stages of the war'.[104] As before, this propaganda was primarily conducted through personal contacts and unofficial emissaries to Ireland.

T HE British intelligence system detected some alarming features in Irish society during the Second World War. During 1940 and 1941 this centred around the amount of support for the Axis powers. There was some basis to this. Czech, Polish and Dutch visitors all commented on a pro-German bias in Ireland at this time; even G2 concluded that a large number of people were so anti-British in 1940 that they would welcome a German invasion.[105] Moreover, there was a widespread feeling that Britain could not win the war: 'England is already conquered', Joseph Walshe flatly wrote in July 1940. 'That is an elementary fact for everyone who has not allowed himself to be overcome by Britain's belief in her permanent invincibility.'[106] Nonetheless, these tendencies should not be exaggerated. The bulk of the country hoped for an Allied victory, while strongly supporting their own country's neutrality. Irish opinion swung more and more behind the Allied cause after the Americans entered the war and the strategic situation changed. Moreover, Irish attitudes were not shaped by Axis propaganda or the intrigues of the German legation. Instead, the chief problem was Ireland's traditional enmity toward Britain, driven by history and the continuance of partition. The war seemed to confirm Maffey's early conclusion that 'anti-British feeling was the dynamic of Irish opinion, always there though often latent.'[107]

Like Axis efforts, British propaganda played little part in causing shifts in Irish opinion. The Ministry of Information struggled to develop a propaganda strategy for southern Ireland. Because of perceived German intrigues, and the strategic importance of southern Ireland, it felt compelled to conduct some propaganda, mostly channelled through the press attaché, John Betjeman, or a stream of British visitors. Yet it shied away from the sort of aggressive, covert activity that it freely undertook in other parts of the world (including the United States). One reason was the belief that such propaganda would be ineffective: to reach an audience it had to be organised; if it was organised, it would appear as blatant British propaganda; in that event it would have little effect on the audience and might be counterproductive. Another reason was the likely reaction of the Irish government. De Valera was prepared to turn a blind eye to clandestine British intelligence operations on Irish soil, but he would not tolerate organised British propaganda, because he regarded it as an attempt to undermine the policy of neutrality. For these reasons, Britain fought a very gentle propaganda war in Ireland.

CHAPTER 13

Leakage of Information

G ATHERING operational intelligence, tackling the Irish fifth column and countering Axis propaganda declined in importance once the war left Ireland behind at the end of 1941. But Ireland presented another challenge that preoccupied the British intelligence community until the final stages of the Second World War: preventing espionage and leakage of information. This was a priority for many reasons. The central tenet of British security policy was to deny the enemy all information of military importance from the United Kingdom – neutral Ireland was a potential spying post because of its geographical position. In addition, southern Ireland was itself a source of valuable information: for example, for forecasting the weather, or for planning an invasion of the country. After 1940 the importance of counter-intelligence went beyond this. As well as denying information, Britain deceived the enemy by supplying false information. It did this by capturing German agents in Britain, 'turning' them and allowing them to operate under British direction – the highly successful Double-Cross (or XX) System. For this operation to remain undetected, two conditions were necessary. First, all German agents sent to Britain had to be quickly apprehended. Second, Germany had to be starved of all other information on the British war effort, so that it would not receive contradictory reports. This raised the stakes of counter-espionage in Ireland. Some of the German spies sent to Ireland had the mission of contacting double-cross agents in Britain, which would have jeopardised the latter's position; besides, information leaked via Ireland might contradict the reports of double-cross agents in Britain, thereby causing Berlin to suspect their *bona fides*.[1] As a result, it was vital to make Ireland as impenetrable to German espionage as Britain itself.

The panic about the fifth column during the summer of 1940 was accompanied by a presumption that Germany must have numerous espionage agents in Britain. However, the capture and interrogation of the unimpressive German pre-invasion agents landed in Britain between September and November did much to reassure MI5, as did the material from decrypted continental Abwehr radio traffic that became available in December 1940. Gradually the British intelligence community realised that the domestic espionage threat was slight. The MI5 internal history notes that 'some time during 1941 it began to be apparent

– contrary to our previous and justified over-estimate of their efficiency – that the Germans had no previously established espionage network of any appreciable size or effectiveness.'[2] J. C. Masterman writes that the XX or Twenty Committee set up to run the Double Cross System in January 1941 quickly began to grasp the truth that they 'actively ran and controlled the German espionage system' in Britain.[3] MI5 progressed from a state of almost total ignorance about the Abwehr's capacities to the position in which its influence over Abwehr's activities was so great that these activities were a serious handicap to Germany for the rest of the war.[4]

The British intelligence community was far slower to come to a similar realisation about the situation in Ireland. For much of 1940 and 1941 it was considered axiomatic that neutral Ireland was the centre of an elaborate German espionage network directed against Britain. This had been MI5's conclusion in April 1940, after the discovery of an illicit wireless transmitter near Dublin, and it was reinforced by supposed evidence of a rampant Irish fifth column during the summer. The Joint Intelligence Committee (JIC) stated on 23 May 1940:

> It can be assumed that intelligence activities favourable to Germany are being carried on from the German Legation in Dublin. The last two German Military Attaches in London are known to have undertaken tours in Eire, probably with the object of organising an intelligence service. It is presumed that a considerable amount of intelligence work is also carried on by business concerns with German connections.[5]

The realisation that Germany had failed to establish an espionage network in Britain intensified the belief that Ireland was its principal base for espionage activity. In September 1940 the Military Intelligence Directorate fumed that 'it was a known fact that the Germans' main source of information was Dublin'. This opinion was shared by Cecil Liddell and MI5.[6] Two months later the JIC was told that there was evidence that Ireland represented 'almost the only point of leakage' about conditions in Britain.[7] Even in August 1941 Churchill complained that there was still 'a pretty good leak' from Ireland.[8] As with the Irish fifth column and Axis subversion, this was an exaggeration. It was not until 1942 – when Britain had a full understanding of the Abwehr's capabilities and a mature intelligence relationship with Ireland – that this threat was put into proper perspective.

Chasing Irish spies

T HE British intelligence community's first response to the threat of German espionage was to institute an array of preventive security measures to
stop sensitive information leaking *to* Ireland from Britain – a 'ringed fence' was
erected between the two countries. A second response was to try to uncover
the German intelligence organisation that was presumed to exist *in* Ireland. The
third measure was to place controls over Ireland's foreign communications to
stop information leaking *from* Ireland – the 'ringed fence' was extended to separate the country from the rest of the world. In doing so, the British government
continued to follow the twin-track approach of covert intelligence activity in
Ireland and collaboration with Irish officials: counter-espionage became a major
task of the SIS network, which investigated hundreds of suspected individuals; at
the same time, preventing the leakage of information was the 'primary function'
of the MI5 Irish section, which pursued co-operation with the Irish authorities.[9]
A dispute over the threat of German espionage was one of the reasons for the
breakdown of the 'Dublin link' in the middle of 1941. However, the relationship
was then resumed on a more satisfactory level and rapidly deepened. Ultimately,
co-operation would prove far more effective than covert activity in neutralising
this threat.

The conviction in April 1940 that southern Ireland was the centre of an elaborate German espionage network led to drastic steps to prevent information
reaching the country. The first step was the imposition of a full censorship on
postal, telegraph and telephone communications between Ireland and Britain.
This was instituted after a test-check, placed on 20 per cent of the mails bound
for Ireland on 20 May, revealed 150 'fairly important indiscretions' after just two
days: these included details of the positions of Royal Navy ships, aerodromes,
anti-aircraft defences and army units.[10] MI5, the armed services and the censorship division were adamant that a full censorship should be imposed on mails
to and from Ireland forthwith. Within a few days a thousand censors had been
turned on to the job. Henceforth all post and telegraph communications were
passed through the censorship department, while all telephone calls were monitored and liable to immediate interruption.[11] These measures stayed in place for
the rest of the war.

Concomitant with the sweeping censorship was the imposition of controls
on the movement of people between Britain and Ireland. The spectre of Irish
fifth columnists slipping into Britain led the JIC to impose new regulations,
requiring all travellers to obtain a visa in Dublin or an exit permit in Belfast.[12]
Captain Collinson's Permit Office was established in Dublin on 7 June 1940, and

it subsequently vetted everyone who intended to travel to Britain. At the same time equally tight controls were imposed on the movement of people *to* Ireland: exit permits had to be obtained in Britain and 'all doubtful cases were submitted to MI5'.[13] The Home Defence (Security) Executive decided that this traffic should be reduced to a minimum. For six months after June 1940 permits were only issued for travel in the case of 'work of national importance', or to Irish members of the armed forces on leave, effectively stopping almost all regular passenger movement.[14] Because of discontent among Irish workers, there was a relaxation of these restrictions in November 1940 to allow anyone with a home in Ireland to return on holidays once every six months.[15] Nevertheless, the tightest control on movement was maintained for the rest of the war.

The restrictions on movement were accompanied by a clampdown on Irish immigrant workers. Between June 1940 and June 1941 few people were given permits to work in Britain. (The only exception was the annual migration of farm workers at harvest time.) In June 1941, however, because of an acute need for labour, the Ministry of Labour pressed for a substantial increase in Irish recruitment. The Home Defence (Security) Executive warned that such an influx posed grave security problems, namely 'the possible infiltration into this country of members of the I.R.A.' and 'subversive and troublesome activities generally'. Churchill also resisted the proposal, writing that it was 'not desirable to bring over large numbers of these hostile people to this island at a time when invasion must be considered more than likely'.[16] It was finally agreed that the demand for labour was so great that the risk would have to be tolerated, but only if recruitment was 'conducted in an orderly fashion with sufficient official supervision to ensure maximum regard to security interests'.[17] The Ministry of Labour established an office in Dublin; there was 'proper vetting from the security angle of every entrant'; and, once in Britain, workers were subject to tight controls.[18] The British could rely on the assistance of the Irish government, which regarded emigration as a safety valve for economic and social pressures. Local Garda checked prospective Irish workers before they received a travel permit, rejecting known IRA sympathisers.[19] Thousands of Irish workers (estimates range from 100,000 to 150,000) flocked to Britain during the war. This threw an enormous burden onto the intelligence services: Captain Collinson's office issued some 170,000 travel permits between 1941 and 1945; and MI5 struggled to monitor the workers after they arrived in Britain.[20]

British security chiefs also tried to control the information that was passed to the Irish government and Irish military. It was feared that information passed to Irish officials might find its way to Germany. On 12 April 1941 Military Mission 18 received the following warning, courtesy of Winston Churchill:

> Owing to the peculiar conditions existing in Eire, there is a grave risk that any information on war matters, which may be communicated to persons connected with the EIRE Government may find its way to the enemy. The Prime Minster has directed that those who may have dealings with officials of the EIRE Government are to be warned that they must not discuss general war matters with those officials.[21]

In November 1941 a conference to devise rules on the disclosure of information to neutral governments confirmed that 'it must be assumed that information given to the Eire Government will sooner or later reach the enemy, though the risk is to some extent dependent on the particular Eire Department concerned.'[22] This reflected British suspicion in the early years of the war that the southern Irish state was riddled with anti-British officials, who would be only too willing to help Germany.

The ringed fence between southern Ireland and Britain had one very frayed end – the Northern Ireland border. The province posed a unique security challenge because the arbitrary, twisting 180-mile land frontier allowed easy communication between the two jurisdictions. Both the military and civil authorities agreed that sealing the border would be impossible; it would require huge numbers of troops, would provoke civil disturbance, and could never be made completely effective.[23] This made it necessary to impose the same travel and censorship restrictions on communications between Britain and Northern Ireland that applied to communications with southern Ireland – there was no attempt to separate north and south. This policy was not without problems. It ruffled unionist political sensitivities because it meant that the province was treated differently from the rest of the United Kingdom. Moreover, it did not safeguard information that originated in Northern Ireland: by 1941 the province was a source of important intelligence in its own right, because of the concentration of convoys off its coast, the development of war industries and German air raids on Belfast. At various times in 1940 and 1941 there were calls for the border to be closed and for a full censorship to be imposed on communications with the south.[24] Security chiefs always came to the conclusion that this would be impractical. Instead, they relied on 'secret selective scrutiny' by the Northern Ireland security forces.[25] Customs officials and the RUC patrolled the border, checking those found crossing it; there was a partial censorship of mail and telegrams passing to the south; and the RUC kept a close surveillance on the nationalist community. The RUC was confident that these measures were sufficient. It had 'a very good knowledge of the dangerous individuals in Northern Ireland', the British Home Secretary wrote, and it could rely on Garda co-operation to provide 'adequate information about espionage activities by persons trying to enter Northern Ireland from Eire'.[26]

The RUC may have been over-confident. The IRA did collect military information in Northern Ireland and attempt to transmit it to German agents in Dublin – this is one of the few actual espionage networks that operated in Ireland during the war. On 20 October 1941 the Irish police discovered a 'Comprehensive Military Report on Belfast' in the handbag of Helena Kelly when she was searched in Dublin. Compiled by the Belfast IRA, the report contained a diagram of the Shortt and Harland aircraft factory, a plan of Sydenham aerodrome, details on the disposition of the British army, the names and addresses of British army officers and a scheme for sabotaging the Belfast telephone system. Its most extraordinary aspect was the advice tendered to German bombers. There was a map showing 'the remaining and most outstanding objects of military significance, as yet unblitzed'. The IRA helpfully suggested that if these objectives were 'bombed by the Luftwaffe as thoroughly as the other areas in recent raids'. Belfast would 'be rendered a negative quantity in Britain's war effort'. Nationalist areas of the city were marked in a special colour so that they could be spared. Thus, just months after horrific bomber raids on Belfast in April 1941 (some of the worst suffered by any city in the United Kingdom), the local IRA was calling down another blitz on the city, while attempting to spare its own community. Little of the intelligence collected by the IRA found its way to Germany. Nonetheless, the fact remains that the IRA collected, and brought to Dublin, information that would have been of use in planning German operations.[27]

Because of the porous nature of the Northern Ireland border and the inevitable movement of servicemen and workers across the Irish Sea, it was impossible to prevent all information reaching neutral Ireland; besides, southern Ireland, like the north, was itself a source of valuable intelligence. Therefore the British counter-espionage strategy had a second dimension: the intelligence community tried to uncover and take action against German espionage agents in Ireland. During 1940 and 1941 the British assumed there was an extensive 'enemy Intelligence organisation' operating in southern Ireland.[28] It was believed that this organisation collected 'scraps of news and gossip' from people returning from Britain, 'which may not in themselves seem very important but which pieced together may give the Germans a fairly clear picture of a situation in which they are interested'.[29] Both SIS, through its clandestine network, and MI5, through its link with G2, investigated scores of suspects in an attempt to uncover this organisation.

The most obvious place to look was the German legation in Dublin. Throughout the war the British public remained convinced that the legation was a nest of spies, largely because of a steady stream of sensationalist press articles.[30] This opinion was initially shared by the British intelligence community. In its long report on the legation in December 1940, SIS warned that the Germans had 'intensified intrigues in the realm of espionage' and had created 'a regular service of agents ... all over Eire' – it consisted of 'German nationals, Irish extremists and other suitable elements'. The Counsellor, Henning Thomsen, was 'the chief organiser of Nazi espionage' and made journeys by car all around the county to meet his 'agents'.[31] The JIC accepted this as accurate, and it caused the Prime Minister to fret over the importation of large numbers of Irish workers. 'Obviously the German Embassy in Dublin can work in any German they wish through this channel', Churchill warned in July 1941. 'This would be the best way to get spies and assassins into the United Kingdom, and special vigilance is required.'[32] As late as December 1941 the Air Ministry warned an American official, preparing for a visit to Ireland, that anything he said 'would get to the German Minister within half an hour' because 'the German Embassy had a staff of about 75 who acted as a spy column' – 'the situation in Ireland was not to be trusted.'[33]

British fears were exaggerated. For fear that it would lead to his expulsion from Ireland, the German Minister was loath to engage in espionage activity, and distanced himself from Abwehr agents sent there. His subordinates were mostly kept on a tight rein. Furthermore, even if the legation staff had wished, they would have struggled to play a more active espionage role, as they were kept under close scrutiny by the Irish security organisations.[34] All calls to the legation were tapped, its letters intercepted, and the building kept under constant surveillance. Joseph Walshe stated that 'the whole British notion of the power of the German Minister in Dublin was greatly exaggerated. He was in truth "just like a man in a cage," whose every movement was watched.'[35] It is true that the legation staff gratefully accepted any useful information on the United Kingdom that came their way and passed it to Berlin. They also associated with pro-German and republican figures, who may have been willing to procure such information. But the standard of information was never high, simply scraps of gossip, often inaccurate, about conditions in the United Kingdom. The notion that the legation was at the centre of a vast German intelligence organisation was unfounded.

The other suspected kingpins of the 'enemy Intelligence organisation' were trained Abwehr operatives. There were solid grounds for British concerns, as the Abwehr despatched two agents to Ireland in 1941. The first was Günther Schütz. Before the war Schütz had spied for the Abwehr in Britain in conjunction with a Portuguese man named Pierce, who later became the successful MI5 double agent 'Rainbow'. Schütz was chosen for an Irish mission in December

1940. His tasks were to transmit weather information and to spy on convoy traffic and economic targets in Northern Ireland. He was dropped by parachute on the night of 12 March 1941. He quickly aroused the suspicion of two local Garda after they cycled by him on a road the next morning. When questioned, he stuck to the prearranged cover story that he was a South African named Hans Marschner, that he had been driving from Dublin to Naas in Co. Kildare when his car had broken down, and that he was now walking home – this was unfortunate, because he was in fact in Co. Wexford, far from his intended drop point and nowhere near the Dublin–Naas road. After the Garda officers discovered a transmitter in his suitcase, he was arrested and brought to Dublin for interrogation by G2.[36] He talked freely of the personnel and procedures of the Abwehr Hamburg station. Full details were supplied to MI5 and to Major Bailey of the War Office, who visited Dublin on 20 March.[37]

The other German agent sent to Ireland in 1941, Joseph Lenihan, had a very different fate: he evaded the Irish authorities but quickly surrendered himself to the RUC. Born in Ennistymon, Co. Clare, Lenihan had various IRA and criminal antecedents. He had moved to Britain in the 1930s and drifted around, until he found himself on the island of Jersey in time for the German occupation. From there, he was recruited by German intelligence, taken to Paris and trained for a mission to Ireland. His instructions were to set up a weather reporting station in Co. Sligo. Lenihan landed by parachute in Co. Meath on 18 July 1941 and successfully made his way to Dublin, where he reacquainted himself with friends and family. After five days he proceeded to Northern Ireland and handed himself in to the RUC, asking to speak to a representative of MI5.[38] He was immediately flown to Camp 020, MI5's interrogation centre, where he was vetted for consideration in the Double-Cross programme. However, he would have had to establish radio communication with the Abwehr from Co. Sligo, which would have required bringing the Irish authorities into the double-cross secret. This was unacceptable, so it was decided not to use Lenihan in this way. Even so, Lenihan was of great use to MI5. Cecil Liddell later wrote:

> though of rough appearance, he was fairly well educated, intelligent and with a phenomenal memory for facts and faces. He gave more fresh and accurate information about the Abwehr in the Netherlands and Paris than any other single agent.[39]

The Schütz and Lenihan cases represented more abject failures by the Abwehr in Ireland. Yet British intelligence had evidence suggesting that two other German agents were working in southern Ireland during 1941. The first was a middle-aged native of Hamburg named Werner Unland. After a spell as a failed businessman and ineffective Abwehr operative in Britain, Unland and his English wife fled to Dublin on the outbreak of the war. From an apartment at 46 Merrion Square he corresponded regularly with Abwehr cover addresses in Europe, inventing a fictitious network of Irish agents in order to obtain German payouts. This correspondence was monitored by G2 and MI5 from the start. The British did not initially realise Unland's deception, believing that he had recruited a circle of minor agents in Ireland to collect information. The truth was only revealed when Unland was arrested and interrogated in April 1941, after his name was found on instructions carried by Günther Schütz.[40] The second, and much more dangerous, Abwehr operative to remain at liberty was Hermann Görtz, who had landed by parachute in May 1940 and was not captured for eighteen months. As we have seen, neither G2 nor MI5 had reliable intelligence on his activities until September 1941, but they knew enough to be concerned. MI5's still incomplete knowledge of the extent of Abwehr operations in Ireland meant that the British intelligence community could not be sure that no other German spies were successfully operating in neutral Ireland. It helped fuel the belief that a German espionage organisation must exist in the country, collecting the information that inevitably leaked from the United Kingdom.

Because of the suspicion that a German intelligence organisation was active in Ireland and the difficulty of preventing information reaching the country, the focus of British security policy began to shift more and more towards preventing information leaking *from* southern Ireland to the outside world. The significance of this was not initially realised. Cecil Liddell admitted that by the end of 1940 MI5 'had not taken any steps at that time to raise the question of the various ways by which information from this country once it reached Eire could be passed on to the enemy'. One reason was that communications from southern Ireland to the outside world were the direct responsibility of SIS: 'this was all part of the failure to visualise the problem as a whole', Cecil Liddell noted.[41] Gradually it was realised that the key to handling the security threat posed by neutral Ireland was controlling its means of external communications: posts and telegraph, movement of individuals, air and shipping services and, most crucially, the communications of the German legation. Steps were taken to extend the 'ringed fence' that had been erected between Ireland and Britain so that it would encircle both islands. It would not matter what secrets leaked into Ireland, so long as no secrets could leak out.

The first step was to impose controls on Ireland's posts and telegrams. Since the beginning of 1940, the Irish government had agreed to send all its continental mails via Britain, which allowed for a full British censorship. Mails were still sent direct from Ireland to the United States, but it was felt that they were adequately dealt with at that end. Telegrams were more dangerous, as they provided a rapid means of communication, and the matter was complicated by the presence of two cable stations in Co. Kerry at the end of international lines. Steps were taken to close this avenue of leakage by cutting the cables landing in Ireland and extending them to Britain. To appease the Irish government, one cable to the United States was left in place, but this went via Newfoundland where the traffic was subject to British censorship.[42] Thus by the end of 1940 British censorship effectively controlled all Ireland's external postal and telegraphic communications.

British surveillance also extended to Ireland's diplomatic communications. As we have seen, GC&CS had first begun decrypting Irish messages after de Valera came to power in 1932. Constrained by limited resources, it seems that British cryptanalysts gave up this task soon after. With the start of the Second World War, however, GC&CS began decrypting Irish diplomatic communications on a regular basis. This was an easy task, as all official Irish telegrams passed through British hands, and Irish ciphers were unsophisticated. (In addition, British officials secretly listened into phone calls between the Irish High Commissioner in London and the Department of External Affairs, and occasionally opened and read the contents of Irish diplomatic pouches.) This revealed whether Irish officials were transmitting important secrets abroad. It also gave an insight into the policy and attitudes of the Dublin government, which was helpful in Britain's handling of Anglo-Irish relations. Most valuable was the information provided by Irish diplomats in Berlin, Rome and occupied Europe, who reported regularly on morale, air raid damage, economic conditions and foreign policy in their countries. In effect, London used Ireland's diplomatic reporting system as an additional source of foreign intelligence. Irish decrypts were frequently shown to Winston Churchill, who eagerly reviewed the most interesting items from Britain's signals intelligence each evening.[43]

As well as supervising all Ireland's post, telegram and telephone communications, MI5 was also determined to control the movement of people between Ireland and the rest of the world. After May 1940 passengers passing through Britain required permits from the British office in Dublin. They were also closely scrutinised by security officers at British ports of entry and departure: for example, the Dublin government was incensed when twenty-nine Irish priests and three Irish nuns were strip-searched and interrogated when returning from Rome through an English port.[44] One of the few ways of avoiding this control was by air travel. In the spring of 1941 the British Overseas Airways Corporation (BOAC) began operating a flying boat service from Foynes in Co. Limerick to Lisbon. A year later, two American companies, American Air Export and Pan

American, were given permission to fly between Foynes and the United States of America. Both services connected with flights to and from Britain. They were used mainly for passengers, generally high-ranking Allied military and government officials, but they also carried mails and diplomatic bags. The British intelligence agencies were determined to impose tight controls on this service, not least because Lisbon was 'known to be full of enemy agents'. Any Irish mails sent or received via the aircraft had first to be sent to Britain for censorship. Any Irish persons wishing to travel on the American service (they were barred from the Lisbon flight) were obliged to obtain a visa from the Permit Office in Dublin; in any case, places were rarely available.[45] As a final control, the air service was scrutinised by an MI5 officer at Foynes, initially a covert appointment, disguised as a BOAC 'passenger welfare officer'. After the Irish authorities allowed the British to appoint an official security representative, Mr F. B. Carruthers took up this post in July 1942 and remained at the airport for the rest of the war. His salary was shared by the Home Office, SIS and MI5. These security measures proved effective: after the war MI5 concluded with some relief that the Germans never made use of the Foynes air service, even though it provided 'an almost ideal means of communication, for it was ... both rapid and regular'.[46]

The greatest challenge thrown up by Irish neutrality was how to control the communications of the German legation in Dublin. The legation's regular communications went by cable via London, where they were subject to a four-day delay. At this stage, Bletchley Park could not read the German diplomatic cipher, so the messages were simply copied and stored away. For security reasons, it would have been desirable to stop this traffic altogether, but this was made impossible by international protocol, the demands of the Irish government and a policy of reciprocity (by which the Axis allowed the passage of British diplomatic communications from neutral countries such as Switzerland). This meant that some information would inevitably escape from Ireland. The value of the intelligence passed on by Hempel was low, but the British intelligence community, unable to read the messages, had no way of knowing this at that time. There was a natural tendency to presume the worst. The one positive aspect was that the four-day delay on telegrams meant that any operational intelligence could probably not reach Germany in time to be useful.

However, if the German legation was able to communicate by wireless then this safeguard would no longer exist: if, for example, legation staff obtained information about convoy movements, it could be put at the disposal of the Luftwaffe and the U-boat fleet within minutes. Eliminating the German legation radio transmitter was the most serious challenge faced by British intelligence agencies in relation to Ireland during the Second World War. It contributed to a 'crisis' in the 'Dublin link' between June and September 1941; conversely, the steps that Dublin took to remedy the situation contributed to the blossoming of relations between MI5 and G2 at the end of 1941.[47]

That it took so long to confirm the existence of the German wireless was itself a major failing of the British intelligence community. Hempel had brought a specially constructed suitcase transmitter back to Dublin in July 1939, which he began using at the outbreak of the war. In April 1940 the British obtained a bearing on a station, south of Dublin, that was working to the German diplomatic control station of Nauen west of Berlin. This discovery led British security chiefs to conclude that Ireland was the centre of the German espionage system. However, they could not prove that this transmitter belonged to the legation, and in June 1940 the taking of the traffic was given up, as GC&CS had no hope of reading it. In December 1940 the JIC again drew attention to the dangers of leakage through the German legation in Dublin, and a special watch was arranged for all German diplomatic broadcasts. However, because the signals were weak, the Dublin transmissions were not picked up. Cecil Liddell later admitted that this problem was not handled well. He wrote that, even though it was an SIS responsibility, MI5 'should have made it their business to find out the exact position of the German Legation W/T at a much earlier stage'.[48] This failure is even more surprising considering that GC&CS had separately concluded that every German legation in Europe was equipped with a transmitter.[49]

The first proof that the legation in Dublin was no exception was received on 1 January 1941. It came not from wireless interception but from decrypted Italian diplomatic traffic. Bletchley Park produced a message from the Italian embassy in Washington instructing the Italian minister in Dublin that he could use the facilities for radio communication possessed by Hempel to send specially secret or urgent messages. This was the sort of cryptographic 'golden egg' so relished by Churchill. A member of the Dominions Office minuted with some satisfaction: 'This appears to afford definite evidence of what we had previously suspected, but of which we here at any rate have no proof, that the Germans have effective wireless communication between Dublin and Berlin.'[50] Unfortunately, the 'most secret' nature of the source meant that this evidence could not be acted on. It was only two months later that alternative proof was obtained: listening stations in Britain finally intercepted the German transmitter and were able to use direction-finding to locate it in a triangle around Dublin.[51] The matter could now be brought to the attention of the Irish government and a demand made for the transmissions to be stopped.

The Irish authorities had always reassured Maffey that there was no reason to suspect the existence of a transmitter in the German legation, so Walshe was 'very disturbed' when presented with evidence that proved otherwise on 14 March 1941.[52] The British expected the Dublin government to secure the removal of the transmitter and to set up a wireless detection service in collaboration with their technical experts. However, over the next six months Walshe went no further than passing a half-hearted warning to Hempel, which led the German Minister to curtail, but not stop, his transmissions. Walshe was also evasive in discussions with Maffey, who suspected the Irish of not 'playing quite straight' with him.[53] As for the proposed wireless detection service, MI5 offered in June 1941 to supply the technical equipment and trained personnel that Colonel Archer claimed was necessary to locate the German transmitter, but this offer was repulsed by the new G2 head, Colonel Dan Bryan, with the excuse that Walshe was on leave and he (Bryan) knew nothing about the matter.[54] The British heard nothing for over two months, and the 'Dublin link' temporarily ceased functioning.

Maffey thought the situation 'most unsatisfactory' and warned the Irish that there would be a 'violent reaction in London' unless they took steps to remove this threat to British interests.[55] The intelligence services in London were even more appalled by the 'cavalier' Irish attitude. 'We have sent the Eire Government through you a great deal of technical information to assist them in the location of this wireless', Colonel Vivian fumed to the Dominions Office, 'and you will no doubt agree that we should not sit down under the sort of treatment that Walshe has meted out to the British Government in this matter.' He wanted to know exactly what the Irish had done to suppress the transmitter. His suspicions were magnified by information, probably from the covert SIS network, that Walshe and Maffey had holidayed with their families at the same hotel in Waterville, Co. Kerry – the two men were 'on the friendliest terms'.[56] MI5 later acknowledged that this case was 'a good example of the limitations of the Security Service link with Colonel Archer, and its control by political superiors'.[57] It drove SIS to consider starting a clandestine wireless detection service in Ireland, although the proposal was dropped because it would be impossible to hide from the Irish authorities.[58]

Vivian was completely justified in his suspicion of the Irish attitude. Indeed, the truth was worse than he thought: G2 had deliberately withheld information from MI5. When the British had first raised the matter of a German transmitter in early 1941, G2 had formed a special signals section and succeeded in locating the set in the legation building. But the Department of External Affairs instructed Colonel Archer to tell the British nothing, despite the latter's persistent pleas for information. Archer's action in feigning ignorance when Guy and Cecil Liddell visited in May 1941 was, therefore, entirely duplicitous.[59] There were a number of reasons for this attitude. First, although G2 was happy to share information about Abwehr operations, it was far more reticent about the activities of the German legation, as it was feared that evidence of wrongdoing would be used by the British to demand its expulsion, thus endangering Irish neutrality. The German diplomats were given a measure of protection. In addition, the unhelpful Irish attitude must be understood in the context of the fluctuating course of the war. Colonel Bryan recalled that 'this incident happened at a period when the Germans after being victorious in the West now looked like being victorious in the East and totally defeating the Russians. This state of affairs undoubtedly had its effect on External Affairs.' According to Bryan, there was much truth in a comment Sir John Maffey made at this time: 'Sure, you have no use going to those people for certain things while they are convinced the Germans have won the war.'[60]

To London's great relief, the difficulties did not persist: in the autumn the Irish authorities proved far more co-operative. On 10 November 1941 Bryan travelled to London for his first meeting as head of G2. He informed the Liddells that the German transmitter had been located and was under constant observation. In response, Colonel Stratton of the Radio Security Service (RSS) visited Dublin in December. He discovered that the Irish technical staff were aware of the location of the German transmitter and were keeping a twenty-four hour watch on it. After agreeing to supply the latest wireless detection equipment to Dublin, he made arrangements for co-operation between the two countries (which continued until after the war). In effect, the Irish Signal Corps agreed to provide RSS with an additional monitoring service in Ireland, sending reports of all intercepted transmissions, while RSS agreed to share its expertise. Almost a year after the German set was first discovered, the British finally had their desired liaison with the Irish wireless detection service.[61] In addition, the end of 1941 saw the resolution of the other major problem that worried British intelligence – the elusiveness of Hermann Görtz. The handling of the Görtz case healed the rift in the 'Dublin link' and heralded a phase of much deeper intelligence co-operation between MI5 and G2.

The arrangements made in December 1941 ensured that German transmissions would be closely monitored, but they did not stop them; the threat of leakage of operational information was therefore still high. Consequently, the British prepared to make a formal demand for the wireless to be removed. The *casus belli* was the escape of the German battleships *Gneisenau* and *Scharnhorst* and the cruiser *Prinz Eugen* through the English Channel in February 1942. The ships took advantage of a storm to evade pursuers at sea and in the air. Advance weather information was vital to this enterprise, and the British press claimed that this information had been sent by wireless from the German legation in

Dublin. This generated another public debate over the threat posed by Irish neutrality. In a way, these accusations were correct. The RSS detected that, after a two-month silence, Hempel used the transmitter on 11 February to transmit a seventy-word message to Berlin; a year later, GC&CS was able to show that this was a weather report. However, it was confirmed after the war that the legation did not play a crucial role, as the weather information had already been supplied by Luftwaffe aircraft on reconnaissance in the Atlantic.[62] Nonetheless, the British immediately protested to the Irish authorities, who summoned the German Minister, told him that the set would be confiscated if any further messages were sent, and warned that this would probably lead to a diplomatic break. The Irish threat had the desired effect: Hempel never used the transmitter again, although he continued to receive inward traffic and was at times urgently instructed to reply.[63]

By the beginning of 1942 Britain had taken effective steps to limit the amount of information reaching southern Ireland, to investigate suspected German espionage agents and to prevent valuable intelligence from being transmitted abroad. As a result, it is possible to detect a change in British assessments of the espionage threat in Ireland. The information emerging from the Görtz interrogation cast doubt on the notion of a sophisticated German network at work in the country: Görtz had been shunned by the German legation, he did not link up with any other German agents, and his attempts to create an intelligence service achieved little. The British intelligence community also developed a more accurate perception of the role of the German legation. When MI5 was asked for evidence implicating Hempel in spying in February 1942, Cecil Liddell prepared a memorandum that showed 'fairly conclusively that the German Legation, as such, is not actively engaged in espionage, although it may be cognisant of what is going on.'[64] In August 1942 Cecil Liddell went further, telling intelligence chiefs that they had 'no evidence that the Germans had set up an information-gathering organisation in southern Ireland or that the Germans had better communications with southern Ireland than with the United Kingdom.'[65] In the early years of the war, London had assumed that a vast German spy network, centred on the German legation in Dublin, was using neutral Ireland to collect information from the United Kingdom. By 1942 this myth had been debunked.

The final proof emerged after January 1943, when GC&CS broke the high-grade German diplomatic cipher. (The codename for this new material was Pandora.) The British could henceforth read all the cables passing between Hempel and Berlin, and would be able to read any wireless messages that Hempel might send. Moreover, as all previous cables and radio messages had been carefully stored for this day, GC&CS set about decrypting Hempel's traffic since 1940.[66]

This gave a complete and mostly reassuring picture of the activities of the German legation. SIS concluded:

> Hempel's policy is definitely <u>not</u> to allow the German Legation to run any organised system of military espionage, or indeed to have <u>any</u> contact with German espionage agents, which might lead the British Government to demand the ejection of the Legation. Similarly, and for the same reason, he begs the German Government not to send further agents ... to Eire for the purpose of exploiting the extremist I.R.A.[67]

After January 1943 the British intelligence community could breathe a lot easier as far as Ireland was concerned, because the last unknown had been removed from the Irish security situation: Britain now controlled and read all of the German legation's communications. Moreover, because of the depth of co-operation between MI5 and G2, London was now confident that the Anglo-Irish security apparatus would be capable of uncovering any new espionage operations that Germany might attempt.

The Irish diving bell

EVEN after MI5 concluded that neutral Ireland was not a base for sophisticated German espionage, rumours of nefarious German plots in Ireland, and among Irish residents in Britain, continued to reach the British government. All were diligently investigated. Faced with fewer real threats, and possessing a well-developed security system, the British could devote impressive resources to addressing the smallest risks. The Special Branch and local police forces stepped up their surveillance of potential IRA members in Britain. The clandestine SIS operation in Ireland reached its peak. MI5 deepened its intelligence relationship with G2, which was henceforth willing to share information unreservedly in an effort to prove that Irish neutrality was not a threat to the Allies: according to one historian, 'from 1942 on, Irish security policy proved to be the cornerstone of military neutrality'.[68] Between 1942 and 1944 MI5 and SIS built up records on hundreds of Irish citizens and foreign residents who might consider working for the Axis. There was no complacency, because British counter-intelligence was preparing for its greatest test: maintaining the secrecy of the planned Allied invasion of France.

Part of the British counter-espionage effort was directed at Irish residents in Britain, whose numbers were swelled by the influx of wartime workers. In early 1942 MI5 became briefly concerned about the IRA organisation in Britain. This was prompted by the Görtz case, which gave the first '100 per cent evidence' of tangible German-IRA co-operation.[69] The Special Branch and local police forces were confident that the IRA in Britain had been broken up and posed little threat, but MI5 believed that the police were 'inclined to be complacent.' Guy Liddell wrote:

> They regard the I.R.A. purely as a sabotage organisation and provided pillar-boxes are not catching fire and so on, they do not feel that they are called upon to investigate matters too closely. They ignore the possibility of the I.R.A. being used as an espionage organisation.[70]

MI5 advanced the hypothesis that, on the outbreak of the war, the Germans had instructed the IRA to stop its bombing campaign and 'go to ground', so that its members could take up legitimate jobs and concentrate on collecting military information in Britain. In support of this view they dug out information from the 1920s regarding IRA espionage on behalf of the Soviets and Germans. Lord Rothschild, the head of MI5's counter-sabotage section, even suggested that IRA men might be preparing to commit acts of sabotage in Britain.[71] These were grave risks because, despite warnings to the armed services and the Ministry of Supply, MI5 was unable to enforce the principle that Irish workers should not be employed on 'secret contracts'. Irishmen were found working in aircraft assembly shops and around critical naval bases during 1942.[72]

A major conference – attended by the Home Office, MI5, the Special Branch, the RUC and police Chief Constables – was held on 10 April 1942 to discuss this issue. Sir Norman Kendal of the Special Branch continued to give an optimistic analysis of the situation, but he agreed to tighten up security. Instructions were issued to police to safeguard explosive stores, and immigration officers were told to look out for 'Irishmen of the intellectual type posing as labourers or industrial workers'.[73] In addition, the Home Office provided a special fund that local police forces could use to recruit extra informers among the Irish community, a procedure that had been used at the height of the bombing campaign in 1939.[74]

MI5's concerns were partly caused by ignorance. In 1931 Sir Vernon Kell had agreed to leave IRA matters in the hands of the Special Branch, and MI5 had stayed well away from this subject ever since; MI5 officers therefore had little knowledge of the IRA.[75] They were also inclined to doubt the competence of the police. They suspected that the Special Branch did not use modern intelligence techniques such as telephone taps and bugging. Moreover, Guy Liddell pointed out that the police dealt with the IRA only in so far as its members transgressed the law; there was no effort to study it as a 'movement', or to discover its organisation and aims. MI5 had supplied this need in the cases of communism and fascism, and now Liddell suggested that it should do the same for the IRA:

'It seems questionable whether in time of war we, as the Security Service, can entirely divest ourselves of responsibility for the activities of what may perhaps be the most dangerous subversive movement that we have in this country.' This was a veiled attempt to take over the last major piece of domestic security that remained in the hands of the Special Branch. It was predictably blocked by the officers of New Scotland Yard, who jealously guarded their turf.[76] (It was not until 1992 that MI5 finally gained responsibility for Irish republican terrorism in Britain.) In any case, MI5's attention drifted away, as increased police surveillance produced no evidence to support its alarming hypotheses about the IRA.

The British intelligence community devoted more energy to investigating individuals in southern Ireland who might be involved in German espionage. One group consisted of suspected 'renegades' – disloyal Allied citizens or officials who had access to military secrets. This included Flight Sergeant Michael Joseph Joyce, an RAF officer and cousin of the infamous Lord Haw Haw, who visited his family home in Co. Mayo at the end of 1942 after escaping from a German prisoner of war camp. London feared that he might give away information on MI9 escape routes in Europe. Another suspect, an official of the Ministry of Aircraft Production, was rumoured to receive visits from members of the German legation when visiting his home in Co. Kildare.[77] A particularly dangerous individual was Francis Hurley-Beresford, a former worker at a De Havilland aircraft factory in Britain. He obtained an exit permit on false pretences, claiming he had a sick mother in Northern Ireland, and then travelled with his wife to Dublin, where he remained for the rest of the war. Though his real object was to avoid conscription, SIS suspected that he had brought plans from De Havilland and wished to supply them to the German legation.[78] The Stubbs agency investigated all these men at the request of Captain Collinson, but found no evidence of treachery. Moreover, the Irish authorities demonstrated their ability to prevent information reaching the Germans: one of the few 'renegades' who did approach the German legation, the Dutch sailor Jan Van Loon, was quickly detected and interned.[79]

British intelligence also scrutinised scores of suspects in southern Ireland who might be collecting information from unsuspecting visitors from the United Kingdom. The most obvious culprits were Axis nationals living in southern Ireland. Almost every member of the small German, Austrian and Italian communities was subject to enquiry by the SIS network, or by MI5 working through G2. For example, Captain Collinson made enquiries into two Dublin cafés owned by the Italians Olimpio and Ernesto Nardone after he was told that they were 'being used as a clearing house for espionage reports for the Axis Legations'.[80] Collinson was on firmer ground when he ordered enquiries into Ernst Weber-Drohl, the circus strongman turned Abwehr agent who had landed in Ireland in February 1940. Since then, Weber-Drohl had revived his strongman act, toured the provinces and fathered another illegitimate child. Although no longer working for the Abwehr, he was finally interned in August 1942 when the Irish authorities learnt (probably from Görtz) that he had illicitly arrived by submarine.[81]

In 1943 SIS became preoccupied with a number of *femmes fatales* who were suspected of extracting information from hapless British and American servicemen. At least five Irish women were investigated. The most exotic was Mary Dunne (whose married name was Mrs Brady). A former employee of the notoriously republican Irish Hospital Sweepstakes, Dunne mixed with a 'bad set' and was on good terms with members of the Axis legations. According to SIS, she had 'the reputation of being an enemy agent' who took pains 'to contact and become intimate with' members of British forces when they were on leave in Dublin and in Northern Ireland. An SIS report described her as:

> Age about 30. Height 5' 8". Hair partly brown and partly blonde effect from bleaching. Eyes brown and closely set – she also knows how to use them. Nose long and irregular at bridge; features irregular and attractive ... Dunne is reported to be an acute and systematic observer and very interested in personalities. Can drink and make love. She also discusses military subjects, mostly those of Eire. Avoids continental travel topics.

An SIS agent learnt from a woman who shared a house with Dunne that the latter was frequently visited by men of a rough type: it was 'thought rather odd that anyone of her attractive appearance should not be able to get hold of something better'. The visits did not last long and the same men rarely returned: over forty had passed through her doors.[82] The threat from women such as Dunne also preoccupied American military officers in Northern Ireland and was the subject of a somewhat hysterical press campaign in the United States. From the stories in American newspapers, G2 wryly noted, 'it would appear that the simple Irish "colleen" has exchanged her green shawl for the black cloak of the spy and spends her time eliciting information from unsuspecting "doughboys".[83] The simpler explanation was that prostitution flourished in Dublin because of the large numbers of American and British servicemen visiting on leave.[84]

The British intelligence community also continued to investigate suspect Irish politicians and civil servants. Of the potential Quislings identified in 1941, both Dan Breen and Frank Aiken repeatedly featured in British intelligence reports in later years. In January 1942 the British received information that Breen was a paid German agent, who had been given a list of questions on military and political topics.[85] After discovering that he was 'a frequent caller' after dark to the home of Thomsen (the Counsellor of the German legation), an SIS agent was 'put on it as a special job to watch the house'.[86] These suspicions were confirmed when the British secured a copy of a letter from Breen, congratulating the Führer on his birthday and hoping that Hitler would live long 'to lead Europe on the road to peace, security and happiness'.[87] Jane Archer, who included a section on Breen in her bi-monthly report on Irish affairs on 1 September 1943, referred to him as 'a paid Intelligence officer of the German Legation'.[88] All the British suspicions about Aiken were confirmed after the German diplomatic code was broken in January 1943: the British discovered a message from Hempel to Berlin that warmly praised the Irish minister as 'in the highest degree a supporter of Germany'.[89] The British were also aware of the unsavoury activities of two Irish diplomats in continental Europe. Charles Bewley, a former Irish minister to Berlin, established himself in Rome, worked on behalf of a German propaganda organisation and offered his services to the Nazi party's security service (the Sicherheitsdienst); he was arrested by the Allied authorities on 17 June 1945 and interned for six months. Leopold Kerney, the Irish minister in Madrid, assisted and concealed the Abwehr's release of Frank Ryan, and had inappropriate discussions with Nazi officials in 1942 and 1943; after discovering these contacts, British intelligence placed him on its Black List.[90] Although the British were confident that the increasingly benevolent Irish government desired an Allied victory, they realised that there were elements within the political élite that retained sympathy for Germany.

During 1942 the Abwehr, while failing to land any agents in Ireland, continued to plan intelligence operations with an Irish angle. Much of its effort surrounded an ill-fated 'Irish Brigade', which the Germans tried to recruit among Irish prisoners of war (just as Sir Roger Casement had attempted in the First World War). Of two hundred Irishmen who joined a special camp set up at Friesack, twelve eventually volunteered for intelligence work but only one, James O'Neill, actually embarked on a mission to Ireland. He did not stay loyal to his new handlers for long; after being brought to the Spanish border he immediately presented himself to British intelligence officers in Madrid. G2 and MI5 worked together to gather intelligence on the members of the Irish Brigade, before the Germans abandoned it as a failure in September 1942.[91]

The Abwehr next tried to exploit Irish merchant shipping, which was one of the few ways to by-pass the tight controls over Ireland's external communications. The German conquests in 1940, and the withdrawal of British-owned vessels from Irish trade in 1941, reduced the number of ships visiting Ireland to a trickle. However, a small number of ships owned by the Irish government traded with the Iberian peninsula. Because Spain and Portugal were important centres of German espionage, the Irish shipping service was a perfect channel for the communication of information to the Germans. In July 1941 and March 1942 decrypted Abwehr messages (Isos) showed that the Germans were interested in smuggling passengers on board these ships and obtaining information from Irish crews. The threat came to the fore in April 1942, when Charles McGuinness, the most successful IRA gunrunner in Germany in 1921 and now a Chief Petty Officer in the Irish Marine Service, approached the German legation, offering to supply information on Allied shipping and to assist the escape of Axis nationals from Ireland. His letter to the German legation was intercepted by the Irish postal censorship, and he was sentenced to seven years' imprisonment. Details of this case were supplied to MI5. SIS also tracked it with interest.[92]

Britain was able to exercise some control over Ireland's maritime trade, for Irish ships had to obtain a special certificate (a 'navicert') before departing and were examined at English ports on their outward and inward journeys. Yet it was impossible to search every ship so thoroughly that every hidden document would be found, and a crew-member could always carry messages by memory. Therefore the British relied heavily on the Irish authorities to root out any ill-disposed individuals among these crews. From the end of 1941 G2 placed informants onboard and ensured that all passengers and crew were searched before departure. Later, it was agreed that navicerts would not be issued to ships until their crew-lists were vetted by the British Permit Office in Dublin – this was another matter in which Anglo-Irish security co-operation became complete.[93]

Even with these precautions, evidence that the Abwehr in Portugal was exploiting Irish shipping surfaced in February 1943. It came almost simultaneously from two different sources. First, Isos decrypts showed that German intelligence in Lisbon had received a cipher message from a cook on the ss *Edenvale*, Christopher Eastwood. The same information came from the SIS station in Lisbon. In a remarkable piece of bad luck, the individual whom Eastwood had selected to carry his message, a Portuguese named Tomas, happened to be an SIS agent. Tomas took the message straight to his British handlers and gave them all Eastwood's subsequent correspondence for photographing. G2 and MI5 decided to allow the traffic to run on, so they could watch developments and discover the identities of the conspirators. They learnt that the messages, written in a cipher used by Görtz, originated with Joseph Andrews, one of Görtz's helpers before his capture. Andrews was promiscuous in his liaisons with the intelligence services of the great powers: he sold information on the international Sweepstakes organisation to the Americans in the late 1930s, unsuccessfully offered his services to the British in 1939, worked with Görtz for much of 1941 and then betrayed the German agent and his radio operator, Anthony Deery, to the Irish authorities. Having mastered Görtz's code, Andrews decided to approach the Abwehr, using Eastwood as a courier. He offered to create a grandiose organisation in southern Ireland to further the German cause. However, despite receiving £100 from the Germans, Andrews did little to fulfil his promises.[94] Colonel Bryan later concluded that Andrews was 'an astute and plausible rogue without any fixed convictions ... mainly actuated by a desire to obtain money rapidly'.[95] SIS referred to him as 'a habitual double-crosser'.[96] MI5 and G2 watched the exchanges until the SIS agent, Tomas, was compromised in August 1943. It was then decided to 'close down the traffic'. Andrews and Eastwood were arrested, their homes searched, and Andrews was interned for the rest of the war.[97]

The Andrews-Eastwood case is significant because it demonstrates the extent of co-operation between G2 and MI5. The two organisations were not simply exchanging information: they were running a joint counter-intelligence operation. This was most apparent in the deciphering of the communications, which was chiefly due to the Irish. The Görtz cipher defeated the mighty Bletchley Park (although it is possible that no great resources were directed at the problem) but was mastered by Dr Richard Hayes, the Director of the National Library in Dublin and G2's cryptographic expert. 'His gifts in this direction amounted almost to genius', Cecil Liddell eulogised. However, the Abwehr key words necessary to read the messages were only possessed by the British. The 'Dublin link' reached a new degree of co-operation when the Irish invited MI5 to bring over an expert, who, armed with the key words, was able to read the messages. Cecil Liddell recorded:

> The real Irish co-operation in this was that they voluntarily agreed to allow the messages to run on, and enabled the British to read them without knowing what they might reveal or what Irish nationals might be compromised; in fact the messages did indicate that the G.O.C. of the 2nd Division of the Eire, who was well known to be anti-British and pro-German, had been in touch with Goertz before his arrest. It need hardly be said that no allusion was ever made to this by either side. There is no doubt that this co-ordination was largely due to Colonel Bryan's enthusiasm as an intelligence officer and to Dr Hayes' cryptographic zeal. It is very doubtful if his military superiors agreed to the passing of the ciphers to the British and certainly his political superiors would not have done so.[98]

The breaking of this cipher yielded further dividends over the coming months. G2 detected attempts by Görtz to communicate with Germany from captivity, intercepted the messages and deceived the agent into making a comprehensive eighty-page report on his earlier activities in Ireland. G2 passed a full copy to

MI5, again with no reservations about what this might reveal about Görtz's eighteen months at liberty.[99]

The Andrews–Eastwood case represented the last significant Abwehr involvement in Ireland during the war. During 1943 there was a power shift in the German intelligence system. Tainted by innumerable mission failures, a handful of defections to the Allies and suspected intrigues against Hitler, the Abwehr was gradually displaced as Germany's foreign intelligence-gathering agency by the Nazi party's security service – the Sicherheitsdienst or SD. Disregarding the history of intelligence blunders, the SD aggressively sought to infiltrate agents into Ireland.

The SD chose two Irishmen for this task: John O'Reilly and John Kenny. By a strange quirk, O'Reilly's father, a sergeant in the Royal Irish Constabulary, had been associated with a more famous German covert operation earlier in the century: he was part of the patrol that arrested Roger Casement after he landed from a U-boat in 1916. This earned him a lifetime nickname, 'Casement O'Reilly'. His son emigrated to Britain, where he briefly studied for the priesthood, and then moved to Jersey to work as a potato harvester. After German troops occupied the island he cultivated good relations with the new rulers and became a familiar voice on Germany's Irish radio service, before offering his services for intelligence work. Kenny, another agricultural labourer on Jersey, was selected to join the mission because he had been expelled from Britain for IRA activities in 1940. A man of 'limited education and limited intelligence', he was entirely unsuited to the task. O'Reilly landed by parachute on 16 December 1943, and Kenny three days later. Despite being native Irishmen, they suffered the same fate as many other German agents – within 24 hours each was in Garda custody. G2 provided full details to London, and MI5 took an active part in the interrogation of the two men, supplying G2 with background information and questions, and receiving full interrogation reports in return. MI5 was also supplied with the results of Dr Richard Hayes' successful attempt to understand O'Reilly's code and cipher systems.[100]

The O'Reilly–Kenny mission marked the final intervention of any German intelligence service in Ireland. It could not have come at a worse time for Eduard Hempel. The Allies were pressing the Irish government to expel the Axis legations, and the landing of these two agents, a flagrant transgression of Irish neutrality, provided powerful ammunition. A furious Hempel made his feelings known to the German Foreign Ministry, which was equally angry because it had been unaware of the SD operation. Fearing that any further incidents would drive Ireland into the Allied camp, Ribbentrop ordered both the SD and the Abwehr to a meeting and placed a ban on any further intelligence activities in the country.[101] SIS was aware of these developments: by early 1944 it had 'reliable independent evidence that the German Military Intelligence have received orders strictly forbidding operations directed against Ireland'.[102]

During 1942 and 1943 all the investigations of suspected German espionage in Ireland had reassuring outcomes. Yet Britain intensified its counter-intelligence operations as it prepared for one of the most decisive events of the Second World War in June 1944: Operation Overlord, the Allied invasion of France. The timing and location of Operation Overlord was the greatest secret of the whole war. On this rested the fate of tens of thousands of lives and the outcome of the entire struggle. Allied planners were adamant that if the Germans got 48 hours notice of the attack, it would probably fail; any more notice and it would definitely fail.[103] An enormous effort was expended in preventing information leaking to Germany. Furthermore, the Allies did not simply deny information to the enemy; they actively supplied misinformation. They mounted the most elaborate and successful campaign of deception in history to convince the Germans that the attack would come in the Calais region, far from Normandy. This relied on an array of dummy installations, false wireless traffic and double agents. It required an absolute control of the channels by which information could pass to the enemy, as any leakage could destroy the deception. Matched only by the neutral legations in London, the greatest perceived threat to the security of Operation Overlord was neutral Ireland. Its Axis legations were perilously close to the zone of preparations. Thousands of Irish workers were employed on Overlord-related contracts, including the construction of the top secret 'Mulberry' harbours, floating temporary structures that would be used in the D-Day landings.[104] By this time British intelligence chiefs had a fairly sound appreciation of the threat of leakage through Ireland and were confident that, with the help of the Irish authorities, they would be able to prevent it. But the stakes were so high that they were determined to close every possible channel.

The greatest danger in Ireland was undoubtedly the radio transmitter still held in the German legation. Though Hempel had not used it since 11 February 1942, there was always the danger that he would resume transmission if he received a vital piece of intelligence. Pandora decrypts in late 1942 and early 1943 revealed that Hempel was in almost constant consultation with Berlin on the subject of devising methods of camouflage for his transmitter, so that he would be able to use it without detection. These discussions also revealed that Hempel was willing to use the radio transmitter without camouflage to communicate information of 'vital importance', even if this resulted in the expulsion of the German legation from Ireland. Warning of an Allied invasion of France qualified as this sort of information.[105]

Worryingly, in the spring of 1943, Pandora decrypts also revealed that Hempel was 'ready to show a greater activity in espionage matters'.[106] With Irish neutrality assured and Abwehr operations prohibited, he agreed to Berlin's instructions to collect 'any possible scraps of information bearing on the British war effort and future military operations'.[107] Hempel's telegrams to Berlin in 1943 and early 1944 contain references to a few 'trusted' and 'reliable' informants: for example, he became 'deeply involved' with an Irishman, 'an intelligent military personage' with connections in England, who speculated on the location of the Allied landing in Europe; he obtained material from an individual in Northern Ireland 'with specialist knowledge' of troop movements; he received two anonymous documents on the composition of the British Home Fleet and the presence of an American airborne division in the south of England. In January 1944 there was a 'considerable increase' in the espionage material forwarded by Hempel. According to SIS, it was 'quite clear' that Hempel was 'using one or more of his "absolutely reliable friends" systematically to extract and note in detail information from Irish workmen, soldiers and others on leave in Ireland from Britain'. This was the first sign that a German system for gleaning information from indiscreet travellers might exist after all. Hempel's activities did not cause undue concern, because the material sent to Berlin was 'poor and scanty', generally little more than 'current gossip in Dublin'. It was often contradictory, and in many cases misleading.[108] However, there was always a chance that Hempel would stumble across some important piece of intelligence relating to Operation Overlord.

There was a long debate in London during 1943 about how to address this threat. In April SIS drew up a detailed memorandum arguing that the Irish government should be pressed to confiscate the German transmitter.[109] MI5 and the Dominions Office were consulted, Maffey was briefed on the Pandora secret, and the SIS memorandum was presented to Churchill. In the end the Deputy Prime Minister and Secretary of State for Dominion Affairs, Clement Attlee, persuaded his colleagues to take no action. At that time Britain and America were working towards a diplomatic move that would bring about a total expulsion of the enemy legations – the presence of the German transmitter would be a useful lever.[110] However, in the autumn MI5 raised this issue more forcefully, and argued that the risks of inaction were too great. At a high-level meeting on 4 November 1943, MI5 asserted:

> while the chances of HEMPEL obtaining vital information as to the 'when and where' of forthcoming operations were perhaps small, nevertheless if he did obtain such information and pass it to Berlin, the results might be

so disastrous that ... we should not take the risk of this happening however small the chances might be.

The arguments of MI5 and SIS convinced British politicians that they should approach the Irish government with a formal request to remove the transmitter.[111]

There was some doubt within the Dominions Office about whether de Valera would accept the British demand. At this point MI5's 'Dublin link' again showed its worth. As with the first Archer–Liddell meeting in May 1940, it acted as a military back channel by which sensitive matters could be discussed and resolved. On 4 November 1943 Cecil Liddell visited Dublin and was invited to dinner by General McKenna, the Irish Chief of Staff. In the course of a long talk Liddell expressed his concerns about the possibility that information on the forthcoming invasion might be sent via the German wireless transmitter. General McKenna was sympathetic, saying that 'it might mean the loss of thousands of lives, and that if there should ever be a suspicion that the leakage of information had occurred in this way, the relations between the two countries, Eire and Britain, would be put back a hundred years.' Somewhat improperly, Liddell informed McKenna about the proposed *démarche* involving the German transmitter. Following this conversation McKenna put the British case to de Valera. The Irish were therefore amenable when Maffey was authorised to raise the matter formally. Any lingering resistance was dispelled by the landing of O'Reilly and Kenny, which gave the Irish a pretext to demand the handover of the transmitter. Hempel relinquished the set on 22 December 1943 and it was placed in the vaults of a Dublin bank. This removed the final major threat to British security in neutral Ireland. Hempel could now only communicate with Berlin by telegram; the British controlled and read this traffic and, if necessary, could stop any messages that contained useful intelligence.[112]

Despite this positive development, in the spring of 1944 the British government adopted a number of additional measures to prevent leakage of information to and from Ireland. On 15 March normal travel between Britain and Ireland (north and south) was suspended. This was accompanied by intensified postal censorship and (from 6 April) a total ban on all telephone calls between the two countries. The other aspect of British policy was to cut Ireland off from the rest of the world, which led to the closing of the few channels by which communication was still possible. The shipping service that operated between Ireland and the Iberian peninsula was stopped. Aer Lingus flights between Dublin and Liverpool were suspended. Steps were taken to control diplomatic communication from Ireland: cables from the German legation incurred a six-day delay, and all diplomatic telegrams and pouches emanating from Ireland, including those from the Dublin government, were subject to British censorship. The sweeping scale of these security measures was epitomised by the new metaphor introduced by the Prime Minister; instead of the 'ringed fence', it was decided to turn Ireland into a 'diving bell', completely sealed from the outside world.[113]

The neutering of the German legation and the imposition of 'diving bell' security measures meant that the British intelligence community was confident that neutral Ireland did not pose much threat to the security of Operation Overlord. Yet on 21 and 22 February 1944 the Americans and British handed diplomatic notes to the Irish government demanding the expulsion of the Axis legations, on the grounds that they posed a serious risk to Allied security – the 'American Note' incident. This has the appearance of a striking contradiction. It implies that the American and British governments did believe that the Axis legations were a serious threat after all. How can this be reconciled with the confident assertion by British intelligence that the opposite was the case?

To understand the American Note it is necessary to understand the history of US intelligence involvement in Ireland. Before 1942 American intelligence on Ireland had been amateur and unreliable. The United States of America did not have a foreign intelligence organisation or a centralised intelligence apparatus; therefore the American diplomatic service played a more active role in the collection of intelligence.[114] In the case of Ireland, this meant the Minister in Dublin, David Gray, and a series of military attachés. Gray at first developed good relations with the Irish government and was not overly gripped by fifth column hysteria, but as American pressure for the ports intensified he developed a marked antipathy towards his hosts and became increasingly obsessed with the danger of Axis and IRA subversion.[115] Even more alarmist reports were provided by the military attachés stationed in Dublin. For example, Major J. W. Wofford was of the opinion that there was enough pro-German sentiment in the country 'for fruitful fifth column activities' in the event of an invasion by Germany. His successor, Reynolds, was even more concerned, suggesting that the Irish government might throw its lot in with German invaders. It was, of course, assumed that German espionage in Ireland was rampant.[116] These reports shaped the opinions of the armed services in Washington, which were increasingly interested in Ireland but had very little information in their files. By 1942 there was a perception of Ireland as a hotbed of German and IRA intrigue that bears a striking similarity to British assumptions about the Irish fifth column two years before. As in that case, an underdeveloped intelligence system, new to Ireland, took indications of republican and pro-German sentiment as a sign that there was a serious security threat to the Irish government and the Allied war effort.

This changed when the new American intelligence system engaged with Irish affairs. In July 1941 Colonel William 'Wild Bill' Donovan was appointed Co-ordinator of Information in Washington. Almost a year later an American foreign intelligence agency, the Office of Strategic Services (OSS), was created under his direction. Between January 1942 and May 1943 Donovan sent four covert agents to Ireland. Their reports did much to overturn the alarming misconceptions in Washington about German and IRA activities.[117] OSS could never be entirely satisfied with the security situation so long as it had no liaison with the Irish authorities, but this too changed in early 1943. Following an invitation from Joseph Walshe, Colonel Bruce (the head of the OSS office in London) travelled to Dublin on 15 March 1943 to meet Colonel Dan Bryan. Following this meeting, one covert OSS agent, Ervin 'Spike' Marlin, emerged from his cover and became the chief liaison to G2. OSS now had its own 'Dublin link' to match that of MI5. At the same time OSS established a counter-espionage branch (X-2) in London that worked closely with Section V of SIS. An X-2 officer, Hubert Will, took over responsibility for Ireland, received briefings on MI5's 'Dublin link' and the SIS network, and obtained full access to British material.[118] From 1944 the British and American intelligence systems handled Ireland jointly. They both agreed that neutral Ireland posed little security threat.

One historian has argued that the American Note came about because the American State Department formed its opinions on the basis of 'Gray's highly coloured reporting from Dublin', rather than the accurate appraisals of OSS. According to this argument, something similar happened in London, where the reliable assessments of the British intelligence community were 'overridden by the personal views of the Prime Minister'. Thus, the impetus for the note's delivery came from people who 'knew little of the actualities of Irish security cooperation' and who ignored 'the views of the Allied agencies most involved with Irish security ... in favour of a juvenile analysis of the issues'.[119] However, this is a simplification. First, Churchill, albeit reluctantly, did give up his long-held assumptions about German intrigue in Ireland after briefings by MI5: he told the War Cabinet that 'he had examined the Security aspect of leaving the Axis Missions in Dublin' and this showed that they would not be justified in basing the proposed demand for their expulsion 'directly on Security'.[120] The Dominions Office echoed these sentiments:

> From the security point of view, we understand that the view is that there is no special advantage to be obtained from the removal of the German Minister. He is not at the moment a very serious danger so long as the Irish are prepared fully to co-operate with us in taking the necessary precautions.[121]

Gray's views had also moderated since 1942, and he never made any great effort to stress the danger of Axis espionage, except when formulating a case for public consumption. Similarly, the OSS in Washington was satisfied that it had adequately briefed the State Department about actual conditions in Ireland in advance of the initiative.[122] Ultimately, Washington and London, intelligence officers and politicians, all agreed that a demand for the expulsion of the Axis legations was not justified on the grounds of security.

The answer to why the note was presented lies not with security but politics, and in particular domestic American politics: the object of the American Note was to neutralise the Irish-American lobby as a factor in Anglo-American relations. Since the beginning of the war, Roosevelt and Gray had developed their policy towards Ireland with this end in mind: 'our Irish policy', Gray wrote to the president, 'should be conducted primarily with reference to political conditions in America and to the end of protecting the Administration from pressure group attacks on our foreign policy.'[123] Initially they hoped to achieve this by wooing Ireland into the Allied camp. By 1943 this had been given up; instead they sought some way of damning the country in the eyes of Irish-America. Gray wanted to place Ireland's unhelpful behaviour 'on the record ... while the war conditions existed' in order 'to prevent the Irish partition issue being injected into post-war American politics by De Valera and exploited by the subversive elements in America.'[124] After toying with the idea of a formal demand for Irish bases, Gray decided that this could be best achieved through a demand for the expulsion of the Axis legations. Thus the American Note was a political tool designed to break the sympathy of Irish-America with Ireland and ensure that Irish-America would not block post-war co-operation with Britain. Further proof lies in the fact that it was never intended that the Irish government should agree to the demand. Maffey, who supported the initiative, explained to London that 'Mr. Gray's whole plan of campaign' was 'based on the confident expectation of a refusal.'[125]

The American Note *démarche* was successful in terms of its principal aim – influencing Irish-American opinion. British diplomats observed that, when the notes were published in early March, there was 'almost 100 per cent support' for the action in the American press. At a press conference the Secretary of State, Cordell Hull, 'used the old argument that lives of American boys were being endangered', while General Marshall said that the threat of Axis 'spying and sabotage via Dublin' was as bad as in Spain.[126] This was a cue for a general attack in the American and British press on Irish neutrality, and a revival of Dublin's image as a viperous nest of spies.[127] On 22 March 1944 the Foreign Office described with some satisfaction how the American Note removed any lingering sympathy for Ireland among Irish-Americans:

> It has been clear for a long time that the Irish Americans have grown much less interested in Ireland and much less hostile to Britain. The principal factors have been the virtual stoppage of immigration in 1921, the education and assimilation of the youth, the substantial concessions made to Ireland in the Treaty and later agreements and, most recently, our lack of interference with Irish neutrality. The State Department and the American press have now done us a considerable kindness by widening still further the gulf between Mr. de Valera's group in Ireland and their former supporters in the U.S.[128]

This satisfactory assessment held for the rest of the war.[129]

In contrast, the American Note had a most unwelcome impact in Ireland. Instead of demurely receiving the Allied demand, de Valera chose to interpret it as an ultimatum. The army was put on full alert and told to expect an imminent Anglo-American invasion, as rumours to this effect swept the country. De Valera publicly faced down Britain and the United States by publishing the notes and condemning their action as an abuse of Irish sovereignty. The effect was to swell his support in the country, which allowed Fianna Fáil to sweep to victory in a snap election a few weeks later. At the official, inter-governmental level, the Irish were understandably incensed. They had done everything to co-operate with the Allies and to thwart German espionage; they knew that the German legation posed no real threat; and yet here was a brazen attempt to condemn the Irish nation in the eyes of the world. De Valera was 'white with indignation' when he met Gray and Maffey. The Irish reaction took both governments aback, and there was some frantic back-pedalling to ensure that no permanent rupture with Ireland ensued.[130]

These developments caused great unease among British and American intelligence organisations. Both MI5 and OSS had been opposed to the American Note initiative from the start. Not only did they regard the removal of the Axis legations as unnecessary, they regarded the Allied demand as a dangerous political move that might destroy the harmonious relations enjoyed with the Irish authorities: Cecil Liddell recorded that 'the presentation of the American note was regarded with great misgivings by the Security Service who feared that, at a most critical moment, the intelligence co-operation with the Irish might be seriously prejudiced'.[131] The initial Irish reaction indicated that this might be the result. Thus, the American Note, which on the surface was intended to improve Allied security, threatened to do it serious damage.

In fact, Anglo-Irish security collaboration proved more resilient than a diplomatic spat. Although in public de Valera condemned the Allied demand as an abuse of sovereignty, in private the Irish authorities moved to appease any remaining Allied security concerns. Joseph Walshe came to London in April 1944 and expressed a 'desire to eliminate all sources of friction in the future' and a 'readiness to be even more helpful in the sphere of intelligence during the critical months ahead'. The Irish government agreed to implement the 'diving bell' security measures in conjunction with the British. Walshe went one step further, with the suggestion that British and American intelligence officers could be stationed in Dublin to oversee the Irish security effort.[132] This was unnecessary, but it was agreed to hold a three-way security conference in Dublin to see if any further measures were required. On 1 May 1944 Colonel Dan Bryan and Garda Superintendent Carroll met with Cecil Liddell of MI5 and representatives of the American intelligence services. The Irish representatives pledged to increase their vigilance still further: all agreed that what was required was not new measures, but 'an intensification of the measures already in force'.[133] The results were most satisfactory. Sir David Petrie of MI5 told the American ambassador in London that 'the Eire Government is making every effort to co-operate on security measures'. Even Churchill thought that the American Note 'had done great good', because 'it had prompted the Irish to pull their socks up'.[134]

The rigorous security measures imposed by the three governments were wholly successful. GC&CS watched with satisfaction as Hempel's reports to Berlin dwindled in the early months of 1944. In the two-week period covering the Normandy landings, Hempel's cables contained no espionage material whatsoever.[135] Thus, no information pertaining to Operation Overlord leaked to the enemy from Ireland. MI5's handling of the Irish problem was thoroughly vindicated. It had succeeded in achieving Churchill's vision of transforming Ireland into a diving bell, hermetically sealed from the outside world and posing no threat to British security.

Increased Anglo-Irish security co-operation in the lead-up to D-Day was accompanied by a winding down of the clandestine SIS operation in Ireland. Until 1944 Britain had pursued its dual approach of covert activity alongside official collaboration. The SIS network was frequently asked to investigate cases that were already being dealt with by G2 in co-operation with MI5: for example, Captain Collinson instructed the Stubbs agency to collect 'full information' on the Dublin associates of Joseph Andrews (even though this case was run as a joint G2–MI5 operation).[136] However, the value of the SIS operation became questionable. On security matters it usually duplicated the work of G2 and MI5, while producing much less reliable information. In addition, because of the decline in the number of security threats, the SIS network began to report more and more on political matters. On one occasion SIS agents were used to conduct an informal opinion poll, asking fifty unsuspecting persons whether food shortages were attributed to Britain, thus creating anti-British feeling. (Most said no.)[137] The Stubbs agency was also asked to investigate individual politicians.[138] By 1944 Jane Archer's bi-monthly reports dealt mostly with political developments in southern Ireland, containing only minor items on subversive movements or Axis intrigues. The problem was that such political matters were already adequately covered by the reports of the United Kingdom Representative, Sir John Maffey – indeed, this was his primary function. Thus, the clandestine SIS network was somewhat redundant.

The British government also worried that Irish discovery of the SIS network would jeopardise Anglo-Irish co-operation. This was the catalyst for a reorganisation of the SIS network in the spring of 1944. Captain Collinson learnt that some of his men were frequenting hotels, flashing money, and openly boasting that they were 'British S.S. agents'. He believed that, as a result, the Irish authorities had discovered the network (although he still thought that they were unaware that he was 'the hub of the organisation'). Matters came to a head when de Valera made a reference to the British secret service in Ireland after the delivery of the American Note – covert intelligence threatened to cause a diplomatic row. On 21 March 1944 Collinson, acting under orders from London, sent out an instruction that all agent activity was to stop. Six days later he travelled to SIS headquarters in London, where it was decided that the whole organisation would be reorganised 'they were going to weed out the undesirables'.[139]

What started as a reorganisation evolved into a full dismantling of the SIS operation. Between April and August 1944 the majority of the SIS agents were 'demobilised', and there was a general tightening up in regard to expenditure. Collinson gave control of the remaining network to William Podesta, the manager of Stubbs Ltd., and told him 'to get a good man' to take charge of each of five centres – Cork, Limerick, Galway, Clare and Donegal. Podesta was to collect the 'dope' from these agents each week, but he was to keep away from the Permit Office as much as possible.[140] There was further retrenchment after SIS headquarters decided in September 1944 'to reduce their organisation in Eire to the pre-1940 level, but to maintain a small nucleus which would be capable of expansion if necessary'.[141] Collinson was called to London on 5 October and informed that his position would be abolished; he left Dublin for good at the end of the month and took up a position in newly liberated Brussels. A member of the Permit Office, F. C. Savage, took over his duties instead. Queries for the Stubbs agency continued to emanate from SIS, although in much smaller quantities.[142]

The decision to fully close down the SIS operation was finally taken in London in March 1945. SIS wrote to MI5, explaining that the Irish service was no longer necessary because the political information in its QRS reports was already contained in Maffey's despatches, while information on suspects and aliens was covered by MI5's link with G2. Cecil Liddell later recalled that 'SIS felt that neither the present nor future requirements would justify the risks that would be incurred by maintaining the nucleus'. MI5 and the Dominions Office agreed. The involvement of the Secret Intelligence Service in Ireland, dating back to 1932, came to an end.[143]

The manner in which the network was shut down was painful to William Podesta. He was called to a meeting at the Permit Office on 4 April 1945, but Savage did not deign to see him, and instead delegated the task to his assistant, Miss Houston. She bluntly informed Podesta that the organisation was being closed down at the end of the month: Stubbs received the final enquiry from the Permit Office (no. 1882) on 25 April 1945. Apparently Podesta felt 'somewhat aggrieved at the abrupt closing down of the work'. At a lunch two weeks later he received a fuller explanation from Miss Houston. She explained that 'the organisation was closing down' because 'their authorities believed now that both the Government and the people here had swung round in their attitude towards the British'. She said that 'all the files had gone to London' and that they had 'nobody else on this side working for them'. Despite Podesta's exhortations about the necessity for maintaining a network in southern Ireland, she said there was little prospect of its being revived in the future, although 'there was a suggestion that P's organisation would keep their ears to the ground and pass on any information of interest'. Houston added that 'a recommendation was being made and would be backed strongly by the Dublin Office for a handsome present for P. and M. [Podesta and Moore]'. This mollified Podesta somewhat, though it is clear that he felt badly treated after so many years of loyal service. His subordinate Moore, who possessed more complex loyalties, naturally passed full details of these conversations to his G2 handlers, who followed the termination of the British covert operation with great interest.[144]

The reduction and final closing down of the SIS network is significant for two reasons. First, it demonstrates that by the middle of 1944 neutral Ireland was no longer regarded as a serious espionage threat. London was happy that the 'Diving Bell' measures would safeguard the security of Operation Overlord. After the invasion of France, Ireland was even less of a threat, as there were few secrets that Berlin could hope to learn from it.[145] Second, the decision to close down the SIS network was a vote of confidence in the Irish authorities. The British were confident that the Irish government, in conjunction with

MI5, would be able to deal with any remaining threats to the security of the United Kingdom. This brought a reconfiguration of the British intelligence community's relationship with southern Ireland. The dual approach that had persisted since the start of the war – covert intelligence activity in parallel with official intelligence co-operation – was finally abandoned. The link between G2 and MI5 would now serve all Britain's intelligence needs. Consequently MI5 finally usurped SIS as the dominant intelligence agency handling Irish affairs.

T HE popular conception that neutral Ireland was a viperous nest of German agents outlived the Second World War: the notion of 'German spies in Ireland' entered the folklore.[146] However, the reality was very different. This was confirmed when the British intelligence community studied captured German documents and interrogated German officials after the end of the war. MI5 concluded that:

> no single case of espionage or sabotage by the I.R.A. or by the Germans through the I.R.A. is known to have occurred. No complete explanation of this has been given, but it was probably due to the breaking up of the organisation here by the police; to the numerous controls which came into force on the outbreak of war, and to the dissension and lack of funds among the I.R.A. themselves, as well as to the repressive measures taken against them by the Eire and Northern Ireland Governments.

As for the thousands of Irish workers in Britain, some leakage did occur through this channel, but it was 'of little value and more often than not incorrect'. The only explanation for this was that 'the enemy had no organised intelligence service in Eire'.[147] Finally, the oft-expressed fears about the German legation proved to be unfounded. Colonel Vivian wrote:

> The documents do show Hempel complicity in the GÖRTZ case and anxiety to assist his Government by all means in his power. But they also showed how his efforts were circumvented and largely frustrated by our own security arrangements and by De Valera's determination to avoid any complications with the British Government arising out of charges that he was allowing Eire to be used as a base for espionage activities against this country.[148]

A senior Abwehr officer, Major-General Lahousen, told the press as much when asked what satisfaction the German intelligence services had gained from Ireland during the war. 'There was no satisfaction', he curtly replied.[149]

CHAPTER 14

Coming to Terms with Irish Independence

BRITAIN'S intelligence relationship with Ireland had come a long way since 1916. From a rebellious territory, the twenty-six counties had evolved into a state with *de facto* independence. For over two decades the British intelligence system had found it uniquely difficult to handle this transition. This had contributed to frequent reversals of British policy. However, by the middle of the Second World War Britain had developed mature, sophisticated mechanisms for collecting and using Irish intelligence. This not only laid the foundation for wiser policy-making; it also helped bring about a more fundamental change in British perceptions of Ireland.

Poor intelligence had been one of the reasons for Britain's capitulation to Sinn Féin and the loss of southern Ireland during the revolutionary period. The old Irish system, organised around the RIC and DMP, struggled to penetrate republican inner circles before 1918, and was then smashed by an audacious IRA guerrilla campaign. New British agencies and personnel intervened in Irish affairs in a disjointed, ignorant and amateurish way. They lost the covert intelligence war and instead had to resort to overt, indiscriminate intelligence methods, which, though yielding information, alienated the Irish population. Of course, the British intelligence system was also hampered by the misguided decisions of policy-makers in Dublin and London, and the frustration of much of the Irish people at the failure to introduce self-government. The importance of this unfavourable political environment was illustrated by Britain's greater success when dealing with the republican movement outside the twenty-six counties: in Northern Ireland, the British could call on the support of the unionist majority and its new government, which quickly took over responsibility for internal security; republican activities in Britain and abroad were tackled more easily by Britain's established domestic and foreign intelligence system (especially when the new government in Dublin agreed to co-operate on security matters during the Civil War). Yet, as well as suffering the consequences, the British intelligence system bore some responsibility for causing the political failures. It was unable to overturn misconceptions in London and inform policy towards Ireland; indeed, intelligence officers were a chief source of partisan, conspiracy-minded advice, which impeded constructive peace efforts.

After 1923 it became even more difficult for Britain to collect intelligence on Ireland. If the newly formed Free State had been a foreign country, the British government would have been represented by an ambassador, the armed services would have exchanged attachés, and SIS could have chosen to run covert intelligence operations on Irish territory. If it had been a loyal Dominion, MI5 would have formed a link with security officials in Dublin, the police and armed services would have co-operated with their Irish counterparts, and Britain would have been represented by a Governor-General or High Commissioner. But the Irish Free State was somewhere in between, a restless, reluctant Dominion always seeking to distance itself from British control. It fell between the cracks of the British intelligence system. London briefly tried using Northern Ireland as a base to spy on the south; it also turned to a range of *ad hoc*, informal sources of information, especially the Protestant loyalist community in the twenty-six counties. Even when SIS began operations in the Free State in 1932, it was little more than a formalisation of these sources. The problem was that this intelligence was sporadic and subject to political bias. As a result, the British government fluctuated between indifference towards Irish affairs and alarm over Irish security threats – in particular over the threat posed by militant republicans and the IRA.

The weakness of Britain's Irish intelligence meant that politics, prejudices and preconceptions had a strong influence on British policy-making. During the years of the Irish revolution, British officials characterised the Sinn Féin movement as a minor, temporary, unrepresentative phenomenon that could be eradicated – it was a 'German plot', an extension of the 'Red Menace', the work of a 'murder gang' imported from America. By denying Sinn Féin political legitimacy, British politicians did not have to face up to the reality of Irish nationalism. Rather than constructing an imaginative political settlement, they could concentrate on restoring law and order. After the Anglo-Irish Treaty was signed, British perceptions of Ireland became somewhat schizophrenic. One school of thought – the 'liberal imperialists' – held out hopes that southern Ireland would realise its affinity for Britain and return to the imperial fold, settling down as a loyal partner within the empire and possibly wooing Northern Ireland into a united state. At the other end of the spectrum 'diehard unionists' stressed the anarchic and violent qualities of the new southern Irish state, predicted a hostile republican takeover and warned that Irish independence would have a calamitous effect on British security. Underlying this view of Ireland were deeply engrained negative stereotypes of the Irish character, often based on crude racial theories – the Irish were seen as irrational, barbaric and inferior to Anglo-Saxon stock. These stereotypes, and the diehard unionist perspective, though only expressed by a minority in normal times, had a tendency to rise to prominence during periods of crisis in Anglo-Irish affairs.

Throughout its history, Britain had rarely faced as great a national crisis as the Second World War. In the first year of the war the British government suffered from some startling misconceptions about neutral Ireland, centred on the notion of an Irish 'fifth column'. London assumed that the IRA was a potent force that would give major assistance to a German invasion of Ireland. Indeed, this assumption was a reason for the certainty that such an invasion would take place – why else would Germany have gone to such trouble to cultivate a fifth column? In the most fantastic form of these scares, the British believed that hidden IRA saboteurs were waiting to strike in Britain, and that the IRA had sufficient power to mount a revolution against the Irish government, either on its own or with the help of a small German contingent. At the same time London tended to exaggerate the extent and success of covert German activities in neutral Ireland. The Admiralty gave credence to reports that U-boats were being 'succoured' on the coasts; MI5 believed that Ireland was the centre of an elaborate espionage system stretching into the United Kingdom; SIS and the Ministry of Information tended to see Axis propaganda and intrigue behind any manifestations of anti-British feeling in Ireland. Finally, British officials had grave suspicion of the trustworthiness of Irish officials and state institutions, especially the armed forces.

These exaggerated fears were caused by deficiencies in Britain's intelligence relationship with Ireland. Because of its neglect of Ireland during the 1930s the British intelligence system started the war with a poor knowledge of Irish affairs. In the first year of the war Irish intelligence co-operation was neither complete nor fully trusted by British officials. Similarly, British intelligence-gathering in Ireland was in its infancy, and produced as much unfounded rumour as reliable information: the SIS network was the chief culprit and did more than any other source to foster the fifth column panic. This would have had less effect if it were not for the absence of a proper system of intelligence assessment in London. Policy was formed not by objective analysis of the information available but by preconceptions and prejudices. Alarmist scares circulated alongside more sober reports (for example, from Sir John Maffey), and British policy-makers picked the facts that coincided with their preconceptions. They used intelligence the way a drunk uses a lamp post – for support rather than illumination.[1] In the case of Ireland, this allowed the cultural and racial stereotypes about the 'wild Irish' to come to the fore. Assumptions about Irish moral cowardice, political instability, bloodthirstiness and treachery contributed to the fear that an Irish fifth column was preparing to stab Britain in the back.

However, the nadir of British intelligence in Ireland was followed by a rapid, continuous improvement. Britain's first step was to enhance greatly its ability to independently collect intelligence in Ireland. Censorship of communications and movement control yielded a mass of information; the armed services and the Ministry of Information sent undercover representatives and appointed attachés in Dublin; SIS expanded and enhanced its clandestine network, using the Stubbs credit agency to investigate rumours. Many other secret agencies – the Government Code & Cipher School, the Special Operations Executive, MI9, British Security Coordination – engaged in Irish affairs, as the full power of the developing British intelligence system was brought to bear. Second, and more important, the British secured an unprecedented level of co-operation from the Irish authorities. MI5 enjoyed a highly productive relationship with G2 – the 'Dublin link'; the service attachés and other military officers worked closely with the Irish armed forces; the RUC collaborated with the Garda to suppress the IRA. All the British intelligence agencies established much closer relations with the RUC. These sources provided the best intelligence on Irish conditions and potential threats to Allied security. The increased flow of intelligence was matched by an improvement in its analysis and use in London. Departments circulated regular intelligence summaries; the Dominions Office reasserted its position as the ultimate arbiter on Irish political affairs; and the centralised intelligence machinery of the Joint Intelligence Committee produced high-level assessments for policy-makers. As with its earlier failings, the great improvement in Britain's Irish intelligence should be seen in the context of the overall performance of the British intelligence system. By 1942 this had reached impressive heights, with the availability of decrypted Axis communications, the success of the Double-Cross System and the production of sophisticated analyses of enemy intentions.

Britain pursued its twin-track approach of covert intelligence-gathering together with official collaboration until remarkably late in the war, although the balance shifted gradually from the former to the latter. Eventually, the British decided that collaboration with the Irish authorities would satisfy all their security needs, and the SIS network was closed down. This was accompanied by a shift in authority on Irish affairs from SIS to MI5. It could be argued that this shift in responsibility should have occurred much earlier, as SIS activities served little purpose in the latter years. But it took time for the Irish to begin sharing information unreservedly, and it took time for the British to develop the necessary trust. The irony is that Britain's intelligence and security relationship with Ireland turned out to be inversely related to constitutional linkages. In the early 1930s, while the Free State was supposedly a Dominion like any other, Britain enjoyed no intelligence co-operation with Dublin and sanctioned covert activity by SIS; in 1945, when southern Ireland had ripped up the treaty and asserted its independence through neutrality, intelligence co-operation was intimate, the SIS operation had shut down, and MI5 managed Britain's intelligence engagement – just as if it was a loyal Dominion. Britain and Ireland only achieved a mature intelligence and security relationship once they had drifted constitutionally apart.

For over two decades the deficiencies in British intelligence had had a damaging effect on British policy towards Ireland. After failing to suppress the Sinn Féin revolt, Britain struggled to deal with the Boundary Commission crisis in the mid-1920s, de Valera's dismantling of the treaty settlement after 1932 and the need to secure its flank from German subversion and attack when the international situation deteriorated in the late 1930s. During the first year of the Second World War, hysteria over the Irish fifth column brought Anglo-Irish relations close to collapse. But after 1940 the improvements in British intelligence provided a much sounder foundation for wise policy-making.

One of the most important achievements of the British intelligence community was to show that, contrary to popular perceptions, neutral Ireland did not pose a major threat to British security. The intimate collaboration between the British and Irish armed services demonstrated that a German invasion of Ireland would be repulsed; in any case, by the middle of 1941 better strategic intelligence indicated that the chances of such a German attack were remote. British intelligence revealed that there were some groups in Ireland willing to assist the Axis, but they were weak, divided and well controlled by the Irish authorities – the fifth column myth of 1940 was debunked. Intelligence reports also showed that Axis propaganda had made little headway, and that by 1942 Irish public opinion had swung decisively behind the Allied cause. The most difficult challenge thrown up by Irish neutrality – preventing espionage and leakage of information – was met by imposing tight controls on Irish communications and actively investigating every possible risk, again with the full collaboration of the Irish security apparatus. As a result, the dangers that had worried British strategists on the outbreak of the war turned out to be groundless. Neutral Ireland did not provide a suitable base for covert operations against the United Kingdom, nor was it a welcoming 'back door' for enemy attack on Britain.

At the same time, good intelligence helped convince London that the Irish could not easily be coerced out of their policy of neutrality. In 1940 and 1941 intelligence assessments deterred the British from undertaking the ultimate act of aggression – using force to seize Irish ports and air bases. Although British forces might be able to steamroller the ill-equipped Irish army, all reports indicated that the vast majority of people would resist a British invasion, leading to a widespread Irish guerrilla campaign. The Joint Planning Sub-Committee warned in July 1940:

> We are advised ... that any attempt to occupy Eire territory would inevitably provoke the hostility of the Irish. In this event, we should become involved in a Military commitment which might well be greater than that which we expect to undertake against a German invasion. We should, in fact, find ourselves faced with the necessity of occupying the whole of Eire, not only to secure it against invasion but also to suppress a general rising similar to that of 1921.

The same analysis held at the end of 1940, when Churchill ordered the army to plan a move south.[2] The British may have scoffed when the Irish boasted of their expertise at hedge-fighting, but it was this prospect that deterred them from military intervention – the revolutionary war twenty years earlier was a nightmare that the British government was determined not to revisit.

British intelligence assessments also tempered Winston Churchill's eagerness to use diplomatic and economic pressure against Dublin. At the end of 1940 the Prime Minister made public speeches on the need for the ports, fostered a hostile press campaign and instructed that 'no attempt should be made to conceal from Mr. De Valera the depth and intensity of feeling against the policy of Irish neutrality'.[3] Most dangerously, he latched onto an anonymous memorandum from an Irish resident that advocated the use of economic pressure to bring down the Irish government. Although the Dominions Office was sceptical about this tendentious document, which characterised de Valera and his cronies as implacable fanatics, Churchill attempted to make it the basis for a reorientation of British policy.[4] He ordered British officials to prepare a scheme for cutting off Irish supplies that would 'bring De Valera to his knees in a very short time' – the Admiralty referred to it as the plan for 'getting the use of the Eire Treaty Ports by economic pressure'.[5] Behind this scheme lay a brief flirtation with the notion that the Irish people could be cajoled out of neutrality, even if de Valera could not. British ministers began labelling the Irish premier as 'intensely rigid and obstinate', 'temperamentally incapable of concession or compromise'.[6] The decline in concern over the Irish fifth column and the unexpected helpfulness of the Irish armed forces led to a mistaken impression that mainstream Irish opinion might be more amenable to British requests for help – perhaps de Valera and his ministers were the extremists after all? There was a deliberate policy to 'baby' the Irish army, while turning up the heat on Irish political leaders.[7] For a time this combination of wishful thinking and selective use of informal intelligence looked like 1932 all over again.

Unlike 1932, however, the British intelligence and policy-making systems were able to counteract Churchill's impetuous scheme by presenting sound analysis of the likely consequences in Ireland. Maffey insisted that de Valera had wide public support and that economic sanctions would only strengthen his position and generate anti-British feeling. MI5 expressed a similar opinion: 'England has not been successful in coercing the Irish in the past by economic or by other means', Cecil Liddell wrote on 13 February 1941. 'We are even less likely to succeed by these methods now.'[8] Intelligence reports from the Ministry of Information and SIS portrayed a country united behind the policy of neutrality. Coercive measures would not only fail to yield up the ports, they also threatened to end the co-operation that was essential to British security. For these reasons, the proposal for an economic blockade was watered down as it passed through the White-hall machinery. This was much to Churchill's annoyance: 'I hope we shall not fall into the error of becoming too tender-footed in this policy', he complained.[9] But although supplies were gradually cut, the British continued to provide basic commodities and characterised the reductions as the inevitable consequence of shipping losses, not punitive measures.[10]

The brief flirtation with the notion that the Irish people might tolerate British occupation was replaced by a more realistic understanding of the Anglophobic dynamics of Irish opinion. British observers realised that Irish entry into the war might have a dangerous impact on the country's political stability and internal security. From the outbreak of the war de Valera had talked up the IRA threat, compared himself to John Redmond in 1916, and argued that neutrality was the only option for his government, as belligerency would split the country and lead to civil war.[11] During the panic of the summer of 1940 de Valera back-pedalled, assuring the British that the *actual* threat from the IRA fifth column was limited; yet, he still stressed the *potential* threat should neutrality be abandoned. He returned to this theme at the end of 1940, repeating that even if he wished to hand over the ports he could not do so, because it would lead to political turmoil and attacks on British forces.[12] British intelligence on Irish opinion largely supported this argument. For example, Elizabeth Bowen reported that there was 'truth in Mr. de Valera's contention. It would be more than hardship, it would be sheer disaster for this country, in its present growing stages and with its uncertain morale, to be involved in war.'[13] By the end of 1941 the Dominions Office had accepted that 'it would be impossible for [de Valera] to bring a united Ireland into the war, and that there would be a substantial minority which would provide at the worst civil war and at the least determined and continuing sabotage.'

The same argument was given by Cecil Liddell in his post-war report on the MI5 Irish section.[14] It is a thesis that has found much support in recent historical writing. For example, Garret Fitzgerald, writing in the *Irish Times*, evocatively concluded that 'neutrality came from fear of ourselves' – Ireland's stance was as much a product of internal division as national unity.[15]

Good intelligence helped steer British policy off the rocks during the tense months of 1940 and 1941. Together with changes in the strategic situation, it then helped cause a reformulation of British policy at the end of 1941. For the first two years of the war the British government had tried to persuade, entice or coerce southern Ireland to abandon its neutrality. Now British policy-makers questioned whether this was wise. On the one hand, Ireland's entry into the war would produce few benefits for the Allies. The importance of Irish ports and air bases had lessened, because of the development of facilities north of the border and greater American involvement; moreover, any advantage from their possession would be largely offset by the need to divert Allied military resources to defend the country from German attack. Manpower advantages would have been slight, as Irishmen were already volunteering in large numbers for the British armed forces (about 150,000 served during the war), while thousands of Irish people were working in British industry and agriculture. Irish entry into the war would have made little difference to Allied security, as the British intelligence community was now confident that the Irish authorities were capable of suppressing German espionage, sabotage and propaganda activities. The only benefit would have been the elimination of the German legation, but this was now seen as a manageable threat. On the other hand, assessments of Irish opinion indicated that entry into the war might split the country and embolden the subversive groups that were then being successfully contained. Furthermore, it might allow Ireland to bring its protest against partition to the peace table, which might complicate relations with the United States.[16] As a result, the British government came to the conclusion that Irish neutrality was preferable to Irish belligerency. Thus, when the Americans began developing a propaganda strategy for Ireland in January 1942 Churchill's intelligence adviser, Major Desmond Morton, informed them that 'H.M.G. would probably not care to take part in propaganda which might be designed to convince Eire to enter war'.[17]

Over the following three years there were some half-hearted attempts to persuade the Irish government to change its policy. These were usually prompted by Winston Churchill, who quixotically wanted to 'try to save these people from themselves' and help 'Ireland to redeem her own soul'.[18] Yet most British military chiefs and politicians had no wish to change the *status quo*. 'Irritating as the present position of Eire as a neutral is to all right-thinking people', a civil servant in the Dominions Office wrote in 1943, 'it cannot be argued that in fact their neutrality is doing us serious practical harm.'[19] The Deputy Prime Minister, Clement Attlee, expressed the relief of many when he remarked that 'at present, for the first time in history, Southern Ireland is being kept quiet, during a war, by an Irish Government with no liability on British arms.'[20]

Instead, British policy was focused on obtaining maximum concessions from the Irish government – Britain sought 'a most benevolent neutrality.'[21] This required some minor favours in return. Maffey stated that 'provided the facade of neutrality is maintained, much can be done. But not if our conduct here is to be governed by a blank policy of negation.'[22] Between November 1941 and February 1942 the British delivered the first significant consignment of military equipment to Dublin since July 1940. It would continue to provide 'sweeteners' such as fuel and raw materials in order to secure Irish goodwill and assistance.[23] This was similar to British policy towards neutral Switzerland, where supplies were given in exchange for Swiss tolerance of Allied intelligence operations against Germany.[24] The British also tried to head off the expected post-war anti-partition campaign by cultivating pro-Allied sentiment in Ireland and neutralising the Irish-American lobby in the United States. British policy towards Ireland was neither vindictive nor generous, but instead based on rational calculation of how to procure the maximum benefits from Irish neutrality. Clement Attlee defined this approach in September 1943:

> At the present time, our treatment of Eire is based on the principle of 'absent treatment.' We deal firmly with such questions as arise on a basis of our own self-interest. We allow them a minimum of necessary supplies and, on the other hand, we receive from them considerable practical help in vital matters affecting the war. Much of this is of a secret nature and cannot be referred to publicly. By pursuing this policy we avoid commitments to Southern Ireland, and at the same time keep our hands completely free to treat them in the post-war settlement as may then be most convenient and useful.[25]

The dividends of this policy came in the form of increased Irish co-operation on a range of issues. At the end of 1941 American entry into the war and German military reverses caused a change in Irish attitudes. When the Secretary of State for Dominion Affairs met de Valera on 19 December 1941 the latter 'was extremely forthcoming in his manner and outspokenly sympathetic to our cause; he said that he had now come to the conclusion that we should win the war.' De Valera was willing to help in any way, so long as it was kept secret.[26] Henceforth the Irish state provided many types of assistance to Allied military operations.

All interned Allied airmen were eventually released; airmen landing in southern Ireland were quietly repatriated; British seaplanes were allowed to fly over Co. Donegal; British-installed wireless stations on the Irish coast provided direction-finding beacons for returning Allied aircraft; and American bombers were allowed to refuel at Rineanna airport. The free flow of people from Ireland to Britain produced even greater numbers of workers and recruits for the armed services. Perhaps most important was the deepening co-operation between Irish and British agencies on intelligence and security matters.[27] While maintaining a façade of neutrality, Ireland became more and more unneutral as the war progressed.

How effective was British policy towards Ireland during the Second World War? In the final days of the conflict British officials began to reflect on the overall impact of Irish neutrality on the British war effort. In particular, Sir John Maffey wished to prepare a comprehensive memorandum on the subject for use as propaganda in Ireland. He was battling an emerging Irish consensus that held that neutrality – including the denial of naval and air bases to the Allies – had no effect on the struggle, and that Ireland – because of its benevolent neutrality – had been as good as in the war. (Irish historians have advanced similar arguments in recent years.)[28] This was the Irish trying to have their cake and eat it: they wanted to enjoy the stature of independence that neutrality had bestowed, weaving a myth of the small nation standing up against the rapacious great powers (*their* 'finest hour'), while proclaiming that they had all the time given plenty of assistance to the right side. The wartime paradox of neutrality in thought, unneutrality in deed made this contorted logic possible. There was also an anti-partition dimension to this argument. The British stated they could not give up Northern Ireland without being guaranteed use of strategic Irish bases during future wars; the Irish were trying to show that these facilities were not important to British security. Maffey hoped to neutralise the threatened campaign against partition by showing how Irish neutrality had damaged the Allied cause and threatened British security.[29]

In June 1946, after crateloads of German documents were examined and dozens of German military officers questioned, the armed services finally produced a memorandum in response to Maffey's request. They concluded that the chief significance of Irish neutrality was that it prevented the Allies from using Irish naval and air bases during the Battle of the Atlantic: it was estimated that the availability of these bases, especially in 1940 and 1941, would have saved 1,200,000 tons of shipping, along with innumerable lives. Although the exact figure was somewhat tendentious, no amount of Irish sophistry could obscure the underlying truth. On the other hand, the report confirmed that Germany had not been able to exploit Irish neutrality to its advantage. There was no proof 'of there having been any naval activities advantageous to the Germans in Eirean waters' or any supply bases for U-boats on the Irish coast. There was little evidence of any successful espionage or sabotage conducted in or through neutral Ireland. The armed services also drew attention to all the ways in which Ireland had assisted the Allied war effort: the provision of operational intelligence to British forces, the different treatment of Allied and German aircraft in Irish territory, the arrangements for thousands of workers to travel to Britain, the permission for thousands more to join the British armed services. Thus, Irish neutrality did not cause as much damage to the Allied war effort as British propagandists might have liked.[30]

The 1946 report highlighted the extent to which Britain had limited the impact of Irish neutrality. Overall, Britain's wartime policy towards Ireland must be judged a success. Britain was never going to obtain Irish bases through persuasion or coercion, while their seizure by force would have entailed an onerous military commitment. However, through firm negotiation with the Irish government, it did gain many benefits from Irish neutrality at little cost. Looking back in 1946, Cecil Liddell described the calculation that underlay British policy:

> Once the British control of Eire had been given up the only alternatives were to re-acquire that control by force, or to obtain as many as possible of the advantages which such control would have given, by fostering good relations with the Government and people of Eire. This latter alternative, tempered on occasion with firmness, has, in fact, been the policy of the British Government since 1938.[31]

The British intelligence system deserves some credit for allowing London to handle the challenge of Irish neutrality so effectively. It tackled those threats that directly affected Britain's security: preparing for possible military operations in southern Ireland; investigating the Irish fifth column; monitoring and countering Axis propaganda; preventing German espionage and leakage of information. It debunked dangerous myths and proved that neutral Ireland did not pose as great a threat to British security as popularly believed. On the other hand, better political intelligence demonstrated that the country would not easily be knocked off its neutral perch. Moreover, British coercion might have the effect of stopping Irish co-operation, not least on intelligence and security matters. Good intelligence, therefore, helped the British come to terms with Irish neutrality and make the most of it.

The experience of the Second World War caused a fundamental change in

British perceptions of Ireland. Both the liberal imperialist and diehard union-ist interpretation of Irish affairs were challenged by Irish behaviour and British intelligence. Reports from SIS, MI5, the Ministry of Information and, above all, Sir John Maffey, pointed out that the southern Irish viewed themselves as an independent nation with no obligations to Britain. 'Englishmen are still inclined to have a sentimental belief in links that have vanished', Maffey wrote. 'The part played by Irishmen in the Great War, or in the Empire and in our common his-tory encourages the delusion that we are really all one happy family and that this regrettable tiff will blow over.' In fact, he asserted, Éire had 'cut free from Eng-land', it was a 'foreign country'. The unwavering attachment to neutrality was 'the final proof of difference, of severance, of independence'.[32] The presence of Axis legations in Dublin – and, he might have added, de Valera's offer of condolences to the German legation on Hitler's death – was 'truly symptomatic of public opinion'.[33] On the other hand, the country's behaviour during the war demon-strated that an independent Ireland would not stab Britain in the back; instead, the Irish government made many concessions that were not strictly compatible with neutrality to safeguard British security. Better intelligence also challenged the crude, negative stereotypes of the Irish; well-informed British observers may have been frustrated by Irish behaviour, but they ascribed it to a differing politi-cal philosophy, not genetic flaws.

Out of the conflicting images of the liberal optimists and diehard unionists emerged a new consensus. Ireland was neither a sister-nation nor a fanatical enemy, but an independent country – with links to the United Kingdom, as well as grievances – pursuing its own interests. This acceptance of Ireland as a for-eign country was as much a psychological readjustment as a political realisation. It was easy for younger politicians who had grown up with the Irish Free State, but harder for older men who had known an undivided Ireland in the Union before 1921 – it was particularly hard for Winston Churchill. However, it con-tained some benefits for Britain. Irish neutrality wiped out any residual guilt over historical British repression or the partition of the island: in Maffey's words, the war allowed the British to 'get the poison of the Irish Question drained out of our system'.[34] Henceforth London could deal with southern Ireland on the basis of self-interest. 'The Irish question now confronts us in a simpler and more man-ageable form than ever before', Maffey elaborated; they could 'talk to Eire on a cold, factual, horse-trading basis'.[35] This produced a new maturity in Anglo-Irish relations. Once Britain gave up its claim on Irish allegiance, the two countries could settle down to an amicable relationship based on equality between two nations and co-operation in pursuit of common interests, with no obligations or favours on either side.

This solid, more realistic, basis for Anglo-Irish relations was illustrated by developments in the years after the war. On the one hand, some of the predictions about post-war complications were borne out. When Cecil Liddell sat down to write his history of the MI5 Irish section in 1946 he noted that there was already 'ample evidence' of the anticipated anti-partition campaign: de Valera was making fiery speeches in Ireland and canvassing support in the United States.[36] Two years later a new coalition government assumed power in Dublin, with the suspected wartime Quisling, Seán MacBride, as Minister of External Affairs. He was instrumental in the government's decision to withdraw southern Ireland from the commonwealth. The long-awaited Irish republic was finally established on Easter Monday, 18 April 1949, thirty-three years to the day after republican revolutionaries launched their insurrection in Dublin.[37] However, this sundering of constitutional ties did not dent Anglo-Irish intelligence cooperation. The 'Dublin link' continued for many years after the war, even surviving MacBride's tenure as Minister of External Affairs. Guy Liddell visited Dublin in 1949 and 1950; he corresponded frequently with Colonel Dan Bryan; and the two men swapped information on communism and the IRA. On one occasion Liddell sent the Irishman a copy of George Orwell's recently published *Animal Farm*, so that he would better understand the Soviet menace.[38] Moreover, the Irish declaration of a republic barely caused a ripple in Britain. There were no accusations of betrayal, no warnings of the terrible consequences for British security; it was viewed as a legal and technical matter that made little difference to Anglo-Irish relations. Because of the experience of the Second World War, Britain had already come to terms with Irish independence. In British eyes, the erstwhile rebels had long ago become a foreign nation.

Notes

Introduction

1 *Intelligence: the acme of skill* (CIA booklet), quoted in J. Der Derian, 'Anti-diplomacy, intelligence theory and surveillance practice', *Intelligence & National Security*, 8, 3 (Jul 1993), p. 29.

2 M. Silvestri, ' "An Irishman is specially suited to be a policeman": Sir Charles Tegart & revolutionary terrorism in Bengal', *History Ireland* (Winter 2000), pp. 40–4.

3 Desmond Morton to Lord Swinton, 8 Jun 1940, TNA, PREM 3/131/2; War Cabinet meeting, 16 Jun 1940, TNA, CAB 65/7.

4 Chamberlain to Churchill, 12 Jun 1940, TNA, PREM 1/131/2.

5 Dan Bryan transcripts (in possession of Prof. Eunan O'Halpin).

6 M. Herman, *Intelligence power in peace and war* (Cambridge, 1996), pp. 1–2, 114–6; S. Kent, *Strategic intelligence for American world policy* (Hamden, CT, 1965 edn), p. xxiii; Der Derian, 'Anti-diplomacy, intelligence theory and surveillance practice', p. 30; R. Hibbert, 'Intelligence and policy', *Intelligence & National Security*, 5, 1 (Jan 1990), pp. 110–29.

7 C. A. Andrew & D. Dilks (eds.), *The missing dimension; governments and intelligence communities in the twentieth century* (London, 1984).

8 C. A. Andrew, *Secret service: the making of the British intelligence community* (London, 1985); W. Wark, *The ultimate enemy: British intelligence and Nazi Germany, 1933–1939* (London, 1985), pp. 23–4.

9 See F. S. L. Lyons, *Culture and anarchy in Ireland, 1890–1939* (Oxford, 1980).

10 Andrew, *Secret service*, pp. 1–6.

11 E. Sparrow, *Secret service: British agents in France, 1792–1815* (Woodbridge, 1999), pp. 176–7, 180.

12 T. Bartlett, 'Informers, informants and information: the secret history of the 1790s re-considered', in T. Bartlett, D. Dickson, D. Keogh & K. Whelan (eds.), *1798: a bicentenary perspective* (Dublin, 2003), pp. 406–22. See also B. Porter, *Plots and paranoia* (London, 1989), pp. 26–38.

13 S. J. Connolly, *The Oxford companion to Irish history* (Oxford, 1998), pp. 163, 491–2.

14 R. V. Comerford, *The Fenians in context* (Dublin, 1985); Andrew, *Secret service*, pp. 16–17; Porter, *Plots and paranoia*, pp. 96–9.

15 L. Burt, *Commander Burt of Scotland Yard* (London, 1959), p. 120.

16 K. R. M. Short, *The dynamite war* (Dublin, 1979); Andrew, *Secret service*, 18–19; B. Porter, *The origins of the vigilant state* (London, 1983), chs. 3–5; Porter, *Plots and paranoia*, pp. 101–10, 116; R. Thurlow, *The secret state: British internal security in the twentieth century* (Oxford, 1994), p. 4.

17 See L. W. McBride, *The greening of Dublin Castle: the transformation of bureaucratic and judicial personnel in Ireland, 1892–1922* (Washington, DC, 1991).

18 Bartlett, 'Informers, informants and information', pp. 406–14.

19 D. Neligan, *The spy in the Castle* (London, 1999), pp. 43, 82.

20 The groundbreaking work of L. P. Curtis in the 1960s has been challenged by Sheridan Gilley and Roy Foster, although later ripostes by F. S. L. Lyons, M. A. G. Ó Tuathaigh, M. J. Hickman and Curtis himself have supported the earlier conclusions. See L. P. Curtis, *Anglo Saxons and Celts: a study of anti-Irish prejudice in Victorian England* (New York, 1968); L. P. Curtis, *Apes and angels: the Irishman in Victorian caricature* (Washington & London, 1997 edn); S. Gilley, 'English attitudes to the Irish in England, 1780–1900', in C. Holmes (ed.), *Immigrants and minorities in British society* (London, 1978); M. A. G. Ó Tuathaigh, 'The Irish in nineteenth-century Britain: problems of integration', in R. Swift and S. Gilley (eds.), *The Irish in the Victorian city* (London, 1985); R. Foster, *Paddy and Mr Punch: connections in Anglo-Irish history* (London, 1993), pp. 171–94; M. J. Hickman, *Religion, class and identity* (Aldershot, 1995). This debate is ably described in D. M. MacRaild, *Irish migrants in modern Britain, 1750–1922* (Basingstoke, 1999), pp. 160–2. It also appears in a recent work by Pittock, who concludes that Curtis's conclusions still stand. M. G. H. Pittock, *Celtic identity and the British image* (Manchester & New York, 1999), p. 45–54.

21 Lyons, *Culture and anarchy in Ireland*, pp. 11–15.

CHAPTER 1
Losing Southern Ireland

1 Many works cover this period. For example, see M. Laffan, *The resurrection of Ireland: the Sinn Féin Party, 1916–23* (Cambridge, 1999); M. Hopkinson, *The Irish war of independence* (Dublin, 2002); P. Hart, *The I.R.A. and its enemies: violence and community in Cork, 1916–1923* (Oxford, 1998); R. Kee, *The green flag: a history of Irish nationalism* (London, 1972).

2 C. Townshend, *Easter 1916: the Irish rebellion* (London, 2005), chs. 3–5.

3 'Record of the rebellion in Ireland and the part played by the army in dealing with it', vol. 2: 'Intelligence', p. 28, London, Imperial War Museum (IWM), Jeudwine Papers, p. 4; hereafter cited as 'Army record of the rebellion'. See also Townshend, *Easter 1916*, pp. 58, 86–9; introduction to P. Hart (ed.), *British intelligence in Ireland, 1920–21: the final reports* (Cork, 2002), p. 5; C. Townshend, 'Policing insurgency in Ireland, 1914–23', in D. M. Anderson & D. Killingray (eds.), *Policing and decolonisation; politics, nationalism and the police, 1917–65* (Manchester, 1992), pp. 23–4; E. O'Halpin, 'British intelligence on Ireland, 1914–1921', p. 58–9, in C. A. Andrew & D. Dilks (eds.), *The missing dimension; governments and intelligence communities in the twentieth century* (London, 1984).

4 Andrew, *Secret service*, pp. 11–27, 35–59, 74–5, 132; A. Judd, *The quest for C: Sir Mansfield Cumming and the founding of the British secret service* (London, 1999), p. 35.

5 Townshend, *Easter 1916*, pp. 85–6.

6 Notes by Eoin MacNeill, Ms. 11437, NLI.

7 J. Dudgeon, *Roger Casement: the Black Diaries – with a study of his background, sexuality, and Irish political life* (Belfast, 2002), pp. 481–6.

8 MI5 note, 4 Nov 1914, & other material in MI5 Roger Casement file, TNA, KV 2/6.

9 MI5 G Branch history, TNA, KV 1/42.

10 Andrew, *Secret service*, p. 60.

11 C. A. Andrew, *For the president's eyes only: secret intelligence and the American presidency from Washington to Bush* (London, 1996 edn), p. 34; P. Beesly, *Room 40: British naval intelligence, 1914–18* (London, 1982).

12 Andrew, *Secret service*, p. 91.

13 N. Hiley, 'Counter-espionage and security in Great Britain during the First World War', *English Historical Review*, 101, 400 (Jul 1986); Andrew, *Secret service*, pp. 177–82.

14 O'Halpin, 'British intelligence on Ireland, 1914–1921', pp. 55–6.

15 Admiralty messages intercepted by IRA, [early 1915], Florence O'Donoghue Papers, NLI, Ms. 31223(1).

16 G Division report on 'Granite' & 'Chalk', 27 Mar & 22 Apr 1916, TNA, CO 904/23/3.

17 Reports from Findlay to FO, 29 Oct 1914 – 13 Jan 1915; anon. note, 8 Aug 1915, TNA, KV 2/6. See also Dudgeon, *Roger Casement*, pp. 432–58.

18 O'Halpin, 'British intelligence on Ireland', pp. 59–61; B. Thomson, *The scene changes* (London, 1939), pp. 241–2, 275–9, 303; article by Basil Thomson in *English Life*, Mar 1925, in TNA, KV 2/10.

19 Townshend, *Easter 1916*, pp. 126–31.

20 Quoted in O'Halpin, 'British intelligence on Ireland', pp. 59–61.

21 Major F. Hall to Major Price, 23 Apr 1916, TNA, KV 2/7; Thomson to Sir E. Blackwell, 18 Jul 1916, TNA, MEPO 1/10664; O'Halpin, 'British intelligence on Ireland', p. 61.

22 Townshend, *Easter 1916*, pp. 143–51, 162–4. See also Laffan, *The resurrection of Ireland*, pp. 36–40; L. O'Broin, *Dublin Castle and the 1916 rising*, 2nd edn (London, 1970).

23 See Townshend, *Easter 1916*, pp. 143–51.

24 C. Townshend, *Political violence in Ireland: government and resistance since 1848* (Oxford, 1983), p. 312. For a similar opinion, see Thurlow, *The secret state*, pp. 89–91.

25 Laffan, *The resurrection of Ireland*, pp. 60–142.

26 Monthly army intelligence reports are in TNA, CO 904/157/1.

27 MI5 G Branch history, TNA, KV 1/42.

28 Thomson, *The scene changes*, p. 326.

29 *Ibid.*, p. 352.

30 *Ibid.*, pp. 352, 366–7; Dudgeon, *Roger Casement*, pp. 483–6.

31 O'Halpin, 'British intelligence in Ireland', pp. 62–4.

32 *Ibid.*, pp. 65–9; Thurlow, *The secret state*, pp. 84–5.

33 D. G. Boyce, 'How to settle the Irish Question: Lloyd George and Ireland 1916–21', in A. J. P. Taylor (ed.), *Lloyd George: twelve essays* (London, 1971), p. 141; N. Mansergh, *The unresolved question: the Anglo-Irish settlement and its undoing, 1912–72* (New Haven & London, 1991), pp. 96–7; Laffan, *The resurrection of Ireland*, pp. 7–8; T. Garvin, *Nationalist revolutionaries in Ireland, 1858–1928* (Oxford, 1987), p. 139.

34 Key works on this period are Hopkinson, *The Irish war of independence*; Laffan, *The resurrection of Ireland*; J. Augusteijn, *From public defiance to guerilla warfare: the experience of ordinary Volunteers in the Irish war of independence, 1916–1921* (Dublin & Portland, OR, 1996); Hart, *The I.R.A. and its enemies*; Kee, *The green flag*.

35 See T. P. Coogan, *Michael Collins* (London, 1990).

36 O. Winter, *Winter's tale: an autobiography* (London, 1955).

37 Quoted in Andrew, *Secret service*, p. 252.

38 Quoted in E. O'Halpin, 'Collins and intelligence, 1919–1923', in G. Doherty & D. Keogh (eds.), *Michael Collins and the making of the Irish state* (Dublin, 1998), p. 71. For a less laudatory analysis of Collins's role in IRA intelligence, see P. Hart, *Mick: the real Michael Collins* (London, 2005).

39 Army record of the rebellion, vol. 2.

40 'A Report on the Intelligence Branch of the Chief of Police from May 1920 to July 1921' by Colonel Winter, undated, TNA, CO 904/156b. Hereafter cited as 'Winter report on intelligence'. These last two reports have been published in Hart, *British intelligence in Ireland*.

41 Paper by Capt. Frank Thornton, undated [1940?], NLI, Leon Ó Broin Papers, Ms. 31655; T. Ryle Dwyer, *The Squad: and the intelligence operations of Michael Collins* (Cork, 2005), pp. 133–4; N. Macready, *Annals of an active life* (London, 1924), p. 551.

42 D. Ferriter, *The transformation of Ireland: 1900–2000* (London, 2004), p. 207.

43 See Ryle Dwyer, *The Squad*, pp. 37–9, 63; Hopkinson, *the Irish war of independence*, p. 69; Neligan, *The spy in the Castle*.

44 J. Borgonovo, *Florence and Josephine O'Donoghue's war of independence: a destiny that shapes our ends* (Dublin, 2006).

45 Ferriter, *The transformation of Ireland*, pp. 205–6.

46 Neligan, *The spy in the Castle*, p. 81.

47 Quoted in J. Dunn, *Paperchase: adventures in and out of Fleet Street* (London, 1938), p. 156.

48 Ryle Dwyer, *The Squad*, pp. 66–8.

49 Augusteijn, *From public defiance to guerilla warfare*, ch. 5; Hart, *The I.R.A. and its enemies*, p. 76; Townshend, 'Policing insurgency in Ireland', pp. 24, 30.

50 Army record of the rebellion, vol. 2, p. 4; Andrew, *Secret service*, p. 53.

51 Hopkinson, *The Irish war of independence*, pp. 8–10.

52 French to Lord Londonderry, 3 Jan 1920, IWM, French papers, Ms. 75/46/12.

53 Hopkinson, *The Irish war of independence*, pp. 9, 32–3. See also Neligan, *The spy in the castle*, pp. 59–61, 65.

54 M. T. Foy, *Michael Collins's intelligence war: the struggle between the British and IRA, 1919–21* (Stroud, 2006), p. 16.

55 C. Ackerman, 'Ireland from a Scotland Yard notebook', *The Atlantic Monthly*, Apr 1922.

56 Ryle Dwyer, *The Squad*, pp. 79–80, 90; Hopkinson, *The Irish war of independence*, p. 56; Thomson, *The scene changes*, pp. 388–9; Neligan, *The spy in the Castle*, pp. 55–6, 64–6. For the A2 Branch, see Porter, *Plots and paranoia*, p. 147; Foy, *Michael Collins's intelligence war*, pp. 75–7. Peter Hart interprets this episode differently: he says that it was 'a most serious breach of IRA security' and that Byrnes and his handlers had 'played it perfectly'. However, the fact remains that Byrnes was killed and the British gained nothing useful from the operation – apart from learning that Collins was growing a moustache. Hart, *Mick*, pp. 224–37.

57 Army record of the rebellion, vol. 2, p. 7; Winter report on intelligence.

58 Hopkinson, *The Irish war of independence*, p. 55; Ryle Dwyer, *The Squad*, pp. 70–3, 98–101; Neligan, *The spy in the Castle*, p. 65.

59 Winter report on intelligence. See also Army record of the rebellion, vol. 2, p. 5.

60 Neligan, *The spy in the Castle*, p. 93.

61 Army Record of Rebellion, vol. 2.

62 Report by Lieut-General A. E. Percival, in W. Sheehan (ed.), *British voices: from the Irish war of independence, 1918–21* (Cork, 2005), p. 131.

63 Macready, *Annals of an active life*, p. 462.

64 Table of Secret Service expenditure, 1 Apr 1921, TNA, HO 317/59. For Kelly see Lieut-General F. Shaw to WO, 14 Apr 1920, TNA, WO 141/42; also report by US military attaché, 26 Nov 1919, USNA, RG 165, MID 2633–1.

65 Army record of the rebellion, vol. 2.

66 K. Strong, *Intelligence at the top: the recollections of an intelligence officer* (London, 1968), pp. 1–5. For Battalion Intelligence Officers, see Lieut-General A. E. Percival, in Sheehan, *British voices*, p. 131.

67 Army record of the rebellion, vol. 2.

68 *Ibid.*, pp. 6–7, 9, 18, 29. For Wilson, see K. Jeffrey, 'British military intelligence following World War I', in K. G. Robertson (ed.), *British and American approaches to intelligence* (London, 1987), pp. 55–84, 71.

69 Memoir of Capt. R. D. Jeune, in Sheehan, *British voices*, pp. 84–6.

70 Winter report on intelligence. See also Winter, *Winter's tale*, p. 294.

71 Neligan, *The spy in the Castle*, p. 100.

72 For secret service expenditures, see correspondence of Sir John Anderson, Jul 1920 – Apr 1921, TNA, HO 317/59.

73 Hopkinson, *The Irish war of independence*, p. 28.

74 E. O'Halpin, *The decline of the union: British government in Ireland, 1892–1920* (Dublin, 1987), pp. 206–9. See also Cope to Anderson, 16 Jun 1920, TNA, HO 317/59.

75 Lord Oranmore, quoted in Hopkinson, *The Irish war of independence*, p. 37.

76 Hopkinson, *The Irish war of independence*, p. 61; introduction in M. Hopkinson (ed.), *The last days of Dublin Castle: the Mark Sturgis diaries* (Dublin & Portland, OR, 1999), pp. 5–7.

77 Macready to Churchill, 15 Apr 1922, CCA, CHAR 22/12B.

78 Thurlow, *The secret state*, pp. 30–1.

79 Hopkinson, *The last days of Dublin Castle*, p. 4.

80 See F. P. Crozier, *Impressions and recollections* (London, 1930), pp. 251–4, 290.

81 Hopkinson, *The Irish war of independence*, p. 74. For casualties, see Laffan, *The resurrection of Ireland*, p. 284.

82 Connolly, *The Oxford companion to Irish histor*, pp. 32, 47; Hopkinson, *The Irish war of independence*, pp. 49–50; Townshend, 'Policing insurgency in Ireland', pp. 32–3.

83 Neligan, *The spy in the Castle*, p. 87.

84 Hopkinson, *The last days of Dublin Castle*, p. 40.

85 Winter, *Winter's tale*.

86 Andrew, *Secret service*, p. 255.

87 Hopkinson, *The last days of Dublin Castle*, p. 32.

88 Winter, *Winter's tale*, ch. x.

89 Hopkinson, *The last days of Dublin Castle*, p. 19.

90 Winter report on intelligence.

91 Winter, *Winter's tale*, pp. 298–9.

92 Winter report on intelligence.

93 Winter, *Winter's tale*, p. 311; Hopkinson, *The last days of Dublin Castle*, p. 60.

94 Tegart to Sir Malcolm Seton, 1 Jul 1920. See also Seton to Macready, 2 Jul 1920; Seton to Anderson, 6 & 21 Aug 1920, 6 Jan 1921; F. W. Duke to Anderson, 12 Oct 1920, TNA, HO 317/59.

95 Winter to Anderson, 6 Jan 1922, TNA, HO 317/59; Winter, *Winter's tale*, p. 296; Jeune memoir, in Sheehan, *British voices*, p. 90. For details on Cameron, see Andrew. *Secret service*, pp. 139–41, 255.

96 Winter report on intelligence; Army record of the rebellion, vol. 2, p. 29.

97 Winter report on intelligence.

98 Jeune memoir, in Sheehan, *British Voices*, p. 88.

99 Winter report on intelligence.

100 Ryle Dwyer, *The Squad*, pp. 137–9; Foy, *Michael Collins's intelligence war*, p. 109; Winter report on intelligence.

101 Frank Thornton paper, NLI, Leon Ó Broin Papers, Ms. 31655.

102 Hopkinson, *The Irish war of independence*, pp. 69, 107; Ryle Dwyer, *The Squad*, p. 15. Captured British documents are in NLI, Florence O'Donoghue Papers, Ms. 31223(2).

103 Foy, *Michael Collins's intelligence war*, pp. 141–77; Hopkinson, *The Irish war of independence*, p. 90; Ryle Dwyer, *The Squad*, pp. 170–5; Hart, *Mick*, pp. 240–1. Porter (*Plots and paranoia*, p. 154) mistakenly states that the victims were 'Winter's men', sent over by the London Bureau. Nigel West makes the even more far-fetched claim that they were members of Cumming's SIS. See N. West, *MI5: British Security Service operations, 1909–1945* (New York, 1981), p. 46.

104 Thornton paper on IRA intelligence, NLI, Leon Ó Broin Papers, Ms. 31655.

105 Army record of the rebellion, vol. 2, p. 28.

106 Jeune memoir, in Sheehan, *British voices*, p. 90.

107 Hart, *The I.R.A. and its enemies*, pp. 21–38.

108 Army record of the rebellion, vol. 2, pp. 26, 33.

109 Cope to Greenwood, 9 Aug 1921, TNA, HO 317/46.

110 Winter report on intelligence; Haldane to Anderson, 28 Jan 1921; Cope to Anderson, 9 Jun 1921, TNA, HO 317/59. Hart mistakenly claims that Winter 'instituted' the Dublin Special Branch. This is not so: it had existed before he arrived in Ireland and was only belatedly transferred to his control. See Hart, *Mick*, p. 240.

111 Neligan, *The spy in the Castle*, pp. 138, 142.

112 Winter, *Winter's tale*, p. 338; Frank Thornton paper, NLI, Leon Ó Broin Papers, Ms. 31655; O'Halpin, 'British intelligence in Ireland, 1914–21', p. 72.

113 Ryle Dwyer, *The Squad*, pp. 213–14.

114 Army record of the rebellion, vol. 2; Strickland to Macready, 22 Jan 1921, IWM, HHW 2/2C/33; Kelly to Lieut Davies, 15 Mar 1921, in NLI, Florence O'Donoghue Papers, Ms. 31228. Hart identifies thirteen informers in Co. Cork at this time. Hart, *The I.R.A. and its enemies*, pp. 306–7.

115 Winter report on intelligence.

116 Neligan, *The spy in the Castle*, pp. 133–55.

117 Frank Thornton paper, NLI, Leon Ó Broin Papers, Ms. 31655.

118 Ryle Dwyer, *The Squad*, pp. 224–5.

119 Winter, *Winter's tale*, pp. 332–4.

120 Percival paper, in Sheehan, *British voices*, pp. 134–6; Ryle Dwyer, *The Squad*, p. 224; N. Hamilton, *Monty: the making of a general* (London, 1981), pp. 160–1.

121 Cope to Greenwood, 9 Aug 1921, TNA, HO 317/46; Hopkinson, *The last days of Dublin Castle*, p. 180. The two officers to commit suicide in later years were Major Cameron and Major Sarigny, one of the leaders of the D Branch in Dublin. Neligan, *The spy in the Castle*, p. 165.

122 Hart, *The I.R.A. and its enemies*, p. 314. See also Macready, *Annals of an active life*, pp. 464–5; Winter, *Winter's tale*, p. 301.

123 Army record of the rebellion, vol. 2.

124 Winter report on intelligence. See also Augusteijn, *From public defiance to guerilla warfare*, pp. 336–7.

125 Strong, *Intelligence at the top*, pp. 1–5.

126 Record Army record of the rebellion, vol. 2, pp. 25, 28.

127 Winter, *Winter's tale*, pp. 295, 303–4.

128 Army record of the rebellion, vol. 2, p. 27.

129 Winter report on intelligence.

130 *Ibid.*; Macready to Greenwood, 27 Apr 1921, IWM, HHW 2/2D/36.

131 Hopkinson, p. 111; captured IRA document with L. K. Lockhart to Hemming, 11 May 1921, TNA, HO 317/60.

132 C. Townshend, *Ireland: the 20th century* (London, 1998), p. 103; Augusteijn, *From public defiance to guerilla warfare*, pp. 138–9; Hopkinson, *The Irish war of independence*, p. 111; Hart, *The I.R.A. and its enemies*, pp. 107–9.

133 Augusteijn, *From public defiance to guerilla warfare*, p. 341; Laffan, *The resurrection of Ireland*, pp. 271–5.

134 Townshend, *Political violence in Ireland*, p. 361; C. Townshend, 'The Irish Republican Army and the development of guerrilla garfare, 1916–1921', *English Historical Review*, 94, 371

(Apr 1979); Laffan, *The resurrection of Ireland*, p. 297.

135 Macready to Wilson, 14 Mar 1921, HHW 2/2C/45; Winter report on intelligence.

136 Neligan, *The spy in the castle*, p. 137.

137 Army record of the rebellion, vol. 2, pp. 10–12. See also Macready to Wilson, 5 May & 16 Jun 1921, IWM, HHW 2/2D/49.

138 Hopkinson, *The last days of Dublin Castle*, pp. 61, 75–6n, 90; Seton to Anderson, 5 Nov, 27 Nov & 3 Dec 1920; Denham to Anderson, 5 & 9 Nov 1920, TNA, HO 317/59.

139 Hart (*British intelligence in Ireland*, pp. 8–9) defends Winter's record in the introduction to his recent book. A full examination of the evidence backs the earlier conclusions of O'Halpin and Andrew.

140 Memo by MPs, undated [Mar 1921]; Hoare to Greenwood, 24 Mar 1921, CUL, Templewood Papers. I am endebted to Dr Peter Martland for these sources.

141 Army record of the rebellion, vol. 2, p. 10. For French's wartime career, see Andrew, *Secret service*, p. 146; M. Occelshaw, *Armour against fate: British military intelligence in the First World War* (London, 1989), appendix; D. French, 'Sir John French's Secret Service on the Western Front 1914–1915', *Journal of Strategic Studies*, 7, 4 (1984).

142 D. George Boyce, *Nationalism in Ireland* (London & New York, 1991 edn), p. 322.

143 Hopkinson, *The Irish war of independence*, pp. 177–85.

144 Army record of the rebellion, vol. 2.

145 Townshend, *Political violence in Ireland*, pp. 346–50.

146 Winter report on intelligence.

147 Ferriter, *The transformation of Ireland*, p. 231; J. J. Lee, *Ireland, 1912–1985: politics and society* (Cambridge, 1989), p. 42; Hopkinson, *The Irish war of independence*, p. 66.

148 J. Campbell, *F. E. Smith: first Earl of Birkenhead* (London, 1983), p. 549.

149 Boyce, 'How to settle the Irish Question', p. 141; Laffan, *The resurrection of Ireland*, pp. 7–8.

150 Report by Sir Warren Fisher, 15 May 1920, Parliamentary Archives London, Lloyd George Papers, F/31/1/33.

151 For a contemporary journalist's perspective on the 'military mind', see H. Martin, *Ireland in insurrection* (London, 1921).

152 Boyle to Hemming, 11 Dec 1920, TNA, HO 317/60. For the Special Branch view, see Lieut-Colonel J. F. C. Carter to Hoare, 27 Oct 1940, CUL, Templewood Papers.

153 R. K. Betts, 'Analysis, war, and decision: why intelligence failures are inevitable', *World Politics*, 31, 1 (1978), p. 61; Herman, *Intelligence power in peace and war*, pp. 227–30. A. Levite, *Intelligence and strategic surprises* (New York, 1987).

154 Macready, *Annals of an active life*, pp. 470–1, 485, 492.

155 'A History of the 5th Division in Ireland', 23 Mar 1922. IWM, Jeudwine Papers, 72/82/2.

156 Macready, *Annals of an active life*, pp. 562–5; Macready to Wilson, 17 Jun 1921, IWM, HHW 2/2E/24. See also Laffan, *The resurrection of Ireland*, p. 295.

CHAPTER 2
Alarms, Excursions and Civil War

1 Macready, *Annals of an active life*, p. 618.

2 *Ibid.*, p. 584.

3 *Ibid.*, p. 584.

4 Cope to Greenwood, 9 Aug 1921, TNA, HO 317/46.

5 Winter, *Winter's tale*, p. 319.

6 British intelligence report on Sinn Fein leaders, 11 Jul 1921, TNA, HO 317/49.

7 Intelligence report marked 'J' [from Winter's London Bureau], 1 Nov 1921, TNA, HO 317/46; B. Murphy, *John Chartres: mystery man of the treaty* (Dublin, 1995), pp. 48–9, 57–8, 67–8.

8 Macready to Wilson, 5 Dec 1921, IWM, HHW 2/2G/19.

9 D Branch intelligence report, 22 Oct 1921; Lieut-Colonel French to Anderson, 31 Oct 1921, TNA, HO 317/46; Macready to Wilson, 26 Nov 1921, IWM, HHW 2/2G/4.

10 T. Jones, *Whitehall diary*, vol. 3: *Ireland, 1918–1925*, ed. K. Middlemas (London, 1971), p. 88.

11 Report by Colonel J. J. Brind, 1 Oct 1921, in appendix to Army record of the rebellion, vol. 1, p. 59.

12 Wilson-Macready correspondence, Jun–Jul 1921, IWM, HHW 2/2E; Macready, *Annals of an active life*, pp. 576–9.

13 Winter to Hemming, 1 Jul 1921, TNA, HO 371/60.

14 Hopkinson, *The last days of Dublin Castle*, pp. 170, 201. For Cope's secretive peace parlays see Macready to Wilson, 19 May 1921, IWM, HHW 2/2D/63.

15 Neligan, *The spy in the Castle*, p. 134; Hopkinson, *The last days of Dublin Castle*, p. 42; Cope to Curtis, 24 Aug 1922, TNA, CO 739/6.

16 H. de Montmorency, *Sword and stirrup: memories of an adventurous life* (London, 1936), p. 356.

17 C. G. Whiskard to Marsh, 22 Jul 1922, & Churchill to Gretton, 25 Jul 1922, TNA, CO 739/15.

18 A. Godley, *Life of an Irish soldier* (London, 1939), p. 275. See also Winter, *Winter's tale*, p. 345.

19 Strickland diary, 17 May 1922, IWM, Strickland papers.

20 Wilson to Macready, 12 Jul 1921, IWM, HHW 2/2E/37.

21 Report on revolutionary organisations by Thomson, 25 Aug 1921, TNA, CAB 24/127; Vice-Admiral E. Gaunt to Macready, 29 Oct 1921, IWM, HHW 2/2F/42.

22 Report by Winter, 2 Aug 1921, TNA, HO 317/60.

23 Macready to Wilson, 12 Sep 1921, IWM, HHW 2/2F/8; Macready to Wilson, 4 Dec 1921, IWM, HHW 2/2G/17.

24 Report on revolutionary organisations by Thomson, 25 Aug 1921, TNA, CAB 24/127.

25 Report by Macready, 8 Nov 1921, TNA, CAB 24/129.

26 Report by Brind, 4 Oct 1921, TNA, CAB 24/128.

27 Macready, *Annals of an active life*, p. 583.

28 Report by Macready, 9 Aug 1921, TNA, CAB 24/127. See also Greenwood report, 29 Sep 1921, & Thomson report, 6 Oct 1921, TNA, CAB 24/128.

29 Report by Brind, 1 Oct 1921, IWM, Jeudwine Papers.

30 Police intelligence report, 2 Dec 1921, PRONI, CAB 6/27/2.

31 Winter to Belfast Local Centre, 3 & 4 Dec 1921, PRONI, CAB 6/27/2. See also intelligence from Winter's D Branch, 1 Nov 1921, TNA, HO 317/46.

32 Report by Brind, 4 Oct 1921, TNA, CAB 24/128.

33 Macready, *Annals of an active life*, p. 562.

34 M. Hopkinson, *Green against green: the Irish civil war* (Dublin, 1988), pp. 15–18. For similar assessments, see J. Regan, 'The politics of reaction: the dynamics of treatyite government and policy, 1922–33', *Irish Historical Studies*, 30, 120 (Nov 1997), pp. 547–8; A. Mitchell, *Revolutionary government in Ireland: Dáil Éireann, 1919–22* (Dublin, 1995), pp. 312–19. In private, Collins warned his colleagues that the IRA would be 'slaughtered' if it had to face the might of the British army. See Hart, *Mick*, pp. 316–22.

35 See Greenwood reports, 6 & 12 Aug, 24 Sep 1921, TNA, CAB 24/127–128; W. Darling to Hemming, 9 Aug & 18 Oct 1921, TNA, HO 316/60.

36 Macready, *Annals of an active life*, p. 601; Macready to Wilson, 25 Oct 1921, IWM, HHW 2/2F/36.

37 Report by Colonel Winter, 2 Aug 1921, TNA, HO 317/60.

38 Entry for 16 Oct 1921, in J. M. McEwen (ed.), *The Riddell diaries, 1908–1923* (London, 1986), p. 353(f). Lord Riddell was the owner of the *News of the World* and a close friend of the Prime Minister.

39 Entry for 22 Oct 1921, in J. Ramsden (ed.), *Real old Tory politics: the political diaries of Sir Robert Sanders, Lord Bayford, 1910–1935* (London, 1984), p. 162.

40 Hopkinson, *Green against green*, pp. 62–8.

41 Cope to Churchill, 12 Feb 1922, TNA, CAB 21/250; Collins to Churchill, 13 Feb 1922, TNA, CO 906/20.

42 Laffan, *The resurrection of Ireland*, pp. 387–411; Hopkinson, *Green against green*, pp. 93–104.

43 Tudor to Churchill, 1 Apr 1922, CCA, CHAR 22/12B/201–3. See also K. Fedorowich, 'The problems of disbandment: the Royal Irish Constabulary and imperial migration, 1919–1929', *Irish Historical Studies*, 30, 117 (May 1996), pp. 98–108.

44 Report by Macready, 14 Feb 1922, TNA, CAB 24/133; report by Brind, 23 May 1922, TNA, CAB 24/136.

45 Minutes of the Provisional Government of Ireland (PGI) Committee, 14 Feb 1922, TNA, CAB 27/153.

46 Greenwood to Winter, 23 Oct 1922, TNA, CO 904/177; Neligan, *The spy in the Castle*, pp. 133–55.

47 Instructions issued by British army, 8 Feb 1922, in appendix XIII to report on army intelligence section in Northern Ireland, 1926, TNA, WO 106/6156.

48 Macready to Wilson, 9 Feb 1922, TNA, HHW 2/2G/52.

49 Minutes of PGI Committee, 3 Apr 1922, TNA, CAB 27/154.

50 Instructions by Brind, 8 Apr 1922, in Appendix No. XV to report on army intelligence section in Northern Ireland, 1926, TNA, WO 106/6156; letter from Brind to Jeudwine, 18 Apr 1922, IWM, Jeudwine 72/82/2; Macready, *Annals of an active life*, pp. 638–9.

51 Memo by Macready, 15 Apr 1922, TNA, WO 32/9530. See also Macready at meeting of

Committee of Imperial Defence Sub-Committee on Ireland, 4 May 1922, TNA, CAB 16/42.

52 Macready to WO, 7 Jul 1922, TNA, WO 35/180C. The Private was J. Brooks. For details on this case see WO to PGI Committee, 28 Sep 1922, TNA, CO 739/11; F. J. R. Hendy to Churchill, 30 May 1922, TNA, CO 739/15; Mulcahy to Loughnane, 12 Oct 1923, TNA, CO 739/19.

53 J. Linge, 'The Royal Navy and the Irish civil car', *Irish Historical Studies*, 31, 121 (May 1998), pp. 60–71.

54 Macready to Churchill, 17 Apr 1922, CCA, CHAR 22/12B/171.

55 See meeting between Collins, Eoin O'Duffy, Cope and Macready, 4 Apr 1922, TNA, CO 739/14.

56 J. McColgan, 'Implementing the 1921 treaty: Lionel Curtis and constitutional procedure', *Irish Historical Studies*, 20, 79 (Mar 1977), p. 313; Jones, *Whitehall diary*, vol. 3, p. 194.

57 P. Canning, *British policy towards Ireland, 1921–41* (Oxford, 1985), pp. 17–22.

58 Wilson Diaries, 6 Dec 1921, IWM, Wilson Papers.

59 Wilson Diaries, 18 Jan 1922, IWM, Wilson Papers; Wilson to Macready, 6 Jan 1922, IWM, HHW 2/2G/35.

60 For his optimistic assessments, see Cope to Churchill, 22 Feb 1922, TNA, CO 906/20; PGI Committee minutes, 20 Mar 1922, TNA, CAB 27/153; Cope to Churchill, 4 Apr 1922, TNA, CO 739/14.

61 Macready to Worthington-Evans, 21 Feb 1922, CCA, CHAR 22/11/104–110.

62 Macready to Wilson, 12 Feb 1922, IWM, HHW 2/2G/56; Macready to Worthington-Evans, 23 Feb 1922, CCA, CHAR 22/11/112–8.

63 Macready to Churchill, 15 Apr 1922, CCA, CHAR 22/12B/164–6.

64 Greenwood report, 7 Dec 1921, TNA, CAB 24/131.

65 Macready to Wilson, 28 Dec 1921, IWM, HHW 2/2G/28; memo by Churchill, 21 Dec 1921, TNA, CAB 27/154.

66 Wilson to Macready, 2 Mar 1922, IWM, HHW 2/2H/5.

67 Draft letter to Provisional Government by Curtis [not sent], 28 Jun 1922, CO 730/6.

68 Cosgrave to Curtis, 19 Nov 1922, TNA, CO 739/2; cabinet paper by Masterton-Smith, 3 Jan 1923, TNA, CAB 24/158; Mulcahy to Loughnane, 12 Oct 1923, TNA, CO 739/19.

69 Macready to Wilson, 27 Feb 1922, IWM, HHW 2/2H/4; WO to CO, 27 Nov 1923, TNA, CO 739/23.

70 Report by Macready, 21 Feb 1922, TNA, CAB 24/133.

71 RIC report, 20 Feb 1922, TNA, CO 906/20; Macready report, 21 Feb 1922, CAB 24/133.

72 Macready to Worthington-Evans, 21 Feb 1922, CCA, CHAR 22/11/104–110.

73 Report by Vice-Admiral Gaunt, 31 Mar 1922, CCA CHAR 22/12A/85–91; report by Cmdr Candy, 31 Mar 1922, & Gaunt to Admiralty, 3 Apr 1922, TNA, ADM 178/100.

74 Macready to Wilson, 6 Apr 1922, IWM, HHW 2/2H/13.

75 Gaunt to Admiralty, 5 Apr 1922, TNA, ADM 178/100.

76 Secret memo by Churchill for cabinet, 4 Apr 1922, CCA, CHAR 22/12B/102–114; list of stores taken from *Upnor*, 5 Jul 1922, TNA, ADM 178/100.

77 Special Branch report on revolutionary organisations, 12 Apr 1922, CP 3939, TNA, CAB 24/136.

78 Report by Brind, containing intelligence reports from Munster, 13 Apr 1922, TNA, CAB 24/136.

79 Report by Capt G. M. Crick for DNI, 6 Apr 1922, TNA, CO 739/3.

80 Macready to Wilson, 6 Apr 1922, IWM, HHW 2/2H/13.

81 Cabinet minutes, 5 Apr 1922, TNA, CAB 23/30.

82 Secret memo by Churchill for cabinet, 4 Apr 1922, CCA, CHAR 22/12B/102–114. See also Sturgis to Churchill, 20 Apr 1922, CO 19760, TNA, CO 739/16.

83 J. C. C. Davidson to R. Dickinson, 11 Apr 1922, in R. Rhodes James (ed.), *Memoirs of a Conservative: J. C. C. Davidson's memoirs and papers, 1910–37* (London, 1969), p. 111.

84 Churchill to Lloyd George, 19 Apr 1922, CCA, CHAR 22/12B/177.

85 Draft letter to Provisional Government by Curtis [not sent], 28 Jun 1922, CO 730/6.

86 Churchill to Collins, 29 Apr 1922, CO 739/14. For lawlessness and sectarian violence, see P. Hart, 'The Protestant experience of revolution in southern Ireland', in R. English & G. Walker (eds.), *Unionism in modern Ireland: new perspectives on politics and culture* (Basingstoke/London, 1996), pp. 81–98; R. B. McDowell, *Crisis and decline: the fate of the southern Unionists* (Dublin, 1997), pp. 119–30; Hopkinson, *Green against green*, pp. 89–92; E. O'Halpin, *Defending Ireland: the Irish state and its enemies since 1922* (Oxford, 1999), pp. 32–3.

87 Paper by deputation of southern loyalists, 25 May 1922, TNA, CAB 43/2.

88 Letter from A. Hodder, 28 May 1922, with Sir L. Scott to CO, 26 Jun 1922, TNA, CO 739/16.

89 Colonel J. Gretton to Churchill, 26 Jun 1922, CO 739/15.

90 Cabinet minutes, 16 May 1922, TNA, CAB 23/30.

91 Curtis to Cope, 1 May 1922, TNA, CO 906/20.

92 Draft letter to Provisional Government by Curtis [not sent], 28 Jun 1922, CO 730/6. The information on Co. Donegal came from a memo by an Anglo-Irish lord. See Lord Leitrim to Churchill, 20 Jun 1922, CO 739/15.

93 Hopkinson, *Green against green*, pp. 97–102.

94 Conference of British signatories to the treaty, 27 May 1922, CAB 43/1.

95 Cabinet minutes, 30 May & 1 Jun 1922, CAB 23/30.

96 See chapter 4 for more details.

97 Curtis to Churchill, 25 Aug 1922, TNA, CO 739/6.

98 Cabinet minutes, 16 May 1922, CAB 23/30.

99 Conference of British signatories to the treaty, 23 May 1922, CAB 43/1.

100 31 May 1922 entry, J. Barnes & D. Nicholson (eds.), *The Leo Amery diaries*, vol. 1: *1896–1929* (London, 1980), p. 286. For a similar assessment, see 2 Jun 1922 entry, J. Vincent (ed.), *The Crawford papers* (Manchester, 1984), pp. 422–3.

101 Conference between Churchill and armed services, 1 Jun 1922, TNA, CAB 16/42.

102 Neville Chamberlain to Ida Chamberlain, 24 Jun 1922, in R. Self (ed.), *The Neville Chamberlain diary letters*. vol. 2: *The reform years, 1921–27* (Ashgate, 2000), pp. 115–16.

103 P. Hart, 'Michael Collins and the assassination of Sir Henry Wilson', *Irish Historical Studies*, 28, 110 (Nov 1992).

104 Memo by Major-General Childs, undated, with Horwood to HO, 7 Jul 1922, TNA, MEPO 2/1974.

105 Conferences of ministers, 22, 23 & 24 Jun 1922, TNA, CAB 21/155. These conferences do not appear in the normal Cabinet papers. A single manuscript record was made by the Cabinet Secretary, Maurice Hankey, and kept in his safe in a sealed envelope. Minutes by Hankey, Curtis and Churchill, [1922], TNA, CAB 21/155.

106 Conference of ministers, 25 Jun 1922, TNA, CAB 21/155.

107 Macready, *Annals of an active life*, pp. 650–1.

108 15 May 1922 entry, Jones, *Whitehall diary*, vol. 3, p. 200.

109 8 Jun 1922 entry, Jones, *Whitehall diary*, vol. 3, p. 212.

110 For positive appraisals of Churchill, see P. Addison, 'The search for peace in Ireland', in J. W. Muller (ed.), *Churchill as peacemaker* (Cambridge, 1997), p. 203. Even Churchill's most critical biographer can find little fault with his handling of Ireland. R. Rhodes James, *Churchill: a study in failure, 1900–1939* (London, 1970), pp. 130–4.

111 O'Halpin, *Defending Ireland*, p. 17.

112 Quoted in Ferriter, *The transformation of Ireland*, p. 297.

113 For general histories of the Irish civil war see Hopkinson, *Green against green*; O'Halpin, *Defending Ireland*; Townshend, *Ireland: the 20th century*.

114 Telegrams between Cope and CO, 28–30 Jun 1922, TNA, CO 906/21.

115 Macready, *Annals of an active life*, pp. 655–9.

116 Colonel Maxwell Scott to Jeudwine, 13 Jul 1922, IWM, Jeudwine 72/82/2.

117 Reports by Macready, 29 Aug & 19 Sep 1922, TNA, CAB 24/138–139.

118 Report by Macready, 29 Aug 1922, TNA, CAB 24/138.

119 Sturgis to Cope, 11 Jul 1922, TNA, CO 906/21.

120 Anon. employee to Sir F. Lewis, 14 Aug 1922, TNA, CO 739/6. This letter was passed to Churchill.

121 Memo by P. Kellaway, 1 Jul 1922, & Curtis to Churchill, 5 Jul 1922, TNA, CO 739/13; intelligence report by Somerville, 31 Jul 1922, & Superintendent, Commercial Cable Co., Kenmare, to Admiralty, 10 Sep 1922, TNA, 739/3; minute by Freeston, 10 Aug 1922, TNA, CO 739/6.

122 Admiralty minute, 14 Sep 1922, TNA, ADM 1/8652/253.

123 Report by G. Purkiss, 4 Jul 1922, & report by Capt. G. Chetwode, 8 July 1922, TNA, CO 739/3.

124 Report by Macready, 8 Aug 1922, CP 4158, TNA, CAB 24/138; intelligence reports by Somerville, Sep–Oct 1922, TNA, CO 739/3.

125 Report by HMS *Vanity*, 18–31 Aug 1922, TNA, ADM 1/8632/173.

126 Intelligence report by Somerville, 9 Aug 1922, TNA, CO 739/3.

127 Intelligence report by Somerville, 2 Oct 1922, TNA, CO 739/3.

128 Intelligence report by Somerville, 8 Aug 1922, TNA, CO 739/3.

129 Macready, *Annals of an active life*, p. 661.

130 Curtis to Tallents, 15 Jan 1923, TNA, CO 739/17.

131 Minutes of Committee of Imperial Defence sub-Committee on Ireland, 29 Jun 1922, TNA, CAB 16/42.

132 Churchill to Collins, 7 Jul 1922, TNA, CO 739/6.

133 Churchill to Collins, 30 Jun 1922, 6.10 pm, CO 906/21.

134 Minutes of PGI Committee, 14 Jul 1922, TNA, CAB 27/153; Macready, *Annals of an active life*, p. 505.

135 Churchill to Craig, 7 Jul 1922, TNA, CO 739/6.

136 Curtis to Churchill, 25 Aug 1922, TNA, CO 739/6; quoted in G. R. Sloan, *The geopolitics of Anglo-Irish relations in the twentieth century* (Leicester, 1997), pp. 188–9.

137 Report by Macready, 15 Aug 1922, TNA, CAB 24/138.

138 British military intelligence summary for week ending 26 Aug 1922, NA, D/T S.1784.

139 Salisbury to Churchill, 27 Jul 1922, enclosing report from Irish informant, TNA, CO 739/16. For other examples see Gretton to Churchill, 5 Jul 1922, TNA, CO 739/15; anon. letter to Edward Marsh, 26 Sep 1922, TNA, CO 739/7.

140 Report by deputation of southern Irish unionists, undated [Oct 1922], TNA, CO 739/15.

141 D. Kennedy, *The widening gulf: northern attitudes to the independent Irish state, 1919–49* (Belfast, 1988), pp. 133–4.

142 Lord Londonderry to Churchill, 17 Jan 1923, CCA, CHAR 2/126/1–2.

143 See chapter 4.

144 Statement by Irish Claims Compensation Association in *Washington Post*, 5 Nov 1922.

145 Memo by Lord Derby and General Staff, 21 Nov 1922, CP 4315, TNA, CAB 24/140; Maxwell Scott to Jeudwine, 6 & 30 Sep 1922, IWM, Jeudwine 72/82/2.

146 British military intelligence summaries for weeks ending 16 Sep & 7 Oct 1922, NA, D/T S.1784.

147 Report by Macready, 29 Aug 1922,
TNA, CAB 24/138; Macready at meeting of
British signatories to treaty, 7 Sep 1922, TNA,
CAB 43/1.

148 Macready to Jeudwine, 8 Sep 1922, IWM,
Jeudwine 72/82/2.

149 Macready to Churchill, 20 Sep 1922, TNA,
CO 739/2.

150 Macready to Jeudwine, 8 Sep 1922, IWM,
Jeudwine 72/82/2. See also Macready, *Annals
of an active life*, pp. 663–4.

151 Meeting of British signatories to the treaty,
7 Sep 1922, TNA, CAB 43/1; letter from 'Joseph'
to 'Seamus', 3 Sep 1922, enclosed with note by
Colonel Carter to Curtis, 5 Sep 1922, TNA, CO
739/13.

152 Curtis to Cope, 7 Sep 1922, TNA,
CO 906/22.

153 Telegrams between Churchill, Cope, and
Sturgis, 1 Jul 1922, TNA, CO 906/21.

154 Telegrams and letters from Cope to
CO, 7 Sep – 14 Oct 1922, TNA, CO 739/2 &
CO 906/22.

155 A. J. P. Taylor, *English history, 1914–1945*
(London, 1977 edn), pp. 191–5; P. Clarke, *Hope
and glory; Britain, 1900–90* (London, 1997 edn),
pp. 109–10, 119–21.

156 Taylor, *English history*, p. 196.

157 Canning, *British policy towards Ireland*,
p. 22.

158 Macready, *Annals of an active life*, p. 665.

159 Note by Macready, 21 Nov 1922, TNA,
CO 739/11; memo by Lord Derby and Gen-
eral Staff, 21 Nov 1922, TNA, CAB 24/140;
Macready, *Annals of an active life*, pp. 671–5.

160 Salisbury to Bonar Law, 22 Oct 1922,
quoted in Canning, *British policy towards
Ireland*, p. 70. See also R. J. Q. Adams, *Bonar
Law* (London, 1999), p. 334.

161 Memo by Duke of Devonshire, 23 Apr
1923, TNA, CAB 27/216.

162 Report by HMS *Danae*, 13 Jul 1922, TNA,
ADM 1/8632/173; memo by Air Staff, 29 Jun
1922, TNA, AIR 8/49.

163 Minute by Maurice Antrobus, 26 Oct 1922,
TNA, CO 739/3.

164 Intelligence reports by Somerville, 19 Sep
& 13 Oct 1922, TNA, CO 739/3.

165 Cope to Curtis, 1 Jul 1922, TNA,
CO 906/21.

166 Curtis to Cope, 3 Jul 1922, TNA,
CO 906/21; meeting of Committee of Imperial
Defence sub-Committee, 10 Jul 1922, TNA,
CAB 16/42.

167 Letter from Admiralty to CO, 31 Jul 1922,
TNA, ADM 1/8652/253.

168 Minute by Admiralty, 14 Sep 1922, TNA,
ADM 1/8652/253; Admiralty to CO, 16 Sep 1922,
TNA, CO 739/3.

169 Admiralty to SNO Haulbowline, 3 Oct
1922, TNA, ADM 1/8652/253; Admiralty to CO,
16 Sep 1922, TNA, CO 739/3.

170 See chapter 3.

171 Report on Intelligence Department of
Free State army, Apr 1923, NA, D/T S.3361.

172 Colonel Carter to Sir Herbert Creedy, 11
Aug 1922, TNA, WO 141/58. For details on
Nolan incident, see telegrams between Sturgis,
Cope, and Whiskard, 11–12 Aug 1922, TNA,
CO 906/21; Whiskard to Masterton Smith,
12 Aug 1922, TNA, CO 739/6.

173 Telegrams between Cope and Sturgis,
27 Jul 1922, TNA, CO 906/21; Somerville to
Admiralty, 29 Jul 1922, TNA, CO 739/3.

174 Curtis to Churchill, 5 Sep 1922, TNA,
CO 739/3. See also telegrams between Freeston,
Curtis, Cope, and Loughnane 30–31 Aug,
4 Sep, 7 Sep 1922, TNA, CO 906/21–22.

175 Memo by Freeston, 25 Oct 1922, TNA,
CO 739/7.

176 PG cabinet minutes, 6 Sep 1922, NA, G 1/3.

177 Mulcahy to O'Hegarty, 14 Oct 1922, UCD,
O'Malley Papers, P17a/197.

178 Report on Intelligence Department of
Free State army, Apr 1923, NA, D/T S.3361.

CHAPTER 3
An International Conspiracy

1 Biographical notes on John T Ryan, undated
[1918], USNA, RG 165, MID 9771–56.

2 Ryan to McGarrity, undated [late March
1922], NLI, McGarrity Papers, Ms. 17486(1).

3 Ferriter, *The transformation of Ireland*, p. 44.

4 E. Delaney, '"Almost a class of helots in an
alien land": the British state and Irish immigration, 1921–45', in D. MacRaild (ed.), *The Great
Famine and beyond: Irish migrants in Britain
in the nineteenth and twentieth centuries* (Dublin & Portland, OR, 2000), p. 241.

5 P. Hart, '"Operations Abroad": the IRA in
Britain, 1919–23', *The English Historical Review*,
115 (2000), pp. 71–102. See also Hopkinson,
The Irish war of independence, pp. 147–9.

6 Ryle Dwyer, *The Squad*, pp. 23–6.

7 Hart, '"Operations Abroad"', pp. 74–77, 85;
Ryle Dwyer, *The Squad*, pp. 53–4, 206–7; Paper
by Capt. Frank Thornton, undated [1940], NLI,
Leon Ó Broin Papers, Ms. 31655.

8 Hart, '"Operations Abroad"', pp. 82–5, 91–4.

9 *Ibid.*, pp. 78, 93–4, 98; MI5 memo, enclosed with Kell to HO, 8 Mar 1939, TNA, KV 4/232. For postal censorship, see Andrew, *Secret service*, pp. 176–7.

10 Conference between Home Secretary, Basil Thomson and police chiefs, 10 Jun 1921, TNA, MEPO 3/465.

11 Special Branch report on revolutionary organisations, 27 Oct 1921 & 24 Nov 1921, TNA, CAB 24/129.

12 Wilson diary, 7 & 8 Dec 1921, IWM, Wilson Diaries, DS/MISC/90.

13 Special Branch report on revolutionary organisations, 17 Nov 1921, TNA, CAB 24/129.

14 Special Branch reports on revolutionary organisations, 24 Nov & 1 Dec 1921, TNA, CAB 24/131; HO minutes, 18 & 22 Nov 1921, & Carter to HO, 21 Nov 1921, TNA, HO 5/11223.

15 Special Branch reports on revolutionary organisations, 14, 20 & 27 Oct, 17 Nov 1921, TNA, CAB 24/129.

16 Major-General Sir Wyndham Childs, *Episodes and reflections* (London, 1930), pp. 65–8, 102–13, 174–82.

17 *Ibid.*, pp. 184–5, 184–6.

18 Special Branch reports on revolutionary organisations, 15 Dec 1921, 9 Feb, 9 Mar, 27 Apr, 1 Jun & 6 Jul 1922, TNA, CAB 24/131, 24/133, 24/137.

19 Special Branch report on revolutionary organisations, 9 Mar 1922, TNA, CAB 24/134.

20 Childs, *Episodes and reflections*, pp. 198–9.

21 Special Branch reports on revolutionary organisations, 4, 11 & 25 May 1922, TNA, CAB 24/136; local police reports, 1 May 1922, TNA, CO 739/11; note from Director of Public Prosecutions, 6 May 1922, TNA, CO 739/11; *Manchester Guardian*, 11 May 1922.

22 Special Branch report on revolutionary organisations, 15 Jun 1922, TNA, CAB 24/137. For an example of successful IRA gunrunning by Con Neenan, see U. MacEoin, *Survivors* (Dublin, 1980), p. 244.

23 Childs, *Episodes and reflections*, pp. 186–8.

24 C. E. Callwell, *Field-Marshal Sir Henry Wilson: his life and times* (London, 1927), p. 341; Commemorative pamphlet by the republican London Memorial Committee, undated [probably 1949], NA, D/T S.1570B; *The Sunday Press*, 14 Aug 1955; K. Jeffrey, *Field Marshal Sir Henry Wilson: a political soldier* (Oxford, 2006).

25 Hopkinson, *Green against green*, pp. 112–14.

26 Hart, 'Michael Collins and the assassination of Sir Henry Wilson', pp. 168–70.

27 R. Popplewell, *Intelligence and imperial defence: British intelligence and the defence of the Indian empire, 1904–1924* (London, 1995), p. 125.

28 Shortt (Home Sec.) to Churchill, 22 Jun 1922, CCA, CHAR 2/123/129–136; conference of ministers with Childs, 23 Jun 1922, TNA, CAB 21/255.

29 Conference of HO and military officials, 1 Jul 1922, TNA, HO 317/56.

30 Commissioner Horwood to HO, 7 Jul 1922, TNA, MEPO 2/1974; memo by Shortt, 17 Jul 1922, TNA, CAB 24/138; Cabinet minutes, 24 Jul 1922, TNA, CAB 23/30; Receiver of Metropolitan Police to Commissioner Horwood, 19 Oct 1922, TNA, MEPO 2/1974; Winter, *Winter's tale*, p. 347.

31 Memo by Childs, enclosed with Horwood to HO, 7 Jul 1922, TNA, MEPO 2/1974.

32 See chapter 2.

33 Curtis to Churchill, 25 Aug 1922, TNA, CO 739/6. For a critical assessment of Fitzgerald's activities see J. F. White to Thomas Johnson, 3 Mar 1924; notes by Johnson on investigation by Committee on Public Accounts, 1924–25; draft speech by Johnson, 1 Aug 1927, NLI, Johnson Papers, Ms. 17160. Another clandestine attempt to purchase military equipment, this time wireless sets, can be found in WO 141/58.

34 Special Branch reports on revolutionary organisations, 12 Oct, 16 Nov & 14 Dec 1922, 4, 11 & 18 Jan 1923, TNA, CAB 24/139, /140 & /158.

35 Hopkinson, *Green against green*, p. 255.

36 Special Branch report on revolutionary organisations, 8 Feb 1923, TNA, CAB 24/158.

37 Special Branch reports on revolutionary organisations, 25 Jan, 22 Feb & 8 Mar 1923, TNA, CAB 24/159.

38 Sturgis to Donnelly, 13 Jan 1923, NA, D/T s.1753; FS cabinet minutes, 13 Jan 1923, NA, G 2/1; O'Halpin, *Defending Ireland*, p. 22.

39 Childs, *Episodes and reflections*, p. 207. See also Special Branch report on revolutionary organisations, 15 Mar 1923, TNA, CAB 24/159. Hopkinson (*Green against green*, p. 25) wrongly states that 160 were arrested.

40 Secretary of FS Government to Cosgrave, 13 Mar 1923; committee of deportees to Home Secretary, 18 Mar 1923, NA, D/T S.2156; O'Hegarty to Cosgrave, 3 Apr 1923, NA, D/T S.2156.

41 See clippings in MEPO 38/111.

42 An excellent review of the case is a memo by Home Sec., 10 Mar 1924, TNA, HO 144/7583. See also Cabinet conclusions, 15 May 1923, TNA, CAB 23/45; telegrams between Loughnane and Sturgis, 15 & 16 May 1923, TNA, CO 739/21; police reports and newspaper clippings in TNA, MEPO 38/111.

43 Moss Twomey to Lynch, 5 Apr 1923, quoted in Hopkinson, *Green against green*, p. 255.

44 Special Branch reports on revolutionary organisations, 29 Mar & 12 Apr 1923, TNA, CAB 24/159. See also memo by C. B. Dutton, 28 Jul 1923, NLI, Joseph H. Fowler Papers, Ms. 27097(7).

45 P. Williamson (ed.), *The modernisation of Conservative politics: the diaries and letters of William Bridgeman, 1904–1935* (London, 1988), pp. 165–6, f.

46 Biographical note on John T. Ryan, Jun 1918, RG 165, MID 9771–56, USNA; biographical note on Jeremiah O'Leary, summer 1918, RG 165, MID P.F.5851, USNA; 'Notes on the Constitution and Activities of the Irish Revolutionary Party in America' by Robert Nathan, Oct 1918, RG 165, MID 9771–56, USNA [hereafter referred to as 'SIS notes on Clan na Gael, Oct 1918'].

47 Reports from British agent ('Z') intercepted by Clan na Gael, 1912–17, NLI, McGarrity Papers, Ms. 17502; Popplewell, *Intelligence and imperial defence*, pp. 147–8.

48 Andrew, *For the president's eyes only*, pp. 32–54; R. B. Spence, 'Englishmen in New York: the SIS American station, 1915–1921', *Intelligence and National Security*, 19, 3 (Autumn, 2004), pp. 511–37.

49 Letter from Guy Gaunt, 22 Aug 1916, TNA, MEPO 2/10664.

50 'Synopsis of the Irish Agitation in the United States'; SIS notes on Clan na Gael, Oct 1918; N. Biddle to W. Phillips, 15 Oct 1918, USNA, RG 165, MID 9771–56.

51 Draft letter from J. O'Brian to F. G. Caffey, 10 Dec 1918 [unsent], USNA, RG 60, 191962–30.

52 C. DeWoody to Caffey, 23 Dec 1919, & O'Brian to Caffey, 9 Jan 1919, USNA, RG 60, 191961–32; correspondence between Bureau of Investigation and MID, Jan 1921, USNA, RG 165, MID 9771-A-100.

53 Hopkinson, *Irish war of independence*, pp. 165–75; A. J. Ward, *Ireland and Anglo-American relations, 1899–1921* (London, 1969), pp. 257–64; F. M. Carroll, *American opinion and the Irish question, 1910–23* (London & New York, 1978), ch.6.

54 Luke Dillon to McGarrity, 2 Feb 1922, NLI, McGarrity Papers, Ms. 17610(1); McGarrity

to Harry Boland, 13 Jan 1921, NLI, McGarrity Papers, Ms. 17424(3).

55 Spence, 'Englishmen in New York', pp. 531–3. See also Popplewell, *Intelligence and imperial defence*, pp. 236–8, 321–4; Andrew, *For the President's eyes only*, p. 65.

56 *Time*, 15 Aug 1930; correspondence between Armstrong and FO, May–Jul 1921, TNA, FO 371/5655.

57 One example is in a telegram from US embassy, London, 4 Feb 1921, USNA, RG 59, 841d.00/298.

58 Memo by Churchill, 21 Jun 1921, TNA, CAB 24/125.

59 Report by Armstrong, 16 Jun 1923, & UK ambassador, Washington to London, 17 Jun 1921, TNA, HO 351/79; report by US Customs, 18 Jun 1921, & US embassy, London to State Dept, 29 Jun 1921, USNA, RG 59, 841d.00/372 & /382; *New York Times*, 17 Jun 1921; FO minute, 27 Jun 1921, TNA, FO 371/5655; report by Roy C. McHenry, 4 Oct 1921, USNA, RG 60, Entry 114AB, Box 11007, File 52-505.

60 Memo by John Crim, 28 Oct 1921, USNA, RG 60, Entry 114AB, Box 11007, File 52–505.

61 T. P. Coogan, *The IRA* (London, 1995 edn), pp. 94–5.

62 Carroll, *American opinion and the Irish question*, pp. 177–86.

63 Prof. T. Smiddy to Gavan Duffy, 4 & 30 May 1922, NA, D/FA, EF Box, 30 File 199(1).

64 McGarrity stated in September 1923 that $200,000 had been sent in the previous twelve months. Before that a further $79,000 is indicated in the McGarrity papers. See speech by McGarrity to Clan convention, 1 Sep 1923, NLI, McGarrity Papers, Ms. 17657.

65 Major Kelly to Walsh, 18 Dec 1922, NYPL, Frank P. Walsh Papers, Box 26, Irish Correspondence 1922 September – December; Armstrong to FO, 19 Mar 1923, NA, D/T S.1976.

66 Special Branch report on revolutionary organisations, 18 Jan 1923, TNA, CAB 24/158; interview between US Consul, Dublin and William Cosgrave, 14 Mar 1923, USNA, RG 59, 841d.00/592.

67 Armstrong to FO, 12 Jan 1923, NA, D/T S.1976.

68 Armstrong to FO, 22 Dec 1921, TNA, FO 371/7266; Capt. Somerville to Admiralty, 5 Jun 1922, & Armstrong to FO, 8 Jun 1922, TNA, FO 371/7272; correspondence between US Shipping Board, US Consulate in London, US Customs Service, Treasury Dept and State Dept, Jun 1922, USNA, RG 59, 841d.00/512–516.

69 Report by Special Branch, 29 Mar 1923, TNA, CAB 24/159.

70 Smiddy to D/FA, 15 Jan 1923, NA, D/FA, EF Box 28, File 185. The identification of these detectives as 'Burns' men' is in Ryan to McGarrity, 23 Apr 1923, NLI, McGarrity Papers, Ms. 17486(2). See also R. P. Weiss, 'Private detective agencies and labour discipline in the United States, 1855–1946', *Historical Journal*, 29, 1 (Mar, 1986), pp. 87–107; http://www.pinkertons.com (accessed 1 Aug 2006).

71 Report by private detective agency, New York, Feb–Jun 1923; Smiddy to Desmond Fitzgerald, 12 May 1923; D/FA to Smiddy, all in NA, D/FA, EF Box 28, File 185.

72 Reports from Gloster Armstrong are in NA, D/T S.1976.

73 Smiddy to Fitzgerald, 12 May 1923, NA, D/FA, EF Box 28, File 186.

74 'A.L.M.' (Smiddy's Secretary) to Smiddy, 8 Jun 1923, NA, D/FA, EF Box 28, File 186.

75 Smiddy to General E. O'Duffy, 12 May 1923, NA, D/FA, EF Box 28, File 189(2).

76 McGarrity to Lynch, 24 Mar 1923, NLI, Ms. 17526(2).

77 McGarrity to A. Stack, 23 Nov 1922, NLI, McGarrity Papers, Ms. 17489.

78 Andrew, *Secret service*, ch.7.

79 Porter, *Plots and paranoia*, pp. 151, 156.

80 Andrew, *Secret service*, ch.7.

81 *Ibid.*, pp. 280–2; Jeffrey, 'British military intelligence following World War I', p. 63.

82 Andrew, *Secret service*, pp. 227–8.

83 Thurlow, *The secret state*, pp. 110–12.

84 Draft treaty with Soviet Union, May 1920; de Valera to Harry Boland, 27 Oct 1920; memo by McCartan on mission to Soviet Union, Jun 1921, in *Documents on Irish foreign policy*, vol. 1: *1919–1922* (Dublin, 1998), pp. 59–63, 98, 148–56; E. O'Connor, *Reds and the green: Ireland, Russia and the Communist Internationals, 1919–43* (Dublin, 2004), pp. 44–7, 74.

85 O'Connor, *Reds and the green*, pp. 16–74.

86 *Nationalism in Ireland*, p. 327; Townshend, *Political violence in Ireland*, pp. 330–1; A. Pimley, 'The working-class movement and the Irish revolution, 1896–1923', in D. G. Boyce (ed.), *The revolution in Ireland, 1879–1923* (Basingstoke & London, 1988); P. Bew, 'Sinn Féin, agrarian radicalism and the war of independence, 1919–1921', *ibid.*

87 R. Dawson, *Red Terror and green* (London, 1920).

88 Nathan to FO, 20 May 1921; Curzon minute, 18 May 1921, TNA, FO 371/6912.

89 Andrew, *Secret service*, pp. 278–9.

90 Monthly reviews of revolutionary movements by Sir Basil Thomson, 1 May & 1 Jun 1921, TNA, CAB 24/125; *Intercourse between Bolshevism and Sinn Fein*, Cmd. 1326, 10 Jun 1921.

91 Wallinger intelligence report enclosed with Seton to Anderson, 8 Oct 1921, TNA, HO 317/59. For information on Chattopadhyaya and Wallinger's Indian intelligence service, see Popplewell, *Intelligence and imperial defence*, pp. 222–8.

92 Special Branch report on revolutionary organisations, 14 Oct 1921, TNA, CAB 24/129.

93 Midleton to Churchill [undated], TNA, Midleton Papers, 30/67/49.

94 Special Branch reports on revolutionary organisations, 1 Sep 1921 & 25 May 1922, CAB 24/127 & /136.

95 Dublin District weekly intelligence summaries, 11 Feb & 11 Mar 1922, TNA, WO 35/92. For a similar analysis, see Brigade-Major Bernard Montgomery to father, 1 Mar 1922, in B. Montgomery, *A field-marshal in the family* (London, 1973), pp. 182–3.

96 Edward Swann to State Dept, 17 Feb 1920, USNA, RG 60, 206924; O'Connor, *Reds and the green*, pp. 80–1.

97 Churchill to Geddes, 3 May 1922, TNA, CO 739/5; State Dept note, 5 May 1922, USNA, RG 59, 841d.00/550. For British efforts in March 1922, see TNA, CO 739/4.

98 Special Branch report on revolutionary organisations, 7 Sep 1922, TNA, CAB 24/138.

99 Special Branch report on revolutionary organisations, 25 May 1922, TNA, CAB 24/136.

100 M. MacWhite to D/FA, 13 Jan 1923, & reports by Michael McDunphy, 19 & 26 Jan 1923, NA, D/T S.3147; Nicholas Klishko to Lord Curzon, 21 Feb 1923, NA, D/T S.2108; O'Halpin, *Defending Ireland*, p. 24.

101 Special Branch reports on revolutionary organisations, 12 Oct & 21 Dec 1922, 15 Feb, 5 Apr & 6 Dec 1923, TNA, CAB 24/162.

102 Childs, *Episodes and reflections*, pp. 198–200.

103 J. M. Roberts, *Europe, 1880–1945*, 3rd edn (Harlow, 2001), pp. 367–73.

104 Murphy, *John Chartres*, pp. 48–9, 57–8; A. Roth, 'Gun running from Germany in the early 1920s', *The Irish Sword*, 22, 88 (2000), pp. 209–20. There is some discrepancy between these two sources on the amount of funds in the possession of Briscoe and McGuinness, but the higher figure appears

more reliable. For Beaumont, see O'Connor, *Reds and the green*, pp. 48–9.

105 Lord D'Abernon to FO, 10 Jul 1922, TNA, FO 371/7531.

106 Major H. A. Strauss to Brig-General M. Churchill, 3 Feb 1920, & reply from Churchill, 10 Feb 1920, USNA, RG 165, MID 9771-A-65.

107 Basil Cave to FO, 24 Feb 1921, TNA, HO 144/1652/214036.

108 Memo by Churchill, 21 Jun 1921, TNA, CAB 24/125.

109 Wallinger report with Seton to Anderson, 8 Oct 1921, TNA, HO 317/59.

110 Roth, 'Gun running from Germany in the early 1920s', pp. 212–13.

111 Memo on information given by Sir Edward Bellingham (Anglo-Irish landowner, former head of British Military Mission in Berlin) to D/FA, 6 Mar 1922, NA, D/FA, EF Box, 23 File 140(2).

112 *Ibid.*

113 Murphy, *John Chartres*, pp. 57–8; Colonel Carter (Special Branch) to Anderson, 21 Oct 1921, TNA, HO 317/59.

114 Quoted in S. M. Lawlor, 'Ireland from truce to treaty: war or peace? July to October 1921', *Irish Historical Studies*, 22, 85 (Mar 1980), p. 56.

115 Murphy, *John Chartres*, pp. 57–8; 67–8; Roth, 'Gun running from Germany in the early 1920s', pp. 213–16.

116 Report by Brind, 1 Oct 1921, in appendix to Army record of the rebellion, vol. 1.

117 Murphy, *John Chartres*, pp. 57–8, 67–8, 115.

118 F. Oliver to FO, 18 Jan 1922, TNA, FO 371/7462; Fitzalan to Churchill, 27 Jan 1922, CCA, CHAR 22/11.

119 James Masterton Smith to FO, 13 May 1922; D'Abernon to German Government, 16 May 1922, TNA, FO 371/7531.

120 FO to D'Abernon, 4 Jul 1922, & reply from D'Abernon, 14 Jul 1922, TNA, FO 371/7532; correspondence between Irish D/FA and John Chartres, 14–19 Jun 1922, NA, D/FA, EF Box, 24 File 143.

121 Roth, 'Gun running from Germany in the early 1920s', pp. 219–20.

122 Min. of Defence to D/FA, 5 Jan 1923, NA, D/FA, EF Box, 23 File 141; D/FA to CO, 3 Feb 1923, NA, D/T S.4107.

123 Commission of Control, Berlin to WO, 2 Nov 1922, TNA, FO 371/6711.

124 Special Branch reports on revolutionary organisations, 23 Nov 1922 & 22 Mar 1923, TNA, CAB 24/140 & /159.

125 Roth, 'Gun running from Germany in the early 1920s', p. 220.

126 Lynch to Seán Moylan, 6 Feb 1923, TNA, CO 739/21.

127 Ryan to McGarrity, 22 Feb 1923, & McGarrity to Ryan, 5 Apr 1923, NLI, McGarrity Papers, Ms. 17637(1); Seán Moylan to Pa Murray, 10 May 1923, NLI, McGarrity Papers, Ms. 17466(1); correspondence from de Valera, Lynch, McGarrity, J. J. O'Kelly, Moylan, and Laurence Ginnell in TNA, CO 739/21.

CHAPTER 4

Security and Sectarianism in Northern Ireland

1 P. Buckland, *James Craig* (Dublin, 1980); D. Fitzpatrick, *The two Irelands, 1912–1939* (Oxford, 1998), p. 103; B. A. Follis, *A state under siege: the establishment of Northern Ireland, 1920–1925* (Oxford, 1995), pp. 1–5.

2 J. Bardon, *A history of Ulster* (Belfast, 1992), p. 494; NI Government statistics, PRONI, CAB 6/28/3.

3 Bardon, *A history of Ulster*, pp. 466–76; Hopkinson, *The Irish war of independence*, pp. 153–7.

4 Hopkinson, *Irish war of independence*, pp. 153–79; J. McColgan, *British policy and the Irish administration, 1920–22* (London, 1983), ch. 2.

5 Report by W. P. Kent, 8 Mar 1922, USNA, RG 59, 841d.00/490.

6 Report by Kent, 31 Aug 1921, USNA, RG 59, 841d.00/426.

7 Craig to Greenwood, 27 Sep 1921, TNA, CAB 24/128; Macready to Wilson, 24 Sep 1921, IWM, HHW 2/2F/24; Follis, *A state under siege*, pp. 82–4.

8 Macready to Worthington-Evans, 8 Mar 1922, TNA, CO 739/11; Macready to Wilson, 14 Mar 1922, IWM, HHW 2/2H/9.

9 Memo by Greenwood, 10 Dec 1921, TNA, CAB 24/131; Follis, *A state under siege*, pp. 85–6.

10 Follis, *A state under siege*, p. 86.

11 Macready to Worthington-Evans, 8 Mar 1922, TNA, CO 739/11; Macready to Worthington-Evans & Wilson, 20 Mar 1922, IWM, HHW 2/2H/11; The local British army commander had a similar opinion. See Major-General Cameron to Macready, 18 Dec 1921, IWM, HHW2/2G/22. The depredations of the

Special Constabulary have been exaggerated by nationalist commentators. Indeed, one recent historian, Follis, has attempted to defend their record. However, contemporary British reports confirm that, especially in the first half of 1922, the Specials often sided with Protestant rioters. For a balanced assessment, see P. Buckland, 'A Protestant state: Unionists in government, 1921–39', in D. George Boyce & A. O'Day (eds.), *Defenders of the Union: a survey of British and Irish unionism since 1801* (London & New York, 2001), p. 214.

12 Minutes of NI cabinet, 14 Mar 1922, PRONI, CAB 4/36; report by Cameron, 7 Mar 1922, with Macready to Worthington-Evans, 8 Mar 1922, TNA, CO 739/11.

13 Macready to Worthington-Evans, 8 Mar 1922, TNA, CO 739/11; Memo by Macready, 28 Mar 1922, TNA, WO 32/9533.

14 Report by Macready, 10 Jan 1922, TNA, CAB 24/132; Macready to Wilson, 5 Jan 1922, IWM, HHW 2/2G/34; Cameron to Craig, 28 Mar 1922, PRONI, CAB 6/28/1.

15 NI Government statistics on casualties, 28 Jun 1922, PRONI, CAB 6/28/3.

16 Brigadier Frederick Clarke memoir, in Sheehan, *British voices*, p. 44.

17 Cameron to Macready, 18 Dec 1921, with Macready to Worthington-Evans, 20 Dec 1921, IWM, HHW 2/2G/22.

18 Macready to Worthington-Evans, 27 Mar 1922, TNA, CAB 27/154; report on army intelligence section in Northern Ireland, 1926, TNA, WO 106/6156.

19 Army record of the rebellion: vol 2, p. 25.

20 Minutes of meeting between Churchill, Craig and military chiefs, 10 Mar 1922, TNA, CO 739/11.

21 Instructions issued by GHQ, Dublin, 8 Feb 1922, in Appendix XIII to report on army intelligence section in Northern Ireland, 1926, TNA, WO 106/6156.

22 NI cabinet conclusions, 16 Feb 1922, PRONI, CAB 4/33.

23 Telegrams between Craig and Churchill, 11–13 Feb & 21 Mar 1922, TNA, CO 906/20; Craig to Churchill, 11 Mar 1922, CCA, CHAR 22/12A/30–34.

24 Collins to Churchill, 21 Mar 1922, TNA, CAB 24/134; Collins to Churchill, 22 Mar 1922, TNA, CO 906/20.

25 É. Phoenix, 'Michael Collins – the northern question, 1916–1922', in G. Doherty & D. Keogh (eds.), *Michael Collins and the making of the Irish state* (Dublin, 1998), pp. 102–4.

26 P. Buckland, *Ulster unionism and the origins of Northern Ireland* (Dublin, 1973), p. 154.

27 NI cabinet conclusions, 13 Mar 1922, PRONI, CAB 4/35; Follis, *A state under siege*, pp. 69–70.

28 Memo by Jones and Curtis, 18 Mar 1922, TNA, CAB 24/134. See also Cope to Anderson, 13 Feb 1922, TNA, CO 906/20; weekly survey by Greenwood, 13 Feb 1922, TNA, CAB 24/133.

29 Report by Macready for cabinet, 28 Mar 1922, TNA, CAB 24/136.

30 Macready to Cavan, 20 Mar 1922, with Macready to Wilson, 20 Mar 1922, IWM, HHW 2/2H/11. For Macready's unhappy time in Belfast, see J. Fergusson, *The Curragh Incident* (London, 1964).

31 Letter from Macready to Wilson, 15 Feb 1922, IWM, HHW 2/2G/62.

32 Macready to Worthington-Evans, 8 Mar 1922, TNA, CO 739/11.

33 For example, see telegrams from Churchill to Collins and Craig, Feb 1922, TNA, CO 906/20.

34 J. Baker, *The McMahon family murders and the Belfast troubles, 1920–22*, Glenravel Local History Project pamphlet (Belfast, n.d. [1995?]), pp. 1–14; Follis, *A state under siege*, p. 95; report by Kent, 29 Mar 1922, USNA, RG 59, 841d.00/495.

35 Weekly survey by Greenwood, 17 Mar 1922, CP 3855, CAB 24/134, TNA.

36 Churchill to British cabinet, 22 Mar 1922, TNA, CAB 23/29; PGI Committee, 24 Mar 1922, TNA, CAB 27/153.

37 Collins to Churchill, 20 Apr 1922, TNA, CO 906/20. See also M. Hopkinson, 'The Craig–Collins pacts of 1922: two attempted reforms of the Northern Ireland government', *Irish Historical Studies*, 27, 106 (Nov 1990), p. 145.

38 Hopkinson, *Green against green*, pp. 77–81; Phoenix, 'Michael Collins – the Northern question', pp. 108–9.

39 Follis, *A state under siege*, pp. 98–9. For murder statistics, see memo by S. Watt & Solly-Flood to Tallents, 27 Jun 1922, PRONI, CAB 6/80.

40 Memo by Solly-Flood, 18 May 1922, PRONI, CAB 6/41; report by Brind, 23 May 1922, TNA, CAB 24/136.

41 Solly-Flood to Tallents, 27 Jun 1922, PRONI, CAB 6/80.

42 Curtis to Churchill, 23 Jun 1922, CO 33108, CO 739/6.

43 Hopkinson, *Green against green*, p. 87.

44 Craig to Churchill, 26 May 1922, TNA, CO 739/14.

45 'Secret notes on southern Ireland', 24 May & 15 Jun 1922, PRONI, CAB 6/88.

46 Circular by Solly-Flood for senior police officers, 24 May 1922, PRONI, CAB 6/41.

47 Richard King to Craig, 23 May 1922, PRONI, CAB 6/28/2; 'Secret & Urgent' note from Craig to Churchill, 24 May 1922, PRONI, CAB 6/28/2; NI cabinet conclusions, 26 May 1922, PRONI, CAB 4/45.

48 Report by Colonel Maxwell Scott, 31 May 1922, CAB 21/254, TNA.

49 Instructions to intelligence officers, 6 Jun 1922, in Appendix XVI to report on army intelligence section in Northern Ireland, 1926, TNA, WO 106/6156.

50 See memo by Curtis, 6 Jun 1922, CHAR 22/13/116–20; report by Brind, 7 Jun 1922, TNA, CAB 24/137; and report by Macready, 13 Jun 1922, TNA, CAB 24/137; report by Commandant Dan Hogan, 7 Jun 1922, CCA, CHAR 22/13/150–62.

51 Jones, *Whitehall diary*, vol. 3, pp. 203–4.

52 Report by Solly-Flood, 7 Apr 1922. & Solly-Flood to WO, Apr 1922, PRONI, CAB 6/41.

53 NI cabinet conclusions, 12 May 1922, PRONI, CAB 4/41.

54 NI cabinet conclusions, 26 May 1922, PRONI, CAB 4/45. For London's support for the NI constabulary see conference on Ireland of ministers and officials & Committee of Imperial Defence sub-Committee on Ireland, 22 May 1922, TNA, CAB 16/42.

55 Conference between Churchill, Macready, and Londonderry, 22 May 1922, TNA, CAB 16/42.

56 Note in Appendix XIV to report on army intelligence section in Northern Ireland, 1926, TNA, WO 106/6156.

57 Instructions for intelligence officers, 6 Jun 1922, in Appendix XVII to report on army intelligence section in Northern Ireland, 1926, TNA, WO 106/6156.

58 The following section is based on this document. See report on army intelligence section in Northern Ireland, 1926, TNA, WO 106/6156.

59 *Ibid.*

60 Macready to Wilson, 4 Jan 1922, IWM, HHW 2/2G/32.

61 Report by Solly-Flood, 7 Apr 1922, PRONI, CAB 6/41; Solly-Flood to Craig, 3 Oct 1922, PRONI, CAB 8G/1.

62 Report by Macready, 2 Sep 1922, TNA, CAB 43/2. See also meeting of Committee of Imperial Defence Sub-Committee, 26 May 1922, TNA, CAB 16/42.

63 Minute by A. Magill, 10 May 1922, PRONI, CAB 6/28/1.

64 News Bulletins issued by Military's Adviser's Press Bureau, 24 Jul – 17 Aug 1922, PRONI, CAB 6/50.

65 Solly-Flood to NI Ministry of Home Affairs, 17 Jul 1922; Clark to Watt (both Home Affairs), 22 Jul 1922; Watt to NI Ministry of Finance, 18 Sep 1922, PRONI, CAB 6/51.

66 Report on army intelligence section in Northern Ireland, 1926, TNA, WO 106/6156.

67 Conference between RUC Inspector Harrison and Childs, 11 Jul 1922, TNA, MEPO 2/1974.

68 Solly-Flood to Craig, 3 Oct 1922, PRONI, CAB 8G/1.

69 L. K. Donohue, 'Regulating Northern Ireland: the Special Powers Acts, 1922–72', *The Historical Journal*, 41, 4 (1998), p. 1092.

70 Solly-Flood to Craig, 12 Aug 1922, quoting letter from NI Cabinet Secretary on 20 Apr 1922, PRONI, CAB/9B/47/1; NI cabinet conclusions, 23 May 1922, CAB 4/43, PRONI.

71 Follis, *A state under siege*, pp. 107–9.

72 NI Government statistics on outrages, Nov 1921 – Dec 1923, PRONI, CAB 6/11.

73 Follis, *A state under siege*, p. 15.

74 Macready to Wilson, 23 Sep 1921, IWM, HHW 2/2F/23; Londonderry to Craig, 14 Aug 1922, PRONI, CAB 6/29.

75 Wickham to Watt, 30 Sep 1922, PRONI, CAB 6/31.

76 Memos by General Ricardo, Colonel Perceval Maxwell and Bob Stevenson, 30 Jun 1922, TNA, CO 906/27.

77 Memo by Solly-Flood, 24 Jul 1922, PRONI, CAB 6/51.

78 Memo by Solly Flood, 22 Jun 1922, PRONI, CAB 6/28/3; Solly-Flood to Craig, 5 Sep 1922, PRONI, CAB 6/30.

79 Craig to Londonderry, 16 Aug 1922, PRONI, CAB 6/29.

80 Solly-Flood to Craig, 22 Aug 1922, PRONI, CAB 6/29.

81 See letters from Solly-Flood to Craig, Sep–Oct 1922, PRONI, CAB 6/29.

82 Tallents to Masterton-Smith, 6 Dec 1922, TNA, CO 739/1; Solly-Flood to Craig, 5 Dec 1922, PRONI, CAB 6/52.

83 Memo by E. Clark, 28 Sep 1922, PRONI, CAB 6/51.

84 Memo by NI ministry of finance, 10 Jun 1922, PRONI, CAB 6/28/3.

85 Board of enquiry into Portadown and Dramore arrests, 4 Sep 1922; RUC County Inspector reports, 26 Sep 1922, PRONI, CAB 6/30.

86 Memo by Dawson Bates, 27 Sep 1922, PRONI, CAB 6/30.

87 Report by RUC Commissioner Gelston, 25 Sep 1922, PRONI, CAB 6/31; Follis, *A state under siege*, pp. 113–14.

88 For praise of the CID see report by Macready, 2 Sep 1922, TNA, CAB 43/2, & report by Solly-Flood, 3 Oct 1922, PRONI, CAB 8G/1.

89 Wickham to Watt, 30 Sep 1922, PRONI, CAB 6/31.

90 Waters-Taylor (for Military Adviser) to NI Min. of Home Affairs, 16 Aug 1922, PRONI, HA/32/1/257; RUC County Inspector reports, 26 Sep 1922, PRONI, CAB 6/30; Wickham to Watt, 30 Sep 1922, PRONI, CAB 6/31.

91 Spender to Craig, 21 Sep 1922, PRONI, CAB 6/29; Dawson Bates to Craig, 23 Nov 1922, PRONI, CAB 6/31.

92 Memo by Wickham, 27 Sep 1922, PRONI, CAB 6/51.

93 Tallents to Masterton-Smith, 6 Dec 1922, TNA, CO 739/1.

94 Spender to Craig, 21 Sep 1922, PRONI, CAB 6/29.

95 R. Megaw to Craig, 1 Sep 1922, PRONI, CAB/9B/47/1.

96 Dawson Bates to Craig, 23 Nov 1922, PRONI, CAB 6/31; Solly-Flood to Craig, 25 Nov 1922, PRONI, CAB 8G/1.

97 Dawson Bates to Craig, 8 Dec 1922, PRONI, CAB 8G/1.

98 Report by Macready, 2 Sep 1922, TNA, CAB 43/2; Lord Derby to Craig, 29 Nov 1922, PRONI, CAB 8G/1.

99 Solly-Flood to Spender, 28 Nov 1922, & Solly-Flood to Dawson Bates, 6 Dec 1922, PRONI, CAB 8G/1; Solly-Flood plan for defence of Ulster, 19 Dec 1922, PRONI, CAB 9G/25.

100 Tallents to Masterton-Smith, 6 Dec 1922, TNA, CO 739/1.

101 Spender to Dawson Bates, 12 Dec 1922, PRONI, CAB 8G/1.

102 Note of conference between NI Government and WO, 20 Dec 1922, PRONI, CAB 8G/1; report by Major-General A. A. Montgomery and Colonel H. Knox on NI constabulary, 12 Feb 1923, TNA, WO 32/5330.

103 PGI Committee meeting, 14 Jul 1922, TNA, CAB 27/153; undated & unsigned memo, [Mar 1923], TNA, CO 739/21; memo by Worthington-Evans, 1 Feb 1925, TNA, WO 32/5308.

104 See RUC reports based on IRA informant, Sep 1923 – 1925, PRONI, CAB 6/110.

105 See return of murders and attempted murders in Northern Ireland, 21 Jun 1923, TNA, HO 267/362.

106 RUC reports based on IRA informant, 30 Oct, 26 Nov & 13 Dec 1923, PRONI, CAB 6/110.

107 Intelligence summary by Wickham, Oct 1925, PRONI, HA/32/1/481.

108 Report by Lieut-Colonel H. D. G. Crerar on visit to Ireland, 22 Jul 1925, TNA, WO 32/5315.

CHAPTER 5
British Images of Ireland

1 Betts, 'Analysis, war, and decision', p. 61. For an excellent synthesis, see Herman, *Intelligence power in peace and war*, pp. 143–5, 227–30. Other works on this subject include T. L. Hughes, *The fate of facts in a world of men: foreign policy and intelligence making* (New York, 1976); R. Jervis, *Perception and misperception in international politics* (Princeton, 1976); Levite, *Intelligence and strategic surprises*; Y. Y. Vertzberger, *World in their minds: information processing, cognition, and perception in foreign policy decisionmaking* (Stanford, 1990).

2 W. Wark, *The ultimate enemy: British intelligence and Nazi Germany, 1933–39* (Oxford, 1986), p. 19. See also E. May, 'Conclusions: capabilities and proclivities', in E. May (ed.), *Knowing one's enemies: intelligence assessment before the two world wars* (Princeton, 1984), p. 529; T. Buchanan, ' "A far away country of which we know nothing?": perceptions of Spain and its civil war in Britain, 1931–1939', *Twentieth Century British History*, 4, 1 (1993).

3 Kennedy, *The widening gulf*, pp. 11–23.

4 P. Bew, 'Moderate nationalism and the Irish revolution, 1916–1923', *The Historical Journal*, 42, 3 (1999), pp. 729–49.

5 Canning, *British policy towards Ireland*, p. 316.

6 B. Bond, *British military policy between the two world wars* (Oxford, 1980), pp. 36–71.

7 Porter, *Plots and paranoia*, pp. 169–71.

8 C. Seymour-Ure, 'The press and the party system between the wars', in G. Peele & C. Cook (eds.), *The politics of reappraisal, 1918–1939* (London, 1975), pp. 233, 239, 241–2.

9 'Seán MacBride', in MacEoin, *Survivors*, p. 121.

10 Paper by Lieut-General A. E. Percival, in Sheehan, *British voices*, p. 98.

11 F. J. Hearnshaw, *Outlines of the history of the British Isles* (London, 1938), pp. 628–9.

12 A. M. Sullivan, *Old Ireland: reminiscences of an Irish K.C.* (London, 1927), p. 246.

13 Macready, *Annals of an active life*, p. 548. See also Winter, *Winter's tale*, p. 101.

14 Macready to Wilson, 14 Apr 1921, IWM, HHW 2/2D/20.

15 Army record of the rebellion, vol. 1.

16 Vice-Admiral H. T. Baillie Grohman, in Sheehan, *British voices*, p. 78.

17 Sir H. A. Robinson, *Memories: wise and otherwise* (London, 1923), p. 323.

18 Sullivan, *Old Ireland*, pp. 286–96.

19 Wilson to Macready, 25 May 1920: HHW 2/2A/13.

20 Winter report on intelligence, undated [1922], TNA, CO 904/156b.

21 See chapter 2.

22 Sir J. O'Connor, *History of Ireland, 1798–1924* (London, 1925). For similar analyses by former residents in Ireland, see Robinson, *Memories*, p. 323; Sir J. Ross, *Pilgrim scrip* (London, 1927), pp. 251, 254; M. Headlam, *Irish reminiscences* (London, 1947), p. 13. It was also the thesis of a contemporary history: W. A. Phillips, *The revolution in Ireland, 1906–1923* (London, 1923).

23 8 May 1924 entry, Jones, *Whitehall diary*, vol. 3, p. 233.

24 Memo by A. S. Hutchinson, 4 Jul 1936, TNA, HO 144/21964. For similar comments by a powerful Foreign Office mandarin, see Lord Vansittart, *The mist procession* (London, 1958), pp. 264–6.

25 Memo by COS, 6 Dec 1929, TNA, CAB 53/17.

26 Headlam, *Irish reminiscences*, p. 13.

27 Report by Major G. White, 22 Jul 1925, TNA, WO 32/5315. See also Sir H. A. Robinson, *Further memories of Irish life* (London, n.d. [1924?]), pp. 256–7.

28 Northern Ireland defence scheme by Major-General Archie Cameron, 4 Jul 1924, TNA, WO 32/5313.

29 Report by White, 22 Jul 1925, TNA, WO 32/5315. See also Lieut-Colonel E. Heathcote Thruston, *Earl of Rosebery: statesman and sportsman* (London, 1928), pp. 207–8, 212.

30 Dublin District military intelligence summary, 2 Dec 1922, TNA, WO 35/92.

31 Headlam, *Irish reminiscences*, p. 221. See also Heathcote Thruston, *Earl of Rosebery*, pp. 207–8.

32 Macready, *Annals of an active life*, p. 444.

33 Pittock, *Celtic identity and the British image*, pp. 3–4.

34 Army record of the rebellion, vol. 2.

35 Montmorency, *Sword and stirrup*, pp. 221–41.

36 Heathcote Thruston, *Earl of Rosebery*, p. 207.

37 Unless otherwise references, the following section draws on R. M. Douglas, 'Anglo-Saxons and Attacotti: the racialization of Irishness in Britain between the World Wars', *Ethnic and Racial Studies*, 25, 1 (Jan 2002), pp. 40–63.

38 C. H. Bretherton, *The real Ireland* (London, 1925), pp. 45, 55, 115. See also Phillips, *The revolution in Ireland*, pp. 3–4.

39 *Morning Post*, 29 May 1916.

40 Jones, *Whitehall diary*, vol. 3, p. 50. See also Neville Chamberlain to Ida Chamberlain, 17 May 1922, in Self, *The Neville Chamberlain diary letters*, vol. 2, p. 110.

41 Barnes & Nicholson, *The Leo Amery diaries*, vol. 1, pp. 515–16.

42 Winston Churchill to Clementine Churchill, 31 Mar 1920, quoted in Hopkinson, *The Irish war of independence*, p. 7.

43 Douglas, 'Anglo-Saxons and Attacotti', pp. 57–8.

44 Major Bernard Montgomery to Major A. E. Percival, 14 Oct 1923, in Sheehan, *British voices*, pp. 151–2.

45 Memo by Ormsby Gore, 9 Jul 1923, TNA, CO 739/20; Campbell, *F. E. Smith*, p. 549.

46 Curtis to Devonshire, undated [1923], TNA, CO 739/8.

47 J. Gibbons, *Ireland – the new ally* (London, 1938), p. 258.

CHAPTER 6
The Cosgrave Years

1 Laffan, *The resurrection of Ireland*; Townshend, *Ireland: the 20th century*, pp. 108, 117–21, 127; Garvin, *Nationalist revolutionaries in Ireland*, p. 175; G. MacMillan, *State, society and authority in Ireland: the foundations of the modern state* (Dublin, 1993), pp. 202–3.

2 Frank Aiken to IRA officers, 28 May 1923, NA, D/T S.1859.

3 The best works on Anglo-Irish relations during this period are D. Harkness, *The restless Dominion: the Irish Free State and the*

British Commonwealth of Nations, 1921–31 (London, 1969); D. McMahon, *Republicans and imperialists: Anglo-Irish relations in the 1930s* (London, 1984); Canning, *British policy towards Ireland*.

4 SIS CX report, 17 Oct 1924, TNA, CO 532/282; Tallents to Alexander Maxwell, 18 Oct 1924, & Millar to Tallents, 20 Oct 1924, TNA, HO 267/274.

5 Follis, *A state under siege*, pp. 153–82.

6 B. B. Cubitt to Treasury, 21 Feb 1923, TNA, T 161/198.

7 Minute by Phillips, 20 Jul 1923, TNA, KV 4/279; WO minute, 27 Apr 1924, WO 32/4851.

8 Minutes by W. A. Phillips and Colonel Eric Holt-Wilson, Jun 1924, TNA, KV 4/279. This question had been raised in 1922, but was put on hold because of the treay split. Memo by Phillips, 3 Feb 1922, TNA, KV 4/279.

9 Minute by L. B. Freeston, 1 Jun 1923, TNA, CO 739/18.

10 Conference between FS Minister for External Affairs, CO and Spencer, 23 Jun 1924, TNA, CO 532/277; O'Halpin, *Defending Ireland*, pp. 75–6.

11 Minute by HO official, 16 Jan 1925, TNA, HO 45/15630; HO memo, 8 Nov 1928, TNA, DO 35/55; MI5 memo on travel control, Oct 1925, TNA, KV 4/279.

12 Minute by HO official, 16 Jan 1925, TNA, HO 45/15630.

13 Neligan to Garda Commissioner, 18 Dec 1924, NA, D/J S.47/23, quoted in O'Halpin, *Defending Ireland*, p. 74.

14 O'Halpin, *Defending Ireland*, pp. 56–7.

15 Follis, *A state under siege*, pp. 156–7, 173; Kevin O'Shiel to Curtis, 29 Jul 1923, TNA, CO 739/20.

16 RUC report based on IRA informant, 26 Nov 1923 & 9 Jan 1924, PRONI, CAB 6/110.

17 Intelligence summary by Wickham, Oct 1925, PRONI, HA/32/1/481; Woolley to Phillips, 22 Feb 1926, TNA, KV 4/279.

18 Tallents to Anderson, 23 Nov 1923, TNA, HO 267/253; Baldwin to Craig, 19 Dec 1923, & Craig to Baldwin, 17 Dec 1923, CUL, Baldwin Papers, vol. 101; Loughnane to Sturgis, 28 Nov 1923, TNA, HO 144/4096.

19 Sturgis to Loughnane, 26 Nov 1923, TNA, HO 144/4096.

20 'Secret notes on southern Ireland', May–Jul 1922, PRONI, CAB 6/88.

21 Report by RUC Inspector E. Gilfillan, 16 Apr 1923, PRONI, CAB 86/14.

22 Capt. Woolley to Phillips, 9 Feb 1926, TNA, KV 4/279.

23 RUC intelligence report, 9 Feb 1926, in appendix to report on army intelligence section in Northern Ireland, 1926, TNA, WO 106/6156; Lieut Brown to Phillips, 17 Feb 1926, TNA, KV 4/279.

24 Tallents to Anderson, 2 Jun 1923, TNA, HO 317/68; report on army intelligence section in Northern Ireland, 1926, TNA, WO 106/6156.

25 Statement by Sergeant Denis Monaghan, Jul 1923, NA, D/FA EF, Box 23 File 141.

26 Report on army intelligence section in Northern Ireland, 1926, TNA, WO 106/6156.

27 Lieut Brown to Phillips, 17 Feb 1926, TNA, KV 4/279.

28 Tallents to Anderson, 3 & 22 Aug 1923, TNA, HO 144/3915.

29 Report on army intelligence section in Northern Ireland, 1926, TNA, WO 106/6156. For an example of the output from this service, see Tallents to Anderson, 17 Mar 1924, TNA, HO 267/257.

30 Report on army intelligence section in Northern Ireland, 1926, TNA, WO 106/6156; Denniston, 'The Government Codes and Cipher School between the wars', *Intelligence & National Security*, 1, 1 (1986), pp. 51–2, 61.

31 Meeting between MI5, WO and CO, 20 Jul 1923, TNA, KV 4/279.

32 Kennedy, *The widening gulf*, pp. 11–23; despatch by American Consul, Belfast, 27 Sep 1922, USNA, RG 59, 841d.00/546.

33 Solly-Flood to Craig, 5 Sep 1922, PRONI, CAB 6/30.

34 RUC report, 20 Oct 1924, PRONI, HA/32/1/441; Intelligence memo by Wickham, Oct 1925, PRONI, HA/32/1/481.

35 RUC reports based on IRA informant, 9 Jan & 11 Aug 1924, PRONI, CAB 6/110.

36 Londonderry to Churchill, 17 Jan 1923, CCA, CHAR 2/126/1–2.

37 O'Halpin, *Defending Ireland*, pp. 45–52; M. Valiulis, *Almost a rebellion: the Irish army mutiny of 1924* (Cork, 1985); Regan, 'The politics of reaction', pp. 554–9.

38 Londonderry to Arthur Henderson, 11 Mar 1924, TNA, PREM 1/43.

39 S. McDougall, 'The projection of Northern Ireland to Great Britain and abroad, 1921–39', in P. Catterall & S. McDougall (eds.), *The Northern Ireland question in British politics* (London, 1996), pp. 29–35.

40 H. A. Gwynne to Craig, 25 Apr 1923, PRONI, CAB 8G/1.

41 Gwynne to Spender, 1 Dec 1923; Gwynne to Craig, 2 Dec 1924, PRONI, CAB 6/99; Gretton to Craig, 2 Feb 1925, PRONI, CAB 6/107; Gretton to Craig, 23 Sep 1925, and reply from Craig, 24 Sep 1925, PRONI, CAB 6/107.

42 On one occasion the Northern Ireland authorities received the same type of report from three different sources. They did not know whether this provided useful corroboration of the information or meant that a paid informant was trying to sell his wares to multiple customers. Correspondence between John McCulloch and C. H. Blackmore, Apr 1925, PRONI, CAB 6/102.

43 Report from E. Moyle to Colonel Lancelot Storr, 7 Aug 1924, CUL, Baldwin Papers, vol. 99.

44 'Strictly confidential' memo sent by Gretton to Craig, 12 Nov 1924; memo sent by Colonel Gretton to Craig, 2 Feb 1925; Gretton to Craig, 10 Jul 1925, PRONI, CAB 6/107; Gretton memo enclosed with McCulloch to Blackmore, 28 Mar 1925, PRONI, CAB 6/102; 'Strictly confidential' memo [probably from Gretton] enclosed with Watt to Wickham, 18 May 1925 Jun 1925, PRONI, HA/32/1/461.

45 Watt to Wickham, 18 May 1925, PRONI, HA/32/1/461.

46 Gwynne to Craig, 25 Apr 1923, PRONI, CAB 8G/1.

47 Special Branch reports on revolutionary organisations, 17 Apr & 7 Aug 1924, TNA, TNA 30/69/220.

48 Memos by Seán Lester, 11 Jun & 19 Oct 1923, NA, D/T S.4386.

49 McDowell, *Crisis and decline*, pp. 131–62; P. Buckland, *Irish unionism: the Anglo-Irish and the new Ireland, 1885–1922* (Dublin, 1972), vol. 1, pp. 284, 290–1, 296–7.

50 N. Brennan, 'A political minefield: southern loyalists, the Irish Grants Committee and the British government, 1922–31', *Irish Historical Studies*, 31 (1997), pp. 406–19.

51 F. S. L. Lyons, 'The minority problem in the 26 counties', in F. MacManus (ed.), *The years of the great test* (Cork, 1967), pp. 99–100. See also McDowell, *Crisis and decline*, ch. 8; Buckland, *Irish unionism*, vol. 1, pp. 296–7; J. C. Beckett, *The Anglo-Irish tradition* (London, 1976), pp. 151–2; P. Dempsey, 'Trinity College Dublin and the new political order', in M. Cronin & J. M. Regan (eds.), *Ireland: the politics of independence, 1922–49* (Basingstoke & New York, 2000).

52 2 May 1934 entry, in A. O. Bell (ed.), *The diary of Virginia Woolf*, vol. 4: *1931–1935* (London, 1982), p. 212.

53 Craig to Churchill, 26 May 1922, TNA, CO 739/14.

54 Follis, *A state under siege*, p. 131.

55 Memo by Seán Lester, 19 Oct 1923, NA, D/T S.4386.

56 Cosgrave to Baldwin, 27 Jun 1923, TNA, CO 739/18.

57 K. Matthews, 'Stanley Baldwin's Irish Question', *The Historical Journal*, 43, 4 (2000), pp. 1027–49.

58 J. Ferris & U. Bar-Joseph, 'Getting Marlowe to hold his tongue: the Conservative Party, the intelligence services and the Zinoviev letter', *Intelligence and National Security*, 8, 4 (Oct 1993), pp. 100–37; G. Bennett, 'A most extraordinary and mysterious business': the *Zinoviev Letter of 1924*, FCO History Notes (London, 1999), pp. 28–9. See also Andrew, *Secret service*, pp. 306–8; Porter, *Plots and paranoia*, pp. 165–7.

59 Amery to Baldwin, 3 Aug 1924, CUL, Baldwin Papers, vol. 99; Neville Chamberlain to Ida Chamberlain, 3 Aug 1924, in Self, *The Neville Chamberlain diary letters*, vol. 2, pp. 240–1. For naval attitudes see report of 28 Jun 1924, TNA, CO 532/279.

60 Report by C. G. Whiskard, 11 Aug 1924, TNA, CO 532/282.

61 Note by Maxwell, 5 Aug 1924, & minute by Whiskard, 6 Aug 1924, TNA, CO 537/1054.

62 Memo by Curtis, 18 Mar 1924, TNA, CO 532/280.

63 Memo by Curtis, 15 May 1924, TNA, CAB 21/281.

64 Neville Chamberlain to Hilda Chamberlain, 20 Sep 1924, in Self, *Neville Chamberlain diary letters*, vol. 2, p. 247; 25 Sep 1924 entry, in Barnes & Nicholson, *The Leo Amery diaries*, vol. 1, p. 387.

65 Memo by Curtis, 15 May 1924, & note by General Staff, 11 Jun 1924, TNA, CAB 21/281.

66 Note by Whiskard, 28 Jul 1924, TNA, CAB 21/281.

67 Tallents to Anderson, 30 Oct 1925, TNA, CO 537/1092.

68 Memo by Curtis, 15 May 1924, TNA, CAB 21/281.

69 Note by the General Staff, 11 Jun 1924, TNA, CAB 21/281.

70 Draft joint memo by Home Secretary and Secretary of State for Dominion Affairs [Oct 1925], TNA, CO 537/1089; Canning, *British policy towards Ireland*, p. 104.

71 Meetings between Irish and British ministers, 1 & 2 Dec 1925, TNA, CAB 27/295.

72 Birkenhead to Lord Reading, 3 Dec 1925, in Earl of Birkenhead, *Frederick Edwin Earl of Birkenhead*: vol.2: *The last phase* (London, 1935), pp. 268–9.

73 Meetings between Irish and British ministers, 26–9 Nov 1925, TNA, CAB 27/295.

74 R. English, *Armed struggle: the history of the IRA* (London, 2003), p. 46; B. Hanley, *The IRA, 1926–36* (Dublin, 2002), pp. 11–12, 28–9.

75 Laffan, *The resurrection of Ireland*, pp. 435–42.

76 Capt. 'Fatty' Woolley to Phillips, 9 Feb 1926, TNA, KV 4/279.

77 Memo by Phillips, 19 Mar 1926, TNA, KV 4/279.

78 Report by Lieut-Colonel H. D. G. Crerar, 22 Jul 1925, TNA, WO 32/5315.

79 GOC, Western Command to WO, 20 Oct 1925; reply by B. B. Cubitt, 5 Nov 1925, WO 32/5315.

80 Orders for destroyers in Irish waters, 28 Mar 1923, TNA, ADM 1/8652/253.

81 Report by Crerar, 22 Jul 1925, TNA, WO 32/5315.

82 Meeting between Holt-Wilson, RUC and NI District command, 1 Dec 1931, TNA, KV 4/279.

83 Minute by DNI, 6 Aug 1930, TNA, ADM 116/2525.

84 For examples of one-sided reporting, see memo by Major Grove White, 22 Jul 1925, TNA, WO 32/5315; Admiral R. W. Bentinck to Admiralty, 6 Apr 1929, TNA, ADM 1/8737/100.

85 Eric Eddison to DO, 12 Mar 1929, TNA, DO 35/76.

86 Sir R. Hodgson to FO, 8 Aug 1927, TNA, FO 371/12605.

87 Sir C. Davis to Dept of Overseas Trade, 2 Dec 1929, TNA, DO 35/76; note by Edward Harding, 9 Apr 1931, TNA, DO 35/243/4.

88 Peters to Harry Batterbee, 25 Sep 1931, & minute by Batterbee, 2 Feb 1934, TNA, DO 35/251/3.

89 Edgcumbe to DO, 16 Mar 1935, & minute by Harding, 29 Apr 1935, TNA, DO 35/251/3; minute by John Stephenson on talk with Braddock (new Trade Commissioner), 2 Sep 1937, TNA, DO 35/894/6.

90 F. H. Hinsley, *British intelligence in the Second World War*, vol. 1: *Its influence on strategy and operations* (London, 1979), p. 45.

91 Minute by Harry Batterbee on talk with Peters, 2 Feb 1934, TNA, DO 35/251/3.

92 E. O'Halpin, 'Financing British intelligence: the evidence up to 1945', in K. G. Robertson (ed.), *British and American approaches to intelligence* (London, 1987), p. 195.

93 *The Security Service, 1908–1945: the official history* (London, 1999), pp. 80, 98–9, 142; Andrew, *Secret service*, pp. 342–50; Wark, *The ultimate enemy*, pp. 21–7; Denniston, 'The Government Codes and Cipher School between the wars', pp. 50–1; Jeffrey, 'British military intelligence following World War I', pp. 75–6; Hinsley, *British intelligence in the Second World War*, vol. 1, pp. 3–11.

94 Woolley to Phillips, 9 Feb 1926, TNA, KV 4/279.

95 Memo by Phillips, 19 Mar 1926, TNA, KV 4/279.

96 Minute by Director of Military Operations & Intelligence, 19 Mar 1926, TNA, KV 4/279.

97 Special Branch report on revolutionary organisations, 6 Aug & 17 Sep 1925, CCA, CHAR 22/82.

98 Laffan, *The resurrection of Ireland*, pp. 444–7.

99 Townshend, *Ireland: the 20th century*, p. 374.

100 Hanley, *The IRA*, pp. 13, 47–8, 52–3, 71–80, 206.

101 Reports by Lieut-Colonel A. Haywood, 22 & 23 Mar, 5 Apr 1924; proceedings of court of enquiry, TNA, WO 32/4850; telegrams from Haywood, Loughnane and naval Cmdr in Chief, Devonport, 22–24 Mar, TNA, CO 739/26; reports by General Eoin O'Duffy, 11 & 22 Apr 1924, NA, D/T S.3693.

102 Letters between WO and CO, 28 Apr, 7 & 15 May 1924, TNA, WO 32/4851; report by Comdt. P. D. Scott, 21 Jun, with J. Brennan to CO, 24 Sep 1924, TNA, CO 532/278.

103 Statements by Jimmy Thomas to House of Commons, quoting from Cosgrave, 24 & 26 Mar 1924, *Hansard*; A. Reid Jamieson to WO, 27 Oct 1924, TNA, WO 32/4850; Ramsay MacDonald to Cosgrave, 26 Mar 1924, TNA, CO 738/26.

104 Report by Crerar, 22 Jul 1925, TNA, WO 32/5315.

105 Lord Cavan at COS meeting, 5 Nov 1925, TNA, CAB 53/1.

106 Minutes by DNI and Admiralty officials, 14 Apr, 12 & 16 Jun 1931, TNA, ADM 116/2525.

107 Memo by CO, 5 Oct 1928, & Lord Lascelles to Amery, 14 Oct 1928, TNA, DO 35/51.

108 Garda report, 31 Oct 1930, NA, D/T S.5864.

109 Gwynne to Craig, 2 Dec 1924, PRONI, CAB 6/99; Gretton to Craig, 10 Jul 1925, PRONI, CAB 6/107.

110 Precis by 'S' [probably Special Branch] on 'Communism in Ireland', 1 Apr 1925, TNA, MEPO 38/19.

111 O'Halpin, *Defending Ireland*, p. 71. See also O'Connor, *Reds and the green*; D. Nevin, 'Radical movements in the twenties and thirties', in T. Desmond Williams (ed.), *Secret societies in Ireland* (Dublin, 1973), pp. 166–79).

112 M. O'Driscoll, 'The economic war and Irish foreign trade policy: Irish–German commerce 1932–39', *Irish Studies in International Affairs*, 10 (1999), pp. 71–89.

113 'Strictly confidential' memo [probably from Gretton], with Watt to Wickham, 18 May 1925, PRONI, HA/32/1/461.

114 Woolley to Phillips, 9 Feb 1926, TNA, KV 4/279.

115 Capt. Edward Twiss to Major Blacker for MI5, 30 Jun 1926; Capt. H. H. Bacon to Whiskard, 16 Jul 1926; minutes by DO officials, Jul 1926; Phillips to Whiskard, 15 Sep 1927; Walter Ellis to Phillips, 27 Sep 1927, TNA, DO 35/17.

116 MI5 memo on travel control, Oct 1925, TNA, KV 4/279.

117 Memo by Phillips, 19 Mar 1926, TNA, KV 4/279.

118 *Ibid.*

119 Reports by IRA officers, 3 Oct 1925, UCDA, FitzGerald Papers, P80/869, quoted in O'Halpin, *Defending Ireland*, pp. 72–3. See also O'Connor, *Reds and the green*, pp. 112–13, 129; Hanley, *The IRA*, p. 173.

120 MI5 note on Krivitsky debriefing, 30 Jan 1940, TNA, KV 2/804; http://en.wikipedia.org/wiki/Walter_Krivitsky.

121 Memo by S.8. (MI5), 8 Mar 1932, TNA, KV 4/279.

122 Special Branch report, 10 Jul 1924, TNA, TNA 30/69/220; Special Branch report, 12 Feb 1925, CCA, CHAR 22/79; Craig to Gretton, 27 Jun 1925, PRONI, CAB 6/107.

123 MI5 note on Special Branch intelligence report, 13 Mar 1925, TNA, KV 2/1185.

124 Special Branch reports, 15 & 29 Oct 1925, CCA, CHAR 22/83.

125 SIS to MI5, 20 Apr 1927, TNA, KV 3/11.

126 MI5 minutes, 20 Apr & 31 May 1927, TNA, KV 3/11.

127 Special Branch report, 8 Mar 1927, TNA, KV 2/1185.

128 Special Branch report, 6 May 1926, CCA, CHAR 22/148.

129 Meeting between Special Branch and MI5, 4 Apr 1928, & undated MI5 memo, TNA, KV 3/17; MI5 documents on Hansen case, Jan 1938, TNA, KV 2/649; Andrew, *Secret service*, pp. 329–30; J. Betteridge, 'The political purposes of surveillance; the rupture of diplomatic relations with Russia, May 1927', at http://www.leedsac.uk/history/e-journal/Betteridge.pdf.

130 Circular from DNI to Naval Recruiting Officers, 28 Apr 1926; Lieut-Colonel Orde to Phillips, 20 Oct 1926; reply from Phillips, 20 Nov 1926, TNA, ADM 1/8705/186.

131 Memos by D/J, 4 Nov 1930 & 12 Nov 1931, NA, D/T S.6091A; Clann na nGaedheal to de Valera, 15 Mar 1934, NA, D/T S.11168.

132 O'Connor, *Reds and the green*, p. 130.

133 MI5 note on Krivitsky debriefing, 30 Jan 1940, TNA, KV 2/804; http://en.wikipedia.org/wiki/Walter_Krivitsky.

134 O'Connor, *Reds and the green*, pp. 127–40.

135 Garda report on revolutionary organisations, 4 Apr 1930, & summary of IRA activity, 15 Sep 1931, NA, D/T S.5864; Hanley, *The IRA*, pp. 13–14, 48–9, 53–58, 79–81; Coogan, *The IRA*, pp. 45–51.

136 J. Regan, *The Irish counter-revolution, 1921–1936: treatyite politics and settlement in independent Ireland* (Dublin, 1999), pp. 279–80, 287; Townshend, *Ireland: the 20th century*, p. 133; D. Keogh, 'De Valera, the Catholic Church and the "Red Scare", 1931–1932', in J. P. O'Carroll & J. A. Murphy, *De Valera and his times* (Cork, 1983), pp. 136–40.

137 Peters to Batterbee, 25 Sep 1931, TNA, DO 35/251/3.

138 Carter to MI5, 13 Nov 1928, TNA, KV 2/1185; Special Branch précis on revolutionary organisations in Ireland, 19 Oct 1931, TNA, MEPO 38/112; Précis of MI5 information on Irish communism, 8 Mar 1932, TNA, KV 4/279; Report by Asst. Superintendent E. Foster, 28 Sep 1932, TNA, KV 2/1185.

139 Minute by Holt-Wilson, 29 Oct 1931, TNA. KV 4/279.

140 Meeting between Holt-Wilson, RUC and NI District command, 1 Dec 1931, TNA, KV 4/279.

141 SIS report entitled 'The USSR and Ireland', 17 Nov 1931, TNA, DO 121/77. For details on actual IRA gunrunning in the 1920s, see Hanley, *The IRA*, p. 33.

142 Boyce, *Nationalism in Ireland*, pp. 344–6; Ferriter, *The transformation of Ireland*, pp. 362–4.

CHAPTER 7
The de Valera Challenge

1 H. T. Baker to FO, 20 Aug 1932, TNA, DO 35/397/12.

2 Minutes by John Stephenson and C. W. Dixon, 17 Aug 1932, TNA, DO 35/397/12.

3 Meeting of Irish Situation Committee, 12 Apr 1932, TNA, CAB 27/523. The best treatment of this period is McMahon, *Republicans and imperialists.*

4 Hanley, *The IRA*, pp. 16, 53–61, 82–92, 177–83; J. Bowyer Bell, *The secret army: the IRA 1916–79* (Dublin, 1979), pp. 100–18; T. P. Coogan, *De Valera: long fellow, long shadow* (London, 1995), pp. 465–6; Coogan, *The IRA*, p. 64; O'Halpin, *Defending Irelan*, pp. 106–8, 121–3.

5 M. Manning, *The Blueshirts* (Dublin, 1970); M. Cronin, *The Blueshirts and Irish politics* (Dublin, 1997); Regan, *The Irish counter-revolution*, pp. 324–72.

6 O'Halpin, *Defending Ireland*, p. 118.

7 Andrew, *Secret service*, pp. 259–60.

8 Decrypts are in TNA, HW 12/154–7. See also E. O'Halpin, ' "Weird prophecies": British intelligence and Anglo-Irish relations, 1932–3', in M. Kennedy & J. Morrison Skelly (eds.), *Irish foreign policy, 1919–66* (Dublin, 2000), pp. 67–73.

9 Denniston, 'The Government Codes and Cipher School between the wars', pp. 50–1.

10 Irish Situation Committee, 5 Aug 1932, TNA, CAB 27/523.

11 MI5 Irish section history, 1946, TNA, KV 4/9/67192.

12 Andrew, *Secret service*, p. 346.

13 *The Security Service*, pp. 103–7.

14 'Most Secret' report on 'Irish Affairs: The Army Comrades Association', marked QRS/28, 24 Nov 1932, TNA, ADM 178/161.

15 SIS QRS report, 28 Nov 1939, TNA, DO 35/1107/11.

16 MI5 Irish section history, 1946, TNA, KV 4/9/67192.

17 Colonel Valentinte Vivian to Guy Liddell, 9 Sep 1938, TNA, KV 4/279.

18 MI5 Irish section history, 1946, TNA, KV 4/9/67192.

19 For a similar analysis, see E. O'Halpin, 'MI5's Irish memories: fresh light on the origins and rationale of Anglo-Irish security liaison in the Second World War', in B. Girvin & G. Roberts (eds.), *Ireland and the Second World War: politics, society and remembrance* (Dublin 2000).

20 Diary of HMS *Amazon* by Lieut-Cmdr W. N. G. Beckett, 15 Aug 1933, TNA, ADM 116/2957.

21 Diary of HMS *Westcott* by Cmdr G. R. B. Back, 24–29 Apr 1934, TNA, Adm 116/2990.

22 Earl of Midleton to Hailsham, 5 Oct 1932, TNA, DO 35/397/13; Gretton to Chamberlain, 25 Jun 1937, & G. Humphreys-Davies to J. J. S. Garner, TNA, DO 35/891/1.

23 Meeting of Irish Situation Committee, 5 May 1932, TNA, CAB 27/523; William Ormsby-Gore, MP, to Baldwin, 10 Jan 1934, CUL, Baldwin Papers, vol. 101. For the biases of opposition politicians, see M. G. Valiulis, ' "The man they could never forgive" – the view of the opposition: Eaman de Valera and the civil war', in J. P. O'Carroll & J. A. Murphy (eds.), *De Valera and his times* (Cork, 1983), pp. 93, 98–9.

24 *Daily Express*, 23 Jul 1932; Harding to Thomas, 23 Jul 1932; reply from Thomas, 23 Jul 1932; minute by Harding, 27 Jul 1932, TNA, DO 35/397/11. See also McMahon, *Republicans and imperialists*, p. 100.

25 McMahon, *Republicans and imperialists*, p. 30. De Valera's MI5 file is in TNA, KV 2/515.

26 M. MacDonald, *Titans & others* (London, 1972), p. 55.

27 27 Feb 1932 entry, in T. Jones, *A diary with letters, 1931–1950* (Oxford, 1954), p. 31.

28 Memo by Major Ralph Glyn, 7 Sep 1932, TNA, PREM 1/132.

29 Ramsay MacDonald to Archbishop of York, 13 Sep 1932, Ramsay MacDonald Papers, TNA, TNA 30/69/701; MacDonald to Sir Abe Bailey, 22 Jul 1932, Ramsay MacDonald Papers, TNA 30/69/1442.

30 Minute by Harker, 12 Mar 1932, TNA, KV 4/279.

31 5 Mar 1932 entry, in Jones, *Diary with letters*, p. 34. For reports by people who met de Valera see Peters to Batterbee, 14 Mar 1932, TNA, DO 35/397/10; memo by Frank Pakenham, 30 Mar 1932, CUL, Baldwin Papers, vol. 101; memo by Thomas and Hailsham, 8 Jun 1932, TNA, CAB 27/525.

32 Meeting of Irish Situation Committee, 6 Mar 1933, TNA, CAB 27/523.

33 Cabinet conclusions, 24 Jun 1932, TNA, CAB 23/71.

34 Note by Harding, 21 Jul 1932, TNA, PREM 1/132.

35 Minute of conversation between Henry Hall and Malcolm MacDonald, 18 Jul 1933, TNA, DO 35/398/3.

36 Memo by S.8. (MI5), 8 Mar 1932, TNA, KV 4/279.

37 Memo by Harker, 12 Mar 1932, TNA, KV 4/279.

38 Memo by S.8. (MI5), 8 Mar 1932, TNA, KV 4/279.

39 Memo by Ralph Glyn, 7 Sep 1932, TNA, PREM 1/132; memo by Professor W. R. Scott, 20 Apr 1934, TNA, DO 35/398/7; memo by Frank Pakenham, 30 Mar 1932, CUL, Baldwin Papers, vol. 101; memo by Thomas on conversation with Capt. Moss and J. B. O'Driscoill, 22 Nov 1932, TNA, CAB 27/526; Crofton to Strathcona, 19 Apr & 7 May 1934, TNA, DO 35/398/7. See also R. Foster, *Modern Ireland, 1600–1972* (London, 1989), p. 536.

40 Hailsham to Capt. Alan Graham, 25 Sep 1934, CCA, HAIL 1/3/5.

41 DO summaries of press comment, 2 & 28 Aug, 25 Sep, 28 Oct 1932, TNA, CAB 27/530–31.

42 Articles on 'Secrets of the I.R.A.', *Evening Standard*, 12–19 Oct 1932.

43 Memos by Glyn, 7 Sep 1932 & 18 Jan 1933, TNA, PREM 1/132. For an example of the positive response of British naval officers to the Blueshirts, see report by Lieut-Cmdr E. O'Connor, 1 Oct 1933, TNA, ADM 116/2958.

44 SIS report, 24 Nov 1932, TNA, ADM 178/161.

45 Diary of HMS *Amazon* by Lieut-Cmdr W. H. Beckett, 15 May – 6 Jun 1933, TNA, ADM 116/2957.

46 Reports by Professor W. R. Scott, 12 Jun & 25 Sep 1933, TNA, DO 35/398/3–4. For the unionist perspective, see Kennedy, *The widening gulf*, pp. 185–93.

47 Harding to Major-General W. H. Bartholomew & Rear-Admiral G. C. Dickens, 20 Jun 1933, and replies from them, 21 Jun 1933, TNA, DO 35/398/3. For a contrasting appraisal, see report by Professor Coupland, undated [Aug 1933], TNA, DO 35/398/3.

48 DO summary of press comment, 10 Aug 1932, TNA, CAB 27/533.

49 Minute by Harding, 11 Aug 1933, TNA, DO 35/398/4.

50 SIS reports, 26 May & 9 Jun 1932, TNA, DO 121/77. For another report, see British Consulate, Antwerp to FO, 11 Jun 1932, TNA, DO 121/77.

51 J. S. Barnes to Harding, 23 Aug 1932, TNA, DO 121/77; British military attaché, Prague to FO, 24 Sep 1932, TNA, FO 371/15955. For Bruno's 1914 activities, see www.wikipedia.org.

52 Admiralty to Cmdr in Chief, Plymouth, 26 May 1932; telegram from unnamed Royal Navy ship to Admiralty, 29 May 1932; Thomas to Dulanty & reply from Dulanty, 27 May 1932, TNA, DO 121/77.

53 DO note on protest by Dulanty, 30 May 1932; Thomas to de Valera & DO note, 10 Jun 1932; minute by Machtig, 14 Jun 1932, TNA, DO 121/77.

54 Barnes to Harding, 23 Aug 1932, TNA, DO 121/77; Admiralty orders for destroyers in Irish waters, 14 Aug 1933, TNA, ADM 178/91.

55 Minutes by Marsh and Harding, 8 Jul 1932, TNA, DO 121/77; Sankey Diary, 24 Aug 1932, quoted in O'Halpin, *Defending Ireland*, p. 108n.

56 Articles on 'Secrets of the I.R.A.', in *Evening Standard*, 12–19 Oct 1932.

57 *Daily Herald*, 30 Jun 1933, contained in TNA, DO 35/473/13. For other stories see DO summary of press comment, 15 Jun 1933, TNA, CAB 27/532.

58 Baikaloff report with SIS to MI5, 28 Jul 1933; MI5 minute, 12 Aug 1933; MI5 note, 6 Jan 1940, TNA, KV 2/819. For information on the Duchess of Atholl see www.spartacus.school-net.co.uk/PRstewartmurray.htm.

59 J. H. Phillips to DO, 10 Jun 1932; Cmdr in Chief, Plymouth to Admiralty, 11 & 12 Jun 1932; Minutes by Machtig, 12, 14 & 15 Jun 1932; report by Vernon Kell, 13 Jun 1932, TNA, DO 121/77.

60 Report by Major J. S. Douglas, 24 Jul 1933; reports by Major R. A. Woods, 12 Jun & 26 Jul, TNA, DO 35/473/13.

61 Reports by Lieut-Cmdr W. N. T. Beckett, 19 & 21 Jun, 31 Jul 1933, TNA, DO 35/473/13; diaries of HMS *Westminster* and HMS *Amazon*, Jun – Aug 1933, TNA, ADM 116/2957.

62 Report by Beckett, 31 Jul 1933; minute by Batterbee, 25 Sep 1933, TNA, DO 35/473/13.

63 Kennedy, *The widening gulf*, pp. 138–9.

64 Memo by Sir Russell Scott, 4 Jul 1932, CUL, Baldwin Papers, vol. 101; Major G. C. Tryon, MP to Thomas, 21 Jun 1932; minute by Antrobus, 29 Jun 1932, TNA, DO 35/397/11.

65 Meeting of Irish Situation Committee, 5 Aug 1932, TNA, CAB 27/523.

66 Minute by Batterbee, 8 Aug 1932, & Batterbee to Sir Patrick Duff, 21 Sep 1932, TNA, DO 35/219/2; Admiralty orders, 14 Aug 1933, TNA, ADM 178/91.

67 Diary of HMS *Crescent*, 11–17 Oct 1933, & diary of HMS *Cygnet*, 5–12 Sep 1933, TNA, ADM 116/2957–58.

68 Report by JPS, 11 Jun 1937, TNA, CAB 53/32.

69 Meeting of Irish Situation Committee, 5 Aug 1932, TNA, CAB 27/523.

70 Intelligence report by commander of HMS *Westminster*, 14 Jun – 21 Jul 1933, TNA, ADM 116/2957. See also diaries of HMS *Westminster*, 19 Jun – 10 Jul 1933 in same file, & Garda report, 23 Jun 1933, NA, JUS 8/434.

71 Diary of HMS *Thanet*, 24 Jul 1933, & diary of HMS *Amazon*, 15 Aug 1933, TNA, ADM 116/2957.

72 Note by Whiskard, 27 Jun 1932, TNA, DO 35/383/4.

73 Lord Midleton to Lord Hailsham, 5 Oct 1932, & Hailsham to Thomas, 10 Oct 1932, TNA, DO 35/397/13.

74 Meetings of Irish Situation Committee, 5 May & 21 Jun 1932, TNA, CAB 27/523; schedule of correspondence between Thomas, Lord Granard and Cosgrave, 13 Nov 1932, TNA, DO 35/384/1; McMahon, *Republicans and imperialists*, p. 54; Canning, *British policy towards Ireland*, p. 143.

75 Thomas at Irish Situation Committee, 23 Nov 1932, TNA, CAB 27/523.

76 Memo by Glyn, 7 Sep 1932, TNA, PREM 1/132; Seán T. O'Kelly speech, in *Irish Press*, 6 Jan 1933; Manning, *The Blueshirts*, pp. 51–2.

77 Report by Peters, 6 Aug 1932, TNA, CAB 27/525; McMahon, *Republicans and imperialists*, pp. 106, 124–5.

78 *Cork Examiner*, 25 & 26 Mar 1936; Diary of HMS *Thanet*, 29 Mar – 3 Apr 1936, TNA, ADM 116/3587.

79 Hanley, *The IRA*, pp. 18–19.

80 Bowyer Bell, *The secret army*, p. 138; J. A. Murphy, 'The new IRA 1925–62', in T. Desmond Williams (ed.), *Secret societies in Ireland* (Dublin, 1973), p. 154. See also Hanley, *The IRA*, pp. 126–44; Coogan, *The IRA*, p. 89–90; O'Halpin, *Defending Ireland*, pp. 124–6; R. Dunphy, *The making of Fianna Fáil power in Ireland, 1923–1948* (Oxford, 1995), pp. 183–9.

81 Note by Batterbee, 29 Jun 1934, TNA, DO 35/398/7.

82 Memo by Cosgrave, sent by Lord Granard to DO, 13 Feb 1934, TNA, DO 35/398/6.

83 Diary of HMS *Cygnet*, 30 Aug – 5 Sep 1933, TNA, ADM 116/2957.

84 Peters to DO, 25 Sep 1934, TNA, DO 35/399/1.

85 Canning, *British policy towards Ireland*, pp. 165–6; McMahon, *Republicans and imperialists*, pp. 165–8.

86 Diary of HMS *Walpole*, 21–7 Feb 1934, & diary of HMS *Westcott*, 27 Feb – 5 Mar 1934, TNA, ADM 116/2990.

87 Diary of HMS *Versatile*, 20–5 Aug 1934, TNA, ADM 116/2996.

88 Report by Professor Scott, 20 Apr 1934, TNA, DO 35/398/7.

89 *Notes from Ireland*, 4, 32 (Nov 1935), in TNA, DO 35/399/3.

90 Hailsham to Graham, 25 Sep 1934, CCA, HAIL 1/3/5;

91 Note by Malcolm MacDonald, 28 Nov 1935, TNA, DO 35/399/3; meetings of Irish Situation Committee, 12 & 25 May 1935 & 16 Jul 1936, TNA, CAB 27/523–4. See also McMahon, *Republicans and imperialists*, pp. 119–21, 163; Canning, *British policy towards Ireland*, pp. 123–4, 130–3, 145–51.

92 Lord Granard to Hailsham, 7 Jun 1934, CCA, HAIL 1/1/1.

93 Lee, *Ireland*, pp. 178–80; Regan, *The Irish counter-revolution*, pp. 377–8.

94 Some recent historians have acknowledged the sinister qualities of Irish politics in the 1930s. For example, Fitzpatrick, *The two Irelands*, p. 195; Townshend, *Ireland: the 20th century*, pp. 141–4; O'Halpin, *Defending Ireland*, p. 120.

95 O'Connor, *Reds and the green*, pp. 173, 191–2.

96 Hanley, *The IRA*, pp. 33–4.

CHAPTER 8
England's Back Door

1 Sloan, *The geopolitics of Anglo-Irish relations*, p. ix.

2 Rear-Admiral G. C. Dickens to Harding, 21 Jun 1933, TNA, DO 35/398/3.

3 Report by COS & JPS, 31 Jul 1936, TNA, CAB 53/28.

4 Memo by Worthington-Evans, 14 Oct 1926, & meeting of Committee of Imperial Defence, 3 Nov 1927, TNA, CAB 16/70; note by Anthony Eden on meeting with Joseph Walshe, 15 Oct 1935, TNA, DO 35/399/3.

5 Hastings Ismay to Batterbee, 2 Aug 1928, TNA, DO 117/113; meeting of Committee of Imperial Defence, 18 Dec 1933, TNA, CAB 2/6.

6 Note by Robert Vansittart at front of Government War Book, 17 Jan 1936, TNA, HO 45/18349.

7 Note by Malcolm MacDonald, 7 Apr 1937, TNA, PREM 1/273. See also meeting of Irish Situation Committee, 9 Jun 1937, Mtg, TNA, CAB 27/524.

8 Chamberlain to Irish Situation Committee, 14 Dec 1937, TNA, CAB 27/524.

9 Ferriter, *The transformation of Ireland*, p. 388. See also McMahon, *Republicans and imperialist*, pp. 233–4, 293.

10 Sloan, *The geopolitics of Anglo-Irish relations*, pp. 180–9.

11 John Cudahy to Franklin D. Roosevelt, 26 Apr 1938, Roosevelt Library, President's Secretary's File, Diplomatic Correspondence, Ireland 1938–39 Box 40.

12 COS meeting, 22 Dec 1937, TNA, CAB 53/8; report by COS, 12 Jan 1938, TNA, CAB 53/35.

13 Meeting of Irish Situation Committee, 1 Mar 1938, TNA, CAB 27/524.

14 COS meeting, 22 Dec 1937, TNA, CAB 53/8; report by COS, 12 Jan 1938, TNA, CAB 53/35.

15 J. R. Clynes, *Memoirs, 1869–1924* (London, 1937), p. 316.

16 Meeting of Irish Situation Committee, 1 Mar 1938, TNA, CAB 27/524.

17 Note by Chamberlain, 24 Sep 1937, TNA, PREM 1/273.

18 Memo by Malcolm MacDonald, 6 Oct 1937, TNA, DO 35/891/4.

19 Note by Edward Harding, 31 Dec 1937, TNA, DO 35/892/4.

20 Memo by Malcolm MacDonald, 6 Oct 1937, TNA, DO 35/891/4.

21 McGarrity to de Valera, 2 Oct 1933, NLI, McGarrity papers, Ms. 17441.

22 Report by Sir John Maffey, 21 Aug 1945, TNA, DO 35/2090.

23 Meeting of Irish Situation Committee, 1 Mar 1938, TNA, CAB 27/524.

24 Quoted in McMahon, *Republicans and imperialists*, p. 282.

25 Meeting of Joseph Walshe with JPS, 4 Feb 1938, TNA, CAB 55/2.

26 Ismay to Batterbee, 30 Aug 1938, TNA, PREM 1/245. See also note by Duke of Devonshire, 12 Oct 1938, TNA, CAB 53/41.

27 O'Halpin, *Defending Ireland*, p. 144.

28 Committee of Imperial Defence memos, 26 May & April 1939, TNA, CAB 5/9; Committee of Imperial Defence meeting, 8 Jun 1939, TNA, CAB 2/8(1).

29 Note by Duke of Devonshire, 18 Oct 1938, TNA, DO 35/894/10.

30 G2 memo on censorship, 28 Mar 1938, IMA, G2/X/0042.

31 Dan Bryan transcripts (in possession of Professor Eunan O'Halpin), p. 3.

32 Memos by COS, 26 & 31 Oct 1938, 4 Jan 1939, TNA, CAB 53/42–43; COS meeting, 1 Nov 1938, TNA, CAB 53/9.

33 Minute by Rear-Admiral John Godfrey, 23 Jun 1939; Dulanty to Godfrey, 29 Jun 1939; DO to Dulanty, 12 Jul 1939; Dulanty to DO, 28 Jul 1939, TNA, ADM 11/10214; minute by P. Liesching, 29 Jul 1939, TNA, DO 35/819/5.

34 Note by Batterbee, 6 Jan 1937, TNA, DO 35/890/11. See also J. Bowman, *De Valera and the Ulster question, 1917–73* (Oxford, 1982).

35 Note by M. MacDonald, 16 Mar 1938, TNA, PREM 1/274.

36 D. Harkness, *Ireland in the twentieth century: divided island* (Basingstoke & London, 1996), p. 65.

37 McDougall, 'The projection of Northern Ireland to Great Britain and abroad'.

38 Memo by DO, Feb 1939, TNA, DO 35/893/7.

39 O'Halpin, *Defending Ireland*, p. 135.

40 Memo by Liesching, 5 Jul 1939, TNA, DO 35/894/1; Admiralty minute, 31 Jul 1939, TNA, ADM 1/10223.

41 MI5 Irish section history, p. 14, 1946, TNA, KV 4/9.

42 Dixon comments, May 1938, TNA, INF 1/528; Malcolm MacDonald at Committee of Imperial Defence meeting, 27 Oct 1938, TNA, CAB 2/8 (1).

43 Inskip to COS meeting, 1 Nov 1938, TNA, CAB 53/9; WO report, 30 Aug 1939, TNA, WO 93/104/1A.

44 Memo on intelligence by Godfrey, 14 Sep 1966, National Maritime Museum, Ms. 80/073.

45 O'Driscoll, 'The economic war and Irish foreign trade policy', pp. 71–89.

46 *Notes from Ireland*, 18 Nov 1935, in TNA, DO 35/399/3; G. Humphreys-Davies to J. J. S. Garner, 2 Jul 1937, TNA, DO 35/891/1.

47 Kell to Vansittart, 12 Jun 1937, enclosing Olsen documents and SIS report of 8 Jun 1937, TNA, CAB 56/3.

48 MI5 Irish section history, pp. 22–4, TNA, KV 4/9.

49 O'Halpin, *Defending Ireland*, pp. 129, 141–2; Dan Bryan transcripts.

50 N. West, *The Guy Liddell diaries*, vol. 1: *1939–42* (Abingdon, 2005), pp. 1–9.

51 Extract from W. Somerset Maughan book, Guy Liddell Diary, 10 Aug 1940, TNA, KV 4/186.

52 Memo by Guy Liddell on talk with Walshe, 1 Sep 1939; MI5 note, 10 Sep 1938; Kell minute, 12 Oct 1938; Memo by Harker, 14 Oct 1938, TNA, KV 4/279. See also MI5 Irish section history, TNA, KV 4/9.

53 *The Security Service*, pp. 109–12, 122–3.

54 M. Hull, *Irish secrets: German espionage in Ireland, 1939–45* (Dublin & Portland, OR, 2003), pp. 29–36, 52–9.

55 MI5 Irish section history, TNA, KV 4/9.

56 Haggard to FO, 28 Jul & 8 Aug 1939, TNA, FO 371/23039.

57 MI5 Irish section history, p. 31, TNA, KV 4/9.

58 Andrew, *Secret service*, p. 413. See also Hull, *Irish secrets*, pp. 8–13.

59 *The Security Service*, pp. 124–5, 128.

60 RUC to Vivian, 10 Oct 1938, TNA, KV 4/279.

61 MI5 Irish section history, pp. 28, 34, TNA, KV 4/9. For Mill-Arden, see G2 report on German activities, IMA, G2/1722.

62 *The Security Service*, p. 126; Dan Bryan transcripts.

63 MI5 Irish section history, pp. 38–9, TNA, KV 4/9; Hull, *Irish secrets*, pp. 49–50.

64 MI5 Irish section history, pp. 34–8, TNA, KV 4/9; O'Halpin, 'MI5's Irish memories', p. 139.

65 Cudahy to State Dept, 6 Apr 1939, USNA, RG 59, 841d.00/1154.

66 Seán Russell to Dr Hans Luther, 25 Oct 1936, NLI, McGarrity Papers, Ms. 17485.

67 Hull, *Irish secrets*, pp. 47–8.

68 *Ibid.*, pp. 55–64; correspondence between McGarrity and Dr Karl Bruch, Nov 1939, NLI, McGarrity Papers, Ms. 17546(1). There was one final Abwehr visitor to Ireland before this occurred, Professor Franz Fromme, although his activities are unclear.

69 F. H. Hinsley & C. A. G. Simkins, *British intelligence in the Second World War*, vol. 4: *Security and counter-intelligence* (London, 1990), p. 17.

70 MI5 Irish section history, pp. 31–2, TNA, KV 4/9.

71 Despatch from John Cudahy on interview with de Valera, 6 Apr 1939, & with P. J. Ruttledge, 17 May 1939, USNA, RG 59, 841d.00/1154 & /1160; O'Halpin, *Defending Ireland*, p. 148.

72 MI5 Irish section history, pp. 6–7, TNA, KV 4/9; Dan Bryan transcripts.

73 MI5 Irish section history, pp. 32–3, TNA, KV 4/9; report from Czech Consul, TNA, FO 371/23039.

74 Special Branch report on revolutionary organisations, 26 Feb 1925, CCA, CHAR 22/79.

75 Special Branch reports on revolutionary organisations, 3 & 17 Apr 1924, TNA, TNA 30/69/220.

76 Special Branch report on revolutionary organisations, 6 Aug 1925, CCA, CHAR 22/82.

77 Hanley, *The IRA*, pp. 171–2.

78 Special Branch report on revolutionary organisations, 10 May 1923, TNA, CAB 24/160.

79 Andrew, *Secret service*, pp. 363–4.

80 *The Security Service*, pp. 101–2.

81 Special Branch report, 1 Nov 1936, TNA, HO 144/21964.

82 Note by Guy Liddell, 12 Apr 1942, TNA, KV 2/233.

83 O'Halpin, *Defending Ireland*, p. 127.

84 *The Sunday Express*, 30 Jul 1939.

85 Russell to McGarrity, 5 Nov 1937, NLI, McGarrity Papers, Ms. 17485; Bowyer Bell, *The secret army*, pp. 145–7; Coogan, *The IRA*, pp. 117–18; R. English, ' "Paying no heed to public clamour": Irish republican solipsism in the 1930s', *Irish Historical Studies*, 28, 112 (Nov 1993).

86 Copy of 'S-Plan', sent by J. Edgar Hoover to Major-General G. Strong, 4 May 1943, USNA, RG 165, Ireland 2700, Box 1685, 'Privilege' Folder.

87 Bowyer Bell, *The secret army*, p. 148; HO circular to Chief Constables, 25 Jan 1939, TNA, KV 4/232.

88 British intelligence memo on IRA, sent by J. Edgar Hoover to Major-General G. Strong, 4 May 1943, USNA, RG 165, Ireland 2700, Box 1685, 'Privilege' Folder.

89 Russell to McGarrity, 21 Sep 1938, NLI, McGarrity Papers, Ms. 17485; Coogan, *The IRA*, pp. 119–21; Bowyer Bell, *The secret army*, p. 152;

90 Copy of 'S-Plan', USNA, RG 165, Ireland 2700, Box 1685, 'Privilege' Folder.

91 Quoted in Coogan, *The IRA*, pp. 124–7.

92 Special Branch review of IRA activity, 13 Apr 1939, TNA, HO 144/21357; Manchester City Police report, 20 Feb 1939, TNA, HO 144/21356.

93 Russell to McGarrity, 25 Jan 1939, NLI, McGarrity Papers, Ms. 17485.

94 Special Branch review of IRA activity, 13 Apr 1939, TNA, HO 144/21357.

95 Minute by Machtig, 19 Jan 1939, TNA, DO 35/893/6; HO minute, 17 Jan 1939, TNA, HO 144/21356.

96 Note by Inskip on conversation with Dulanty, 16 Feb 1939, TNA, DO 35/893/6.

97 *New York Sun*, 1 Dec 1938.

98 Special Branch review of IRA activity, 13 Apr 1939, TNA, HO 144/21357; R. Allason, *The Branch* (London, 1983), pp. 97–8.

99 HO memo, 18 Jan 1939, TNA, HO 144/21356; Special Branch review of IRA activity, 13 Apr 1939, TNA, HO 144/21357; British intelligence memo on IRA, 1943, USNA, RG 165, Ireland 2700, Box 1685, 'Privilege' Folder; *Daily Telegraph & Morning Post*, Feb 1939.

100 H. Montgomery Hyde, *United in crime* (London, 1955), p. 104.

101 HO circular, 25 Jan 1939, TNA, KV 4/232; Allason, *The Branch*, p. 105.

102 List of protective duties on 21 Feb 1939, TNA, MEPO 3/1911.

103 HO notes, 15 Feb & 3 Mar 1939, TNA, HO 144/21356–21357.

104 Norman Kendal to HO, 1 Aug 1939, TNA, MEPO 2/8258.

105 Tomo Costelloe interview, in U. MacEoin, *The IRA in the twilight years, 1923–48* (Dublin 1997), pp. 473–4.

106 Kell to Chief Constables, 9 Feb 1939, TNA, KV 4/232.

107 Kell to Holderness, 9 May 1939, & reply from Holderness, 5 Jun 1939, TNA, HO 144/21358.

108 HO minute, 1 Aug 1939; reports by Detective Inspector Brooks, 14 & 27 Jul, 16 Aug 1939, TNA, HO 144/21358.

109 The following is taken from Special Branch reviews of IRA activity, 13 Apr, 4 May & 1 Sep 1939; memo by Sir E. Holderness, 20 Dec 1939, TNA, HO 144/21357–21358; *Irish Bulletin*, 8 Jul 1939, in TNA, DO 35/894/2; *Evening News*, 29 Mar 1939; Coogan, *The IRA*, p. 127.

110 Burt, *Commander Burt of Scotland Yard*, pp. 120–1.

111 R. Fanning, '"The rule of order": Eamon de Valera and the I.R.A., 1923–40', in J. P. O'Carroll & J. A. Murphy (eds.), *De Valera and his times* (Cork, 1983), pp. 168–9; Canning, *British policy towards Ireland*, p. 236.

112 Dulanty to Inskip, 16 Feb 1939, & note by Inskip, 16 Feb 1939, TNA, DO 35/893/6.

113 Note by Inskip, 5 Apr 1939, TNA, DO 35/893/7.

114 Memo by P. Liesching, 5 Jul 1939, TNA, DO 35/894/1.

115 Despatch by John Cudahy, 25 Aug 1939, USNA, RG 59, 841d.00/1221.

116 Holderness to Stephenson, 1 Sep 1939, TNA, DO 35/894/2.

117 Major M. J. Egan to HO, 10 Oct 1939, TNA, DO 35/894/2.

118 Memo by Liesching, 5 Jul 1939, TNA, DO 35/894/1. There had been no change by the end of 1939. See memo by Holderness, 20 Dec 1939, TNA, HO 144/21358.

119 Russell to McGarrity, 30 Nov 1936, NLI, McGarrity Papers, Ms. 17485.

120 Note by Dan Bryan, 16 Sep 1939, IMA, G2/X/0058.

121 *New York Daily News*, 13 Feb 1939.

122 *Irish Bulletin*, 8 Jul 1939, in TNA, DO 35/894/2.

123 Special Branch review of IRA activity, 13 Apr 1939, TNA, HO 144/21357.

124 *Sunday Express*, 22 Jan 1939.

125 *Irish Bulletin*, 8 Jul 1939, in TNA, DO 35/894/2; despatch from John Cudahy, 6 Apr 1939, USNA, RG 59, 841d.00/1154.

126 MI5 Irish section history, pp. 31–2, TNA, KV 4/9.

127 Report by Florence O'Donoghue, 23 Nov 1943, IMA, G2/X/0093.

128 Dan Bryan to Joseph Walshe, 4 Apr 1946, NAI, D/FA, A20/4.

129 Conference between HO, MI5 and police, 5 Apr 1939; Kendal to Holderness, 29 Apr 1939, TNA, HO 144/21357.

130 Memo by Holderness, 25 Apr 1939, TNA, HO 144/21357.

131 Memo by Liesching, 5 Jul 1939, TNA, DO 35/894/1.

132 Enclosed with Special Branch to K. Hill, 9 Mar 1939, CCA, CHAR 1/351/70.

133 British intelligence memo on IRA, 1943, USNA, RG 165, Ireland 2700, Box 1685, 'Privilege' Folder; Bowyer Bell, *The secret army*, pp. 160–2; Coogan, *The IRA*, pp. 128–9.

134 Special Branch review of IRA activity, 1 Sep 1939.

135 Burt, *Commander Burt of Scotland Yard*, p. 122.

136 Memo by Holderness, 20 Dec 1939, TNA, HO 144/21358.

137 British intelligence memo on IRA, 1943, USNA, RG 165, Ireland 2700, Box 1685, 'Privilege' Folder.

138 O'Donovan diary, 23 Aug 1939, quoted in M. Hull, 'German Military Intelligence Operations in Ireland, 1939–45' (PhD diss., University College Cork, 2000), p. 67.

139 Meeting of Irish Situation Committee, 6 Mar 1933, TNA, CAB 27/523.

140 Memo by MacDonald, 6 Oct 1937, TNA, DO 35/891/4; note by Chamberlain, 25 Mar 1939, TNA, DO 35/893/7.

141 Note by Chamberlain, 25 Mar 1939, TNA, DO 35/893/7.

142 *Los Angeles Examiner*, 15 May 1939.

143 Lindsay to FO, 20 May 1939, TNA, DO 35/893/7.

144 State Dept memo, 8 Jun 1939, USNA, RG 59, 841d.00/1186.

145 Lindsay to FO, 5 Jun 1939, TNA, DO 35/894/1.

146 McGarrity to Minnie Marshall, 24 Jun 1939, NLI, McGarrity Papers, Ms. 17546(4).

147 AARIR circulars, 28 Dec 1937 & 31 Jan 1938, NYPL, Frank P. Walsh Papers, Box 26, Irish Correspondence 1938.

148 Reports of meeting in Philadelphia, 19 Feb & 2 Apr 1939; NLI, McGarrity Papers, Ms. 17546(3); Report of Clan na Gael convention, 6 May 1939, NLI, McGarrity Papers, Ms. 17546(7).

149 Memo by Hoare and Inskip, undated [Apr 1938], TNA, PREM 1/386.

150 Memo by MacDonald, 6 Oct 1937, TNA, DO 35/891/4.

151 Note by Devonshire, 4 Oct 1938, TNA, DO 35/893/5.

152 Note by Chamberlain, 4 Oct 1938, TNA, PREM 1/349.

153 Note by Devonshire, 4 Oct 1938, TNA, DO 35/893/5.

154 Note by Devonshire, 18 Oct 1938, TNA, DO 35/894/10.

155 Despatch by John Cudahy, 13 Feb 1939, USNA, RG 59, 841d.00/1151; memo by Joseph Green, USNA, RG 59, 841d.24/6.

156 Note by Chamberlain, 25 Mar 1939, TNA, PREM 1/349.

157 Despatch by John Cudahy, 25 Aug 1939, USNA, RG 59, 841d.00/1221. See also Cudahy despatches on 20 Jan & 17 May 1939 in 841d.00/1148 & /1160.

158 Inskip to Chamberlain, 21 Apr 1939, TNA, DO 35/893/7.

CHAPTER 9
The Irish Fifth Column

1 Memo by Maffey, 20–22 Sep 1939, TNA, DO 35/1107/9.

2 R. Fisk, *In time of war: Ireland, Ulster and the price of neutrality, 1939–45* (Dublin, 1983), p. 106.

3 NID monograph on Eire by Rear-Admiral J. Godfrey, 17 Jun 1948, NMM, Godfrey Papers, Ms. 80/073; Guy Liddell to WO, 13 Sep 1939, TNA, KV 4/279.

4 E. Wilson, 'British intelligence and fear of a "fifth column" in 1940' (unpublished MPhil dissertation, Cambridge University, 1999), p. 4.

5 Winston Churchill at War Cabinet, 17 & 24 Oct 1939, TNA, CAB 65/1; Churchill to Lord Halifax, 20 Oct 1939, in M. Gilbert (ed.), *The Churchill war papers*, vol. 1: *At the Admiralty: September 1939 – May 1940* (London, 1993), p. 270.

6 Churchill to Eddie Marsh, 17 Sep & 11 Nov 1932, CCA, CHAR 8/311/23; correspondence between Churchill, Gretton and Gwynne, Jul 1935, CCA, CHAR 2/236/94.

7 David Gray to Roosevelt, 8 Apr 1940, Roosevelt Library, President's Secretary's File, Diplomatic Correspondence, Ireland 1940, Box 40.

8 Eden & Chamberlain at War Cabinet, 24 Oct 1939, TNA, CAB 65/1.

9 David Gray to J. Dulanty, 13 Apr 1940, Roosevelt Library, Gray Papers, Correspondence, Box 1; Canning, *British policy towards Ireland*, p. 257.

10 Churchill to Admiral Pound, 5 & 24 Sep 1939, in Gilbert (ed.), *The Churchill war papers*, vol. 1, pp. 28–9, 143.

11 Dan Bryan transcripts (in possession of Prof. Eunan O'Halpin).

12 Memos by Maffey, 14 & 22 Sep 1939, TNA, DO 35/1107/9; Maffey to DO, 12 Oct 1939, TNA, ADM 116/4600.

13 P. Beesly, *Very special admiral: the life of Admiral J. H. Godfrey* (London, 1980), preface, p. xix.

14 Memo by Naval Staff for War Cabinet, 21 Nov 1939, TNA, CAB 66/3.

15 See chapter 1. For a reference to Hall's earlier activities see minute by J. Phillips, 11 Sep 1939, TNA, ADM 1/10366.

16 Report of proceedings of HMS *Tamura*, 27 Feb-11 Mar 1940, TNA, ADM 199/1829; Fisk, *In time of war*, pp. 131–40.

17 Beesly, *Very special admiral*, p. 137.

18 G2 notes on activities of British agents, undated [mid-1941], IMA, G2/x/1091.

19 Churchill to Godfrey, 6 Sep 1939, in Gilbert (ed.), *The Churchill war papers*, vol. 1, p. 37.

20 Memo by Naval Staff for War Cabinet, 21 Nov 1939, TNA, CAB 66/3.

21 Correspondence between Godfrey and Admiral Sir Hugh Sinclair ('C'), May–Nov 1939, TNA, ADM 223/486; Guy Liddell Diary, 27 Nov 1939, TNA, KV 4/185.

22 SIS 'QCW' reports, 26 Apr, 8 & 26 May 1940, TNA, KV 4/280; Beesly, *Very special admiral*, pp. 137–8.

23 Monograph on 'Methods' by Godfrey, Nov 1947, NMM, Godfrey Papers, Ms. 80/073.

24 G2 notes on activities of British agents, undated [mid-1941], IMA, G2/X/1091; Dan Bryan transcripts; correspondence between Maffey, DO and NID, Nov–Dec 1939 TNA, DO 130/4.

25 Greig to Slade, 28 Nov 1939, & Slade reply, 1 Dec 1939, TNA, DO 130/4; report by Greig, 18 Nov 1939, TNA, DO 130/7; NID monograph on Eire, 17 Jun 1948, NMM, Godfrey Papers, Ms. 80/073.

26 Beesly, *Very special admiral*, p. 138.

27 Guy Liddell Diary, 18 Jan 1940, TNA, KV 4/186. See also anon. report by Irish loyalist, Jan 1940, TNA, Hankey Papers, CAB 63/147.

28 Admiralty minutes, May 1940, TNA, ADM 116/4600.

29 NID monograph on Eire, 17 Jun 1948, NMM, Godfrey Papers, Ms. 80/073.

30 Beesly, *Very special admiral*, p. 138; draft JP report on Eire, 29 May 1940, TNA, CAB 84/14.

31 Hinsley & Simkins, *British intelligence in the Second World War*, vol. 4, pp. 11–12.

32 *The Security Service*, pp. 155–6.

33 Dan Bryan transcripts.

34 MI5 report, undated [Nov 1939], TNA, CAB 76/14.

35 COS meeting, 16 Sep 1939, TNA, CAB 79/1; report by MOI, 16 Sep 1939, TNA, INF 1/528.

36 Churchill to Admiral Pound, 28 Oct 1939, TNA, ADM 205/2.

37 Memo by Godfrey, 28 Oct 1939, TNA, ADM 205/2.

38 MI5 report, undated [Nov 1939], TNA, CAB 76/14.

39 Leakage of Information Committee meeting, 1 Nov 1939, TNA, CAB 76/14.

40 Note by Lord Hankey, 15 Dec 1939, TNA, CAB 76/14; C. J. Radcliffe to E. Crutchley, 21 Mar 1940, TNA, INF 1/528; G2 minute, 13 Nov 1939, IMA, G2/X/0042; Dan Bryan transcripts.

41 West, *The Guy Liddell diaries*, vol. 1, pp. 1–3; E. O'Halpin (ed.), *MI5 and Ireland, 1939–45: the official history* (Dublin, 2003), p. 3.

42 MI5 Irish section history, p. 6, TNA, KV 4/9.

43 Guy Liddell Diary, 6 Dec 1939, TNA, KV 4/185.

44 Dan Bryan transcripts.

45 *Sunday Dispatch*, 31 Mar 1940; *Daily Mail*, 1 Apr 1940; *News Review*, 2 May 1940.

46 J. Betjeman to Pugh, 17 Oct 1942, TNA, DO 35/1011/4.

47 Note by Eden on talk with Walshe and Dulanty, 3 May 1940, TNA, DO 35/1107/12.

48 Minute by John Stephenson, 5 Apr 1940, & minute by Eden, 13 Apr 1940, TNA, DO 35/1107/12.

49 Guy Liddell Diary, 15, 17 & 21 Feb 1940, TNA, KV 4/185.

50 MI5 memo, 2 May 1940, TNA, KV 4/280.

51 John Stephenson to Machtig, 5 Apr 1940, TNA, DO 35/1107/72. See also Kell to Lord Hankey, 29 Apr 1940, TNA, KV 4/280, & JIC report, 9 Apr 1940, TNA, CAB 81/96.

52 MI5 memo, 2 May 1940, TNA, KV 4/280.

53 Hinsley, *British intelligence in the Second World War*, vol. 1, p. 31.

54 Special Branch report on IRA, 2 Feb 1940, TNA, HO 45/25550. For Behan see *New York Times*, 8 Feb 1940.

55 Guy Liddell Diary, 20 Sep 1940, TNA, KV 4/186. See also Kell to Godfrey, 27 Dec 1939, TNA, ADM 1/10223.

56 HO circulars for Chief Constables, 17 Aug 1939 & 8 Jan 1940, TNA, HO 144/21358.

57 J. M. Ross to W. C. Tame, 3 Feb 1940; inter-departmental conference on Irish labour, 29 Feb 1940, TNA, DO 35/721/1; history of naval intelligence by Charles Morgan, Aug 1944, TNA, ADM 223/464.

58 Memo by Frank Pakenham, 23 Oct 1939, TNA, DO 35/1005/10. See B. Barton, 'Northern Ireland: the impact of war, 1939–45', in B. Girvin & G. Roberts (eds.), *Ireland and the Second World War: politics, society and remembrance* (Dublin, 2000), pp. 71–2.

59 RUC Commissioner Harrison to Wickham, 4 Sep 1939, PRONI, CAB 9CD/129.

60 Report by Pollock, 2 Sep 1939, PRONI, CAB 9CD/129; memo by Pollock, 16 Sep 1939, TNA, WO 166/1172/1.

61 Guy Liddell diary, 7 Feb 1940, TNA, KV 4/185.

62 Memo by Major R. A. Curtis, 11 Feb 1940, TNA, WO 166/1172/1.

63 Internal security scheme for 53rd (Welsh) Division, Apr 1940, TNA, WO 166/1172/1.

64 O'Halpin, *Defending Ireland*, pp. 200–3; summary of IRA activities during war, 1946, NAI, D/T, S.11564; report on IRA [probably by G2], with Hoover to Strong, 4 May 1943, USNA, RG 165, Ireland 2700, Box 1685.

65 Summary of IRA activities during war, 1946, NAI, D/T, S.11564.

66 Bowyer Bell, *The secret army*, p. 175; Coogan, *The IRA*, pp. 171–2.

67 Dan Bryan transcripts.

68 Summary of IRA activities during war, 1946, NAI, D/T, S.11564.

69 G2 report, 19 Jan 1940, & Bryan to G2 Southern Command, 30 May 1940, IMA, G2/X/0058.

70 Coogan, *The IRA*, pp. 146–7, 177; summary of IRA activities during war, 1946, NAI, D/T, S.11564; report on IRA [probably by G2], with Hoover to Strong, 4 May 1943, USNA, RG 165, Ireland 2700, Box 1685.

71 Hull, *Irish secrets*, pp. 66–9.

72 *Ibid.*, pp. 69–75.

73 *Ibid.*, pp. 90–2.

74 For Weber-Drohl see SIS summary of German legation decrypts, 29 May 1943, TNA, DO 121/87.

75 O'Halpin, *Defending Ireland*, pp. 193–4.

76 Cmdr Wyatt (US naval attaché, Madrid) to Office of Naval Intelligence, 21 Dec 1939 & 3 Jan 1940, USNA, RG 59, 841d.24/13 & 841d.00/1246.

77 John Stephenson to Maffey, 27 Jan 1940, TNA, DO 130/8.

78 Anon. report, Jan 1940, TNA, Hankey Papers, CAB 63/147.

79 SIS report on Irish Affairs, 28 Nov 1939, TNA, DO 35/1107/11.

80 Guy Liddell Diary, 20 Mar 1940, TNA, KV 4/186.

81 SIS QRS reports, 20 Mar & 9 Apr 1940, TNA, DO 35/1107/12; Guy Liddell Diary, 26 Apr 1940, TNA, KV 4/186.

82 Maffey to Machtig, 18 Dec 1939, TNA, DO 35/1107/11.

83 Maffey to Eden, 8 Feb 1940, TNA, DO 130/12.

84 Maffey to Parkinson, 22 Apr 1940, TNA, DO 130/12. For his reaction to the 28 Nov 1940 QRS report see Maffey to Machtig, 18 Dec 1939, TNA, DO 35/1107/11.

85 Guy Liddell Diary, 17 May 1940, TNA, KV 4/186.

86 FO minute, 12 Feb 1940, TNA, FO 371/25222. See also J. Colville, *The fringes of power: Downing Street diaries, 1939–1955* (London, 1985), p. 81; Malcolm MacDonald to Chamberlain, 5 Feb 1940, TNA, PREM 1/416.

87 Hinsley, *British intelligence in the Second World War*, vol. 1, p. 3. See also R. Bennett, 'Intelligence and strategy in World War II', in

K. G. Robertson (ed.), *British and American approaches to intelligence* (London, 1987), p. 136.

88 *The Security Service*, pp. 145–9, 160–3, 373. See also Hinsley & Simkins, *British intelligence in the Second World War*, vol. 4, p. 10.

89 R. Cecil, 'Five of Six at war: Section V of MI6', *Intelligence & National Security*, 9, 2 (1994); K. Benton, 'The ISOS years: Madrid 1941–3', *Journal of Contemporary History*, 30 (1995).

90 Andrew, *Secret service*, pp. 433–9, 467.

91 Beesly, *Very special admiral*, pp. 100, 106–9; memo by Godfrey, 14 Sep 1966, NMM, Godfrey Papers, Ms. 80/073.

92 Andrew, *Secret service*, p. 442. See also E. Thomas, 'The evolution of the JIC system up to and during World War II', in C. Andrew & J. Noakes (eds.), *Intelligence and international relations, 1900–1945* (Exeter, 1987).

93 The latter is the title of a chapter in Hinsley & Simkins, *British intelligence in the Second World War*, vol. 4.

94 Report by Naval Staff, May 1943, TNA, ADM 1/15572.

95 H. Umbreit, 'Churchill's determination to continue the war' & 'Plans and preparations for a landing in England', in Militärgeschichtliches Forschungsamt (ed.), *Germany and the Second World War* (Oxford, 1991), pp. 361–3, 366–74; P. Schenk, *Invasion of England, 1940: the planning of Operation Sealion* (London, 1990); Hinsley, *British intelligence in the Second World War*, vol. 1, pp. 159–64.

96 Wilson, 'British intelligence and fear of a "fifth column" in 1940', pp. 8–20.

97 N. A. Robb, *An Ulsterwoman in England, 1924–1941* (Cambridge, 1942), p. 118.

98 Quoted in Wilson, 'British intelligence and fear of a "fifth column" in 1940', p. 26.

99 JP report, 5 May 1940, TNA, CAB 84/13. See also JIC reports, 2 & 21 May 1940, TNA, CAB 81/96; COS report, 10 May 1940, TNA, CAB 66/10.

100 Note on fifth column, 29 Jun 1940, TNA, INF 1/251.

101 Thurlow, *The secret state*, pp. 223–5, 230.

102 War cabinet memo, 28 May 1940, TNA, CAB 66/8; J. A. Cross, *Lord Swinton* (Oxford, 1982), pp. 224–31.

103 Hinsley & Simkins, *British intelligence in the Second World War*, vol. 4, p. 32.

104 Security Intelligence Centre meeting, 15 Jun 1940, TNA, CAB 93/5.

105 Hull, *Irish secrets*, pp. 75–95.

106 *Ibid.*, pp. 107–19, 121–6; MI5 Irish section history, p. 46, TNA, KV 4/9.

107 Hinsley & Simkins, *British intelligence in the Second World War*, vol. 4, p. 91; *The Security Service*, p. 176.

108 Hull, *Irish secrets*, pp. 126–38.

109 *Ibid.*, pp. 96–100; G2 Southern Command intelligence summary, 31 Aug 1940, IMA, G2/X/0093.

110 Irish cabinet committee, 3 & 6 Jun 1940, NAI, D/T, S.11992. See also O'Halpin, *Defending Ireland*, p. 202.

111 Summary of IRA activities during war, 1946, NAI, D/T, S.11564; report on IRA [probably by G2], with Hoover to Strong, 4 May 1943, USNA, RG 165, Ireland 2700, Box 1685; Coogan, *The IRA*, pp. 144–5.

112 Hull, *Irish secrets*, p. 96–100; O'Halpin, *Defending Ireland*, p. 222.

113 F. McGarry, *Eoin O'Duffy: a self-made hero* (Oxford, 2005), pp. 329–30.

114 Stephen Hayes confession, [Sep 1941], p. 20, NAI, D/FA, A34.

115 Fisk, *In time of war*, p. 357.

116 MI5 Irish section history, pp. 47, 52, TNA, KV 4/9.

117 C. Cox, 'Militär geographische Angaben über Irland', *An Cosantóir* (Mar 1975); Hull, *Irish secrets*, p. 106–7, 140.

118 NID monograph on Eire, 17 Jun 1948, NMM, Godfrey Papers, Ms. 80/073.

119 Reports by Censorship Dept, 24 & 28 May 1940, TNA, CAB 76/14.

120 Report by JIC on ' "Fifth Column" activities in the United Kingdom', 2 May 1940, TNA, CAB 81/96.

121 JIC minutes, 1 & 15 May 1940, TNA, CAB 81/87.

122 Guy Liddell Diary, 8 & 17 Jun 1940, TNA, KV 4/186.

123 Morton to Swinton, 8 Jun 1940, TNA, PREM 3/131/2.

124 Note by MI5, 8 Jul 1940, TNA, KV 4/232.

125 COS report, 18 May 1940, TNA, CAB 66/11.

126 Sir John Anderson at Leakage of Information Committee, 2 May 1940, TNA, CAB 76/14; Machtig minute, 24 May 1940; Antrobus to John Stephenson, 27 May 1940; Hutchinson to Garner, 1 Jun 1940, TNA, DO 35/894/3.

127 *Cavalcade*, 20 Jul 1940. Earlier examples are *News Review*, 2 May 1940, & *Daily Mirror*, 11 May 1940.

128 *Daily Mail*, 23 Jul 1940.

129 Report by Prof. Hancock, 16 May 1940, TNA, PREM 4/53/2; report by Colonel Commandant, Gloucestershire Special Constabulary, 18 May 1940, TNA, DO 130/12; Lord Rotherham to Churchill, 24 Jun 1940, TNA, PREM 4/53/2. For Rotherham, see entry in *Who Was Who* (London, 2006).

130 Lady Beatrix Dunalley to Henry Morris-Jones, MP, 23 May 1940; Morris-Jones to Churchill, 25 May 1940, TNA, DO 35/1008/8. For information on Dunalley, see C. Kavanagh, 'Neutrality and the volunteers: Irish and British government policy towards the Irish volunteers', in B. Girvin & G. Roberts (eds.), *Ireland the Second World War: politics, society and remembrance* (Dublin, 2000), p. 84.

131 Antrobus to Boland, 1 Jun 1940, NAI, D/FA, A3. See also résumé of talks between de Valera and MacDonald, 17 Jun 1940, NAI, D/FA, P13.

132 Major M. H. Pryce to Colonel Conyers-Baker, 13 Jul 1940, TNA, WO 106/6043.

133 See report from British embassy, Ankara, 16 Jul 1940; FO minute, 5 Aug 1940; report from British embassy, Belgrade, 5 Aug 1940, TNA, FO 371/24384; report by JIC, 6 Jun 1940, TNA, CAB 81/97.

134 Fisk, *In time of war*, p. 224; NID synopsis of invasion threat, undated, TNA, ADM 223/484.

135 Major A. F. L. Clive to Pryce, 19 Jul 1940; Conyers-Baker to Pryce, 25 Jul 1940, TNA, WO 106/6043.

136 Note by Herbert, 24 May 1940, TNA, CAB 76/14.

137 Report by Maxwell, 23 Sep 1940, TNA, DO 35/1011/3.

138 Report by Godfrey, 24 May 1940, TNA, ADM 223/486.

139 Popplewell, *Intelligence and imperial defence*, pp. 114–15.

140 Silvestri, ' "An Irishman is specially suited to be a policeman" ', pp. 40–4.

141 Morton to Swinton, 8 Jun 1940, TNA, PREM 3/131/2. This is confirmed by Admiral Godfrey in his monograph on Eire, 17 Jun 1948, NMM, Godfrey Papers, Ms. 80/073.

142 HD(S)E meeting, 29 May 1940, TNA, CAB 93/2.

143 Minutes of Security Intelligence Centre, 7 Aug 1940, TNA, CAB 93/4; HD(S)E meeting, 19 Aug 1940, TNA, CAB 93/2.

144 Morton to Swinton, 8 Jun 1940, TNA, PREM 3/131/2.

145 HD(S)E meeting, 29 May 1940, TNA, CAB 93/2; Ismay to Churchill, 29 May 1940,

TNA, PREM 3/130; Antrobus to Boland, 1 Jun 1940, NAI, D/FA, A3.

146 Maffey to Machtig, 4 Oct 1939, TNA, DO 35/548/25.

147 Morton to Swinton, 8 Jun 1940, TNA, PREM 3/131/2.

148 COS instructions, 20 May 1940, & JP memo on Ireland, 23 May 1940, TNA, CAB 84/14; JIC reports on Ireland, 23 & 24 May 1940, TNA, CAB 81/97.

149 Churchill to Ismay, 25 May 1940, TNA, PREM 3/129/1; note by Churchill for COS, 31 May 1940, TNA, CAB 80/12; Defence (Operations) Committee, 19 Jul 1940, TNA, CAB 69/1.

150 Reports by JIC, 6, 12 & 15 Jun 1940, TNA, CAB 81/97; COS meeting, 7 Jun 1940, TNA, CAB 79/4.

151 JP report on 'Eire', 17 Jun 1940, TNA, CAB 84/15.

152 Report by JIC, 16 Jul 1940, TNA, CAB 81/97.

153 JP reports on Ireland, 23 & 29 May 1940, TNA, CAB 84/14.

154 Report by JIC, 23 May 1940, TNA, CAB 81/97.

155 JIC report on invasion of United Kingdom, 15 Jun 1940, TNA, CAB 81/97.

156 Air Commodore Carr to Air Ministry, 30 Jul 1940, TNA, AIR 2/5130.

157 Meeting between DO & armed service officials, 28 May 1940, TNA, PREM 3/130.

158 Memo by Directorate of Military Operations, undated [mid-May 1940], TNA, WO 193/761; WO memo for GHQ Home Forces, 6 Jun 1940, TNA, WO 199/906.

159 War Cabinet minutes, 30 May 1940, TNA, CAB 65/7.

160 Memo by CIGS for COS, 23 May 1940, TNA, CAB 80/11.

161 JIC meeting, 15 May 1940, & report by JIC, 25 May 1940, TNA, CAB 81/87; Ismay to Churchill, 29 May 1940, TNA, PREM 3/130.

162 C-in-C Home Fleet to HMS *Newcastle* & HMS *Sussex*, 9 Jun 1940, TNA, WO 193/761; memo by Assistant CIGS, 18 Jun 1940, TNA, WO 193/761.

163 J. M. Hailey to Pryce, 30 Jun 1940, TNA, WO 106/6043.

164 Defence Committee (Operations) meeting, 3 Jul 1940, TNA, CAB 69/1; memo by J. Walshe on 'Moments of Special Crisis during the War', 1945, NAI, D/FA, A2.

165 Pryce to Conyers-Baker, 9 Jul 1940, TNA, WO 106/6043; Admiralty minutes, 25 & 30 May 1940, TNA, ADM 223/486; C-in-C Plymouth

to Flag-Officer-in-Charge, Belfast, 19 Jul 1940, TNA, ADM 199/1200.

166 Dan Bryan transcripts.

167 Hull, *Irish secrets*, p. 112, 116–17; MI5 Irish section history, p. 46, TNA, KV 4/9; HD(S)E Liaison Officers' conference, 17 Jul 1940, TNA, CAB 93/4.

168 Meetings of Irish and British representatives, 23 & 24 May 1940; meeting of DO and Service depts, 28 May 1940, TNA, PREM 3/130.

169 Note by JP secretary, enclosing telegram from Maffey, 23 May 1940, TNA, CAB 84/14.

170 Meeting of DO and Service depts, 28 May 1940, TNA, PREM 3/130.

171 Note of talk between de Valera and MacDonald, 17 Jun 1940, TNA, DO 35/1008/8.

172 Report by Pryce, 8 Jun 1940, TNA, WO 106/6043. See also meeting of Irish and British representatives, 24 May 1940, TNA, PREM 3/130.

173 Admiralty weekly intelligence reports, 5 & 19 Jul 1940, TNA, ADM 223/147.

174 JP report, 29 May 1940, TNA, CAB 84/14.

175 JP report, 29 May 1940, TNA, CAB 84/14; JIC report, 23 May 1940, TNA, CAB 81/97; directive to GOC, Northern Ireland District, 25 Jun 1940, TNA, CAB 80/13.

176 Notes of talks between de Valera and MacDonald, 17 & 22 Jun 1940, TNA, DO 35/1008/8. See also Pryce to Conyers-Bakers, 13 Jul 1940, TNA, WO 106/6043.

177 Guy Liddell diary, 29 May, 4 & 12 Jun 1940, TNA, KV 4/186; Morton to Lord Swinton, containing information from Sir Charles Tegart, 8 Jun 1940; Chamberlain to Churchill, 12 Jun 40; Chamberlain to de Valera & Craigavon, 12 Jun 1940, TNA, PREM 3/131/2. See also War Cabinet minutes, 16 Jun 1940, TNA, CAB 65/7.

178 Notes by Malcolm MacDonald for RTE interview, 1 May 1979, Durham University Library, Malcolm MacDonald Papers, 10/6/5; note of talk between MacDonald, de Valera, Aiken and Lemass, 27 Jun 1940, TNA, DO 35/1008/8.

179 Carr to Air Ministry, 30 Jul 1940, TNA, AIR 2/5130.

180 Minutes by J. C. Cole & Director of Plans, Air Staff, 23 Jun 1940, TNA, AIR 2/5130.

181 Memo by O. G. Sargent, 13 Jun 1940, TNA, CAB 80/13.

182 Minutes by J. C. Cole and Director of Plans, 23 Jun 1940, TNA, AIR 2/5130. See also Chamberlain at War Cabinet, 28 Jun 1940, TNA, CAB 65/7.

183 Colonel Balfour-Davey to Lieut-Colonel MacLean, 20 Jun 1940, TNA, WO 193/761.

184 Field-Marshal the Viscount Montgomery, *The memoirs of Field-Marshal the Viscount Montgomery* (London, 1958), p. 70.

185 Director of Air Plans to Brigadier I. Playfair & Capt. C. S. Daniel, 7 Jul 1940, TNA, AIR 2/5130.

186 JP report on Eire, 11 Jul 1940, TNA, CAB 84/16.

187 David Gray to State Dept, 23 Jul 1940, USNA, RG 59, 841d.00/1275.

188 Clive to Pryce, 17 Oct 1940, TNA, WO 106/6044.

189 NID monograph on Eire, 17 Jun 1948, NMM, Godfrey Papers, Ms. 80/073. See also memo by Walshe, 25 Jul 1940, NAI, D/FA, A2; Walshe to Dulanty for Lord Caldecote, 17 Jul 1940, NAI, D/FA, A6; Pryce to Conyers-Bakers, 13 Jul 1940, TNA, WO 106/6043; A. J. P. Taylor (ed.), *W. P. Crozier: off the record: political interviews, 1933–1943* (London, 1973), p. 180.

190 Report by Garda Superintendent T. Donovan, 4 Jul 1940, IMA, G2/X/0266.

191 Pryce to Conyers-Baker, 16 Jul 1940, TNA, WO 106/6043.

192 Walshe memo, 15 Jul 1940, NAI, D/FA, A2.

193 Maffey to Machtig, 16 Jul 1940, TNA, DO 130/12; 'Notes on Eire' by Elizabeth Bowen, 13 Jul 1940, TNA, DO 35/1011/3.

194 MI5 Irish section history, p. 6, TNA, KV 4/9.

195 NID monograph on Eire, 17 Jun 1948, NMM, Godfrey Papers, Ms. 80/073.

196 MI5 Irish section history, pp. 42–4, TNA, KV 4/9.

197 Chamberlain to Churchill, 12 Jun 1940, TNA, PREM 1/131/2.

CHAPTER 10

Operational Intelligence

1 JIC report, 30 Oct 1940, TNA, CAB 81/98; Defence (Operations) Committee meeting, 31 Oct 1940, TNA, CAB 69/1.

2 JP report, 27 Sep 1940, TNA, CAB 84/19; JP directive to GOC and AOC, Northern Ireland, 5 Oct 1940, TNA, CAB 84/20.

3 Memos by Chief of Naval Staff for COS, 25 Oct & 1 Nov 1940, TNA, CAB 80/21; memo by CIGS for COS, 29 Oct 1940, TNA, CAB 80/21; B. Bond (ed.), *Chief of Staff: the diaries of Lieutenant-General Sir Henry Pownall, 1940–1944* (London, 1974), vol. 2, pp. 6–10.

4 WO weekly intelligence summaries for 1–8 & 16–23 Jan 1941, TNA, WO 208/2258. See also memo by naval Director of Plans, 9 Jan 1941, TNA, ADM 1/11317; memo by CIGS, 30 Jan 1941, TNA, CAB 80/25; COS meeting, 1 Feb 1940, TNA, CAB 79/8.

5 Memo by Vice CIGS, 26 Feb 1941, & report by COS, 5 Mar 1941, TNA, CAB 80/26; minute by Assistant Chief of Naval Staff, 31 Mar 1941, TNA, ADM 1/11330.

6 Sloan, *The geopolitics of Anglo-Irish relations*, pp. 208–10.

7 Memo by Admiralty officer, 5 Oct 1940, TNA, ADM 116/5631. See also memo by Chief of Naval Staff, 1 Nov 1940, TNA, CAB 80/21.

8 G. Roberts, 'Three narratives of neutrality: historians and Ireland's war', in B. Girvin & G. Roberts (eds.), *Ireland the Second World War: politics, society and remembrance* (Dublin, 2000), pp. 165–9.

9 Defence (Operations) Committee meeting, 31 Oct 1940, TNA, CAB 69/1.

10 Churchill to WO, 12 Nov 1940, & minute by Churchill, 3 Dec 1940, TNA, PREM 3/327/2.

11 JPS memo, 30 Aug 1940, TNA, CAB 81/98.

12 WO to Pryce, 25 Jun 1940, TNA, WO 106/6043.

13 Memo by Boyle, 9 Jul 1940, TNA, AIR 2/5172.

14 NID monograph on Eire by Godfrey, 17 Jun 1948, NMM, Godfrey Papers, Ms. 80/073.

15 Memo by Boyle, 9 Jul 1940, TNA, AIR 2/5172.

16 Patrick J. Lundon to de Valera, 3 Dec 1940, IMA, G2/X/0266.

17 Pim report, 20 Jul 1940, TNA, PREM 3/129/2.

18 Memo by Colonel Archer, 13 Jul 1940, & Lord Caldecote to Maffey, 16 Jul 1940, NAI, D/FA, A5; Pryce to Conyers-Baker, 18 Jul 1940, TNA, WO 106/6043.

19 Report on 'Q' (Movements) branch, Sep 1939 – Jun 1945, quoted in Fisk, *In time of war: Ireland*, p. 240.

20 MI5 Irish section history, pp. 3–4, TNA, KV 4/9.

21 NID monograph on Eire by Godfrey, 17 Jun 1948, NMM, Godfrey Papers, Ms. 80/073.

22 Report by Godfrey, 21 Oct 1940, in NID monograph on Eire, 17 Jun 1948, NMM, Godfrey Papers, Ms. 80/073.

23 Lieut-Comdr Ewen Montagu to DNI, 2 Dec 1940, TNA, ADM 1/11104; *Who Was Who* (London, 2006).

24 Godfrey monograph on Inter Service Topographical Department, [1947–48], NMM, Ms. 80/073; Beesly, *Very special admiral*, pp. 206–13.

25 Conyers-Baker to Pryce, 24 Jul 1940, TNA, wo 106/6043; JIC report, 5 Dec 1940, TNA, CAB 81/99.

26 Clive to Pryce, 23 Jul 1940, TNA, wo 106/6043.

27 Papers in TNA, CAB 104/184.

28 MI5 Irish section history, pp. 49–50, TNA, KV 4/9.

29 M. R. D. Foot & J. M. Langley, *MI9* (London, 1979), pp. 116–17. See also Garda report, 26 Jun 1941, NA, JUS 8/876; report by Colonel R. McNally, 26 Jun 1941, enclosing letter from escapee, NA, D/FA P.44.

30 Maffey to Machtig, 16 Feb 1942, TNA, DO 35/1109/2; SIS enquiry, 7 Nov 1942, IMA, G2/X/1091; Garda report, 18 Sep 1942, NA, JUS 8/876.

31 WO instructions for Pryce, 3 Jun 1940, TNA, wo 106/6043.

32 Report by Lywood, [mid-Jun 1940], TNA, AIR 2/5130.

33 Report by Pryce, 8 Jun 1940, TNA, wo 106/6043; Pryce to Clive, 11 Oct 1940, TNA, wo 106/6044.

34 Report by Carr, 14 Oct 1940, TNA, AIR 2/5130.

35 Reports by Pryce, 11 & 14 Jun 1940, TNA, wo 106/6043.

36 Pryce to J. M. Hailey, 27 Jun 1940, TNA, wo 106/6043.

37 Pryce to Conyers-Baker, 20 Jan 1941, TNA, wo 106/6045.

38 Pryce to WO, 9 Aug 1940, TNA, wo 106/6044.

39 Pryce correspondence for Jun–Jul 1940, TNA, wo 106/6043.

40 Report Lywood, undated [mid-Jun 1940], TNA, AIR 2/5130; Pryce to Hailey, 27 Jun 1940, TNA, wo 106/6043.

41 Pryce to Conyers-Baker, 7 Aug 1940, TNA, wo 106/6043; war diary of Military Mission 18, Aug–Oct 1940, TNA, wo 178/2; Pryce to WO, 19 Dec 1940, TNA, wo 106/6045.

42 Pryce to Conyers-Baker, 9 Jul 1940, TNA, wo 106/6043; reports by Garda and G2, 25 Oct 1940 & 13 Feb 1941, IMA, G2/X/0266.

43 O'Donoghue journal, 13 Jan 1942, NLI, Florence O'Donoghue Papers, Ms. 31348.

44 Reports and correspondence by Pryce, 18 Sep 1940, 23 Oct 1940, 23 Dec 1940, 10 Feb 1941 & 14 Oct 1941, TNA, wo 106/6044–45.

45 M. S. Alexander 'Introduction: knowing your friends, assessing your allies – perspectives on intra-alliance intelligence', *Intelligence and National Security*, 13, 1 (1998).

46 Meetings of Irish and British representatives, 23 & 24 May 1940, TNA, PREM 3/130.

47 Reports by Pryce, 13 Jun & 9 Jul 1940, TNA, wo 106/6043; Antrobus to John Stephenson, 20 Feb 1941, & M. J. Dean to Stephenson, 22 Apr 1941, DO 35/1109/11.

48 Reports and correspondence by Pryce, 9 & 27 Jul 1940, 20 Jan 1941, TNA, wo 106/6043 & 106/6045; minute by Costar, 23 Mar 1944, TNA, DO 35/2117.

49 Conyers-Baker to Pryce, 21 Sep 1940, TNA, wo 106/6044.

50 War diary of Military Mission 18, Jun–Oct 1940, TNA, wo 178/2.

51 Pryce to Conyers-Baker, 28 Aug 1940, TNA, wo 106/6044.

52 Directive to C-in-C, BTNI, 9 Oct 1940, CAB 80/19.

53 War diary of Military Mission 18, TNA, wo 178/2; report by Carr, 14 Oct 1940, TNA, AIR 2/5130.

54 Report by Lieut-Colonel John Reynolds, 19 Jan 1942, USNA, RG 319, 381 Ireland, Box 779; note by Godfrey, 19 Aug 1941, TNA, CAB 79/13.

55 MI5 Irish section history, pp. 3–4, TNA, KV 4/9. Descriptions of holidaying British officers are in IMA, G2/X/0266.

56 War diary of Military Mission 18, 17 Jul 1942, TNA, wo 178/2.

57 Memo by CIGS, 7 May 1941, TNA, CAB 80/27.

58 Air Staff minute, 8 Feb 1941, TNA, AIR 2/5172.

59 Andrew, *Secret service*, pp. 475–7.

60 N. Wylie, 'Ungentlemanly warriors or unreliable diplomats? Special Operations Executive and "Irregular Political Activities" in Europe'. *Intelligence and National Security*, 20, 1 (Mar 2005), 99–100. See also M. R. D. Foot, 'The IRA and the origins of SOE', in M. R. D. Foot (ed.), *War and society: historical essays in honour and memory of J. R. Western, 1928–1971* (London, 1973), pp. 57–70.

61 E. O'Halpin, ' "Toys" and "Whispers" in "16-land": SOE and Ireland, 1940–1942', *Intelligence & National Security*, 15, 4 (2000), pp. 6–10; MI5 Irish section history, p. 3, TNA, KV 4/9; papers in TNA, HS 6/305.

62 JIC report, 18 Dec 1940, TNA, CAB 81/99.

63 'Ireland: Air Intelligence Notes', Nov 1940, TNA, AIR 10/3990.

64 *Ibid.*; 'Short notes on Eire' by HQ, BTNI, undated [spring 1941?], TNA, WO 106/6045.

65 Report by Major J. W. Wofford, 8 Jul 1941, USNA, RG 319, 353.5 Ireland, Box 779.

66 Duff Cooper to Viscount Caldecote, 29 Jul 1940, TNA, DO 35/1107/12; Cabinet meeting, 26 Jul 1940, TNA, CAB 65/8; John Stephenson to Cavendish Bentinck, 26 Sep 1940, TNA, CAB 21/881; Walshe report, 18 Oct 1940, NAI, D/FA, A2.

67 Minutes of conference, 15 Dec 1940, IMA, EDP 1/2; C. Mangan, 'Plans and operations', *The Irish Sword*, 19, 75 & 76 (1993–4), pp. 50–2; O'Halpin, *Defending Ireland*, p. 178.

68 Memo by Walshe, 14 Mar 1941, NA, D/FA, A2; memo by Maffey, 20 Jun 1941, TNA, DO 35/1109/6.

69 Sloan, *The geopolitics of Anglo-Irish relations*, pp. 213–18.

70 Attlee to Churchill, 12 & 23 Mar 1942, TNA, DO 121/10B; Churchill minute, 6 Jun 1942, TNA, PREM 3/13.

71 WO to Admiralty, 22 Apr 1943, TNA, ADM 1/13032.

CHAPTER 11
Debunking the Fifth Column

1 MI5 Irish section history, p. 5, TNA, KV 4/9.

2 Florence O'Donoghue journal, 10 Apr 1942, NLI, Florence O'Donoghue Papers, Ms. 31348. For his date of appointment see report by Major J. W. Wofford, 1 May 1941, USNA, RG 165, Ireland 3840, Box 1687.

3 Report by Superintendent T. Donovan, 4 Jul 1940, IMA, G2/X/0266; O'Donoghue journal, 28 Nov 1941, NLI, Florence O'Donoghue Papers, Ms. 31348; G2 notes on 'British Activities in Eire', 13 Jul 1944, IMA, G2/X/0266; G2 notes on interview with Moore, 5 Oct 1944, IMA, G2/X/1091;.

4 Memoirs of Sir Richard Pim, PRONI, T/3620/1.

5 G2 'Notes on the activities of British agents' [mid-1941]; report by Superintendent Donovan, 4 Jul 1940; report by Florence O'Donoghue, 26 Jun 1941; report by Capt. Lordan, 19 May 1944, IMA, G2/X/0266; O'Donoghue journal, 17 Mar 1942, NLI, Florence O'Donoghue Papers, Ms. 31348.

6 G2 memo on British activities, undated, IMA, G2/X/0266; memo of meeting at Kinnaird House, 27 Jun 1940, TNA, CAB 104/184; MI5 Irish section history, pp. 49–50, TNA, KV 4/9.

7 G2 notes on British activities, IMA, G2/X/0266.

8 O'Donoghue journal, 15 & 25 Nov 1941, NLI, Florence O'Donoghue Papers, Ms. 31348; report by Major O'Connell, 12 Jan 1942, & Ms. G2 note on British activities, undated, IMA, G2/X/0266.

9 G2 notes on Moore information [Nov–Dec 1941], IMA, G2/X/1091; O'Donoghue journal, 7 & 12 Jan 1942, NLI, Florence O'Donoghue Papers, Ms. 31348.

10 SIS query for Stubbs, 15 Jun 1942; report by Colonel Archer, 30 Jul 1941; G2 note on Moore information [Oct 1941]; report by Moore, 8 Feb 1942, IMA, G2/X/1091; report by Commandant Harrington, 28 Aug 1942, IMA, G2/X/0266.

11 G2 notes on Moore information [Nov–Dec 1941], IMA, G2/X/1091.

12 Notes by Moore, undated [Dec 1941] & 17 Apr 1944; SIS query for Stubbs, 15 Jun 1942; notes by Colonel Archer, 5 Dec 1941, 12 Jan 1942, & undated, IMA, G2/X/1091.

13 O'Halpin, 'Financing British intelligence', p. 209; *Thom's Directory* (Dublin, 1940); G2 papers in IMA, G2/X/1091.

14 MI5 Irish section history, p. 5, TNA, KV 4/9.

15 Report by Superintendent Donovan, 4 Jul 1940, IMA, G2/X/0266.

16 K. Philby, *My silent war* (New York, 2002 edn), pp. 105–6. Guy Liddell Diary, 18 Nov & 6 Dec 1940, 22 Oct 1941, TNA, KV 4/185 & /188. See also S. Dorrill, *MI6: inside the covert world of Her Majesty's Secret Intelligence Service* (New York, 2000), ch. 1.

17 MI5 Irish section history, p. 98, TNA, KV 4/9.

18 Report by SIS, 7 Jan 1941, ADM 223/486. See also Pim report, 20 Jul 1940, TNA, PREM 3/129/2.

19 O'Donoghue journal, 28 Nov 1941, NLI, Florence O'Donoghue Papers, Ms. 31348.

20 *Ibid.*, p. 4.

21 Ms. G2 note on British activities, undated, IMA, G2/X/0266.

22 Dan Bryan transcripts (in possession of Prof. Eunan O'Halpin).

23 Report by Superintendent Donovan, 4 Jul 1940, IMA, G2/X/0266.

24 O'Halpin, *Defending Ireland*, p. 166; O'Donoghue journal, 28 Nov 1941 & 10 Apr 1942, & memo by O'Donoghue, 27 Dec 1942, NLI, Florence O'Donoghue Papers, Ms. 31348 & Ms. 31350.

25 G2 notes, 5 & 17 Oct 1944, IMA, G2/X/1091.

26 NID monograph on Eire by Godfrey, 17 Jun 1948, NMM, Godfrey Papers, Ms. 80/073.

27 Report by Commandant S. Hayes, 24 Feb 1942, IMA, G2/X/1091; G2 notes on Moore, 27 Dec 1944, 5 & 22 Jan 1945, IMA, G2/X/1091.

28 MI5 Irish section history, pp. 4–5, TNA, KV 4/9.

29 Maffey to Machtig, 8 Jan 1944, TNA, DO 35/2078.

30 Reports by Pryce, 8 & 13 Jun 1940; Clive to Pryce, 19 Jul 1940; Conyers-Baker to Pryce, 25 Jul 1940, TNA, WO 106/6043. For the significance of the yellow jumper, see Wilson, 'British intelligence and fear of a "fifth column" in 1940', p. 43.

31 Pryce to Balfour-Davey, 18 Jun 1940, & report by Pryce, 10 Jul 1940, TNA, WO 106/6043.

32 Pryce to Clive, 22 Aug 1940, TNA, WO 106/6044.

33 Pryce to Clive, 2 Aug 1940, TNA, WO 106/6043. See also report by Pryce, 16 Jul 1940, TNA, WO 106/6043.

34 Guy Liddell to Wing-Cmdr Elliot, 20 May 1940, TNA, CAB 104/184; MI5 Irish section history, pp. 43–4, TNA, KV 4/9.

35 Guy Liddell Diary, 20 Oct 1940 & 21 May 1941, TNA, KV 4/187.

36 Cecil Liddell to DO, 29 Jan 1942, TNA, KV 4/280.

37 SIS report, 17 Apr 1943, TNA, DO 121/84.

38 MI5 Irish section history, pp. 42–4, TNA, KV 4/9; O'Halpin, *Defending Ireland*, p. 227.

39 MI5 Irish section history, p. 1, TNA, KV 4/9.

40 Sir David Petrie to J. Curry, 12 Feb 1946, TNA, KV 4/9.

41 Guy Liddell Diary, 3 Dec 1940, TNA, KV 4/187.

42 Curry to Petrie, 8 Feb 1946, TNA, KV 4/9.

43 *The Security Service*, pp. 56–8; Hinsley & Simkins, *British intelligence in the Second World War*, vol. 4, ch.8.

44 Pim report, 20 Jul 1940, PREM 3/129/2. Referred to in the records as 'Pim's report', this consists of four different documents. The first is a four-page summary, whose author would appear to be Capt. Richard Pim, a former RIC officer and Northern Ireland civil servant who was in charge of the Prime Minister's Map Room in 1940. (However, this is not certain. See Fisk, *In time of war*, p. 143.) The second is a three-page report on Northern Ireland; the third document is an eight-page report by the RUC officer on his talks with Garda personnel; the fourth is a county-by-county survey of suspected fifth column and U-boat activity,

probably by SIS. Put together, these four documents comprise one of the most comprehensive and interesting intelligence reports on Ireland, and it is a pity that its interpretation is complicated by uncertainties over authorship.

45 Cecil Liddell to Vivian, 2 Sep 1940, TNA, KV 4/280.

46 MI5 report on Northern Ireland, 4 Sep 1940, TNA, CAB 93/3. See also Guy Liddell Diary, 28 Nov 1941, TNA, KV 4/188.

47 Cecil Liddell to Vivian, 2 Sep 1940, TNA, KV 4/280.

48 Wickham to MI5, 2 Oct 1940, TNA, KV 4/280.

49 Note by Godfrey, 19 Aug 1941, TNA, CAB 79/13.

50 NID monograph on Eire, 17 Jun 1948, NMM, Godfrey Papers, Ms. 80/073.

51 *Ibid.*

52 Balfour-Davey to Pryce, 11 Jun 1940, TNA, WO 106/6043. For NID reports see USNA, RG 226, Entry 16, No. 7157 (M1499, Roll 22).

53 Opinion of Maffey recorded in Pryce to Conyers-Bakers, 13 Jul 1940, TNA, WO 106/6043.

54 Maffey to Machtig, 1, 11 & 16 Jul 1940, TNA, DO 130/12; memo by CIGS on talk with Maffey, 20 Jul 1940, TNA, CAB 80/15.

55 Guy Liddell Diary, Aug-Sep 1940, TNA, KV 4/186; Hinsley & Simkins, *British intelligence and the Second World War*, vol. 4, p. 59.

56 Hinsley, *British intelligence in the Second World War*, vol. 1, pp. 183–90, 261–4.

57 Andrew, *Secret service*, pp. 448–51.

58 Beesly, *Very special admiral*, pp. 186–7.

59 Thomas, 'The evolution of the JIC system'; Herman, *Intelligence power in peace and war*, p. 27; Andrew, *Secret service*, pp. 483–4.

60 F. H. Hinsley, *British intelligence in the Second World War: abridged edition* (London, 1993), pp. 115–20.

61 Note by MI5 (Section B9), 6 Jan 1941, TNA, KV 4/232.

62 MI5 weekly intelligence summary, 19 Dec 1940, TNA, KV 4/122.

63 E. Montagu to DNI, 2 Dec 1940, TNA, ADM 1/11104.

64 'Ireland: Air Intelligence Notes', Nov 1940, TNA, AIR 10/3990; 'Short notes on Eire for Junior Commanders' by HQ, BTNI, undated [spring 1941], TNA, WO 106/6045.

65 JP report, 2 Oct 1940, TNA, CAB 84/19; JIC report, 18 Sep 1940, TNA, CAB 81/98.

66 Chief Superintendent P. Carroll to Colonel Archer, 6 Nov 1940, IMA, G2/x/0058.

67 Memo on meeting between Walshe, McKenna, Archer, Harrison and Pryce, 17 Feb 1941, NAI, D/FA, A3.

68 MI5 weekly intelligence summary, 19 Dec 1940, TNA, KV 4/122.

69 Hull, *Irish secrets*, pp. 47–8.

70 Report by SIS, 14 Jan 1941, TNA, ADM 223/486; Pryce to Skrine, 20 Jul 1940, TNA, WO 106/6043.

71 Report by SIS, 14 Jan 1941, TNA, ADM 223/486.

72 *Ibid*. For other references to Aiken see minute by Clive, undated [Oct 1940], TNA, WO 106/6044; minute by Admiralty Director of Plans, 25 Oct 1940, TNA, ADM 116/6207.

73 Report by SIS, 28 Mar 1941, TNA, ADM 223/486.

74 British memo on Aiken, with Hoover to Berle, 12 Jun 1941, USNA, RG 59, 862.20241D/4; J. L. Rosenberg, 'The 1941 mission of Frank Aiken to the United States: an American perspective', *Irish Historical Studies*, 22, 86 (Sep 1980), pp. 162–77.

75 SIS query, 21 Jul 1942, IMA, G2/x/1091.

76 Memo by J. Betjeman, 21 Mar 1942, TNA, DO 130/30. See also O'Halpin, *Defending Ireland*, p. 223; report on Continental political ideologies in Irish political life, 1943, USNA, RG 226, Entry 196, Box 6, File 13.

77 Report by Moore, 27 Apr 1942, IMA, G2/x/1091; SIS reports on 'Irish Affairs', 1 Sep 1942, 1 Mar & 1 Jul 1943, TNA, DO 121/85.

78 SIS query for Stubbs, 20 Jul 1944, IMA, G2/x/1091. For widespread suspicion of this organisation, see K. B. Nowlan, 'Conclusion', in T. D. Williams (ed.), *Secret societies in Ireland* (Dublin, 1973), pp. 184–6.

79 Betjeman to MOI, 14 Mar 1941, TNA, INF 1/786; minute by Antrobus, 3 Nov 1941, TNA, DO 35/1011/6.

80 Memo by Betjeman, 21 Mar 1942, TNA, DO 130/30; HD(S)E meeting, 2 Jul 1941, TNA, CAB 93/2.

81 Report by SIS, 29 Apr 1941, TNA, ADM 223/486.

82 Report by SIS, 24 Dec 1940, TNA, ADM 223/486.

83 Report on IRA [probably by G2], with Hoover to Strong, 4 May 1943, USNA, RG 165, Ireland 2700, Box 1685. See also summary of IRA activities, 1946, NAI, D/T, S.11564; Coogan, *The IRA*, pp. 144–5.

84 Report on IRA [probably by G2], with Hoover to Strong, 4 May 1943, USNA, RG 165, Ireland 2700, Box 1685.

85 Tarlach O'hUid, quoted in Coogan, *The IRA*, p. 156.

86 Coogan, *The IRA*, p. 158; O'Halpin, *Defending Ireland*, p. 249.

87 Note by Godfrey, 19 Aug 1941, TNA, CAB 79/13.

88 Admiralty weekly intelligence report, 31 Oct 1941, TNA, ADM 223/152.

89 'W.2 Plan', 15 Jan 1942, TNA, WO 166/668.

90 Report on IRA [probably by G2], with Hoover to Strong, 4 May 1943, USNA, RG 165, Ireland 2700, Box 1685; memo on IRA, undated [1946], NAI, D/T, S.11564A; Bardon, *A history of Ulster*, pp. 582–3; Coogan, *The IRA*, pp. 158–9, 179, 183–90.

91 SIS query for Stubbs, 7 Nov 1942, IMA, G2/x/1091; SIS report, 1 Jan 1944, TNA, DO 121/85.

92 SIS report, 1 May 1942, TNA, DO 121/85.

93 SIS report, 4 Jul 1942, TNA, DO 121/85.

94 Dan Bryan transcripts.

95 G2 reports on IRA, 13 Mar 1943, IMA, G2/x/0058; SIS report, 1 Mar 1943, TNA, DO 121/85.

96 SIS report, 1 Mar 1944, TNA, DO 121/85.

97 MI5 Irish section history, pp. 85–9, and appendix I, TNA, KV 4/9.

98 Hull, *Irish secrets*, pp. 144–6; O'Halpin, *Defending Ireland*, p. 245; *Irish Times*, 8 Sep 1947; Dan Bryan transcripts.

99 Report by Cecil Liddell, 6 Aug 1943, TNA, DO 121/86.

100 Hull, *Irish secrets*, pp. 141–4, 148–51, 170–3.

101 G2 precis, undated [Sep 1941], IMA, G2/x/0058.

102 Memos by Joe Stephenson, 25 Sep 1941, & R. T. Reed, 30 Sep 1941, TNA, KV 2/1323.

103 G2 precis, undated [Sep 1941], G2, IMA, G2/x/0058; O'Donoghue journal, 8 Sep 1941, NLI, Florence O'Donoghue Papers, Ms. 31348.

104 Guy Liddell Diary, 16 Jul 1941, TNA, KV 4/188.

105 SIS report, 17 Apr 1943, TNA, DO 121/84.

106 Liddell to Bryan, 30 Sep 1941, IMA, G2/1722; note on Goertz by Cecil Liddell, 14 Oct 1941, TNA, KV 2/1321; Guy Liddell Diary, 10, 12 & 28 Nov 1941, TNA, KV 4/188.

107 SIS report, 1 Nov 1943, DO 121/85; note by Colonel Archer, 5 Dec 1941, IMA, G2/x/1091; Garda reports, 1 & 8 Dec 1941, IMA, G2/x/0093 & G2/x/1091.

108 Guy Liddell Diary, 6 Jan 1942, TNA, KV 4/189. See also MI5 note, 8 Dec 1941, TNA, KV 4/1321.

109 SIS reports, 4, 8 & 16 Dec 1941, TNA, KV 2/1321.

110 Correspondence between Liddell and Bryan, Jan–Mar 1942, IMA, G2/X/1722.

111 MI5 Irish section history, pp. 8, 54, TNA, KV 4/9.

112 'Irish-German-American Notes' by G2, 18 Mar 1941, NAI, D/FA, A12; Hermann Görtz in *Irish Times*, 7 Sep 1947; Hayes confession; D/EA to Kerney, 6 Aug 1941, & Bryan to Boland, 8 Aug 1941, NAI, D/FA, A20; reports in IMA, G2/3010.

113 G2 report on Russell and Ryan, undated [1946?], IMA, G2/X/0093; Hull, *Irish secrets*, pp. 186–90.

114 MI5 report on Frank Ryan, 15 Dec 1941, TNA, KV 2/1291; 'Irish-German-American Notes' by G2, 18 Mar 1941, NA, D/FA, A12.

115 9 Jun 1942 entry, West, *The Guy Liddell diaries*, vol. 1.

116 Conference between MI5, Special Branch and Lancashire police, 6 Mar 1942, TNA, KV 2/23; correspondence between Liddell and Bryan, Jan 1942, IMA, G2/X/1722.

117 Memo by Godfrey, 21 Mar 1942, TNA, ADM 223/486.

118 Pryce to Clive, 3 Sep 1940, TNA, WO 106/6044; Cecil Liddell in MI5 weekly intelligence summary, 13 Feb 1941, TNA, KV 4/122.

CHAPTER 12
Opinion and Propaganda

1 M. Balfour, *Propaganda in war, 1939–1945* (London, 1979); I. C. B. Dear & M. R. D. Foot (eds.), *The Oxford companion to the Second World War* (Oxford, 1995), pp. 1084–90; D. C. Watt, 'The proper study of propaganda', *Intelligence and National Security*, 15, 4 (2000), pp. 143–64.

2 *The Security Service*, p. 122.

3 P. Addison, *The road to 1945: British politics and the Second World War* (London, 1994 edn), pp. 64–5. See also M. Donnelly, *Britain in the Second World War* (London, 1999), p. 70; Balfour, *Propaganda in war*, pp. 53–71.

4 MOI organisational table, undated [1939], TNA, INF 1/28; report by Pakenham, 23 Oct 1939, TNA, DO 35/1005/10.

5 Maffey to Parkinson, 22 Apr 1940, TNA, DO 130/12; Canning, *British policy towards Ireland*, p. 250.

6 Maffey on talk with de Valera, 24 Dec 1941, TNA, DO 130/17.

7 Maffey to Machtig, 16 Feb 1940, TNA, DO 35/894/3.

8 M. J. Graham to Maffey, 8 Jan 1940, TNA, DO 35/1011/3.

9 General V. Pollock to DMI, 17 Feb 1940, TNA, DO 35/1011/3.

10 SIS report on German propaganda, Sep 1940, TNA, ADM 223/486.

11 D. O'Donoghue, *Hitler's Irish voices: the story of German radio's wartime Irish service* (Dublin, 1998); A. Roth, 'Francis Stuart's broadcasts from Germany, 1942–44: some new evidence', *Irish Historical Studies*, 32, 127 (2001).

12 Graham to Maffey, 8 Jan 1940, TNA, DO 35/1011/3; Thurlow, *The secret state*, pp. 235–6.

13 O'Donoghue, *Hitler's Irish voices*, p. 50; MI5 Irish section history, pp. 45, 53, TNA, KV 4/9.

14 SIS reports on German propaganda, Sep & 24 Dec 1940, TNA, ADM 223/486.

15 Summary of decrypted German legation messages, 29 Apr 1944, TNA, DO 121/87; MOI 'Plan of propaganda to Eire', 10 Feb 1943, TNA, INF 1/562.

16 SIS query for Stubbs, 19 Oct 1943, IMA, G2/X/1091.

17 SIS queries, 19 Oct 1943, 7 & 18 Sep 1944, IMA, G2/X/1091; Maffey to Machtig, 3 Feb 1942, TNA, DO 35/1011/4; SIS summary of decrypted German legation messages, 30 May – 12 Jun 1943, TNA, DO 121/87.

18 Summary of IRA activities during war, 1946, NA, D/T, S.11564; Bryan to Walshe, 22 May 1943, NA, D/FA, A.12.

19 Transcript of IRA broadcast, Dec 1939, NAI, D/T, S.11564; BTNI security summary, 30 Apr 1941, TNA, WO 166/1172/2; Dan Bryan transcripts (in possession of Prof. Eunan O'Halpin).

20 John Stephenson to Maffey, 18 Apr 1940, TNA, DO 130/8; Cecil Liddell to Jebb, 21 Mar 1940, TNA, FO 371/25222.

21 Leaflet enclosed with Maffey to Machtig, 8 Feb 1940, TNA, DO 130/8.

22 H. V. Hodson to John Stephenson, 10 & 25 Jun 1940, TNA, DO 35/1011/3.

23 Roy Foster notes that she was 'a kind of spy'. See Foster, *Paddy and Mr Punch*, p. 117. See also O'Halpin, 'MI5's Irish memories', p. 139.

24 Antrobus to John Stephenson, 27 Jul 1940; Cranborne to Churchill and Eden, 19 Nov 1940, TNA, DO 35/1011/3.

25 Report by Arnold Lunn, 19 Aug 1940, TNA, INF 1/404.

26 Report by Betjeman, 21 Jun 1940, TNA, INF 1/528.

27 Reports by Bowen, 31 Jul, 14 Aug & 9 Nov 1940, TNA, DO 35/1011/3.

28 Report by Maxwell, 23 Sep 1940, TNA, DO 35/1011/3.

29 Report by Bowen, 9 Nov 1940, TNA, DO 35/1011/3.

30 Clive to Pryce, 29 Aug 1940, TNA, WO 106/6044.

31 Report by SIS, 8 May 1941, TNA, ADM 223/486.

32 Report by SIS, 26 Jul 1941, TNA, ADM 223/486.

33 D. Ó Drisceoil, *Censorship in Ireland, 1939–45: neutrality, politics and society* (Cork, 1996); D. Ó'Drisceoil, 'Censorship as propaganda: the neutralisation of Irish public opinion during the Second World War', in B. Girvin & G. Roberts (eds.), *Ireland and the Second World War: politics, society and remembrance* (Dublin, 2000).

34 Report by C. Hollis, Mar 1942, TNA, INF 1/786.

35 MOI 'Plan of propaganda to Eire', 10 Feb 1943, TNA, INF 1/562; note by Maffey, 21 Mar 1945, TNA, DO 35/2086.

36 F. S. L. Lyons, *Ireland since the Famine* (London, 1973 edn), pp. 557–8.

37 Memo by Shaw, 1 Jan 1941, FO 371/29108; memo by Maffey, 20 Jun 1941, TNA, DO 35/1109/6. See C. Willis, *That neutral island: a cultural history of Ireland during the Second World War* (London, 2007), p. 7.

38 MOI 'Plan of propaganda to Eire', 10 Feb 1943, TNA, INF 1/562.

39 R. Cole, ' "Good relations": Irish neutrality and the propaganda of John Betjeman, 1941–43', *Eire-Ireland*, 30, 4 (1996), p. 33.

40 Memo by C. R. Price on interview with Pakenham, 14 Oct 1939, TNA, DO 35/1005/10.

41 Hodson to MOI Director-General, 18 Oct 1940, TNA, INF 1/28.

42 General Pollock to DMI, 17 Feb 1940, TNA, DO 35/1011/3.

43 John Stephenson to Maffey, 18 Apr 1940, TNA, DO 130/8; Cecil Liddell to Jebb, 21 Mar 1940, TNA, FO 371/25222.

44 MOI, HO and DO meetings and correspondence, Apr–May 1940, TNA, INF 1/404.

45 Clive to Pryce, 11 Aug 1940, TNA, WO 106/6043.

46 Clive to Pryce, 17 Oct 1940, TNA, WO 106/6044.

47 Report by Betjeman, 21 Jun 1940, TNA, INF 1/528.

48 Minute by John Stephenson, 1 Oct 1940, TNA, DO 35/1011/3.

49 Hodson to John Stephenson, 23 Sep 1940; minute by Stephenson, 1 Oct 1940; Machtig to Maffey, 3 Oct 1940, TNA, DO 35/1011/3; Clive to Pryce, 10 Nov 1940, TNA, DO 106/6045.

50 G2 report, undated [1941], IMA, G2/X/0680.

51 Report by Betjeman, 17 Oct 1942, TNA, DO 35/1011/4.

52 G2 reports, undated [1941] & 14 Jul 1941, IMA, G2/X/0680.

53 Quoted in *The Guardian*, 22 Apr 2000.

54 Betjeman to R. B. Pugh, 5 Jun 1941, TNA, DO 35/1011/3; Cole, ' "Good relations": Irish neutrality and the propaganda of John Betjeman, 1941–43', pp. 43–4.

55 Report by Betjeman, 17 Oct 1942, TNA, DO 35/1011/4.

56 Betjeman to MOI, 14 & 22 Mar 1941, TNA, INF 1/786; MOI 'Plan of propaganda to Eire', 10 Feb 1943, TNA, INF 1/562.

57 Prof. Harlow to Sir Maurice Peterson, 16 Jun 1941, TNA, INF 1/539.

58 *Daily Mail*, 14 Oct 1941; Betjeman to MOI, 14 Mar 1941, TNA, INF 1/786; Mansergh to Betjeman, 1 Nov 1941; minutes by Antrobus & Machtig, 3 Nov 1941; Machtig to Maffey, 4 Nov 1941; Maffey to Machtig, 6 Nov 1941, TNA, DO 35/1011/3.

59 Note by Pugh, 11 May 1942, TNA, DO 35/1011/4.

60 *Sunday Independent*, 16 Apr 1978. One historian dismissed this as 'preposterous. See Fisk, *In time of war*, p. 441.

61 Channel 4 documentary, 23 Apr 2000; *The Guardian*, 22 Apr 2000.

62 Harlow to Peterson, 16 Jun 1941, TNA, INF 1/539; Maffey to Machtig, 24 Dec 1941, TNA, DO 35/1011/4.

63 Betjeman to Mansergh, 29 Jul 1942, TNA, DO 130/30.

64 SIS report, 1 Sep 1942, TNA, DO 121/85.

65 K. Young (ed.), *The diaries of Sir Robert Bruce Lockhart: 1939–1965* (London, 1980), vol. 2, pp. 19–24.

66 MOI 'Plan of propaganda to Eire', 10 Feb 1943, TNA, INF 1/562.

67 Summary of decrypted German legation messages, 8–21 Aug 1943, TNA, DO 121/87.

68 Note for Pryce, 8 May 1941, enclosing letter to Roddy Keith, TNA, HS 6/307.

69 SOE note on 'Eire whispering'; D/Q to AD/P (both SOE), 27 Feb 1942, TNA, HS 6/305; SOE minutes, Jul 1941, TNA, HS 6/307.

70 D/Q10 to AD/P, 13 Oct 1942, TNA, HS 6/307. See also O'Halpin, '"Toys" and "Whispers" in "16-land"', pp. 10–13.

71 Lord Lothian to Lord Halifax, 21 Sep 1939; FO minute, 6 Oct 1939, TNA, FO 371/22831; meeting of HO, DO and MOI officials, 15 Apr 1940, TNA, DO 35/1011/3; N. J. Cull, *Selling war: the British propaganda campaign against American 'neutrality', in World War II* (Oxford, 1995), pp. 33–68; S. Brewer, *To win the peace: British propaganda in the United States during World War II* (Ithaca & London, 1997), p. 236.

72 *British Security Coordination: the secret history of British intelligence in the Americas, 1940–45* (London, 1998), p. 85; memo by Prof. T. North Whitehead (FO), 29 Nov 1940, TNA, FO 371/24232.

73 C. Hargrove to North Whitehead, 13 Jun 1941; J. Balfour to Hargrove, 25 Jun 1941, TNA, FO 371/26185.

74 Brewer, *To win the peace*, pp. 45–6.

75 There is much literature on the activities of BSC, not all of it reliable. H. Montgomery Hyde, *The quiet Canadian: the Secret service story of Sir William Stephenson* (London, 1962) [published in USA as *Room 3603: William Stevenson, a man called Intrepid: the secret war* (New York, 1976)]; T. F. Troy, *Wild Bill and Intrepid: Donovan, Stephenson and the origin of CIA* (New Haven, CT, 1996); D. M. Charles, 'American, British and Canadian intelligence links: a critical annotated bibliography', *Intelligence and National Security*, 15, 2 (2000), pp. 259–69.

76 *British Security Coordination*, pp. 85–7.

77 Brennan to D/FA, 15 Sep, 4 Oct, & 12 Nov 1941, NAI, D/FA, P.52; note by Major O'Connell, 18 Mar 1942, IMA, G2/X/0825.

78 Rodgers to Lord Davidson, 10 Jun 1941, TNA, INF 1/539.

79 Rodgers to Newbold, 25 Jan 1941; meeting at Guinness headquarters, 29 Jan 1941; Rodgers to Davidson, 10 Jun 1941, TNA, INF 1/539.

80 Hingeley to Rodgers, 27 Jan 1941, TNA, INF 1/539.

81 Harlow to Peterson, 16 Jun 1941, TNA, INF 1/539.

82 E. Rawdon Smith to Rodgers, 21 Jul & 26 Aug 1941; Betjeman to Rodgers, 15 Aug 1941, TNA, INF 1/539.

83 Meeting between DO and MOI, 4 Dec 1941, TNA, DO 35/1011/4.

84 Mansergh to Harlow, 10 Feb 1942, TNA, INF 1/539.

85 Willis, *That neutral island*, pp. 194–203.

86 Report by Betjeman, 17 Oct 1942, TNA, DO 35/1011/4.

87 *Ibid.* See also meeting between DO and MOI, 4 Dec 1941, TNA, DO 35/1011/4.

88 Report by Christopher Hollis, Mar 1942, & Betjeman to Hollis, 11 Sep 1942, TNA, INF 1/786.

89 MOI 'Plan of propaganda to Eire', 10 Feb 1943, TNA, INF 1/562.

90 *Ibid.*

91 Memo by Godfrey, 21 Mar 1942, TNA, ADM 223/486.

92 SIS report, 1 Nov 1943, TNA, DO 121/85.

93 MOI 'Plan of propaganda to Eire', 10 Feb 1943, TNA, INF 1/562.

94 *Ibid.*

95 SIS report, 1 Jan, 1 Jul & 1 Nov 1943, TNA, DO 121/85.

96 MOI 'Plan of propaganda to Eire', 10 Feb 1943, TNA, INF 1/562.

97 Memo by Maffey, 21 Aug 1945, TNA, DO 35/2090.

98 Memo by Maffey, 17 Apr 1943, TNA, DO 121/84.

99 O'Halpin, *Defending Ireland*, p. 223.

100 Report on continental political ideologies, probably by G2, undated [1943], USNA, RG 226, Entry 196, Box 6, File 13.

101 Report by G2 Southern Command, 6 Nov 1943, IMA, G2/X/0266.

102 SIS reports, 1 Jul & 1 Nov 1943, 1 Jan, 1 May, 31 Aug, 31 Oct & 31 Dec 1944, TNA, DO 121/85.

103 Note by Maffey, 10 Nov 1944; anon. DO minute, 17 Nov 1944; note of conference between Cranborne, Maffey and Machtig, 15 Dec 1944, TNA, DO 35/2080.

104 MOI 'Plan of propaganda to Eire', 10 Feb 1943, TNA, INF 1/562.

105 McGarry, *Eoin O'Duffy*, pp. 327–8; G2 Southern Command intelligence summary, 31 Aug 1940, IMA, G2/X/0093.

106 Memo by Walshe, 11 Jul 1940, NAI, D/FA, A2.

107 Memo by Maffey, 24 Dec 1941, TNA, DO 130/17.

CHAPTER 13

Leakage of Information

1 *The Security Service*, pp. 245–57.

2 *Ibid.*, pp. 222–3.

3 J. C. Masterman, *The double cross system* (London, 1973), p. xii.

4 Hinsley & Simkins, *British intelligence in the Second World War*, vol. 4, p. 87.

5 JIC report on importance of Eire, 23 May 1940, TNA, CAB 81/97. See also Morton to Swinton, 8 Jun 1940, TNA, PREM 3/131/2; *The Security Service*, pp. 167, 175.

6 L. Grant to Pryce, 29 Sep 1940; minute by Clive, undated, TNA, WO 106/6044.

7 Memo by Air Ministry, 29 Oct 1940, in appendix to note by JIC secretary, 6 Nov 1940, TNA, CAB 81/98.

8 Churchill to Home Secretary, 31 Aug 1941, TNA, PREM, 4/53/3. For similar concerns, see Twenty Committee meeting, 9 Oct 1941, TNA, KV 4/64.

9 MI5 Irish section history, p. 1, TNA, KV 4/9.

10 Note by Herbert, 24 May 1940, TNA, CAB 76/14.

11 HD(S)E meetings, 29 May & 5 Jun 1940, TNA, CAB 93/2; memo by Duff Cooper for Churchill, 5 Apr 1941, TNA, PREM 4/6/7; memo by Inter-Services Security Board for JIC, 7 Jun 1940, TNA, CAB 81/97.

12 JIC minutes, 3 & 15 May 1940, TNA, CAB 81/87; MI5 Irish section history, pp. 44–5, TNA, KV 4/9.

13 HD(S)E meeting, 29 May 1940, TNA, CAB 93/2.

14 Memo by Assistant Chief of Air Staff, 28 Mar 1941, & memo by DMI, 8 May 1941, TNA, CAB 81/101.

15 Memo by HD(S)E, 19 Nov 1940, TNA, CAB 93/3.

16 H. Gee to Churchill, 18 Jun 1941, TNA, PREM 4/53/3; HD(S)E meeting, 25 Jun 1941, TNA, CAB 93/2; Churchill minutes, 19 & 26 Jun 1941, TNA, PREM 4/53/3.

17 John Anderson to Ernest Bevin, 10 Jun 1941, TNA, PREM 4/53/3.

18 Bevin to Churchill, 23 Jun 1941, TNA, PREM 4/53/3; HD(S)E meeting, 25 Jun 1941, TNA, CAB 93/2.

19 Conference of MI5 regional officers, 21 Apr 1942, TNA, KV 2/233.

20 T. Connolly, 'Irish workers in Britain during World War Two', in B. Girvin & G. Roberts (eds.), *Ireland and the Second World War: politics, society and remembrance*

(Dublin, 2000), pp. 122–3. See also MI5 Irish section history, p. 51, TNA, KV 4/9.

21 Colonel Conyers-Baker to Pryce, 12 Apr 1941, TNA, WO 106/6045.

22 Note by Sir Herbert Creedy, 21 Nov 1941, TNA, CAB 93/3.

23 MI5 Irish section history, p. 12, TNA, KV 4/9.

24 For parliamentary agitation see question by Sir William Davison, 3 Jul 1941, TNA, FO 371/26580. For the response, see report by Creedy, 10 Jun 1941, TNA, CAB 93/3; HD(S)E meetings, 11 Jun & 16 Jul 1941, TNA, CAB 93/2; memo by Home Secretary, 15 Aug 1941, TNA, CAB 66/18.

25 HD(S)E meeting, 6 Sep 1940, TNA, CAB 93/2.

26 Memo by Home Secretary, 15 Aug 1941, TNA, CAB 66/18.

27 Report by Garda, 23 Oct 1941, containing IRA 'Comprehensive Military Report on Belfast', undated [1941], IMA, G2/1722; Dan Bryan transcripts. Other IRA men were found with similar documents. See the case of James Rice (in Fisk, *In time of war*, p. 377) and Henry Lundborg (in Hull, *Irish secrets*, p. 247). For a description of the German bombing, see Bardon, *A history of Ulster*, pp. 564–74.

28 Memo by Air Ministry, 29 Oct 1940, TNA, CA 81/98.

29 Memo by Assistant Chief of Air Staff, 28 Mar 1941, TNA, CAB 81/101.

30 See *Evening Standard*, 7 Aug 1941.

31 Report by SIS, 24 Dec 1940, TNA, ADM 223/486.

32 Churchill minutes, 6 Jul & 31 Aug 1941, TNA, PREM 4/53/3; MI5 Irish section history, p. 55, TNA, KV 4/9.

33 Memo by William Ziff, 19 Dec 1941, USNA, RG 226, Entry 116, Microfilm M1642, Roll 123, Frames 1081–90.

34 Report by Colonel Bryan, 7 Dec 1940, NAI, D/FA, A41; MI5 report, 29 Oct 1943, TNA, DO 121/84.

35 Report by C. Hollis, Mar 1942, TNA, INF 1/786.

36 Hull, *Irish secrets*, pp. 229–35.

37 MI5 Irish section history, pp. 41, 49, TNA, KV 4/9; Pryce to Major J. V. Bailey, 28 Mar 1941, TNA, WO 106/6045.

38 Hull, *Irish secrets*, pp. 179–83.

39 MI5 Irish section history, pp. 52–3, TNA, KV 4/9.

40 Report on Unland by MI5, 6 Mar 1941, TNA, KV 2/1295; Hull, *Irish secrets*, pp. 162–9.

41 MI5 Irish section history, p. 55, TNA, KV 4/9.

42 Memo by Irish Minister for Posts & Telegraph, 4 Jul 1940, NAI, D/T, S.3157.

43 E. O'Halpin, ' "According to the Irish minister in Rome … "; British decrypts and Irish diplomacy in the Second World War', *Irish Studies in International Affairs*, 6 (1995), pp. 95–107. For phone tapping, see memo by John Godfrey, 21 Mar 1942, TNA, ADM 223/486.

44 Guy Liddell Diary, 6 Aug 1942, TNA, KV 4/190.

45 Joint memo by MI5, SIS & Director of Postal and Telegraph Censorship [Apr 1941]; memo by MI5 for Security Executive, 28 Mar 1942, TNA, CAB 93/3; MI5 Irish section history, pp. 65–7, TNA, KV 4/9.

46 MI5 Irish section history, pp. 66, 68–9, TNA, KV 4/9; report by Capt. Hewitt (G2) on Carruthers, 27 Jul 1942, NAI, D/FA, A60.

47 Dan Bryan transcripts.

48 MI5 Irish section history, p. 55, TNA, KV 4/9.

49 Denniston, 'The Government Code and Cipher School between the wars', p. 58.

50 John Stephenson to Colonel Vivian, 7 Jan 1941, TNA, DO 121/84.

51 Vivian to John Stephenson, 25 Jan & 10 Mar 1941, TNA, DO 121/84.

52 MI5 Irish section history, p. 55, TNA, KV 4/9; Maffey to John Stephenson, 14 Mar 1941, TNA, DO 121/84.

53 Maffey to John Stephenson, 16 & 21 May 1941, TNA, DO 121/84.

54 John Stephenson to Maffey, 24 Jun 1941, TNA, DO 121/84.

55 Maffey to John Stephenson, 9 Jun 1941, TNA, DO 121/84.

56 Vivian to John Stephenson, 18 Sep 1941, TNA, DO 121/84.

57 MI5 Irish section history, p. 57, TNA, KV 4/9.

58 Both SIS and SOE considered such a scheme. See E. O'Halpin, ' "Toys" and "Whispers" in "16-land" ', p. 13; Maffey to Stephenson, 9 Jun 1941, TNA, DO 121/84.

59 Dan Bryan transcripts; O'Halpin, *Defending Ireland*, p. 188.

60 Dan Bryan transcripts.

61 *Ibid.*; Cecil Liddell to John Stephenson, 13 Nov 1941, & N. Archer to Stephenson, 3 Dec 1941, TNA, DO 121/84; MI5 Irish section history, p. 58, TNA, KV 4/9.

62 SIS report on German wireless transmitter, 17 Apr 1943, & Vivian to John Stephenson, 13 Apr 1943, TNA, DO 121/84.

63 MI5 Irish section history, p. 59, TNA, KV 4/9.

64 Guy Liddell Diary, 21 Feb 1942, TNA, KV 4/189.

65 Security Executive meeting, 27 Aug 1942, TNA, CAB 93/2.

66 See instructions by Denniston to GC&CS, 2 Feb 1943, TNA, HW 36/5.

67 Summary of decrypted German legation messages, 8–20 Feb 1943, TNA, DO 121/87.

68 O'Halpin, *Defending Ireland*, p. 183.

69 Conference between MI5, Special Branch and Lancashire police, 6 Mar 1942, TNA, KV 2/233.

70 Guy Liddell Diary, 5 Mar 1942, TNA, KV 4/189.

71 Conference between MI5, Special Branch, RUC, HO and Chief Constables, 10 Apr 1942, TNA, KV 2/233. For 1920s IRA espionage see Cecil Liddell to Jane Archer, 26 Apr 1942, TNA, KV 4/233.

72 MI5 Irish section history, p. 51, TNA, KV 4/9; memo by MI5, 17 Apr 1942, TNA, CAB 93/3; Security Executive meeting, 22 Apr 1942, TNA, CAB 93/2.

73 Conference between MI5, Special Branch, RUC, HO and Chief Constables, 10 Apr 1942, TNA, KV 2/233.

74 HO to Petrie, 9 Jun 1942, TNA, KV 4/232.

75 Rothschild to Cecil Liddell, 25 Mar 1942, TNA, KV 4/232.

76 Guy Liddell to Sir David Petrie, 12 Apr 1942, TNA, KV 2/233.

77 Hankinson to F. H. Boland, 10 Nov 1942, NAI, D/FA, A60; SIS query for Stubbs, 28 Aug 1943, IMA, G2/X/1091.

78 SIS queries, 28 Jul 1942 & 7 Sep 1944, IMA, G2/X/1091.

79 Hull, *Irish secrets*, pp. 183–6.

80 SIS query for Stubbs, 27 Apr 1943, IMA, G2/X/1091.

81 Hull, *Irish secrets*, pp. 177–8, 238–40; undated SIS query for Stubbs, [early 1942], IMA, G2/X/1091.

82 Collinson notes, 8 Feb, 11 & 21 May 1943, IMA, G2/X/1091. The other four suspicious women were Betty Krampt, Coleen Kivlehan, Marion Charlotte Eager and Sheila McDonnell. See SIS queries, 3 Feb, 3 Jul 1943, 10 Aug & 22 Sep 1943, IMA, G2/X/1091.

83 G2 note on American opinion, Nov 1942, IMA, G2/X/0825.

84 Willis, *That neutral island*, p. 323.

85 David Gray to State Dept, 18 Jan 1942, USNA, RG 59, 841d.00/1323; G2 notes on Moore report, 24 Feb & 1 Mar 1942, IMA, G2/X/1091.

86 Moore reports, 13 & 21 May 1942, IMA, G2/X/1091.

87 Breen to Hempel, 20 Apr 1943, USNA, RG 226, Entry 141A, Box 2, File 3.

88 SIS report, 1 Sep 1943, TNA, DO 121/85.

89 Summary of decrypted German legation messages, 19 Sep – 2 Oct 1943, TNA, DO 121/87.

90 For Bewley see Hull, *Irish secrets*, pp. 190–1, 209; SIS note on summary of decrypted German legation messages, 16–29 May 1943, TNA, DO 121/87; Colonel Bryan to Walshe, 12 Dec 1945, NAI, D/FA, P17. For Kerney, see D. Keogh, *Ireland and Europe, 1919–48* (Dublin, 1988), pp. 166–71; O'Halpin, *Defending Ireland*, p. 217; Hull, *Irish secrets*, pp. 127–8, 190–3.

91 MI5 Irish section history, pp. 48, 64–5, TNA, KV 4/9; Hull, *Irish secrets*, pp. 217–26. For G2 files, see IMA, G2/X/0154, G2/X/0947, G2/X/1164. The O'Neill incident is described in Benton, 'The ISOS years', p. 385.

92 Hull, *Irish secrets*, pp. 232–3; SIS report on 'Irish Affairs', 1 Sep 1942, TNA, DO 121/85.

93 MI5 Irish section history, pp. 59–61, TNA, KV 4/9; N. Archer to Machtig, 18 Oct 1941, TNA, DO 121/84; Sir David Petrie to Findlater Stewart, 15 Feb 1944, TNA, CAB 113/18.

94 MI5 Irish section history, p. 70, TNA, KV 4/9; SIS summary of decrypted German legation messages, 1 May 1943, TNA, DO 121/87; report by Cecil Liddell and Jane Archer, 6 Aug 1943, TNA, DO 121/86; G2 note, 24 Sep 1943, IMA, G2/1091. See also Hull, *Irish secrets*, pp. 196–9.

95 G2 summary, Sep 1945, IMA, G2/3261.

96 SIS report, 1 Nov 1943, DO 121/85.

97 MI5 Irish section history, p. 70, TNA, KV 4/9.

98 *Ibid.*, pp. 69–71. See also unsigned note [probably by B1H, MI5], 4 Apr 1943, TNA, KV 2/1323.

99 Hull, *Irish secrets*, pp. 243–9.

100 MI5 file on John Francis O'Reilly and John Kenny, TNA, KV 2/119; MI5 Irish section history, pp. 78–9, TNA, KV 4/9; Hull, *Irish secrets*, pp. 199–207, 261–6.

101 Hull, *Irish secrets*, p. 207; MI5 Irish section history, pp. 78–9, TNA, KV 4/9.

102 Summaries of decrypted German legation messages, 5–18 Mar & 19 Mar – 1 Apr 1944, TNA, DO 121/97.

103 See papers on Operation Overlord in TNA, CAB 113/18.

104 MI5 Irish section history, p. 51, TNA, KV 4/9.

105 SIS report, 17 Apr 1943, TNA, DO 121/84.

106 John Stephenson to Machtig, 12 Apr 1943, DO 121/84.

107 SIS summary of decrypted German legation messages, 21 Mar 1943, TNA, DO 121/87.

108 SIS summaries of decrypted German legation messages, May 1943 – Jan 1944, TNA, DO 121/87.

109 SIS report on German wireless transmitter, 17 Apr 1943, TNA, DO 121/84.

110 Clement Attlee to Churchill, 3 May 1943, TNA, DO 121/10B. See also MI5 Irish section history, pp. 63–78, TNA, KV 4/9.

111 Note of meeting on German wireless transmitter, 4 Nov 1943, TNA, DO 121/84.

112 MI5 Irish section history, pp. 72–8, TNA, KV 4/9; minute by John Stephenson, 16 Dec 1943, & Maffey to Machtig, 8 Jan 1944, TNA, DO 35/2078.

113 Papers of Overlord Preparations committee, Feb–Mar 1944, TNA, DO 35/2119; report by J. L. Hathaway, 21 Apr 1944, USNA, RG 319, 092. Ireland, Box 779; MI5 Irish section history, p. 81, TNA, KV 4/9.

114 Philby, *My silent war*, p. 76.

115 'Notes on Axis activities in Ireland' by Gray, Jul 1941, Roosevelt Library, Gray Papers, Subject Files, Box 9, Ireland (1938–47).

116 Report by Wofford, 5 May 1941, USNA, RG 165, MID 2657-A-330–1; reports by Lieut-Colonel Reynolds, 24 Mar 1942 & 1 Jun 1942, USNA, RG 319, 000.24 Ireland, Boxes 778 & 779.

117 They were a former US consul named Patterson; an Irish emigrant, Roland Blenner-Hassett; Ervin 'Spike' Marlin, who was attached to the legation as a special assistant to the Minister; and Martin Quigley, who travelled under the cover of a representative of an American film distribution company.

118 See history of OSS activities in Eire, 12 Oct 1945 (copy in author's possession). For collaboration between X-2 and Section V, see T. J. Naftali, 'X-2 and the apprenticeship of American counterespionage, 1942–44' (PhD thesis, Harvard University, 1993); Hinsley & Simkins, *British intelligence in the Second World War*, vol. 4, p. 187.

119 E. O'Halpin, 'Irish-Allied security relations and the "American note" crisis: new evidence from British records', *Irish Studies in International Affairs*, 11 (2000), pp. 71–2.

120 War cabinet meeting, 4 Feb 1944, TNA, CAB 65/41.

121 Minute by John Stephenson, with agreement of Machtig and Cranborne, 8 Feb 1944, TNA, DO 35/2108.

122 See Gray to Roosevelt, 13 Dec 1943, Roosevelt Library, President's Secretary's File, Diplomatic Correspondence, Ireland 1943, Box 40; history of OSS activities in Eire, 12 Oct 1945.

123 Gray to Roosevelt, 2 Oct 1944, Roosevelt Library, President's Secretary's File, Diplomatic Correspondence, Ireland 1944, Box 40.

124 Gray to State Dept, 13 Sep 1943, USNA, RG 59, 841d.01/203.

125 Maffey to Machtig, 3 Jan 1944, TNA, DO 35/2108.

126 Weekly policy summary by UK Washington embassy, 18 Mar 1944, TNA, DO 35/2108.

127 See *The Times*, 13 Mar 1944.

128 Minute by I. G. Donnelly, 22 Mar 1944, TNA, FO 371/38540.

129 Donnelly to M. E. Allen, 7 May 1945; Darvall to Pugh, 23 Jan 1945, TNA, FO 371/50364.

130 Gray to State Dept, 21 Feb 1944, USNA, RG 59, 841d.01/244; Maffey to DO, 22 Feb 1944, TNA, DO 35/2108; Cranborne to Churchill, 17 & 21 Mar 1944, TNA, DO 121/10A.

131 MI5 Irish section history, pp. 80–1, TNA, KV 4/9. For OSS opposition see memo by Colonel Donovan for Roosevelt, 30 Mar 1944, Roosevelt Library, PSF safe, OSS folder.

132 Memo by Walshe on visit to London, 30–1 Apr 1944, NAI, D/FA, A2.

133 Note by Cecil Liddell, 9 May 1944, TNA, KV 4/280; MI5 Irish section history, pp. 85–9 & appendix I, TNA, KV 4/9.

134 Winant to State Dept, 15 & 20 Apr 1944, USNA, RG 59, 841d.01/333 & /344.

135 Summaries of decrypted German legation messages, May–Jul 1944, TNA, DO 121/87; SIS report, 1 Jul 1944, TNA, DO 121/85.

136 G2 note, 24 Sep 1943, IMA, G2/X/1091.

137 SIS report, 1 Jul 1943, TNA, DO 121/85.

138 Note by Moore, 17 Apr 1944, & query for Stubbs, 26 Feb 1945, IMA, G2/X/1091.

139 Note by Moore, 17 Apr 1944, IMA, G2/X/1091; Cranborne to Churchill, 17 Mar 1944, TNA, DO 121/10A; SIS (probably Jane Archer) to Cecil Liddell, 7 Nov 1944, TNA, KV 4/281.

140 G2 memo on 'British Activities in Eire', 13 Jul 1944, IMA, G2/X/1091.

141 MI5 Irish section history, pp. 97–8, TNA, KV 4/9.

142 G2 notes on interview with Moore, 5 & 17 Oct 1944, IMA, G2/X/1091; MI5 Irish section history, p. 4, TNA, KV 4/9.

143 MI5 Irish section history, pp. 97–100, TNA, KV 4/9.

144 G2 notes on interview with Moore, 5 & 21 Apr 1945, IMA, G2/X/1091.

145 The only aspects that attracted attention were preventing information on V1 and V2 rocket attacks from leaking to Germany, the post-war handling of 'Irish renegades' who had assisted the Nazis and the fate of German diplomats and intelligence agents in Ireland. MI5 Irish section history, pp. 90–105, TNA, KV 4/9.

146 Foster, *Modern Ireland*, p. 560.

147 MI5 Irish section history, pp. 47, 52, TNA, KV 4/9.

148 Vivian to John Stephenson, 31 Dec 1945 & 2 Aug 1946, TNA, DO 121/89.

149 Associated Press interview with Major-General Lahousen, *Irish Independent*, 15 Dec 1945.

CHAPTER 14
Coming to Terms with Irish Independence

1 Hughes, *The fate of facts in a world of men*, p. 24.

2 JP report on Eire, 11 Jul 1940, TNA, CAB 84/16. For similar assessments some months later see COS report, 6 Nov 1940, TNA, CAB 80/22; COS meeting, 6 Nov 1940, TNA, CAB 79/7; minutes of First Lord's meeting with Cmdrs-in-Chief, 30 Oct 1940, TNA, ADM 223/484.

3 Churchill minute, 31 Jan 1941, TNA, PREM 3/131/3.

4 Anon. memo, enclosed with Cranborne to Churchill, 22 Nov 1940, TNA, PREM 3/128.

5 Diary entry for 3 Dec 1940, Colville, *The fringes of power*, p. 306fs; Admiralty note, 17 Dec 1940, TNA, ADM 116/5631. See also Sir Kingsley Wood to Churchill, 20 Feb 1941, TNA, PREM 3/128.

6 Memo by Cranborne, 3 Dec 1940, TNA, PREM 3/128.

7 Maffey to Cranborne, 26 Jul 1941, in COS paper, 14 Aug 1941, TNA, CAB 80/29.

8 Cecil Liddell in MI5 weekly intelligence summary, 13 Feb 1941, TNA, KV 4/122.

9 Churchill minute, 17 Feb 1941, TNA, PREM 3/128.

10 Note by Cranborne, 21 Jan 1941, TNA, PREM 3/128.

11 Memo by Maffey, 14 Sep 1939, & memo by Eden, TNA, DO 35/1107/9.

12 Notes of conversations between de Valera and MacDonald, 17 & 22 Jun 1940, TNA, DO 35/1008/8; report by Maffey, 20 Nov 1940, TNA, PREM 3/127/1.

13 Report by Bowen, 9 Nov 1940, TNA, DO 35/1011/3.

14 Minutes of meeting between Cranborne, Maffey, Gray, Antrobus & Stephenson in Dublin, 16 Dec 1941, TNA, DO 130/17; MI5 Irish section history, p. 15, TNA, KV 4/9. It appears to have been a general cultural perception. See G. B. Shaw to Lord Alfred Douglas, 9 & 14 Nov 1940, in D. H. Laurence (ed.), *Bernard Shaw: collected letters, 1926–1950* (London, 1988), pp. 586–8.

15 *Irish Times*, 6 May 1995. For similar assessments see J. A. Murphy, 'Irish neutrality in perspective', in B. Girvin & G. Roberts (eds.), *Ireland and the Second World War: politics, society and remembrance* (Dublin, 2000), pp. 12–13; O'Halpin, *Defending Ireland*, pp. 151–3.

16 Memo by DO, 11 Feb 1943, TNA, DO 35/2062.

17 Colonel W. J. Donovan to Roosevelt on talk with Desmond Morton, 19 Jan 1942, Roosevelt Library, President's Secretary's File, Box 147, OSS reports. For Irish military volunteers, see Willis, *That neutral island*, p. 110.

18 Churchill to Attlee, 5 May 1943, TNA, PREM 3/131/7B; Churchill to Attlee, 17 Sep 1943, TNA, DO 35/2076.

19 Machtig to Attlee, 18 Sep 1943, TNA, DO 35/2076.

20 Memo by Attlee, 30 Apr 1943, TNA, CAB 66/36.

21 Maffey to Machtig, 3 Feb 1942, DO 121/113.

22 Maffey to Cranborne, 26 Jul 1941, TNA, CAB 80/29.

23 Memo by CIGS, 24 Nov 1941, TNA, CAB 80/60; Attlee to Churchill, 9 Jun 1942, TNA, DO 121/10B.

24 N. Wylie, ' "Keeping the Swiss sweet": intelligence as a factor in British policy towards Switzerland during the Second World War', *Intelligence & National Security*, 11, 3 (1996), pp. 445–51.

25 Memo by Attlee, 16 Sep 1943, TNA, DO 35/2076.

26 Cranborne to Churchill, 19 Dec 1941, TNA, PREM 3/131/6.

27 MI5 report, appendix to report by Sir Findlater Stewart, 18 Mar 1944, TNA, DO 35/2119.

28 It has been analysed, and challenged, in a recent article. See Roberts, 'Three narratives of neutrality', pp. 165, 178.

29 Maffey to Machtig, 2 Aug 1945, TNA, DO 35/2089.

30 Memo by Admiralty and Air Ministry, 17 Jun 1946, TNA, DO 35/2089; minute by Sir John Stephenson, 19 Aug 1946, TNA, DO 35/2060.

31 MI5 Irish section history, p. 13, TNA, KV 4/9.

32 Memo by Maffey, 23 Jun 1941, TNA, DO 35/1109/6.

33 Maffey to Machtig, 25 Feb 1943, TNA, DO 35/2068.

34 *Ibid.*

35 Memo by Maffey on 'The Irish Question in 1945', 21 Aug 1945, TNA, DO 35/2090.

36 MI5 Irish section history, pp. 98–9, TNA, KV 4/9.

37 C. Reeves, ' "Let us stand by our friends": British policy towards Ireland, 1949–59', *Irish Studies in International Affairs*, 11 (2000), pp. 85–102.

38 Liddell–Bryan correspondence, 1949–50, TNA, KV 4/281. See also O'Halpin, *Defending Ireland*, pp. 277–80.

Bibliography

Unpublished sources

Detailed references to file classes and documents consulted are found in the notes.

I *Official records*

The National Archives, London
Public Records Office of Northern Ireland, Belfast
National Archives of Ireland, Dublin
Irish Military Archives, Dublin
US National Archives, Washington, DC

II *Private Papers*

Stanley Baldwin	Cambridge University Library
Joseph H. Fowler	National Library of Ireland
Lord French	Imperial War Museum, London
Admiral John. H. Godfrey	National Maritime Museum, Greenwich
Viscount Hailsham	Churchill College Archives, Cambridge
Maurice Hankey	The National Archives, London
Major-General Sir Hugh Jeudwine	Imperial War Museum, London
Thomas Johnson	National Library of Ireland
David Lloyd George	Parliamentary Archives, London
Malcolm MacDonald	Durham University Library
Ramsay MacDonald	The National Archives, UK
Joseph McGarrity	National Library of Ireland
Florence O'Donoghue	National Library of Ireland
Ernie O'Malley	University College Dublin
Gerald O'Reilly	New York University, Robert F. Wagner Labor Archive
Sir Richard Pim	Public Records Office of Northern Ireland, Belfast
Franklin D. Roosevelt	Roosevelt Library, Hyde Park, New York
Viscount Templewood [Sir Samuel Hoare]	Cambridge University Library
Frank P. Walsh	New York Public Library

III *Miscellaneous*

Dan Bryan transcripts	In possession of Prof. Eunan O'Halpin
History of OSS activities in Eire, 12 Oct 1945	Copy in author's possession

Published sources and theses

References to newspapers, contemporary periodicals, parliamentary debates and papers, television documentaries and websites appear in the notes.

Ackerman, C., 'Ireland from a Scotland Yard notebook', *The Atlantic Monthly*, Apr 1922.

Adams, R. J. Q., *Bonar Law* (London, 1999).

Addison, P., *The road to 1945: British politics and the Second World War* (London, 1994 edn).

—— 'The search for peace in Ireland', in J. W. Muller (ed.), *Churchill as peacemaker* (Cambridge, 1997).

Alexander, M. S., 'Introduction: knowing your friends, assessing your allies – perspectives on intra-alliance intelligence', *Intelligence and National Security*, 13, 1 (1998).

Allason, R., *The Branch* (London, 1983).

Andrew, C. A., *Secret service: the making of the British intelligence community* (London, 1985).

—— *For the president's eyes only: secret intelligence and the American presidency from Washington to Bush* (London, 1996 edn).

—— & D. Dilks (eds.), *The missing dimension: governments and intelligence communities in the twentieth century* (London, 1984).

Augusteijn, J., *From public defiance to guerilla warfare: the experience of ordinary Volunteers in the Irish war of independence, 1916–1921* (Dublin & Portland, OR, 1996).

Baker, J., *The McMahon family murders and the Belfast troubles, 1920–22*, Glenravel Local History Project pamphlet (Belfast, n.d. [1995?]).

Balfour, M., *Propaganda in war, 1939–1945* (London, 1979).

Bardon, J., *A history of Ulster* (Belfast, 1992).

Barnes, J. & D. Nicholson (eds.), *The Leo Amery diaries*, vol. 1: *1896–1929* (London, 1980).

Bartlett, T., 'Informers, informants and information: the secret history of the 1790s re-considered', in T. Bartlett, D. Dickson, D. Keogh & K. Whelan (eds.), *1798: a bicentenary perspective* (Dublin, 2003).

Barton, B., 'Northern Ireland: the impact of war, 1939–45', in B. Girvin & G. Roberts (eds.), *Ireland and the Second World War: politics, society and remembrance* (Dublin, 2000).

Beckett, J. C., *The Anglo-Irish tradition* (London, 1976).

Beesly, P., *Very special admiral: the life of Admiral J. H. Godfrey* (London, 1980).

—— *Room 40: British naval intelligence, 1914–18* (London, 1982).

Bell, A. O. (ed.), *The diary of Virginia Woolf*, vol. 4: *1931–1935* (London, 1982).

Bennett, G., *'A most extraordinary and mysterious business': the Zinoviev Letter of 1924*, FCO History Notes (London, 1999).

Bennett, R., 'Intelligence and strategy in World War II', in K. G. Robertson (ed.), *British and American approaches to intelligence* (London, 1987).

Benton, K., 'The ISOS years: Madrid, 1941–3', *Journal of Contemporary History*, 30 (1995).

Best, A., ' "This probably over-valued military power": British intelligence and Whitehall's perception of Japan, 1939–41', *Intelligence & National Security*, 12, 3 (1997).

Betts, R. K., 'Analysis, war, and decision: why intelligence failures are inevitable', *World Politics*, 31, 1 (1978).

Bew, P., 'Sinn Féin, agrarian radicalism and the war of independence, 1919–1921', in D. G. Boyce (ed.), *The revolution in Ireland, 1879–1923* (Basingstoke & London, 1988).

—— 'Moderate nationalism and the Irish revolution, 1916–1923', *The Historical Journal*, 42, 3 (1999).

Birkenhead, Earl of, *Frederick Edwin Earl of Birkenhead*, vol. 2: *The last phase* (London, 1935).

Bond, B., *British military policy between the two world wars* (Oxford, 1980).

—— (ed.), *Chief of Staff: the diaries of Lieutenant-General Sir Henry Pownall, 1940–1944* (London, 1974).

Borgonovo, J., *Florence and Josephine O'Donoghue's war of independence: a destiny that shapes our ends* (Dublin, 2006).

Bourke, J., 'Effeminacy, ethnicity and the end of trauma: the sufferings of "shell-shocked" men in Great Britain and Ireland, 1914–39', *Journal of Contemporary History*, 35, 1 (2000).

Bowman, J., *De Valera and the Ulster question, 1917–73* (Oxford, 1982).

Bowyer Bell, J., *The secret army: the IRA 1916–79* (Dublin, 1979).

Boyce, D. G., *Nationalism in Ireland* (London & New York, 1991 edn).

—— 'How to settle the Irish Question: Lloyd George and Ireland, 1916–21', in A. J. P. Taylor (ed.), *Lloyd George: twelve essays* (London, 1971).

Brennan, N., 'A political minefield: southern loyalists, the Irish Grants Committee and the British government, 1922–31', *Irish Historical Studies*, 31 (1997).

Bretherton, C. H., *The real Ireland* (London, 1925).

Brewer, S., *To win the peace: British propaganda in the United States during World War II* (Ithaca & London, 1997).

British Security Coordination: the secret history of British intelligence in the Americas, 1940–45 (London, 1998).

Buchanan, T., ' "A far away country of which we know nothing?": perceptions of Spain and its civil war in Britain, 1931–1939', *Twentieth Century British History*, 4, 1 (1993).

Buckland, P., *Irish unionism: the Anglo-Irish and the new Ireland, 1885–1922* (Dublin, 1972).

—— *Ulster unionism and the origins of Northern Ireland* (Dublin, 1973).

—— *James Craig* (Dublin, 1980).

—— 'A Protestant state: Unionists in government, 1921–39', in D. George Boyce & A. O'Day (eds.), *Defenders of the Union: a survey of British and Irish unionism since 1801* (London & New York, 2001).

Burt, L., *Commander Burt of Scotland Yard* (London, 1959).

Callwell, C. E., *Field-Marshal Sir Henry Wilson: his life and times* (London, 1927).

Campbell, J., *F. E. Smith: first Earl of Birkenhead* (London, 1983).

Canning, P., *British policy towards Ireland, 1921–41* (Oxford, 1985).

Carroll, F. M., *American opinion and the Irish question, 1910–23* (London & New York, 1978).

Cecil, R., 'Five of Six at war: Section V of MI6', *Intelligence & National Security*, 9, 2 (1994).

Charles, D. M., 'American, British and Canadian intelligence links: a critical annotated bibliography', *Intelligence and National Security*, 15, 2 (2000).

Childs, W., *Episodes and reflections* (London, 1930).

Clarke, P., *Hope and glory: Britain, 1900–90* (London, 1997 edn).

Clynes, J. R., *Memoirs, 1869–1924* (London, 1937).

Cole, R., ' "Good relations": Irish neutrality and the propaganda of John Betjeman, 1941–43', *Eire-Ireland*, 30, 4 (1996).

Colville, J., *The fringes of power: Downing Street diaries, 1939–1955* (London, 1985).

Comerford, R. V., *The Fenians in context* (Dublin, 1985).

Connolly, S. J., *The Oxford companion to Irish history* (Oxford, 1998).

Connolly, T., 'Irish workers in Britain during World War Two', in B. Girvin & G. Roberts, *Ireland and the Second World War: politics, society and remembrance* (Dublin, 2000).

Coogan, T. P., *Michael Collins* (London, 1990).

—— *De Valera: long fellow, long shadow* (London, 1993).

—— *The IRA* (London, 1995 edn).

Cox, C., "Militär geographische Angaben über Irland," *An Cosantóir* (Mar 1975).

Cronin, M., *The Blueshirts and Irish politics* (Dublin, 1997).

Cross, J. A., *Lord Swinton* (Oxford, 1982).

Crozier, F. P., *Impressions and recollections* (London, 1930).

Cull, N. J., *Selling war: the British propaganda campaign against American 'neutrality', in World War II* (Oxford, 1995).

Curtis, L. P., *Anglo-Saxons and Celts: a study of anti-Irish prejudice in Victorian England* (New York, 1968).

—— *Apes and angels: the Irishman in Victorian caricature* (Washington & London, 1997 edn).

Dawson, R., *Red Terror and green* (London, 1920).

De Montmorency, H., *Sword and stirrup: memories of an adventurous life* (London, 1936).

Dear, I. C. B., & M. R. D. Foot (eds.), *The Oxford companion to the Second World War* (Oxford, 1995).

Delaney, E., ' "Almost a class of helots in an alien land": the British state and Irish immigration, 1921–45', in D. MacRaild (ed.), *The Great Famine and beyond: Irish migrants in Britain in the nineteenth and twentieth centuries* (Dublin & Portland, OR, 2000).

Dempsey, P., 'Trinity College Dublin and the new political order', in M. Cronin & J. M. Regan (eds.), *Ireland: the politics of independence, 1922–49* (Basingstoke & New York, 2000).

Denniston, A. G., 'The Government Codes and Cipher School between the wars', *Intelligence & National Security*, 1, 1 (1986).

Der Derian, J., 'Anti-diplomacy, intelligence theory and surveillance practice', *Intelligence & National Security*, 8, 3 (Jul 1993).

Documents on Irish foreign policy, vol. 1: *1919–1922* (Dublin, 1998).

Donnelly, M., *Britain in the Second World War* (London, 1999).

Donohue, L. K., 'Regulating Northern Ireland: the Special Powers Acts, 1922–72', *The Historical Journal*, 41, 4 (1998).

Dorrill, S., *MI6: inside the covert world of Her Majesty's Secret Intelligence Service* (New York, 2000).

Douglas, R. M., 'Anglo-Saxons and Attacotti: the racialization of Irishness in Britain between the World Wars', *Ethnic and Racial Studies*, 25, 1 (Jan 2002).

Dudgeon, J., *Roger Casement: the Black Diaries – with a study of his background, sexuality, and Irish political life* (Belfast, 2002).

Duggan, J., *A history of the Irish army* (Dublin, 1991).

Dunn, J., *Paperchase: adventures in and out of Fleet Street* (London, 1938).

Dunphy, R., *The making of Fianna Fáil power in Ireland, 1923–1948* (Oxford, 1995).

English, R., *Armed struggle: the history of the IRA* (London, 2003).

—— '"Paying no heed to public clamour"; Irish republican solipsism in the 1930s', *Irish Historical Studies*, 28, 112 (1993).

Fanning, R., 'Irish neutrality – an historical review', *Irish Studies in International Affairs*, 1, 3 (1982).

—— '"The rule of order"; Eamon de Valera and the IRA, 1923–40', in J. P. O'Carroll & J. A. Murphy (eds.), *De Valera and his times* (Cork, 1983).

Fedorowich, K., 'The problems of disbandment: the Royal Irish Constabulary and imperial migration, 1919–1929', *Irish Historical Studies*, 30, 117 (May 1996).

Fergusson, J., *The Curragh Incident* (London, 1964).

Ferris, J., & U. Bar-Joseph, 'Getting Marlowe to hold his tongue: the Conservative Party, the intelligence services and the Zinoviev letter', *Intelligence and National Security*, 8, 4 (Oct 1993).

Ferriter, D., *The transformation of Ireland, 1900–2000* (London, 2004).

Fisk, R., *In time of war: Ireland, Ulster and the price of neutrality, 1939–45* (Dublin, 1983).

Fitzpatrick, D., *The two Irelands, 1912–1939* (Oxford, 1998).

Follis, B. A., *A state under siege: the establishment of Northern Ireland, 1920–1925* (Oxford, 1995).

Foot, M. R. D., 'The IRA and the origins of SOE', in M. R. D. Foot (ed.), *War and society: historical essays in honour and memory of J. R. Western, 1928–1971* (London, 1973).

—— 'A comparison of SOE and OSS', in K. G. Robertson (ed.), *British and American approaches to intelligence* (London, 1987).

—— & Langley, J. M., *MI9* (London, 1979).

Foster, R., *Modern Ireland, 1600–1972* (London, 1989).

—— *Paddy and Mr Punch: connections in Anglo-Irish history* (London, 1993).

Foy, M. T., *Michael Collins's intelligence war: the struggle between the British and IRA, 1919–21* (Stroud, 2006).

French, D., 'Sir John French's Secret Service on the Western Front, 1914–1915', *Journal of Strategic Studies*, 7, 4 (1984).

Garvin, T., *Nationalist revolutionaries in Ireland, 1858–1928* (Oxford, 1987).

Gibbons, J., *Ireland – the new ally* (London, 1938).

Gilbert, M. (ed.), *The Churchill war papers*, vol. 1: *At the Admiralty, September 1939 – May 1940* (London, 1993).

Gilley, S., 'English attitudes to the Irish in England, 1780–1900', in C. Holmes (ed.), *Immigrants and minorities in British society* (London, 1978).

Godley, A., *Life of an Irish soldier* (London, 1939).

Hamilton, N., *Monty: the making of a general* (London, 1981).

Hanley, B., *The IRA, 1926–36* (Dublin, 2002).

Harkness, D., *The restless Dominion: the Irish Free State and the British Commonwealth of Nations, 1921–31* (London, 1969).

—— *Ireland in the twentieth century: divided island* (Basingstoke & London, 1996).

Hart, P., *The I.R.A. and its enemies: violence and community in Cork, 1916–1923* (Oxford, 1998).

—— (ed.), *British intelligence in Ireland, 1920–21: the final reports* (Cork, 2002).

—— *Mick: the real Michael Collins* (London, 2005).

—— 'Michael Collins and the assassination of Sir Henry Wilson', *Irish Historical Studies*, 28, 110 (Nov 1992).

—— 'The Protestant experience of revolution in southern Ireland', in R. English & G. Walker (eds.), *Unionism in modern Ireland: new perspectives on politics and culture* (Basingstoke/London, 1996).

—— '"Operations abroad": the IRA in Britain, 1919–23', *The English Historical Review*, 115 (2000).

Headlam, M., *Irish reminiscences* (London, 1947).

Hearnshaw, F. J., *Outlines of the history of the British Isles* (London, 1938).

Heathcote Thruston, E., *Earl of Rosebery: statesman and sportsman* (London, 1928).

Herman, M., *Intelligence power in peace and war* (Cambridge, 1996).

Hibbert, R., 'Intelligence and policy', *Intelligence & National Security*, 5, 1 (Jan 1990)

Hickman, M. J., *Religion, class and identity* (Aldershot, 1995).

Hiley, N., 'Counter-espionage and security in Great Britain during the First World War', *English Historical Review*, 101, 400 (Jul 1986).

Hinsley, F. H., *British intelligence in the Second World War*, vol. 1: *Its influence on strategy and operations* (London, 1979).

—— *British intelligence in the Second World War: abridged edition* (London, 1993).

—— & Simkins, C. A. G., *British intelligence in the Second World War*, vol. 4: *Security and counter-intelligence* (London, 1990).

Hopkinson, M., *Green against green: the Irish civil war* (Dublin, 1988).

—— (ed.) *The last days of Dublin Castle: the Mark Sturgis diaries* (Dublin & Portland, OR, 1999).

—— *The Irish war of independence* (Dublin, 2002).

—— 'The Craig–Collins pacts of 1922: two attempted reforms of the Northern Ireland government', *Irish Historical Studies*, 27, 106 (Nov 1990)

Hughes, T. L., *The fate of facts in a world of men: foreign policy and intelligence making* (New York, 1976).

Hull, M., 'German Military Intelligence Operations in Ireland, 1939–45' (PhD diss., University College Cork, 2000)

—— *Irish secrets: German espionage in Ireland, 1939–45* (Dublin & Portland, OR, 2003).

Jeffrey, K., *Field Marshal Sir Henry Wilson: a political soldier* (London, 2006).

—— 'British military intelligence following World War I', in K. G. Robertson (ed.), *British and American approaches to intelligence* (London, 1987).

Jervis, R., *Perception and misperception in international politics* (Princeton, 1976).

Jones, T., *A diary with letters, 1931–1950* (Oxford, 1954).

—— *Whitehall diary*, vol. 3: *Ireland, 1918–1925*, ed. K. Middlemas (London, 1971).

Judd, A., *The quest for C: Sir Mansfield Cumming and the founding of the British secret service* (London, 1999).

Kavanagh, C., 'Neutrality and the volunteers: Irish and British government policy towards the Irish volunteers', in B. Girvin & G. Roberts, *Ireland the Second World War: politics, society and remembrance* (Dublin, 2000).

Kee, R., *The green flag: a history of Irish nationalism* (London, 1972).

Kennedy, D., *The widening gulf: northern attitudes to the independent Irish state, 1919–49* (Belfast, 1988).

Kent, S., *Strategic intelligence for American world policy* (Hamden, CT, 1965 edn).

Keogh, D., *Ireland and Europe, 1919–48* (Dublin, 1988).
—— 'De Valera, the Catholic church and the "Red Scare", 1931–1932', in J. P. O'Carroll &
J. A. Murphy, *De Valera and his times* (Cork, 1983).
Laffan, M., *The resurrection of Ireland: the Sinn Féin Party, 1916–23* (Cambridge, 1999).
Laurence, D. H. (ed.), *Bernard Shaw: collected letters, 1926–1950* (London, 1988).
Lawlor, S. M., 'Ireland from truce to treaty: war or peace? July to October 1921', *Irish
Historical Studies*, 22, 85 (Mar 1980).
Lee, J. J., *Ireland, 1912–1985: politics and society* (Cambridge, 1989).
Levite, A., *Intelligence and strategic surprises* (New York, 1987).
Linge, J., 'The Royal Navy and the Irish civil car', *Irish Historical Studies*, 31, 121 (May
1998).
Lyons, F. S. L., *Ireland since the Famine* (London, 1973 edn).
—— *Culture and anarchy in Ireland, 1890–1939* (Oxford, 1980).
—— 'The minority problem in the 26 counties', in F. MacManus (ed.), *The years of the
great test* (Cork, 1967).
MacBride, S., 'Reflections on intelligence', *Intelligence & National Security*, 2, 1 (1987).
MacDonald, M., *Titans & others* (Collins, 1972).
MacEoin, U., *Survivors* (Dublin, 1980).
—— *The IRA in the twilight years, 1923–48* (Dublin, 1997).
MacMillan, G., *State, society and authority in Ireland: the foundations of the modern
state* (Dublin, 1993).
MacRaild, D. M., *Irish migrants in modern Britain, 1750–1922* (Basingstoke, 1999).
Macready, N., *Annals of an active life*, 2 vols. (London, 1924).
Mangan, C., 'Plans and operations', *The Irish Sword*, 19, 75 & 76 (1993–4).
Manning, M., *The Blueshirts* (Dublin, 1970).
Mansergh, N., *The unresolved question: the Anglo-Irish settlement and its undoing,
1912–72* (New Haven & London, 1991).
Martin, H., *Ireland in insurrection* (London, 1921).
Masterman, J. C., *The double cross system* (London, 1973).
Matthews, K., 'Stanley Baldwin's Irish Question', *The Historical Journal*, 43, 4 (2000).
May, E., 'Conclusions: capabilities and proclivities', in E. May (ed.), *Knowing one's
enemies: intelligence assessment before the two world wars* (Princeton, 1984).
McBride, L. W., *The greening of Dublin Castle: the transformation of bureaucratic and
judicial personnel in Ireland, 1892–1922* (Washington, DC, 1991).
McColgan, J., *British policy and the Irish administration, 1920–22* (London, 1983).
—— 'Implementing the 1921 treaty: Lionel Curtis and constitutional procedure', *Irish
Historical Studies*, 20, 79 (Mar 1977).
McDougall, S., 'The projection of Northern Ireland to Great Britain and abroad,
1921–39', in P. Catterall & S. McDougall (eds.), *The Northern Ireland question in
British politics* (London, 1996).
McDowell, R. B., *Crisis and decline: the fate of the southern Unionists* (Dublin, 1997).
McEwen, J. M. (ed.), *The Riddell diaries, 1908–1923* (London, 1986).
McGarry, F., *Eoin O'Duffy: a self-made hero* (Oxford, 2005).
McMahon, D., *Republicans and imperialists: Anglo-Irish relations in the 1930s*
(London, 1984).
McMahon, P. 'Covert operations and official collaboration: British intelligence's dual
approach to Ireland during World War II', *Intelligence and National Security*, 18, 1
(Spring 2003).

Mitchell, A., *Revolutionary government in Ireland: Dáil Éireann, 1919–22* (Dublin, 1995).

Montgomery, B., *A field-marshal in the family* (London, 1973).

Montgomery, Viscount, *The memoirs of Field-Marshal the Viscount Montgomery* (London, 1958).

Montgomery Hyde, H., *United in crime* (London, 1955).

—— *The quiet Canadian: the secret service story of Sir William Stephenson* (London, 1962) [published in USA as *Room 3603: William Stevenson, a man called Intrepid: the secret war* (New York, 1976)].

Murphy, B., *John Chartres: mystery man of the treaty* (Dublin, 1995).

Murphy, J. A., 'The new IRA, 1925–62', in T. Desmond Williams (ed.), *Secret societies in Ireland* (Dublin, 1973).

—— J. A. Murphy, 'Irish neutrality in perspective', in B. Girvin & G. Roberts (eds.), *Ireland and the Second World War: politics, society and remembrance* (Dublin, 2000).

Naftali, T. J., 'X-2 and the apprenticeship of American counterespionage, 1942–44' (PhD thesis, Harvard University, 1993).

Neligan, D., *The spy in the Castle* (London, 1999).

Nevin, D., 'Radical movements in the twenties and thirties', in T. Desmond Williams (ed.), *Secret societies in Ireland* (Dublin, 1973).

Nowlan, K. B., 'Conclusion', in T. Desmond Williams (ed.), *Secret societies in Ireland* (Dublin, 1973)

Ó Broin, L., *Dublin Castle and the 1916 rising*, 2nd edn (London, 1970).

Occelshaw, M., *Armour against fate: British military intelligence in the First World War* (London, 1989).

O'Connor, E., *Reds and the green: Ireland, Russia and the Communist Internationals, 1919–43* (Dublin, 2004).

O'Connor, J., *History of Ireland, 1798–1924* (London, 1925)

O'Donoghue, D., *Hitler's Irish voices: the story of German radio's wartime Irish service* (Dublin, 1998).

Ó Drisceoil, D., *Censorship in Ireland, 1939–45: neutrality, politics and society* (Cork, 1996).

—— 'Censorship as propaganda: the neutralisation of Irish public opinion during the Second World War', in B. Girvin & G. Roberts, *Ireland and the Second World War: politics, society and remembrance* (Dublin, 2000).

O'Driscoll, M., 'The economic war and Irish foreign trade policy: Irish–German commerce 1932–39', *Irish Studies in International Affairs*, 10 (1999).

O'Halpin, E., *The decline of the union: British government in Ireland, 1892–1920* (Dublin, 1987).

—— *Defending Ireland: the Irish state and its enemies since 1922* (Oxford, 1999).

—— *MI5 and Ireland, 1939–45: the official history* (Dublin, 2003).

—— 'British intelligence in Ireland, 1914–21', in C. Andrew & D. Dilks (eds.), *The missing dimension: governments and intelligence communities in the twentieth century* (London, 1984).

—— 'Financing British intelligence: the evidence up to 1945', in K. G. Robertson, *British and American approaches to intelligence* (London, 1987).

—— ' "According to the Irish minister in Rome …": British decrypts and Irish diplomacy in the Second World War', *Irish Studies in International Affairs*, 6 (1995).

—— 'Collins and intelligence, 1919–1923', in G. Doherty & D. Keogh (eds.), *Michael Collins and the making of the Irish state* (Dublin, 1998).

—— 'Irish-Allied security relations and the "American note" crisis: new evidence from British records', *Irish Studies in International Affairs*, 11 (2000)

—— 'MI5's Irish memories; fresh light on the origins and rationale of Anglo-Irish security liaison in the Second World War', in B. Girvin & G. Roberts (eds.), *Ireland and the Second World War: politics, society and remembrance* (Dublin, 2000).

—— ' "Toys" and "Whispers" in "16-land": SOE and Ireland, 1940–1942', in *Intelligence & National Security*, 15, 4 (2000).

—— ' "Weird prophecies": British intelligence and Anglo-Irish relations,1932–3', in M. Kennedy & J. Morrison Skelly (eds.), *Irish foreign policy, 1919–66* (Dublin, 2000).

Ó Tuathaigh, M. A. G., 'The Irish in nineteenth-century Britain: problems of integration', in R. Swift and S. Gilley (eds.), *The Irish in the Victorian city* (London, 1985).

Philby, K., *My silent war* (New York, 2002 edn).

Phillips, W. A., *The revolution in Ireland, 1906–1923* (London, 1923).

Phoenix, É., 'Michael Collins – the northern question, 1916–1922', in G. Doherty & D. Keogh (eds.), *Michael Collins and the making of the Irish state* (Dublin, 1998).

Pimley, A., 'The working-class movement and the Irish revolution, 1896–1923', in D. G. Boyce (ed.), *The revolution in Ireland, 1879–1923* (Basingstoke & London, 1988).

Pittock, M. G. H., *Celtic identity and the British image* (Manchester & New York, 1999).

Popplewell, R., *Intelligence and imperial defence: British intelligence and the defence of the Indian empire, 1904–1924* (London, 1995).

Porter, B., *The origins of the vigilant state* (London, 1983).

—— *Plots and paranoia* (London, 1989).

Ramsden, J. (ed.), *Real old Tory politics: the political diaries of Sir Robert Sanders, Lord Bayford, 1910–1935* (London, 1984).

Regan, J., *The Irish counter-revolution, 1921–1936: treatyite politics and settlement in independent Ireland* (Dublin, 1999).

—— 'The politics of reaction: the dynamics of treatyite government and policy, 1922–33', *Irish Historical Studies*, 30, 120 (Nov 1997).

Reeves, C., ' "Let us stand by our friends": British policy towards Ireland, 1949–59', *Irish Studies in International Affairs*, 11 (2000).

Rhodes James, R. (ed.), *Memoirs of a Conservative: J. C. C. Davidson's memoirs and papers, 1910–37* (London, 1969).

—— *Churchill: a study in failure, 1900–1939* (London, 1970).

Robb, N. A., *An Ulsterwoman in England, 1924–1941* (Cambridge, 1942).

Roberts, G., 'Three narratives of neutrality: historians and Ireland's war', in B. Girvin & G. Roberts (eds.), *Ireland the Second World War: politics, society and remembrance* (Dublin, 2000).

Roberts, J. M., *Europe, 1880–1945*, 3rd edn (Harlow, 2001).

Robinson, H. A., *Memories: wise and otherwise* (London, 1923).

—— *Further memories of Irish life* (London, n.d. [1924?])

Rosenberg, J. L., 'The 1941 mission of Frank Aiken to the United States: an American perspective', *Irish Historical Studies*, 22, 86 (Sep 1980).

Roskill, S., *Churchill and the admirals* (New York, 1978).

Ross, J., *Pilgrim scrip* (London, 1927).

Roth, A., 'Gun running from Germany in the early 1920s', *The Irish Sword*, 22, 88 (2000).

—— 'Francis Stuart's broadcasts from Germany, 1942–44: some new evidence', *Irish Historical Studies*, 32, 127 (2001).

Ryle Dwyer, T., *The Squad: and the intelligence operations of Michael Collins* (Cork, 2005).

Schenk, P., *Invasion of England, 1940: the planning of Operation Sealion* (London, 1990).

The Security Service, 1908–1945: the official history (London, 1999).

Self, R. (ed.), *The Neville Chamberlain diary letters*, vol 2: *The reform years, 1921–27* (Ashgate, 2000).

Seymour-Ure, C., 'The press and the party system between the wars', in G. Peele & C. Cook (eds.), *The politics of reappraisal, 1918–1939* (London, 1975).

Sheehan, W. (ed.), *British voices: from the Irish war of independence, 1918–21* (Cork, 2005).

Short, K. R. M., *The dynamite war* (Dublin, 1979).

Silvestri, M., ' "An Irishman is specially suited to be a policeman": Sir Charles Tegart & revolutionary terrorism in Bengal', *History Ireland* (Winter 2000).

Sloan, G. R., *The geopolitics of Anglo-Irish relations in the twentieth century* (Leicester, 1997).

Sparrow, E., *Secret Service: British agents in France, 1792–1815* (Woodbridge, 1999).

Spence, R. B., 'Englishmen in New York: the SIS American station, 1915–1921', *Intelligence and National Security*, 19, 3 (Autumn, 2004).

Strong, K., *Intelligence at the top: the recollections of an intelligence officer* (London, 1968).

Sullivan, A. M., *Old Ireland: reminiscences of an Irish K.C.* (London, 1927).

Tarpey, M. V., 'The role of Joseph McGarrity in the struggle for Irish independence' (PhD thesis, St John's University, New York, 1969).

Taylor, A. J. P (ed.), *W. P. Crozier: off the record: political interviews, 1933–1943* (London, 1973).

—— *English history, 1914–1945* (London, 1977 edn).

Thomas, E., 'The evolution of the JIC system up to and during World War II', in C. Andrew & J. Noakes (eds.), *Intelligence and international relations, 1900–1945* (Exeter, 1987).

Thom's Directory (Dublin, 1940).

Thomson, B., *The scene changes* (London, 1939).

Thurlow, R., *The secret state: British internal security in the twentieth century* (Oxford, 1994).

Townshend, C., *Political violence in Ireland: government and resistance since 1848* (Oxford, 1983).

—— *Ireland: the 20th century* (London, 1998).

—— *Easter 1916: the Irish rebellion* (London, 2005).

—— 'The Irish Republican Army and the development of guerrilla garfare, 1916–1921', *English Historical Review*, 94, 371 (Apr 1979).

—— 'Policing insurgency in Ireland, 1914–23', in D. M. Anderson & D. Killingray (eds.), *Policing and decolonisation: politics, nationalism and the police, 1917–65* (Manchester, 1992).

Troy, T. F., *Wild Bill and Intrepid: Donovan, Stephenson and the origin of CIA* (New Haven, CT, 1996).

Umbreit, H., 'Churchill's determination to continue the war' & 'Plans and preparations for a landing in England', in Militargeschichtliches Forschungsamt (ed.), *Germany and the Second World War* (Oxford, 1991).

Valiulis, M. G., *Almost a rebellion: the Irish army mutiny of 1924* (Cork, 1985).

—— ' "The man they could never forgive" – the view of the opposition: Eaman de Valera and the civil war', in J. P. O'Carroll & J. A. Murphy (eds.), *De Valera and his times* (Cork, 1983).

Vansittart, R., *The mist procession* (London, 1958).

Vertzberger, Y. Y., *World in their minds: information processing, cognition, and perception in foreign policy decisionmaking* (Stanford, 1990).

Vincent, J. (ed.), *The Crawford papers* (Manchester, 1984).

Ward, A. J., *Ireland and Anglo-American relations, 1899–1921* (London, 1969)

Wark, W., *The ultimate enemy: British intelligence and Nazi Germany, 1933–39* (Oxford, 1986).

Watt, D. C., *How war came: the immediate origins of the Second World War, 1938–39* (London, 1989).

—— 'An intelligence surprise; the failure of the Foreign Office to anticipate the Nazi–Soviet Pact', *Intelligence & National Security*, 4, 3 (1989).

—— 'The proper study of propaganda', *Intelligence and National Security*, 15, 4 (2000).

Weiss, R. P., 'Private detective agencies and labour discipline in the United States, 1855–1946', *Historical Journal*, 29, 1 (Mar 1986).

West, N., *MI5: British Security Service operations, 1909–1945* (New York, 1981).

—— *The Guy Liddell diaries*, vol. 1: *1939–42* (Abingdon, 2005).

Wheale, A., *Renegades* (London, 1994).

Who Was Who (London, 2006).

Williamson, P. (ed.), *The modernisation of Conservative politics: the diaries and letters of William Bridgeman, 1904–1935* (London, 1988).

Willis, C., *That neutral island: a cultural history of Ireland during the Second World War* (London, 2007).

Wilson, E., 'British intelligence and fear of a "fifth column" in 1940' (unpublished MPhil dissertation, Cambridge University, 1999).

Winter, O., *Winter's tale: an autobiography* (London, 1955).

Wylie, N., 'Ungentlemanly warriors or unreliable diplomats? Special Operations Executive and "Irregular Political Activities" in Europe'. *Intelligence and National Security*, 20, 1 (Mar 2005)

—— ' "Keeping the Swiss sweet": intelligence as a factor in British policy towards Switzerland during the Second World War', *Intelligence & National Security*, 11, 3 (1996).

Young, K. (ed.), *The diaries of Sir Robert Bruce Lockhart, 1939–1965* (London, 1980).

Index

(Northern Ireland *cont.*)
(internal security *cont.*)
RIC 136, 137–8, 139, 152, 158
sectarian violence (1922) 104, 134–5, 136,
139–40, 155
partition 52, 134
post-WWII IRA threat 390
relations with British government (1921–39)
Boundary Commission crisis 177–8, 189,
192–3
British debate intervention (1922) 135, 140–2
British support Belfast government 145–6,
153, 159, 167, 193–4, 250
relations with southern Ireland (1923–39) 163,
176
anti-partition campaign by Dublin
(1938–9) 250, 276
base to spy on Free State (1923–5) 178, 181–4,
195–6, 427
intelligence on south (1922–5) 77, 86, 89, 144,
149, 153, 155, 181–2, 184–5, 189
intelligence on south (1932–9) 218, 231–2, 237
threat of southern attack 166–7, 232, 278–9,
299, 301, 302
and Second World War
base to spy on south 331, 332, 335–6, 353
border controls 294, 396–7
British army 329, 330, 336, 341
internal security 296–7, 363
Ministry of Information activities 378, 386
treatment of Catholic minority 157, 166, 181,
194, 250
See also Royal Ulster Constabulary; Special
Constabulary
Northern Whig 184, 231
Northumberland 267
Norway 19, 229, 292, 304, 316, 318, 319

O'Brennan, Kathleen 119, 124
O'Brien, Art 103, 107, 108, 262
O'Callaghan, Colonel Les 345
O'Connell, Colonel J. J. 336
O'Connell, M. J. 94–5
O'Connor, Sir James 165
O'Connor, Maurice 309
O'Connor, Rory 64–5
O'Cunningham, Gerald 389
O'Donnell, Peadar 211
O'Donoghue, Florence 28, 40, 348
O'Donovan, James 260–1, 265, 266, 275, 299
O'Duffy, General Eoin
and Blueshirts (1930s) 217, 224, 239
Second World War 309, 358, 374
O'Higgins, Kevin 81, 175, 194, 202
O'Leary, Jeremiah 110, 111
O'Neill, James 411
O'Reilly, John 372, 414, 417
O'Shea, Michael 268
O'Shiel, Kevin 181
Obed, Henry 308
Observer, The 225
Offences Against the State Act (Ireland) 271
Office of Strategic Services (OSS) 419
Olivier, Laurence 380
Olsen, Udo 252–3, 254
Omagh, Co. Tyrone 226

Operation Overlord (Allied landing in
France) 407, 415, 416, 417, 422
Operation Sealion 329
Orgesch 126, 128, 129, 132
Ormsby Gore, William 172–3
Orwell, George 438
OSS *See* Office of Strategic Services
Oxford University 35, 69, 269, 332

Pakenham, Frank 371, 378
Palace Bar (Dublin) 361, 380
Palestine 1, 66, 315
Pan American airline 401–2
Pandora 406, 415, 416 *See also* codebreaking
Paris 4, 29, 73, 113, 124, 219, 229, 304, 309, 399
Parks, Major 331
partition *See* Northern Ireland
Passage, Co. Cork 84
Passport Control Office *See under* Secret
Intelligence Service
Pearl Harbor 298, 341
Pearse, Padráig 16
Pearson, Norman 334
Pearson, Captain Stuart 290
Penapa 309, 310
Peoples National Party 309
Peters, William 198–9, 211–12, 214, 221, 236
Petersen, Dr Carlheinz 256, 361, 373, 380, 388
Petrie, Sir David 307, 351, 422
Pettigo, Co. Donegal 145
Philadelphia 113, 277
Philby, Kim 220, 347
Phillips, Charles Bernard Compton 258
Phillips, Major W. A. 196, 207
Phoenix Park, Dublin 6, 8, 66, 298
Pierce (double agent 'Rainbow') 398
pigeons 337
Pinkerton's detective agency 110
Pitt, William (the Younger) 4, 237
Podesta, William A. 346, 348, 349, 423, 424
Poges, Major 43
poison gas 61, 62
Poland 34, 261, 284, 286, 350, 387
Political Warfare Executive 370, 382
Pollack, Major-General R. V. 297
Portugal 300, 359, 368, 401, 402, 411–12
Preetz, Wilhelm 308, 320
press
in Britain
campaign against Irish neutrality
(WWII) 324, 340
exaggeration of subversive forces
(1932–3) 225, 227
German support for IRA bombing campaign
(1939) 272–3
hunt for Irish spies (WWII) 294, 313, 345,
380–1, 398, 420
IRA campaign in Britain (1918–21) 98, 99
in Ireland 68, 83, 373, 377, 380–1
in Northern Ireland 145, 150, 185
Prevention of Violence (Temporary Provisions)
Act (1939) 274
Price, Major Ivor H. 16, 21
propaganda 110, 241, 328, 430
by Americans in Ireland (WWII) 387
by Axis in Ireland (WWII) 372–7, 381, 391

Printed and bound by CPI Group (UK) Ltd, Croydon, CR0 4YY

23/05/2024

14506022-0002